Electronic Discovery and Evidence

Michael R. Arkfeld

Member of the State Bar of Arizona

2006–2007 ed.
Law Partner Publishing, LLC
Phoenix * Arizona

Subscription Notice

This Law Partner Publishing, LLC product is updated on a periodic basis with supplements to reflect changes in the subject matter. If you obtained this product directly from Law Partner Publishing, we have recorded your purchase for the update service.

However, if you purchased this product from a bookstore or other organization and wish to receive future updates and password protected web site access please contact Law Partner Publishing at (602) 993-1937 or send your name, company name (if applicable), address and the title of the product to Law Partner Publishing, LLC, 9602 North 35th Place, Phoenix, Arizona 85028 (www.lawpartnerpublishing.com) or e-mail us at sales@lawpartnerpublishing.com.

Citation to Book

Michael R. Arkfeld, *Electronic Discovery and Evidence,* § ___, _____ (2006).

Disclaimer

Copyright

ISBN # 0-9669347-1-7

Library of Congress Control Number: 2003098824

ABOUT THE AUTHOR

Michael R. Arkfeld is a practicing attorney, speaker, consultant and author.

As a former assistant United States Attorney for the District of Arizona Michael handled multimillion-dollar cases involving personal injury, medical malpractice, wrongful termination and a host of other tort claims. He has appeared before both federal and state appellate courts and has extensive experience in jury (over 30 trials) and bench trials. His case duties include comprehensive case management plans, investigation and deposing of expert and lay witnesses, pretrial preparation of witnesses and document organization, pretrial filing of documents, and appearances for motion hearings, pretrial conferences, trials, and appellate arguments.

Since 1985, Michael has incorporated personal computers extensively in his legal practice and lectures and consults throughout North America and overseas on the impact of technology to the practice of law and the discovery and admission of electronic evidence.

Michael was the recipient of 2004 E-Evidence Thought Leading Scholar Award and was presented the President's Award from the State Bar of Arizona in 1996.

Michael is a licensed attorney in the state of Arizona. He presently serves on the Electronic Discovery Committee for the State Bar of Arizona. Michael is the past chairman of the Task Force on Integrating Technology into the Justice System for the State Bar of Arizona.

Michael has been the editor of the E-Discovery Supplement to the American Lawyer and Corporate Counsel magazines published by American Lawyer Media. He is a past columnist for the Arizona Attorney magazine and a contributing writer to the American Bar Association Journal and a variety of other legal publications. Michael received his J.D. from the University of Nebraska College of Law in 1975. Michael is also the author of *The Digital Practice of Law (5th Ed.): A Practical Reference for Applying Technology Concepts to the Practice of Law.*

Michael can be reached by e-mail at *Michael@Arkfeld.com*. His web sites, Electronic Discovery and Evidence Center (www.edecenter.com) and Arkfeld and Associates (www.arkfeldandassociates.com), feature electronic discovery and other litigation and law office resources.

ACKNOWLEDGEMENTS

A special acknowledgement to my family and supporters for their assistance as I continue my journey down the road applying technology to the practice of law and the justice system. To Ruth, my wife and best friend. To my daughter Dawn, whose love of animals and persistence in life is always admired. To my son Adam, whose search for adventure is inspirational. To my son Colby, whose sensitivity keeps me reminded of the important things in life.

To Alexandra Lukic for your editing, insightful comments and joyful spirit. To David C. Lieb for your thorough and timely research assistance. To Tim Murray for your formatting and editorial comments. To Adam Arkfeld for your assistance with graphics design.

SUMMARY OF CONTENTS

TABLE OF CONTENTS

Chapter 2
Creation and Storage of Electronic Information

Chapter 3
Structure and Type of Electronic Information

Chapter 4
Computer Forensics, Experts and Service Bureaus

Chapter 5
Collecting, Processing and Searching Electronic Information

Chapter 7
Court Procedural Rules and Case Law

Chapter 8
Admissibility of Electronic Evidence

Specific Type of Computer Evidence

PREFACE

My experiences as a trial attorney and computer enthusiast have convinced me of the necessity, obligation and importance of discovering electronic evidence. We have changed from a paper-based to an electronic-based information society. Now, every use of a computer (or other electronic device) creates potential electronic evidence.

As practitioners, we are being challenged to apply procedural rules and case law to the discovery and subsequent admission of electronic information. It will not be an easy transformation. Not only will we have to understand how electronic information is generated, stored and retrieved; but we will also have to understand authentication, hearsay and other evidentiary obstacles for its admission.

Disclosing electronic information will require new skills to prevent sanctions from being imposed on you and your clients. New issues will have to be addressed such as when does the duty to preserve arise, what electronic information needs to be retained and what obligation does outside counsel have to ensure that their client actually preserves the data. You will discover that even the simple act of booting up a computer destroys electronic information.

However, there is a new "mini-industry" of forensic specialists who are willing to assist in the discovery and disclosure of electronic information. Their level of expertise varies, but they can assist in your discovery efforts.

Eventually, electronic discovery standardization will occur. Just as standards and procedures were developed for the taking of videotaped depositions, so will the discovery and disclosure process for electronic discovery.

One immense benefit that will also eventually be derived from this transition is the realization that a computer's capacity to store, assemble, retrieve and manipulate information and images will provide an advantage for the attorneys who use it in their cases. It decreases the amount of time spent organizing your case and instead, allows attorneys to focus on the analysis and presentation of their cases.

Without a doubt, electronic discovery is here to stay. We will not be going back to earlier paper-based discovery – we are firmly entrenched in the future.

My hope is this book will assist, in some way, to lesson the changeover obstacles to electronic discovery. If so, then my efforts will have been rewarded.

Chapter 1

Electronic Information in Litigation

§ 1.1   TRANSITION TO ELECTRONIC INFORMATION

The ubiquitous use of computers for creating electronic information has dramatically changed discovery and admission of case information. Whether in business, government or at home, information is created in an electronic format. "According to a University of California study, 93% of all information generated during 1999 was generated in digital form, on computers. Only 7% of information originated in other media, such as paper." *In re Bristol-Myers Squibb Securities Litigation,* 205 F.R.D. 437, 440 n.2 (D.N.J. 2002). Not only is this a pervasive change, it has occurred quickly.

In a short period of time technology, computers, and the Internet have radically changed the way we create and transmit information. In 1975 the first microcomputer was introduced which replicated the power of larger computers into a small desktop. This breakthrough was the result of the miniaturization of new microprocessor technologies called semiconductors. These were followed by the introduction of the first word processing software in 1978, which enabled people to easily write and change text and graphics. Over the next 20 years, computers found their way into millions of households and businesses. One commentator noted, "[i]n 1991 companies for the first time spent more on computing and communications gear . . . than on industrial, mining, farm, and construction machines. Infotech is now as vital . . . as the air we breathe." Thomas A. Stewart, *The Information Age in Charts,* Fortune, April 4, 1994, at 75–79.

Coupled with the introduction of the Internet, which allowed information transfer in an electronic format, information created by computers could easily be transmitted worldwide in seconds. This combination laid the foundation for the societal change commonly known as The Digital Age, The Information Age, or the Multimedia Revolution.

Now people use computers in all facets of their lives. Computers are used to design graphics, produce full motion video projects, compose music, create and revise business documents, transmit business information through e-mail, make airline or hotel reservations and even participate in online chat rooms for business or pleasure. These activities are made possible by the advances made in this Digital Age.

[A]   Discovery Changes

The discovery of evidence has undergone a profound change. One author noted:

> The courtroom is the crucible of the law, where the fire of litigation tests the intellectual and political forces that inform social policy. Discovery - the process by which litigants identify and assemble their evidence - provides the fuel for the fire. Indeed, not long ago most of the evidence that the discovery process produced was, quite literally, flammable: boxes upon boxes of paper documents. No longer is this the case. Computer technology has taken us from a world of paper to a world of digital media. It has changed almost everything about our relationship with information: how we create it, how much of it we create, how it is stored, who sees it, how and when we dispose of it.

James Gibson, *A Topic Both Timely and Timeless,* 10 Rich. J.L. & Tech. 49 (2004), at http://law.richmond.edu/jolt/v10i5/article49.pdf.

Prior to the 1990s, most cases involved the discovery of paper documents. It was, and still is to a large extent, the norm to obtain printed discovery material, then copy and recopy, categorize, *Bates* number, and file. However, in today's legal world, most discovery consists of technologically-based information: it is estimated that more than 30 percent of corporate communications never appear in printed form and more than 97 percent of information is created electronically. Peter V. Lacouture, *Discovery and Use of Computer-Based Information in Litigation,* 45 R.I.B.J. (1996); John H. Jessen, *Special Issues Involving Electronic Discovery,* 9 Kan. J. L. & Pub. Pol'y 425, 442 (2000).

Now it is required to discover not only printed materials, but also electronic information that has not been reduced to hard copy. In addition to searching for paper documents in corporate archives, file cabinets, branch offices and other physical locations, to keep up with the times, one must seek information contained on hard drives, removable storage media, cell phones, and other electronic storage devices.

With the availability of these new technologies discovery materials should be obtained in an electronic "native" file format in order to discover metadata that is contained in all computer files. Metadata is electronic information that is hidden in an electronic file and may contain valuable data relevant to your case.

In addition, receiving discovery materials in electronic format will assist you later in searching for specific information using standard litigation support software. Using full text search and retrieval software and/or a database, one can search and retrieve information about a particular person or issue in thousands of e-mail in seconds.

There have been several high profile stories — such as the Microsoft antitrust lawsuit, Monica Lewinsky, and Oliver North's "deleted" e-mail — that detail the immense value of electronic information. Even though much publicity has been given to discovering the "smoking gun" from the opposing party, your client's electronic information can also support their claims or defenses. Your client's e-mail, office memos, and other communications can often support the factual basis of their case

The process of discovering, producing, and presenting electronic information is different and will initially be more difficult than handling paper documents. Instead of worrying about how many copies of a document will be made, the focus will shift to electronic information; the file format in which you wish to either receive or disclose information, processing and searching software, and ultimately, its presentation in the courtroom. As the electronic discovery process matures, the methodology of discovering and producing electronic information will become commonplace. The paper discovery model served as a basis during the analog era, the electronic model will serve as the foundation during the digital era.

For most attorneys, their practice of law has not changed nor kept pace with computer technology and discovery rules. They still discover paper documents, even though most documents today are in an electronic format, and a significant percentage of communications, such as e-mail, are never printed out. The fact-finding process is beginning to focus on uncovering electronic messaging systems, Internet usage, word processing revisions, metadata, and other electronic information relevant to your case. This electronic information discovery process is a critical change and requires attorneys to understand and educate themselves about electronic discovery in order to incorporate it into their normal case preparation process.

§ 1.2   UNIQUE CHARACTERISTICS

Digitized information takes on very different characteristics. As set out below electronic information is different and in many ways contains information of greater value than paper information. Always remember that electronic information is not just text or data, but also includes audio, video, and graphics.

[A]   Informal Nature

Because of its informal nature, electronic mail has encouraged senders to write unguarded, unwise, and often inappropriate comments. Although people would never make certain malapropos comments to another person directly or write them down in a letter, a person is more likely to use e-mail to write admissions that are subsequently used in litigation. Part of the reason for this informality is that "[y]ou've got more people who are lower down the chain of command putting things in writing than you did when it was a system of official memos. People are less discreet when they're doing emails." Phil Harris, *Electronic Discovery,* Of Counsel (April 2001).

Another reason is that businesses and other users usually do not realize that e-mail and other electronic data oftentimes create a permanent record. They treat e-mail as a verbal communication that can be simply deleted after it is read. In truth, the specific e-mail may be stored in many different locations and "undeleted" by using computer forensics. In two recent examples, business users have been reminded of the evidentiary nature of e-mails.

> Also driving the desire for electronic discovery are the much-publicized e-mails that can make a case--such as Frank Quattrone's e-mail to Credit Suisse First Boston staff following notice of a grand jury subpoena, reminding them of the company's document-destruction policy, or the e-mail from former Salomon Smith Barney telecommunications analyst Jack Grubman, linking a research report he issued with his desire to obtain the help of Citigroup, Inc.'s CEO, Stanford Weill, in obtaining admission for his daughters to an exclusive preschool.

Walter, *Plaintiffs' Law Firms No Longer As Disadvantaged,* National Law Journal, July 5, 2004, at S3.

This informal nature of comments also applies to word processing documents that have been revised by one or many authors. Within each word processing file there is what is commonly called metadata that stores the previous revisions and comments. The metadata can be opened and reviewed for unguarded comments by the authors of the documents.

[B] Metadata

Electronic data files contain what is commonly referred to as "metadata," "hidden data," or "embedded data." Metadata is additional, and often valuable, information about the electronic data, which does not appear on a printed copy of the electronic file. Computers of all types generate hidden data that is embedded in software files. Metadata is found in e-mail messages, word processing documents, spreadsheets, and other computer files. In word processing documents it may contain prior revisions, dates of revisions, authors and other information. E-mail metadata may contain who was blind copied on a message, which computer created or generated a message, and who opened and viewed a message. Computers can also contain information about Internet usage such as which websites were visited, though discovering it generally requires the assistance of a forensic specialist. Metadata may be more valuable then the more traditional forms of evidence in building or defending a case as it is often not consciously created by a user and is less vulnerable to manipulation after the fact. *See,* § § 3.7, *Metadata, Hidden, or Embedded Information* and 7.7[B][2], *Metadata.*

[C]   Preservation

Litigants have an obligation to preserve electronic evidence in lawsuits and prevent its spoliation. However, electronic information can be changed, overwritten, or obliterated by normal everyday use. The simple acts of booting up a computer, opening a file, adding new data onto a hard disk, or running a routine maintenance program on a network can alter or destroy existing data without the user's knowledge. Ken Withers, *Computer Based Discovery in Civil Litigation,* 2000 Fed. Cts. L. Rev. 2 (2000).

This is unlike the preservation of information in paper-based discovery, where the information is generally physically stable. Preservation of electronic information can be a difficult task when considering the volume and potential numerous locations where it can be found. Because of the easy destruction of electronic information, special attention should be paid to the preservation of a client's relevant information that has to be produced.

If the opposing side delays the discovery process and the data is destroyed, they may have to contend with several court decisions imposing sanctions and outright default judgment for those who fail to preserve electronic information. The courts are not reluctant to impose sanctions for failing to preserve data. In *In re Prudential Ins. Co. of Am. Sales Practices Lit.,* 169 F.R.D. 598, 615 (D.N.J. 1997), the Court fined *Prudential* $1 million for its "haphazard and uncoordinated approach to document retention" and not acting quickly to prevent the destruction of electronic data. *See,* § 7.09[D], *Duty to Preserve.*

[D]   Deletion

It is a myth that deleting a computer file, such as a word processing document, will cause it to be destroyed. When a computer user pushes the delete key to erase a document, one is not destroying the document data, but instead merely removing the pointer or computer address of the document. The data remains, until it is overwritten by new data. Depending on its usage, this could take minutes or years. In fact, since the computer data that corresponds to a specific word processing document or other electronic file may be located on different parts of a hard drive, remnants of a word processing document may be found even though other parts of it have been overwritten. However, attempting to retrieve deleted documents may be costly, time-consuming, and the results less than satisfying. *See,* § 3.5[E], *Deletion of Electronic Information.*

[E]   Storage Locations

Electronic information can be stored in any location in the world and on devices, ranging from pen drives (resembling a ballpoint pen) to mainframe computers. Since electronic information is generally disorganized, it may reside on local business storage media or on computers thousands of miles away. This is dissimilar from paper-based discovery, where file cabinets, folders, and documents are generally stored in organized and concrete locations. The portability of electronic information presents an additional issue since information can be easily transferred from one location to another. Searching and locating electronic information in a modern, distributed business-computing environment can be a challenging task. *See,* Chapter 2, *Creation and Storage of Electronic Information.*

[F]   Disorganized

Electronic information is disorganized. It is the exception for electronic information to be accurately stored in directories, subdirectories, and folders. Generally, since computer files can be found by searching for specific words or other data, users store electronic information in various unrelated computer systems or directories. Many organizations do not have an electronic information custodian, and therefore information can be lost or misplaced. Even in small organizations, vast amounts of information generated over years of business can result in an inconsistent and chaotic filing system.

For example, in *McPeek v. Ashcroft,* 212 F.R.D. 33, 35 (D.D.C. 2003) the magistrate recognized the disorganization of electronic data on backup tapes and stated:

> [t]he frustration of electronic discovery as it relates to backup tapes is that backup tapes collect information indiscriminately, regardless of topic. One, therefore, cannot reasonably predict that information is likely to be on a particular tape. This is unlike the more traditional type of discovery in which one can predict that certain information would be in a particular folder because the folders in a particular file drawer are arranged alphabetically by subject matter or by author.

However, performing general searches on computer directories can often generate significant information instantaneously relevant to the claims or defenses of a case. Be aware that the producing party may not make the effort to locate disorganized electronic information and will reply that it was never created, does not exist any longer, or cannot be found. This assertion can be risky for the producing party since information previously thought not to be in existence may be uncovered in later depositions of employees or cross-referenced in paper or other electronic documents.

[G]   Volume

The growth of new electronic information that may have some relevance to litigation is staggering. Through normal routine use and the immense storage capabilities of today's computers, there are millions of new electronic items created on a daily basis. It is:

> estimate[d] that new stored information grew about 30% a year between 1999 and 2002. . . . Print, film, magnetic, and optical storage media produced about 5 exabytes of new information in 2002. Ninety-two percent of the new information was stored on magnetic media, mostly in hard disks. How big is five exabytes? If digitized with full formatting, the seventeen million books in the Library of Congress contain about 136 terabytes of information; five exabytes of information is equivalent in size to the information contained in 37,000 new libraries the size of the Library of Congress book collections.

Peter Lyman & Hal R. Varian, *How Much Information*, University of California at Berkeley, School of Information Management and Systems (Oct. 27, 2003) available at http://www.sims.berkeley.edu/how-much-info-2003.

At first blush, it may seem that the amount of electronic information in your case is controllable and finite. This is simply not correct. For example, the use of e-mail geometrically increases the amount of information available in your case. The number of e-mail messages for an employee may number between 30 and 60 a day. Assuming that you have 10 employees, between 300 and 600 e-mail messages may be received daily. This can eventually lead to anywhere from 60,000 to 120,000 messages per year (assuming 200 workdays). If you add to this number, word processing documents, spreadsheets and other computer files, electronic information can grow to unprecedented proportions.

With more employees, the numbers increase rapidly. A company of 100,000 employees generates 22 million e-mail messages per week alone. John H. Jessen, *Special Issues Involving Electronic Discovery,* 9 Kan. J.L. & Pub. Pol'y. 425, 427-428 (2000).

Today, electronic information is copied, recopied, forwarded, backed up, archived, and inadvertently duplicated in other directories and computer locations on storage media that can hold a vast amount of information. "On a single, ten square inch hard drive, more information can be stored than would fit on an entire floor of a building." Kimberly D. Richard, *Electronic Evidence: To Produce or Not to Produce, That is the Question,* 21 Whittier L. Rev. 463 (1999); Grace V. Bacon, *Fundamentals of Electronic Discovery,* 47 Boston Law Journal 18 (2003).

The large volume of electronic information raises serious challenges to the cost of locating, reviewing for privileges, and producing information to the requesting party. This is unlike paper-based discovery where the physical nature of paper, folders, and file cabinets limits the amount of information stored. *See,* § 3.5[A], *Volume & Obsolescence.*

[H]   Redundancy – Archived and Backup Copies

Since computer storage is inexpensive and easy, electronic information is constantly and consistently being backed up or archived to ensure recovery in the event of loss of data or a disaster. It is commonplace to backup important computer information on a daily, weekly, monthly, or other periodic basis. In anticipation of potential hardware and user failures, backup copies can be permanent or semipermanent. These backup files may contain previously deleted e-mail and early drafts of documents, strategic plans and other information. In addition, when e-mail or a document is mailed to several people the document may be saved repeatedly. For this reason, there may be several duplicates of e-mail or other types of electronic information. *See,* § 3.5[C], *Replication - Archived and Backup Copies.*

[I]   Searching Electronic Information – Costs

Computer-based electronic information is easier to search and provides a lower cost for retrieving and managing case information than paper documents. One of the critical features that distinguish electronic information from paper is that information contained in an electronic format can be searched for particular words, phrases, concepts and dates, and the results are retrieved instantaneously. This is similar to searches in case law-based systems such as Westlaw or LEXIS. In *Zubulake v. UBS Warburg LLC,* 217 F.R.D. 309, 318 n.50 (S.D.N.Y. 2003), the court noted that "[b]y comparison [to the time it would take to search through 100,000 pages of paper], the average office computer could search all of the documents for specific words or combination[s] of words in a minute, perhaps less."

There has already been substantial development of "electronic discovery" software to process electronic information into databases, full text, and images. This development will continue and provide cost-effective and efficient methods of searching and controlling electronic information.

Information in conventional discovery is generally produced in a paper format, even though a computer created the information in an electronic format. Many firms, once they receive the paper, try to convert it into an electronic format by using optical character recognition software, abstracting and/or scanning an image of the paper document.

However, it can be quite expensive to scan, abstract and OCR paper documents. It is more cost-efficient to obtain the same discovery material in an electronic format, since electronic information does not have to be converted from paper and can be instantly searched.

[J]   Encryption

Electronic information can be encrypted, thus precluding access to its content. In conventional paper-based discovery, encryption is not a problem. Information on a document or a manual is viewable and readable without the necessity of decrypting the information.

Many business organizations set up security for their electronic information by encrypting their information. If encrypted, it is necessary to obtain the passwords to access the information. Encrypted word-processing documents, spreadsheets, and e-mail can be viewed once the encryption code or key is used to unlock the file. Yet it is not always that easy. Encryption software is available that encrypts e-mail, and then the encryption code is automatically destroyed after a set amount of time. If the code is unavailable, it may be impossible to view the contents of the encrypted material. *See,* § 3.5[H], *Computer Security Protocols.*

[K]   Quality

Electronic information can be reproduced as many times as necessary without any degradation in quality. Obviously, this is not the case with paper-based discovery. Often second, third or fourth-generation copies of paper are often illegible.

[L]   Alterations

Alterations to electronic documents are difficult to detect, if not impossible. Numeric and textual data can be altered without a trace. In addition, computer files containing audio, video, or photographs can be altered in ways that are difficult to discover. *See,* § 3.5[G], *Alteration of Electronic Information.*

§ 1.3   IMPORTANCE OF UNDERSTANDING ELECTRONIC DISCOVERY

The only way to service your client's legal needs and to maintain a competitive edge is to understand computer technology and information management systems. There are several reasons why it is necessary for you to understand the electronic discovery process.

[A]   Discovering Electronic Information

Computers, and the various media on which computer generated information is stored, provide a unique opportunity to view an individual or company's correspondence, strategies, business plans and other data.

However, in order to conduct electronic discovery of this valuable data, one will need to understand how electronic information is generated, stored and where it might be located. It will be necessary to understand the different features and characteristics of electronic information such as e-mail and word processing documents. For example, if you are involved in a case with an Internet component, then electronic information found in listservs, newsgroups or chat rooms might be important. Also, you will need to know whether the data contains metadata that may be useful to your case.

Discovery of electronic information will become a central focus since case information is increasingly in an electronic format, and, more significantly, much electronic information is no longer printed to paper. "Discovery of electronically stored data is essential because litigants would not find much of this information through traditional paper discovery processes. . . . stating that 90% of all businesses with over 1000 employees rely on e-mail, but individuals never print 20 to 30% of electronically stored data." Corinne L. Giacobbe, *Allocating Discovery Costs in The Computer Age: Deciding Who Should Bear the Costs of Discovery of Electronically Stored Data,* 57 Wash. & Lee L. Rev. 257 (2000).

Most courts recognize and support the discovery of electronic information realizing that it is simply keeping pace with changes in business and technological advances.

- "The law is clear that data in computerized form is discoverable even if paper 'hard copies' of the information have been produced. . . . [T]oday it is black letter law that computerized data is discoverable if relevant." *Anti-Monopoly, Inc. v. Hasbro, Inc.,* 1995 WL 649934 (S.D.N.Y. Nov. 3, 1995); *see also, McPeek v. Ashcroft,* 202 F.R.D. 31 (D.D.C. 2001); *Linnen v. A.H. Robins Co.,* 1999 WL 462015 (Mass. Super. Jun. 16, 1999); *Crown Life Ins. Co. v. Craig,* 995 F.2d. 1376 (7th Cir. 1993).

- "It would be a dangerous development in the law if new techniques for easing the use of information became a hindrance to discovery or disclosure in litigation. The use of excessive technical distinctions is inconsistent with the guiding principle that information which is stored, used, or transmitted in new forms should be available through discovery with the same openness as traditional forms." *Daewoo Electronics Co. v. United States,* 650 F. Supp. 1003, 1006 (Ct.Int'l Trade 1986).

- "This court need not dwell on the benefits computers provide over traditional forms of record keeping. The revolution over the last fifteen years speaks for itself. From the largest corporations to the smallest families, people are using computers to cut costs, improve production, enhance communication, store countless data and improve capabilities in every aspect of human and technological development. Computers have become so commonplace that most court battles now involve discovery of some type of computer-stored information." *Bills v. Kennecott Corp.,* 108 F.R.D. 459, 462 (D. Utah 1985).

- "Rules 26(b) and 34 of the Federal Rules of Civil Procedure instruct that computer-stored information is discoverable under the same rules that pertain to tangible, written materials." *In re Brand Name Prescription Drugs Antitrust Litigation,* No. CIV.94-897, 1995 WL 360526, at *1 (N.D. Ill. Jun. 15, 1995).

• FED. R. CIV. P. 26(a)(1)(B) requires that a party provide to other parties "a copy of, or a description by category and location of, all *documents, data compilations,* and tangible things in the possession, custody, or control of the party and that the disclosing party may use to support its claims or defenses, unless solely for impeachment." (emphasis added). Documents include all forms of computer data. *See,* § 7.7[B], *"Document"* - *Definition.*

In essence, lawyers need to integrate the discovery of electronic information into the litigation process in the same way as traditional paper discovery.

[B]   Producing Electronic Information

Not only will you be discovering electronic information, you can be assured that you will receive production requests seeking electronic information from your clients. Once the requests are received, you will need to provide proactive advice to your client as to the preservation and disclosure of electronic information. Preservation of data will need to be done in a timely, cost-effective, and defensible manner. In addition, clients will need to know what affects, if any, it will have on their continuing business operations.

Under conventional paper-based discovery, attorneys responsible for producing documents would visit their client's business and walk through their building to determine relevance in response to a production request. Often, the attorney would inspect file cabinets, record centers, employee files, off-site storage areas, and any other place where paper documents would be kept. Generally, these record storage areas would contain correspondence files, drawings, invoices, accounting records and other business documents that may be material to the case. In the past, one could count on this type of inspection to locate all the documents that were relevant to the discovery requests. This is no longer the case.

Now the production process of electronic information will require you to understand how computers generate and store electronic information as well as how information technologies are used in your client's personal and business life. Some of the legal issues will involve the scope of disclosure, form of production, privilege, and alleged spoliation of data.

Location and production of e-mail and other electronic information are no longer reserved for the "exceptional" case. As one Court recently noted, "[a]t some point, a party and/or its attorneys must be held responsible for knowing what documents are discoverable and where to find them, since certainly neither the party's opponent nor the Court can answer those questions." *Danis v. USN Communications, Inc.,* No. CIV.98-7482, 2000 WL 1694325, at *49 (N.D. Ill. Oct. 20, 2000). In *Danis,* the Court found that once the duty to preserve arises that this duty covers discoverable information that a party "knows or reasonably should know" may be relevant to the pending or impending litigation. *Id*. at 32.

Now when you visit your client's business you will no longer walk through their building but instead will walk through their information infrastructure and communication system. You will need to know the technical terms to enable you to communicate effectively with those who manage the data and communication systems. You will discover that many businesses have very few policies and procedures regarding the creation, storage, and retention of electronic information.

In order to effectively discuss discovery requests and document retention policies with your clients, you will need to be able to discuss document management systems, e-mail systems, Internet usage, voice answering services, and any other electronic media or storage devices that may contain electronic information relevant to the case. It is not expected that you become a computer expert, but it is mandatory that you have a thorough working knowledge of how electronic information is created and stored in your client's technology systems, since production of information and costs will often depend on your knowledge of these systems.

[C]   Costs

There can be astounding costs associated with production of electronic information because of the volume. As previously stated, the number of e-mail can easily run into the tens of thousands, even for a small business organization.

Understanding what data is available in your client's system may enable you to favorably negotiate compliance with the requesting party and significantly lower the cost for your client.

If you are discovering electronic information, the costs of searching electronic data can be substantially reduced. Instead of manually searching paper documents, a computer can immediately search and locate vital information relevant to your case.

[D]   Sanctions for Failure to Disclose

The failure to investigate your client's information management system can lead to potentially catastrophic results. There are many cases where the courts have not hesitated to impose sanctions, default judgment or spoliation instructions for failure of a party to preserve electronic information or to disclose electronic information in their possession. *See,* § 7.9, *Sanctions*. Failure to investigate a client's information system can be especially challenging when your client has in his possession arcane and obsolete data. Investigating clients' information systems goes beyond simply asking or entrusting them to produce relevant electronic information in the case, but requires proactive diligence in ensuring all information has been disclosed. *See,* § 7.9[F], *Affirmative Continual Obligation to Preserve and Disclose.*

[E]   Providing Advice on Technology Issues

Understanding your client's technology information system will provide you the ability to advise your clients on legal technology matters. For example, you may be called upon to render legal advice on employees who attempt to damage or destroy computer-related information. This may require you to understand what harm computer viruses can do as well as other techniques for intentionally destroying electronic information.

You may also be asked to provide legal advice and obtain computer evidence from former employees who have moved to a competitor and stolen trade secrets from your clients. In such a case, it may be necessary to undelete computer files on the former employee's computers. You may also need to subpoena e-mail storage records from Internet service providers to support your client's case. These types of issues will become routine in your daily legal practice as the transition to electronic information continues.

You will also need to keep abreast of changing information technologies, so that you can anticipate the impact of such changes on your client's business. Your client may be materially affected from a financial and business interruption perspective if you fail to provide timely and accurate advice.

[F]   Client's Document Retention Policies

In addition, it is necessary to provide proactive technology advice to your client as you advise them of preventive measures in running their business.

Retention of electronic information in any organization will have a significant effect in any future litigation. For example, if your client is accused of anticompetitive actions then stored e-mail communications may become a focal point of discovery requests. In such a case, if your client has preserved e-mail for the past ten years, then the e-mail, if relevant, may mandate review and disclosure. If the client had successfully implemented a document retention policy of preserving e-mail for only a certain amount of time, then the cost of locating, reviewing and disclosing such e-mail would be substantially less. *See,* §§ 6.2[D], *Document Retention Policy Before Litigation*, 7.9[D], *Duty to Preserve and* 7.09[H], *Document Retention Policy - Prior to Litigation.*

[G]   Leverage

Lawyers who have taken the time to understand electronic discovery realize that even the threat of electronic discovery against an uneducated and unprepared opposing party provides a powerful negotiating tool. "Instead of taking the time to learn about technology and electronic discovery, many lawyers have chosen not only to ignore requesting electronic information but also have been intimidated by the thought of opposing counsel obtaining such information from their clients. The simple threat of forcing a corporation to review thousands of files or backup tapes has become . . . 'an incredible bargaining chip' [that] has leveraged countless settlements in the last decade." Bruce Rubenstein, *Somebody Destroyed the Evidence: Electronic Discovery Costs are Leveraging Settlements: Corporate Law Department Stung by Mishandling E-Mail,* Corp. Legal Times, Sept. 1997, at 1.

One court noted:

> If the likelihood of finding something was the only criterion, there is a risk that someone will have to spend hundreds of thousands of dollars to produce a single e-mail. That is an awfully expensive needle to justify searching a haystack. It must be recalled that ordering the producing party to restore backup tapes upon a showing of likelihood that they will contain relevant information in every case gives the plaintiff a gigantic club with which to beat his opponent into settlement. No corporate president in her right mind would fail to settle a lawsuit for $100,000 if the restoration of backup tapes would cost $300,000. While that scenario might warm the cockles of certain lawyers' hearts, no one would accuse it of being just.

McPeek v. Ashcroft, 202 F.R.D. 31, 34 (D.D.C. 2001).

During discovery, an attorney may find out that their client has error-prone systems and procedures in place for document (including e-mail) retention and management. These shortcomings, though avoidable, may increase the cost of production to a point where settlement is the only option. *See generally,* Steven C. Bennett & Thomas M. Niccum, *Two Views from the Data Mountain,* 36 Creighton L. Rev. 607 (2003); Daniel B. Garrie et al, *Electronic Discovery and the Challenge Posed by the Sarbanes-Oxley Act,* 2005 UCLA J. L. & Tech. 2 ("'[e]-discovery blackmail' describes a process by which a litigant capitalizes on e-discovery cost disparities by forcing another litigant to settle a claim that the settling litigant would otherwise defend if not for the enormous costs of e-discovery.").

[H]   Organize, Search and Analyze Case Information

Another important reason for understanding electronic information is that it will provide you with a significant advantage in controlling and managing case information using standard litigation support software. Whether it is your client's or the opposing party's data, it will permit you to organize, search and analyze electronic information quickly and efficiently. Litigation support software such as searchable databases, full text, and outliners provide control tools for electronic information that can substantially reduce the cost and time necessary to locate and manage vital case information. Now instead of obtaining paper documents from the opposing party and then scanning, coding and performing optical character recognition on paper documents, one would merely obtain electronic information from opposing counsel and import it directly into the litigation support software as a searchable database or full text. Instead of a legion of attorneys and legal assistants working on a case, a smaller technology-oriented staff could effectively manage case information by using litigation support tools. *See, § 5.2, Value of Collecting Information in an Electronic Format.*

[I]   Evidentiary Considerations

In general, the Federal Rules of Evidence apply to computerized data as they do to other types of evidence. However, the questions and answers to lay a proper foundation for the admission of electronic information will be different. You will continue to ask questions as to authentication, reliability, and trustworthiness and whether it is the original document. Though these admissibility issues may be addressed in pretrial stipulations or agreements, if they are challenged, it will be necessary to understand and provide the court with the necessary foundational evidence for admission of electronic data.

In addition, it may be necessary to educate the court, by experts and pleadings, about the factual and legal computer issues that may be relevant in your case. For example, technology oriented testimony or other evidence must support a burdensome objection to a discovery request for computer data. Likewise, appropriate expert or other evidence must be presented to oppose any such objections. *See,* Chapter 4, *Computer Forensics, Experts and Service Bureaus.*

§ 1.4   EVIDENTIARY VALUE OF ELECTRONIC EVIDENCE

Documentary evidence has always been compelling evidence in a criminal or civil case. Important facts and communications are often contained in documentary evidence. Paper documents can provide a wealth of information in any case, whether they are used in civil cases involving wrongful employment dismissals, sexual or racial discrimination, or in criminal matters involving drug transactions or money laundering. This paper evidence has been the norm for hundreds of years, and to some extent, will continue. However, a new source of evidence (electronic information) will become as important, if not more important, and very persuasive to the factfinder for several additional reasons. *See,* Chapter 8, *Admissibility of Electronic Evidence.*

[A]   Informal Nature of Evidence

Electronic information may expose the innermost thoughts, schemes and motives of individuals, and therefore are usually informal in composition. For example, individuals often treat the writing of e-mail similar to a telephone conversation, assuming that the e-mail will disappear once the recipient has read the message. The reason for this notion is that e-mail is easy to create and send. However, people's perception of the impermanence of email is hugely incorrect. Once e-mail is created, it is virtually impossible to delete all of the stored and archived copies. This may allow you to reconstruct the history and pattern of changes to business documents and the strategies and motives behind an individual or organization's actions. In actuality, electronic information often completes the gaps in the fact chronology of a case.

[B]   Growth and Type of Evidence

The type and amount of electronic evidence that is being created, distributed, stored and destroyed on a daily basis in the United States and throughout the world is unbelievable. There are many different types of computer evidence being created. These include text, graphics, photographs, television programs, movies, x-rays, CDs, CAT scans, e-mail, spreadsheets, etc. Other types of computer evidence include business accounting records, stock trades, budgets, check registers, telephone records, bank records, tickets, and bills of lading. They are being created, saved, edited, and distributed in an electronic format. Nearly every event in our personal and financial life is being saved electronically. Much of this information may be relevant in a lawsuit and subject to civil discovery.

[C]   Metadata – Hidden Evidence

Modern technology has created new types of computer evidence called metadata that previously did not exist. Such hidden data is generally not viewable on a printout. Instead, this metadata is contained in the electronic file of a word processing document, e-mail, spreadsheet, and other electronic information formats. For example, metadata may provide information about prior document versions, authors of documents, date of revisions, date when a document was last accessed, on which computer and other possible relevant information.

The computer user is usually not aware that metadata is being created, as the computer data is being created and revised. For example, we see attorneys sending settlement documents and other case information to opposing counsel unaware that their previous comments, revisions and other information are being sent along with the final word processing document. Many times this data is not accessible to the average computer user making it difficult to erase or delete before sending. As a result, this metadata in e-mail, word processing documents, and other electronic files can become a valuable source of evidence. *See,* §§ 3.7, *Metadata, Hidden, or Embedded Information* and 7.7[B][2], *Metadata.*

[D]   Case Examples

Electronic data discovery is becoming more commonplace and often reveals an incriminating trail by the participants. There have been several recent (and not so recent) litigation and high profile matters that have turned on electronic evidence discovered by the opposing party. These cases make the point that electronic discovery applies to all cases involved in litigation. *Zubulake v. UBS Warburg, L.L.C.,* 217 F.R.D. 309, 317 (S.D.N.Y. 2003) (U.S. District Judge Shira Scheindlin opined that "virtually all cases" involve the discovery of electronic data.).

The recent plethora of electronic discovery cases suggests that she is right. Whether it is a high-profile case such as the Microsoft antitrust trial, investigation of President Clinton, police brutality involving Rodney King or the attempted deletion of files by Oliver North, participants have not learned from others' experiences. Even with these publicly embarrassing examples, e-mail and other electronic information is still being generated containing information that can be either personally damaging or harmful to a business.

[1]   Antitrust - Microsoft

In the government's high profile antitrust case against Microsoft, the significant impact of electronic information was present throughout the trial. In this case, the government collected e-mail and other electronic information from Microsoft. Commentators noted that e-mail undermined the credibility of Microsoft's witnesses and provided the basis for the antitrust ruling.

> Indeed, the proliferation of records was perhaps nowhere more startlingly and ironically seen than in *United States v. Microsoft*, where the government collected in discovery more than three million documents, many of them e-mails, to use against the software giant. Ken Auletta, *World War 3.0: Microsoft and Its Enemies* 55, 389 (2001). Though Microsoft argued that the government's case "relie[d] heavily on snippets of Microsoft e-mail messages that are taken out of context," id. at 67, these e-mails provided support for the district court's liability findings, upheld on appeal, because "[e]ven in context, to read many of Microsoft's internal e-mails is to be struck by their arrogance." *Id.* at 73. These e-mails became important ingredients in spicing up the government's proofs of anticompetitive behavior, intent, and lack of credibility of Microsoft's witnesses. *Id. See also id.* at 209 (quoting trial judge as stating, "Truth be told, a lot of Microsoft's witnesses were not credible. They were testifying in the teeth of e-mails that said something else. . . .").

James P. Flynn & Sheldon M. Finkelstein, *A PRIMER ON E-VIDE-N.C.E.,* 2 Litigation 34, 35 (Winter 2002).

[2]   Presidential Indiscretion - Monica Lewinsky

One case that should be viewed as a constant reminder of the ineffectiveness of deleting e-mail and other electronic information is the investigation by Ken Starr of President Clinton and Monica Lewinsky's affair. In the case Monica Lewinsky had deleted (what she thought were permanently erased) e-mail to her friends regarding the President. One of the e-mails stated: "The Big Creep didn't even try to call me on V-day (Valentine's Day)." Another read: "I want to hug him so bad right now I could cry." It was also computer evidence that helped identify the now infamous 'Blue Dress' in the Clinton impeachment hearings. June Kronholz & Rebecca Quick, *The Lewinsky Story Is a Tale Spun Out of Cyberspace: And Therein Lies a Drawback of E-Mail: It's Difficult to Ever Really Delete It,* The Wall St. J., Sept. 22, 1998, at A1.

[3]   Police Brutality - Rodney King

E-mail admissions are not limited to business litigation. This was clearly shown in the e-mail admission by police officer Laurence Powell minutes after assaulting Rodney King where he stated: "Oops, I haven't beaten anyone this bad in a long time." M.A. Stapleton, *Discovery 'Paper Chase' Transforming Bit by Byte as Attorneys Target Computer Data,* Chi. Daily L. Bull, Nov. 25, 1994, at 1; Wendy J. Rose, *The Revolution of Electronic Mail,* The Legal Intelligencer, Jan. 21, 1997, at 9.

[4]   Deleted Files Restored - Oliver North

One of the first episodes of e-mail supposedly deleted was the high-profile case of Oliver North. In the mid-1980s, the Tower Commission used back-up files of Colonel Oliver North's deleted e-mail to chronicle the Iran-Contra scandal. North thought he had deleted electronic messages regarding his assistance in providing arms to Nicaraguan rebels, but it turned out that he had neglected to eliminate the back-up copies. Seven hundred and fifty-eight (758) e-mail messages were sent, involving him in the Iran-Contra affair, and every one of them was recovered. Frank Conley, *Service with a Smiley: The Effect of E-Mail and Other Electronic Communications on Service of Process,* 11 Temp. Int'l. & Comp. L.J. 407 (1997); Geanne Rosenberg, *Electronic Discovery Proves an Effective Legal Weapon,* N.Y. Times, Mar. 31, 1997, at D5.

[5]   Sexual Harassment and Retaliation

One of the most fertile areas for incriminating e-mail communications involves employment cases such as sexual harassment or retaliation. In one of the leading electronic discovery cases in the country, the court, in a wrongful discrimination case, found that the defendants had willfully failed to preserve relevant e-mail archived on the computers of the defendant's human resource personnel. The Court granted the plaintiff's motion for sanctions including an adverse inference instruction and monetary sanctions. *Zubulake v. UBS Warburg LLC,* No. CIV.02-1243, 2004 WL 1620866 (S.D. N.Y. July 20, 2004). Eventually, the case went before a jury who awarded the plaintiff 29 million dollars in damages.

In another case, this time involving sexual harassment, the mirror image of a hard drive was made and files were undeleted to establish that the ex-boss had a history of propositioning women under his supervision. This discovery came after the employee was fired from her job for alleged poor performance. Chris *Santella, Technolawyer.Com: The Growing Importance of Computer Forensics,* Lawyer's PC (April 1, 2002).

In a retaliation case, the defendant unsuccessfully moved to exclude from evidence certain e-mail messages generated by a Microsoft employee, which contained inappropriate sexual and gender-related comments. *Strauss v. Microsoft Corp.,* No. CIV.91-5928, 1995 WL 326492 (S.D.N.Y. Jun. 1, 1995).

[6]   Race Discrimination

E-mail has also played a substantial role in race discrimination lawsuits. The Washington Post reported,

> In the past four months, three major U.S. corporations - R.R. Donnelley & Sons Co., Morgan Stanley & Co. and Citicorp's Citibank N.A. - have been sued by black employees alleging discrimination as a result of messages sent via e-mail. Lawyers and technology experts say they believe the suits are the beginning of a wave of litigation in which employees produce e-mail evidence of sex, race or age discrimination. Also, lawyers searching for ways to prove or disprove discrimination routinely are asking companies to retrieve e-mail from their computer systems.

Michelle Singletary, *E-Mail Humor: Punch Lines Can Carry Price Jokes Open Employers to Discrimination Suits,* Washington Post, Mar. 18, 1997, at A1.

[7]   Securities Fraud

In a recent 1.4 billion dollar securities fraud case that "shook the china in boardrooms," the Court granted the plaintiff's motion for adverse inference due to e-mail destruction and failure to comply with the judge's discovery order. Because of deleted e-mail and failure to disclose backup tapes, the Court permitted the plaintiff to argue an adverse inference regarding the concealment of evidence and shifted the burden of proof to the defendant as to certain elements of the cause of action. *Coleman (Parent) Holdings, Inc. v. Morgan Stanley & Co., Inc.,* 2005 WL 67071 (Fla. Cir. Ct. Mar. 1, 2005).

In a securities fraud suit concerning Siemens' acquisition of an ARCO subsidiary, Siemens discovered e-mail messages in the subsidiary's computer system. These e-mails demonstrated that while ARCO was concerned about serious flaws in its subsidiary's products, it neglected to disclose those concerns to Siemens in due diligence. *Siemens Solar Industries v. Atlantic Richfield Co.,* No. CIV.93-1126, 1994 WL 86368, at *2 (S.D.N.Y. Mar. 16, 1994).

[8]   Trademarks and Trade Secrets

Electronic document discovery is also making a difference in cases involving the theft of corporate trade secrets. In one case, a court-appointed forensic expert determined that one of the parties had randomly inserted data in customer and address fields in an attempt to prevent a competitor from approaching customers to determine whether they had actually made the purchases reflected in the records. *D. Cerruti 1881 S.A. v. Cerruti, Inc.,* 169 F.R.D. 573 (S.D.N.Y. 1996).

In *Dodge, Warren & Peters Ins. Services, Inc. v. Riley,* 105 Cal. App. 4th 1414, 130 Cal. Rptr. 2d 385 (4th Dist. 2003) the Court granted the employer's request for a preliminary injunction prohibiting employees from destroying electronic evidence in a misappropriation of trade secrets case. In addition to photocopying thousands of documents, employees copied many of the employer's computer files onto discs and took them offsite for later use at a new agency.

[9]   Domestic Relations

In a matrimonial action, the wife took a laptop computer that was owned by her husband's employer and gave it to her attorney. The plaintiff argued that the laptop was used for business as well as for personal family financial matters. The Court held that the computer memory is similar to a file cabinet. Since the wife could have access to contents of a file cabinet left in the marital residence, she should have access to the computer contents. The Court ordered that the parties' computer experts should meet at a mutually agreeable time for downloading memory files of the computer. *Byrne v. Byrne,* 168 Misc. 2d 321, 650 N.Y.S.2d 499 (1996).

[10]   Bankruptcy Suit

In a bankruptcy case, the debtor sought protection under Chapter 7 in an attempt to discharge a $4 million defamation judgment. The debtor's notebook computer had been seized pursuant to a writ of execution levied on the debtor's assets to satisfy the $4 million judgment. The Court denied relief from bankruptcy partly because of letters found on the debtor's personal computer that substantiated a $500 accounts receivable fraud on the bankruptcy court. *In re Trost,* 164 B.R. 740 (W.D. Mich. 1994).

§ 1.5   ETHICAL OBLIGATIONS

[A]   Generally

The discovery and production of electronic information have significant ethical and legal implications for the practitioner. If lawyers ignore case information available in electronic form, they risk (1) losing an otherwise winnable case; (2) imposition of sanctions; (3) disciplinary action and/or (4) malpractice claims. Pooley & Shaw, *What's There: Technical and Legal Aspects of Discovery,* 4 Tex. Intell. Prop. L.J. 57, 60 (1995). *See also,* § 7.2[B], *FED. R. CIV. P. 11* (discussing sanctions for failure to make a reasonable inquiry before filing a lawsuit.). Of important concern is that most law firms and lawyers today are not competent to handle the discovery and production of electronic information. Michael A. Clark, *EDD Supplier Landscape, Electronic Discovery in Litigation Series,* October 28, 2004. (When suppliers were asked "[w]hat percentage of AmLaw 200 firms has the requisite knowledge and experience to professionally handle a complex EDD matter?" There was a broad consensus that the answer was not more than 25%).

Several questions must be addressed to determine our ethical obligations regarding electronic data in litigation.

- As technology changes and influences the practice of law, how does it affect the scope of liability for our actions?

- Do we have an obligation to discover electronic information within the possession of the opposing party?

- Do we have an obligation to counsel our clients as to their present-day electronic information retention policies and preservation obligations?

- Do we have an obligation to search our client's computer systems for production of discoverable electronic information?

- What are our obligations when we inadvertently or intentionally receive electronic evidence, including metadata, from the opposing party or another source that is privileged?

Ethical Principles

There are several principles set forth in ethic rules that effect a practitioner's handling of electronic data. The following are derived from the American Bar Association's *Model Rule of Professional Conduct.* However, most states have professional responsibility rules requiring attorneys to perform legal services with competence, diligence, faithfulness, good judgment and not to obstruct access, destroy or conceal paper or electronic information having potential evidentiary value.

- *ABA Model Rule of Professional Conduct* 1.1 provides that "A lawyer shall provide competent representation to a client. Competent representation requires the legal knowledge, skill, thoroughness and preparation reasonably necessary for the representation."

- *ABA Model Rule of Professional Conduct* 1.3 provides that "A lawyer shall act with reasonable diligence and promptness in representing a client."

- *ABA Model Rule of Professional Conduct* 1.6 provides that "(a) A lawyer shall not reveal information relating to the representation of a client unless the client gives informed consent . . ."

- *ABA Model Rule of Professional Conduct* 3.4(a) provides that "a lawyer shall not unlawfully obstruct another party's access to evidence or unlawfully alter, destroy or conceal a document or other material having potential evidentiary value [and] . . . shall not counsel or assist another person to do any such act. . . ."

- *ABA Model Rule of Professional Conduct* 8.4(c)-(d) proscribes "dishonesty, fraud, deceit, or misrepresentation [or] conduct that is prejudicial to the administration of justice."

Discovery of Electronic Information

Attorneys have an obligation to understand how to ask the proper questions to uncover relevant and critical electronic evidence, such as e-mail and word processing documents. Prudent counsel seeking discovery should immediately send a "duty to preserve" letter to the opposing party specifically setting forth that certain electronic data, which might otherwise be deleted in the ordinary course of business, be preserved. *See,* Chapter 6, *Discovery and Production Process.*

Preservation of Electronic Information

Almost all of your clients, individuals and businesses, maintain their records and communications on computers. It is their primary method of preserving communications, financial data, and other records. Because of the huge volume of e-mails and other electronic data, most clients have informal or formal policies for deleting and destroying electronic records. These policies can cause ethical problems when it is reasonably anticipated that litigation is imminent and data is destroyed. It is a lawyer's ethical obligation to make sure that all relevant evidence is disclosed and a client preserves all responsive electronic records involved in the litigation.

Under the Federal Rules of Civil Procedure, electronic data is discoverable and needs to be preserved. *Anti-Monopoly, Inc. v. Hasbro, Inc.*, 1995 WL 649934 (S.D.N.Y. Nov. 3, 1995) ("Today it is black letter law that computerized data is discoverable if relevant."); *Zubulake v. UBS Warburg, LLC*, 220 F.R.D. 212, 217 (S.D.N.Y. 2003) ("The duty to preserve attached at the time that litigation was reasonably anticipated."); *Danis v. USN Communications*, No. CIV.98-7482, 2000 WL 1694325 (N.D. Ill. Oct. 20, 2000) (The Court found that a party to pending litigation has a duty to preserve and produce discoverable evidence that a party knows or reasonably should know may be relevant to the pending or impending litigation.).

However, clients generally do not understand this obligation. "[I]n a 2000 American Bar Association membership survey, 83 percent of the respondents said that their corporate clients had no established protocol to deal with discovery requests for electronic data." Ashby Jones, *"What a Mess!, For Corporations, Pileup of Electronic Data Could Be Trouble Waiting to Happen,"* National Law J. (Dec. 2, 2002) at C6. "This problem is compounded by the fact that many in-house lawyers 'are very uncomfortable' with the technical aspects of document management." *Id.* at C7.

Attorneys have an ethical duty to comply with discovery obligations. Upon notice of "reasonably anticipated litigation" you need to confer with your client to identify and preserve responsive data. All destruction of responsive data should cease. Be aware that many document retention policies automatically destroy electronic data and need to be put on hold until responsive data can be identified and segregated. It is strongly suggested that a "certification" of the scope and extent of your search for electronic records is prepared to avoid any allegations of improper concealment of responsive electronic information. *See,* Chapter 6, *Discovery and Production Process* and § 7.09[D], *Duty to Preserve*.

The courts expect counsel to ensure their clients comply with discovery requests and are less sympathetic to attorneys who fail to fulfill their discovery obligations. For example in *Danis v. USN Communications, Inc.*, No. CIV.98-7482, 2000 WL 1694325, at *1 (N.D. Ill. Oct. 20, 2000) the Court stated:

> The duty of disclosure finds expression not only in the rules of discovery, but also in this Court's Rules of Professional Conduct, which prohibit an attorney from 'suppress[ing] any evidence that the lawyer or client has a legal obligation to reveal or produce,' *Rules for the Northern District of Illinois,* LR 83.53.3(a)(13), or from 'unlawfully obstructing another party's access to evidence . . . *Id.* LR 83.53.4(1). This duty of disclosure would be a dead letter if a party could avoid the duty by the simple expedient of failing to preserve documents that it does not wish to produce. Therefore, fundamental to the duty of production of information is the threshold duty to preserve documents and

other information that may be relevant in a case. That duty, too, finds expression in this Court's Rules of Professional Conduct. *See Rules for the Northern District of Illinois,* LR 83.53.4(1) (a lawyer shall not unlawfully alter, destroy, or conceal a document or other material having potential evidentiary value).

In another case, *Metropolitan Opera Ass'n., Inc. v. Local 100,* 212 F.R.D. 178, 181, 222-223, 231 (S.D.N.Y. 2003), *adhered to on reconsideration,* 2004 WL 1943099 (S.D.N.Y. Aug. 27, 2004), the Court found liability against the defendant and noted that defendants' lawyers "completely abdicated their responsibilities under the discovery rules and as officers of the court" and defendants "lied and, through omission and commission, failed to search for and produce documents and, indeed, destroyed evidence--all to the ultimate prejudice of the truth-seeking process." In particular, the Court noted that outside counsel:

(1) never gave adequate instructions to their clients about the clients' overall discovery obligations, what constitutes a "document" . . . (2) . . . never implemented a systematic procedure for document production or for retention of documents, including electronic documents; (3) delegated document production to a layperson who . . . did not even understand . . . that a document included a draft or other non-identical copy, a computer file and an e-mail; (4) never went back to the layperson designated to assure that he had establish[ed] a coherent and effective system . . . and (5) . . . failed to take any action to remedy the situation or supplement the demonstrably false responses . . . The court concludes that . . . its counsel failed in a variety of instances to conduct any reasonable inquiry into the factual basis of its discovery responses. . . . Such an inquiry would have required, at a minimum, a reasonable procedure to distribute discovery requests to all employees and agents of the defendant potentially possessing responsive information, and to account for the collection and subsequent production of the information to plaintiffs.

Because Rule 3.4(a) of the *Rules of Professional Responsibility* prohibits the unlawful alteration or destruction of material that has potential evidentiary value this case could have easily resulted in the initiation of disciplinary proceedings.

Metadata

Metadata is "embedded" information that is stored in electronically generated materials, but which is not visible when a document or materials are printed. Metadata is information used by the computer to manage and often classify the computer file from which it originated. It is often thought of as computer information that exists beyond the visible data viewed in an application software program. This is significantly different from paper information, where all of the information is set out before you. Paper discovery discloses only what the creator or author wishes the reader to view.

For example, if a user creates a document using a word processing software such as Microsoft Word metadata is also included in each document. Some of the metadata that may be created would include the author's name, initials, company's name, computer name, directory where the document was saved, other authors, document revisions, versions, comments, hidden text and other information.

From an ethical perspective, metadata affects you depending on whether you are sending documents containing metadata or whether you are receiving electronic files containing metadata. If you are disclosing electronic documents to the opposing party, the metadata may contain attorney-client communications, work product, or trade secrets. For example, if you send an electronic settlement letter to the opposing side, the metadata may contain client comments regarding the settlement limits for the case. This would obviously bring your ethical obligations regarding confidentiality of your client's communications into question.

If you receive electronic files or metadata from the opposing side or another source that contain attorney-client communications, work product or trade secrets then the issue is what is your ethical obligation respecting this confidential information? If you receive these files from the opposing party, the New York State Bar Association's Committee on Professional Ethics held, in its Ethics Opinion 749, that it was unethical for a lawyer to inspect and use metadata from a word processing e-mailed from opposing counsel.

The Committee also held that sending the e-mail was not a violation since it was unclear how to remove the data. However, since the date of this opinion, there have been significant research and writings on the process of removing metadata from electronic files. J. Brian Beckham, *Production, Preservation, and Disclosure of Metadata*, 7 Colum. Sci. & Tech. L. Rev. 1(2005-2006); Campbell C. Steele, *Attorneys Beware: Metadata's Impact on Privilege, Work Product, and the Ethical Rules,* 35 U. Mem. L. Rev. 911 (2005); and Hon. Steve Leben, *Considering the Inadvertent Disclosure of Metadata*, 75-APR J. Kan. B.A. 26 (2006).

Clawback Agreements

In addition, ethical issues can arise where parties agree to "clawback" or "quick peek" agreements that provide for nonwaiver of confidential protection of disclosed electronic information even though confidential data has been inadvertently disclosed. The issue arises of whether or not it is ethical to enter into such an agreement. *See,* Laura Catherine Daniel, *The Dubious Origins and Dangers of Clawback and Quick-peek Agreements: An Argument Against Their Codification in the Federal Rules of Civil Procedure,* 47 Wm. & Mary L. Rev. 663 (Nov. 2005) and § 7.4 [I][1], *Nonwaiver or Clawback Agreements.*

Receipt of Privileged Electronic Information

An ethical issue arises when counsel receives privileged information that was inadvertently disclosed by the opposing counsel. In *Knitting Fever, Inc. v. Coats Holding Ltd.,* No. CIV.05-1065, 2005 U.S. Dist. LEXIS 28435, at *4-5 (D.N.Y. Nov. 14, 2005) the Court held that upon receipt of privileged documents, counsel for plaintiffs had a clear ethical responsibility to notify defendants' counsel and either follow the latter's instructions with respect to the disposition of the documents or refrain from using them pending ruling by the court. The Court affirmed the magistrate's order which: (1) directed plaintiffs' principal to appear with his "laptop, his PDA, his cell phone, and all his desktops" at the courthouse so that defendants could conduct a forensic search regarding plaintiffs' receipt of certain privileged documents, outside of the discovery process. *See also, United States v. Rigas*, 281 F. Supp. 2d 733 (S.D.N.Y. 2003) ("Am. Bar Ass'n. Standing Comm. on Ethics and Prof. Resp., Formal Op. 92-368 (1992) . . . 'A lawyer who receives materials that on their face appear to be subject to the attorney-client privilege or otherwise confidential, under circumstances where it is clear they were not intended for the receiving lawyer, should refrain from examining the materials, notify the sending lawyer and abide the instructions of the lawyer who sent them.'").

Malpractice

In addition, attorneys are facing exposure to malpractice claims for their handling of electronic data. In *TIG Insurance Co. v. Giffin Winning Cohen & Bodewes, P.C.*, 2006 WL 890763 (7th Cir. April 7, 2006) an insurance company brought a malpractice claim against a law firm claiming that it was negligent in the untimely production of electronic information (gender equity studies) in the underlying employment cases. The Court eventually held that the damages of 1.2 million dollars for legal fees paid to another firm for defending against sanctions was not reasonably foreseeable. *See also, Phoenix Four, Inc. v. Strategic Resources Corp.,* No. CIV. 05-4837, 2006 WL 1409413 (S.D.N.Y. May 23, 2006) where the Court found defendant counsel's deficiencies constituted "gross negligence" for failure to discover that its client's server contained a substantial amount of discoverable data until a few months before trial.

[B]   Reported Cases

* *In matter of Michael Ward,* No. 20050092, 2005 WL 1713924 (N.D. July 25, 2005). The Court sanctioned an attorney under Professional Conduct rule 1.15(f) for failing to provide billing records when the attorney claimed that a virus destroyed the electronic backup of his records.

- *United States v. Castellano,* 610 F. Supp. 1151, 1164-65 (S.D.N.Y. 1985). The criminal defense attorney was disqualified from representing a RICO defendant for violating Rule 3.4(a), partially based on his destruction of records that were relevant to an imminent judicial proceeding. *See also, Harlan v. Lewis,* 982 F.2d 1255, 1262 (8th Cir. 1993) (sanctioning an attorney for concealing information having possible evidentiary relevance).

- *Briggs v. McWeeny,* 796 A.2d 516 (Conn. 2002). An attorney was disqualified from representing a municipality in construction litigation for violating Rule 3.4(a) because of an attempted concealment of an expert report adverse to her client's position.

- *White v. Office of the Public Defender for the State of Maryland,* 170 F.R.D. 138, 153 (D.Md. 1997). The plaintiff-lawyer was referred to the court's disciplinary committee based on spoliation of evidence in the case.

- *Idaho State Bar v. Gantenbein,* 986 P.2d 339 (Idaho 1999). In a personal injury case, an attorney was charged with violating Rule 3.4(a) for altering a medical report and submitting it to opposing counsel.

- *Jones v. Goord,* No. CIV.95-8026, 2002 WL 1007614, *6 (S.D.N.Y. May 16, 2002). The Court denied plaintiffs request for electronic data for failure to seek discovery in a timely manner. The plaintiffs (prisoner inmates) had sought databases from prison officials. The court stated, ". . . [a]s electronic mechanisms for storing and retrieving data have become more common, it has increasingly behooved courts and counsel to become familiar with such methods, and to develop expertise and procedures for incorporating 'electronic discovery' into the familiar rituals of litigation."

- *State v. Braidic,* No. 28952-1-II, 2004 WL 52412, *2 (Wash. Ct. App. Jan. 13, 2004) (unpublished). The Court denied the defendant's claim of *ineffective assistance of counsel* based on failure to object to e-mail evidence as hearsay and best evidence. The trial court originally allowed the admission of e-mail under the present sense impression hearsay in criminal trial. The Appellate Court reversed the basis of admitting the e-mail finding that the e-mail was not hearsay since it was not offered to prove the truth of the statements.

- *Cobell v. Norton,* 206 F.R.D. 324 (D.D.C. 2002). The defendant's motion for a protective order to clarify duty to produce e-mail was not appropriate and denied which led to discovery sanctions against the plaintiff's counsel. The defendants had raised the same issue in two previous pleadings.

- Justice Holmes stated in *Texas & Pac. Ry. v. Behymer,* 189 U.S. 468, 470 (1903): "What usually is done may be evidence of what ought to be done, but what ought to be done is fixed by a standard of reasonable prudence, whether it usually is complied with or not."

• In *The T.J. Hooper,* 60 F.2d 737, 740 (2d Cir. 1932) case Justice Hand stated:

> Indeed in most cases reasonable prudence is in fact common prudence; but strictly it is never its measure; a whole calling may have unduly lagged in the adoption of new and available devices. It never may set its own tests, however persuasive be its usages. Courts must in the end say what is required; there are precautions so imperative that even their universal disregard will not excuse their omission.

• The Seventh Circuit in a "duty to browse" decision seems to impose a duty on litigants to "browse" the Internet for specific financial information. *Whirlpool Financial Corporation v. GN Holdings, Inc.,* 67 F.3rd 605, 610 (7th Cir. 1995). The Court stated:

> Moreover, once the significant discrepancies between the projections and actual results placed *Whirlpool* on notice regarding the possibility of fraud, the information *Whirlpool* says it needed to uncover the alleged fraud was in the public domain. In today's society, with the advent of the information superhighway, federal and state legislation and regulations, as well as information regarding industry trends, are easily accessed. A reasonable investor is presumed to have information available in the public domain, and therefore *Whirlpool* is imputed with constructive knowledge of this information.

[C]   Other Authorities

• Peter Brown, *Discovery and Spoliation: Internet and Electronic Media Issues,* 80 PLI/ NY 391, 400 (Aug. 2000). "It is the attorney's duty to instruct the client on appropriate record preservation policies. Attorneys must zealously advocate for their clients, but in doing so they must recognize that while technology changes, certain ethical obligations remain fixed."

• Campbell C. Steele, *Attorneys Beware: Metadata's Impact on Privilege, Work Product, and the Ethical Rules,* 35 U. Mem. L. Rev. 911 (Summer 2005).

• J.T. Westermeier, *Ethical Issues for Lawyers on the Internet and World Wide Web,* 6 RICH. J.L. & TECH. 5 (1999). "To keep pace with the law of legal ethics in the United States . . . one must have the ABA/BNA Lawyers Manual on Professional Conduct, the Model Code of Professional Responsibility, Rules of Professional Conduct, Hazard and Hodus' The Law of Lawyering, local statutes and opinions from applicable local ethics rules committees and local bar counsel."

• David Hricik & Robert R. Jueneman, *The Transmission and Receipt of Invisible Confidential Information,* 15 The Professional Lawyer no. 1, p. 18 (Spring 2004). "To comply with their duty of confidentiality, lawyers should take steps to remove metadata from documents exchanged with opposing counsel or disclosed to the public."

- MacLachlan, *Gandy Dancers on The Web: How the Internet Has Raised the Bar on Lawyers' Professional Responsibility to Research and Know the Law,* 13 Geo. J.L. Eth. 607 (2000).

- Brian J. Simpson & Reed F. Simpson, *Computer Discovery Techniques: Legal Malpractice,* 39 Orange Cty. Lawyer 12 (Aug. 1997).

§ 1.6   JUDICIAL ROLE

Judges are becoming more sophisticated about computer-based discovery and will be actively involved in managing the process and the foundational issues regarding the admissibility of electronic evidence. Under federal and state procedural and evidentiary rules, the court has available judicial tools such as pretrial conferences and appointing special masters to administer the discovery and production of electronic information. *See,* Chapter 7, *Court Procedural Rules and Case Law.* However, it still is imperative that you also provide the court, through briefings or expert testimony, the necessary factual and legal basis to support your client's position in electronic discovery.

§ 1.7   CONCLUSION

Computers are found in all segments of society, from the home to the business office. Though they are in widespread use, most legal professionals are unaware of how they work in creating and storing electronic information. Just as it is necessary to understand some of the basic features of an automobile to prosecute an automobile case, it is necessary to learn the basic features of computers and software to effectively discover, produce, and admit electronic information.

We are firmly in a world of electronic records and communications. It is no longer acceptable for attorneys to ignore the enormous quantities of discoverable information on computer disks and tapes. In today's environment, a computer is often the best — and, more often, the only — source of evidence. The discovery of electronic information may yield the "smoking gun" that may win your case.

It is vital that attorneys working on discovery learn the technology, the law, and language of this new world. With fuller understanding, litigants will be able to request the appropriate electronic information from the opposing party as well as advise their clients as to their production obligations.

Chapter 2

Creation and Storage of Electronic Information

§ 2.1   GENERALLY

Computers play a central role in the creation, storage, and retrieval of electronic information. In order to discover and respond to requests for electronic information, one will have to understand the basics of computers and how they create and store information.

Failure to understand computer systems and the unique issues they present can have unfortunate consequences for you and your clients. The courts are not reluctant to impose sanctions against counsel and their clients for failure to preserve or disclose relevant electronic information. In addition, it is necessary to understand the fundamentals of computers, software, and data files to lay a factual predicate for admission of electronic information. For this reason, knowing how a computer operates and stores information will enable an attorney to make educated decisions in the discovery, production, and admissibility of electronic information.

This chapter catalogues a wide range of potential media, devices, and locations of electronic evidence. Each of these sources should be considered in creating a discovery plan for either the discovery or production of electronic data. In addition, new sources of electronic data are constantly being created, such as instant and text messaging. Given the constant change in this area, it is important for lawyers to keep current on evolving technologies.

§ 2.2   CREATING ELECTRONIC INFORMATION

Creating electronic information is now the norm for businesses and individuals. Set out below is an explanation of the main computer components, hardware and software, that form the foundation for creating electronic information.

[A]   Computers

A fundamental characteristic of a computer is its ability to create, store and retrieve electronic information at lightning speed and its reliability and storage capacity. "The relevant dictionary meaning of 'computer' is '[a] device that computes, especially a programmable electronic machine that performs highspeed mathematical or logical operations or that assembles, stores, correlates, or otherwise processes information.'" *Diagnostic Group, LLC v. Benson Medical Instruments Co.,* No. CIV.02-777, 2005 WL 715935, at *8 (D. Minn. Mar. 28, 2005).

[1]   Hardware

Hardware is the physical equipment that comprises a computer system. The monitor, keyboard, printer, and other components are the hardware of a personal computer (PC). The hardware works with software to perform tasks on the computer. The software is the program that tells the computer what to do with the hardware and how to process data. The main piece of a PC is the system unit. Inside are dozens of hardware parts. These include the microprocessor, which acts as the brains of the computer, memory chips that store data as it is being processed, hard drives and more. Hardware peripherals reside outside the system unit and include printers, scanners, keyboards, etc. Expansion cards fit within the main system and are installed to operate different hardware parts such as a modem or CD-ROM. The microcomputer connotes a computer designed for use by one person. The terms "microcomputer," "PC," and "personal computer" are interchangeable.

The programs that run computer hardware are the operating system and application software. System software, such as Windows XP, is designed to run the general operation of a computer. Application software runs a specific software application, such as a word processing program like WordPerfect. *See,* § 2.2[C], *Software.*

[2]   Types and Description

Computers exist in a wide range of sizes and levels of power. The Court in *Global Maintech Corp. v. I/O Concepts, Inc.,* No. CIV.05-1340, 2006 LEXIS 11017, at *8-9 (Fed. Cir. May 2, 2006) (unpublished) observed that a "computer system . . . may take many forms. For example, the computer system may be a data center, an enterprise computing system, a network of computers, a mainframe computer, a minicomputer, a server, a workstation, and/ or a personal computer."

Because of miniaturization, computers are now embedded within the circuitry of many appliances, such as televisions, wristwatches, refrigerators and even the air bags in automobiles. These types of computers are programmed for a specific task such as recording TV usage, keeping accurate time, or recording the impact speed of an automobile at the time of a collision. Since computers are increasingly being embedded in mechanical and electrical devices, you should always be asking yourself whether the information or data recorded in these devices is pertinent in your cases.

Programmable computers vary significantly in their power, speed, memory, and physical size. Generally, the smallest of these computers can be held in one hand and is called a personal digital assistant (PDA). PDAs are used as calendaring systems, notepads, address books and, if equipped with a cellular Internet connection, can be connected to the Web and receive e-mail.

The most widely used programmable computers are desktop PCs and laptops. These are used in businesses and at home for word processing, e-mail and a host of other electronic information applications. They can store (using hard drives or other storage media) huge amounts of electronic information and hundreds of programs and documents. They are generally equipped with a keyboard, mouse, and a video display monitor. A PC can be standalone or networked with hundreds of other computers. Laptops generally have the same capability as PCs, but are more compact.

One Court described the personal computer, hardware, and operating system as follows:

1. A "personal computer" ("PC") is a digital information processing device designed for use by one person at a time. A typical PC consists of central processing components (e.g., a microprocessor and main memory) and mass data storage (such as a hard disk). A typical PC system consists of a PC, certain peripheral input/output devices (including a monitor, a keyboard, a mouse, and a printer), and an operating system. PC systems, which include desktop and laptop models, can be distinguished from more powerful, more expensive computer systems known as "servers," which are designed to provide data, services, and functionality through a digital network to multiple users.

United States v. Microsoft Corp., 84 F. Supp. 2d 9, 12 (D.D.C. 1999), *aff'd in part & rev'd in part,* 253 F.3d 34 (D.C. Cir. 2001), *cert. denied,* 122 S. Ct. 350 (2001); *People v. Rivera,* 182 Ill. App. 3d 33, 42, 537 N.E.2d 924, 931 (1989) (Court concluded that the trial "judge correctly held that he could take judicial notice that IBM is a 'standard, reliable computer'".).

Computers known as "workstations" generally have greater memory and more computing power, though are similar to desktop PCs. They are often found in industrial, scientific, and other business environments that require high levels of computational capability such as a computer aided design (CAD) application.

There has been a recent resurgence of mainframe computers that have more memory and speed capabilities than workstations and can be shared by multiple users through a series of interconnected computers. The most powerful mainframe computers, called supercomputers, process complex and very time-consuming mathematical calculations, such as the prediction of weather patterns. Among their largest users are the military, large corporations and scientific institutions whose computational requirements are significant.

Besides these computers, there are many other electronic computerized devices such as facsimile machines, tablet PC's, electronic video games and pagers that contain electronic information that may be of relevance to your case. *See,* § 2.5, *Storage Devices.*

[3]   Uses

The scope of computer use by your client or the opposing party will dictate the extent of your electronic information discovery and production. For example, if the litigation involves product inventories with bar codes, then bar code scanners and database information will be relevant to your lawsuit. If the credit status of your client is at issue, then the database credit information from credit reporting agencies will be relevant. If the actual event and time of occurrence are important to your case, then a home security system may provide this information. Since computers are used in so many appliances and programmable computer devices, it is important that one brainstorm the possible data sources relevant to your case.

Set out in the following sections is a list of storage media, storage devices, and storage locations that should be considered for all of your lawsuits. Many of them may not have relevance to the issues in your case, but should be reviewed to ensure that all electronic information is discovered or produced.

[B]   How a Computer Works

[1]   Bits and Bytes – 1's and 0's

Computers create, process and store electronic information in the form of binary digits or bits. Bits (binary digits) are the building blocks for all information processing that occurs inside digital computers. A bit is a basic unit of information in a computer. These bits have two possible representations, 0 or 1. Bits are then combined into larger units called bytes. A byte is composed of eight bits. To the computer these are all 1's and 0's. *Universal City Studios v. Reimerdes,* 111 F. Supp. 2d 294, 306 (D.N.Y. 2000) ("The smallest unit of memory in a computer, a 'bit', 'is a switch with a value of 0 (off) or 1 (on).' . . . A group of eight bits is called a byte and represents a character--a letter or an integer.").

A byte is the basic unit of storage measurement. A byte can store enough information, and in enough patterns, to represent a letter of the alphabet, a numeric digit, a punctuation mark and other characters.

A kilobyte (1,024 bytes) can store more than one thousand characters; a megabyte about one million characters; a gigabyte about one billion and a terabyte about one trillion. Shira A. Scheindlin & Jeffrey Rabkin, *Electronic Discovery in Federal Civil Litigation: Is Rule 34 Up to the Task?,* 41 B.C. L. Rev. 327, 334 (2000) ("Computer storage capacity is usually measured in thousands (or millions) of bytes of information. Although it might appear cumbersome to translate letters and decimals into zeros and ones, computers do it at lightning speed and can store an enormous volume of bits.").

These terms are used to rate the storage capacities of diskettes and hard drives. *See,* § 2.3[B], *Unit of Measurement - Storage Unit.* Besides text, these bytes together can generate a photograph, video, recording, and other digital information.

In its native or "raw" form (1's and 0's) electronic information is unintelligible. Computer operating and application software are required to decipher the 1's and 0's into understandable information. These 1's and 0's are then deciphered in application programs, such as Microsoft Word, and are then displayed as comprehensible information. Application programs interpret and transform the 1's and 0's into something we can understand and use.

If you do not have the application software or conversion software to convert native or raw data into understandable information, then you are essentially provided no information. This may become an issue if a company has archived electronic information, but has not retained the necessary software programs to process the raw data into an understandable format. Often companies will argue that the conversion of this "raw data" into understandable information should be at the cost of the requesting party. However, the courts are reluctant to impose these costs on the requesting party, since the organization chose to create and store information in this format that they are now claiming is inaccessible. *See,* §§ 7.7[D], *Translated Into Reasonably Useful Form* and 7.7[G], *Form of Production of Computer-based Data.*

[2] Microprocessor and Micro Controller

Computers create electronic information using a microprocessor. Commands are sent through a keyboard, mouse, voice recognition microphone or other input device to the microprocessor. For example, if you press a letter key on your keyboard, a byte of information is created and subsequently processed and stored on a storage device such as a hard drive. All information processed by a computer can be expressed as a binary notation.

A microprocessor (which is the central processing unit (CPU)) acts as the computer's brain and carries out the software commands, performs calculations and communicates with the different hardware components needed to operate the computer. It performs the system's arithmetic, logic, and control operations. The processor speed is the speed of the microprocessor chip in your computer. Modern microprocessors operate with data widths of 32 bits (**b**inary dig**its**, or units of information represented as 1s and 0s), meaning those 32 bits or 4 bytes of data can be transferred at the same time.

A different kind of integrated circuit, a micro controller, is a complete computer on a chip, containing all of the elements of the basic microprocessor along with other specialized functions. Micro controllers are used in video games, videocassette recorders (VCRs), automobiles, and other devices.

[3] Storage

The computer memory or storage media can store binary information created by the computer. The measurement storage unit of media is bytes. Some common storage media are floppy disks, hard drives, and CD-ROM disks.

[C] Software

Software is a set of computer programs and related documentation associated with a computer system. "[S]oftware is the 'totality of programs usable on a particular kind of computer, together with the documentation associated with a computer program, such as manuals, diagrams, and operating instructions.'" *Former Employees of Electronic Data Systems Corp. v. U.S. Secretary of Labor,* 350 F. Supp.2d 1282, 1293 (Ct. Int'l. Trade Dec. 1, 2004).

There are two basic types of software: system (or operating software) and application software.

[1] Operating System Software

System software controls and coordinates the operation of the various types of equipment and operating system in a computer. The most important type of system software is a set of programs called the operating system. The operating system controls the activity of a computer whether it is a desktop, laptop, PDA or other type of computing device.

When a computer is turned on, it searches for instructions in its memory. Usually, the first set of these instructions is a special program called the operating system, which is the software that makes the computer work. It prompts the user (or other machines) for input and commands, reports the results of these commands and other operations, stores and manages data, and controls the sequence of the software and hardware actions. Popular operating systems, such as Microsoft Windows and the Macintosh operating system (Mac OS), have a graphical user interface (GUI), that is, a display that uses tiny pictures or icons to represent various commands. To execute these commands, the user clicks the mouse on the icon or presses a combination of keys on the keyboard.

DOS, which stands for Disk Operating System, was one of the first software operating systems. Windows 3.1 and 3.11 are not operating software, but are graphical interfaces between the operating software DOS and application software. As technology improved, the Windows graphical interface was combined with the DOS operating system to create the first windows operating software, Windows 95. This was succeeded by Windows 98, Windows 2000 and, the most recent, Windows XP. The Macintosh operating system is Mac OS X. UNIX is the name of an operating system used with mainframe computers and other high-end computers. Windows Server is a network operating system. The prevalent personal computer operating system is Windows based.

A federal Court defined an operating system as "a software program that controls the allocation and use of computer resources (such as central processing unit time, main memory space, disk space and input/output channels). The operating system also supports the functions of software programs, called 'applications,' that perform specific user-oriented tasks". *United States v. Microsoft Corp.,* 84 F. Supp. 2d 9, 12 (D.D.C. 1999), *aff'd in part & rev'd in part*, 253 F.3d 34 (D.C. Cir. 2001), *cert. denied*, 122 S. Ct. 350 (2001).

There are many desktop and server based operating systems. In *Global Maintech Corp. v. I/O Concepts, Inc.,* No. CIV.05-1340, 2006 U.S. Dist. LEXIS 11017, at *8-9 (Fed. Cir. May 2, 2006) (unpublished) the Court observed that "the computer system may be an MVS operating system-based computer (or one of its derivative like IBM's OS/390), a UNIX operating system-based computer, an IBM AS400 computer, a Microsoft Windows operating system-based computer, an Apple Macintosh operating system-based computer, an OS/2 operating system-based computer, or a DOS-based computer. . . ."

For a computer to operate properly, the application software or program must be compatible with the particular operating system of the computer on which the program is to be used. For example, software designed for the Windows based operating system will not run on a Macintosh computer and vice versa because the two utilize different operating systems. *Appforge, Inc. v. Extended Systems, Inc.*, No. CIV.04-704, 2005 WL 705341, *1 (D.Del. Mar. 28, 2005). In addition, different versions of the same operating system, such as Windows, are not always compatible with each other. Many application programs require a particular operating system version and will not run on a computer with a different operating system version. For example, Microsoft Office Word 2003 will not run on a DOS operating system.

[2]   Application Software

Application software programs have specific uses, such as processing text, calculating numbers, organizing large amounts of data, etc. Application software includes word processors, spreadsheets, database managers, graphics, money managers, and games. They are developed using programming languages such as BASIC, C++, or Delphi that result in the "source code" for the program. "The term 'source code' means the [non-machine] language used by a computer programmer to create a program." *Davidson & Associates, Inc. v. Internet Gateway, Inc.* 334 F. Supp.2d 1164, 1171 n.4 (E.D.Mo. 2004). "The source code of a program is its operating instructions in a format that a computer programmer can read and use to maintain and revise a program." *Liu v. Price Waterhouse LLP,* 302 F.3d 749, 752 n.1 (7th Cir. 2002).

The following is the most common application software and examples of them:

- Word processing programs are designed to allow the user to create letters, briefs, memos and other written documents. Examples of these programs are Microsoft Word and WordPerfect.

- Spreadsheet programs are used to manipulate numbers, perform calculations, handle mathematical formulas, and organize data. Quattro Pro, Lotus 123 and Microsoft Excel are examples of spreadsheet programs.

- Database programs are used to organize large quantities of data. They are generally used to compile business indexes, accounting or personnel information, case management and more. Database programs include Microsoft Access, Paradox, and Filemaker Pro.

- Graphics programs are used for drawing and designing on the computer. Exhibits, charts, graphs, and bulleted items can be created using graphics programs. Microsoft PowerPoint, Corel Draw, Paintbrush, and Visio are some graphic programs.

- Game programs are designed for fun. They include action/adventure, flight simulation, golf, and others. SIMS, Quest, and Microsoft Golf are just some of the many game programs available.

These application programs generate electronic information that is then saved in computer files. These files contain the actual information formatted for that specific program and often have a specific file extension, which are the last three or more letters following the file name and period, such as "smith.PST" for a Microsoft Outlook file (PST) relating to a person named "Smith." These extensions correspond to the application program. For further information on file formats *see* § 3.4, *Directories, Files and File Formats*.

[3] Reported Cases

- *David L. Aldridge Co. v. Microsoft Corp.,* 995 F. Supp. 728, 732 (S.D.Tex. 1998). "Computers only perform operations when told to do so. An operating system is a program that coordinates activities among the various components of the computer and controls the flow of data among them. It is a computer's operating system, for example, that instructs the computer to download data from memory to a disk or to execute the necessary procedures to open a program when requested to do so by the user. While personal computer users could conceivably write their own customized operating system programs, commercially available operating systems are far more desirable to most users."

- *United States v. Maali,* 346 F. Supp.2d 1226, 1234 n.9 (M.D.Fla. 2004). In a tax evasion case the search warrant requested, "15. 'Computer software,' which refers to digital information which can be interpreted by a computer and any of its related components to direct the way computer systems work. Software is stored in electronic, magnetic, optical, or other digital form. It commonly includes programs to run operating systems, applications (such as word processing, graphics, or spreadsheet programs), utilities, compilers, interpreters, and communications programs; 16. 'Computer-related documentation,' which refers to written, recorded, printed, or electronically stored material that explains or illustrates how to configure or use computer hardware or computer software, or related items."

- *Williams v. Sprint/United Mgmt. Co.,* 230 F.R.D. 640, 647 (D. Kan. 2005). The Court observed that "metadata varies with different [application software] . . . At one end of the spectrum is a word processing application where the metadata is usually not critical to understanding the substance of the document. The information can be conveyed without the need for the metadata. At the other end of the spectrum is a database application where the database is a completely undifferentiated mass of tables of data."

§ 2.3   STORAGE AND RETRIEVAL OF ELECTRONIC INFORMATION

[A]   How Information Storage and Retrieval Works

Information storage and retrieval describe the organization, storage, location, and retrieval of electronic information in computer systems.

In order to store or retrieve information in a computer system, the CPU processes information and temporarily stores it in Random Access Memory (RAM) in the form of bits that make up files. When this temporary storage of information needs to be stored permanently or semi-permanently, the CPU locates unused space on the storage media, such as a hard drive or floppy disk. The CPU instructs the computer to begin to make changes to the storage media. When computer data is written to a floppy or hard disk a mechanical device called a head is used to write the data. The data is stored electronically in magnetic patterns (for magnetic storage media) of binary ones and zeros. The patterns are in the form of sectors, which are written consecutively in concentric rings called tracks. The device then transmits bits and bytes of information onto the media.

This process is reversed when the CPU needs access to some piece of electronic information. The CPU will determine by specific addresses where the information is located on the physical media and it will then direct the read/write head to position itself at that location on the media and read the information stored there and then transmits it to the RAM in the form of bits.

[1]   Reported Cases

• The Court in *United States v. Triumph Capital Group, Inc.*, 211 F.R.D. 31, 46 nn.5-7 (D. Conn. 2002) described the storage process of computer files,

> [a] file is made up of a whole number of clusters that are not necessarily contiguous. When a computer user creates a file to be saved, the computer's "file allocation table" ("FAT") assigns or allocates a cluster or clusters to store that file. The clusters are not necessarily contiguous because the FAT assigns data to whatever available clusters it finds on the hard drive. Saved files that occupy allocated clusters are called 'active files.'

> The FAT is similar to a road map or a table of contents. The computer's operating system uses the FAT to track the specific cluster or clusters that are allocated to each active file and the clusters that are free, or available for storage of new data. When a document or data is stored in an active file, the FAT assigns a number to each cluster that is allocated to that document or file. When the user opens that document or file, the FAT tells the operating system the numbers of the clusters

that contain, or store the document or file and gathers the clusters into one contiguous file that the user can open.

*   *AOL v. St. Paul Mercury Insurance Co.*, 347 F.3d 89 (4th Cir. 2003). In an insurance claim case, the Court discussed the difference between software and the hard drive of a computer.

[B]   Unit of Measurement - Storage Unit

Information storage memory is generally quantified in terms of bits, bytes, kilobytes (KB), megabytes (MB), gigabytes (GB) and terabytes (TB). A byte is composed of 8 bits (a bit is the smallest unit of measurement for electronic data). A kilobyte is equivalent to 1,024 bytes. A megabyte is 1,048,576 bytes. A gigabyte is 1,073,741,824 bytes or 1024 megabytes. A terabyte is about one trillion bytes or more precisely 1,099,511,627,776 bytes.

[C]   Information Storage

Information storage can be categorized as temporary, semipermanent or permanent. Temporary storage is storage of information often associated with random access memory (RAM) chips. It can then be written to semipermanent storage such as a floppy disk or permanent storage such as a CD-ROM.

Information can also be categorized as having been stored to or retrieved from primary or the secondary memory. Primary memory, also known as main or internal memory, is a computer's RAM. The primary memory is memory that is accessed directly by the central processing unit (CPU) - the main circuitry or brains within which the computer processes information. All information that is processed by a computer first passes through primary memory. Secondary or external memory is any form of memory, other than the primary computer memory. This includes hard drives, floppy disk, CD-ROMs and magnetic tapes.

[1]   Temporary, Semipermanent and Permanent Storage

[a]   Temporary Storage

Generally, temporary information storage is used as an intermediate process between permanent or semipermanent storage and a computer's central processing unit (CPU). Temporary storage in the form of memory chips called RAM is the primary memory in a computer. Information is stored in the primary memory or RAM while the CPU is processing it. After processing, it is transferred to a permanent or semipermanent form of memory such as a hard drive. This type of memory in the form of RAM chips is also known as volatile memory because it must have power supplied to it continuously or the RAM chip or memory loses its contents. When a computer loses its power, electronic information can be lost that has not been transferred to semipermanent or permanent storage. *David L. Aldridge Co. v. Microsoft Corp.,* 995 F. Supp. 728, 732 n.1 (S.D.Tex. 1998).

[b]   Semipermanent Storage

Semipermanent storage is storage that is not permanent. For example, semipermanent storage material is a floppy disk or hard drive. Once information is transferred to these storage devices, it will generally remain until the computer overwrites it. This type of storage media can be rewritten many times. However, with a floppy disk, a tab can be removed which locks the disk to prevent further overwriting on the floppy disk. Once the tab is replaced, the write protection is gone and the information can be overwritten once again.

For electronic discovery purposes, the computer storage capacity refers to the amount of data that can be stored electronically. This data will be stored even though the power source to the computer is disconnected. Typically, the storage capacity of semipermanent storage is measured in units of megabytes or gigabytes. A gigabyte is 1000 megabytes (MB) or one billion bytes. If the stored data is compressed, this allows more data to reside on the storage media, such as backup tapes.

[c]   Permanent Storage

Information is considered to be stored permanently if the storage media can only be written on once, such as a CD-ROM (**C**ompact **D**isc - **R**ead **O**nly **M**emory). Another form of permanent storage is ROM (read-only memory). ROM are chips in the primary memory that stores basic information that the computer needs in order to function. ROM cannot be overwritten, thus, is considered permanent storage.

[2]   Primary and Secondary Memory

A computer's memory can refer to either the primary or the secondary memory of a computer system.

In *WeddingChannel.Com, Inc. v. The Knot, Inc.,* No. CIV.03-7369, 2005 WL 165286, at *8 (S.D.N.Y. Jan. 26, 2005) the Court discussed the difference between the two types of memory and stated:

> The Microsoft Computer Dictionary . . . defines 'memory' as follows: A device where information can be stored and retrieved. In the most general sense, memory can refer to external storage such as disk drives or tape drives; in common usage, it refers only to a computer's main memory, the fast semiconductor storage (RAM) directly connected to the processor.

[a]   Primary Memory

The primary memory of a computer is either random access memory (RAM), which can be changed, or read-only memory (ROM), which can be read by the computer, but not altered. RAM is used by the CPU as it processes information and is a temporary storage area the system uses to hold the programs or files that are currently open on your machine. ROM memory is used to store the basic set of instructions called BIOS (basic input-output system) that the computer needs to run when it is first turned on. This information is permanently stored on computer chips in the form of hardwired electronic circuits.

[b]   Secondary Memory

Secondary or external storage devices, such as a floppy disk or hard drive, store electronic information that has been processed and transmitted from the CPU or primary memory. A floppy disk can store about 1.44 megabytes of information, hard drives can store thousands of megabytes, CD-ROMs can store approximately 640 megabytes and DVDs (digital video discs) can store 8.5 gigabytes. Storage media types are explained further in § 2.04, *Storage Media.*

[D]   Types of External Storage Technology - Magnetic, Optical, Magneto-Optical and Flash

Secondary or external memory is classified as either magnetic or optical, or a combination called a magneto-optical and flash memory. A magnetic storage device uses materials and mechanisms similar to those used for audiotape, while optical storage materials use lasers to store and retrieve information from a plastic disk. Magneto-optical memory devices use a combination of optical storage and retrieval technology coupled with a magnetic media.

"With any type of [magnetic or optical] media, the data is recorded in tracks. These tracks take various forms, depending on the type of media. Data tracks on disks may be formed in concentric circles. On magnetic tape, the data tracks are formed longitudinally or sometimes helically. Data storage capacity of any media depends in large part upon how closely together the data tracks are written." *Storage Technology Corp. v. Quantum Corp.*, No. CIV.03-672, 2005 WL 1172737, *7 (D. Colo. May 17, 2005).

[1]   Magnetic Media

Magnetic storage media, such as a floppy disk, hard disk, or tape, store the information microscopically in a magnetic format. Distinct spots are magnetized on the media, corresponding to binary 1's and 0's created by the CPU. For example, on a hard disk, the disk spins and as the disk spins a read/write head scans the surface of the disk reading and writing magnetic spots in concentric circles. A magnetic disk is classified as either hard or floppy, depending upon the flexibility of the material from which they are made. A floppy disk is made of a flexible plastic with magnetic material on the surface. A hard drive is made of rigid material. *Storage Technology Corp. v. Quantum Corp.,* No. CIV.03-672, 2005 WL 1172737, *7 (D. Colo. May 17, 2005).

One of the most common types of magnetic media is tape, which is most commonly used for backup storage.

[2]   Optical Media

An important form of storage media is the optical disk. It was created by the same kind of laser technology as the compact disc (CDs), which revolutionized the music business. An optical disk provides tremendous storage capabilities at an inexpensive price. As a result, technologies that have large storage requirements such as databases or document images can easily be backed up and stored on an optical disk such as a digital video disk (DVD).

Data is recorded on an optical disk by using a laser device to burn minuscule holes into the surface of a hard plastic disk. Because the spots are so small, extremely high data density can be achieved on the disk. Once data has been burned onto the surface of certain optical disks, they cannot be changed. To read the data, a low-power laser light is beamed across the surface. This burned area reflects lights, which are interpreted as 1 and 0 bits.

[a]   Reported Case

- *Storage Technology Corp. v. Quantum Corp.,* 370 F. Supp.2d 1116, 1124 (D. Colo. May 17, 2005). "Another category of recording media is optical data storage media. Compact disks ('CDs') and digital video disks ('DVDs') are examples of optical storage media. Optical storage devices operate with drives that detect variations in the optical properties of the media surface."

- *Quinby v. WestLB AG,* No. CIV.04-7406, 2005 U.S. Dist. LEXIS 35583 (D.N.Y. Dec. 15, 2005), *aff.,* 2006 U.S. Dist. LEXIS 1178 (D.N.Y. Jan. 11, 2006). "The e-mails are stored on optical storage media, which are more accessible than back-up tapes. . . . n6 As described in *Zubulake,* optical storage media typically consists of a robotic storage device (robotic library) that houses removable media, uses robotic arms to access the media, and uses multiple read/write devices to store and retrieve records. Access speeds can range from as low as milliseconds if the media is already in a read device, up to 10-30 seconds for optical disk technology, and between 20-120 seconds for sequentially searched media, such as magnetic tape. Examples include optical disks."

[3]   Magneto-Optical Media

Magneto-optical technology combines optical and magnetic phenomena. Magneto-optical (MO) devices write data to a disk with the help of a laser beam and a magnetic write-head. There are two main types of magneto-optical drives; **WORM** drive, which stands for **W**rite **O**nce **R**ead **M**any, and **WMRM** drive, **W**rite **M**any **R**ead **M**any. WORM drives can hold up to 2.6 gigabytes of data and can only be written on once, but can be read many times. WMRM drives can be written on many times and read many times. These portable media are often used for backup storage.

[4]   Flash Memory

Another type of storage media, called flash memory, traps small amounts of electric charge in "wells" on the surface of a chip. To rewrite to flash memory, the charges in the wells must first be drained. Such drives are useful for storing information that changes infrequently.

[5]   New Developments

Although magnetic and optical technologies continue to increase in storage density, a variety of new technologies are emerging. Redundant Arrays of Independent Disks (RAIDs) are storage systems that look like one device, but are actually composed of multiple hard disks. These systems provide more storage and read data simultaneously from many drives.

Since the inception of computer storage, the capacity of internal and external memory devices has grown steadily at a rate that leads to a quadrupling in size every three years. Computer industry analysts expect this rapid rate of growth to continue unimpeded.

§ 2.4   STORAGE MEDIA

Floppy Disk	Magnetic Tape Drive
Hard Drive	DAT (Digital Audio Tape)
CD-ROM	Compact Flash Card
DVD (Digital Video Disk)	Smart Card
Jaz and Zip Disk	Microfilm/Microfiche
LS −120 (SuperDisk)	Micro Drive
PC Card (PMCIA Card)	Memory Stick

MD (Minidisk)   Bernoulli Drive

Pen or Thumb Drive

Storage media is used to store data from an electronic device. *Digeo, Inc. v. Audible, Inc.*, No. CIV. 05-464, 2006 U.S. Dist. LEXIS 22715, at *27-28 (D. Wash. Mar. 27, 2006) ("'electronic storage media' means 'memory configured to store information in a format that an electronic device can read'").

Many devices today have capabilities for both fixed (internal) storage/memory and the ability to store data simultaneously to removable storage media. Information is stored on many different types of media, the most common being floppy disks, hard drives, CD-ROMs and magnetic tape. Storage media come in many variations, and more are being introduced into the market on a regular basis.

One area that has seen a significant change is the development of different types of removable storage media. Traditionally, the only types of removable storage media were floppy disks (5 1/4" disks and 3 1/2" disks) on workstations and magnetic tape on mainframe computers. Now there are all sorts of removable media including CD-ROMS, Zip drives, DVD's, pen drives, etc. There are numerous types of removable storage media that should be considered for potential discovery. For example in the case of *In re Amato*, 2005 WL 1429743, *3 (D.Me. Jun. 17, 2005) the plaintiff sought "c. Any magnetic, electronic or optical storage device capable of storing data, such as floppy disks, hard disks, tapes, CD-ROMs, CD-R, CD-RWs, DVDs, optical disks, printer or memory buffers, smart cards, PC cards, memory calculators, electronic dialers, electronic notebooks, and personal digital assistants; d. Any documentation, operating logs and reference manuals regarding the operation of the computer equipment, storage devices or software."

The type and accessibility of storage media will determine whether the Courts will order disclosure and/or cost allocation to the sought after electronic evidence. *See*, §§3.06[B], *Classification of Data* and 7.04 [G][2], *Pending Rule 26(b)(2) Amendment*.

Some of the more common and well-established media storage types found in the consumer and commercial marketplace are outlined below.

[A]   Floppy Disk

A floppy, also called a disk or diskette, is a removable storage device used to store computer files. Floppy disks come in two sizes, 5 1/4" and 3 1/2". The larger floppy holds between 360 kilobytes and 1.2 megabytes, depending on the density of the disk. They are obsolete, but may contain data historically relevant to your case. The smaller floppy, 3 1/2" disk, can store between 720 kilobytes and 1.44 megabytes, depending on the disk density.

Before writing on a floppy disk, it must be formatted. Floppy drives actually have the read/write heads touch the surface of the material. Floppy diskettes can potentially be tied to a computer that wrote data to them. Data on a floppy, if deleted, is still recoverable, if it has not been overwritten. *See,* § 3.5[E], *Deletion of Electronic Information.*

Floppy disks can be written on many times. However, with a floppy disk, a tab in the upper corner of the disk can be removed or shifted which would prevent further overwriting on the floppy disk. Once the tab is replaced or shifted back the write protection is gone.

Floppy disks are most often used to store material that is not accessed frequently, to transfer files or to back up files contained on a computer's hard drive.

[1]   Reported Cases

- *Four Seasons Hotels and Resorts v. Consorcio Barr,* 267 F. Supp. 2d 1268, 1300 (S.D. Fla. 2003). The forensic expert was able to establish based on the serial number on the defendant's floppy disks that they had not been manufactured as of the date that the defendant alleged that the information had been provided to him on disk.

[B]   Hard Drive (External or Internal)

One of the most often-discovered secondary storage devices is the hard disk drive. Also, called a "hard drive" or "HDD." In 2002, 92 percent of all newly recorded information was stored on magnetic media (primarily hard disks), whereas only 0.01 percent was originally recorded on paper. Peter Lyman & Hal R. Varian, *How Much Information,* University of California at Berkeley, School of Information Management and Systems (Oct. 27, 2003) available at http://www.sims.berkeley.edu/how-much-info-2003.

Most computers have a hard drive and are designed to read and write data as well as retrieve stored data. Hard drives have tremendous storage capacity and are increasing in size. It is common to find hard drive capacities of 20 GB or more. The normal sizes of a hard drive are 5-1/4 inches for a desktop computer and 3-1/2 inch for a laptop.

A hard drive consists of a rigid circular magnetic platter that is sealed in a metal box with read/write heads. Though usually internal to a computer, external hard drives are common. Most hard drives have multiple platters stacked on top of one another to store data. Hard drives are sealed to prevent contaminants from interfering with the read/write function.

In hard drives, the read/write mechanism floats slightly above the hard drive platter surface. If the computer is dropped or an electrical malfunction occurs the read/write mechanism may touch the surface of the hard drive. If this occurs, then this is called a head or hard drive crash, and generally results in the loss of data where the surface becomes scratched. However, the portion of the hard drive not affected by the crash still contains data that is recoverable.

Hard drives are most often used to store information such as the operating system or an application program and its data that are frequently accessed by the user.

[1]   Reported Cases

- *United States v. Triumph Capital Group, Inc.*, 211 F.R.D. 31 n.4 (D. Conn. 2002). The Court described a hard drive:

    A hard drive is the primary means of data storage on a personal computer. Its surface is divided into concentric circles that are further divided into sectors. A group of sectors is called a cluster. A cluster is the minimum amount of space a file can occupy, regardless of the size of the file. The computer's operating system assigns a number to each cluster and keeps track of which clusters a file occupies. Occupied clusters are called "allocated." Clusters that are available for use (even if they contain data from previous files) are unallocated or free.

- *State v. Martin*, 674 N.W.2d 291, 303 (S. Dak. 2003). "Furthermore, we agree that [a] computer hard drive is much more similar to a library than a book; the hard drive can store literally thousands of documents and visual depictions."

- *Zubulake v. UBS Warburg LLC,* 217 F.R.D. 309, 318 (S.D.N.Y. 2003). For cost allocation purposes, the Court categorized hard drives as accessible and stated: "1. Active, online data: On-line storage is generally provided by magnetic disk. It is used in the very active stages of an electronic records [sic] life--when it is being created or received and processed, as well as when the access frequency is high and the required speed of access is very fast, i.e., milliseconds.' Examples of online data include hard drives."

- *United States v. Vig,* 167 F.3d 443, 447 n.5 (8th Cir. 1999), *cert. den.,* 528 U.S. 859. "The computer used by the defendants contained two hard drives, the 'C' and the 'D.' All the computer image files listed in Count I of the indictment against Tom Vig were taken from the 'C' drive of the computer and all the computer image files listed in Count II against Donovan Vig were found on the 'D' drive."

- *United States v. Frabizio,* 341 F. Supp.2d 47, 48 (D. Mass. Oct. 27, 2004). The defendant was charged with receiving and/or possessing child pornography and moved for production of discovery. The Court granted the production request and ordered the FBI to provide "a 'bit stream' copy of all electronically-stored data on the hard drive" and Encase files.

- *Williams v. Massachusetts Mut. Life Ins. Co.,* 226 F.R.D. 144, 146-147 (D. Mass. Feb. 2, 2005). The Court ordered defendants "to preserve all documents, hard drives and e-mail boxes which were searched by their forensic expert in response to Plaintiff's motion."

[2]   Other Authorities (reserved)

[3]   Discovery Pointers

• Data may still be on a hard drive that has been "reformatted." When a hard drive is reformatted, the internal address tables a computer uses to keep track of data are reassigned, however, the underlying data is generally unaffected. Data can oftentimes be recovered, unless specialized tools "shred" the data and render the computer data unrecoverable.

• Data can also be found on hard drives that are "broken." A forensic expert may be able to retrieve data from nonfunctioning hard drives.

• Hard drives can be found in a variety of devices including the popular iPod. The iPod hard drive can store not only music files but also any type of computer file. In your request for disclosures, include this as one of the electronic discovery devices that may contain electronic information.

[C]   CD-ROM (Compact Disc-Read Only Memory)

One of the most common information storage mediums is the CD-ROM.

A CD-ROM (Compact Disc-Read Only Memory) is an injection-molded aluminized disc, which stores digital data (such as text, audio, video and software) in high-density microscopic pits. It is the same size, and uses the same technology as musical CD disks. Once written to, the contents cannot be deleted or changed by the user. A multi-session CD-ROM allows for additional data to be added after the initial CD is "burned" with data. Many people are familiar with the compact disc as an audio device for playing music, but it can hold a large amount of text, graphics, images, animation, video and sound data. The 4.72-inch compact disk stores approximately 650 megabytes (650 million characters) on a single side, compared to only 1.44 megabytes on a 3.5-inch floppy disk. "A CD-ROM's storage capacity is 650 megabytes, the equivalent of 325,000 typewritten pages" or 15,000 document page images. *Hagemeyer North America, Inc. v. Gateway Data Sciences Corp.*, 222 F.R.D. 594, 601 (E.D.Wis. 2004).

The process of "burning" a CD-ROM is relatively easy. A blank CD-ROM, containing a reflective layer of gold or aluminum, as well as a layer of organic dye, is inserted into a CD-R (CD Recorder). Information is embedded onto the disc via a laser in the CD recorder. This is the so-called "burning" process.

CD-ROMs are a type of storage medium that is capable of being written to only once, but read many times. They are useful for storing a large amount of information that does not need to be changed or updated by the user. This storage medium is usually purchased with information already written to them, although special types of CD drives, called WORM (write once, read many) drives, allow the user to write data to a blank CD once, after which it is a CD-ROM.

This type of CD is referred to as a CD-R ("CD Recordable") and CD-RW ("CD-Rewritable") disks. CD-R disks can only have data written on them once as opposed to a CD-RW disks that allows a user to write data many times on the same disk.

Most desktops and laptops have a CD drive that can create or "burn" a CD-ROM, CD-RW or CD-R disc depending on the disk drive.

[1]   Reported Case

- *Davison v. Eldorado Resorts LLC,* No. CIV.05-0021, 2006 U.S. Dist. LEXIS 12598, n.1 (D. Nev. Mar. 10, 2006). The Court noted, "[t]he CD at issue is a CD-R, as opposed to a CD-RW. . . . The key difference between the two is that files placed onto a CD-R cannot be modified or overwritten . . . Files that are placed onto a CD-RW may be overwritten."

- *Graham v. James,* No. CIV.91-800, 1992 WL 10844, *1 (W.D.N.Y. Jan. 17, 1992). "A CD ROM disk, or CD ROM, is identical in appearance to the compact disks used in audio players but, rather than storing music decipherable by a compact disk player, stores data which can be read by a laser into a computer via a CD ROM disk drive, just as a computer reads information off of a floppy disk through a disk drive. The main advantage of CD ROM disks over floppy disks is their larger storage capacity; one CD ROM holds roughly the same amount of information as 1,000 floppies."

- *In re Lorazepam and Clorazepate Antitrust Litigation,* 300 F. Supp. 2d 43, 47(D.D.C. 2004). The Court ruled that the plaintiff had to take the discovery that was provided on "23 CD-ROM's . . . to a company that specializes in computer forensics or electronic discovery to ascertain whether the information on the 23 CDROM's can be either read and searched by a commercially available software or whether it can be converted to a format that will render it capable of being read and searched by commercially available software."

- *See also,* § 2.3[D][2], *Optical Media.*

[D]   DVD - Digital Versatile (Video) Disk

"Digital Versatile Discs" or "DVDs" is the next-generation optical disk standard that has a storage capacity upward of 8.5 gigabytes of data and can store two hours of a movie on each side. It is designed to be backward compatible, which will enable current CD-ROM's to be played on a DVD player.

There are several different DVD formats. Two of the most popular are the DVD-VIDEO and DVD-ROM. A DVD-VIDEO format is used for home entertainment and a DVD-ROM format is used for storing computer data. Compared to a CD-ROM, the DVD, because of its size and access speed, provides for better graphics, resolution and increased storage capacity. The DVD recording device is becoming increasingly popular and can hold up to 17 gigabytes of data, which is twenty times as much information than is on a CD-ROM. It will eventually replace the CD-ROM for storage of electronic data.

Many desktops and laptops have a DVD drive that can "burn" a DVD disk, and are frequently used to store or transfer electronic data.

[1]   Reported Cases

- *Universal City Studios, Inc. v. Corley*, 273 F.3d 429, 436 (2nd Cir. 2001). "Movies in digital form are placed on disks, known as DVDs, which can be played on a DVD player (either a stand-alone device or a component of a computer). DVDs offer advantages over analog tapes, such as improved visual and audio quality, larger data capacity, and greater durability."

- *Charles Schwab & Co., Inc. v. Carter*, No. CIV.04-7071, 2005 WL 351929, *2 (N.D.Ill. 2005). In this trade secret case the defendant was alleged to have arrived at Schwab with a laptop computer capable of burning large amounts of information onto DVDs.

- *See also*, § 2.3[D][2], *Optical Media*.

[E]   Jaz and Zip Disk

The newly developed group of "super floppies" can store 100 MB to more than 20 GB of data in removable storage cartridges. They are similar in appearance to a floppy disk. These cartridges fit into disk drives that can be external or internal. Some of the more popular brands are the Jaz and the Zip disk by Iomega (www.iomega.com).

[1]   Reported Cases

- *State v. Anderson*, 2004 WL 413273, *5 (Ohio 2004). The defendant in a child pornography case extensively used Jaz disks to transfer and backup images.

- *United States v. Maxwell*, 386 F.3d 1042, 1045-1046 n.2 (11th Cir. 2004). In a child pornography case "[the agent] . . . described zip disks [as] . . . removable devices that are used to store computer files, much like standard floppy disks. The technology that facilitates storage is slightly different for zip disks than it is floppy disks, and zip disks therefore can only be used in computers that are equipped with a zip drive. Zip disks are capable of storing substantially more information than floppy disks."

- *LEXIS-NEXIS v. Beer*, 41 F. Supp. 2d 950 (D. Minn. 1999). In this action for breach of a covenant not to compete, the defendant prior to quitting had copied an ACT! customer database onto a ZIP disk along with some e-mails.

[F]   LS-120 (SuperDisk)

Imation 120MB SuperDisk (www.imation.com) diskettes have 83 times more storage space than regular floppies. These diskettes are the same size and shape as regular diskettes, but hold up to 120MB of data. Special Imation SuperDisk Drives are needed to read the data. The drives have since been discontinued.

[1]   Reported Case

• *United States v. Barth,* 26 F. Supp.2d 929, 934 (W.D.Tex. 1998). The agent in a criminal case seized ". . . eight LS 120 computer disks, each of which can store 120 megabytes of data . . . "

[G]   PC Card (PMCIA Card)

PC Cards, formerly called PCMCIA (**P**ersonal **C**omputer **M**emory **C**ard **I**nternational **A**ssociation) cards, are small-covered circuit boards that can be inserted into special slots on laptops. These slots, available on a number of portables, permit plug and play functionality for different products. PC cards are usually about the size of a credit card and about three to ten mm (about 0.1 to 0.4 in.) thick. Computers designed to accept PC cards have slots in the outside case to accommodate the cards.

PC Cards can be hard drives, modems, network adapters, RAM (random access memory), sound cards, SCSI or cellular phone connectors and flash memory.

Of special interest for discovery is that hard disks and flash memory PC Cards can hold many megabytes of stored information. The information stored on these cards is "nonvolatile," meaning that the data is maintained even if the memory card is removed from the laptop or PDA.

[1]   Reported Case

• *In re Two Admin. Subpoenas Duces Tecum,* No. CIV.05-29, 2005 U.S. Dist. LEXIS 11867, at *10-11 (D. Me. Jun. 17, 2005). While investigating defendant for alleged health care fraud, FBI agents served defendant with two subpoenas duces tecum requiring the production of "[a]ny magnetic, electronic or optical storage device capable of storing data, such as floppy disks, hard disks, tapes, CD-ROMs, CD-R, CD-RWs, DVDs, optical disks, printer or memory buffers, smart cards, *PC cards,* memory calculators, electronic dialers, electronic notebooks, and personal digital assistants. . . . (emphasis added)."

[H]   MD (Minidisk)

Minidisk is a 2 1/2″ floppy disk that records and stores either digital audio or data. Minidisks are similar in appearance, but smaller, compared to a 3 1/2″ floppy disk. They can store 140MB of data or 74 minutes of audio.

[I]   Pen or Thumb Drive

The pen or thumb drive device fits into the USB port of your computer, is half the size of a pen, and may store upwards of one gigabyte of information. They are also referred to as a flash drive, USB hard drives, key chain drives, key chain memory, pocket drives, USB minidrives, USB Memory Keys, or simply removable flash disk drives. They are best described as portable hard drives that fit on a key chain or in your pocket. You simply plug them into USB ports where they are automatically recognized as another external drive and are ready to use in seconds. Data can be easily stored and transferred to another computer using this device. They are similar to a hard drive, but much smaller and easily transportable.

[J]   Magnetic Tape Drive

A magnetic tape drive can be external or internal and is generally used as a backup device. Magnetic tape can hold significant amounts of computer information – between 100 MB and 20 GB and higher.

Magnetic tape has served as a storage medium since the 1950s and is composed of strong plastic embedded with metallic particles that become magnetized. It is generally used for archival storage of electronic data for mainframe computers since it can hold large amounts of data and is inexpensive to store. However, it is also available to store data from servers, personal computers and laptops. The smaller magnetic tapes resemble audiocassette tapes. These tapes are written on sequentially from the beginning to the end of the tape. Since the data is stored in a sequential fashion, access to the data can be slow. In addition, the magnetic media will degrade over time, reducing the life expectancy of the electronic data. They can be reused and data recorded over prior recorded data.

Since magnetic tapes come in various sizes and can be reused, it may be beneficial to determine if there is data on the end of the tape that may not have been overwritten. For example, if magnetic tape has been used to back up a computer that involved 400 MB of information, and the tape was later reused to back up a different computer involving only 200 MB of information, then 200 MB of information from the first computer may be available for discovery.

For discovery purposes, when you obtain the tape you will need to know the specific type of tape, the manufacturer's name and model number of the tape drive and the manufacturer's name, program name and version number of the software used to write the data to the tape. It may also be necessary to know the specific parameters controlling the program's various operational capabilities. *See also,* § 2.6[C], *Backups – Computer Files.*

[1]   Reported Cases

• *Storage Technology Corp. v. Quantum Corp.*, No. CIV. 03-672, 2005 WL 1172737, at *1-2 (D. Colo. May 17, 2005). The Court described DLT and SDLT tape systems.

> DLT tape drive systems record data in a linear pattern on magnetic tape. Each data track goes the entire length of the tape, which may be as long as 1800 feet. During recording, the first set of tracks is recorded on the length of the tape. When the end of the tape is reached, the heads are repositioned to record another set of tracks, lengthwise in the opposite direction, and this process is repeated until the tape reaches full capacity . . . SDLT tape products, introduced by Quantum in 2001, are the latest generation of the DLT technology. SDLT drives and tape . . . are designed for the recording of longitudinal data tracks. Data is recorded on the front surface of the tape which is coated with a material containing magnetic particles. SDLT drives have magnetic heads that read and write data tracks. . . . Tape automation libraries are large systems that hold magnetic tape cartridges and tape drives and have robotic devices that can automatically select and mount a cartridge into a tape drive.

• *Zubulake v. UBS Warburg LLC,* 217 F.R.D. 309, 319 (S.D.N.Y. 2003). For cost allocation purposes the Court categorized magnetic tape according to its accessibility. One of the categories was its use as a backup media:

> *4. Backup tapes:* "A device, like a tape recorder, that reads data from and writes it onto a tape. Tape drives have data capacities of anywhere from a few hundred kilobytes to several gigabytes. Their transfer speeds also vary considerably . . . The disadvantage of tape drives is that they are sequential- access devices, which means that to read any particular block of data, you need to read all the preceding blocks." As a result, "[t]he data on a backup tape are not organized for retrieval of individual documents or files [because] . . . the organization of the data mirrors the computer's structure, not the human records management structure." Backup tapes also typically employ some sort of data compression, permitting more data to be stored on each tape, but also making restoration more time-consuming and expensive, especially given the lack of uniform standard governing data compression.

[K]   DAT (Digital Audio Tape)

DAT (Digital Audio Tape) is a standard medium and technology for the digital recording of audio or data on tape. A DAT drive is a digital tape recorder with rotating heads similar to those found in a video deck. It is often used as an archiving medium. It can store 2 to 24 gigabytes of data and support data transfer rates of about 2 Mbps. Like other types of tapes, DATs are sequential-access media.

[L]   Compact Flash Card

A Compact Flash (CF) card is a popular memory card developed by SanDisk (www.sandisk.com) and uses flash memory to store data on a very small card. The card can easily provide additional storage for a wide variety of computing devices, including digital cameras and music players, desktop computers, personal digital assistants (PDAs), digital audio recorders and photo printers. It is about the size of a matchbook and has storage capacity between ten megabytes and one gigabyte and higher. Because flash is nonvolatile memory, stored data is retained even when a device's power source is turned off or lost.

[M]   Smart and Magnetic Stripe Cards

A smart card is a standard credit card-sized plastic card within which a microchip has been embedded. The chip can be loaded with data and when placed in a specialized card reader, the card's data can be read and updated. There are two basic types of smart cards. The first is a memory only card that is a digital storage device capable of holding a large amount of information. The second type is a microprocessor card that is basically a small computer with the capability of processing data and performing calculations. A smart card holds more data than a magnetic stripe card. Smart cards currently are used in telephone, transportation, banking, health care transactions and Internet applications. For example, smart cards can contain medical histories of patients, food stamp allocations, satellite TV programming, prepaid telephone calling authorization and for electronic cash payments on college campuses for buying lunches, dinners and other items. Some smart cards do not require a reader and send the information wirelessly to computer devices.

A black or brown stripe that runs across the back of a card identifies a magnetic stripe card. The stripe is made up of tiny iron-based magnetic particles in a plastic-like film. Account or user information can be stored on numerous tracks embedded on the magnetic stripe. As you "swipe" a credit card through a reader or insert it in a reader at the gas station pump the information on the stripe is read. Magnetic stripe cards are used for ATM access, subway access, driver licenses, security door passes and many other uses.

Information that may be found on smart cards and magnetic stripe cards:

- Debit and credit card information;
- Medical records;
- Food allowances;
- Passport information; and
- Room key information.

[1]   Reported Case

- *MasterCard International Inc. v. First National Bank of Omaha,* No. CIV.02-3691, 2004 WL 326708, at *1, 6 (S.D.N.Y. Feb. 23, 2004). "A smart card is typically a plastic card containing a computer chip that enables the holder to purchase goods and services, to access financial or other records, and to perform other operations requiring data stored on the chip."

- *Leighton Technologies LLC v. Oberthur Card Systems, S.A.,* 358 F. Supp.2d 361, 364 (S.D.N.Y. 2005).

  [A] "smart card," [is] a plastic card that includes an electronic element (such as a computer chip) and a reader, and that is used in numerous common applications including security swipe cards, credit/debit cards, mass transit access, toll collection (EZ-Pass), and government identification. . . . Smart cards come in three forms. As the name suggests, a "contactless" smart card transmits a signal when it is placed near the reading device, even if the card is contained in a purse or wallet. A "contact" smart card requires contact between a magnetic strip on the card and the reading device. A "dual function" card works with or without contact.

- *C.F.T.C. v. Sterling Trading Group, Inc.,* No. CIV.04-21346, 2004 WL 2005617, at *1 (S.D.Fla. Jun. 9, 2004). "For the purposes of this Order, the following definitions apply: 1. The term 'document' is synonymous in meaning and equal in scope to the usage of the term in Federal Rule of Civil Procedure 34(a), and includes, but is not limited to, writings, drawings . . . *smart cards* . . ." (emphasis added).

[N]   Microfilm/Microfiche

Although computer-generated documents are usually stored as files on magnetic tape or disks, both computer documents and paper documents may be stored on microfilm or microfiche. Documents are stored on microfilm and microfiche to reduce the space needed for paper storage.

Microfilm is a continuous roll of photographic film, used for storage of miniaturized text which can be read only with magnification by a reader/printer machine. In some libraries, back files of periodicals are routinely converted to microfilm to save space. Handling and retrieval is simplified by use of microfilm equipment, which photographically reduces images, producing miniature transparencies that can then be magnified for viewing or printing.

Microfiche are miniaturized photographic document images arranged in horizontal rows and vertical columns that form a grid pattern on a card-size transparent film sheet. The text itself can be read and copied only with the aid of a microform reader/printer machine.

[1] Reported Case

- *Zubulake v. UBS Warburg, LLC*, 217 F.R.D. 309, 318 (S.D.N.Y. 2003). Court stated that microfiche is an example of a document that may be in an inaccessible format and not easily readable.

[O] Micro Drive

Micro Drive is an ultra-miniature hard disk technology from IBM that uses a single one-inch diameter platter to provide storage between 170 MB and 1 GB. The Micro Drive uses hard disk drive (HDD) technology to store information.

[P] Memory Stick

Developed by Sony, the Memory Stick is digital data storage technology with more than 10 times the storage capacity of a 3.5" diskette. Memory Stick is a way to share and transfer pictures, sound and other data between different compact electronic devices such as digital cameras, PDA's and camcorders. About the size of a flat AA battery, Memory Sticks are available from 4MB to 64MB with larger sizes being developed. These small plastic inserts can store several hours of audio or hundreds of photographs (depending on the pixel and storage size).

[1] Reported Case

- *M & G Electronics Sales Corp. v. Sony Kabushiki Kaisha,* 250 F. Supp.2d 91, 95 E.D.N.Y. 2003). "Sony began selling a computer storage card device, marketed under the registered trademark MEMORY STICK. Each MEMORY STICK is less than 1 inch wide, 2 inches long and less than 1/8 inch thick. The MEMORY STICK fits into MEMORY STICK-compatible products, including computers, camcorders, personal digital assistants and WALKMAN products."

[Q]   Bernoulli Drive

This storage device is similar in capacity to a hard drive and is primarily used as a backup device. This unusual storage device operates on the principle of air flowing under flexible material and as it spins, data is recorded on it. The drive can be removed just like a floppy. It is no longer being produced.

[R]   Other Resources

A dictionary of storage networking terminology can be located at the Storage Network Industry Association's website located at www.snia.org. For storage specific information, visit SearchStorage.com located at www.searchstorage.com.

§ 2.5   STORAGE DEVICES

Mainframe Computer	Printer
Server (Networking)	Copier
Personal Computer	Compact Disc Duplicator
Laptop	Cameras/Camcorder (Digital)
Personal Digital Assistant (PDA)	Electronic Game Devices
Cellular Telephone	Home Electronic Devices
Cordless Telephone	Global Positioning System (GPS)
Voice Mail and Answering Machine	Security Systems
Caller ID Device	Vehicle Computer Devices
Paging Device	RFID
Facsimile Transmission (Faxes)	Biometric
Smart and Magnetic Stripe Cards	Other New Devices
Scanner	

There are many different types of storage devices that use the storage media discussed in § 2.4, *Storage Media*, and more devices are being developed daily. The most commonly used devices use hard drive, magnetic tape and optical media for their storage needs.

[A] Mainframe Computer

As noted, mainframe computers have more memory and speed capabilities than workstations and can be shared by multiple users through a series of interconnected computers. Most of these mainframes are found in businesses and industrial facilities and are used for heavy computational requirements.

Mainframe computers are commonly networked. They are often connected to PCs, workstations or terminals that have no computational abilities of their own. These "dumb" terminals can be used to enter data or receive data from the central computer, however, they are unable to perform calculations or store data.

Information that may be found on a mainframe. Generally, the electronic data discussed in § 3.3, *Business Software Applications* and the data types discussed in § 3.6 can be found on a mainframe. Consider also whether the computer is being used as another device such as a voice mail or caller ID device. For a list of devices *see* § 2.5, *Storage Devices.*

[1] Reported Cases

- *In re American Academy of Science Tech Center,* 367 F.3d 1359, 1365-66 (Fed. Cir. 2004). The Court discussed the difference between a mainframe computer and distributed network system similar to a Local Area Network (LAN).

- *Resqnet.com Inc. v. Lansa Inc.,* 346 F.3d 1374, 1375-76 (Fed. Cir. 2003). The Court discussed mainframes, dumb terminals and the changeover to PC's that process information.

[B] Server (Networking)

[1] Server

A server, on a local area network (LAN), is a computer (or computers) that controls access to the network and its resources (such as hard drives, e-mail and printers). Information on servers is generally stored on hard drives or optical disks. Depending on the type of server, they are often the targets of discovery requests because of the electronic information stored on them. There are many types of "servers" to consider when requesting discovery of electronic information. However, the most common are file, Web, e-mail, fax and application servers. These may exist as separate, stand-alone server computers or they may be contained within the same server computer. Servers are part of a networking system called client/server.

They are generally high-powered machines, since they are required to handle the computing needs of many client workstations. Client computers, at the worker's desk, can also be powerful machines, but a variety of low or high-powered machines are often connected to the network.

Network servers may hold tremendous amounts of information. *Hagemeyer North America, Inc. v. Gateway Data Sciences Corp.*, 222 F.R.D. 594, 601 (E.D.Wis. 2004). ("[some] computer networks create backup data measured in terabytes-1,000,000 megabytes-which is the equivalent of 500 billion typewritten pages.").

A server provides a specific kind of service to a client computer. For example, a Web server can store and provide content for clients if they are using an Intranet or Extranet. A server host can have several different packages or applications running on it, thus providing many different services to network clients. Services to a network client can include e-mail, fax, word processing, spreadsheets and so on. Since they need to handle computing requests from several computers at once, they must run an advanced operating system.

[2]   Networking, LAN and WAN

Computer links and local area networks (LANs) are the means by which computers exchange data and talk to each other. LANS allow linked computers to share data, programs, storage and printers.

Networking is commonly defined as connecting computers together by cables, wire, or wireless devices to share information and hardware resources. These resources, located on servers, include data sharing, printers, storage disk drives, modems, CD-ROMs, communication equipment and so on. Being connected on a network is like being connected to the hard drive of many other computers. One can access files on other computers, as if they were on their own computer.

The type of network can often determine the location of electronic information. There are two types of networks, LAN and WAN. A LAN (local area network) is several computers connected together in the same general vicinity, such as an office building. Computers connected together within a city, state or worldwide, but not in the same general vicinity, are referred to as a WAN (Wide Area Network). Computers on a WAN can be connected by modems and communication lines or by satellite. A computer connected to a network such as a LAN or WAN is called a node.

A local area network (LAN) consists of several PCs or workstations connected to a special computer called the server (unless it is a peer-to-peer setup, which requires no server). The server stores and manages programs and data. A server often contains all of a networked group's data and enables LAN workstations to be set up with or without storage capabilities.

A LAN has a file server that acts as the central computer for the system, network-operating software and application programs such as word processing, e-mail and calendars. The network operating system, like Windows Server, runs on top of the individual PC's operating system (such as Windows 95/98/00/XP). The network operating system manages file transfers, the control of peripherals and other network tasks. A LAN generally has an administrator who handles the network and ensures that things are run properly. A PC is connected to the network with a network interface card that fits into a computer's expansion slot or by a wireless connection.

As mentioned previously, wide area networks (WANs) are networks that span large geographical areas. Computers can connect to another city or country. For example, a person in Los Angeles can browse through the computerized archives of the Library of Congress in Washington, D.C. The largest WAN is the Internet, a global consortium of networks linked by common communication programs.

[a]   Reported Cases

- *Massachusetts v. Microsoft Corp.*, 373 F.3d 1199, 1222 (Fed. Cir. 2004). "A network typically involves interoperation between one or more large, central computers (the servers) and a number of PCs (the clients). By interoperating with the server, the clients may communicate with each other and store data or run applications directly on the server. The district court found that servers may use any of several different operating systems . . . but most clients run a version of Windows."

- *In re American Academy of Science Tech Center*, 367 F.3d 1359, 1365-66 (Fed. Cir. 2004). The Court discussed the difference between a mainframe computer and distributed network system similar to a local area network.

- *Cobell v. Norton*, No. CIV.96-285, 2001 WL 1555296, at*4 n.16 (D.D.C. Dec. 6, 2001). "A wide area network (WAN) is a geographically dispersed telecommunications network. The term distinguishes a broader telecommunication structure from a local area network (LAN). A wide area network may be privately owned or rented, but the term usually connotes the inclusion of public (shared user) networks."

- *Dynacore Holdings Corp. v. US Philips Corp.*, 363 F.3d 1263, 1268 (Fed. Cir. 2004). In this patent case the Court discussed nodes, topologies (serial, parallel and tree) and defined a LAN as "a collection of computers and/or peripheral devices in close geographic proximity interconnected to allow communication. Like most aspects of computer technology, LANs combine physical characteristics with software capabilities. The geometry describing a LAN's physical layout is referred to as its 'topology.' A LAN's defining software embodies its 'communication protocols.'"

[3]   Client/Server

Client/server is a type of computing that divides tasks between clients and servers. Client/server networks use a dedicated computer called a server to handle file, print and other services for client users. The client (usually the less powerful machine) requests information from the servers. The server (usually the more powerful machine) accepts the client's request, performs computations, satisfies clients' requests and sends responses. The client is sometimes referred to as the front-end component and the server is referred to as the back-end component.

A client/server network may have several server computers to handle the server needs for the client group. Computers connected to the server network are called clients. Client computers are at the worker's desk. There are several types of servers such as a fax server that allows one to fax documents from a client computer or save faxes to a fax server. As the network system grows, separate servers for print, file, Web and e-mail can be connected. Servers called redundant file servers can be connected to the primary server to backup data instantly.

[a]   Reported Cases

- *New York v. Microsoft Corp.* 224 F. Supp.2d 76, 121-122 (D.D.C. 2002). The Court discussed the client/server computing environment.

- *Tilberg v. Next Mgmt. Co.,* No. CIV.04-7373, 2005 U.S. Dist. LEXIS 24892, at *2-4 (D.N.Y. Oct. 24, 2005). The Court allowed the employee full access to search the employer's e-mail server, central server, and individual workstations.

- *Physicians Interactive v. Lathian Systems, Inc.,* No. CIV. 03-1193, 2003 WL 23018270, at *1 n.2, 11 (E.D.Va. Dec. 5, 2003). The Court granted the plaintiff's request to make a "mirror image" of the defendant's computer server and noted that a "'File server' is defined as, 'a computer in a network that stores application programs and data files accessed by other computers.' *See,* Microsoft Encarta College Dictionary 533 (1st ed. 2001)."

- *In re Priceline.com Inc. Sec. Litig.,* 233 F.R.D. 88, 89-90 (D. Conn. 2005). In a securities case the Court noted that "The data stored in the snapshot is created and stored on three different types of servers: production database servers, which contain the raw transactional information of customer bids and offers; development servers, which contain quality-control and other 'test' data; and corporate file servers, which contain e-mails, memoranda, letters, and all other office-type documents. . . ."

[4]   Peer-to-Peer Network

The primary idea behind a peer-to-peer network is that each computer can be both a client and a server. Therefore, each computer can share its resources and borrow resources from other computers. For example, if one computer has a laser printer attached, a peer can request access rights to the laser printer and print a document on that printer. Similarly, if another computer has work product on it, then one can access the peer "server" as a "client" to locate specific information.

In order to discover information on a peer-to-peer network, one would have to request the files from each of the connected workstations.

[a]   Reported Case

• *MGM Studios Inc. v. Grokster, Ltd.,* 125 S. Ct. 2764, 2770 (2005). The Court in this copyright infringement case discussed the advantages of peer-to-peer networks.

> Respondents . . . distribute free software products that allow computer users to share electronic files through peer-to-peer networks, so called because users' computers communicate directly with each other, not through central servers. The advantage of peer-to-peer networks over information networks of other types shows up in their substantial and growing popularity. Because they need no central computer server to mediate the exchange of information or files among users, the high-bandwidth communications capacity for a server may be dispensed with, and the need for costly server storage space is eliminated. Since copies of a file (particularly a popular one) are available on many users' computers, file requests and retrievals may be faster than on other types of networks, and since file exchanges do not travel through a server, communications can take place between any computers that remain connected to the network without risk that a glitch in the server will disable the network in its entirety. Given these benefits in security, cost, and efficiency, peer-to-peer networks are employed to store and distribute electronic files by universities, government agencies, corporations, and libraries . . .

• *Metro-Goldwyn-Mayer Studios, Inc. v. Grokster Ltd.,* 380 F.3d 1154, 1158 (9th Cir. 2004), *rev'd on other grounds,* 2005 WL 1499402 (U.S. Jun. 27, 2005). "In a peer-to-peer distribution network, the information available for access does not reside on a central server. No one computer contains all of the information that is available to all of the users. Rather, each computer makes information available to every other computer in the peer-to-peer network. In other words, in a peer-to-peer network, each computer is both a server and a client."

[5]   Network Components

A network has three layers of components; network software, network hardware and application software.

Network software is the operating system selected to run the network. This system enables the computer to exchange information and ensure correct data transmission. The network operating system (NOS) is the controlling software that enables a server to accommodate multiple clients and provide the communication network between them.

Network operating systems manage various network functions, such as file storage, application software and printer use. Some types of network operating software include Novell NetWare and Windows Server. Some server protocols are TCP/ISP and IPX/SPX.

Network hardware is made up of the physical components that connect computers. The physical components are network topology and network connecting devices, which include network interface cards, cabling, routers, bridges, hubs and all other hardware connected to computers, including the cabling.

A network can be connected by cable or by wireless connections. The wide use of notebook and other portable computers has driven the advances in wireless networks. Wireless networks use either infrared or radio frequency transmissions to link mobile computers to networks. Infrared wireless LANs work only within a room, while wireless LANs based on radio-frequency transmissions can penetrate most walls. Wireless communications for WANS use cellular telephone networks, satellite transmissions or dedicated equipment to provide regional or global coverage.

Application software consists of computer programs that interface with network users and permit the sharing of information, such as files, graphics, video and other resources such as printers and disks. Word processing, e-mail and spreadsheets are run by network application software such as WordPerfect, Microsoft Outlook and Microsoft Excel.

[6]   Web-Based Networking - Intranet and Extranet

Most businesses operate an internal network version of the Internet, known as "Intranets." Technically speaking, an *Intranet* is an internal network that operates using Internet "open standards." The "open standards" consist of the key standard TCP/IP (the network protocol), HTML (WWW programming language), POP3 and SMTP (E-mail standards), HTTP (Web server language), FTP (file transfer protocol) and others. *Intel Corp. v. Hamidi,* 1 Cal. Rptr.3d 32, 38 n.1 (S.Ct. Cal. Jun. 30, 2003) ("[a]n 'intranet' [is] . . . 'a network based on TCP/IP protocols (an internet) belonging to an organization, usually a corporation, accessible only by the organization's members, employees, or others with authorization.'").

An *Intranet* is a private network inside an organization, which uses browser software like that used on the Internet. It is for internal use, can be walled off and does not have to be part of the Internet for total security. It generally is located on an organization's networked computer system. They are based on "open" Internet standards and have seen exceptional growth.

Within a company many departments and individuals may have their own websites on the company's Intranet. Companies use Intranets to manage projects, provide employee information, distribute data and information and for many other uses. For example, the human resource's department may have their own website where they post employment related notices, policies and/or procedures. A different department may set up a collaborative platform for other departments and employees to provide feedback on a given project.

Intranets are a huge repository for information. In addition to web postings, it may have electronic mail capabilities and formal or informal chat groups. The material on the Intranet may be accessible to everyone within an organization. However, communications and other material on a company's Intranet may not be privileged and work product or other legal material sent utilizing an Intranet may result in a waiver of such privileges.

An *Extranet* is a private "Internet" for two or more firms or organizations. An *Extranet* is a private network that uses Internet technology to enable sharing and collaboration between businesses, organizations, government entities, educational units and others.

The importance of understanding *Intranets* and *Extranets* is that through the use of Web servers and other storage devices, they contain significant amounts of electronic information that may be of value to your case. An *Intranet* or *Extranet's* data is found on servers that are located within or outside of an organization's physical structure. These intranets can be discovered by requesting a HTML version of the site where a snapshot of the site is captured for later viewing using a web browser. In addition, many organizations will maintain an archive of their changes made to an Intranet.

[a]   Reported Cases

- *Campbell v. General Dynamics Government Systems Corp.,* 407 F.3d 546, 556 (1st Cir. 2005). The Court discussed the posting of employment notices on the company's Intranet, e-mail delivery and paper notice.

- *Battagliola v. National Life Ins. Co.,* No. CIV.03-8558, 2005 WL 101353, at *3 (S.D.N.Y. Jan. 19, 2005). "In 1999, UnumProvident established this 'legal extranet system' ('LES') to allow in-house counsel and outside counsel representing Unum to access and share information about legal claims and strategies."

[7]   Server Types

Application software and data files for databases, word processors, faxes, e-mail, etc. can be located on one or multiple servers. There may be several different types of servers on a computer network.

- *File Server.* A file server is a file storage device on a LAN that is generally accessible to all users on the network. A file server stores, manages and maintains data files for users on the system. They serve as central data depositories for networks of desktop computers. They are more powerful and efficient then desktop computers and allow multiple users to update documents and share computer files. Files can include word processing, database, spreadsheet or other application software data.

- *E-mail Server.* An e-mail server is a device on a LAN that sends, receives and stores e-mail.

- *Fax Server.* A fax server is a device on a LAN that is capable of sending, receiving and storing facsimile documents.

- *Web Server.* A Web server is a device on a LAN that handles and stores Web pages and other Web information on Intranets, Extranets and the World Wide Web. For example, an organization's Intranet may contain the organization's policies and procedures regarding sick leave, retirement, etc.

- *Application Server.* An application server generally contains application programs, such as Microsoft Word, for use by networked client computers.

   Information that may be found on a server:

   Generally, the electronic data discussed in § 3.3, *Business Software Applications* and the data types discussed in §§ 3.6–3.19 can be found on a server. In addition, you should consider whether the computer is being used as another device such as a voice mail or caller ID device. For a list of devices *see* § 2.5, *Storage Devices.*

   Activity on a server may be recorded by server logs. *Lynch v. Omaha World-Herald Co.,* 300 F. Supp. 2d 896 (D. Neb. 2004) (web server logs available detailing user activity); *See also,* § 2.06[G], *Audit Trails and Logs.*

   [8]   Reported Case

- *Center for Democracy & Technology v. Pappert,* 337 F. Supp.2d 606, 614 (E.D.Pa. 2004). "To make a web site available on the World Wide Web, a web publisher must place the content or web pages onto a computer running specialized web server software. This computer, known as a Web Server, transmits the requested web pages in response to requests sent by users on the Internet."

- *Verizon Online Services, Inc. v. Ralsky,* 203 F. Supp.2d 601, 606 (E.D.Va. 2002). "An e-mail server processes every e-mail that is addressed to the ISP's customer. In other words, once the e-mail is transmitted, it must first pass through the ISP's computer server to reach its ultimate destination--the subscriber's computer."

- *Keir v. UnumProvident,* No. CIV.02-8781, 2003 WL 21997747, at *4 (S.D.N.Y. Aug. 22, 2003). The Court discussed at length the discovery process involved and noted, "[s]ince August 2000, IBM has provided email, file server, and electronic data related disaster recovery services to UnumProvident. . . . UnumProvident has approximately

888 computer servers supported by tape libraries at five locations: Chattanooga, Columbia, Portland, Burlington, and Worcester."

- *Arista Records, Inc. v. Sakfield Holding Co. S.L.,* 314 F. Supp.2d 27 (D.D.C. 2004). The Court denied the defendant's motion to dismiss for lack of personal jurisdiction and found that "[p]laintiffs' expert determined that a program designed to erase electronically stored information had been run over 50 times from a remote location in an effort to erase all electronic information on the [web] servers."

[C]   Personal Computer

Desktop, personal computers or PC's can be found in virtually all offices and businesses. *See,* § 2.2[A][2], *Types and Description* for a court definition and other information regarding a PC.

Information that may be found on a personal computer:

Generally, the electronic data discussed in § 3.03, *Business Software Applications* and the data types discussed in §§ 3.06-3.19 can be found on a personal computer. In addition, you should consider whether the computer is being used as another device such as a voice mail or caller ID device. For a list of devices see § 2.5, *Storage Devices.*

[D]   Laptop

See, § 2.2[A][2], *Types and Description* for information regarding a laptop.

Information that may be found on a laptop:

Generally, the electronic data discussed in § 3.3, *Business Software Applications* and the data types discussed in §§ 3.6-3.19 can be found on a laptop. In addition, you should consider whether the computer is being used as another device such as a voice mail or caller ID device. For a list of devices *see* § 2.5, *Storage Devices.*

[1]   Reported Case

- *Byrne v. Byrne,* 168 Misc. 2d 321, 650 N.Y.S.2d 499 (1996). In this domestic relations case the Court held that computer memory is similar to a file cabinet. Since the wife could have access to contents of a file cabinet left in the marital residence, she should have access to the computer laptop contents.

- *Ranta v. Ranta,* 2004 WL 504588 (Conn. Super. Feb. 25, 2004). The Court issued an order setting forth procedures re privilege, etc. for the wife in a domestic relations case to turn over her laptop computer to the court for review of responsive data.

[E]   Personal Digital Assistant (PDA)/Handheld Computer

A Personal Digital Assistant (PDA) is a small, general purpose, battery powered hand-held computer that helps with such tasks as calendaring, contact management, taking notes, paging, sending and receiving faxes and electronic mail as well as database and Web access. There are hundreds of "custom made" and "off the shelf" software programs that exist for PDAs including Word, Excel and Quicken.

Most PDAs can connect to other computers either through telephone lines, radio waves or a computer cable. Many have PC card slots for attaching storage, modems and other auxiliary devices. Most PDAs are capable of at least limited handwriting recognition, allowing users to enter notes into the computer with a special pen-like device rather than with a keyboard.

The hardware is small in size and usually has a small liquid crystal display (LCD). Like a desktop, a handheld computer has a specific operating system and application software designed for the system. Many PDAs utilize the Palm or the Windows CE operating system and input can be by using a stylus or keyboard.

PDAs provide users with much of the functionality of a full-size personal computer, but are small in size. They can also serve as a portable phone, fax machine, electronic mailbox, pager, voice recorder and some have a built-in camera. Devices may be stand-alone or be networked, at the office, at home or at an off-site location.

This category can also include so-called "smart phones" which are devices that combine the PC-like capabilities of handheld devices and mobile telephone technology.

One of the most popular messaging devices is the Blackberry Handheld PDA which is primarily used for wireless e-mail. They generally do not have as many applications as a PDA but may contain an address book, a personal scheduler and have pager capability.

Many of these handheld devices have some form of an input or output to synchronize with a desktop or laptop computer using a wired or wireless connection.

Some PDAs will lose all of their data if the battery is not kept charged. If you take possession of a PDA, ensure that a power supply is available to prevent any loss of data.

Information that may be found on a PDA/Handheld Computer:

- Calendars;
- Contact information;
- Notes and to-do lists;
- Paging information;

- Bar code scanner;
- GPS capability;
- Voice recorder;
- Pictures;
- Internet and Web access information;
- E-mail;
- Faxes;
- Personal finances; and
- Stored data - text, images, audio, video, etc.

[1]   Reported Case

- *Hopson v. Mayor & City Council of Baltimore,* 232 F.R.D. 228, 245 (D. Md. 2005). Citing to the Civil Discovery Standards for the American Bar Association Section on Litigation the court noted that the parties should discuss "the scope of the electronic records sought . . . i.e. e-mail, voice mail, archived data, back-up or disaster recovery data, laptops, personal computers, *PDA's . . .*" (emphasis added).

- *United States v. Curtin,* 443 F.3d 1084, 1088 (9th Cir. 2006). The police searched the defendant's digital assistant and found 140 stories of child pornography.

- *Mathias v. Jacobs*, 197 F.R.D. 29 (S.D.N.Y. 2000), *vacated on other grounds,* 167 F. Supp. 2d 606 (2001). In this business lawsuit, the defendant had requested calendars, electronic organizers, schedules, diaries, etc. from the plaintiff. The plaintiff produced a number of documents but objected to the production of the Palm Pilot. The Court ordered the production of the Palm Pilot that contained the information the defendant sought, and the Court also considered spoliation and preservation rulings.

- *Nationwide Equipment Co. v. Allen,* No. CIV.305-236, 2005 WL 1228360, at *5 (M.D.Fla. May 24, 2005). The plaintiff claimed that it invested significant resources to keep its customer list secret but the Court noted that its "primary customer contact database was maintained on his palm pilot, as opposed to any password protected computer program . . ."

- *NTP, Inc. v. Research In Motion, Ltd.* 392 F.3d 1336, 1334 (Fed. Cir. 2004). In ruling upon a possible patent infringement the Court described in detail the process of receiving e-mail using a Blackberry.

- *C.F.T.C. v. Sterling Trading Group, Inc.,* No. CIV.04-21346, 2004 WL 2005617, at *1 (S.D.Fla. Jun. 9, 2004). "For the purposes of this Order, the following definitions apply: 1. The term 'document' is synonymous in meaning and equal in scope to the usage of the term in Federal Rule of Civil Procedure 34(a), and includes, but is not limited to . . .

personal digital assistants such as Palm Pilot computers, as well as printouts or readouts from any magnetic storage device) . . ." (emphasis added).

[2]   Other Authorities

• Wayne Jansen & Rick Ayers, *Guidelines on PDA Forensics*, NIST Special Publication 800-72 (2004) available at http://csrc.nist.gov/publications/nistpubs/ on July 17, 2006. This article provides an in-depth look at the forensic collection of information from PDAs.

[3]   Discovery Pointer

Interrogatory/Request to produce:

• List and provide all diaries, appointment books, calendars, schedules, electronic organizers and itineraries of any kind, in any form, from _____ to _____ and all telephone directories, Rolodex cards, diaries, organizers, electronic organizers, personal digital assistants (PDAs) and documents of any kind listing the names, addresses, or phone numbers of any people or entity Plaintiff has contacted in any way from _____to _____.

[F]   Cellular Telephone

A cellular (wireless telephone) or a cell phone combines their portable radio capability with the wired, or wireless, telephone network to provide mobile users with access to the rest of the public telephone system used by nonmobile callers. Cell phones use various protocols such as CDMA, TDMA, GSM, etc.

Cellular mobile phones use a system that divides a service area into a grid of cells. From each cell, low powered portable phones can be accessed and connected to the main telephone network.

Cell phones have many capabilities including acting as a voice mail depository, sending and receiving e-mail and faxes, text messaging, acting as a paging device, accessing the Web, taking and sending pictures, acting as organizers and many other electronic functions.

Text messaging refers to sending short text messages from one cellular phone to another cellular. It is less intrusive and less expensive then a phone call. Oftentimes text messages are saved on the provider's computer storage system.

Enhanced 911 is a requirement imposed by the Federal Communications Commission (FCC) mandating that cellular telephone service providers provide GPS capabilities on cellular phones. This will allow physical tracking of 911 calls by a transmitter device in the phone.

Information that may be found on a cellular telephone:

- Numbers called;
- Numbers stored for speed dialing;
- Names and addresses;
- Caller ID for incoming calls;
- Log of missed and received calls;
- Phone/pager numbers;
- Pictures and PIN numbers;
- Voice mail access numbers;
- Voice mail password;
- Recorded memos and conversations;
- Debit and credit card numbers;
- Calling card numbers;
- E-mail (text and picture)/Internet access information;
- Fax information;
- Service provider information;
- Personal data assistant (PDA) capabilities;
- Video clips; and
- Financial and retail transactions.

[1]   Reported Cases

- *In re Pen Register & Trap/Trace Device with Cell Site Location Auth.,* 396 F. Supp. 2d 747, 755 (D. Tex. 2005). The Court partially granted the United States request to compel a cell phone company to disclose records of a customer's cell phone use. Among the records that were sought was "cell site data." This "cell site data" included the location of cell site/sector at call origination, call termination, and, if reasonably available, during the progress of a call. In addition, the Court noted "[i]n December 1997, the Federal Communications Commission issued final 'Enhanced 911' (E911) rules requiring cellular service providers to upgrade their systems to identify more precisely the longitude and latitude of mobile units making emergency 911 calls. By the end of 2005, carriers using handset-based location technology will be required to locate cell phones within 50 meters for 67% of calls, and 150 meters for 95% of calls. See 47 C.F.R. § 20.18(h) (2005)."

- *United States v. Forest,* 355 F.3d 942, 947 (6th Cir. 2004). In a criminal case federal agents were able to track defendants by dialing the defendant's "cellular phone (without allowing it to ring) several times that day and used Sprint's computer data to determine which cellular transmission towers were being 'hit' by Garner's phone. This 'cell-site data' revealed the general location of Garner."

- *Pinney v. Nokia, Inc.,* 402 F.3d 430, 439-440 (4th Cir. 2005). The Court extensively discussed the technology involving a cellular phone including base stations, Electronic Serial Numbers (ESN) and so forth. *See also, United States v. Brady,* 13 F.3d 334, 335-336 (10th Cir. 1993).

- *State v. Tillett,* No. 21163-1-III, 119 Wash. App. 1013, 2003 WL 23221519, at *7-8 (Wash. 2003)(unpublished). The Court reviewed the foundation for admission of cell phone company data tracking records under the business record exception to the hearsay rule.

[2]   Other Authorities

- Timothy J. Duva, Comment *You Get What You Pay For . . . And So Does The Government: How Law Enforcement Can Use Your Personal Property to Track Your Movements,* 6 N.C. J. L. & Tech. 165 (Fall 2004). This article discusses how cellular phones can be used to track your movements.

[G]   Cordless Telephone

A cordless telephone allows a user the freedom of moving with the telephone as long as the user remains within range of the telephone base station. The base station is the connection between the cordless handset and the wire connection for telephone service. Cordless telephones operate on various frequencies (900 MHz, 1.2 GHz, etc.).

Information that may be found on a cordless telephone:

- Numbers called;
- Numbers stored for speed dialing;
- Caller ID for incoming calls;
- Phone/pager numbers;
- Names and addresses (can serve as a PDA);
- PIN numbers;
- Voice mail access number;
- Voice mail password;
- Debit or credit card numbers;
- Calling card numbers; and
- Onscreen image may contain other information.

[1]   Reported Case

•   *State v. DeLaurier,* 488 A.2d 688, 690 (R.I. 1985). The police using a standard AM radio picked up the phone conversations from a cordless phone.

[H]   Voice Mail and Answering Machine

[1]   Generally

Voice mail is an advanced computerized communication tool, functioning primarily as a telephone answering system. *Voice Systems and Services, Inc. v. VMX, Inc.,* No. CIV.91-88, 1992 WL 510121, at *1 (N.D. Okl. Nov. 5 1992) (description of a voice mail system). *See also, Fraser v. Nationwide Mut. Ins.* Co., 135 F. Supp. 2d 623, 635 (E.D.Pa. 2001), *aff'd in part, vacated in part,* 352 F.3d 107 (3rd Cir. 2003).

The use of voice mail is commonplace and allows parties to exchange information when direct conversation is not needed or possible. Voice mail is easy to use and versatile, similar to e-mail. Most phone companies in the United States offer voice mail service to business and residential customers. Be advised that many companies are starting to switch over to Internet telephone service. *Data Race, Inc. v. Lucent Technologies, Inc.,* 73 F. Supp. 2d 698, 736 (W.D.Tex. 1999) (court discussed the Internet technology involved in Voice over Internet Protocol (VoIP) technology which sends and receives phone calls using the Internet instead of traditional methods). In addition, many companies provide voice mail service in-house, often-storing voice mail on backup tapes or optical disks.

There has been an increase in discovery of voice mail. One commentator noted,

> It used to be voice mail wasn't a big risk in discovery because it resided on third-party proprietary platforms. You couldn't get to it, it got overwritten effectively, and it was hard to deal with. Today every major voice mail system, every one [sic], is a computer program running on a regular old computer, which means the voice mail messages are digital files sitting on computers, which make all of the rules of discovery, of recoverability, of review, et cetera, fall right into place. We routinely find thousands, tens of thousands, in one case, a quarter million, voice mails showing up from various backups and computer platforms.

John H. Jessen, *Special Issues Involving Electronic Discovery,* 9 Kan. J. L. & Pub. Pol'Y 425, 442 (2000).

Voice mail has evolved from tape recordings to digitized records. Voice mail (that can include video if a camera is used) converts audio messages to digital data and stores them on computer hard disks. You can then access and listen for the messages.

Also, because of their digital format, voice mail can be stored, manipulated and treated like e-mail. Voice mail can be easily attached as files to an e-mail message.

"According to recent studies by research firm Gartner Group, e-mail and voice mail systems are converging rapidly. E-mail is now accessible via telephone voice mail systems and voice mail is now being sent to recipients by e-mail." Madden et al., *Caught on Tape: The Next Frontier in Electronic Discovery,* Law Journal Newsletters (May 2004).

Voice mail can also be stored on simple, inexpensive answering machines. These devices store messages on analog tape or in digital storage memory.

[2]   Evidentiary Impact

Voice mail is persuasive evidence. The actual sound of an oral message from a witness, with speaker tone and inflection, provides a much more realistic depiction of what happened, than say e-mail. It provides a sense of "you are there" as you listen to real life conversations. Words from a document or e-mail cannot capture the tone, sarcasm, negativity, emphasis or other clues provided by the spoken word.

Voice mail has already figured prominently in several headline cases.

•   Lucy Morgan, *Gov's Daughter Charged with Fraud*, St. Petersburg Times (Jan. 30 2002). The Governor's daughter was arrested at a Walgreen's and charged with falsifying a prescription after leaving a voice mail from a "doctor" that was identified as from her.

•   Noah Adams, *All Things Considered,* National Public Radio, 2001 WL 9433961 (Mar. 13, 2001). On trial for criminal charges, a voice mail was left from Sean "Puffy" Combs offering to make a potential witness and his family "comfortable."

[3]   Discovery Considerations

Request for voice mail records can have a major impact on discovery in litigation. The cost of locating and reviewing relevant voice mail for disclosure, usually without the aid of computerized search tools, can put significant pressure on a party to settle.

Voice mail accounts "may be maintained in several locations: in-house, through an application service provider, or through a telephone carrier, which may make retrieval even harder." Michael S. Kridel, *Bytes That Bite: The Discovery of Electronic Evidence,* InfoTech Update, 2001 WL 16996545 (May 2001). Since voice mail may reside in a number of locations, ensure that the voice mail is not destroyed through routine document retention policies.

The primary targets of voice mail records are the likely recipients of the voice message. The voice mail accounts for the likely recipients will generally contain the voice mail messages. Generally, even though voice mail records are archived, it may be difficult and time consuming to identify the dates, duration and the number of calls for a particular recipient. Unless the company has implemented archiving technologies that date/time stamps the recipient's messages and the action taken on the voice mail, they may be inaccessible except by manually reviewing each voice mail.

After locating voice mail it may take a significant amount of time to listen to and review the tapes for proprietary information and privileges. Voice mail files can be converted to WAV files for categorizing and played on a Windows Media Player or other software.

Voice mail in an audio format does not have internal search capabilities. Unless voice mail is converted to searchable computer text, it is not possible to conduct efficient searches of the content for relevance, privilege or proprietary information. It can literally take weeks of listening to segregate relevant and nonprivileged voice mail. In addition, it may require trained listeners (if the files are properly archived) to determine who the speaker was, whether the information is privileged and how to handle unintelligible voice mail. However, new voice mail developments include the capability to store messages as digital files that can be easily forwarded to multiple parties or sent via e-mail as attachments. In addition, voice mail archiving technologies have progressed and now metadata, such as a date and time stamp and sender and recipient information is being added to the voice message which makes voice mail easier to access and search.

Some new technologies are available that may lessen the burden of searching voice mail. *Fast-Talk and Esquire Deposition Services Sign Licensing Agreement,* Bus. Wire, Aug. 14, 2002. This news article discusses Fast-Talk's (now Nexidia - http://www.nexidia.com/) "Voicenetics" software that permits phonetic searches of audio material. This system is designed to allow users to "extract specific information from logged phone conversations, voice mail messages, and audio-based data." For additional white papers on searching voice mail visit http://www.nexidia.com/technology/whitepapers.html.

[4]   Voice Mail Capabilities

Voice mail systems differ in their capabilities. The following are some of the possible features you should be aware of when seeking or disclosing voice mail data.

- Number of phone lines that access the voice mail system.

- Amount of analog or digital storage available (80 hours or more).

- Forwarding voice mail messages to another's e-mail systems and inserting "header" comments to accompany them.

- Live and remote call screening allows one to monitor calls as they are recorded into your mailbox using a telephone speaker, handset or a cordless phone.

- Two-way transfer provides the capability to record a live phone conversation into the mailbox of a third person.

- External message delivery allows one to prerecord a phone message that will be delivered to a specific phone on a specific date and time. Passwords can be employed for content sensitive data.

- Message notification is a system where one can be notified of some new messages by a message lamp that lights or that provides a "stuttered" type dial tone. It may also be a pager alert that can display a caller's telephone number or the system can call the recipient at a preset number.

- Caller ID messages can be provided to certain callers after they are identified. The feature allows for a specific prerecorded message to be played for that individual and a response can be directed to a special voice mailbox.

- Voice mail can have password protection.

- Distribution lists are available to send a message to a voice mail list and/or ad hoc distribution lists.

- Transfer messages to another person or group of persons.

- Phone call origination identification.

- Accessibility to voice mail messages - phone, e-mail, pager or other devices.

Information that may be found on voice mail and answering machines.

- Incoming and outgoing messages (audio, text and/or video);
- Some answering machines double as a telephone;
- Home computer systems are becoming a voice mail recording device;
- Numbers called;
- Numbers stored for speed dialing;
- Caller ID for incoming calls;
- Phone/pager numbers;
- Names and addresses;
- PIN numbers;
- Voice mail access number;
- Voice mail password;
- Debit and credit card numbers;
- Calling card numbers;
- Onscreen image may contain other information; and
- See the above voice mail capability section for possible additional information.

[5]   Reported Cases

- *Hopson v. Mayor & City Council of Baltimore,* 232 F.R.D. 228, 245 (D. Md. 2005). Citing to the Civil Discovery Standards for the American Bar Association Section on Litigation the Court noted that the parties should discuss "the scope of the electronic records sought . . . i.e. e-mail, *voice mail,* archived data, back-up or disaster recovery data, laptops, personal computers, PDA's." (emphasis added).

- *Kleiner v. Burns,* No. 00-2160, 2000 WL 1909470, at *4 (D. Kan. Dec. 15, 2000). "As used by the advisory committee, 'computerized data and other electronically-recorded information' includes, but is not limited to: *voice mail messages and files, back-up voice mail files* . . ." (emphasis added).

- *Stevenson v. Union Pacific R. Co.,* 354 F.3d 739 (8th Cir. 2004). An adverse inference instruction was granted for the destruction of voice records and track maintenance records after an accident pursuant to the railroad's document retention policy. The document retention policy provided that voice tapes between a train crew and dispatchers were routinely overwritten every 90 days.

- *United States v. Smith,* 155 F.3d 1051 (9th Cir. 1998) *cert. denied, Smith v. United States,* 525 U.S. 1071 (1999). In an insider trading action, a defendant's voice mail disclosed his stock trading intentions and knowledge of insider information. The conviction was upheld even though the court held that the information was obtained illegally from an employee who hacked into defendants' account.

- *Bayer Corp. v. Roche Molecular Systems, Inc.,* 72 F. Supp. 2d 1111, 1121-22 (N.D. Cal. 1999). The Court ordered a former employee in a trade secret case to produce "all existing data, including telephone messages, and [w]ith respect to the fourth quarter [future voice mail] . . . shall transcribe or otherwise preserve all voicemails that he receives on these subjects and they too must be produced."

- *Wiginton v. Ellis,* No. CIV.02-6832, 2003 WL 22439865 (N.D. Ill. Oct. 27, 2003). A preservation letter from the plaintiff requested that voice mail not be destroyed.

[6]   Other Authorities

- Baker & Daniels, *Beware: Technology in the Workplace Is a Source of Liability,* 11 Ind. Empl. L. Letter 3 (2001).

- John H. Jessen, *Special Issues Involving Electronic Discovery,* 9 Kansas J.L. & Pub. Pol. 425, 436 (2000) (This article describes the development of voice mail systems).

- Madden et al., *Caught on Tape: The Next Frontier in Electronic Discovery,* Law Journal Newsletters (May 2004).

- Steven C. Bennett, *Voicemail: The Latest Front in the E-Discovery Wars,* N.Y.L.J., Nov. 4, 2002, Tech. Trends at 1.

- For a description of the Voice over Internet Protocol (VoIP) visit the Federal Communication Commission website at http://www.fcc.gov/voip/.

[7]   Discovery Pointers

- Ensure that your client has reasonable voice mail retention policies in place, preferably prior to litigation occurring. Deliberate or negligent destruction of voice mail after litigation will likely result in sanctions.

[I]   Caller ID Device

A caller ID (**Caller I**dentification **D**evice) device collects and displays caller information. Caller ID permits the calling party's number to be displayed to the receiver on special equipment before the call is answered. Caller ID devices (such as a telephone, computer or separate standalone device) displays the automatic number identification (ANI) service and converts the calling number into a firm or individual's name. After identifying the caller some newer systems allow you to accept the call, redirect the call to a secretary or to voice mail, send an electronic message to your secretary to take a message or play a specific predetermined audio message. Some services permit the calling party's telephone number to be hidden or blocked from a caller ID device. These devices can also record the number of recent incoming calls.

Caller ID information can be "spoofed." "Phone spoofing is a practice by which a caller causes a phone number other than their own to appear on a caller ID or similar display. Testimony concerning H.R. 5126, the Truth in Caller ID Act of 2006 available at http://www.epic.org/privacy/iei/hr5126test.pdf.

Information that may be found on caller ID devices:

- May contain telephone and subscriber information from incoming telephone calls;
- Date and time of incoming calls; and
- Number of calls.

[1]   Reported Cases

- *Klump v. Nazareth Area Sch. Dist.,* CIV.04-03606, 2006 U.S. Dist. LEXIS 15328, at *25 (D. Pa. Mar. 30, 2006). "Caller identification on a cellular phone is similar to the function of a paging device: it records the identity of the caller, but does not allow for the communication of any information."

- *See,* § 8.20, *Caller ID*, for other cases relating to caller ID.

[J]   Paging Device

Pagers provide beep, numeric or full text messages, e-mail sending and receiving, voice mail and/or Internet access. Some pagers are capable of a two-way messaging between parties.

The Court in Wycoff v. Motorola, Inc., No. CIV.96-3052, 1997 WL 812996, at *1 (D.Neb. Dec. 18, 1997) stated:

> Pagers are small, battery-operated radio receivers commonly used for personal communication generally consisting of two components, a receiver and a decoder. In order to personalize their use, pagers operate on a "selective-call" basis. Each pager is assigned a unique address. Radio signals containing an address and a message are transmitted. The receiver collects the radio signal and selectively responds only when the decoder determines that the signal contains that pager's unique address.

Pagers monitor specific radio frequencies used by the service providers. If the pager is switched on and is within range of the radio tower, the pager will recognize the coded signal. The pager then converts the signal to data, alerting the owner with a beep, tone or vibration that a page has been sent. The transmission of the page is encoded so that only the intended recipient of the page can receive and decode the message. Most pagers have liquid-crystal displays that can show the number of the calling party or short messages. The owner of the pager can respond to the page by sending a reply through certain types of pagers, by telephoning the paging party or calling the paging company to retrieve the message.

Pager messages are stored on a remote computer terminal that may later be accessed to disclose the history and substance of the digital pager messages.

There are several types of pagers.

- Tone only pagers beep when called. The user responds by calling a predetermined place for the message;

- Numeric display pagers receive only numeric digits (usually a callback number or special code);

- Alphanumeric pagers receive numbers and letters and can display short written messages (some are equipped to receive and send e-mail and access the WWW). Messages to the pager can originate by dialing a designated 1-800 number, using software or a page-entry device;

- Voice pagers that can transmit voice communications; and

• 2-way pagers that can receive and transmit incoming and outgoing messages.

Information that may be found in paging devices:

• Paging messages
• Time and date stamp of when the message arrived;
• Faxes;
• E-mail;
• Internet data;
• Address books;
• Voice mail notification – After a caller leaves a message on your voice mail, your pager will notify you that there is a recording on your voice mail. You may then phone into your voice mail to hear the pager message.

[1]   Reported Case

• *Bohach v. The City of Reno*, 932 F. Supp. 1232 (D. Nev. 1996). Police officers filed an action to attempt to stop investigation regarding their misuse of departments' computerized paging system. The Court held that since the city provided this service they were entitled to access text messages that were stored on the city's computer system.

[K]   Facsimile Transmission (Faxes)

Facsimile transmission is a communication system that scans, sends and receives documents by way of telephone lines or by wireless means. A fax machine scans a piece of paper, digitizes it to an image and then sends it as electronic signals over transmission lines to another fax machine. The receiving machine recreates the image. Faxing is a method of communication that allows people to share exact copies of important papers by duplicating and sending them on one end, and then receiving and reproducing them on the other.

Fax technology is becoming more integrated with computers allowing one to fax a document directly from a word processing or other application program. In addition, computers can now send, receive and store faxes. *See,* § 3.13, *Faxes.*

Information that may be found in the memory component of fax machines:

• Speed dial list;
• Stored faxes (incoming and outgoing);
• Fax transmission logs (incoming and outgoing);
• Header line; and

- Clock setting.

[1]   Reported Cases

- *United States v. Reich,* 420 F. Supp. 2d 75 (D.N.Y. 2006). In this criminal proceeding the Court recounted the expert testimony regarding fax transmissions, headers and other fax data.
- *Goldberg v. Empire Mortg., Inc.,* 2004 WL 3237126 (Ohio Com. Pl. Dec. 7, 2004). "'Mr. Linder had received all of the faxed transmissions at his place of employment and that OCSEA had a computer server for faxes that receives and distributes incoming faxes to recipients by email . . .'"
- *See also,* § 8.19, *Fax* for admissibility issues regarding fax transmissions.

[L]   Scanner

A scanner processes documents or other items placed on the scanner bed into an electronic or digital image format. It converts items such as photographs into binary information that the computer can manipulate. Scanners work by pulling in sheets of paper, which are scanned as they pass over a stationary scanning mechanism, as in the common office fax machine. Scanners can also be copiers, printers and facsimile machines.

Scanning software is needed to operate a scanner. Copies of scanned documents or other material may be found in the storage directory for the software used with the scanner.

Information that may be found in the memory component of scanners:

- Stored copies of documents;
- Data files (complete images or documents from computers in a network environment); and
- Scanning logs.

[1]   Reported Case

- *In re Bristol-Myers Squibb Securities Litigation,* 205 F.R.D. 437, 439 (D.N.J. 2002). "'Scanning' is the process of transforming paper copies (photos, documents, diagrams, charts, and graphs) into digital files."

[M]   Printer

A printer allows for the paper creation of items generated by computers. There are many printer technologies including laser, inkjet, thermal die and dot matrix. A print spooler or "spooler file" on a hard drive can contain copies of documents that have been printed. Some printers are also copiers, scanners and facsimile machines.

Most computer network systems use a technique called "print buffering." Once you direct the computer to print a document, the computer stores the document in a temporary file. Generally, once the information is printed, the buffer file is deleted. However, sometimes the printed document files are maintained in the computer system for later retrieval.

Information that may be found in the memory component of printers:

- Stored print copies;
- Copy logs;
- Data and buffer files (complete copies of printed documents from computers in a network environment); and
- Printers can also be integrated with scanners, copiers and facsimile machines.

[1]   Reported Case

- *In re Amato,* No. CIV.05-29, 2005 WL 1429743, at *3 (D.Me. Jun. 17, 2005). The prosecutor issued a subpoenas duces tecum seeking among other things "printer or memory buffers."

[N]   Copier

A copier allows for duplication of items placed on the copying surface. Laser photocopiers, commonly found in offices and classrooms, use electric charges to transfer the image of an original document to a plain piece of paper.

Information that may be found in the memory component of a copier:

- Stored copies;
- Data files (complete images or documents from computers in a network environment);
- Copy logs;
- Clock setting; and
- Copiers can also be scanners, printers and facsimile machines.

[1]   Reported Cases (reserved)

[2]   Other Authorities

- Michael J. Tonsing, *Cyberian Security: Is There a Leaky Copier in Your Office?*, 51 FEDRLAW 12 (2004). This article discusses that printers and copiers generally have digital hard drives on which electronic copies of paper are stored making it vulnerable to hackers seeking business or personal information.

[O]   Compact Disc Duplicator

A compact disc duplicator allows for the mass creation of compact discs (CD's).

Information that may be found on a duplicator:

- Type and date of duplication;
- Number of discs duplicated;
- Information placed on the discs; and
- Title of duplicated discs.

[P]   Camera/Camcorder (Digital)

A camera and camcorder can record pictures and video in a digital or analog format. Digital photography is a method of taking pictures without the use of conventional photographic film. Digital cameras record the picture information as pixels or digital dots of color. These devices can store data directly to an internal fixed memory and/or removable media. Most digital cameras are able to transfer their computer picture files directly into a computer for storage. Others accept a disc or similar portable storage unit to achieve the same purpose. If you transfer the pictures to a computer, they can be easily changed and transmitted worldwide via the Internet. This poses special evidentiary authentication problems.

Digital camcorders, similar to cameras, record events in a digital format. They are located at many cities' busy intersections to record accidents or to monitor traffic. Camcorders are also used to record home movies, sporting events, in high crime areas, college campuses and other public, and in some cases, private areas. Cameras and camcorders can be found as portable and fixed devices, but usually can be easily moved. Some of these devices may have basic personal computing functions.

Information that may be found in a digital camera/camcorder:

- Graphics;
- Audio;
- Video; and
- Time and date of creation of audio, video and graphic files.

[1]   Reported Cases

- *Cottrill v. MFA, Inc.,* 443 F.3d 629 (8th Cir. 2006). Employees, who brought an action alleging sex discrimination, set up a camera and obtained evidence of another worker "peeping" on women in the restroom.

- *Brown v. Bradshaw,* No. CIV. 04-1727, 2006 U.S. Dist. LEXIS 8339, at *5-6 (D. Ohio Mar. 3, 2006). Though the camera was not working, the inference of the existence of a tape from a surveillance camera was used to obtain a confession from a murderer.

- *Paramount Pictures Corp. v. Davis,* 234 F.R.D. 102, 105-106 (D. Pa. 2005). "Digital copies of motion pictures are very large computer files and take anywhere from several hours to several days to download from one network user to another."

- *See also,* § 8.16, *Photographs* for admissibility issues regarding photographs.

[Q]   Electronic Game Devices

There are two classes of electronic games: video games, which are designed for specific video game systems and handheld systems, such as PlayStation, Nintendo and Xbox; and computer games, which are designed and played on personal computers. Players can use a variety of joysticks, trackballs or steering wheels to control the game. Devices may be standalone or networked via Internet by wire or wireless communication. Electronic game systems are adding computer functions that are capable of storing data, accessing the Internet, sending and receiving e-mail.

Information that may be found on electronic gaming devices:

- Stored data - text, graphics, audio and video;
- Internet access information;
- E-mail; and
- Other basic personal computer data.

[R]   Home Electronic Devices

Home electronic devices provide users with the capability of interacting with other devices, holding messages, keeping an inventory of food items and other personal items, controlling kitchen appliances and will eventually send and receive e-mail and be able to perform other computer functions. The devices range from interactive televisions to smart kitchen appliances, such as a microwave that stores messages for other family members or a kitchen refrigerator that keeps track of food in its inventory list when food items are used.

Information that may be found on home electronic devices:

*   Stored data - text, images, audio, video, etc.;
*   Internet access information;
*   E-mail;
*   Telephone capabilities;
*   Basic personal computing functions; and
*   Devices may be standalone or networked within the home or at an off-site location.

[S]   Global Positioning System (GPS)

Global Positioning System (GPS) is a satellite space-based radio-navigation system that provides users with accurate information about their position and velocity, as well as the time, anywhere in the world and in all weather conditions. *United States v. Bennett,* 363 F.3d 947, 952 (9th Cir. 2004) ("A GPS device uses global positioning satellites to track and record the location of the device and, therefore, the location of any object to which it is attached."). They may also have 2-way radio, messaging and telephone capabilities. Though owned by the U.S. Department of Defense, GPS devices have been created for a variety of private consumer and business uses. These include tracking trucks, rental cars, stolen vehicles, wildlife habitation, people, boats, traffic and other things.

Information that may be found on GPS devices:

*   Internet access information;
*   Routes, marked locations;
*   Time and timelines; and
*   Stored data – text and images/maps.

[1]   Reported Cases

*   *Morgan v. U.S. Xpress, Inc.,* No. CIV.03-88, 2006 WL 1548029 (M.D. Ga. Jun. 2, 2006). Plaintiff sought GPS data showing that the defendant's truck was in the area and involved in an automobile-truck accident. The defendant had not preserved the GPS data and the Court issued an adverse inference instruction.

- *City of Oxford v. FAA,* 428 F.3d 1346, 1354 n.18 (11th Cir. 2005). "GPS is a satellite based navigational system. It works through a receiver that decodes information from a series of satellites. This information allows the receiver to measure the distance between it and the satellites and, thus, to determine its latitude, longitude and height."

- *United States v. Bennett,* 363 F.3d 947, 952 (9th Cir. 2004). The Court noted that a GPS may be equipped with a "backtrack" feature that can graph a boat's journey from previous days. The court also suggested that it may be possible for GPS data to be downloaded and saved to other software programs.

- *United States v. Perez,* 440 F.3d 363, 366 (6th Cir. 2006). After the DEA's electronic device stopped working, the defendants' vehicle was located after a court order was "issued authorizing 'OnStar' to use its global positioning system to find the location of the Escalade."

- *McMaster v. Coca-Cola Bottling Co. of California,* No. CIV.04-4642, 2005 WL 289982 (N.D.Cal. Feb. 04, 2005). "Each morning, account managers use GPS-tracked phones to receive customer and job information for that day's travel route. Using a Coca-Cola van, they travel from customer to customer, checking stock and fulfilling other duties."

- *United States v. Knotts,* 460 U.S. 276, 103 S.Ct. 1081, 75 L.Ed.2d 55 (1983). The police inserted a tracking device in a container of chloroform and used the device to track the movement of the container to the location of a factory where a suspected drug factory was in operation.

- *United States v. Dellas,* 355 F. Supp.2d 1095 (N.D.Cal. 2005). Agents used GPS tracking technology to locate a suspected marijuana growing operation.

- *See,* § 8.17, *GPS Device* for cases re admissibility of GPS data.

[2]   Other Authorities

- Richard B. Langley, *In Simple Terms, How Does GPS Work?* (Mar. 27, 2003), available at http://gge.unb.ca/Resources/HowDoesGPSWork.html (last visited July 21, 2006).

- Timothy J. Duva, Comment *You Get What You Pay For . . . And So Does the Government: How Law Enforcement Can Use Your Personal Property to Track Your Movements,* 6 N.C. J. L. & Tech. 165 (Fall 2004). This article discusses the ways that GPS technology can be used to track your movements including cellular phone, electronic tolls and car monitoring.

[T]   Security Systems

Most organizations have some type of security system. They range from using a physical key to sophisticated electronic systems to monitor employees and nonemployees.

For example, video cameras may be installed as a protective measure and are often positioned in strategic home or business locations. These devices may be standalone or networked via the Internet or a private network. Video can be saved as analog data on a videotape or directly to a digital storage device like a hard drive.

Information that may be found on security systems:

*   Stored data - text, graphics, audio, and video; and
*   Time and date information.

[1]   Reported Case

*   *Velikonja v. Mueller,* 362 F. Supp.2d 1, 20 (D.D.C. 2004). In this employment action the Court found admissible evidence of "electronic door logs" that were then compared with the plaintiff's time sheets.

[U]   Vehicle Computer and Listening Devices

There are several electronic devices or systems located in vehicles that can provide critical electronic information relevant to your cases.

Vehicle Monitoring System. This computer electronic system can provide an owner with information about the automobile and monitor and control vehicle systems. A computer-monitored vehicle may disclose information whether major systems are running properly or are in need of maintenance.

Vehicle Onboard Computer System. Besides monitoring an automotive system, an onboard vehicle computer can enable a driver to send and receive e-mail, locate addresses and provide directions to a destination (using a GPS system) and other basic computer functions.

Crash Data Recorder. Many cars provide electronic data regarding accidents through a "crash data recorder." This electronic system records information in the event of a crash and can play a key role in a motor vehicle crash investigation. The types of crash data available varies from vehicle to vehicle but may include vital crash information such as preimpact and impact speed, impact severity, breaking inputs, engine RPM, driver restraint use status and air bag usage.

Vehicle Communication Devices. Some automobiles are equipped with OnStar or similar dashboard computing systems that allow drivers to communicate with automobile service personnel. They were developed for safety reasons to assist motorists who were stranded or had their vehicles stolen.

Information that may be found in vehicle computer devices:

- Stored data - text, images, maps, audio, etc.;
- Internet access information;
- Telephone capabilities;
- Routes, marked locations;
- Timelines;
- Collision information;
- Engine performance; and
- E-mail.

[1]   Reported Cases

- *Padilla v. Price Toyota,* No. CIV.04-3422, 2005 U.S. Dist. LEXIS 25720 (D.N.J. Oct. 28, 2005). The Court granted plaintiff's motion to compel, pursuant to FED. R. CIV. P. 26, information from the plaintiff parent's automobile electronic data storage unit or "black box." The defendant was ordered to provide the data since it may contain information about the crash pulse, vehicle speed, brake application, throttle position and seat belt status.

- *United States v. Redditt,* 87 Fed. Appx. 440, at *2 (6th Cir. 2003). "However, Krebsbach's Cadillac was equipped with an OnStar Navigation System, allowing police officers to locate the vehicle, which they did at another nearby Memphis apartment complex."

- *In re U.S. for an Order Authorizing Roving Interception of Oral Communications,* 349 F.3d 1132, 1133-34 (9th Cir. 2003). "Such [onboard] systems operate via a combination of GPS (global positioning system, using satellite technology) and cellular technology . . . One feature of the System allows the Company to open a cellular connection to a vehicle and listen to oral communications within the car. This feature is part of a stolen vehicle recovery mode that provides assistance to car owners and law enforcement authorities in locating and retrieving stolen cars. The same technology that permits the interception of the conversations of thieves absconding with the car also permits eavesdropping on conversations within the vehicle."

- *Brill-Edwards v. Ryder Truck Rental, Inc.,* No. CIV.01-1768, 2003 WL 23511733, at *1 (D. Conn. Jan. 24, 2003). In an automobile accident case the Court refused to allow the deposition of a non testifying expert who "retrieved a sensing diagnostic module (data recorder) installed in the Aurora and generated a printout of the data contained in the recorder ['Vetronic' and 'Crash Data Retrieval System (CDR)']."

- *See also,* § 8.21, *Crash Data Recorder.*

[2]   Other Authorities

- Nat'l. Highway Traffic Safety Admin., *Event Data Recorder (EDR) Research History,* available at http://www-nrd.nhtsa.dot.gov/edr-site/history.html (last visited July 17, 2006).

- Ronald G. Bredemeyer, *Make or Break Your Trucking Case With 'Black Box' Data,* 40 JTLATRIAL 50 (Nov. 2004). This article discusses the different type of truck data available in black boxes including speed, braking events, and a host of other trip statistics.

- Jonathan Lawrence, *Crash Data Recorders in Motor Vehicles*, Trial Lawyers of British Columbia, Verdict, Issue #95 (Jan. 2003).

- Lawrence, Heinrichs & Wilkinson, *The Accuracy of Pre-Crash Speed Captured by Event Data Recorders*, available at http://www.sae.org/.

- Lawrence at al., T*he Accuracy and Sensitivity of Event Data Recorders in Low-Speed Collisions* available at http://www.sae.org/.

[V]   RFID (Radio Frequency Identification Device)

RFID is a term for technologies that use radio waves to automatically identify people or objects. The system is based on a technology known as **r**adio **f**requency **id**entification (RFID) and is designed to track the location of everyday objects such as razors and shoes for inventory purposes, files in law offices or for electronic tolls or parking passes. Special microchips are embedded into physical objects such as clothing, credit cards, passports, animals or even human beings. These systems are capable of tracking and collecting information about people or objects. Among retailers Wal-Mart is one of the largest proponents and users of RFID technology.

An RFID system consists of a tag and an antenna (microchip) and a reader with an antenna. The reader sends out electromagnetic waves that are received by the microchip and then receives back digital data from the microchip. The data is then stored in a computer that can be used to track the object and the owner.

In one of its most talked about applications the microchip will contain an Electronic Product Code (EPC) with sufficient capacity to provide unique identifiers for all consumer or other items produced worldwide. When an RFID reader emits a radio signal, tags on items in the vicinity respond by transmitting their stored data to the reader. With passive RFID tags, they can be read from less than an inch to 30 feet away. Active (battery-powered) tags can have a much farther read range.

[1]   Reported Case

• *Bynum v. District of Columbia,* 412 F. Supp. 2d 73, 83-84 (D.D.C. 2006). The Court observed that the Department of Corrections "is requesting capital funds in FY 07 to install a wireless LAN at the DC Jail and an RFID system. The latter system will allow DOC to track inmate movements and locations electronically, conduct real-time counts, and assure positive identification."

• *Checkpoint Systems, Inc. v. Check Point Software Technologies, Inc.,* 104 F. Supp. 2d 427, 435 (D.N.J. 2000). "The resulting 'intelligent tags' [RFID tags] carry, among other things, information about a product's history from initial manufacturing through distribution, sale, and, ultimately, consumer record keeping . . . Such tags surpass traditional bar codes in their ability to store and communicate information concerning specific items and do not have bar coding's line of sight limitations on data capture. . . . The proprietary information generated is entered into a database server and can be transmitted virtually anywhere that the user wishes via computer. . . . The RFID products are not only directed to retail applications, but also to libraries and commercial and industrial applications."

[2]   Other Authorities

• Reuven R. Levary, et al, *Radio Frequency Identification: Legal Aspects*, 12 RICH. J.L. & TECH. 6 (2005), at http://law.richmond.edu/jolt/v12i2/article6.pdf. "Radio frequency identification (RFID) is a wireless technology that identifies objects without having either contact or sight of them. Unlike optically read technologies such bar codes, RFID tags can be read despite fog, ice, snow, paint or widely fluctuating temperatures. 1 Additionally, RFID can identify moving objects. 2 Data in an RFID tag is stored in an integrated circuit, and sent to the reader via an antenna. 3 An RFID reader is essentially a radio frequency receiver controlled by a microprocessor or digital signal processor. The reader uses an attached antenna to capture the data transmitted from the tag and sends the information to a computer, where the data is processed."

• Sheila C. Stark & Euza P. Nagle, *Full Speed Ahead With DOD Identification Requirements: Next Stop, Radio Frequency Identification*, 40 PROCLAW 1140 (Fall 2004). This article describes how RFID tags work and the different way they are being utilized by the DOD.

[W]   Biometric Devices

The use of biometric provides another source of electronic data. For example, biometric timecards are being used in businesses to track the work hours of employees.

Instead of the old-fashioned method of "punching in" to a time clock you place your finger or other biometric information and a scanner records the time and identity of the person being scanned.

Biometric describes the automated use of an individual's physiological or behavioral characteristics to determine or verify their identity. The different types of biometric technology include fingerprint-scan, iris-scan, retina-scan, hand-scan, and facial recognition. An individual's characteristics can be measured by an optical reader which converts the data into electronic form and verifies the person after comparing the data to previously stored information on that person.

Traditionally, because of the hardware and other requirements, biometric was primarily used to secure access to physical locations. With recent advances and miniaturization their use has expanded from accessing computers via keyboard identification to e-commerce applications.

[1]   Reported Case

• *United States v. Newsome,* 439 F.3d 181, 184 (3d Cir. 2006). In a sentence enhancement case the Court stated, "[t]he referenced definition of 18 U.S.C. § 1028(d)(4) is currently codified at 18 U.S.C. § 1028(d)(7) . . . The term 'means of identification' means any name or number that may be used, alone or in conjunction with any other information, to identify a specific individual, including any . . . *(B) unique biometric data, such as fingerprint, voice print, retina or iris image, or other unique physical representation. . . ."* (emphasis added).

[X]   Other New Devices

There are several new innovative electronic devices (and many more are being developed), which store electronic information that may be useful to your case. Determine if any of these new devices contain electronic information relevant to your case.

• Wristwatches - now have built in pagers, organizers, calendars that can send and receive e-mail and access the web.

• Digital "Pens" - can store up to 40 pages of your handwriting for importing into a computer.

§ 2.6   STORAGE LOCATIONS

Service Providers	Residual Data
Internet	Internet Storage Locations

Application   World Wide Web
Satellite   Web Pages
Pager   Chat Room
Telephone   Newsgroups
Cellular   Listserv
Financial Institution /Credit Card Issuer   Cookies
Cable Service Provider   I nternet History Log
Gas Utility   Cache Files
Electric Utility
Water Utility   **Firewalls**
                                         Audit Trails and Logs
Backups - Computer Files   **Other Lawsuits**
Archived Data   **Storage Media**
Legacy Data   **Storage Devices**

[A]   Generally

One of the most challenging issues involved in electronic discovery is actually pinpointing the "physical" location of electronic information. In small and large companies, a single computer command can send a business document or e-mail to a different part of the world within seconds. That document or e-mail can then be downloaded to a home computer or PDA and carried away. The rapid movement of electronic information or case material to locations throughout a global economy within seconds results in substantial challenges in discovery.

In traditional paper-based discovery, most individuals and organizations have centrally located physical files or a limited number of file and paper locations. Generally, an attorney responsible for producing documents could go to his client's physical location and inspect file cabinets, record centers, record storage, access employee files and all the other places where documents are kept. These locations and the type of record keeping vernacular (correspondence files, chronology files, archives and accounting records) are well known to the practitioner.

This has changed. In both large and small organizations, network servers connect and store data for many employees' desktop computers in locations throughout the world. Each employee may also have access to a laptop computer and/or PDA and numerous removable storage media and data devices. All of these devices and storage media may contain information relevant to your case.

Retention Policies

In paper-based systems, documents that were outdated or had no business relevance were routinely destroyed. Record managers would maintain records in data or business record order for subsequent storage and destruction based upon retention policies. However, in today's electronic computing environment, there is generally not a similar electronic record retention system or if there is one, it likely is not followed. Electronic copies of documents are routinely distributed to various individuals and business units and rarely purged or destroyed when they become irrelevant or outdated.

Portability

Another significant issue is the portability of electronic information. A simple floppy disk can contain hundreds of pages of electronic information and can easily be carried home or transferred to other computers. Electronic mail can circle the globe in seconds, and be stored on multiple servers as it is sent throughout an Internet network system. Backup tapes, for archival or disaster recovery purposes, are also being created on a daily or weekly basis to ensure that everything on a company's computer system is duplicated. These backup tapes are often transported to offsite locations ensuring their safekeeping. In effect, electronic information can be easily distributed, stored and moved using the Internet and removable storage media.

Unorganized

Electronic information is generally not kept in a manner that is readily accessible and organized. It may be intermixed with other privileged data that can result in significant review time. The cost for locating, reviewing and disclosing electronic information can be significant - especially when organizations fail to implement information retention policies. Then, much of the information in a client's electronic storage system is possibly subject to discovery, or at least review, depending upon its relevance to the case.

Global

We are challenged with the global distribution of computer-based documents that may exist on a variety of storage media, CD-ROMs, pen drives, Zip drives, etc., and immediately distributed worldwide through local and wide area networks, Intranets, Extranets and the Internet. This creation, storage and distribution of electronic information pertains not only to the large organization, but also to a sole proprietor with a single personal computer.

In a multinational company or sole proprietorship, the issuance of a single computer command can send a one hundred-page document literally around the world in seconds. That document may then be transferred to a disk and then loaded on a home computer or downloaded to a personal data assistant. This significant expansion of the places where discoverable materials may be found has substantial consequences for the legal system, particularly in the area of discovery.

Because of this, for the producing attorney, it is difficult to determine whether all the information has been located and disclosed to the opposing party. This places a significant burden upon lawyers and others who risk spoliation and legal sanctions for failure to disclose.

[B]   Service Providers

Electronic information obtained from consumers and businesses can be stored at many different service providers such as telephone companies, Internet service providers (ISP), financial institutions and cable TV companies. For example, an ISP may provide e-mail services to individuals and businesses. Then, if e-mail is deleted from a business's computer, it may still be available on the storage media of the ISP. Service providers can also provide service and billing records, user and other information.

However, be aware that "time may be of the essence" in requesting preservation since electronic information may be routinely overwritten within a certain period of time.

[1]   Internet Service Provider (ISP)

Internet service providers such as EarthLink, Microsoft Network (MSN) and America Online provide access to the Internet and store, send and receive e-mail. Civil discovery orders are often served upon these Internet service providers for electronic information pertaining to specific individuals or businesses. As we continue to utilize the Internet for group computing, more and more electronic information of businesses will reside on storage networks supported by Internet service providers. One of the things to consider when discovering electronic information is whether the opposing party utilized ISP's for e-mail and document service, data storage or other online services. In addition, many ISP's only keep subscriber data for a short period of time so time is of the essence in discovering this data. *See also*, §§ 3.9, *Internet*, § 3.8[K][2], *Internet Service Provider (ISP)* and 7.10, *Obtaining Data From Third Parties*.

A list of Internet Service Providers (ISPs) can be found at:

* The List (http://thelist.internet.com/); and

* The Directory (http://www.thedirectory.org/).

[a]   Reported Cases

- *United States v. Extreme Associates, Inc.* 352 F. Supp.2d 578, 580 (W.D.Pa. 2005). "Internet service providers ('ISPs') allow subscribers to access the Internet through the subscriber's personal computer by using a telephone modem, broadband, including a cable modem or digital subscriber line (DSL), and dedicated access, such as a T1 line. Most ISPs charge a monthly fee in the range of $15.00 to $50.00, but some provide their users with free or very low-cost Internet access. Every ISP has a Terms of Service Agreement with those customers that desire to host content, in the form of a web site, on the ISP's network. . . . Subscribers who do not host a web site, but utilize the ISP to access the Internet, also enter into a Terms of Service Agreement which may limit certain activities."

- *Center For Democracy & Technology v. Pappert,* 337 F. Supp.2d 606, 613 (E.D.Pa. 2004). "A communication over the Internet will commonly travel up the 'tree' or hierarchy of networks of one or more backbone providers and then back down to its destination. A hypothetical communication (from an employee of a corporation) might originate on the user's computer, travel through the corporation's network, then through a regional ISP's network, then to a backbone provider, then to another backbone provider, then back down to a regional ISP, then, in some cases, through the network of a smaller ISP, and then to the corporate network of the destination, and finally to the computer of the intended recipient of the communication."

[2]   Application Service Provider (ASP)

ASP, an acronym that stands for **A**pplication **S**ervice **P**rovider, is a technology company that provides software or service "application" through the Internet directly to your computer. Instead of the software or service application residing on your computer or network, it resides on a "mainframe" or "server" computer at a remote location and you connect to the software application or service through the Internet. For electronic discovery purposes you need to determine whether the sought-after electronic information resides on an application service provider's storage network. For example, *Employease* (www.employease.com) provides human resources applications for employers. They provide on-line computer applications for centralized databases, benefits administration, payroll interface, compensation analysis, compliance tools and more. You can obtain a sample listing of service providers by visiting the website of ASPStreet.com (www.aspstreet.com).

Of special note is that businesses frequently store their electronic data including documents or backups of documents on ASP computer systems located in remote locations. These ASP's specialize in data storage and can be located across the street or in a different part of the world. These services provide an online, centralized storage platform that gives subscribers access to their digital data regardless of location used to access the Internet. Services include automatic backup and data security. This data is discoverable since a party is under an obligation to produce records in its possession, custody, or control pursuant to FED. R. CIV. P. 34. *See*, §§ 7.7, *Request to Produce and Inspect* and 7.10, Obtaining Data From Third Parties.

[a]   Reported Cases

• *Hugger-Mugger, L.L.C. v. Netsuite, Inc.,* No. CIV.04-592, 2005 U.S. Dist. LEXIS 33003, at *4 (D. Utah Sept. 12, 2005). "Generally speaking, an ASP is a third-party that manages and distributes software-based services and solutions to customers across a wide area network (e.g., the Internet) from a central data center."

• *Sutra, Inc. v. Ice. Express, EHF,* No. CIV.04-11360, 2005 U.S. Dist. LEXIS 14280, at *1-2 (D. Mass. July 14, 2005). A Massachusetts application service provider software company that developed a computerized flight reservation system brought this action against the defendant for breach of contract and misappropriation of trade secrets.

[3]   Satellite Service Provider

Satellite communications allow for the sending of television or telephone signals to small satellite dishes (as small as 12 inches) attached to the roof of a building or home. Subscribers can receive and transmit digital data as well as view TV programming. The satellite provider service company stores the history of usage of the satellite services, either the Internet connection or the TV programming. Depending on the services obtained by the subscriber; e-mail, Internet usage, access times, TV viewing habits and other information may be available for discovery.

[a]   Reported Case

• *DIRECTV Inc. v. Budden,* 420 F.3d 521 (5th Cir. 2005). The Court affirmed summary judgment for piracy of TV transmissions from a satellite service provider.

[4]   Pager Service Provider

A pager service provider provides paging services to individuals or businesses, usually on a subscription basis. The different types of paging services available are described under § 2.5[J], *Paging Device.* Pager data is stored in an electronic format on a digital storage system. This information, including the time and date of pages, the content, etc., is available on the pager service provider's storage systems.

[5]   Telephone Service Provider

Telephone or cable companies provide a variety of services to telephone users. These can include voice mail, caller ID, long distance, numbers dialed, Internet and a host of other communication services. These records are generally in an electronic format and stored in the regular course of business.

Some companies are replacing traditional telephone service with Internet Telephony. Internet telephony uses specialized hardware, software and an Internet network connection that permit the user's computer to act as a traditional telephone. This is accomplished by connecting to another computer or to a "gateway" that connects to the real phone system.

[6]   Cellular Service Provider

Cellular phone companies provide various communications services to their subscribers: voice communication, text messaging, voice mail, paging, Internet, e-mail, etc. The service providers store this information in electronic storage systems.

[7]   Financial Institution/Credit Card Issuer

Financial institutions provide a variety of financial services to their customers. These can include mortgages, online or offline checking and savings accounts, stock market transactions, home and commercial loans, car loans and a host of other business and personal related financial services. These transactions, especially credit card transactions, are routinely kept in an electronic format and stored by the financial institution.

[8]   Cable Service Provider

Cable service providers generally provide cable TV programming to their subscribers. Recently, however, they have also been providing local and long distance telephone service as well as Internet. Information about subscribers viewing habits and telephone usage can be obtained through discovery of this electronic information.

[9]   Gas Utility Service Provider

Gas utility service providers monitor the usage of gas by their customers. The amount of gas and time of usage, as well as other information relating to gas consumption is contained within computerized electronic records.

[10]   **Electric Utility Service Provider**

Similarly, electric utility service providers monitor electronically the consumption of electricity by their customers. Kilowatt usage, time of usage and other pertinent electricity consumption data is recorded.

[11]   **Water Utility Service Provider**

In addition to water, this utility provider takes care of waste collection from individuals and businesses in some regions. Water consumption is generally monitored by electronic computer network systems. Usage and other information can be obtained from these providers.

[C]   **Backups – Computer Files**

[1]   **Generally**

A backup is a duplicate storage copy of a computer program, disk or data. It is made for archiving purposes or for safeguarding valuable files from loss should the active copy be damaged or destroyed. *United States ex rel. Tyson v. Amerigroup Ill., Inc.,* No. CIV.02-6074, 2005 U.S. Dist. LEXIS 24929 (D. Ill. Oct. 21, 2005) ("The data on a backup tape are not organized for retrieval of individual documents or files, but for wholesale, emergency uploading onto a computer system.").

Generally, a backup copy is made periodically of the entire computer system, not just individual computer files.

Backup copies are made by using operating system commands or by using specially designed backup utility software. A backup copy usually compresses the data resulting in a larger volume of information being stored on a smaller amount of storage space. To restore the data one has to "decompress" the data to its original size.

The most common backup storage media is magnetic tape which is available in different formats. *See,* § § 2.3[D], *Types of External Storage Technology - Magnetic, Optical, Magneto-Optical and Flash and* 2.4[J], *Magnetic Tape Drive.* Vast amounts of data, generally compressed, can be stored on these tapes.

Individual Files

Generally, users save individual computer files in two ways. One, they use application software or operating system commands to save a file to a different storage media such as a floppy or pen drive. These can be saved at regular or irregular intervals depending on the needs of the user. Two, most application software programs such as Microsoft Word or Excel make automatic file backups, either temporary or permanent, to prevent loss of information due to a power loss or improper shut down. It is generally unknown to the user that the computer automatically creates a second file which matches the first during the time the file is being worked on. These files are provided different extension file names such as BAK or TMP. Depending on the application software the second file may be an exact replica of the first or may be the prior version of the file. These automatic files may be able to be configured to automatically backup based on a time interval or when the original file is saved. The purpose of the backup file is to allow the user to get back to where he or she started. This is important if the operator makes a serious mistake, or in the event of a major loss of random access memory because of a power shutdown.

Backup Tapes

Most businesses and individuals now maintain some sort of backup or disaster recovery system to protect them in the event of data loss, natural disaster or other catastrophic loss. In the event the business loses valuable data or its primary computer center becomes unavailable, the business or individual can continue with its operations by restoring the applications and data from the backup tapes. These backup tapes may actually be located at a different location to insure a rapid and seamless transition to utilize this back up system. For electronic discovery purposes this may be the primary or alternate source for obtaining evidence that has been deleted, overwritten or purged from the business's primary computer system. *See also,* § 2.4[J], *Magnetic Tape Drive; Zubulake v. UBS Warburg, LLC,* 217 F.R.D. 309, 319 (S.D.N.Y. 2003) (description of backup tapes); *Quinby v. WestLB AG,* No. CIV.04-7406, 2005 U.S. Dist. LEXIS 35583 (D.N.Y. Dec. 15, 2005), *aff.,* 2006 U.S. Dist. LEXIS 1178 (D.N.Y. Jan. 11, 2006) (defendant's vendor (Kroll) had previously restored e-mails from backup tapes to a readily accessible format but then archived the data making the data once again inaccessible.)

Backup tapes contain electronic information such as e-mail messages, word processing documents and spreadsheets. They often will also contain copies of the operating and application software system files. Though at first glance the volume of "backup tapes" may seem staggering, the amount of relevant electronic information contained on the tapes may be quite manageable. Many attorneys will attempt to persuade a judge that the "huge" volume of backup data should support a burdensome ruling. However, the data population may be able to be significantly reduced by limiting the data sought to particular users or date ranges or by sampling. *See,* § 7.04[G][5], *Sampling.*

Backup copies are made at frequent and regular intervals. Many companies use a backup "cycle" to ensure duplication of all relevant information while conserving storage resources. Companies generally employ individuals whose responsibility it is to ensure that electronic information, on networked systems or personal PCs are backed up on a regular schedule.

Computer backup copies are a fertile source of electronic discovery. However, backup copies of computer data do not preserve all the electronic information on a computer system. Generally, when you backup a computer it will only backup active documents and data files that are stored on a computer's hard disk. It does not backup deleted files and other "residual" data that may still be on a computer's hard drive. In order to restore residual data or deleted files not saved on a backup one has to request access to a party's actual computer storage system, in order to make a forensic image copy of the original storage media such as a hard drive. *See also*, §§ 2.06[F], *Residual Data - Slack Space, File Slack and Swap File* and 3.5, [E], *Deletion of Electronic Information*.

In order to determine the amount and type of data available on a backup tape you will have to determine the type of backup that was performed and the cycle of the backups. These backup cycles can vary depending on the organization and type of backup media used. Since the cost of magnetic and optical media has dropped dramatically, multiple types of media and time frames are used in a backup rotation. Most organizations have backup computer-based information available for preceding days, weeks, months and/or years. Data that has been added, deleted or even written over in the normal course of business on the company's main computer system may be recovered from backup tapes and disks. However, since data files are rarely kept in a coherent and organized manner, most backups and archives contain electronic information in a disorganized fashion. Backup media are generally poorly cataloged for review and restoration of the information. Many times they are organized in a fashion to restore "the entire computer system" in case of a disaster, and not just individual files. *Rowe Entertainment, Inc. v. William Morris Agency, Inc.*, 205 F.R.D. 421, 429 (S.D.N.Y. 2002), *aff'd*, 2002 WL 975713 (S.D.N.Y. May 9, 2002); *United States ex rel. Tyson v. Amerigroup Ill., Inc.,* No. CIV.02-6074, 2005 U.S. Dist. LEXIS 24929 (D. Ill. Oct. 21, 2005).

[a]   Reported Cases

- *McPeek v. Ashcroft,* 212 F.R.D. 33, 35 (D.D.C. 2003). The magistrate stated,

     [t]he frustration of electronic discovery as it relates to backup tapes is that backup tapes collect information indiscriminately, regardless of topic. One, therefore, cannot reasonably predict that information is likely to be on a particular tape. This is unlike the more traditional type of discovery in which one can predict that certain information would be in a particular folder because the folders in a particular file drawer are arranged alphabetically by subject matter or by author.

- *Hagemeyer North America, Inc. v. Gateway Data Sciences Corp.*, 222 F.R.D. 594, 601 (E.D.Wis. 2004).

The data on a backup tape are not organized for retrieval of individual documents or files, but for wholesale, emergency uploading onto a computer system. (citation omitted) In case the system "crashes," and all the information created since the previous backup is lost, the contents of the tape can be loaded onto the system, restoring the lost information. *See, Zubulake v. U.B.S. Warburg LLC,* 217 F.R.D. 309, 314 (S.D.N.Y. 2003)("Zubulake I"). Since crashes presumably occur infrequently, backup tapes need not be as convenient to access as, say, a CD-ROM. At the same time, backup tapes must have the capacity to store large amounts of information since they are relied upon to replace all the information contained on a computer system after a crash. It is understandable, then, that backup tapes sacrifice accessibility for storage capacity, since to have both would be impractical and costly. (citation omitted) Indeed, one court has revealed a correlation between the inaccessibility of backup tapes and the cost of searching them. *Zubulake I,* 217 F.R.D. at 318-320.

- *See also, United States ex rel. Tyson v. Amerigroup Ill., Inc.,* No. CIV.02-6074, 2005 U.S. Dist. LEXIS 24929, at *11-12 (D. Ill. Oct. 21, 2005).

[2]   Disaster Recovery Plan

Disaster recovery is a term given to the process of recovering and/or protecting your hardware, software and data after it has been damaged or destroyed. A disaster recovery plan is the procedure that will be implemented to restore information-processing operations that have been halted by destruction or by accident. Most companies have a disaster recovery plan that describes how to restore computer data from backup files, which are usually stored off site.

[3]   Backups – Types

[a]   Systemic Backup

When requesting backups in discovery, you will find that organizations use a "cycle" or "system" to backup their electronic information. A cycle is used to conserve on storage resources, while backing up relevant data. These cyclical backups can be tailored for a specific type of backup - full, selective or incremental - and for specific time periods. Most organizations perform a combination of these backup types. They will also recycle or reuse the tapes to conserve resources.

A full backup will back up all of the data on a system - operating system files, application software and data files (files that contain the e-mail messages, word processing documents, etc.). Though it is simple to perform this method, it uses a significant amount of storage space.

A selective backup will backup specific files and/or directories. The user generally will designate which files or directories (usually containing data files) will be backed up. This requires less storage space and the backup data usually will not include operating system or application software files.

The final type of backup is an incremental backup. This backup will copy only those computer files that have changed since the last backup. This type of backup saves time and space while ensuring that any recently used files such as word processing documents are saved.

Backups may be performed on a daily, weekly or monthly basis. Most businesses perform backup at the end of each business day, each week and at the end of a month.

A backup cycle usually follows a specific backup policy. For example, on every Friday, a complete backup copy may be made of every file on the computer system. Using a different set of backup storage media, a company may backup daily only those active files that have changed. Then, if the computer system fails on Tuesday, the company would use the weekly backup from the prior Friday, as well as the daily backups from Saturday, Sunday and Monday for the active files that have changed. The company may also back up the system on a monthly and/or yearly basis. After the end of the retention period the tapes will be reused and overwritten.

An effective backup strategy will allow for restoration of deleted, corrupted or destroyed files from any point in time.

Companies may employ other strategies. Some companies will store weekly backup materials into perpetuity because of the low-cost of magnetic and optical storage media.

One of the recurring discovery problems is the failure to direct an organization's IT staff to stop recycling relevant backup tapes once a duty to preserve arises. If they continue to recycle using previously used backup tapes then the old data is overwritten, which can lead to spoliation claims from the opposing party.

Deleted or residual data provides unique problems:

• If a user deletes an e-mail between backups then the e-mail will not be available on a subsequent backup, but may be available on an earlier one.

• Residual data will not be transferred to these backup tapes.

If you obtain backup copies of electronic data then this will permit you to recover e-mail, word processing documents and other electronic information that may have been deleted or lost by the opposing party. For this reason, backup procedure and policy questions should be commonplace in your discovery requests.

[i]   Reported Cases

• *Kleiner v. Burns,* No. 00-2160, 2000 WL 1909470, at *4 n.7 (D. Kan. Dec. 15, 2000). The Court stated:

The disclosing party shall take reasonable steps to ensure that it discloses any back-up copies of files or archival tapes that will provide information about any 'deleted' electronic data.

Back-up copies of files may be available as a result of formal or informal preservation of information. Formally, companies often make timed back-ups of all of the information stored on a computer network at given points. These archival tapes may be preserved for short periods of time as a source of memory in the event of an emergency such as accidental deletion or loss of important data. Subsequently, such tapes may be recycled for further archiving or other use. Archival tapes may also be preserved for longer periods of time either because of government-mandated recordkeeping requirements or simply for purposes of historical preservation. Informally, employees may make their own random back-up copies of files to guard against accidental deletion or system failure. These back-ups may employ different file names. Indeed, different versions of evolving documents may be saved under different file names.

- *In re Tyco Sec. Litig.*, No. 00-MD-1335, 2000 WL 33654141, at *3 (D.N.H. Jul. 27, 2000). The Court stated:

Further . . . [plaintiff] has produced evidence that large corporations typically overwrite and thereby destroy electronic data in the course of performing routine backup procedures . . . In accordance with defendant's normal operating procedures, every week the computer system is backed up and saved, thereby deleting the backup from the prior week. After one week, therefore, historical information is unavailable from the computer system.

[b] "Snapshot"

A "snapshot" or "restore point" is a copy of a set of files and directories as they were at a specific time. *Quinby v. WestLB AG,* No. CIV.04-7406, 2005 U.S. Dist. LEXIS 35583, at *5-6 (D.N.Y. Dec. 15, 2005), *aff.,* 2006 U.S. Dist. LEXIS 1178 (D.N.Y. Jan. 11, 2006). Oftentimes, they are used to save the state of an operating system and data so that if future changes to a computer system cause a problem, you can restore the operating system and data to the way it was before changes were made. When a "snapshot" is established the computer creates a backup of all the operating and application software data at that particular time. There are different types of snapshots depending upon the needs of the user. Some "snapshots" only create a backup of the operating system or are only scheduled when a new program is installed that could potentially make the system unusable. Some computer systems routinely create "snapshots" to back up their data such as the tables in a database that are frequently used. The "snapshots" of the computer system settings are typically maps of the disk sectors.

For electronic discovery purposes "snapshots" are taken to copy a set of files and directories at a specific time. However, snapshots can be problematic since they do not provide computer files that may be relevant and reside on backup tapes for past periods of time.

[i]   Reported Cases

- *Hagemeyer North America, Inc. v. Gateway Data Sciences Corp.*, 222 F.R.D. 594, 601 (E.D.Wis. 2004). "Backup tapes record a "snapshot" of the contents of the computer system at the moment the backup is run."

- *In re Priceline.com Inc. Sec. Litig.*, 233 F.R.D. 88, 89-90 (D. Conn. 2005). In a motion to compel production of electronic discovery the Court in a securities case stated,

  > The data at issue is stored in two forms. First, defendants have a 'snapshot,' which is the equivalent of a full back-up of all the material that existed on priceline's corporate file servers in February 2002 (the time the snapshot was taken), reaching back to the beginning of the Company. . . . The data stored in the snapshot is created and stored on three different types of servers: production database servers, which contain the raw transactional information of customer bids and offers; development servers, which contain quality-control and other 'test' data; and corporate file servers, which contain e-mails, memoranda, letters, and all other office-type documents. . . . The files on this snapshot are in native format and do not need to be restored, but, because the snapshot is a reproduction of the way files are stored on computer hardware by the computer system, the files are arranged in an essentially random configuration. In order to find responsive information, the files must be searched, and the substantial number of duplicate files must be identified and eliminated. Defendants can generate a spreadsheet listing 'the contents of the snapshot and the quantity of electronic material contained on it.' . . . Defendants also have certain backup tapes containing e-mail data from former employees in the same format files are maintained on the snapshot.

- *Kier v. UnumProvident Corp.*, No. CIV.02-8781, 2003 WL 21997747, at *13 (S.D.N.Y. Aug. 22, 2003). The Court in a detailed opinion regarding backup systems criticized defendant for loss of e-mail because "[i]f UnumProvident had been as diligent as it should have been . . . many fewer [backup] tapes would have been inadvertently overwritten." UnumProvident's IT staff decided to take a "snapshot" of its servers which did not save the relevant e-mail, instead of restoring backup tapes.

- *Quinby v. WestLB AG*, No. CIV.04-7406, 2005 U.S. Dist. LEXIS 35583 (D.N.Y. Dec. 15, 2005), *aff.*, 2006 U.S. Dist. LEXIS 1178 (D.N.Y. Jan. 11, 2006). The Court noted, "[f]inally, defendant also stores data on back-up tapes. . . . Bigelow describes the data stored on back-up tapes as 'essentially a 'snapshot' of all the e-mails in each employee's e-mail account at the time the 'snapshot' is taken' . . . Because the back-up tapes are 'snapshots,' taken at a particular point in time, e-mails that are sent or received and then deleted between snapshots will not be captured onto back-up tapes. For example, if the back-up tapes are created every night at 11:00 and on a particular afternoon an employee receives and then immediately deletes an e-mail, all before 11:00, that e-mail will not be stored on a back-up tape. . . ."

[c] Inadvertent Backup

Much computer-based electronic information is backed up inadvertently. "Informally, employees may make their own random back-up copies of files to guard against accidental deletion or system failure. These back-ups may employ different file names. Indeed, different versions of evolving documents may be saved under different file names." Mark D. Robins, *Computers and the Discovery of Evidence - A New Dimension to Civil Procedure*, 17 J. Marshall J. Computer & Info. L. 411, 416-17 (1999).

Sources of inadvertent backups include:

- An employee's hard drive, floppy disks or other storage media;

- Employees who work from home or who take their work home;

- Application software that automatically backs up electronic data. These backup systems periodically (for example every 10 minutes) and automatically back up user files in case the computer "crashes." On most networked systems, file backups of this type are saved on the user's hard drive rather than to the centralized network file server and are generally not deleted. Many users are unaware that they exist on their computer systems;

- Data file sharing by different employees of relevant documents and other electronic material; and

- Computer suppliers and outside consultants when they are hired to work on a computer system.

[d] Sampling and Restoration

Sampling involves conducting test runs of data to determine statistically the volume of relevant data available in computer files. The process involves the restoration of a small number of tapes from a larger collection representing specific time periods, custodians or other criteria. Once restored data from the tapes is searched using search terms that are usually agreed upon, to locate relevant information and determine the costs and results. This will provide proof of the cost and time necessary to restore backup tapes or legacy data. After performing the sampling, parties are required to present their findings to the Court for determination of whether production should be ordered, and if so, whether a cost-shifting analysis should be applied. *See also,* § 7.04[G][5], *Sampling.*

[i]   Reported Cases

*   *In re Priceline.com Inc. Sec. Litig.,* 233 F.R.D. 88, 90 (D. Conn. 2005). The Court in ruling upon plaintiff's motion to compel electronic information from 223 backup tapes stated,

    [d]ata is not accessible from these backup tapes; in order to view the files stored on the backup tapes, the files must first be restored to their native formats. Once the files have been restored, as with the snapshot, the files must be searched and culled for duplicates. The process of viewing the files stored as computer data is expensive and time-consuming. The parties have estimated that the cost of restoring a backup tape will range from $200 to $800 per tape, if it is even at all possible. The cost of restoration is in addition to the cost of searching the files, culling for duplicate files, and converting responsive files for production. These costs are exclusive of attorneys' fees associated with reviewing and producing the amount of information that could be responsive.

*   *Medtronic v. Michelson,* No. CIV.01-2373, 2003 WL 21212601, *1 (W.D. Tenn. May 13, 2003). The Court stated, "[i]f, however, the allegedly discoverable information is contained on backup tapes, a preliminary step must be performed. All data on each backup tape must be restored from the backup tape format to a format that the standard computer can read. In the case of a large data volume on multiple tapes like this case presents, the restored files from each tape must be compared to the restored files from every other tape and duplicate files eliminated. The restored data files that are not duplicates must be converted to a common format so that a search program may seek information within them."

*   *Wiginton v. CB Richard Ellis, Inc.,* No. CIV.02-6832, 2004 WL 1895122 (N.D.Ill. Aug. 10, 2004). The plaintiffs filed a class action complaint alleging a nationwide pattern and practice of sexual harassment against the defendants. The Court in reaching their decision on a motion for cost allocation examined in detail the process of restoring a sampling of backup tapes, determining search terms and the review and search software involved in the data review.

[e]   Location of Backups

There are several locations where backup data may be found:

- Off-site storage locations. To guard against catastrophes, many companies' backup their computer systems and store the backup media off site. The off site storage facility may be a vault of an outside vendor, a different physical location within the company or in the home of a senior management employee. The disaster and backup plan for a company may disclose the locations of this backup storage as well as the list of business functions and methods of handling a computer disaster.

- On-line storage vendor. When a backup needs to occur, the company will transmit the backup data through wire or wireless Internet communication to a storage facility. The data will then reside on the storage device and media of an on-line storage facility. "Small [and large] businesses and individuals can back up their computer files by sending them over the Internet to a third party's computer. Several Internet companies even offer computer users free storage space on their Web sites." Gregory Johnson, *A Practitioner's Overview of Digital Discovery,* 33 Gonz. L. Rev. 347, 364 (1997-1998).

- Held in escrow in business transactions;

- Other lawsuits;

- Copies sent to licensees;

- Outside computer consultants;

- An employee's personal backup copies; and

- An employee's alternate storage devices (pen drives, laptop computers, PDA's, etc.).

[i]   Reported Case

- *Lorillard Tobacco Co. v. Montrose Wholesale Candies & Sundries, Inc.,* No. CIV.03-4844, 2005 U.S. Dist. LEXIS 28917, at *29-31 (D. Ill. Nov. 8, 2005). The plaintiff subpoenaed the defendant's computer records from his computer consultant.

- *Linnen v. A.H. Robins Co.,* No. 97-2307,1999 WL 462015 (Mass. Super. Ct. Jun. 16, 1999). " . . . [D]eposition testimony of the defendant's staff revealed that nearly 1,000 backup tapes had been set aside *for unrelated litigation.* By the time of the disclosure, tapes covering a relevant four-month period had been destroyed in the routine course of business." (emphasis added).

[f]   Backups of Networked and Standalone Computer Systems

If you are requesting backups, focus on the organization's computer system setup. Some of the things to consider include:

- Does the organization have a centralized computer network environment system? Are all of the computers for the organization part of a network system? What is the backup protocol for the organization? Is the backup protocol part of a company's standard operating procedure?

- Does the organization have computers - desktop computers, such as laptops or home computers - that are not part of the networked system? If so, are these computers regularly backed up? If so, where are the backups stored?

[g]   Objections to Production

Some companies may object to disclosure of backup electronic information arguing that their retention policies provide that specific information (such as e-mail messages) are not kept more than 30 days. Though this may be accurate in terms of their general backup policy, most employees (and companies) preserve their e-mail correspondence longer in either a printed or an electronic format.

Companies may also argue that they do not have prior versions of specific software products and hardware, and therefore, cannot provide access to the backed up or archived data in question. The courts are not generally sympathetic to this argument reasoning that the decision to automate was a business decision and this is the cost of doing business. As one Court noted, "[t]he normal and reasonable translation of electronic data into a form usable by the discovering party should be the ordinary and foreseeable burden of a respondent in the absence of a showing of extraordinary." *See,* § § 7.04[G][6][b], *Traditional Cost Allocation Approach* and 7.04[G][4][c], *Cases - Burdensome Objection Denied.*

[h]   Discovery Pointers

- Most software programs have an automatic backup feature that creates an extra copy of the file on which a user is working, maintaining both the current and prior versions on storage media. The user may not be aware that an extra copy has been preserved, and therefore may not know to disclose the backup copy.

- Initially, obtain a copy of the opposing party's recycle schedule for backup tapes. Some company's information service departments keep backup tapes longer then mandated by their own document retention schedules.

- Be aware that if you provide your opponent with a "forensic copy" of your client's hard drive, an expert may be able to recover "deleted" and residual electronic information from the disk.

- Sample request to produce questions:

— Provide complete copies of any data backups performed for any person, machine or server for the time period_____ and for any data for the following people_____. (This does not include application or system software).

— Provide all written procedures and policies concerning backup tapes, disaster recovery or archived storage.

— Provide copies of archived data and the means to view and export the data.

— Provide copies of any paper-based source documents that are maintained for archival purposes in a different format such as microfilm, microfiche or digital format.

[D]   Archived Data

As electronic information increases, many organizations will store or "archive" outdated or outmoded information. When an organization archives electronic information, it generally will use software that compresses the data. These archive files conserve storage space, sometimes up to 80 percent. Because these files have been compressed, it requires a decompression method to restore the information. When electronic information has been archived, compressed or encrypted, it creates a single "outer" file. These files generally cannot be searched until they are unarchived or uncompressed. If the decompression software is unavailable, it may be expensive and time-consuming to extract the data. Often, data compressed samples will be processed to determine the cost of decompressing and restoring archival data.

Depending upon the organization, archived documents may be organized for identification and retrieval. If properly managed, electronic information should be archived in a method that allows for easy access to the data. In reality, however, such data is rarely managed for retrieval purposes in a readily identifiable manner. Many organizations use unorganized backup tapes as a substitute for organized archival files.

Not only is electronic data archived, but paper documents can also be archived in an electronic format. Today, organizations often dispose of their original paper documents and capture images of the documents on a variety of media. Although, microfilm or microfiche has been used in the past, it is now more common for them to be stored in an electronic image format on a magnetic or optical storage media such as a CD-ROM.

The cost of retrieving archival data can become an issue. One commentator noted, "[a]s a producing party, he may want to require the requesting party to pay for the cost of retrieving this archival information. However, be prepared for an argument that since your business client chose to maintain the computer information in an obsolete system that it is his

obligation to provide the computer data in a format that is useful to the requesting party."
Bruce Rubinstein, *Electronic Discovery Costs are Leveraging Settlements*, 7 Corporate Legal
Times 26 (Sept. 1997).

[1]   Reported Cases

- *Zubulake v. UBS Warburg LLC,* No. CIV.02-1243, 2004 WL 1620866 (S.D. N.Y. July
  20, 2004). The Court found defendants had failed to preserve relevant e-mail archived
  on the computers of human resources personnel. Key documents had been "archived"
  on the staff's hard drive, but had not been backed up on the centralized network backup
  system. The Court also noted that the defendants had failed to follow their own
  document retention policies for backup tapes.

- *Zubulake v. UBS Warburg, LLC,* 217 F.R.D. 309, 318 (S.D.N.Y. 2003). The Court
  stated:

  > 3. *Offline storage/archives:* "This is removable optical disk or magnetic tape
  > media, which can be labeled and stored in a shelf or rack. Off-line storage of
  > electronic records is traditionally used for making disaster copies of records and
  > also for records considered 'archival' in that their likelihood of retrieval is
  > minimal. Accessibility to off-line media involves manual intervention and is
  > much slower than on-line or near-line storage. Access speed may be minutes,
  > hours, or even days, depending on the access-effectiveness of the storage
  > facility." The principled difference between nearline data and offline data is that
  > offline data lacks "the coordinated control of an intelligent disk subsystem," and
  > is, in the lingo, JBOD ("Just a Bunch Of Disks").

- *McPeek v. Ashcroft, et al.,* 202 F.R.D. 31 (D.D.C. 2001). A plaintiff sued his employer
  claiming retaliation for having accused his supervisor of sexual harassment. The
  plaintiff requested the employer to search a computer backup system for evidence of
  retaliation. The Court wrote a detailed analysis regarding the employer's computer
  system and the archival backup system that were used during this period of time as well
  as a cost allocation analysis for the production of the information. The Court noted the
  complex nature of this discovery request and response and ruled that the employer
  would be required to perform backup restoration of e-mail connected to the plaintiff
  supervisor's computer for one year following the letter to a different supervisor
  complaining of retaliation.

- *Alexander v. FBI,* 194 F.R.D. 305 (D.D.C. 2000). The Court ordered the production of
  computer service records regarding the computers operated by an employee, documents
  pertaining to the archiving, erasing, and servicing of the computer's hard drives, the

"archival database" and the inventory tracking database to show the computer then utilized by the employee.

[E]   Legacy Data

Legacy data is generally electronic information that has been used in prior software and hardware configurations. Often, when a company transitions to a new software and/or hardware configuration the "legacy" data may or may not be converted or imported into the new software application. This legacy data may have little or no value to a company because of its age or because of change of business processes brought on by technology. The issue in electronic discovery is how to access this relevant legacy data, if the hardware and software needed to access the electronic information has been discarded. This can present a substantial issue, especially when the cost is significant and when the legacy data is pertinent to the claims or defenses of the case.

When faced with producing legacy electronic files there are several considerations involved in disclosing this information. Initially, the files should be organized and identified as to which individual documents, e-mail, records, etc. are available from these disks. Hopefully, this data has been transferred to newer information systems implemented by the business. If it has not, then special problems exist. The data may be impossible to read using current hardware and software and if it is converted to contemporary media than certain database fields may be lost. This could lead to problems of information being taken out of context or authenticity of the documents.

[1]   Reported Cases (reserved)

[2]   Other Authorities

• Peter Brown, *Discovery and Use of Electronic Evidence*, 734 PLI/PAT 391, 393 (Mar. 2003).

> "Legacy" formats are those utilizing obsolete technology. Although the electronic documents themselves may not be damaged, the unavailability of the equipment necessary to read the electronic medium or programming language used to store the documents may make the recovery process prohibitively expensive or impossible. For example, in 2002 it would be difficult to access electronic files stored on 8-track tapes or requiring a SNOBOL programming language compiler. In addition, as technologies become outmoded and fewer technology professionals are available to effect translations from old technology to new technology, labor costs for electronic document recovery can rise dramatically, as evidenced by the premiums paid to COBOL programmers during the recent Y2K scare.

[3]   **Discovery Pointers**

• One possible method of responding to a request for legacy data is to create or conduct a random sample of the legacy data to determine the statistical likelihood of finding relevant information. Then, faced with significant cost for converting legacy data into usable information one can argue to the court the likelihood of finding relevant data and the anticipated cost. *See,* § 7.4[G][5], *Sampling.*

[F]   **Residual Data - Unallocated or Slack Space, File Slack and Swap File**

Residual or ambient data may be a significant source of electronic evidence depending on the nature of your case. Such data is partial data that is still available on a hard drive after a file has been "deleted," and that has not been overridden by new data. There are other "hidden" storage areas where data may be found on a hard drive such as the swap files used by a Windows operating system or unallocated space on a hard drive. This data may be in the form of e-mail fragments, word processing fragments and other data types that have been generated by the computer. This residual or "ambient" data generally refers to data that is not generally available to the computer user. It has been defined as follows:

> Residual Data: Residual Data (sometimes referred to as "Ambient Data") refers to data that is not active on a computer system. Residual data includes (1) data found on media free space; (2) data found in the file slack space; and (3) data within files that have functionally been deleted in that it is not visible using the application with which the file was created, without use of undelete or special data recovery techniques.

The Sedona Principles (2004), Glossary.

The Court in *United States v. Triumph Capital Group, Inc.,* 211 F.R.D. 31, 46 nn.5-10 (D. Conn. 2002) described the search efforts of the government investigator as he "mirrored" a hard drive and then searched for *"*active files, free space, slack space, recovered deleted files, directory structures, link files, file attributes, software programs and properties, image files such as internet cache files and temporary directories." The Court described these components as follows:

> A file is made up of a whole number of clusters that are not necessarily contiguous. When a computer user creates a file to be saved, the computer's "file allocation table" ("FAT") assigns or allocates a cluster or clusters to store that file. The clusters are not necessarily contiguous because the FAT assigns data to whatever available clusters it finds on the hard drive. Saved files that occupy allocated clusters are called "active files."

* * *

"Unallocated" or "free space" is comprised of clusters that are available for storage of active files. Free space may contain remnants of, or entire files that were previously deleted.

"Slack space" is the unused space at the logical end of an active file's data and the physical end of the cluster or clusters that are assigned to an active file.

Deleted data, or remnants of deleted data can be found in the slack space at the end of an active file and may consist of relatively small, non-contiguous and unrelated fragments that may have come from any number of previously deleted files. A normal computer user does not see slack space when he opens an active file. Forensic tools are required to extract and view slack space.

"Deleted files" are part of the free space. When a user deletes a file, the data in the file is not erased, but remains intact in the cluster or clusters where it was stored until the operating system places other data over it. When a file is deleted, the computer's operating system tells the FAT to release the clusters that were assigned to it so that the clusters can be used to store new files and data. To indicate that a file has been deleted, the operating system alters the first character of the file's name in the directory structure.

The data in a deleted file remains in a cluster's slack space until it is overwritten by new data. Unless there is sufficient data in a new document or file to overwrite all of the deleted data in the cluster, the cluster will contain remnants of formerly deleted data in the cluster's "slack space"-the space between the end of the new data and the end of the cluster. When all the clusters of a deleted file remain unused by the computer's operating system, it is possible to recover the deleted file in its entirety. Portions of deleted files may be recovered even if portions of the clusters the file occupied are being used by new files.

Also, the Windows swap file is a special operating system file that can hold fragments of e-mail, Internet browsing activity, word processing, passwords and network logons. Most computers have a limited amount of RAM memory to execute programs and store data and will use portions of the hard drive as "virtual memory." These areas of the hard disk are known as "swap files" because they exchange data as needed with the RAM processor. These swap files can be large and may contain e-mail fragments, Internet browsing history and other electronic data. Because the information can be lost once a computer is turned on, it is advisable to retain the services of a forensic expert to preserve this data by mirror imaging the hard drive.

[1]   Reported Cases

- *Williams v. Sprint/United Mgmt. Co.,* 230 F.R.D. 640, 650 (D. Kan. 2005). In an age discrimination suit the Court ruled that metadata was discovererable and in dicta noted that residual data may also be discoverable depending on the circumstances of the case.

- *United States v. Gourde,* 440 F.3d 1065, 1067-1068 (9th Cir. 2006). In denying the defendant's motion to suppress the Court in reviewing the evidence noted "if a computer had ever received or downloaded illegal images, the images would remain on the computer for an extended period. That is, even if the user sent the images to 'recycle' and then deleted the files in the recycling bin, the files were not actually erased but were kept in the computer's 'slack space' until randomly overwritten, making even deleted files retrievable by computer forensic experts."

- *Balboa Threadworks, Inc. v. Stucky,* No. CIV.05-1157, 2006 U.S. Dist. LEXIS 29265 (D. Kan. Mar. 24, 2006). In this copyright litigation the Court stated, "[i]t is not unusual for a court to enter an order requiring the mirror imaging of the hard drives of any computers that contain documents responsive to an opposing party's request for production of documents. (citation omitted) . . . A 'mirror image' is generally described as 'a forensic duplicate, which replicates bit for bit, sector for sector, all allocated and unallocated space, including slack space, on a computer hard drive.'"

- *State v. Myrland,* No.A03-1646, 2004 WL 1381267 (Minn. Ct. App. Jun. 22, 2004). The Court of Appeals reversed the defendant's conviction for child pornography because evidence showed that the Internet access code was the same for all the teachers on all school computers. In addition, the forensics expert admitted that all of the illegal images were retrieved from "unallocated space" on the school's hard drive and there was no way to tell who had viewed the images or if they had been viewed at all.

- *United States v. Bass,* 411 F.3d 1198, 1200-1201 (10th Cir. 2005). The Court denied the criminal defendant's appeal and noted that a "computer forensic search using two programs, 'ENCASE' and 'SNAGIT.' ENCASE recovered over 2000 images of child pornography, and SNAGIT recovered 39 images in the computer's unallocated space . . . He also admitted he used Window Washer and History Kill to make sure his mother would not see the images he was viewing."

- *United States v. Welch,* 401 F. Supp. 2d 1172, 1174-1175 (D. Kan. 2005). The Court stated "[i]n conducting this search for images, he searched the so-called unallocated portion of the hard drive, which he described as an area of the hard drive that does not have a folder structure and contains deleted files and images."

- *Zubulake v. UBS Warburg LLC,* 217 F.R.D. 309, 313 n.19 (S.D.N.Y. 2003). "Deleted data may also exist because it was backed up before it was deleted. Thus, it may reside on backup tapes or similar media. Unless otherwise noted, I will use the term 'deleted' data to mean residual data, and will refer to backed-up data as 'backup tapes.'"

[G] Audit Trails and Logs

Many computerized business systems provide network, audit, version and configuration trails and logs. Audit trails are computer files that record a variety of system usage information. This may include when a user logs in, the location of the user at the time of login, and what activities the user engages in while using the computer. Whenever a user accesses a computer system an audit trail or log is created. This allows computer access and data entries to be traced.

These audit logs are typically utilized by IT managers to detect and guard against unauthorized access to an organization's data. Electronic auditing systems are becoming a source of electronic information about a variety of different types of data important in a lawsuit. For example, in a trade secret misappropriation case it may be vital to know if a certain employee accessed company data and whether the information was downloaded. In addition, they are often used to authenticate electronic data since they provide a link between the individual computer user and the computer activity. As with any type of computer data, it is possible to produce a false audit trail or log.

You can usually find an audit trail and log in an accounting, financial or engineering computer system. However, many businesses provide audit trails and audit logs so that all data entries, including changes made to the system's data, can be traced.

Your discovery plan should include discovery of audit trails since they can provide critical information in your case. The use of a network system is recorded by the network logging software. It logs information as to when, where and which user accesses the system. Depending on the sophistication of the logging software it may pinpoint the exact computer used, the date, time and whether the user modified or deleted any files. They are frequently used to monitor unauthorized attempts to access certain files or folders in a computer system. It may also indicate when and by whom files were downloaded at a particular location, copied, printed out or deleted.

Besides network logging capabilities, many organizations install specially designed software to monitor employees' computer usage and activities. This software will monitor and record information such as what programs they used, Internet sites visited, files accessed, e-mail sent and received and any other user computer activity.

See also, § 8.20, Computer, Audit and Access Logs.

[1]   Reported Cases

- *Liebert Corp. v. Mazur,* 357 Ill. App. 3d 265,283 827 N.E.2d 909, 929 (Ill. App. Ct. 2005). In this trade secret case the Appellate Court reversed the lower court's denial for a preliminary injunction and stated, "[a]lthough [defendant] Mazur attempted to explain many things, he never explained why he deleted an application log that would have conclusively shown whether he burned the price books onto a CD. If [the defendant] believed he had a valid reason to copy the information for his former teammates, why would he attempt to hide his efforts to do so?"

- *Hugger-Mugger, L.L.C. v. Netsuite, Inc.,* No. CIV.04-592, 2005 U.S. Dist. LEXIS 33003, at *17-18 (D. Utah Sept. 12, 2005). The Court found that evidence of "a summary of a computer log of computer transactions . . . supports [defendant's argument] that [the plaintiff's employee] . . . did in fact click on the button. [Plaintiff's employee's testimony] . . . simply does not stand up to reliable computer documentation of transactions . . ."

- *Cobell v. Norton,* 394 F. Supp. 2d 164, 184, 207 (D.D.C. 2005). The Appellate Court affirmed the trial court's preliminary injunction disconnecting the agency's computers from the Internet. In discussing the security issues the Court noted, "[a]dministrator privileges also allows a user to disable what are called 'audit controls,' or the mechanisms by which user activity on a system is recorded . . . explaining that the ability to disable or delete what are called 'audit logs' or 'audit trails' allows a user to 'remove the traces' of operations or transactions he or she performs on a system . . . one or both organizations should analyze audit logs at predetermined intervals to detect and track unusual or suspicious activities across the interconnection that might indicate intrusions or internal misuse,' and 'automated scanning tools should be used to scan for anomalies, unusual patterns, and known attack signatures.'"

- *Touhy v. Walgreen Co.,* No. CIV.05-135, 2006 U.S. Dist. LEXIS 41724, at *5-8 (D. Okla. Jun. 21, 2006). The Court denied plaintiff's request for:

  all computer log files or audit trails that relate to any computer records you have concerning Plaintiff, including any records that identify, evidence or summarize any persons who have accessed Touhy's records, 'all documents that identify, evidence or summarize any 'sign on' or user/system identification or authorization codes that your computer system indicates were used to access any information housed on any Walgreens computer system that concerns Plaintiff,' 'all documents that identify, evidence and summarize any 'sign on', user ID or other employee access code assigned to Whitlock or for any other employee who accessed any records that you maintain concerning Plaintiff at any time after November 2003,' 'any logs or accounting of disclosures you are required to maintain pursuant to HIPPA regarding each time Plaintiff's records were accessed, reviewed, disclosed or displayed,' and 'all manuals concerning any computer system or program where you house any information concerning Plaintiff.'

In response, defendant stated that 'all relevant computer records pertaining to Plaintiff have been produced by Walgreen' and that 'Walgreen has agreen [sic] to provide a copy of its pharmacy code of conduct, confidentiality and privacy policy and Walgreen's computer usage policy to Plaintiff upon execution of an appropriate Protective Order.' . . . Further, Defendant asserts that 'the Walgreen computer system simply 'does not track the identity of employees who merely access a customer's pharmacy records without making an affirmative entry,' and that '[t]he Walgreen computer system 'can identify those employees who entered data during the intake and review of a prescription, but does not provide an audit trail of each employee who updates a specific patient record.' Rather Intercom Plus can only identify the last person who entered/updated patient registration information.' . . . Finally, Defendant asserts that 'the Intercom Plus system cannot be queried to identify those individuals who have accessed a particular customer's pharmacy records or to determine whether a specific employee accessed a particular customer's pharmacy records, beyond those situations identified above.

- *Lynch v. Omaha World-Herald Co.,* 300 F. Supp. 2d 896 (D. Neb. 2004). The plaintiff brought an action for malicious prosecution and other torts for allegedly hacking into defendant newspaper's website and posting sexual material. Court denied defendant's summary judgment. One of the grounds for denying the defendant's summary judgment motion was the failure of the defendant to give the electronic version of the firewall logs and the Web server logs to the FBI - initially stating that the web server log did not exist and then providing inaccurate web log information.

- *Campbell v. General Dynamics Government Systems Corp.,* 321 F. Supp.2d 142, 144 (D. Mass. Jun. 3, 2004). In this employment action the employer was seeking to establish that the plaintiff had notice of changed legal procedures by showing that the plaintiff received an e-mail which included links to other documents. The Court noted that the employer "present[ed] as evidence a 'tracking log' . . . which indicated that [plaintiff] opened the email at 1:56 p.m. on April 30, 2001. (The email was sent at 1:54 p.m. on that day.) However, defendants offer no evidence to support, nor do they even suggest, that Campbell clicked on either link, or that he read the text of the email."

- *Chrimar Systems, Inc. v. Cisco Systems, Inc.,* 318 F. Supp.2d 476, 484 (E.D. Mich. 2004). "The patent generally provides for a network security system for detecting the unauthorized removal of remotely located electronic equipment."

- *United States v. Simons,* 206 F.3d 392, 396 (4th Cir. 1999). A vendor contracted with a government agency for the management of the government's computer network, including monitoring for any inappropriate use of computer resources. The vendor employee entered the keyword "sex" into the firewall database [log files] and found a large number of Internet "hits" originating from the defendant's computer.

- *Sony Music Entertainment Inc. v. Does 1-40,* 326 F. Supp.2d 556, 559 (S.D.N.Y. 2004). "In support of their application for expedited discovery, plaintiffs argued, inter alia, that good cause existed because ISPs typically retain *user activity logs* for only a limited period of time before erasing data." (emphasis added).

- *Kramer v. Cash Link Systems,* No. CIV.03-80109, 2004 WL 2952561, at *3 (S.D. Iowa Dec. 17, 2004). "Second, the CIS mail servers automatically produced log files showing the activity on each of CIS's three mail servers. These log files show the computer from which incoming mail originated, the e-mail address of the mail sender, and the e-mail addresses to which the messages were sent."

- *In the Matter of Rebecca Arlene Ware,* 112 P.3d 155 (Kan. 2005). In an attorney disciplinary proceeding, the Supreme Court imposed disciplinary action in part based on evidence from the company's IT expert that the attorney had deleted a case tracking log from her computer.

[2]   Other Authorities

- Beryl A. Howell, *Digital Forensics: Sleuthing on Hard Drives and Networks,* 31-FALL Vt. B.J. 39, 41 (Fall 2005) (discusses the various types of information that can be discovered using computer forensics).

- Murphy, *The Discovery of Electronic Data and Litigation: What Practitioners and their Clients Need to Know,* 27 Wm. Mitchell L. Rev. 1825, 1828 (2001).

   [S]ome operating systems maintain 'system history files' that may retain such information as the dates on which the documents were created or deleted or on which passwords were changed. At a minimum, most systems retain the date and time that each file was last updated. E-mail files may retain such valuable information as file names, comments appearing in headers or footers, indices, distribution lists, and the time the message was last accessed. In addition some software companies employ 'version control programs,' which maintain original versions of the source code in which the programs are written and which store each new version of a program as deletions, insertions and amendments to the original program.

- Kevin W. Chapman, Comment, *I Spy Something Read! Employer Monitoring of Personal Employee Webmail Accounts,* 5 N.C. J. L. & Tech. 121 (Fall, 2003). "New technology now allows employers to monitor [employees'] web-based accounts. This technology allows them to monitor e-mail messages, record keystrokes, and even take screenshots of what appears on an employee's computer screen."

- Leanna Marchand, *Discovery of Electronic Medical Records,* 1 Ann. 2001, ATLA-CLE 429 (2001).

[3] Discovery Pointers

- Organizations generally will have guidelines for the storage and retention period for these audit logs. Unfortunately some organizations do not properly set up and maintain audit logs and, therefore, they may not be available.

- On a cautionary note an audit trail only identifies the computer that sent the message or document, not the sender, a user can program a computer to produce a false audit trail, also an audit trail may not provide evidence if a document has been altered.

- Depending upon the sophistication of the auditing program the following information may be available for a discovery request.

  System Information:

  — Networked or standalone systems;

  — Networks connected to the Internet or other publicly accessible networks;

  — User and password information required to log onto system;

  — Terminal connections (Telnet) to and from external systems;

  — Access to the system, including successful and failed login attempts, and logouts;

  — Date, time and users associated with each event; and

  — Inbound and outbound file transfers.

- Application Software Information

  — Attempts made to access a program and by whom

- User Information

  — What programs the user accessed;

  — Location of the user;

— How long the user remained in a program;

— Whether the user edited, changed or downloaded specific files;

— Whether e-mail messages were sent or received;

— Which websites the user accessed;

— Websites visited, including uniform resource locators (URLs) of pages retrieved; and

— What files did the user download from the Internet?

• Access control lists

— Provide information of what access rights are available to a user to certain sensitive files or software programs.

[H]   Other Lawsuits – Information Preserved

If electronic data has allegedly been destroyed pursuant to a company's retention policy, it may still be available in unrelated cases where the data has been preserved for litigation.

[1]   Reported Case

• *Quinby v. WestLB AG,* No. CIV.04-7406, 2005 U.S. Dist. LEXIS 35583 (D.N.Y. Dec. 15, 2005), *aff.,* 2006 U.S. Dist. LEXIS 1178 (D.N.Y. Jan. 11, 2006). The Court refused to issue sanctions for failure of the defendant and their attorneys to disclose that some of the sought after data was located with their electronic discovery vendor Kroll. The Court stated, "The Kroll Archives [were] . . . back-up tapes maintained by Kroll that contain data collected from defendant's Database as a result of earlier projects Kroll performed for defendant. The data collected for those projects had been in a readily accessible format, but, after the projects ended, Kroll archived the data onto Kroll's own back-up tapes, making the data inaccessible." *But see, Treppel v. Biovail Corp.,* 233 F.R.D. 363, n.4 (D.N.Y. 2006) ("One of my colleagues recently declined to sanction a party for converting data to an inaccessible format, taking the position that there is no obligation to preserve electronic data in an accessible form, even when litigation is anticipated. (citation omitted) I respectfully disagree."

• *Newby et al. v. Enron et al.,* CIV.05-20462; 2006 WL 649988 (5th Cir. Mar. 16, 2006). The court of appeals affirmed the trial court's ruling permitting a state agency (Texas State Board of Public Accountancy) to intervene in a class action securities case to obtain discovery of electronic and other information relevant to the agency's regulatory investigation. The agency sought documents to determine if any of it members may have violated any of the agency's rules.

* *Lorillard Tobacco Co. v. Montrose Wholesale Candies & Sundries, Inc.,* No. CIV.03-4844, 2005 U.S. Dist. LEXIS 28917 (D. Ill. Nov. 8, 2005). In this trademark violations case, the plaintiff subpoenaed a backup file of defendant's computer records from the defendant's computer consultant which produced several databases.

* *Mosaid Technologies Inc. v. Samsung Electronics Co., Ltd.* 348 F. Supp.2d 332 (D.N.J. 2004). The plaintiff in a commercial litigation case moved for sanctions, for spoliation of evidence after the defendant announced that requested e-mails had been destroyed pursuant to procedure for management of electronic data. In an attempt to ward off sanctions the defendants offered electronic data from a different lawsuit. In response the Court stated that they were "neither impressed nor moved by Samsung's belated efforts to retrieve e-mails that were allegedly retained by a 'litigation hold' imposed for a different lawsuit."

* *Mackey v. IBP, Inc.* 167 F.R.D. 186, 190 (D. Kan. 1996). A plaintiff sought damages for an alleged retaliatory discharge for the "anticipated exercising of rights by the plaintiff." In this case the Court referred to other *nonrelated* cases where the defendant had disclosed information using computer analysis and found their reasoning persuasive.

[I]   Storage Devices

See, § 2.5 above.

[J]   Storage Media

See, § 2.4 above.

[K]   Other Authorities

* E. Garrison Walters, *The Essential Guide to Computing* (2001).

* *Microsoft Computer Dictionary,* (5th ed. 2002).

* *Best Practices for Seizing Electronic Evidence* (2002).

* Douglas Downing & Michael Covington, *Dictionary of Computer and Internet Terms* (8th ed. 2003).

This page intentionally left blank.

Chapter 3

Structure and Type of Electronic Information

§ 3.1   UNDERLYING COMPUTER SETUP

[A]   Generally

Whether requesting or responding to requests for electronic discovery, litigants must be familiar with their own and the opposing party's computer systems. When the requesting party has sufficient knowledge of the responding party's computer systems, it will shape the discovery request. Such an approach avoids unnecessary confusion and conflict regarding what is being asked for, and may enable the parties to resolve areas of disagreement.

At a minimum, the knowledge of your opposing party's computer system should include information about the computer software and hardware system configuration, application software and backup procedures. The opposing party should identify and describe every software application, data repository and hardware system, or devices used to create, manage, interpret or store responsive electronic data. For a useful checklist of computer configuration questions *see* § 7.3[D], *Electronic Discovery Checklist - Pretrial Agenda*.

[B]   Reported Cases

- *Bills v. Kennecott Corp.,* 108 F.R.D. 459, 462 (D. Utah 1985). The Court stated:

  [I]n many instances it will be essential for the discovering party to know the underlying theory and the procedures employed in preparing and storing the machine-readable records. When this is true, litigants should be allowed to discover any material relating to the record holder's computer hardware, the programming techniques employed in connection with the relevant data, the principles governing the structure of the data, and the operation of the data processing system.

- *Zubulake v. UBS Warburg, LLC,* 217 F.R.D. 309, 324 (S.D.N.Y. 2003). "*First,* it is necessary to thoroughly understand the responding party's computer system, both with respect to active and stored data."

- *GTFM, Inc. v. Wal-Mart Stores, Inc.,* 2000 WL 335558, at *2 (S.D.N.Y. 2000). The Court criticized Wal-Mart's counsel for representing in writing that "Wal-Mart does not have the centralized computer capability to track [the relevant transactions]." Later, in a deposition, it became known that the information did exist when it was requested, but had subsequently been deleted from the computer. Sanctions were imposed against the attorney by the Court.

- *Danis v. USN Communications, Inc.,* No. CIV.98-7482, 2000 WL 1694325, at *4 (N.D. Ill. Oct. 20, 2000). The Court criticized the parties for failure to communicate and gain "complete mastery of what types of documents were generated [by defendant] in the ordinary course of business, how they were used, or their significance."

- *Simon Property Group L.P. v. mySimon, Inc.*, 194 F.R.D. 639, 641 (S.D. Ind. 2000). The Court held that discoverable computerized data may include operating systems, applications, computer-generated models and other sets of instructions found in computer memory, and not just the actual information sought.

- *Dunn v. Midwestern Indem.*, 88 F.R.D. 191, 194 (S.D. Ohio 1980). "In many instances it will be essential for the discovering party to know the underlying theory and the procedures employed in preparing and storing machine-readable records."

[C]   Other Authority

- Gregory S. Johnson, *A Practitioner's Overview of Digital Discovery*, 33 Gonz.L.R. 347, 359 (1997-1998). "Digital discovery is not for neophytes. Hence, those who do not possess a comprehensive working knowledge of computers, and the manner in which they store data, should associate with a firm that has this expertise or retain a qualified expert that can guide them through the process."

[D]   Discovery Pointers

- Determine whether the opposing party has upgraded and purchased new computers or software to replace ones that were used during the critical time period. Ensure from discussions that you are talking about the same computers that were in use at the critical time in question.

- Have your opponent designate people most knowledgeable within the company to answer questions concerning network systems, system maintenance, upgrades, performance, data storage, etc.

- Explore all possible electronic storage options: hard drives, back-up tapes, or removable media such as pen drives. *See,* § § 2.4, *Storage Media* and 2.5, *Storage Devices.*

- Consider the number of different geographic locations in which the target of the search maintains operations. Most IT departments are not standardized. Each separate location may be running different hardware and software and will have a different backup and rotation schedule.

- Evaluate the number of users who are the targets of the search, as well as the number of devices to which each user has access. For example, an individual employee may have access to a desktop computer, laptop, home computer, PDA, etc.

- Explore all storage locations for each individual user. Identify where that user has access and stores electronic documents and files. With e-mail as an example, some corporations allocate only a limited amount of storage space on the server and the remainder is stored locally in a Microsoft Outlook PST file on the user's desktop.

- Determine whether any other individuals have access to an individual's mailbox.

- Determine access rights to directories, files, databases, etc. for different individuals.

§ 3.2   ORGANIZATIONAL STRUCTURE AND POSITIONS FOR HANDLING INFORMATION TECHNOLOGY

[A]   Generally

In addition to understanding the underlying computer setup, it is important to understand your client's organizational structure and the staff positions within their IT department. This also applies to the organization of which you are requesting discovery. This will assist you in the drafting of interrogatories, requests for production and depositions of key technology staff.

Data processing departments are generally referred to as MIS (Management Information Services), IT (Information Technology), or some name with the word INFORMATION in it. Recently, data processing departments have started to appear with the word KNOWLEDGE included in the title, such as Chief Knowledge Officer or Knowledge Department. Within these departments are network management and system administration units, which manage the complex system of interconnected computers and resources.

Employees in your client's information technology department may be able to assist in understanding the opposing party's computer systems and their capabilities. Relationships with these employees should be established *prior* to any litigation, in order to advise your client on retention policies and other legal issues pertaining to the generation and storage of electronic information. Since the opposing party will likely depose your client's technology personnel and question them about their computer data policies, it would be beneficial for you to develop a relationship beforehand with these key technology people.

[B]   Information Technology Staff Positions

Within a business organization there may be several information technology staff positions that will pertain to your discovery or production of electronic information. The following is a description of the most common positions.

- A *chief information officer* is generally the manager of a business information management system. This person understands the goals, objectives and operation of the entire business as well as the computer technology used to implement these goals.

Brown v. Miss. Dep't. of Health, No. CIV.05-109, 2006 U.S. Dist. LEXIS 25531 (D. Miss. Feb. 3, 2006) ("'Chief Information Officer,' or simply 'CIO.' The CIO position involved managing information technology personnel and planning information technology projects, among other duties.").

- *Systems analysts* look at the entire scope of the company's information processing activities, the data, the people, the way work is organized and how information is produced. Systems analysts devise computer approaches to improve productivity and deliver better service. They may have programming skills, but programming is not their chief responsibility. *Liebenguth v. Liberty Life Assur. Co.,* No. CIV.05-0482, 2006 U.S. Dist. LEXIS 16228, at *2-3, (D. Tex. Mar. 22, 2006) ("[s]ystems Analyst's job [was described] as 'fulfill[ing] leadership, mentorship and subject matter expert roles in the life cycle of acquiring/developing, implementing, and maintaining information technology solutions.").

- A *system or network administrator* is the person (or team of people) responsible for configuring the computer and the software for a network. For example, the system administrator may install network software and configure a server's file system so client computers can access shared files. *Bobadilla v. MDRC,* No. CIV.03-9217, 2005 U.S. Dist. LEXIS 18140 (D.N.Y. Aug. 24, 2005) ("network administrator duties [include] network analysis, design, configuration, and modification . . . ").

- *Programmers* follow systems analysts' recommendations for customized software solutions. They create and test custom computer programs that precisely fit an organization's needs.

- A *network manager* is the person (or team of people) responsible for configuring the network so that it runs efficiently. For example, the network manager might need to connect computers that communicate frequently to reduce interference with other computers.

- *Database administrators* ensure that data is entered correctly, develop procedures for the analysis of data, and ensure database security.

- *Computer operators* keep computer equipment functioning on a day-to-day basis.

- *Computer repair technicians* fix breakdowns in computers and related equipment.

- *Data entry personnel* enter data into computers from various documents.

§ 3.3   BUSINESS SOFTWARE APPLICATIONS

Most businesses today use computer processing to handle many business functions. Generally, within most business organizations there are different departments to handle specific functions. The most common functions include production, accounting and finance, marketing and sales, human resources, and information technology systems.

There are many different types of business software to assist these departments in the fulfillment of their responsibilities. For example, if your case involves a production or operations factual issue, then it is necessary to focus on any computer production system that processes the purchasing, scheduling and shipping of goods and services.

There are many different types of electronic information control systems. Below are different types of computer business software and information systems that may be relevant to the claims and defenses of your case.

[A]   Calendars, Personal Information Managers (PIMs) and Scheduling Software

If meetings or appointments of an individual(s) are important to your case then questions and disclosure of information pertaining to electronic calendars, personal information managers and/or scheduling software need to be obtained. This type of software assists individuals or companies in storing and organizing the details of a business or personal information scheduling system. The data generally includes a list of customers, clients or other individuals who are important to a company. One of the most frequently used contact manager and scheduler is Microsoft Outlook. This PIM software can be used for individuals as well as enterprise organizations.

Universal Inbox or Unified Messaging. The concept of a universal inbox is a computer capable of receiving messages from multiple sources in multiple formats. Voice mail, e-mail, faxes and pager messages are all delivered to the same inbox. It would list all incoming messages and the user could listen to, read, reply, delete or file the messages.

[B]   Financial Software

Accounting and finance are among the most important functions within a business. Keeping track of the inflow and outflow of money is essential to a business operation. A proper accounting is necessary to comply with tax laws and other legal and regulatory requirements. Specialized accounting software packages are available such as QuickBooks to automate accounting tasks. The accounting software packages usually contain separate modules that make up the accounting function. They generally include a general ledger, accounts payable, accounts receivable and a payroll module. They can also include inventory control and order entry modules.

Many individuals use tax preparation software to calculate their taxes and file their tax returns. Personal finance programs are capable of managing a checkbook, credit cards, investments, bill payments and helping to keep track of income and expenses.

[C]   Document and Record Management Systems

Many companies use computer document and record management systems, which perform a variety of management controls over both paper and electronic business information. They are capable of handling different document data formats such as computer files, imaging, faxes, audio, video, e-mail and can centralize control of data in a specific depository.

Some primary things to consider are whether the system:

* Controls computer files, such as word processing;
* Controls access to documents through security passwords;
* Maintains a history of changes;
* Archives old documents and restores documents as one needs them;
* Searches documents by profiles or other indexing and/or through full text searching;
* Generates labels for paper files;
* Scans and converts paper documents to images;
* Receives, sends, stores and indexes faxes;
* Accesses documents through a LAN, WAN or Internet;
* Provides for bar code tracking of paper files and documents;
* Sorts profile data of documents, such as by author, client, etc.;
* Publishes documents to an Extranet or Intranet;
* Routes documents through a workflow system;
* Provides tools to mark up documents; and
* Automatically archives or deletes files and other materials based on retention schedules.

[1]   Reported Case

* *In re CV Therapeutics, Inc., Sec. Litig.,* No. CIV.03-03709, 2006 U.S. Dist. LEXIS 38909 (D. Cal. Apr. 6, 2006). "The 'eRoom' was a form of communication at CVT used like e-mail, and it was a place where people could work together electronically, and post, share, comment upon, and edit documents. . . . 'Documentum' is CVT's database management system which, among other things, stores FDA communications. . . . All four sources contain primarily non-email documents types, such as Word, PowerPoint, Excel and Adobe Acrobat."

[D]   Project and People Management Tools

Software is available to plan and control projects. This type of software allows you to schedule tasks, calculate amounts of time to finish a project, allocate resources, order priorities and develop a budget. You can construct a project and analyze performance against expected results. Gantt and PERT are two chart types that businesses use to manage projects.

People management software is used to track activities of employees in connection with the performance of a particular project. Programs of this nature can set up a company or department and assign goals and objectives to individuals or groups. These goals can be scored and a deadline set to ensure that goals are met. They can also provide other information such as descriptions, feedback and progress of the project.

[E]   Personnel Records

Human resource systems include personnel records systems that are used to keep track of information on employees and their positions, as well as development systems to keep track of employees' skills. They are also used to track training courses, materials and systems that manage complex benefit packages such as pension and health care programs. Word processing copies and drafts of these documents can often be found on desktops, laptops, servers, backup tapes and attached to e-mail. They can provide an insight into the corporate thought process pertaining to the issues in the case.

Policy and procedure manuals are now commonly found on Intranets, servers, Internet and on other storage media such as CD disks. They can be found in a word processing, HTML, or PDF format, and can be easily searched and compared to previous versions of the same document.

[F]   Marketing and Sales

This type of software identifies customers, keeps track of prospective customers, generates reminders on sales, processes orders, and provides point-of-sale and credit authorization systems.

Mapping software combines' text and graphics, database management and other capabilities to display business data geographically. It can provide data as to locations of customers and competitors, boundaries between sales territories, routes for deliveries, and so on.

[G]   Workflow Software

Workflow software is designed to provide workflow analysis for routine, ad hoc or complex work processes of a business.

[H]   CAD, CAM, CAE and CIM

The business uses of computer-assisted design and engineering software has eliminated dependence on printed blueprints and specifications. These documents are important in construction, manufacturing, chemical and electronic engineering. Oftentimes, these electronic files and the various versions are not printed except for final or approved designs. Usually, the specific software is needed to restore and view the documents.

- CAM stands for **C**omputer **A**ided **M**anufacturing software. Computers and other information technologies are used to automate the manufacturing process with CAM. CAM systems can control specific tools, machines and robots on a factory floor to assist in manufacturing the product.

- CAD stands for **C**omputer-**A**ided **D**esign. Production designers and engineers use CAD to draw product or process designs on the screen.

- CAE stands for **C**omputer-**A**ssisted **E**ngineering.

- CIM stands for **C**omputer **I**ntegrated **M**anufacturing.

[I]   Custom Software

Many businesses will develop or customize software for their specific business needs. When discovering custom software it is important to obtain user manuals, operator manuals, data dictionaries, metadata, programmer names and other information disclosing the creation, operation, and use of this software.

One of the trends in the software industry is for programmers to obtain a license to use a specific application software "engine," such as a database like Microsoft Access, and then design a customized interface that uses the engine. This approach is taking the place of the development of an original database program because a programmer uses all or part of the underlying "engine" and ensures that the customized program is built on an industry standard that can be used in networks and enterprise computing.

[J]   Integrated Software

Another important trend is the "integration" of various software applications such as word processing, databases and spreadsheets that share the data entered into one of the programs. This is accomplished using Dynamic Data Exchange (DDE) or Object Linking and Embedding (OLE). For example, once information is entered into a database program, that same data could be accessed and shared by a word processing document or a spreadsheet. The important point here is that you should be cognizant of "linked" data during the discovery process.

For this reason, it may be necessary to discover word processing documents as well as a database that holds the names and addresses linked with the documents.

§ 3.4   DIRECTORIES, FILES AND FILE FORMATS

Storage media typically contain directories that list the names of the files that are stored on the disk. A directory may also contain information about the file name, file size, when the file was created, when it was last modified and the type of file. This information is usually visible to the user. The computer also keeps track of where the files are physically located on the storage medium, although this information is generally hidden from the user. Even though files appear next to each other in the directory, it is unlikely they are physically located together on the disk. The file in the directory is the location where the underlying data is stored. If the file is deleted, the underlying data is still stored in the same physical location. However, the computer now considers that this space is available for storing new data. When new data is stored at this location it then overwrites the old data which is then generally lost.

[A]   Directory and Subdirectory

The main directory or point of entry in a disk-based hierarchical directory structure is called the root directory. The root directory is identified by the backslash character (\), and is the main directory on drive C. Branching out from the root directory are multiple directories and subdirectories, each of which contain files or other subdirectories. The illustration below depicts a directory structure. Beneath the root directory are a number of directories, one of which is named *My Documents*. This contains two additional directories, *Access Databases* and a subdirectory named *legal*. The name of subdirectories is shown within the directory. To the right of the highlighted subdirectory are the names of files within the subdirectory folder. In addition, the size, type, date and time last modified will be displayed for individual files within the directory or folder.

The folder is equivalent to a directory in that it can hold both files and additional folders/directories. It is symbolized on the screen by a graphical image of a file folder.

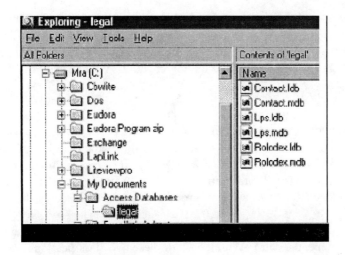

[1] Reported Cases

- *Cisco Systems, Inc. v. Alcatel USA, Inc.* 301 F. Supp.2d 599, 605 (E.D.Tex. 2004). "Alcatel blames its belated findings on Cisco's late production of voluminous electronic data. . . . [Alcatel] discovered that Cisco did not include a directory structure. Cisco provided Alcatel the directory structure in late March, 2002, as well as an additional set of back-up tapes."

- *In re Telxon Corp. Securities Litigation,* No. CIV.98-2876, 2004 WL 3192729, at *16 (N.D. Ohio Jul. 16, 2004). "The core files in the database are arranged in directories, sub-directories, and folders in outline form."

- *United States v. Triumph Capital Group, Inc.,* 211 F.R.D. 31 n.9 (D. Conn. 2002). The Court described directories, "A hard drive is divided into several logical drives, i.e., C:*, D:*, E:*. These drives are further divided into directories. The directories contain the user's files and folders. A directory listing contains the name, size, modification time and starting cluster of each of its files or subdirectories. The term directory structure means a list or inventory of files on the hard drive."

- *Armstrong v. Executive Office of the President, Office of Admin,* 1 F.3d 1274, 1285 (D.C. Cir. 1993). "Our discussion assumes that directories, distribution lists, etc. become part of an electronic record when they are incorporated in that record to specify senders and receivers of documents. We believe such an assumption is warranted as the most natural way of understanding the relation between the substance of a message and its origin and destination."

- *Momah v. Albert Einstein Medical Center*, 164 F.R.D. 412 (E.D. Pa. 1996). The Court allowed discovery of one computer record, specifically, the computer "list files" screen. The "list files" screen would display different information about documents created on the computer including the dates on which each document was created and last edited.

[B]   Files

Generally, information is stored in computers in the form of files. Files store data or information in an electronic format. These files reside on storage media such as hard drives, CD-ROMs and floppy disks. *See also, § 2.4, Storage Media.* The central processing unit (CPU) of the computer writes and reads data from a file. The CPU temporarily stores the file in its random access memory (RAM) in order to process data, and then stores the file on storage media.

Files are usually classified as data files (those containing data) and program files (files that instruct or manipulate the data). Within each of these two classifications are many types of files, depending upon the operating or application software. The files are generally named according to the extension attached to the end of each filename. An example of a file extension is PST for a Microsoft Outlook data file. When saving a file, a user can give any name to the file within the rules of the operating system. Filenames must be unique within the same directory. However, files can have the same name if contained in a different location or subdirectory.

Through linked or embedded objects, an electronic document may consist of information stored in different files and, potentially, on computers at different locations. The linked files may contain information in text, graphic, audio and even video formats.

[1]   Reported Case

- *United States v. Triumph Capital Group, Inc.*, 211 F.R.D. 31, 46 nn.5-10 (D. Conn. 2002). The Court described a file:

  A file is made up of a whole number of clusters that are not necessarily contiguous. When a computer user creates a file to be saved, the computer's "file allocation table" ("FAT") assigns or allocates a cluster or clusters to store that file. The clusters are not necessarily contiguous because the FAT assigns data to whatever available clusters it finds on the hard drive. Saved files that occupy allocated clusters are called "active files."

- *Williams v. Sprint/United Mgmt. Co.*, 230 F.R.D. 640, 646 (D. Kan. 2005). The Court noted that "[m]etadata . . . is defined as 'information describing the history, tracking, or management of an electronic document.'. . . Some examples of metadata for electronic documents include: a file's name, a file's location (e.g., directory structure or pathname), file format or file type, file size, file dates (e.g., creation date, date of last data modification, date of last data access, and date of last metadata modification), and file permissions (e.g., who can read the data, who can write to it, who can run it). Some metadata, such as file dates and sizes, can easily be seen by users; other metadata can be hidden or embedded and unavailable to computer users who are not technically adept."

•   *Davison v. Eldorado Resorts LLC,* No. CIV.05-0021, 2006 U.S. Dist. LEXIS 12598 (D. Nev. Mar. 10, 2006). The Court noted the testimony of an expert who stated that "an operating system such as Windows logs three time stamps when a file is saved. . . . The first stamp is titled 'created' and keeps track of the date and time the file was first saved. . . . The second stamp, 'modified,' shows the last time the file was opened and changed. . . . Finally, the last stamp, 'accessed,' displays the date and time the file was most recently opened regardless of whether any changes were made to the file. . . . Thus, when a file is saved to a CD, the 'created' date will be the same as the 'modified' date, and cannot change on a finalized CD."

[C]   File Formats

Computer application software programs generally maintain their data in proprietary file formats commonly referred to as "native file" format. *See,* § 5.03, *Electronic Data Formats.* These proprietary data file formats generally determine which software program can read the data file and contain the file's metadata. However, many programs, within a specific application group, have conversion utilities that may convert the data to formats that the host software program can read. This is commonplace in a word processing program such as Microsoft Word that can convert a WordPerfect file format to one that can be read by Microsoft Word. Often, formatting and other specific information is not converted 100 percent. This can result in loss of metadata, formatting instructions, and other information in the data file.

Generally, it is not necessary for one to have the original version of the application software that created the data files in order to view and analyze the data in the file. Many companies have developed and continue to develop "electronic discovery" software that permits the processing of "native file" application data in its original format for subsequent searching and viewing in litigation support software. *See,* § 5.7, *Extraction and Conversion.*

For discovery purposes, electronic information produced may be in many different file formats. File formats generally define the way the data is stored and subsequently displayed on a screen or in print. For example, the format of the file that contains plain ASCII text can be simple to display. However other file formats, such as TIFF (tag image file format) or RTF (rich text format) can be complex and have various types of instructions or codes for use by programs, printers and other devices, and can be difficult to view without specific application or "electronic discovery" software.

There are thousands of computer file formats. File formats are generally grouped according to specific application software, such as word processing, spreadsheets, graphic images, e-mail, etc. Files with an extension ending of EXE or COM normally run a program and are called "executable files." Files with an extension of SYS, INI and DLL are referred to as "system files." Files that contain words, sentences and paragraphs are generally referred to as "text" files. For text or word processing, common file formats are DOC, WPK, and TXT. For graphic programs that depict images and pictures, TIFF, BMP, JPG and EPS are some of the common "graphic" extension formats.

If you are unsure of the originating software program for a file format and know its extension, you can check the following websites for assistance:

- Webopedia (www.webopedia.com);
- Filext (http://filext.com/); and
- Wotsit's Format (www.wotsit.org).

Be aware that users may attempt to hide files by changing the file extension. The extension appended to a file name is generally used to identify the program that created the file. For example, a word processing document for Microsoft Word usually has an extension of DOC. However, a user can easily change the file extension to BMP depicting a graphic file or to a SYS extension representing a system file. If you request a search of all files with an extension of DOC then if the file extension has been changed, you will not locate the file. However, a file often contains "metadata" that will identify the file type even if the file extension has been changed. This metadata is in the form of a "file header" which contains the characteristics of known file types. The file header will remain unchanged even if the extension placed on the file is changed. In this instance it would be necessary to search the metadata of all files to attempt to discover their origin. *See also,* § 3.5[H][1], *Encryption and Steganography.*

[1]   Reported Cases

- *United States v. Harding,* 273 F. Supp. 2d 411, 423-424 (S.D.N.Y. 2003). "7. Files stored on personal computers each have file names. 8. In DOS, various versions of Windows, and other operating systems, file names typically are in the format [file name].XXX. 9. The portion of the file name following the period and indicated in paragraph 8 by the characters XXX is referred to as a file extension. 10. The file extension may consist of any three or, in some operating systems, more letters. 11. By convention, files often are assigned file extensions suggesting the nature of their contents. For example, WordPerfect and Word, two commonly used word processing programs, normally assign the file extensions 'wpd' and 'doc,' respectively, to documents created by them. Similarly, graphics files created or saved in the JPEG format normally are assigned names that include the file extension 'jpg.' 12. Notwithstanding the conventions referred to in paragraph 11, personal computers typically allow a user to assign any desired three letter file extension to any file, regardless of the nature of the content of the file. 13. A personal computer user could assign file names including file extensions, such as 'jpg,' that conventionally are used to indicate graphic data files to files that contain text."

- *United States v. Grimmett,* 2004 WL 3171788, at *2 (D.Kan. Aug. 10, 2004). "Kanatzar used a software program known as 'EnCase' to examine the contents of the hard disk drive. He first looked at the directories displayed on the disk drive. He opened each of the directories to view the files in them. He opened a number of files to consider the contents. Primarily, he was interested in a given file based upon the name given it or the extension at end of the name. Suggestive names are usually indicators of child pornography. Computer extensions also provide clues about what is in the file. For example, extensions such as '.jpg,' '.bmp,' or '.gif' commonly contain child pornography. In addition, files with extensions such as '.imp,' and '.rm' refer to movies and may also contain child pornography. Agent Kanatzar discovered a number of files with the aforementioned extensions that contained child pornography on the seized hard disk drive. He did not open every file. In fact, he specifically excluded all files with extensions of '.exe' and '.dll.'"

- *United States v. Maali,* 346 F. Supp.2d 1226, 1265 (M.D.Fla. 2004). "The . . . agent also explained that he could not rely on file names for purposes of determining what was responsive. . . . (citation omitted) . . . 'Few people keep documents of their criminal transactions in a folder marked 'crime records.''"

- *United States v. Hill,* 322 F. Supp.2d 1081, 1090-1091(C.D.Cal. 2004). The Court found that the "Defendant's proposed search methodology [was] . . . unreasonable. 'Computer records are extremely susceptible to tampering, hiding, or destruction, whether deliberate or inadvertent.' (citation omitted) Images can be hidden in all manner of files, even word processing documents and spreadsheets. Criminals will do all they can to conceal contraband, including the simple expedient of changing the names and extensions of files to disguise their content from the casual observer. Forcing police to limit their searches to files that the suspect has labeled in a particular way would be much like saying police may not seize a plastic bag containing a powdery white substance if it is labeled 'flour' or 'talcum powder.' There is no way to know what is in a file without examining its contents, just as there is no sure way of separating talcum from cocaine except by testing it. The ease with which child pornography images can be disguised--whether by renaming sexyteenybop persxxx.jpg as sundayschoollesson.doc, or something more sophisticated--forecloses defendant's proposed search methodology."

[D]   Operating Software and Program File Types

When a computer is turned on, it searches for instructions in its memory. Usually, the first set of these instructions is a special program called the operating system, which is the software that makes the computer work. It prompts the user (or other machines) for input and commands, reports the results of these commands and other operations, stores and manages data and controls the sequence of the software and hardware actions. Some common operating system file format extensions are COM, EXE, INI and SYS. *See also,* § 2.2[C], *Software*.

[E]   Data Compression and Encoding File Format

Data compression or compaction are terms applied to various methods of compressing electronic information for more efficient transmission of data or for storage purposes. It is used to compress data communications, database management files, facsimile transmissions, word processing documents and other electronic information. Compression is a method of removing repetitive elements from a computer file in order to save storage space. One compression technique that is often used is called "keyword encoding" that replaces frequently used words, such as the word "here," with a smaller replacement token word that is smaller in size. This saves at least a byte of storage each time the word is used.

All forms of digital data can be stored in compressed forms. Text, graphics, audio, video, spreadsheets, database and most other computer files can be compressed for storage and more efficient transmission. After compressing, files generally need to be decompressed or restored in order to use or view them. If you use the correct decompression software, these files will decompress for viewing and analysis. However, if the decompression software is unavailable, it can be a significant task for a computer forensics specialist to expand computer files back to their original format.

[1]   Reported Cases

• *In re Priceline.com Inc. Sec. Litig.,* 233 F.R.D. 88, 89 (D. Conn. 2005). "[N]ative files can be compressed to facilitate storage. In order to view the files after compression, the files must be restored to their native format."

• *Zubulake v. UBS Warburg, LLC,* 217 F.R.D. 309, 319 (S.D.N.Y. 2003). "Backup tapes also typically employ some sort of data compression, permitting more data to be stored on each tape, but also making restoration more time-consuming and expensive, especially given the lack of uniform standard governing data compression."

• *Storer v. Hayes Microcomputer Products, Inc.,* 960 F. Supp. 498, 501 (D. Mass. 1997). "Data compression is the process of reducing the size of the representation of a string of electronic data in order to permit it to be transmitted or stored more efficiently and later to be reconstructed without error."

[2]   Other Authority

• Mark Jones & John D. Martin, *Electronic Discovery - Developing Solutions to New and Complex Challenges*, 15 S.C. Law. 15 (May 2004). "These back-up systems sometimes 'archive' the data in such a way that allows it to be compressed into as small a storage space as possible, which requires the data to be unarchived or restored before it can even be searched. The process of restoring archived electronic media into readable form and searching it can take skilled technologists lengthy periods of time, even if they know precisely what they are trying to find, and costs astonishing sums of money. For example, in *Linnen v. A.H. Robins,* 1999 WL 462015 (Mass. Super. 1999), the expense of restoring backup tapes cost an estimated $1.75 million."

[F]   Other Data and File Formats

There are literally thousands of file formats reflecting the hundreds of software programs that have been developed over the years. Many of these programs have updated versions and hence updated file formats. In addition, many software programs no longer exist. Extraction of data from these files may present significant forensic challenges.

§ 3.5   SPECIAL ISSUES - ELECTRONIC INFORMATION

[A]   Volume & Obsolescence

The volume of information in an electronic format is substantial, and can be overwhelming. As the Court noted in *United States v. Triumph Capital Group, Inc.*, 211 F.R.D. 31, 46 (D. Conn. 2002), "[t]he storage capacity of the hard drive is 1.6 GB or approximately 453,000 pages of text. The hard drive actually contained approximately 1 GB, or 250,000 pages of data, including 18,768 active files and 1,800 recovered deleted files." The reason why there is such a large volume of active and stored data is that "the costs of storage are virtually nil. Information is retained not because it is expected to be used, but because there is no compelling reason to discard it." *See also, Rowe Entertainment, Inc. v. William Morris Agency, Inc.*, 205 F.R.D. 421, 429 (S.D.N.Y. 2002), *aff'd,* 2002 WL 975713 (S.D.N.Y. May 9, 2002); § 1.02[G], *Volume.*

Backup media can contain boxes of information. "[A] single eight-millimeter backup tape can maintain the equivalent of 1500 boxes of paper." Corinne L. Giacobbe, *Allocating Discovery Costs in the Computer Age: Deciding Who Should Bear the Costs of Discovery of Electronically Stored Data*, 57 Wash. & Lee L. Rev. 257, 263 (1999).

Routine interoffice communications, such as e-mail can be sent, replied to, revised, forwarded, etc. many times and can increase geometrically depending upon the number of users and locations. Contrast this with paper copies that are physically limiting to the user because of the need to make photocopies and the number of storage locations required such as folders, filing cabinets, storage rooms, etc. Paper copies can be routinely destroyed pursuant to a document retention policy. Electronic information, however, can be easily replicated many times over and can exist in many different locations. In addition, it is unusual to find an electronic document retention policy that is followed. This provides an opportunity for electronic information to be available on backup tapes, archives and inadvertent backups.

However, the amount of responsive information is substantially less than the amount of data available. For example, the Court in *Wiginton v. CB Richard Ellis, Inc.*, No. CIV.02-6832, 2004 WL 1895122, at *2 (N.D.Ill. Aug. 10, 2004) found that the actual responsive data ranged from an estimate of 1.64% to 6.5% for a previously filtered group of documents.

This volume of electronic information includes not only available computer files, but may also include "deleted" documents and metadata. Deleted files may exist on a computer and be subject to discovery with the assistance of forensic specialists. *See,* § 3.5[E], *Deletion of Electronic Information.* "Metadata" or "hidden" data associated with all word processing documents, e-mail, databases, etc. is also available. *See also,* § 3.7, *Metadata, Hidden, or Embedded Information.*

Changing technology has created obsolescence of computer hardware and software systems. *Greyhound Computer Corp., Inc. v. IBM,* 559 F.2d 488, 491 (9th Cir. 1977). The upgrading and changeover to newer computer hardware and software create difficulties in producing electronic documents. It is usual for an organization to have relevant data where the software that created it or the hardware that processed it is no longer available. In addition, the IT staff who may have understood the migration path that was used on part of the data during the migration may no longer be with the company. This legacy data, if it can be accessed at all, will likely be expensive to convert to usable data.

[1]   Reported Cases (reserved)

[2]   Other Authorities

- Shira A. Scheindlin & Jeffrey Rabkin, *Electronic Discovery in Federal Civil Litigation: Is Rule 34 Up to the Task?,* 41 B.C. L. Rev. 327, 334 (2000). "Today's CD-ROM disks can store approximately 325,000 pages of text. The average PC hard disk can store up to two million pages of text. The sheer volume of discoverable electronic evidence--and the trend towards ever greater computer storage capacity--poses logistical challenges to lawyers, litigants and the courts."

- *See also,* THE MANUAL FOR COMPLEX LITIGATION, FOURTH, § 11.446.

[B]   Disorganized & Dynamic

The lack of organization of computer-based evidence results in potential difficulties in discovery and disclosure. Electronic information relevant to a specific case can often be found in many different directories and computers within a business. Since directories and other file management techniques are physically invisible to the user, an organized list of electronic information is not a priority. This is different from paper management, where papers are usually filed in folders and kept in file cabinets or other storage containers in specific areas.

Computer backup and archival copies of information may be properly cataloged. However, this is rarely the case with individual backups of electronic data. An additional problem with improperly catalogued computer files is assuring that only relevant, nonprivileged material is produced.

Electronic information, unlike paper, may change over time. For example, many web page advertisements change by the minute. Word processing documents that are autodate formatted may be changed if the file is reopened. Document assembly database information may be updated which would change the address or other information in a letter to a business. For this reason, many types of electronic documents are never in final form. *See also,* § 1.2[F], *Disorganized.*

[C]   Replication - Archived and Backup Copies

Since electronic information can be easily replicated there are usually several redundant or duplicate copies of discovery information available. These duplicate copies are created to "back up" computer systems, archive information and documents that may have already been disclosed in other lawsuits. Backup copies may contain less or more information than the originals depending on when they were backed up or archived. Redundant data may be kept for months or years. In anticipation of hardware (and users) failures, redundant "backup" copies of important data files are usually made on removable media such as magnetic or optical media. These backup copies may end up being scattered around an office or stored at physically separate locations. *See also,* § 2.6[C], *Backups – Computer Files.*

[D]   Preservation

Because of the uniqueness of electronic information, there are special challenges relating to document preservation. Unlike that encountered in traditional paper-based discovery, we seldom have to worry about the destruction of paper or microfilm during the course of litigation since natural disasters are a rare occurrence. This is not the case with electronic information. Electronic information can be easily overwritten, changed or destroyed by normal everyday use of the computer. This applies whether it is a single desktop computer or an enterprise-wide system. Just using the computer may actually destroy electronic information. Booting up a computer, saving a file onto a disk or running a simple program like a defragmentation utility can alter and destroy information without the user being aware. *See also,* § 7.9[D], *Duty to Preserve.*

[E]   Deletion of Electronic Information

[1]   Generally

One of the most fundamental issues about electronic discovery is how a court should respond to requests for electronic materials that have been "deleted." Courts consistently have held that discoverable electronic information includes files that have been "deleted." *Zubulake v. UBS Warburg, LLC,* 217 F.R.D. 309, 313 n.19 (S.D.N.Y. 2003); *Antioch Co. v. Scrapbook Borders, Inc.,* 210 F.R.D. 645, 652 (D. Minn. 2002); *See also,* §§ 7.7[B], *"Document" - Definition* and 7.07[H], *Inspection of Opposing Party's Computer System.* Deleted data, if restored, can be invaluable for exposing patterns of conduct, behavior or motives behind the deletion of that data. However, it may be necessary to present evidence of the relevance of the "deleted" data or the Courts may label the request a "fishing expedition." *See,* §§ 7.04[F], *Relevancy and Overbroad Concerns - Rule 26(b)(1)* and 7.4[G][4], *Objection on the Ground of Undue Burden or Expense.*

Computer users think that when they press the "delete" key that the computer's data has been destroyed, but this is simply not the case. When a file is "deleted" from a disk, whether it is a word-processing, database or spreadsheet file, it is not actually erased. Instead, the "address" of the file is simply deleted. The file data is still there, but the "address" is open for new data. Until new data is actually written over this area, the electronic information is still on the computer storage media. Computers can only "delete" information by overwriting it with new data.

As one judge noted, "[i]t is becoming widely known that a computer's *delete* key represents an elaborate deception. The deception is pure, and inheres in the key's name: When the *delete* key is used, nothing is deleted. It is now clear that relatively simple devices can recover almost everything that has been 'deleted.' This durability of computerized material compounds itself, because once a computer file is generated - let alone disseminated - internal and external copies proliferate. And each is impervious to deletion." James M. Rosenbaum, *In Defense of the Delete Key,* 3 Green Bag 2d 393, 393 (2000), *available at* http://www.greenbag.org/rosenbaum_deletekey.pdf (last visited on July 21, 2006).

The primary reason for the concern over whether data has been overwritten is that software tools are available to "undelete" data that was thought to have been destroyed. A forensic specialist is needed to properly recover and authenticate deleted information.

Deleted information cannot be restored from a backup tape unless a forensic copy of the data was made.

Deleted documents may be reconstructed from hard drives of personal computers, from the network server's storage media or generally from other storage devices.

The question is often asked when electronic information will be overwritten resulting in its permanent loss. This process can take seconds, months or years. It all depends on the activities that occur on the computer as one continues to use it. Obviously, if you choose not to process any other information on a system then the data will remain on the hard drive or other storage media. Also, the data may not be entirely overwritten since the file data usually resides in different clusters on a disk. For example, a 10-page word processing computer file may reside on different clusters. Through normal use of the computer, four pages in separate clusters may have been overwritten, leaving six pages available for recovery.

Another commentator noted, "[i]n the conventional paper-based world, once a document is shredded, incinerated, or buried in a landfill, it is no longer subject to discovery as a practical matter. The routine 'deletion' of a computer-based document does not, however, actually destroy the data. Hitting the 'delete' key merely renames the file in the computer, marking it as available for overwriting if that particular space on the computer's hard disk is needed in the future. The data itself may remain on the hard disk or on removable storage media for months or years, or may be overwritten only incrementally." Kenneth J. Withers, *Computer-Based Discovery in Federal Civil Litigation*, Practical Litigator (Nov. 2001).

There are generally four ways to destroy 'deleted' information on storage media. First, you can destroy the data if you continue to use the computer and create new documents or database files or install new software and the data is overwritten. Second, there are software packages that are able, with varying levels of success, to wipe or clean the information off a disk by overriding the entire disk with random data that the computer recognizes. However, even though the data may not be recoverable, an expert may be able to determine when the disk was wiped clean. Third, it may be deleted if you run a special software utility such as defragmentation that results in the massive rewriting of information on the disk. Finally, one can physically damage or destroy the storage media itself.

[2] Cost of Restoring Deleted Information

Though one can restore or recover deleted data, it may be expensive and lead to uncertain results. These costs may or may not be chargeable to the requesting party. When a producing party has failed to preserve electronic information that applies to the claims or defenses, if under a duty to do so, then the cost could very well be shifted to the disclosing party. However, if a party decides to seek the deleted information without any basis for believing that it exists, then the requesting party may bear the cost. Counsel should be prepared to demonstrate recovery of deleted files is necessary and germane to the case, and is not a fishing expedition. *See,* § 7.4[F], *Relevancy and Overbroad Concerns - Rule 26(b)(1)* and § 7.4[G][6], *Cost Allocation.*

[3]   Reported Cases

*   *See,* §§ 7.07[B], *"Document" - Definition and* 7.07[H], *Inspection of Opposing Party's Computer System.*

*   *Kleiner v. Burns,* No. 00-2160, 2000 WL 1909470, at *4 (D. Kan. Dec. 15, 2000). The court ruled that "computerized data . . . includes . . . deleted e-mail."

*   *Paramount Pictures Corp. v. Davis,* 234 F.R.D. 102 (D. Pa. 2005). After tracing infringement activity through the defendant's IP address it was discovered that the defendant intentionally wiped his computer's hard drive clean in order to avoid detection of his infringing activities.

*   *Zhou v. Pittsburg State University,* 2003 WL 1905988, *2 (D. Kan. Feb. 5, 2003). The disclosing party should take "reasonable steps to ensure that it discloses any back-up copies or files or archival tapes that will provide information about any 'deleted' electronic data."

*   *Adobe Sys., Inc. v. Sun South Prod., Inc.,* 187 F.R.D. 636 (S.D. Cal. 1999). The Court in denying an ex parte TRO in a computer piracy suit held, "[m]anual or automated deletion of that software may remove superficial indicia, such as its icons or presence in the user's application menu. However, telltale traces of a previous installation remain, such as abandoned subdirectories, libraries, information in system files, and registry keys . . . Even if an infringer managed to delete every file associated with Plaintiffs' software, Plaintiffs could still recover many of those files since the operating system does not actually erase the files, but merely marks the space consumed by the files as free for use by other files."

*   *Kemper Mortg., Inc. v. Russell,* No. CIV.06-042, 2006 U.S. Dist. LEXIS 20729, at *5-7 (D. Ohio Apr. 6, 2006). The Court ruled plaintiff was entitled to an adverse inference when the defendant "caused to be installed on his laptop computer a program called 'Window Washer' . . . which prevents the forensic recovery of deleted electronic files by overwriting them."

*   *Zubulake v. UBS Warburg, LLC,* 217 F.R.D. 309, 313 n.19 (S.D.N.Y. 2003). The Court noted, "The term 'deleted' is sticky in the context of electronic data. 'Deleting' a file does not actually erase that data from the computer's storage devices. Rather, it simply finds the data's entry in the disk directory and changes it to a 'not used' status - thus permitting the computer to write over the 'deleted' data."

- The Court in *United States v. Triumph Capital Group, Inc.,* 211 F.R.D. 31 nn.7-8 (D. Conn. 2002) described the search efforts of the government investigator as he "mirrored" a hard drive and then searched for "active files, free space, slack space, recovered deleted files, directory structures, link files, file attributes, software programs and properties, image files such as internet cache files and temporary directories." The Court described deleted files.

  Deleted data, or remnants of deleted data can be found in the slack space at the end of an active file and may consist of relatively small, non-contiguous and unrelated fragments that may have come from any number of previously deleted files. A normal computer user does not see slack space when he opens an active file. Forensic tools are required to extract and view slack space.

  "Deleted files" are part of the free space. When a user deletes a file, the data in the file is not erased, but remains intact in the cluster or clusters where it was stored until the operating system places other data over it. When a file is deleted, the computer's operating system tells the FAT to release the clusters that were assigned to it so that the clusters can be used to store new files and data. To indicate that a file has been deleted, the operating system alters the first character of the file's name in the directory structure.

  The data in a deleted file remains in a cluster's slack space until it is overwritten by new data. Unless there is sufficient data in a new document or file to overwrite all of the deleted data in the cluster, the cluster will contain remnants of formerly deleted data in the cluster's "slack space", the space between the end of the new data and the end of the cluster. When all the clusters of a deleted file remain unused by the computer's operating system, it is possible to recover the deleted file in its entirety. Portions of deleted files may be recovered even if portions of the clusters the file occupied are being used by new files.

- *Playboy Enterprises, Inc. v. Welles,* 60 F. Supp. 2d 1050 (S.D. Cal. 1999). The Court granted the plaintiff's request for access to the defendant's hard drive after the plaintiff learned that it was the defendant's practice and custom to delete e-mail after sending or receiving e-mail. The Court appointed a computer expert who specialized in the field of electronic discovery to create a "mirror image" of the defendant's hard drive.

- *Vermont Microsystems, Inc. v. AutoDesk, Inc.,* 138 F.3d 449 (2d Cir. 1998). The plaintiff sued one of its competitors, *AutoDesk*, alleging that one of its former engineers took proprietary programs when he left to go to work for *AutoDesk.* The key evidence was a group of computer file names that the engineer thought had been permanently erased. Computer experts, however, were able to recover the file names on *AutoDesk* computer disks, and file names were shown to be the same as the ones that the plaintiff alleged the engineer and *AutoDesk* misappropriated.

- *United States v. White,* 244 F.3d 1199, 1206-07 (10th Cir. 2001). As the Tenth Circuit observed, "software is presently available to erase from a computer's hard drive the names of sites visited. A sophisticated Internet user can circumvent any barrier with knowledge of programming."

[4]   Other Authorities

- Brenner, Frederiksen, *Computer Searches and Seizures: Some Unresolved Issues,* 8 Mich. Telecomm. & Tech. L. Rev. 39, 66 (2002). "During normal computer use, many temporary files are created and deleted by the operating system. Additional files are created, deleted, or modified by specific actions [orders] of the user. If the computer system is in continual use, older information will be overwritten with newer information. The more the system is used, the more evidence will be lost. The simple act of starting a Microsoft Windows system will destroy more than 4,000,000 characters of evidence, and the spoliation will be far greater if the system is used to run any programs."

- Marron, *"Discoverability of 'Deleted' E-mail: Time for a Closer Examination,"* 25 Seattle U. L. Rev. 895, 897 (2002). "As applied to deleted e-mails, the current rules are the equivalent of requiring a litigant to first dig through their garbage for huge amounts of shredded and discarded paper correspondence and then expend considerable resources to repair the letters and documents found. These documents are then handed over to a litigant's opponent and may appear as evidence in a civil case."

[5]   Discovery Pointers

- Always check to determine if data, even though deleted from a computer, may still be available on a backup tape.

- If you are requesting the court to restore deleted data ensure that you have evidence that data was actually deleted. This evidence would come from a witness who can testify that e-mail is deleted on a daily basis or from information that a corporation's document destruction policy has not been suspended.

[F]   Defragmentation and Reformat

Fragmentation on a disk occurs when parts or pieces of a single file are distributed to many different locations on a disk. For example, a word processing document that has been stored on a hard drive is actually saved at a number of different locations on the disk. When this occurs, it increases the time for the file to be accessed by the computer. To solve the problem of slow access times, one generally will run a defragmentation program. This program will go through the hard drive track by track and rearrange sectors for each file so that they can be accessed more quickly.

This writing and rewriting of the hard disk will prevent access to "deleted" files, since the deleted file information will be overwritten by the defragmentation program.

Sometimes an operating system will become corrupted because of computer viruses or other software problems. To revert it to its "factory settings" or a "clean state" the disk is reformatted. This prepares a hard disk or other storage media for use and the reinstallation of the operating system. "When a computer is reformatted, it is essentially reset to its original factory settings such that all information created by the user and extra programs installed by the user are deleted." *Davison v. Eldorado Resorts LLC,* No. CIV.05-0021, 2006 U.S. Dist. LEXIS 12598, n.5 (D. Nev. Mar. 10, 2006). However, reformatting usually causes the loss of data files and "deleted" data that has been overwritten by the reinstallation of the operating system and other application software.

[1]   Reported Cases

- *Krumwiede v. Brighton Assocs., L.L.C.,* No. CIV.05-3003, 2006 U.S. Dist. LEXIS 31669, at *14-15 (D. Ill. May 8, 2006). "Defragmentation utility programs pull file fragments together and are supposed to make computers function faster and more efficiently. . . . When file fragments are pulled together they may use unallocated space in the computer and, in the process, write over previously deleted files (which are often moved to the unallocated space on the computer) . . . The result is that deleted files may no longer be recoverable. . . . According to [the forensic expert] . . . he has been trained to look for use of defragmentation utility because it is a common tool used for covering up file transfers and deletions."

- *RKI, Inc. v. Grimes,* 177 F. Supp. 2d 859, 870, 875 (N.D. Ill. 2001). In this case evidence of defragmentation was used to prove misappropriation of trade secrets. The Court stated, "[D]efragmentation is also a method to cover up deletions of data by eliminating all traces of deleted data. . . . [defendant never explained] why he defragmented his home computer four times in ten days in November, 2001, when no mechanical or engineering reason required it."

- *Zubulake v. UBS Warburg,* LLC, 217 F.R.D. 309, 319 (S.D.N.Y. 2003). The Court stated:

    5. *Erased, fragmented or damaged data:* "When a file is first created and saved, it is laid down on the [storage media] in contiguous clusters . . . As files are erased, their clusters are made available again as free space. Eventually, some newly created files become larger than the remaining contiguous free space. These files are then broken up and randomly placed throughout the disk." Such

broken-up files are said to be "fragmented," and along with damaged and erased data can only be accessed after significant processing.

- *MPCT Solutions Corp. v. Methe,* No. CIV.99-3736, 1999 WL 495115, at *1 (N.D.Ill. Jul. 2, 1999). After ordering preservation of computer data the Court found that on "June 13, Mr. Methe's laptop computer was 'defragged,' preventing the retrieval of deleted documents. . . . According to Mr. Methe, his wife [also] defragged the computer as part of a weekly defragging routine . . . We also know that the deleted information and other possible evidence is no longer recoverable because the computer was . . . defragged."

- *Electronic Planroom, Inc. v. McGraw-Hill Companies, Inc.* 135 F. Supp.2d 805, 812 n.7 (E.D. Mich. 2001). "This process of defragmentation makes it more difficult, if not impossible, to recover deleted data from the hard drive."

- *PFS Distribution Co. v. Raduechel,* 332 F. Supp.2d 1236, 1242 (S.D. Iowa 2004). Defendants ran a "defrag" program on their computers to destroy the data.

[G]   Alteration of Electronic Information

One of the major shortcomings of electronic information is the capability to alter a word processing document, a computer image, audio recording, graphics, video recording, etc., in ways that are difficult to detect without using computer forensic techniques. Electronic information is not the same as analog information. It is difficult for an individual to alter paper or other analog data. There are forensic tools to discover such attempts at falsification.

This is not the case with electronic information. For example, one can "alter" or edit a document without rekeying all the words by just copying the text to another document, change numbers and calculations in spreadsheets and change photographs, audio and video data. These alterations may be undetectable.

We have seen examples of altered information. In the 1994 political campaign of John Warner and Mark Warner in Virginia, a photograph was altered to show that Mark Warner was more of an insider then he actually was. A photograph showed him with the President and the governor. It was false. One of John Warner's campaign managers had inserted the head of Mark Warner in the photograph on top of Charles Robb's body. The falsification was discovered because on Charles Robb's arm was a metal watch, which Mark Warner had never worn. Charles Bierbauer, *Head Games in Virginia Senate Ad Draw Fire,* CNN, *available at* http://www.cnn.com/ALLPOLITICS/1996/news/9610/10/ bierbauer.warner/index.shtml (last visited on July 21, 2006).

There are software programs that will "hash" electronic information to lock in the data in order to prevent changes. *Williams v. Sprint/United Mgmt. Co.,* 230 F.R.D. 640, 655 (D. Kan. 2005) (Court found that using "hash marks" would ensure that a computer file has not been altered or manipulated.); *See also,* §5.05[G], *Chain of Custody, Audit Reports and Hash Values.*

[H]   Computer Security Protocols

Computer security incorporates various protocols to protect single computers and network-linked computer systems from accidental or intentional harm. *Cobell v. Norton,* 394 F. Supp. 2d 164 (D.D.C. 2005). These protocols protect a computer against destruction of hardware and software, physical loss of data, deception by computer users and the deliberate invasion of databases by unauthorized individuals.

For electronic discovery purposes, these various methods will set up barriers to access discoverable information, but may assist in authenticating the discovered evidence, since only authorized users will have access to the system.

Some computer security methods include encryption, limiting access rights to approved users, firewalls and security servers.

[1]   Encryption and Steganography

Encryption

Encryption is the process of converting electronic information, such as messages or data, into a form that is unreadable by anyone, except the intended recipient. Although the technical details of encryption are rather complicated, encryption is basically the scrambling and alteration of data until it is no longer readable by anyone who does not have the proper decrypting tool. Generally, encryption uses algorithms to convert electronic data into an encrypted form of data. Most encryption systems are almost unbreakable. The encrypted data must be decrypted, in order to be read by the recipient.

There are several different types of encryption techniques that users and senders can implement to protect their information. One of the most popular cryptography systems, Pretty Good Privacy (PGP) (www.mcafee.com), uses public-key encryption. In this system, each person gets two keys, a public key and a private key. The keys allow a person to either encrypt (lock) a message or decipher (unlock) an encoded message. Each person's public key is published and the private key is kept secret. Below are the most common encryption techniques.

To guarantee originator, single lock

- Sender creates an electronic document and prepares it for transmission.
- Document is encrypted with sender's private key, known only to sender.
- Sender's public key is obtainable by anyone and is distributed through various websites.

- Recipient can open the document by using the sender's public key. The link between the two keys is proof that the sender sent the transmission.

To guarantee recipient, single lock

- Sender creates a document to be read only by designated recipient.
- Document is locked prior to transmission with designated recipient's public key and transmitted.
- Because it is locked with a public key, it can only be opened with designated recipient's private key.
- Designated document is opened by recipient's private key; thereby proving the document's security and that recipient opened it.

To guarantee originator and recipient, double lock

- Sender creates a document only to be read by designated recipient.
- Document is locked with recipient's public key, and sender's private key, and then transmitted.
- Since the document is locked with recipient's public key and sender's private key the transmitted document can be opened only with designated recipient's private key and the sender's public key. This proves document security and the authenticity of the sender and receiver.

Encryption will become easier and will integrate into the normal transmission of e-mail and other electronic information over the next several years. This obviously will challenge the practitioner and courts to figure out solutions to this problem.

Resources

- Introduction to Public Key Encryption - IPlanet (http://docs.sun.com/source/816-5572-10/app_b_cr.htm)(available on July 21, 2006).
- Frequently asked questions on cryptography (Visit http://www.rsasecurity.com/ and insert the word "cryptography" in the search box)(last visited on July 21, 2006).

Encryption Products
- PGP (Pretty Good Privacy) (www.pgp.com).
- RSA Data Security Public Key Crytosystem (www.rsasecurity.com/).

Steganography

        Steganography (from the Greek word for "covered writings") is the science of hiding the existence of a message within another message or computer file. *United States v. Heiser,* No. CR.04-270, 2006 U.S. Dist. LEXIS 27886, at *14 (D. Pa. Apr. 26, 2006) ("Steganography is the art and science of writing hidden messages in such a way that no one apart from the intended recipient knows of the existence of the message; this is in contrast to cryptography, where the existence of the message itself is not disguised, but the content is obscured.").

        One of today's popular methods is to hide the contents of a message within a graphic image. A text message can be hidden within a graphic image without affecting the outward appearance of the image. Steganography is a branch of cryptography. "Cryptography defined as 'the science and study of secret writing' concerns the ways in which communications and data can be encoded to prevent disclosure of their contents through eavesdropping or message interception, using codes, ciphers, and other methods, so that only certain people can see the real message." Yaman Akdeniz, *Cryptography & Encryption,* (Aug. 1996).

        In order to determine whether steganography has been used a steganalysis is performed to detect embedded hidden information. Using steganography one could hide financial records or trade secret documents inside a photo of a company picnic. Any type of storage device such as an iPod, MP3 player or PDA can be used to transfer images or other files carrying this hidden information. A file can be hidden in many of the popular file image formats such as BMP, JPG and ZIP. The ratio of size of the hidden file to the image or other file will vary according to the product used.

        An example of a steganography product is Steganos Security Suite 6 *available at* http://www.steganos.com/.

[a]   Reported Cases

• *See also,* §§ 7.07[G], *Form of Production of Computer-based Data,* 7.07[E], *Kept in the Usual Course of Business,* and 7.07[D], *Translated Into Reasonably Useful Form.*

• *United States v. Pearson,* No. CR.04-CR-340, 2006 U.S. Dist. LEXIS 32982, at *12-14 (D.N.Y. May 24, 2006). The FBI conducted a limited forensic examination and "found a number of encrypted files within a file labeled 'steganosencryptionsafes,' but did not review any text files from this computer. . . . an email dated March 18, 2004, from 'steganos.asknet.de' to 'Peall20056@aol.com' in which 'a password and serial number necessary for downloading software capable of encrypting files were provided.'"

• *In re Amato,* 2005 WL 1429743, *3 (D.Me. Jun. 17, 2005). The plaintiff sought "f. Any physical keys, encryption devices, dongles and similar physical items that are necessary to gain access to the computer equipment, storage devices or data; and g. Any passwords, password files, test keys, encryption codes or other information necessary to access the computer equipment, storage devices or data[.]"

- *Four Seasons Hotels and Resorts B.V. v. Consorcio Barr, S.A.,* 267 F. Supp.2d 1268, 1296 (S.D.Fla. 2003). "Of the 92 recovered e-mails, 38 of them contained encrypted spreadsheet files attached to them. . . . Utilizing a system of 25 powerful computers to carry out what is called a distributed network attack against the file whose password was encrypted, Ashley was able to crack the password of the first file. . . . It took *between two to three weeks to complete the decryption of all 38 files.*" (emphasis added).

- *In re Network Associates, Inc., Securities Litigation,* No. CIV.99-01729, 2000 WL 33376577, at *5 (N.D.Cal. Sept. 5, 2000). "Pretty Good Privacy was a pioneer in email-encryption technology and developed PGP, a worldwide de facto standard for Internet email and file encryption."

- *State v. Levie,* 695 N.W.2d 619, 623 (Minn. App. May 3, 2005). In a child pornography case the Court held that evidence of a defendant's internet usage and the existence of an encryption program (PGP) on the defendant's computer was sufficiently relevant to be admissible.

[b]   Other Authorities

- Anderson, *Transmitting Legal Documents Over the Internet: How to Protect Your Client and Yourself,* 1 Rutgers Computer & Tech. L. J. 1, 32 (2001):

  Cryptography is 'the art and science of keeping messages secure . . . [, and] the process of disguising a message in such a way as to hide its substance is called 'encryption.' Through encryption, one can convert standard text, or 'plaintext,' into unreadable gibberish, or 'ciphertext.' Encrypted documents are unreadable until they are 'decrypted.'

  The more basic form [of cryptography] is called 'private-key' encryption. Private-key encryption uses the same key to encrypt messages from plaintext to ciphertext and then to decrypt the messages back into plain text.

  Public-key encryption uses a pair of mathematically related keys: a public key that encrypts data, and a corresponding private key that decrypts data. The public key is published, often on a website or through a trusted third party known as a certification authority, while the private key is available only to the sender. Even though the keys are mathematically related, it is 'computationally infeasible' to ascertain the private key from the public key.

[c] Discovery Pointers

- It can be costly to decrypt files protected by passwords and other encrypting methods. If the producing party opposes paying for the decryption it may be necessary to file a motion to compel citing to the requirement in Rule 34 that the data must be in a "reasonably usable form." *See*, § 7.07[D], *Translated Into Reasonably Useful Form.*

- If a computer file or message has been encrypted to protect its information, the code will have to be broken for discovered material. This may endanger the confidentiality of other documents using the same encryption. However, confidential documents may be protected by a court protective order. *See*, §§ 7.3[E], *Discovery and Preservation Orders - Rule 16(c)* and 7.4[I], *Protective Orders - Rule 26(c).*

[2] Limiting Access Rights to Approved Users

Most software programs provide the capability of limiting access to the software data. Access-control software verifies computer users and limits their privileges to view and alter files. Audit records may be made of the files accessed, thereby providing a trail of all those who accessed the software.

Passwords are confidential sets of letters, numbers or other characters that allow users access to computers. Most businesses require typing in a password to gain access to the computer system. Some are requiring passwords to be a mixture of letters, numbers and other characters and no less than a certain length.

Problems arise when you have discovered electronic data that has been password protected by a user. If the user is unavailable and the opposing party has not kept the passwords, then the services of a forensic specialist will be required to try to gain access to the data. There are tools available to "crack" the passwords such as Advanced Office XP Password Recovery (www.crackpassword.com) to recover Microsoft Office XP data. Password recovery software is available for most popular e-mail, spreadsheets, instant messaging and other software applications.

New types of access protections such as biometric identification and tokens are being implemented to make it more difficult to gain access to computer data. Tokens are tamper-resistant plastic cards with microprocessor chips that contain a stored password that automatically and frequently changes. Biometric identification methods use unique personal characteristics, such as fingerprints, retinal patterns, skin oils, deoxyribonucleic acid (DNA), voice variations and keyboard-typing rhythms to allow access.

[a]   **Reported Cases (reserved)**

[b]   **Discovery Pointers**

As encryption and passwords become more commonplace, additional issues will surface regarding discovery of encrypted information.

- Often, employees are given the option of selecting their own encryption keys or passwords which they may frequently change. Is a log kept of these changes?

- If the employee has terminated his employment with the company, has he or she disclosed their encryption keys or passwords before leaving?

- Will an ex-employee cooperate by furnishing the decryption keys to access the data?

- Will the producing party argue that the encryption material is privileged or irrelevant to the case and therefore should not be disclosed?

- Will it become necessary for the court to become involved in requiring the parties to disclose encryption keys and passwords in order to unlock the contents of these electronic files?

Sample Interrogatories:

- Set forth the date and guidelines for issuing passwords to employees.
- In addition to general user access passwords, are individual files or types of files password-protected at the file level?
- Who decides what level of access to grant to an individual employee?
- What areas/directories are off limits to employees of certain departments?
- Have you implemented encryption programs?
- Is their documentation on firewalls and security servers?

[3]   **Firewalls**

Firewalls and security servers block unauthorized access to an organization's local area network (LAN). *Checkpoint Sys. v. Check Point Software Techs., Inc.,* 104 F. Supp. 2d 427, 440 (D.N.J. 2000) ("[a] firewall is software that resides at a network's connection point (or points) to the Internet. The firewall analyzes data streams, either allowing or disallowing data to pass based on a series of network security policies or rules."); *Cobell v. Norton,* 394 F. Supp. 2d 164, 166, n1 (D.D.C. 2005); *Visto Corp. v. Sproqit Techs., Inc.,* No. CIV.04-0651, 2006 U.S. Dist. LEXIS 35467 (D. Cal. Feb. 7, 2006). A firewall can reside on a Web server that acts as the LAN's gateway to the Internet or it can be a dedicated computer placed between the LAN and the Internet. The firewall can keep track of files entering or leaving the LAN. This is done to protect against viruses and other problems. For electronic discovery purposes, it may provide evidence of Internet usage, file transfer and other information relevant to that usage. *United States v. Simons*, 206 F.3d 392, 396 (4th Cir. 1999) (the Court noted that the manager's duties include, "monitoring Internet connections through a device called a firewall. . . . The firewall logs all traffic going outside of the network, and it shows which computers have accessed the outside."); *See also, §§ 3.9[F][4], Firewalls and 2.6[G], Audit Trails and Logs.*

[4]   Content Scraping Programs

Content scraping software programs are used to "scrape" or extract information off a website. For example if a website displays airplane fares a scraping program could be programmed to extract the fare information off the website based on date, travel locations and other pertinent information.

[a]   Reported Cases

- *Cairo, Inc. v. Crossmedia Servs.*, No. CIV.04-04825, 2005 U.S. Dist. LEXIS 8450, at *7-9 (D. Cal. Apr. 1, 2005). The Court enforced the venue clause in a terms of use agreement that involved a dispute that the defendant was "scraping" or copying promotional material off the plaintiff's site and posting a version on its competing site.

- *Southwest Airlines Co. v. Farechase, Inc.* 2004 WL 690897 (N.D. Tex. Mar. 19 2004). In this case the defendant extracted fare scheduling information using a "scraping program" even though the website's use agreement specifically prohibited the use of such a program.

[I]   Computer Viruses

A computer virus is a computer program that infects other programs by replicating itself. A virus consists of two parts, a replication code, which spreads the virus, and the payload, which is the prank or destructive part. One new virus is created each day and there are more than 8,000 signature viruses. Viruses can be transferred on a floppy disk, e-mail attachment, downloading a file off the Internet, shrink-wrapped software, from another computer on your network or even on CD-ROM. You can also pick up a virus from your home computer after your kids have played on it.

Once you open the infected file program, the replication code is activated and will spread by copying itself to other drives on your computer. A virus may lie dormant for months and become triggered by a specific coded date. They come in all sizes and shapes, some are harmless and others replicate on their own destroying valuable data.

After obtaining electronic discovery it is important to check the data for computer viruses or otherwise it may jeopardize the contents of your electronic discovery computer and network.

[1]   Reported Cases

- *Expert Bus. Sys. v. Bi4ce, Inc.,* 411 F. Supp. 2d 601, n5 (D. Md. 2006). "[A] Trojan horse is a program in which malicious or harmful code is contained inside apparently harmless programming or data in such a way that it can get control and do its chosen form of damage, such as ruining the file allocation table on your hard disk. . . . A Trojan horse may be widely redistributed as part of a computer virus. . . . A Trojan Horse neither replicates nor copies itself, but causes damage or compromises the security of the computer. A Trojan Horse must be sent by someone or carried by another program and may arrive in the form of a joke program or software of some sort. The malicious functionality of a Trojan Horse may be anything undesirable for a computer user, including data destruction or compromising a system by providing a means for another computer to gain access, thus bypassing normal access controls."

- *United States v. Duronio,* No. CR.02-933, 2006 U.S. Dist. LEXIS 32313, n.5 (D.N.J. May 23, 2006). "A logic bomb is similar to a computer virus, except that its execution is delayed pending satisfaction of certain criteria, such as a date or time. This logic bomb was . . . instructed to delete all files from computers on which it operated."

- *United States v. Morris,* 928 F.2d 504, 505 n.1(2nd Cir. 1991). "In the colorful argot of computers, a 'worm' is a program that travels from one computer to another but does not attach itself to the operating system of the computer it 'infects.' It differs from a 'virus,' which is also a migrating program, but one that attaches itself to the operating system of any computer it enters and can infect any other computer that uses files from the infected computer."

§ 3.6   DATA TYPES

E-mail	Spyware
Internet	Database
Web pages	Spreadsheet
Chat room	Word processing
Newsgroups	Faxes
Listserv	Graphics
Cookies	Multimedia

Internet history logs	**Presentation**
Cache files	**Video**
Firewalls	**Conferencing**
Web logs	**Audio**

[A] Data Types - Generally

There are many different data types that may contain electronic information relevant to your case. These different file types are discoverable. As stated in *Kleiner v. Burns,* No. 00-2160, 2000 WL 1909470, at *4 (D. Kan. Dec. 15, 2000):

> As used by the advisory committee, 'computerized data and other electronically-recorded information' includes, but is not limited to: voice mail messages and files, back-up voice mail files, e-mail messages and files, backup e-mail files, deleted e-mail, data files, program files, backup and archival tapes, temporary files, system history files, Web site information stored in textual, graphical or audio format, Web site log files, cache files, cookies, and other electronically-recorded information.

The Court noted that they did not intend the list to be exhaustive. *Id.* at *4 n.6.

[B] Classification of Data

Electronic information is classified according to its type, intended use or as to the means by which such information can be accessed. Understanding the classifications of electronic information is important in mastering electronic discovery principles.

How information is classified may have a determinative effect on how the courts decide a cost-shifting request. For example, the court in the seminal decision *Zubulake v. UBS Warburg LLC,* 217 F.R.D. 309, 319-320 (S.D.N.Y. 2003) identified five categories of electronic information and classified each as to the accessibility of the information.

> Whether electronic data is accessible or inaccessible turns largely on the media on which it is stored. Five categories of data, listed in order from most accessible to least accessible, are described in the literature on electronic data storage:
>
> 1. Active, online data: "On-line storage is generally provided by magnetic disk. It is used in the very active stages of an electronic records [*sic*] life--when it is being created or received and processed, as well as when the access frequency is high and the required speed of access is very fast, i.e., milliseconds." Examples of online data include hard drives.

2. Near-line data: "This typically consists of a robotic storage device (robotic library) that houses removable media, uses robotic arms to access the media, and uses multiple read/write devices to store and retrieve records. Access speeds can range from as low as milliseconds if the media is already in a read device, up to 10-30 seconds for optical disk technology, and between 20-120 seconds for sequentially searched media, such as magnetic tape." Examples include optical disks.

3. Offline storage/archives: "This is removable optical disk or magnetic tape media, which can be labeled and stored in a shelf or rack. Off-line storage of electronic records is traditionally used for making disaster copies of records and also for records considered 'archival' in that their likelihood of retrieval is minimal. Accessibility to off-line media involves manual intervention and is much slower than on-line or near-line storage. Access speed may be minutes, hours, or even days, depending on the access-effectiveness of the storage facility." The principled difference between nearline data and offline data is that offline data lacks "the coordinated control of an intelligent disk subsystem," and is, in the lingo, JBOD ("Just a Bunch of Disks").

4. Backup tapes: "A device, like a tape recorder, that reads data from and writes it onto a tape. Tape drives have data capacities of anywhere from a few hundred kilobytes to several gigabytes. Their transfer speeds also vary considerably . . . The disadvantage of tape drives is that they are sequential- access devices, which means that to read any particular block of data, you need to read all the preceding blocks." As a result, "[t]he data on a backup tape are not organized for retrieval of individual documents or files [because] . . . the organization of the data mirrors the computer's structure, not the human records management structure." Backup tapes also typically employ some sort of data compression, permitting more data to be stored on each tape, but also making restoration more time-consuming and expensive, especially given the lack of uniform standard governing data compression.

5. Erased, fragmented or damaged data: "When a file is first created and saved, it is laid down on the [storage media] in contiguous clusters . . . As files are erased, their clusters are made available again as free space. Eventually, some newly created files become larger than the remaining contiguous free space. These files are then broken up and randomly placed throughout the disk." Such broken-up files are said to be "fragmented," and along with damaged and erased data can only be accessed after significant processing.

Of these, the first three categories are typically identified as accessible, and the latter two as inaccessible. The difference between the two classes is easy to appreciate. Information deemed "accessible" is stored in a readily usable format. Although the time it takes to actually access the data ranges from milliseconds to days, the data does not need to be restored or otherwise manipulated to be usable. "Inaccessible" data, on the other hand, is not readily usable. Backup tapes must be restored using a process similar to that previously described, fragmented data must be de-fragmented, and erased data must be reconstructed, all before the data is usable. That makes such data inaccessible.

When conversing with a computer forensic specialist or others, the following classifications are generally used. Grace V. Bacon, *The Fundamentals of Electronic Discovery,* 47 Boston Law Journal 18 (2003).

A. DATA FILES

Data files are the basic information that computer systems store. There are four general types of data files: (1) active data; (2) replicant data; (3) backup data; and (4) residual data.

1. Active Data

"Active data" is the information currently accessible on a computer, such as word processing documents, spreadsheets, databases, e-mail messages and electronic calendars. Generally, active data is relatively simple to access through the use of a computer's file manager program. It can be found on an individual's office desktop computer, laptop, home computer, an assistant's computer, a PDA and the network file server. Moreover, because users frequently create special files or folders in which to store e-mails or other electronic documents that pertain to a particular subject matter, active data will usually be fairly easy to sort for relevant information. Most computer programs also contain search engines that can be used to narrow the scope of potentially relevant documents.

2. Replicant Data

"Replicant data" (or "archival data") is the information a computer automatically backs up as you work on a file. These backed up files are created and saved in order to recover data that may be lost due to a malfunction or power loss. Replicant data is useful because it creates a copy or several copies of a document that the user may not erase. In fact, the user may not even be aware of these "file clones" because they are generally stored in a different directory than active data. On most networked systems, this replicant data is stored on the hard drive as opposed to a centralized network file server. Consequently, a document, or part of it that was purged from a server, may be retrievable from a user's hard drive.

3. Backup Data

"Backup data" is information copied to a removable medium in the event of a system failure. Most businesses have their networks backed up on a routine schedule, while individual users may or may not backup their information. Thus, one can find backup data on system-wide backup tapes, recovery backup tapes that may be stored off site, and on personal backups such as computer disks.

Backup data is particularly useful in that it provides historical snapshots of the data stored on a system on the specific day the backup was made, allowing one to obtain information regarding the progress of a matter. On the flip side, because backup tapes contain a large amount of data, it is frequently time consuming and expensive to restore this data in order to review the material pertinent to your case.

4. Residual Data

Unlike general "paper" discovery, electronic documents thought to be lost or destroyed are more often than not recoverable, yielding what is often an untapped source of information in a case. Simply pressing the "delete" button does not mean that the document is no longer on the computer. "Residual data" is information that is actually recoverable even though an attempt has been made to "delete" the document. When a file is "deleted," the computer makes the space occupied by that file available for new data. Unless that space is "re-written," the so-called deleted document is generally recoverable by using "undelete" or "restore" commands contained in some systems' operating software or through other programs."

[Residual Data: Residual Data (sometimes referred to as "Ambient Data") refers to data that is not active on a computer system. Residual data includes (1) data found on media free space; (2) data found in the file slack space; and (3) data within files that have functionally been deleted in that it is not visible using the application with which the file was created, without use of undelete or special data recovery techniques. The Sedona Principles (2004), *Glossary.*]

In addition, the following classifications of electronic information may be important in your cases.

*   Ambient data - generally referred to as "residual data." See the description above.

*   Archival and legacy data - usually stored on backup tapes in formats that may or may not be easy to access. *See also,* §§ 2.6[C], *Backups - Computer Files,* 2.6[D], *Archived Data* and 2.6[E], *Legacy Data.*

- Forensic, mirror or clone copy - is an exact bit-by-bit copy of a hard drive of a computer system. *See also,* §§ 5.5[F], *Forensic Copy of Storage Media* and 7.7[H][5], *Obtaining Forensic or Mirror Image Copy of Storage Media.*

- System data - "System data, or information generated and maintained by the computer itself. The computer records a variety of routine transactions and functions, including password access requests, the creation or deletion of files and directories, maintenance functions, and access to and from other computers, printers, or communication devices." THE MANUAL FOR COMPLEX LITIGATION, FOURTH, § 11.446; *See also,* § 2.06[G], *Audit Trails and Logs.*

- *See also,* § 7.07[B], *"Document" - Definition.*

[1]   Reported Cases (reserved)

[2]   Other Authorities

- Dort & Spatz, *Discovery in the Digital Era: Considerations for Corporate Counsel,* Computer and Internet Lawyer (Sept. 2003).

- Carey Sirota Meyer & Kari L. Wraspir, *E-Discovery: Preparing Clients for (and Protecting Them Against) Discovery in the Electronic Information Age,* 26 Wm. Mitchell L. Rev. 939, 946 (2000).

- Thompson, Todd N., *The Paper Trail Has Gone Digital: Discovery in the Age of Electronic Information,* 71-MAR J. Kan. B.A. 16, 17 (Mar. 2002).

[C]   Compound Documents

Usually we think of an "electronic file" as constituting all the information about a document. This may be true in some instances such as in a memo or a spreadsheet document. However, in some cases an electronic document may be composed of information stored in different electronic files that may even be located on different servers in different parts of the country. For example, a compound document may display elements from one or many different computer application sources. A compound document may include text from a word processing program, a graphic from a graphics program, and a chart from a database or spreadsheet program. For example, a word processing program that creates a letter may be linked to a database program to merge the recipient's address and other information while at the same time linking to a chart regarding the financial performance of a company from a spreadsheet program.

§ 3.7   METADATA, HIDDEN, OR EMBEDDED INFORMATION

[A]   Generally

Metadata is information used by the computer to manage and often classify the computer file from which it originated. *Madison River Mgmt. Co. v. Business Mgmt. Software Corp.*, 387 F. Supp. 2d 521, 528 n5 (D.N.C. 2005) ("[m]etadata means, literally, data about data. It describes 'how and when and by whom a particular set of data was collected, and how the data is formatted.'"). Metadata is "embedded" information that is stored in electronically generated materials, but which is not visible when a document or materials are printed.

It is often thought of as computer information that exists beyond the visible data viewed in an application software program. This is significantly different from paper information, where all of the information is set out before you. Paper discovery discloses only what the creator or author wishes the reader to view.

There are two types of metadata that are maintained by a computer system about a particular computer file, "file system" and "embedded" metadata.

"File system" metadata.

> Metadata, or 'data about data,' is maintained about each file both by the operating system and in the file itself. Recent versions of the Windows operating system maintain three date and time stamps for each file: the creation date, when the file was first saved on the hard drive upon creation, downloaded from the Internet, or transferred from another media source; the last modified date, when the data within the file was last changed; and the last accessed date, when the file was last opened and viewed. These date/time stamps are known as 'file system metadata' and are generally hidden from view, but can be accessed in Windows by clicking 'File,' then 'Properties.' The act of checking the 'Properties' of a file, even if the file is not opened, will actually modify the system metadata of the file reviewed, absent the use of forensic tools.

> The file system metadata stamps are applied to each file according to the computer clock, which can be reset or may not be accurate.

Beryl A. Howell, *Digital Forensics: Sleuthing on Hard Drives and Networks,* 31-FALL Vt. B.J. 39, 41 (Fall 2005).

"Embedded" metadata.

As opposed to file system metadata, the other type of metadata, called "embedded metadata" is generally automatically generated and stored when electronic materials, such as a word processing document, e-mail or a spreadsheet are created. "For instance, many documents' file properties can reveal the date the document was created, the author of the document, subsequent edit dates to the document, which users have access to revise the document, as well as the number of versions of the document." Carey Sirota Mayer & Kari L. Wraspir, *E-Discovery: Preparing Clients for (and Protecting Them Against) Discovery in the Electronic Information Age*, 26 Wm. Mitchell L. Rev. 939, 946-48 (2000). In addition, document headers and footers may provide important information but may not be seen on a printout, while spreadsheet printouts show lots of numbers but not their formula. If you want to determine whether a particular person was copied on e-mail – then the metadata would disclose the person copied as well as who was blind copied on the e-mail message. This type of metadata follows the file even if it is copied to another computer.

Be aware, however, that metadata can be easily falsified. For example, Creative Element Power Tools (http://www.creativelement.com/powertools/) is software that allows a user to rename multiple files, change file dates, and change the 'created,' 'modified,' and 'accessed' dates.

The metadata of an electronic file may include the prior versions of a written document as well as other information of which the current author was unaware. Comparing the different versions may provide insight into the decision processes connected with a particular document. For example, discovery of metadata may show that the document was falsified or altered, without the author being aware that such information was being recorded.

The opposing party may make an offer to print or convert e-mail or other electronic information to images or paper. However, this "open and print" type of disclosure does not disclose metadata. Opening a computer file and printing its contents, either in a paper or image format, effectively redacts possible important metadata information. However, TIFF images and/or PDF files may be an acceptable disclosure image format, if the metadata is unimportant.

In addition, if opposing counsel "exports" computer data from an e-mail database and provides it to you in a database format, such as a comma delimited or other format, you may lose the metadata that is available. Instead, request the native computer data files for the application.

[B]   Obtaining and Viewing Metadata

Generally, to view metadata you must obtain the native computer file. *See,* §§7.4[K], *Meet and Confer - Rule 26(f)* (discussion of need to meet and confer re metadata) and 7.7[B][2], *Metadata* (definition of "document" includes metadata). After obtaining the file, the metadata can be extracted by using special conversion software. Once extracted, the metadata can be viewed using a database or a full text software program. *See,* § 5.3, *Electronic Data Formats.*

The type and availability of metadata may be found in documentation for a specific software application. If you are seeking metadata, include requests for the documentation of the application software programs.

See, §§ 3.8–3.19 for specific metadata associated with specific types of computer files such as word processing documents, spreadsheets, etc. and § 5.4, *Searching Electronic Information.*

§ 3.8   E-MAIL

[A]   Generally

E-mail has become one of the primary and essential means of communication for most businesses and individuals. It is estimated that 90% of documents created today are in electronic format, including the more than 25 billion e-mails created each day in the United States alone. Peter Brown, *Discovery and Use of Electronic Evidence,* 734 Practicing L. Inst. 391, 398 (2003).

Messages and other electronic information can be transmitted from one computer to another using telephone lines, communication satellites, microwave links, cable and other telecommunications equipment. The same e-mail can be sent to one or several different addresses simultaneously. Generally, in a business organization, e-mail systems use a central computer (sometimes the server) to store messages and data and to send them to the appropriate destination. All that is needed to send messages is a PC, modem and e-mail connection. E-mail messages can contain text, graphics, audio and/or video.

E-mail has become one of the most sought-after pieces of electronic evidence. "Like ghosts from the past, these forgotten electronic blips can come back to haunt a litigant, since computer data bases are subject to civil discovery requests." Goldstein, *Electronic Mail: Computer Messages Present Knotty Issues of Discovery,* New York L. J. (Feb. 8, 1994) at 1.

The reason for its desirability stems from misconceptions that employees and others have about e-mail. Users assume that deleting a message on their computer makes it disappear permanently. However, once an e-mail message is sent, it is usually stored in several locations. These locations can consist of backup tapes, Internet server provider storage media, the recipient's computer, etc. Further, the act of deleting any electronic information does not delete the information from the storage media. All that is done is that the address or location of the electronic data is opened for other electronic data. If this open address has not been overwritten by other data, then the e-mail can be restored to its original state. *See,* § 3.5[E], *Deletion of Electronic Information.*

Employees and others think that e-mail is private. Employees are generally surprised to learn that their imprudent messages are discoverable and admissible in legal proceedings. With the casual nature and easy use of e-mail, users have become very complacent about the content of many of their communications. As one commentator has suggested, "[d]escriptions of e-mail communication styles include freewheeling, candid, unfiltered, not modulated, raw and off the cuff . . . these very attributes, which lend themselves to easy, casual and seemingly efficient communication have stung many companies and individuals whose transmissions have returned to haunt them." Wendy J. Rose, *The Revolution of Electronic Mail*, The Legal Intelligencer, Jan. 21, 1997, at ¶3. As a result, discovery and admission of e-mail evidence are often contested.

Because of the informal nature of an employee or individual's e-mail comments and ease of creation, discovery of e-mail is an excellent source of case information.

[B]   Description

Electronic mail systems allow you to send data (a message), attachments (computer files) and provide pointers (hypertext links to information on the Internet) to other e-mail users. Attachments can include text, sound, graphics or video. *Joao v. Sleepy Hollow Bank*, 418 F. Supp. 2d 578, 584 (D.N.Y. 2006) ("electronic mail [message is a] . . . digital text message that is sent over an communications network from one device to another.").

The receiver of the message does not have to be located at his or her computer to receive the message, but can retrieve it later from any location and with many different devices. One can also "broadcast" a message to one or multiple recipients by the press of a button. Communication can be with customers, business associates, suppliers, staff, witnesses and others. It is becoming as commonplace as the phone system.

"E-mail is essentially a method of communicating and doing business over the Internet. It 'enables an individual to send an electronic message - generally akin to a note or letter - to another individual or to a group of addressees. The message is generally stored electronically, sometimes waiting for the recipient to check her 'mailbox' and sometimes making its receipt known through some type of prompt.' *Reno*, 521 U.S. at 851, 117 S.Ct. 2329." *Verizon Online Services, Inc. v. Ralsky*, 203 F. Supp. 2d 601, 605 (E.D. Va. 2002).

An e-mail address contains the name and location protocol to where the e-mail will be sent. It has a user's name, the @ (at) sign, the name of the user's domain or computer, a period and the type of organization. For example, an e-mail address might be FrankJones@aol.com. The user's name is Frank Jones, the @ sign, the user's domain or computer is AOL and the COM stands for commercial.

No two e-mail names or addresses are alike. Internet addresses can come in all sizes and shapes. Some addresses are long and contain a variety of symbols such as percent signs, exclamation points and so on. Many people have more than one e-mail address.

The e-mail itself consists of electronic data that is contained in a database. When you view the electronic message, you are actually viewing the presentation of a database record. There is generally a sender, recipient, subject, carbon copy recipient and the message – all are database record fields. There also may be other data that is contained in separate fields in e-mail. Once you obtain an e-mail database, you can import it into standard litigation support software to search, organize, code and then convert it into an electronic image (or printout), such as TIFF, for presentation in the courtroom. For further information on databases *see* § 3.10, *Database*.

[C]   Process of Sending E-mail

The process of sending e-mail using most e-mail software applications is simple and straightforward.

To send e-mail one would first open the e-mail software application, such as Microsoft Outlook. Though the commands may be different depending on the program, the general steps are as follows. The user will click on the e-mail menu selection labeled "New" and an e-mail screen will appear that usually will consist of a header and the body of the e-mail.

The header will consist generally of a line for the recipient's address, sender's e-mail address, a line to which a message has been cc'ed (copied) or bcc'ed (blind copied) and a subject line. One can address and transmit a message to one or more people. The Internet e-mail address consists of the user name or pseudonym and host, "Username@hostname." Another line is provided for the subject, brief summary or title of the message.

After filling in the header, the sender will write the body of the message and then can add an attachment or pointer to a website. After completing the message, the sender will click on the send button. The program then routes the message through a series of computer networks connecting the sender with the recipient(s). Internet service providers assist in transmitting the message. The message can be sent through a number of different servers before ending up in the recipient's inbox. When the recipient opens up their e-mail software program, they will be notified that they have new mail. The recipient can then open and read the message. When e-mail is received, it contains header or metadata information. *See,* § 3.8[J], *Metadata and Headers*. The header information will vary depending upon the route of the e-mail but will generally include the name of the sender, sender's IP address, IP addresses of the computers through which the e-mail traveled, message number, the name of the recipient and the date and time the message was sent. The recipient can then reply to the message by clicking the reply button and drafting a reply. The reply is then sent back to the sender or other parties who have been copied on the message.

Description of an e-mail address and the role of an Internet Service Provider (ISP) is set forth in the case of *Verizon Online Services, Inc. v. Ralsky*, 203 F. Supp. 2d 601, 605-606 (E.D. Va. 2002):

To send or receive e-mail to or from other Internet users, one must obtain Internet access through an ISP. . . . An ISP operates a computer communication service through a proprietary network. In addition to allowing access to the content available within its own network, an ISP provides its subscribers with a doorway to the Internet. Subscribers use the ISP's domain name, *e.g.,* "verizon.net," together with their own personal identifier to form a distinctive e-mail mailing address, *e.g.,* "tmarshall@verizon.net." The subscriber's e-mail address is used to send and receive e-mail from other Internet users throughout the world. An e-mail address does not contain any geographic designation, nor does it correspond to any geographic location. The ISP subscriber can retrieve her e-mail using any computer connected to the Internet from anywhere in the world.

However, e-mail transmitted to an ISP subscriber is processed and stored on the ISP's e-mail computer servers. The e-mail server is located in a discrete geographic location. An e-mail server processes every e-mail that is addressed to the ISP's customer. In other words, once the e-mail is transmitted, it must first pass through the ISP's computer server to reach its ultimate destination -- the subscriber's computer.

[1]   Reported Case

•   *NTP, Inc. v. Research In Motion, Ltd.,* 392 F.3d 1336, 1340 (Fed. Cir. 2004). The Court in a patent infringement case reviewed in detail the process of how e-mail is created and delivered using ISPs.

[D]   History

Electronic mail systems have evolved over the past several years and are now more sophisticated then just sending and receiving messages. The first generation supported simple interpersonal communication. Messages were usually short, did not support text enrichment, and were not intended to be saved. They were intended to convey short, timely information.

The second generation of e-mail included the ability to attach binary or textual files. This enabled users to send attached documents and other computer files containing scientific, educational or business correspondence.

The third generation of e-mail focused on the capability of enabling the user to enhance the e-mail message itself. With this advancement rich text format and embedded objects could be part of the message. More important was the capability of the e-mail software to store and organize e-mail materials. Now folders or other systems could be set up to save e-mail for particular projects or cases. This, along with the capability to broadcast e-mail to casual users, increased e-mail use.

The fourth generation of e-mail sees a convergence of e-mail with other workgroup computing applications. E-mail is part of workgroup computing applications such as database linking, voice mail, Internet links to World Wide Web pages and a host of other integrated applications. A key feature of this 4th generation e-mail growth is the compatibility and accessibility by remote users.

[E]   E-mail Features

Depending upon the e-mail program that is being used, there are several features that one should consider when discovering e-mail. Many e-mail programs have the capability to use filtering techniques to prioritize and/or filter out e-mail. These programs may also contain an address book to keep e-mail addresses and distribution lists for different groups of users. For example, an e-mail distribution group may be set up for a team working on a merger or acquisition. Anytime the sender of e-mail wants to communicate with the entire group they would select the distribution group name and send out the message to all individuals on the list. The address and distribution lists should be requested in discovery. Templates are also available for repetitive responses and folders are available for organizing e-mail. These folders may show how a project was divided by chronology or by other criteria. In addition, some e-mail programs like Microsoft Outlook saves any e-mail attachments within the e-mail computer file or they may be archived. Other programs may create a separate directory for attachments that should be obtained during discovery.

[1]   Reported Cases

• *United States v. Shields,* No. CIV.01-0384, 2004 WL 832937, at *6 (M.D.Pa. Apr. 14, 2004). "Second, all members of the [Candyman] Egroup were immediately added to the Candyman email list. Every e-mail sent to the group was distributed to every member automatically."

[F]   Importance and Characteristics

Electronic mail is a new phenomenon in the conventional paper-based world. There are several characteristics that make e-mail both problematic and a fertile source of discovery.

Volume

Most individuals and employees communicate via e-mail with their co-workers, business and personal contacts. Because of the ease of creation and transmission, the volume of statements, admissions and conflicting information has increased dramatically over the last several years. One commentator noted that, "[t]he sheer volume can be staggering, even for a small company or individual. . . . One Internet market research company estimates that the average American processes 26.4 messages per day, one-third of which (8.8 per day) they generate." Kenneth J. Withers, *Computer-Based Discovery in Federal Civil Litigation*, Federal Courts Law Review, October 2000.

The total number of e-mail is in the billions. "In 2000 fewer than 10 billion e-mail messages were sent per day worldwide. By 2005, the number of e-mails sent per day is projected to surpass 35 billion, according to industry analyst IDC." Walter, *Plaintiffs' Law Firms No Longer As Disadvantaged,* National Law Journal, July 5, 2004, at S3.

This volume increases the likelihood of discovering a "smoking gun" or collaborating evidence of employee or employer conduct.

Duplicates

There are generally duplicates of electronic information, such as e-mail, within data collections. Backup tapes, depending on the backup system and frequency, may contain numerous identical electronic messages sent by the same person or that has been sent to several recipients. This is especially true with electronic mail and attachments. For example in the *Zubulake v. UBS Warburg LLC*, 216 F.R.D. 280, 282 (S.D.N.Y. 2003) case the Court stated, "Pinkerton was able to restore each of the backup tapes, yielding a total of 8,344 e-mails. That number is somewhat inflated, however, because it does not account for duplicates. Because each month's backup tape was a snapshot of Chapin's server for that month--and not an incremental backup reflecting only new material--an e-mail that was on the server for more than one month would appear on more than one backup tape. For example, an e-mail received in January 2001 and deleted in November 2001 would have been restored from all five backup tapes. With duplicates eliminated, the total number of unique e-mails restored was 6,203."

In addition, "[m]ost e-mail programs automatically save a copy of every message sent and received by an e-mail account. Therefore, upon transmittal, one copy of the message is saved by the sender's e-mail program, another copy is saved by the recipient, and another copy is stored by the recipient's server. Thus, multiple copies of an e-mail message are saved on the computer of both the sender and the recipient, even if the message is 'deleted' by both." Rasin, Moan, *Fitting a Square Peg into a Round Hole: The Application of Traditional Rules of Law to Modern Technology Advancements in the Workplace,* 66 Mo. L. Rev. 793, 801 (2001).

It can be very time-consuming and costly to review duplicate electronic information. However, there are several "electronic discovery" software conversion programs that use specialized criteria to weed out duplicate e-mail messages. If necessary, these "duplicates" are available for review. *See,* § 5.8, *Filtering and Deduplication.*

Organization

Electronic mail systems, either for business or for personal use, are rarely organized in a coherent fashion. Important business related e-mail messages could be found alongside private personal e-mail messages.

Informal Nature of Comments

Perhaps the most important characteristic of e-mail is its informal, casual nature. Employers and employees will say things in e-mail that they would not say in a written memorandum. They often believe that their comments are confidential and nonpermanent. To the contrary, e-mail messages are not confidential and can be stored in several locations after the messages are sent. In fact, "e-mail is increasingly being treated as the ultimate window into the true thoughts of executives and the inner workings of an enterprise." Harmen, *Corporate Delete Keys Busy as E-Mail Turns Up in Court,* New York Times, Nov. 11, 1998, at A1, C2; *United States v. Quattrone,* 441 F.3d 153, 165 (2d Cir. 2006) (Appellate Court found e-mail could be used to show intent for criminal conviction); *Sonista, Inc. v. Hsieh,* No. CIV.04-04080, 2005 U.S. Dist. LEXIS 31397 (N.D. Cal. Nov. 21, 2005) (Court granted summary judgment after several e-mail were discovered by a forensic expert showing that the defendant had performed numerous tasks in setting up and incorporating a competing company before resigning from his employment).

Private comments in casual e-mail messages are commonplace in many business organizations. *See also,* § 1.2[A], *Informal Nature.* These comments can create enormous legal risk since they are often used to prove patterns of behavior. They are likened to telephone calls in their informal and spontaneous nature. Unlike a telephone conversation, however, e-mail messages are written and generally remain available for subsequent review.

In *Rowe Entertainment, Inc. v. William Morris Agency, Inc.*, 205 F.R.D. 421, 429 (S.D.N.Y. 2002), *aff'd,* 2002 WL 975713 (S.D.N.Y. May 9, 2002), the Court discussed privacy concerns in e-mail.

> The defendants' concern about privacy is also unavailing. To the extent that the corporate defendants' own privacy interests are at issue, the [*sic*] are adequately protected by the confidentiality order in this case. To the degree the defendants seek to assert the privacy concerns of their employees, those interests are severely limited. Although personal communications of employees may be [*sic*] appear in hard copy as well as in electronic documents . . . the defendants made no effort to exclude personal messages from the search of paper records conducted by plaintiffs' counsel. Moreover, an employee who uses his or her employer's computer for personal communications assumes some risk that they will be accessed by the employer or by others.

E-mail Strands

Oftentimes users of e-mail will set their e-mail editors to permit the previous message to be appended to the bottom of their reply. This can result in a lengthy and valuable history of the particular subject of the e-mail. In *In re Universal Serv. Fund Tel. Billing Practices Litig.*, 232 F.R.D. 669, n2 (D. Kan. 2005) the Court stated, "an e-mail strand (or string) occurs where the printed e-mail actually consists of more than one message, usually formatted with the most recent message first."

Credibility

Because of their informality and truthfulness, e-mail messages can make particularly credible evidence at trial. The credibility concept is derived from the perception that the writer is off guard and the truth emerges when a more informal, spontaneous type of communication is asserted. In addition, signature tags provide credibility that the electronic message was sent on behalf of the company. Though they may represent only the personal view of the sender, e-mail is often argued as representing the official position of the company.

Ease of Distribution

With the click of a button, one can send informal, offensive, defamatory or privileged information to one individual, hundreds or thousands of people thus exposing the company to possible lawsuits. It literally takes seconds to create and distribute an e-mail message.

Not Printed Out

E-mail is generally not reduced to hardcopy. In *Rowe Entertainment, Inc. v. William Morris Agency, Inc.*, 205 F.R.D. 421, 429 (S.D.N.Y. 2002), *aff'd*, 2002 WL 975713 (S.D.N.Y. May 9, 2002) the Court noted the unlikelihood of e-mail being reduced to hard copy:

> Furthermore, the supposition that important e-mails have been printed in hard copy form is likewise unsupported. In general, nearly one-third of all electronically stored data is never printed out. Here, the defendants have not alleged that they had any corporate policy defining which e-mail messages should be reduced to hard copy because they are "important." Finally, to the extent that any employee of the defendants was engaged in discriminatory or anti-competitive practices, it is less likely that communications about such activities would be memorialized in an easily accessible form such as a filed paper document. (citation omitted).

[G]   Attachments

E-mail software permits you to send computer files, generally called attachments, along with the e-mail. These attachments can be text, voice mail, graphic, spreadsheet, video and other types of computer files. Once the recipient receives the e-mail with the attachment it can be opened if the recipient has the appropriate software on their computer.

For example, an executive may send a contract in a word processing format to his business partner. His business partner can open the attachment, if his system has the proper software, and edit the document and resend it with his edits.

These attachments can be a fertile source of discovery if the documents are not available from other sources. When you send an e-mail with an attachment, the attachment is saved in the sender's separate e-mail "sent" folder. Also, when the recipient receives the e-mail and attachment it is saved in a separate recipient attachment file directory.

Attachments to e-mail should always be reviewed for copies of files that may not be available from any other source. When a file is attached and sent by e-mail, the e-mail program generally stores a copy of the message and the attachment in a "sent" folder or directory. This copy of the document is separate from the original. If the original is deleted and cannot be recovered by an undelete program or from a backup tape, the copy may still exist in the "sent" folder or directory.

For discovery purposes, it is important to keep the e-mail message and attachment together so that the proof of a particular legal fact is together. Once the message and attachment link are broken, it may be difficult, or nearly impossible, to connect up the message to the attachment later. It is important that data paths and directories be requested and identified in your interrogatories or request for production so that one can keep the message and attachment together. These links may be broken if the data is exported to a different database format. It is advisable to obtain the opposition's e-mail in its native format along with its attachments.

[1]   Reported Case

- *United States v. Maxwell,* 45 M.J. 406, (U.S. Armed Forces, 1996). "A user can send attachments to an e-mail message. Anything that a user can store on a computer, including detailed graphics, can be sent attached to a piece of e-mail."

- *Purdy v. Burlington Northern and Santa Fe Ry. Co.,* No. CIV.98-00833, 2000 WL 34251818 (D. Minn. Mar. 28, 2000). "Sheri Owen is a contractor for the Railroad who assists in the budgeting process. In that capacity, Ms. Owen sent an e-mail message to Roberta Lund, a Railroad employee, on March 12, 2000, via Ms. Lund's work e-mail account, 'roberta.lund@bnsf.com' (the 'Lund e-mail'). Attached to the Lund e-mail message was a password-protected document which included the salaries and social security numbers for approximately 800 Railroad employees."

[H]   Printouts are Not Exact Duplicates of E-mail

A paper or image printout of e-mail is *not* an exact duplicate of the original electronic message file, unless a printout of all available metadata is also included. Electronic copies of e-mail contain more data than a paper copy of the same e-mail. If your request for production asks for electronic originals and you are provided printouts or images without the metadata, you will not be getting all of the significant e-mail data.

[1]   Reported Case

•   *Armstrong, et al. v. Executive Office of the President*, 1 F.3d 1274, 1283 (D.C. Cir. 1993). The Court found that a printed copy of e-mail did not contain the same information as an electronic copy. The Court stated:

> [T]he mere existence of the paper printouts does not affect the record status of the electronic materials unless the paper versions include all significant material contained in the electronic records. Otherwise, the two documents cannot accurately be termed "copies" - identical twins - but are, at most, "kissing cousins."

[I]   E-mail Web Pointers

E-mail messages can now contain e-mail Web pointers that permit you to jump to a Web page when you click on the pointer. These pointers can be linked to business and personal Web information, which can be a picture, text, video or any other type of electronic data. For example, an e-mail advertisement for a product may point or be linked to the features and warranties of the product on the company's website. If the product fails to perform as advertised, then the e-mail pointer and warranty section of the website may be relevant to your case.

[1]   Reported Case

•   *Verizon Online Services, Inc. v. Ralsky*, 203 F. Supp.2d 601, 605 (E.D. Va. 2002). "In addition to text, an e-mail can contain hyperlinks to websites located on the World Wide Web. The World Wide Web is a communications platform that allows Internet users to search for and retrieve information stored in remote computers connected to the Internet."

- *Campbell v. General Dynamics Government Systems Corp.,* 321 F. Supp.2d 142, 144 (D. Mass. Jun. 3, 2004). In this employment action the employer was seeking to establish that the plaintiff had notice of changed legal procedures by showing that the plaintiff received an e-mail which included links to other documents. The Court noted that the employer "present[ed] as evidence a 'tracking log' . . . which indicated that [plaintiff] opened the email at 1:56 p.m. on April 30, 2001. (The email was sent at 1:54 p.m. on that day.) However, defendants offer no evidence to support, nor do they even suggest, that Campbell clicked on either link, or that he read the text of the email."

- *F.T.C. v. Phoenix Avatar, LLC,* No. CIV.04-2897, 2004 WL 1746698, at *2 (N.D.Ill. Jul. 30, 2004). In support of a preliminary injunction one of the witnesses "testified that an e-mail consists of two parts, a header and a body. (PX 1.) Among other things, the header usually contains identifying information fields such as the intended recipient, the sender of the e-mail, the date, and a subject line. Oftentimes, the e-mail body will contain a hyperlink, which is a link to a specific Web site on the Internet. When a user 'clicks' on a hyperlink, that user's Internet browser opens up on the specified Web site."

[J]   Metadata and Headers

Metadata may be important to authenticate or establish the route taken by an e-mail. *See,* § 8.12[C], *Foundation.* There are many metadata or "header" elements available in e-mail. E-mail headers and metadata are important because they contain valuable information about the message. The table below outlines the most common header elements contained in an e-mail message. Forensic experts can use this information to determine whether the message was forged, spoofed or falsified and to identify the sender or the computer from which the message was created. *See also,* §§ 3.7, *Metadata, Hidden, or Embedded Information* and 2.6[G], *Audit Trails and Logs.*

BCC	This acronym stands for blind copied and means a recipient of e-mail whose name is not visible to other recipients of the e-mail. It will not appear on a printout unless it is the sender's e-mail copy that is printed.
CC	Additional recipients who received the e-mail.
Date	The date on which the message was sent.
Encrypted	Methodology used to encrypt the e-mail.
From	Sender's e-mail identity.
In-Reply-To	Identifies previous e-mail answered by this message.

Message-ID	Unique machine ID for this particular e-mail. May be useful to authenticate e-mail.
Received	Shows the time when the recipient received the message and the route traveled from the sender's computer to the recipient's computer. This information may assist with authenticating e-mail. In addition, it may indicate if other storage devices should be examined to locate e-mail.
References	Identifies previous e-mail referenced by this message. May be useful in authentication and validation check of whether other e-mail have been disclosed.
Resent	Provides information if the e-mail has been resent - bcc, cc, date, from, sender, path, etc.
Return-Path	Shows the address and route back to sender of e-mail.
Time and Date	Shows when e-mail was sent.
Sender	Shows the address of the user who sent the e-mail.
Subject	Displays the subject of the e-mail.
To	Shows the primary recipients of the e-mail.

In some instances the header information may be erased by e-mail software on the server or on the recipient's computer.

These header elements or metadata may be able to be viewed through your e-mail software. *See,* Earthlink (How to access extended header information) (http://help.mindspring.com/features/emailheaders/extended.htm).

For an explanation of how to decipher e-mail header information the following websites are useful:

- EarthLink - Explanation of e-mail headers (http://help.mindspring.com/features/emailheaders/index.htm)(last visited on July 21, 2006);

- In depth analysis on how to read e-mail headers (http://www.stopspam.org/email/headers.html)(last visited on July 21, 2006); and

- Specifications for e-mail, including metadata, can be found in the *Standard for the Format of ARPA Internet Text Messages* (Aug. 1982) (http://www.faqs.org/rfcs/rfc822.html) (last visited on July 21, 2006).

[a]   Reported Cases

- *State v. Heckel,* 24 P.3d 404, 407 (Wash. 2001).

    Each e-mail message, which is simply a computer data file, contains so-called "header" information in the "To," "From," and "Received" fields. When an e-mail message is transmitted from one e-mail address to another, the message generally passes through at least four computers: from the sender's computer, the message travels to the mail server computer of the sender's Internet Service Provider (ISP); that computer delivers the message to the mail server computer of the recipient's ISP, where it remains until the recipient retrieves it onto his or her own computer. Every computer on the Internet has a unique numerical address (an Internet Protocol or IP address), which is associated with a more readily recognizable domain name (such as "mysite.com"). As the e-mail message travels from sender to recipient, each computer transmitting the message attaches identifying data to the "Received" field in the header. The information serves as a kind of electronic postmark for the handling of the message. . . . It is possible for a sender to alter (or "spoof") the header information by misidentifying either the computer from which the message originated or other computers along the transmission path.

- *F.T.C. v. Bryant,* No. CIV.04-897, 2004 WL 2504357, at *3 (M.D.Fla. Oct. 4, 2004). "I. 'Header information' means the source, destination, and routing information attached to an electronic mail message, including the originating domain name and originating electronic mail address, and any other information that appears in the line identifying, or purporting to identify, a person initiating the message."

- *Armstrong v. Executive Office of the President,* 1 F.3d 1274, 1280 (D.C. Cir. 1993) (per curiam). The Court discussed the various types of "metadata" available in e-mail.

- *Air-Products and Chemicals, Inc. v. Inter-Chemical, Ltd.,* No. CIV.03-6140, 2005 WL 196543, at *4 n.3 (E.D.Pa. Jan. 27, 2005). "The full email 'header' contains technical information that more accurately reveals the sender of the email than the more easily manipulated 'from' field, which simply recites an email address associated with the sender. This technical information includes the IP address assigned to the sender by his or her internet service provider, as well as the name of the computer from which the email was sent."

[K]   Storage Locations

E-mail can be stored in many different locations. For example, e-mail can reside on the sender's computer, e-mail server, backup storage media and the sender's Internet service provider's computer. *See,* § 7.10, *Obtaining Data From Third Parties.* It can also reside on the recipient's computer, e-mail server, recipient's Internet service provider's computer and backup system. For this reason e-mail is generally never "deleted."

A determination should be made at the outset as to whether a company's e-mail system is centralized or decentralized. If the company's e-mail system is decentralized then the e-mail is not centrally stored and managed from a central location. Instead the e-mail may reside on an individual employee's desktop computer, laptop and even PDA devices, and there may be more than one type of e-mail program being used. Under these circumstances it is more burdensome for a company to locate, accumulate and review e-mail for production purposes, especially since a single search for relevant e-mail cannot be done.

[1]   Offline vs. Online

When e-mail is sent, a copy of the e-mail is stored on intermediate computers that receive the message and is then forwarded to the next intermediate computer or recipient of the message. For discovery purposes, e-mail is generally located on a company's e-mail or Internet Service Provider (ISP) server, and also on the user's computer. The e-mail server can be located internally or externally to the business organization. For example, if a company has an ISP that handles e-mail, the message may be located on the ISP's server. If the company has an internal e-mail server then the message would be located on the company's server. The user may also download all of the messages to their computer where they are then stored.

E-mail messages are sent and received through various devices such as a desktop computer, laptop, pager, PDA and cell phone. When instructed, the e-mail device connects to a remote e-mail server that handles the sending and receiving of e-mail.

E-Mail - Server Based

When e-mail is sent to an individual, it is first stored on an e-mail server awaiting a retrieval request from the recipient. An e-mail server controls and manages the e-mail communications for people within the organization. It controls (by user-defined rules) who may send and receive e-mail within an organization, directs internal and external e-mail to the proper users, stores users' e-mails on the server's hard drive and so on. The user-defined rules determine how the mail server should react when determining the destination of a specific message, or possibly react to the sender of the message. For example, specific e-mail addresses can be barred, or certain users can be restricted to only sending messages within the company. Most mail servers operate automatically - waiting for messages to be sent to the server and collecting messages from other e-mail servers to be delivered.

The list of users is usually managed by an IT person and is contained in a database of user accounts on the mail server. There may be two or more e-mail servers processing mail depending upon the number of users sending and receiving e-mail.

The e-mail server may be located within a business organization or at an Internet Service Provider (ISP). Once the message is delivered to the server it is ready to be delivered to the recipient through the use of e-mail client software. Typically, the protocol for transporting e-mail across the Internet is SMTP and POP3 for delivering it to your desktop. *United States v. Councilman,* 418 F.3d 67, 69-70 (1st Cir. 2005).

The number of e-mail processed by a server or servers can be significant depending upon the size of an organization. The Court in *Wiginton v. Ellis,* 2003 WL 22439865 at *2 (N.D. Ill. Oct. 27, 2003) stated, "[t]o understand what was destroyed, it is necessary to briefly discuss CBRE's network infrastructure. The infrastructure consists of approximately 125 network servers assigned to various offices. Four routing servers maintained at corporate IT headquarters in Newport Beach route all incoming e-mail to the local servers. The four routing servers redistribute up to 8,000 incoming e-mails each hour to local servers."

E-mail Client Software - User Based

When you access an e-mail server from your computer device you are using an e-mail client. An e-mail client is software that allows you to read and send e-mail through your account by connecting to the server. E-mail client software such as Microsoft Outlook allows you to download e-mails from remote servers and then store them on your computer. With client software one can download, read, write and then send e-mail to the e-mail server. It is the user interface to the e-mail system. Some of the most common e-mail clients are Eudora, Mac OS X Mail, Outlook, and Outlook Express.

The client usually consists of a text editor, address book, file folders and a communications module. The text editor allows the user to create the message itself, and usually includes spell checking and some formatting capabilities. The address book allows the user to store e-mail addresses in an accessible location, thus reducing the chance for addressing errors. It also provides the capability to insert "attachments" (text, graphic, audio or video files) to be delivered with the e-mail message. The file folder allows for the filing and storage of e-mail messages. Both sent and received e-mail messages can be filed. In addition, there is typically a search function to locate particular e-mails. The communications module connects the client to the server e-mail application.

E-mail Client Software - Web-Based

When you access web-based e-mail the "client" software is typically located on the website. *United States v. Councilman,* 418 F.3d 67, 69-70 (1st Cir. 2005) (introduction to Internet-based e-mail). Its functions are similar to a "user based" system. It gives the user the capability to edit messages, create message file folders, insert addresses into an address book and allows for searching to retrieve e-mail.

Employees generally will use their personal web-based e-mail accounts, such as Yahoo, Hotmail, Earthlink, and Gmail, for personal use while at work. Web-based e-mail allows users to send and receive e-mail using a Web browser instead of specific e-mail software. Company e-mail accounts store e-mail messages on the company's server. Web-based e-mail is generally stored on the Internet company's server that provides or hosts the account. *Curto v. Medical World Communs., Inc.*, No. CIV.03-6327, 2006 U.S. Dist. LEXIS 29387 (D.N.Y. May 15, 2006) (court found "[p]laintiff did take reasonable precautions to prevent inadvertent disclosure in that she sent the e-mails at issue through her personal AOL account which did not go through the Defendants' servers.").

If an employee wishes to access their personal account at work, they will generally use their employer's computer and Internet connection.

Retrieval of E-mail

Once an e-mail message is delivered and stored on the e-mail server it is ready to be retrieved by the recipient. There are several basic ways to retrieve e-mail; online, offline or a combination of both.

If the online model is used, the user connects to the e-mail server and processes the e-mail. The e-mail is NOT downloaded to the recipient's computer, unless specifically directed. The e-mail resides on the server and is only accessible when the recipient has an online connection to the e-mail server. The user can then edit, store, forward, delete and perform other functions with the e-mail. The user can generally access the e-mail from any location or from several different types of computer devices.

An example of an online model is a web-based e-mail system such as AOL. E-mail can be accessed from any Internet-connected computer and viewed "online" from the AOL mail server. When viewing e-mail online one can edit, send and store messages on the user's computer, if instructed to do so. Deleted messages are generally sent to the "trash" can where it is automatically emptied at different intervals. Once deleted by the user or by the automatic destruction by preset retention periods, the e-mail is generally unrecoverable. For this reason "time is of the essence" when you are submitting preservation letters and subpoenas to companies or individuals that subscribe to online or web-based e-mail server systems. You will want the contents of the e-mail server where the majority of the e-mail would reside, so a discovery request or subpoena for the contents of the e-mail server would be appropriate. In addition, request any e-mail downloaded and saved to the recipient's computer.

If the offline model is used, the client's software connects to the mail server and downloads all messages and attachments for that particular recipient. After the messages are downloaded, the messages are generally erased from the server. Then, the only copy of the e-mail, if it has not been stored on another server or computer, is on the recipient's computer.

The user can then process the e-mail by reading, editing, forwarding, filing or deleting the e-mail. Microsoft Outlook is an example of client offline software. Each time you open Microsoft Outlook, it checks the server for new messages. During this time, it will deliver new messages to your inbox send messages and clear them from the mail server, if instructed to do so.

For an offline model, it is important to determine whether e-mail messages, mailbox folders and attachments are all stored in a single computer file or whether in separate individual files. For example, Microsoft Outlook stores e-mail, attachments and file message folders in a single PST file. However, Eudora stores its attachments in a separate attachment folder selected in the preference menu. If the attachment folder is not provided in discovery, the attachments will be missing from the messages.

Under an offline model it is critical that you request discovery of e-mail on the recipient's computer since the messages may have been erased from the e-mail server, after they were downloaded. In a large organization, the preservation and recovery of e-mail under this system can be burdensome because of the number of separate computers that likely contain e-mail.

Finally, there are other alternative systems available that use a combination of the online and offline models. In these models the recipient connects to a mail server and retrieves the e-mail. The user then disconnects from the e-mail server and processes e-mail offline. Once the user is finished with the messages, the user once again connects to the mail server and uploads any changes. With this model, the mail server acts as the main repository of the user's e-mail.

[a]   Reported Cases

* *Northern Light Technology v. Northern Lights Club,* 97 F. Supp.2d 96, 101-102 (D. Mass. 2000). "FlairMail is a web-based email, all the email sent to FlairMail users is stored on servers located in Alberta even though it may be accessed from anywhere."

[2]   Internet Service Provider (ISP)

A fertile source of discovery is the computer records from the Internet service provider that the opposing party uses for e-mail delivery. Often the Internet service provider maintains storage and backup copies of subscribers' e-mail. *See,* §§ 2.6[B][1], *Internet Service Provider (ISP)* and 7.10, *Obtaining Data From Third Parties.*

Below is an example of an e-mail service agreement that provides for disclosure of e-mail upon a "legal request."

EARTHLINK INTERNET SERVICE AGREEMENT

5. MONITORING THE SERVICES.

EarthLink has no obligation to monitor the Services, but may do so *and disclose information regarding use of the Services for any reason if EarthLink, in its sole discretion, believes that it is reasonable to do so, including to: satisfy laws, regulations, or governmental or legal requests;* operate the Services properly; or protect itself and its Members. (emphasis added).

Some of the major web-based and traditional e-mail providers are:

- Hotmail (www.hotmail.com);
- Microsoft Network (www.msn.com);
- Google (www.google.com);
- Yahoo! (www.yahoo.com);
- EarthLink (www.earthlink.com); and
- AOL - America Online (www.aol.com).

[3]   Reported Cases

- *In Verizon Online Services, Inc. v. Ralsky,* 203 F. Supp. 2d 601, 606 (E.D.Va. 2002). The Court described an ISP server: "ISP Server - However, e-mail transmitted to an ISP subscriber is processed and stored on the ISP's e-mail computer servers. The e-mail server is located in a discrete geographic location. An e-mail server processes every e-mail that is addressed to the ISP's customer. In other words, once the e-mail is transmitted, it must first pass through the ISP's computer server to reach its ultimate destination-the subscriber's computer."

- *Sony Music Entertainment Inc. v. Does 1-40,* 326 F. Supp.2d 556, 559 (S.D.N.Y. 2004). The Court "issued an order granting plaintiffs' ex parte application to serve a subpoena upon non-party Cablevision to obtain the identity of each Doe defendant by requesting the name, address, telephone number, email address, and Media Access Control address for each defendant. In support of their application for expedited discovery, plaintiffs argued, inter alia, that good cause existed because ISPs typically retain user activity logs for only a limited period of time before erasing data."

- *United States v. Bach,* 310 F.3d 1063 (8th Cir. 2002). The Court of Appeals reversed the trial court and held that search and seizure of the defendant's e-mail files from the server of the ISP by technicians of the ISP was reasonable under the Fourth Amendment.

- *Doe v. Ashcroft,* 334 F. Supp.2d 471, 509 (S.D.N.Y. 2004).

  The evidence on the record now before this Court demonstrates that the information available through a § 2709 NSL [subpoena] served upon an ISP could easily be used to disclose vast amounts of anonymous speech and associational activity. For instance, . . . it imposes a duty to provide "electronic communication transactional records," a phrase which, though undefined in the statute, certainly encompasses a log of email addresses with whom a subscriber has corresponded and the web pages that a subscriber visits . . . Those transactional records can reveal, among other things, the anonymous message boards to which a person logs on or posts, the electronic newsletters to which he subscribes, and the advocacy websites he visits. . . . impose a duty on ISPs to provide the names and addresses of subscribers, thus enabling the Government to specifically identify someone who has written anonymously on the internet.

[4]   Other Authorities (reserved)

[5]   Discovery Pointers

• Internet service providers (ISP) generally have set retention periods and storage limitation on e-mail and attachments. Take immediate action if you want to obtain e-mail from an ISP.

[L]   E-mail Retention Policies

To reduce risks associated with improperly managed e-mail, many companies have begun to establish e-mail retention policies regarding the creation, retention, organization and destruction of e-mail in compliance with administrative regulations and "litigation holds." *See,* § 7.9[H], *Document Retention Policy - Prior to Litigation.* They will often correlate with policies in place for paper documents. However, since the characteristics of electronic information are vastly different from paper-based information, it is difficult to implement retention and destruction policies for electronic mail. Because e-mail is stored on each computer it passes through, it is nearly impossible to destroy an e-mail message that has been sent.

Companies use different methods to ensure that e-mail is deleted. Many companies have a thirty-day retention policy on e-mail, in which the e-mail will be automatically deleted after this period of time from the server. Many employees circumvent the policy by saving their e-mail on separate storage media such as their hard drives. Users may also disable the automatic purge function of their e-mail folder. For example, after Microsoft demanded Netscape's e-mail from a discussion list, Netscape found that its 90-day destruction policy had not been followed. Wendy Leibowitz, *As E-Mail Boxes Overflow, Employment Law Issues Proliferate*, Nat'l L.J. Sept. 14, 1998 at B4.

Businesses are using different methods to manage e-mail. Many businesses are warning their employees that e-mail is similar to a letter or an internal memorandum and may be used in litigation or for other purposes. Some companies are including archival e-mail in the e-mail retention and destruction policies. Corporations are also instituting a purge protocol and instructing employees what material is not to be contained in e-mail. However, some servers will backup and store e-mail even though the users have requested their deletion.

Most of the prominent high profile e-mail cases contained derogatory information that had been supposedly deleted. For this reason, corporations are clamping down on e-mail that are in violation of their policies. For example, "[t]o make sure everyone was paying attention, the Times disclosed that it has just fired more than 20 employees for sending 'inappropriate and offensive' e-mail messages." Howard Kurtz, *Not Fit to Print or Transmit New York Times Fires 20 Workers for Sending Offensive E-Mail*, The Washington Post, December 1, 1999, at C3.

To uncover violations, some companies use specific software programs to scan e-mail messages for specific words or phrases. Once inappropriate e-mail messages are located, they are deleted and employees counseled. During discovery, it is important to determine whether or not a corporation has such a self-censorship policy and the type of technical capability to enforce the policy. In addition, determine whether or not flagged e-mail is saved and retained in a separate file.

[1]   Reported Cases

- *See,* § 7.9[H], *Document Retention Policy - Prior to Litigation.*

[2]   Other Authorities (reserved)

[3]   Discovery Pointers

- Often the opposing party will refuse to disclose e-mail arguing that their corporate policy requires that e-mail is not retained more than 30 days. However, it is almost certain that employees will retain e-mail for a longer period of time using secondary storage media and devices such as the hard drive of the user's computer.

- If you are outside counsel, then you should develop a clear understanding of your client's e-mail systems. This would include the capability and methods available to search the client's e-mail for relevant information and to determine the number of e-mail that would be retrieved based on the searches. You need to know whether backup and archived e-mail files are retained. If e-mail is to be retained, they should be organized in a uniform, descriptive manner in order to shorten the time to review e-mail for relevance, privilege, etc.

- After litigation has commenced, clients should always consult their attorneys if they intend to destroy any electronic information that may have relevance to the case.

- Always keep in mind that though e-mail may be deleted from the e-mail server or user's computer that it may be available on backup tapes or on other e-mail devices used by the recipient. For example, many e-mail servers permit the user to download all of the e-mail to a desktop computer, but also leave a copy on the server. If the same user connects to the server using a different computer such as a laptop, then the same e-mail can be downloaded to the laptop.

- Many users are unaware that even though they download all of their e-mail from a server, the server still retains a copy. Until the server is specifically directed by the user or by the server administrator to remove e-mail from the server, it will continue to reside there.

- When negotiating discovery of e-mail, the discovering party generally makes a broad request for it since e-mail is often not organized and can be located on different directories and storage media. Using inexpensive search software, one can locate relevant e-mail to accommodate a production request. However, if you are representing the disclosing party, the problem is that a broad request may generate thousands of e-mail and require you to review all of it for privilege, trade secrets, etc. This may strain your budget and time. One alternative is to agree to a limited date range and subject matter search protocol (keywords, names, and phrases) of the disclosing party's computer. *See,* § 6.2[C], *Production Response Plan.*

- If a corporation has a short retention policy, such as 14 days, it may be a sign that the corporation has had to disclose electronic records in an unrelated case. Determine if e-mail has been preserved in an unrelated lawsuit.

- Determine how many e-mail addresses are available for each person related to the litigation and whether or not he or she changed e-mail addresses or ISPs during the relevant time.

- In order to prevent the waiver of the attorney-client privilege by the inadvertent disclosure of confidential e-mail, attorneys should agree in advance with their clients about the use of attorney-client e-mail. An attorney should instruct the client never to forward, copy or use sections of attorney e-mail correspondence. "Confidential" headers should be used on e-mail. Neither the attorney nor the client should back up confidential e-mail as part of an enterprise-wide system backup routine. Electronic message systems that allow anyone in the client's business to read confidential messages should not be used.

[M] Encryption and Self-Destroying E-mail Programs

Some organizations may use a self-destroying e-mail program. These programs permit one to send encrypted, self-destructing messages to almost any e-mail system. One of the programs, called Email Control by Liquid Machines (www.liquidmachines.com) works with Microsoft Outlook and permits users to send secure messages that are set to expire or "disappear" and become unreadable at a certain date. These include any copies of the e-mail that have been forwarded or backed up. This program uses a method of making e-mail unreadable by destroying an encryption key after a set period of time. However, by using a forensic expert, part of the message, such as the sender, recipient, etc. may still be recoverable. *See also,* § 3.5[H][1], *Encryption and Steganography.*

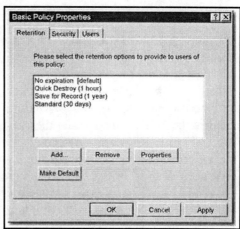

E-mail Control™ by Liquid Machines permits the user to determine the life of e-mail.

[N] Falsification of E-mail

Falsification of e-mail has been and will continue to be a problem. The ability to log into another person's computer system, the lack of an authenticated signature on messages and spoofing has made e-mail susceptible to fraud. Since e-mail can be considered to be evidence in employment cases (sexual harassment, age discrimination, etc.) and other litigation, some employees may attempt to falsify e-mail.

One form of e-mail falsification is e-mail spoofing. E-mail spoofing can take many forms. Just as people can try to pretend to be someone they are not, so can computers. This is called spoofing.

E-mail spoofing is generally used to convince individuals to provide personal or financial information that enables another to commit credit card, bank fraud or other forms of identity theft. Spoofing often involves falsely using the trademark of a business in an "e-mail spoofing" to make it appear that the e-mail originated from the legitimate business.

Another form of spoofing is where the spoofer uses the recipient's address and configures his machine to emulate the recipient's machine. When data comes along the network, which is intended for the actual recipient, the spoofer receives it instead and automatically sends a packet to the sender, which makes the sender believe that the message was properly received. In fact, the spoofer can read the e-mail, concoct a reply and send it back to the unsuspecting person who is unaware that he is communicating with an impostor. More subtly, the spoofer can alter the original e-mail and then relay it to the intended recipient.

"IP spoofing," is when one falsifies IP information. The IP address in the header information is fabricated and the e-mail is sent to the recipient. The message appears in all respects to be authentic, but has not been sent from the purported sender.

A different form of spoofing is the sender inserting a fictitious sender name in the header information. This is a form of an "anonymous remailer." An anonymous remailer is a mail server that after receiving incoming messages, removes the header information that identifies the original sender, and then sends the message to the intended recipient. This effectively hides the name of senders of e-mail messages. There are several different variations of anonymous remailers. For more information on anonymous remailers visit the following websites: http://www.free-definition.com/Anonymous-remailer.html or http://email.about.com/cs/remailers/. Depending on the complexity of the spoofed mail, a forensic expert may be able to assist in tracking down who sent the mail.

As one article noted, "[i]t is fairly easy for knowledgeable computer users to create e-mail messages that falsify this [header] information." Hon. Shira A. Scheindlin & Jeffrey Rabkin, *Electronic Discovery in Federal Civil Litigation: Is Rule 34 Up to the Task?,* 41 B.C. L. Rev. 327, 337,339 (2000).

Of course, it is also possible for someone to gain access to another's password and use that person's computer to send out authentic messages. This is a common method of spoofing. This points out that effective confidentiality and privacy is no stronger than the weakest link in a chain. If counsel, staff, consultants or others have physical access to a computer or password and send e-mail, sufficient authentication will be required for admission of e-mail. *CSX Transp., Inc. v. Recovery Express, Inc.,* 415 F. Supp. 2d 6 (D. Mass. 2006) (non-employee who had access to the corporation's e-mail account and sent a message using the corporation's domain name did not create apparent authority).

There are other methods for fabricating e-mail. *See, Investigative Responses - Methods of Faking E-mail,* available at http://faculty.ncwc.edu/toconnor/426/426lect05.htm

[1]   Reported Cases

• *F.T.C. v. Brian D. WESTBY,* No. CIV.03-2540, 2004 WL 1175047 (N.D.Ill. Mar. 4, 2004). "'Spoofing' means the practice of disguising a commercial e-mail to make the e-mail appear to come from an address from which it actually did not originate. Spoofing involves placing in the 'From' or 'Reply-to' lines, or in other portions of e-mail messages, an e-mail address other than the actual sender's address, without the consent or authorization of the user of the e-mail address whose address is spoofed."

- *Internet Doorway, Inc. v. Parks,* 138 F. Supp. 2d 773 (S.D. Miss. 2001). The plaintiff alleged that the defendant falsified the "from" header to make e-mail appear to have been sent from a plaintiff's ISP service.

- *Munshani v. Signal Lake Venture,* 2001 WL 1526954, (Mass. Super. Oct. 9, 2001). The Court found that plaintiff had fabricated documents based upon testimony of a court-appointed forensic consultant who revealed fraud in creation of e-mail evidence.

- *Jiminez v. Madison Area Technical College,* 321 F.3d 652, 655 (7th Cir. 2003). The Court of Appeals affirmed the dismissal of this racial discrimination case and imposed Rule 11 sanctions on the plaintiff and her attorney. The e-mails and letters were "obviously fraudulent."

- *Premier Homes and Land Corp. v. Cheswell, Inc.,* 240 F. Supp. 2d 97 (D. Mass. 2002). As a party was obtaining a mirror copy of the opposing party's hard drive, he admitted to fabricating e-mail and lease addendum by pasting false header information and changing the subject line information. The Court, for fraud, dismissed the case.

- *People v. Lee,* C-38925 (Calif. Super. Ct. Jan. 30, 1997). A woman falsified an e-mail message in an attempt to get a $100,000 settlement in a sexual harassment claim against Oracle Corp. The disgruntled former employee sent a fake e-mail message from her boss to support her case. She was later convicted of perjury for falsifying documents.

[2]   Other Authorities

- Greenberg, *Threats, Harassment, and Hate On-line: Recent Developments,* 6 B.U. Int.L.J. 673 (Spring 1997).

[3]   Discovery Pointers

- If you think that an e-mail message has been falsified by spoofing or some other method, hire a forensic expert to examine the header, metadata and other e-mail characteristics.

[O]   Costs to Search and Waiver Issues

E-mail will generally be disclosed in an electronic format. The advantage of receiving information in an electronic format is that you will be able to electronically search and analyze the data instantly, and for very little cost. If the e-mail is produced in its native file format, it can be exported to a standard litigation support package for easy searching or left in its native format and searched by a program such as dtSearch (www.dtSearch.com). In an electronic format, one can conduct electronic searches for words, phrases, names, dates and other issues of interest. If necessary, you can easily convert e-mail to a TIFF format or print it out for courtroom presentation.

If you request e-mail in a hardcopy format or it is produced in an unsearchable image format, your search will have to be manually done by reading each e-mail.

Screening e-mail messages for attorney-client communication privilege, attorney work-product protection, trade secrets or other privileged material is necessary because inadvertent production of e-mail messages may result in the waiver of the privilege in part or in whole. If you are producing e-mail, screening for relevance and privilege can be costly and time-consuming. One way of lowering the screening cost is to use computer search techniques to identify and filter messages addressed to or authored by legal personnel, corporate officers and others who may have confidential communications. However, the results of such searches will be far from precise.

The better practice is to also negotiate an agreement for the nonwaiver of inadvertent production of privileged e-mail messages and have it endorsed as an order from the court. By producing documents under such a court order, the parties may limit their confidentiality exposure to each other and to possible third parties. *See,* § 7.4[H], *Work Product Doctrine, Attorney Client Privilege and Trade Secrets.*

[P]   Reported Cases

Rule 34 Includes E-mail

•   *Mosaid Technologies Inc. v. Samsung Electronics Co., Ltd.*, 348 F. Supp.2d 332, 336-337 (D.N.J. 2004). In a commercial litigation case the defendant failed to preserve e-mail and argued that the plaintiff failed to use the word "e-mail" in its discovery request. The Court rejected the argument and said it was implied when it asked for correspondence and other communications.

Agency Records

•   *York Hosp. v. Dep't. of Human Services,* 869 A.2d 729, 733 (Me. 2005). The Court in remanding for further action ruled that a state agency should have considered whether to include its e-mail communications in the agency record denying a certificate of need for a radiation therapy facility. The court noted "[e]lectronic mail communications are correspondence more similar to a letter than a telephone conversation and would ordinarily be included in the record if such communications carried substantive information."

Discovery of Deleted E-Mail

- *Playboy Enterprises, Inc. v. Welles,* 60 F. Supp. 2d 1050 (S.D. Cal. 1999). The plaintiff was entitled to discover deleted e-mail contained on the defendant's computer hard drive. *See also,* § 3.5[E], *Deletion of Electronic Information.*

Searching Both Backup Tapes and Individual's E-Mail

- *In re Amsted Industries, Inc. "ERISA" Litigation,* No. CIV.01-2963, 2002 WL 31844956, at *2 (N.D. Ill. Dec. 18, 2002). The Court granted additional keyword search request because of enlargement of subject matter of litigation and also ruled producing party, who had already searched the backup tapes, must search "the in-box, saved, and sent folders of any relevant individual's e-mail in the same manner."

Burdensome E-mail Argument

- *Medtronic v. Michelson,* 2003 WL 21468573 at *9 (W.D. Tenn. May 13, 2003). The Court refused to shift costs, and ordered the defendant, at its own cost, to search through 300 gigabytes of individual user e-mails, using Boolean search terms provided by plaintiff's counsel. *See also,* § 7.4[G][6], *Cost Allocation.*

Form of Disclosure

- *Overseas Private Inv. Corp. v. Mandelbaum,* No. CIV.97-1138, 1998 WL 647208 (D.D.C. Aug. 19, 1998). This case involved a breach of contract action between two companies. The Court ordered disclosure of e-mail that were in a database and listed the database fields. The Court opinion set out a database report format for disclosure of the e-mail in dispute. These included the addresses, author, number of e-mail, recipients and nature of the document. *See also,* § 7.7[G], *Form of Production of Computer-based Data.*

Attorney-client Privilege Waived

- *United States v. Keystone Sanitation Co., Inc.,* 885 F. Supp. 672 (M.D. Pa. 1994). The Court held that the attorney-client privilege had been waived because two e-mail had been inadvertently disclosed in a massive production of documents. *See also,* § 7.4[H], *Work Product Doctrine, Attorney Client Privilege and Trade Secrets.*

Federal and State Records Acts

- *Armstrong, et al. v. Executive Office of the President,* 1 F.3d 1274 (D.C. Cir. 1993). E-mail messages are considered to be "records" under the Federal Records Act. As such, the government is required to preserve e-mail messages in accordance with the Federal Records Act. *See,* Federal Records Act, 44 U.S.C. §§ 2101 *et seq.*

- Many state governments have statutes providing that e-mail are government records. For example, Alabama law stipulates that any document is a government record when a government employee, using government resources in the course of conducting public business, creates it. Code of Alabama 1975, Section 41-13-1.

Sanctions for Failure to Disclose

- *Zubulake v. UBS Warburg LLC,* 220 F.R.D. 212 (S.D.N.Y. 2003). The defendant failed to preserve backup tapes that contained missing e-mail. The judge found that the plaintiff was unable to establish that the lost evidence would have supported her claims and, therefore, an adverse inference instruction would not be authorized. However, *see, Zubulake v. UBS Warburg LLC,* No. CIV.02-1243, 2004 WL 1620866, (S.D.N.Y. July 20, 2004) where the Court subsequently ordered an adverse inference instruction after a nexus was found. *See also,* § 7.9[K], *Spoliation.*

Evidentiary Proof

- *Ouzts v. USAir, Inc.,* No. CIV.94-625, 1996 WL 578514, at *20 (W.D. Pa. July 26, 1996), *aff'd,* 118 F.3d 1577 (3d Cir. 1997). The Court found that "based on this 'e-mail,' no reasonable jury could find that USAir 'regarded' plaintiffs as disabled . . . and [therefore the] court concludes that plaintiffs have failed to raise a material issue of fact in connection with [their claim under the Americans with Disabilities Act]."

- *Smyth v. Pillsbury,* 914 F. Supp. 97 (E.D. Pa. 1996). An at-will employee who sent e-mail messages from home was dismissed for transmitting inappropriate and unprofessional comments over the employer's e-mail system.

- *See also,* § 8.12, *E-mail* for admissibility issues and § 7.3[E], *Discovery and Preservation Orders - Rule 16(c).*

[Q]   Other Authorities:

- Hon. Shira A. Scheindlin & Jeffrey Rabkin, *Electronic Discovery in Federal Civil Litigation: Is Rule 34 Up to the Task?,* 41 B.C. L. Rev. 327 (2000).

- Samuel A. Thumma & Darrel S. Jackson, *The History of Electronic Mail in Litigation,* 16 Santa Clara Computer & High Tech. L.J. 1 (1999).

- Staib, *Absence of Proper Guidelines for E-Mail Use Can Create Client Headaches During Discovery,* 21 Litigation News 4 (1996).

- Sherry L. Talton, *Mapping the Information Superhighway: Electronic Mail and the Inadvertent Disclosure of Confidential Information*, Note, 20 Rev. Litig. 271 (2000).

- Amy M. Fulmer Stevenson, *Making a Wrong Turn on the Information Superhighway: Electronic Mail, The Attorney-Client Privilege and Inadvertent Disclosure*, 26 Cap.U.L.Rev. 347 (1997).

- Marnie H. Pulver, *Electronic Media Discovery*, 21 Cardozo L. Rev. 1379 (2000).

- Joshua M. Masur, *Safety in Numbers: Revisiting the Risks to Client Confidences and Attorney-Client Privilege Posed by Internet Electronic E-mail*, 14 Berkeley Tech. L.J. 1117 (1999).

- *E-Mail Rules, Policies and Practices Survey (2003)*, American Management Association (available at http://www.amanet.org/research/) (subscription required).

[R]   Discovery Pointers

- *Request for Production and Interrogatories.* The discovery request needs to be specifically drawn to define "communications" as to include e-mail messages in paper form and/or stored on any computer, floppy disk, magnetic tape or other storage media or devices. If seeking information from AOL or another third-party e-mail provider, time is of the essence as the storage media at these operations are constantly writing and overwriting e-mail content.

- E-mail for Individuals, Attachments, Pointers and Number of Years.

    — List all e-mail addresses used by _____(name) within the last _____ years.

    — Provide e-mail and attachments from any server, whether owned by the _____ (plaintiff/defendant) or outside service providers that have e-mail related to this case. Include with the e-mail associated attachments and directory locations and pointers.

    — Is the corporation's e-mail provided internally or via a third party vendor?

    — List all Internet service providers or employer e-mail servers that may have been used.

    — List all e-mail systems used by _____ (name) within the last 5 years.

    — Has the e-mail system in question changed during the relevant time period?

— If so when, what was the change and who within the organization was responsible for implementing the change?

— If so, how do you propose restoring it for discovery purposes and where are the tapes kept with the information from the old system?

• Form of Disclosure - File Formats

— Provide the e-mail both in native file format including attachments and pointers as well as either ASCII comma delimited or Microsoft Access™ formats.

— Provide all database fields of the e-mail (including metadata and headers).

• Deposition Notice

Designate "one or more" representatives to testify regarding the:

— System of files maintained to store, protect, and preserve documents including audio and videotape recordings, computer files, and electronic mail sent, received, forwarded, and transmitted, etc. from _____ until _____.

— Systems used since _____ to create, store, retrieve, and delete electronic mail;

— Systems for recording the acquisition, location, and/or disposition of personal electronic computers operated by any official, employee, detailee, resident, volunteer, intern, visitor or overnight guest.

§ 3.9   INTERNET

[A]   Generally

The Internet is an international network of computers that links thousands of businesses, governments, educational institutions, individual users, law firms and clients. These links transport and store digital information (video images, sounds, graphics, animations and text) from computer to computer until it reaches its final destination.

"[T]he Internet is currently believed to connect more than 159 countries and close to 322 million users worldwide. . . . Because the Internet merely links together numerous individual computers and computer networks, no single entity or group of entities controls all of the material made available on the Internet or otherwise limits the ability of others to access such materials." *United States v. Extreme Associates, Inc.,* 352 F. Supp.2d 578, 580 (W.D.Pa. 2005).

A federal Court has defined the Internet as follows:

11. The Internet is a global electronic network, consisting of smaller, interconnected networks, which allows millions of computers to exchange information over telephone wires, dedicated data cables, and wireless links. The Internet links PCs by means of servers, which run specialized operating systems and applications designed for servicing a network environment.

United States v. Microsoft Corp., 84 F. Supp. 2d 9, 13 (D.D.C. 1999), *aff'd in part & rev'd in part*, 253 F.3d 34 (D.C. Cir. 2001), *cert. denied*, 122 S. Ct. 350 (2001); *See, e.g., Reno v. American Civil Liberties Union*, 521 U.S. 844, 849-853, (1997) (discussing the history and fundamental architecture of the Internet); *Paramount Pictures Corp. v. Davis,* 234 F.R.D. 102, 104 (D. Pa. 2005) (discussing infringing activities on the Internet).

Wire, microwave, satellite and telephone lines interconnect the Internet. There are several commercial online Internet service providers (ISP), such as America Online and Microsoft Network, who provide access for individuals and businesses to the Internet. *See,* § 2.6[B][1], *Internet Service Provider (ISP).* Local area networks (LANs) and wide area networks (WANs) use similar wire and wireless means to transfer digital information. In turn, these systems interconnect to the Internet. Thus, this worldwide-interconnected network is able to carry digital signals throughout the world instantaneously.

Electronic evidence can be found on the Internet in several possible data locations; WWW pages and data files, Internet Relay Chat (IRC) or instant messaging, newsgroups and listservs. The location of the data can be part of an individual or company's computer storage devices or off-site on a third party provider's computer system. In addition, on an individual's computer, Internet usage and data can be found in "cookies," Internet history logs, "cache" files and residual data.

[1]   Reported Case

- *National Cable & Telecommunications Ass'n. v. Brand X Internet Services,* 2005 WL 1498860, at *1 (U.S. Jun. 27, 2005).

    Consumers traditionally access the Internet through "dial-up" connections provided via local telephone lines. Internet service providers (ISPs), in turn, link those calls to the Internet network, not only by providing a physical connection, but also by offering consumers the ability to translate raw data into information they may both view on their own computers and transmit to others connected to the Internet. Technological limitations of local telephone wires, however, retard the speed at which Internet data may be transmitted through such "narrowband" connections. "Broadband" Internet service, by contrast, transmits data at much higher speeds. There are two principal kinds of broadband service: cable modem service, which transmits data between the Internet and users' computers via the network of television cable lines owned by cable companies, and Digital Subscriber Line (DSL) service, which uses high-speed wires owned by local telephone companies. Other ways of transmitting high-speed Internet data, including terrestrial- and satellite-based wireless networks, are also emerging.

[B]   World Wide Web

[1]   Description

The World Wide Web, also referred to as "the Web" or by the initials "WWW," is part of the Internet. It is the most commercialized part of the Internet. The Web is made up of millions of "pages" formatted in **H**yper**T**ext **M**arkup **L**anguage (HTML) and is embedded with cross-references known as hyperlinks. Hyperlinks can link to data, graphics, sounds, videos, text, services and other files on the Web. "Links may also take the user from the original website to another website on a different computer connected to the Internet, a computer that may be located in a different area of the country, or even the world." *United States v. Extreme Associates, Inc.,* 352 F. Supp.2d 578, 580-581 (W.D.Pa. 2005); *Hubbert v. Dell Corporation,* 2995 WL 1968774 (Ill. App. Ct. Aug. 12, 2005) (court found an online arbitration clause enforceable holding that "blue hyperlinks" entitled "terms and conditions of sale" was sufficient notice that the arbitration clause was contained in an online contract).

The dominant protocol for transmitting information over the Internet is the Transmission Control Protocol/Internet Protocol or TCP/IP. It allows two hosts to transmit and receive data. All computers connected to the Internet have installed a copy of the TCP/IP program. The TCP/IP protocol controls the compiling and recompiling of data into packets that are sent over the Internet.

A general description of the World Wide Web and its many components are set forth in the case of *United States v. Microsoft Corp.*, 84 F. Supp. 2d 9, 13 (D.D.C. 1999), *aff'd in part & rev'd in part*, 253 F.3d 34 (D.C. Cir. 2001), *cert. denied*, 122 S. Ct. 350 (2001):

12. The World Wide Web ("the Web") is a massive collection of digital information resources stored on servers throughout the Internet. These resources are typically provided in the form of hypertext documents, commonly referred to as "Web pages," that may incorporate any combination of text, graphics, audio and video content, software programs, and other data. A user of a computer connected to the Internet can publish a page on the Web simply by copying it into a specially designated, publicly accessible directory on a Web server. Some Web resources are in the form of applications that provide functionality through a user's PC system but actually execute on a server.

13. Internet content providers ("ICPs") are the individuals and organizations that have established a presence, or "site," on the Web by publishing a collection of

Web pages. Most Web pages are in the form of "hypertext"; that is, they contain annotated references, or "hyperlinks," to other Web pages. Hyperlinks can be used as cross-references within a single document, between documents on the same site, or between documents on different sites.

14. Typically, one page on each Web site is the "home page," or the first access point to the site. The home page is usually a hypertext document that presents an overview of the site and hyperlinks to the other pages comprising the site.

15. PCs typically connect to the Internet through the services of Internet access providers ("IAPs"), which generally charge subscription fees to their customers in the United States. There are two types of IAPs. Online services ("OLSs") such as America Online ("AOL"), Prodigy, and the Microsoft Network ("MSN") offer, in addition to Internet access, various services and an array of proprietary content. Internet service providers ("ISPs") such as MindSpring and Netcom, on the other hand, offer few services apart from Internet access and relatively little of their own content.

16. A "Web client" is software that, when running on a computer connected to the Internet, sends information to and receives information from Web servers throughout the Internet. Web clients and servers transfer data using a standard known as the Hypertext Transfer Protocol ("HTTP"). A "Web browser" is a type of Web client that enables a user to select, retrieve, and perceive resources on the Web. In particular, Web browsers provide a way for a user to view hypertext documents and follow the hyperlinks that connect them, typically by moving the cursor over a link and depressing the mouse button.

Web browser programs include Microsoft Explorer, Netscape Navigator, Opera, and Mozilla. In addition, many ISPs like Earthlink and America Online provide their own proprietary browsers.

[2]   Website Domain Name

Every website has a specific address on the WWW, called a Uniform Resource Locator (URL) or a domain name and an IP address. A domain name is an identity tag of the Internet. For example, "www.sears.com" is a domain name. Domain names consist of two domains, the first being a "top level" domain indicating the type of organization using the name (e.g., ".edu" for educational, ".com" for commercial and ".gov" for government agencies). The "second-level" domain, although appearing before the top-level domain, is typically the name of the company maintaining the Internet site. *Panavision International, L.P. v. Toeppen,* 945 F. Supp. 1296, 1299 (C.D. Cal. 1996) (discusses the structure and purpose of domain names); *Center for Democracy & Technology v. Pappert,* 337 F. Supp.2d 606, 614-615 (E.D.Pa. 2004) (explaining domain names, shared domain names, hosting and other Internet components); *Sunlight Saunas, Inc. v. Sundance Sauna, Inc.,* 427 F. Supp. 2d 1032, n6 (D. Kan. 2006) ("A domain name is 'any alphanumeric designation which is registered with or assigned by any domain name registrar, domain name registry . . . as part of an electronic address on the Internet.' 15 U.S.C. § 1127. Essentially, it is the website address.").

Every domain name has a unique IP address. An IP address consists of four groups of digits separated by periods that indicate the network, subnetwork, and local address. For example, an Internet address might read 231.35.1.19. *Paramount Pictures Corp. v. Davis,* 234 F.R.D. 102, 105 (D. Pa. 2005) ("[a]n IP address is a unique numerical identifier that is automatically assigned to a user by its Internet Service Provider each time a user logs on to the network. . . . Therefore, if provided with a user's IP address and the date and time of the infringing activity, an ISP can use its user logs to identify the name and address of the ISP subscriber who was assigned that IP address at that date and time.").

[3]   Web Pages

Web pages are used for a variety of business, governmental and personal purposes. These include e-commerce, personal Web pages, want ads, business data depositories, legislation, statutes, etc. Web pages are generally text that originates from files on a directory or from a Web page generator. In addition to text, websites may include photographs, illustrations, video, music, animations or computer programs. They often contain hypertext links to other sites in the form of highlighted or colored text that the user can click on with their mouse, instructing their computer to jump to a new Web page.

A website's content is generally contained in a directory containing data files located on a hard disk or other storage media. The hard disk or other storage media can be located on the user's machine or part of a hard disk managed by a third party such as an Internet service provider. Under the directory is a collection of Web text files in HTML (Hyper-Text Markup Language) format or a Web page generator. Hyper-Text Markup Language (HTML) is a relatively simple cross-platform formatting language that defines how text and images will be displayed by a Web browser

If it is a collection of HTML files, each Web page is a separate file. These pages may contain links to graphics, sound, video or other computer files in the same or different directories or subdirectories. If it is a Web page generator, then a software application takes raw data from a database or other informational source file and produces a HTML file dynamically.

When discovering Web page information, you need to determine whether the Web data is contained in static Web files or whether the data is dynamic and generated from a Web page generator. When requesting information on a website, request the directory, subdirectories and files of the relevant part of the website. Also, request that all raw data and any Web page generator be produced. The target of your search may be the database that supplies the data for the Web page generator. *See,* § 3.10, *Database for additional information regarding databases and* § 8.15, *Web Page Content for admissibility of web content.*

[4]   Reported Cases

- *Gonzales v. Google, Inc.,* 234 F.R.D. 674 (D. Cal. 2006). The Court granted the government's motion for disclosure of a listing of 50,000 URLs in its database. However, the Court denied the request for the search engine company to disclose search queries of its users.

- *Kleiner v. Burns,* No. CIV.00-2160, 2000 WL 1909470 (D. Kan. Dec. 15, 2000). Court issued stern warning for Yahoo to disclose information off its websites.

- *State v. Brown,* 119 Wash. App. 1073, at *5 (Wash. App. Jan. 6, 2004). A computer forensics investigator discovered website pages located in temporary internet folders that were subsequently used to show the defendant's intent to commit identity theft. The investigator "testified that she recovered internet pages saved to temporary internet folders in the laptop . . . These pages contained information about changing identities, assuming other identities, magnetic strip card reader/writer devices, hologram printers, and stolen credit card information."

- *Giardina v. Lockheed Martin Corp.,* No. CIV.02-1030, 2003 WL 1338826 (E.D. La. Mar. 14, 2003). The plaintiff sought a list of all "non-work related Internet sites" accessed by sixteen different company computers to show co-workers visited pornography websites. The Court granted disclosure of website visits and awarded attorney fees.

- *Columbia Ins. Co. v. Seescandy.com,* 185 F.R.D. 573 (N.D. Cal. 1999). The Court permitted plaintiff to conduct discovery, prior to filing of the action, to obtain the identity of certain domain name registers that infringed upon the plaintiff's trademark.

- *Coniglio v. City of Berwyn,* No. CIV.99-4475, 1999 WL 1212190, at *3 (N.D. Ill. Dec. 16, 1999). The Court held that the plaintiff stated a claim for hostile work environment when the defendant's comptroller used his work computer, which was in view of others, to access pornographic websites and to download and print pornographic images. The comptroller also allegedly called her into his office while the pornographic images were still on his screen and attempted to elicit a reaction from her. After she complained of his conduct, she began receiving unsolicited e-mail from pornographic Internet sites.

- *Scott v. Plaques Unlimited, Inc.*, 46 F. Supp. 2d 1287, 1289 (M.D. Fla. 1999). The Court held that an employee stated a claim of sexual harassment based, in part, on her allegation that she had found her supervisor and a customer looking at pornography on the Internet.

- *Charles E. Hill & Assocs. v. Compuserve, Inc.,* 2003 WL 22327827 (S.D. Ind. Sept. 26, 2003). This case provides an extensive description and history of the Internet, HTML programming, how users interact with the WWW sites using browsers, cache files and other general information regarding the Internet and how it functions.

[5]   Discovery Pointers

- If you are looking for prior versions of a particular website you might find it on the archived web pages on the WayBack Machine website available at www.archive.org/web/web.php. It has stored approximately 30 billion web pages archived from 1996 to the present.

- Request to Produce:

  — Provide all Web page files or Web page source files from the computers of every person and every server that contains Web page files or Web page source files related to this case.

  — Provide Internet usage logs, history files and cache files from every person and computer related to this case.

  — Provide the files with complete paths or uncompressed in separate folders for each person, machine or server with complete paths.

[C]   Internet Relay Chat (IRC), Chat Room and Instant Messaging

Chat or "instant messaging" (also known as "IM" or "IMing") is the real-time simultaneous communication between two or more people using a computer. One person types a message on their keyboard and the people with whom they are "chatting" can see the message appear on their monitors and respond immediately. A user is notified of an instant message by a sound or window that indicates that someone is trying to reach them. The user can then accept or reject that message. IM allows multiple users to be online at the same time. These chats or "instant messaging" capabilities, as they develop, will include the use of audio, graphics and video in the communication process.

Chat (IRC) requires that each user be connected to the Internet or other electronic network at the same time. You can be connected to a local area network, a wide area network within a business or the Internet. Users need specialized software to participate in any chat session. America Online (AOL) Instant Messenger, Yahoo and Microsoft Chat are three of the most popular chat systems. *Universal City Studios v. Reimerdes,* 111 F. Supp. 2d 294, 307 (D.N.Y. 2000) ("Internet Relay Chat ('IRC') is a system that enables individuals connected to the Internet to participate in live typed discussions. Participation in an IRC discussion requires an IRC software program, which sends messages via the Internet to the IRC server, which in turn broadcasts the messages to all participants. The IRC system is capable of supporting many separate discussions at once."); *United States v. Helder,* 2006 U.S. App. LEXIS 15995, n.2 (8th Cir. Jun. 26, 2006) ("Yahoo!'s instant messaging service allows for direct, private chats between two people").

Subscribers to the same service can then exchange real-time text messages.

Chat *rooms* are different in that participants view the conversation between the different parties to the session. *Chivers v. Cent. Noble Cmty. Schs.,* 423 F. Supp. 2d 835, n.1 (D. Ind. 2006) ("Like a chat room, IM is used to send messages back and forth through the Internet to a specific user. It is like a chat room in the way that you can communicate, but unlike most chat room communications, the information that is being typed is sent directly to the user and is not viewed by anyone else.").

Though initially used for social interaction, chat sessions are becoming popular with business and educational institutions. Since these chat sessions can be carried on, like a regular conversation, over the Internet with anyone located anywhere in the world, they have become popular and are inexpensive to use.

Many employees are unaware of the use of IM in the workplace. However, a recent IM survey found that 31% of employees use instant messaging at work. Survey respondents admitted: sending jokes, gossip, rumors or disparaging remarks, 16%; confidential information about the company, a co-worker or client (9%); and sexual, romantic or pornographic content (6%). AMA/ePolicy Institute Research 2004 *Workplace E-Mail and Instant Messaging Survey Summary,* available at: http://www.epolicyinstitute.com/survey/survey04.pdf (last visited on July 21, 2006).

In some cases the IM or chat room conversations are saved. "Unless one of the parties to an on-line chat is recording the conversation by storing the text, once the 'chat window' is closed, it is extremely difficult (if not impossible) to recreate the conversation, know whether it ever occurred, or identify the parties to the 'chat'." *United States v. Johnson,* No. CR.97-0206, 2005 WL 22680, at *9 n.9 (N.D.N.Y. Jan. 5, 2005); *Zerega Ave. Realty Corp. v. Hanover Ins. Co.,* No. CIV.04-9651, 2006 U.S. Dist. LEXIS 30034 (D.N.Y. May 17, 2006) (court noted there was "no record of the computer 'chat' exists to corroborate [testimony].").

If chat room discussions are relevant to your case then discovery orders to the major chat rooms, AOL and Microsoft, may prove beneficial. Conversations can also sometimes be downloaded and saved on an individual's computer. Since businesses and educational institutions are using chat rooms and instant messaging, discovery inquiries should include questions regarding the use of business owned chat rooms and storage procedures regarding these conversations.

[1]   Reported Cases

• *State v. Bouse,* 150 S.W.3d 326, 329, n.1-2 (Mo.App. W.D. 2004). "Chat rooms are online forums in which individuals are able to communicate with other people via the

Internet. A person entering a chat room is able to see the user name of every person in the online room. Messages are transmitted instantaneously and can be seen by everyone in the on-line chat room. . . . Instant messaging is a form of computer communication in which individuals hold an online conversation via the Internet. When a person sends an instant message to another person online, that message is transmitted instantaneously to the recipient, opening a window that allows both parties to see the message and to respond immediately. The window, while open, contains a complete history of all messages sent and received during the online conversation."

- *United States v. Root*, 296 F.3d 1222, n1-3 (11th Cir. 2002). At trial a law enforcement official testified that "a chat room is 'a place for people to meet on-line that have similar interests . . . where they can actually type and talk real time.' He explained that when a user logs on to AOL, he or she can select from a list of chat rooms organized by category. When a user enters a chat room, all other people in that room are advised. . . . Instant messaging permits users to exchange private e-mails in quick succession. . . . instant messages is 'like a private chat room . . . It's a message that one person sends directly to another AOL screen name, and no one else can see it.' These messages, he stated, can be sent back and forth so as to replicate a conversation."

- *Zubulake v. UBS Warburg LLC*, No. CIV.02-12432004, WL 1620866, *14 n.117 (S.D.N.Y. July 20, 2004). The Court noted that one of the defendant's document retention policies was entitled "Use of Electronic Mail, Chat and Text Messaging."

- *In re F.P.*, 2005 WL 1399264, *1 n.2 (Pa. Super. Ct. Jun. 15, 2005). The Court noted that "'[i]nstant messaging differs from e-mail in that conversations happen in realtime.' http://en.wikipedia.org. 'Generally, both parties in the conversation see each line of text right after it is typed (line-by-line), thus making it more like a telephone conversation than exchanging letters.'"

- *United States of America v. Daniel Von Loh*, 417 F.3d 710, 711-712 (7th Cir. 2005). In this criminal case where the defendant was convicted of engaging in sex with a minor the Court observed, "[the defendant] subscribed to Internet Service Providers ('ISP'), which offers computer-related communication services. ISP subscribers can communicate with other ISP subscribers through e-mail and instant messaging. Typically, a user assigns himself a screen name, by which he identifies himself to other users of the service. [The defendant] created several private accounts with ISP and used the screen names 'Dan_the_man_4u,' 'Curious_about_u,' 'Music_lover_1980,' 'Ericluvsu,' and 'Baseballstarr69.'"

- *Raytheon Co. v. John Does 1-21*, No. 99-816 (Super. Ct. Middlesex Cty., Mass. 1999). Unidentified Internet users posted confidential engineering information belonging to Raytheon in chat rooms and bulletin boards. Initially, Raytheon could not identify the Internet users because they used pseudonyms. Through subpoenas to Yahoo! and other

ISPs, Raytheon eventually identified the users through their pseudonyms, such as "Ratheonveteran," "Ditchraytheon" and "Rayman-Mass."

• *Blakey v. Continental Airlines, Inc.*, 164 N.J. 38, 59, 751 A.2d 538, 550 (N.J. 2000). In this case the plaintiff alleged her co-workers had sexually harassed her through statements in a "chatroom" set up by the employer. Court remanded case to determine "whether the [chat room] was such an integral part of the workplace that harassment on [it] should be regarded as a continuation or extension of the pattern of harassment that existed in the Continental workplace."

• *State v. Townsend*, 57 P.3d 255 (Wash. 2002). The Court discussed chat technology where the participants talk in "real-time" and whether the messages are stored for later use.

• *Quon v. Arch Wireless Operating Co., Inc.* 309 F. Supp.2d 1204 (C.D.Cal. 2004). Police officers sued the provider of the city's pager service for the unauthorized release to city officials of electronic text messages sent and received by officers.

[2]   Other Authorities

• Gregory S. McCurdy & Martha J. Dawson, *Are Instant Messages Discoverable? Is This Digital Medium More Like E-Mails or Phone Calls?*, The National Law Journal, Jun. 7, 2004, § 1, col. 2, available at http://www.prestongates.com/images/pubs/ Dawson%20NLJ.pdf (last visited on July 21, 2006).

• Charles P. Morrison, *Instant Messaging for Business: Legal Complications in Communication*, 24 J.L. & Com. 141 (Fall, 2004) (discussing business implications of IM in the workplace).

[3]   Discovery Pointers

• If you are using text or instant messaging to communicate with your client, recognize that they raise the core privileges on which attorneys regularly rely: the attorney-client privilege and the work product doctrine. If you are using these tools ensure that the privileges are not waived by inadvertent disclosure.

[D]   Newsgroups (Usenet)

Newsgroups are topic specific forums on the Internet or on local networks where people can post questions, news, comments and/or read and respond to such postings left by other users. *Parker v. Google, Inc.,* 422 F. Supp. 2d 492 (D. Pa. 2006). Newsgroup users can send messages which include text, video, audio and photographs. These informally organized discussion areas attract people from all over the world who meet and discuss various topics ranging from the arts to zoos. Usenets operate through servers which are maintained by education institutions, corporations and individuals. These newsgroups can be viewed online. For detailed information about newsgroups visit Internet Gurus - What Are Usenet Newsgroups? available at net.gurus.com/usenet; or to locate groups visit Google (www.google.com) and search under "Groups."

Newsgroup postings and comments are generally saved on a computer network and, therefore, are available for discovery. Recently, "binary" newsgroups are being used with increasing frequency. Binary newsgroups allow a user to send non-text files such as pictures, music and software applications along with the text message. These non-text files are encoded to ASCII (text) and then sent to a user who decodes the ASCII, turning it back into its original file format. For example, someone could use this method to post an image (JPG or GIF), a music file (MP3) or any type of binary (non-text) files.

[1]   Reported Cases

- *Ellison v. Robertson,* 357 F.3d 1072, 1074 (9th Cir. 2004). "A news-group is an online forum for USENET users to discuss, read about, or post messages on a particular topic. News-groups are commonly organized around a particular shared interest, such as science fiction or politics."

- *ACLU v. Reno*, 929 F. Supp. 824, 834-35 (E.D.Pa. 1996), *aff'd*, 521 U.S. 844 (1997). The Court described newsgroups:

  25. *Distributed message databases.* Similar in function to listservs - but quite different in how communications are transmitted--are distributed message databases such as "USENET newsgroups." User-sponsored newsgroups are among the most popular and widespread applications of Internet services, and cover all imaginable topics of interest to users. Like listservs, newsgroups are open discussions and exchanges on particular topics. Users, however, need not subscribe to the discussion mailing list in advance, but can instead access the database at any time. Some USENET newsgroups are "moderated" but most are open access. For the moderated newsgroups, all messages to the newsgroup are forwarded to one person who can screen them for relevance to the topics under discussion. USENET newsgroups are disseminated using ad hoc, peer to peer connections between approximately 200,000 computers (called USENET "servers") around the world. For unmoderated newsgroups, when an individual user with access to a USENET server posts a message to a newsgroup, the message is automatically forwarded to all adjacent USENET servers that furnish access to the newsgroup, and it is then propagated to the servers adjacent to those servers, etc. The messages are temporarily stored on each receiving server, where they are available for review and response by individual users. The

messages are automatically and periodically purged from each system after a time to make room for new messages. Responses to messages, like the original messages, are automatically distributed to all other computers receiving the newsgroup or forwarded to a moderator in the case of a moderated newsgroup. The dissemination of messages to USENET servers around the world is an automated process that does not require direct human intervention or review.

26. There are newsgroups on more than fifteen thousand different subjects. In 1994, approximately 70,000 messages were posted to newsgroups each day, and those messages were distributed to the approximately 190,000 computers or computer networks that participate in the USENET newsgroup system. Once the messages reach the approximately 190,000 receiving computers or computer networks, they are available to individual users of those computers or computer networks. Collectively, almost 100,000 new messages (or "articles") are posted to newsgroups each day.

• *State v. May,* 829 A.2d 1106, 1110 (N.J.Super. 2003). The Court found that "news groups . . . are Internet sites devoted to specific topics and which were described at trial as functioning '[m]uch like the bulletin board at your local supermarket.' News groups allow a person to post messages and files on a site for other persons to read, and they allow a person to read and download messages and files posted on the site by other persons."

[E]   Listserv (Mailing List)

Listserv is a discussion group, similar to newsgroups, where people exchange information about a variety of subjects. However, a listserv uses standard Internet e-mail to exchange messages. In effect, when you subscribe to a listserv, you are adding your name to a mailing list. When a user sends a message, it is automatically sent to everyone in the group or the messages can be sent in an aggregate format. There are thousands of listserv groups.

Similar to newsgroups, the postings and distribution of e-mail comments are generally saved. Comments on a listserv may be available for discovery and, sometimes, are available simply by searching the World Wide Web using a search engine such as Google (www.google.com).

[1]   Reported Case

• *ACLU v. Reno,* 929 F. Supp. 824, 834-35 (E.D.Pa. 1996), *aff'd,* 521 U.S. 844 (1997), defined listservs:

24. *One-to-many messaging.* The Internet also contains automatic mailing list services (such as "listservs"), [also referred to by witnesses as "mail exploders"]

that allow communications about particular subjects of interest to a group of people. For example, people can subscribe to a "listserv" mailing list on a particular topic of interest to them. The subscriber can submit messages on the topic to the listserv that are forwarded (via e-mail), either automatically or through a human moderator overseeing the listserv, to anyone who has subscribed to the mailing list. A recipient of such a message can reply to the message and have the reply also distributed to everyone on the mailing list. This service provides the capability to keep abreast of developments or events in a particular subject area. Most listserv-type mailing lists automatically forward all incoming messages to all mailing list subscribers. There are thousands of such mailing list services on the Internet, collectively with hundreds of thousands of subscribers. Users of "open" listservs typically can add or remove their names from the mailing list automatically, with no direct human involvement. Listservs may also be "closed," *i.e.,* only allowing for one's acceptance into the listserv by a human moderator.

- *United States v. Coreas,* 419 F.3d 151, 152 (2d Cir. 2005). "After becoming a member of [the listserv] by clicking the 'join' button on its website, Agent Binney was presented with three options for receiving e-mail from the group: (1) he could receive each e-mail automatically; (2) he could receive a digest of each day's e-mails; or (3) he could receive no automatic e-mails whatever, leaving it to his personal discretion to visit the website and determine what individual messages he wished to read and what individual files he wished to download."

[F]   Other Locations of Internet Information

[1]   Cookies

When an Internet user visits a website, a file may be automatically created and stored on the hard disk containing information about the site visited and the user. *BEA Sys. v. Web Balance, Inc.,* No. CIV. 03-11755, 2006 U.S. Dist. LEXIS 15030 (D. Mass. Mar. 31, 2006). This file is referred to as a "cookie." The cookie file contains information about the person's present and previous visits to the website and allows the website "to remember" the user. The user may not have intended to create the "cookie" file and may not know they exist. In electronic discovery, these cookies can contain important information as to Internet sites an individual visits.

[a]   Reported Cases

- *In re Double-click, Inc. Privacy Litigation,* 154 F. Supp.2d 457, 502-503 (S.D.N.Y. 2001). "Cookies are computer programs commonly used by Web sites to store useful information such as usernames, passwords, and preferences, making it easier for users to access Web pages in an efficient manner."

• *Chance v. Avenue A, Inc.,* 165 F. Supp.2d 1153, 1156 (W.D. Wash. Sept. 14, 2001). The Court stated: "[c]ookies are data files placed on a computer's hard drive by a web site, or more properly the web site's server. Cookies enable much of the information exchange that occurs on the Internet by allowing the interactions between a specific computer and a web server to develop a memory of the communications between the two parties. Many web sites use cookie technology to create a memory of such common activities as a user's login or electronic shopping. . . . Any cookie that is placed on a computer can only be read by the web site that created it or an affiliated site."

• *In re Pharmatrak, Inc. Privacy Litigation,* 220 F. Supp.2d 4 (D. Mass. 2002), *rev'd on other grounds,* 329 F.3d 9 (1st Cir. 2003). The Court described a "cookie" and that it is used to capture detailed private information about the plaintiffs, including their names, addresses, telephone numbers, dates of birth, sex, insurance status, medical conditions, education levels, occupations and e-mail content.

[b]   Other Authorities

• Alan Brill, *The Technologies of Privacy and Privacy Invasion: An Introduction,* 748 PLI/Pat 85 (June 2003). The article discusses cookies, web bugs, history files, Internet cache files and keystroke capture devices.

[2]   Internet History Logs

Users who "surf" the Web leave a trail on their computer as to which websites they visited along with other information. A hard disk stores files that detail Internet activity by the user of the computer. Generally, only the history of websites accessed from an individual's computer within a certain time period (often the three most recent weeks) may be accessed. However, Internet "access logs" may be available for longer periods of time. *Doe v. Gonzales,* 126 S. Ct. 1 (2005). For example, to show that a workplace exhibits a harassing atmosphere, an employee may rely on evidence of repeated visits to Internet sites with pornographic content by another employee. On the other hand, an employer, to show that an employee wasted time, rather than doing their job, may offer evidence detailing the employee's Internet visits to unrelated work sites. However, such logs can be erased. *United States v. Richards,* 401 F. Supp. 2d 834, 841 (D. Tenn. 2005) ("the desktop had an icon for washer.exe which runs in conjunction with Microsoft and is used to either overwrite or delete cookies and temporary internet files and to erase evidence of Internet usage."). *See also,* § 2.6[G], *Audit Trails and Logs.*

[a]   Reported Cases

• *Lynch v. Omaha World-Herald Co.,* 300 F. Supp.2d 896 (D. Neb. 2004). The Court denied the defendant's summary judgment motion for failure to give the electronic version of the firewall logs and the Web server logs to the FBI - initially stating that the web server log did not exist and then providing inaccurate header information.

[3]   Cache Files

A computer creates cache files to temporarily store information about application programs and other information, such as visits to different World Wide Web sites. These cache files store this information so that the computer can operate more efficiently since it has already stored prior information regarding the application program or website. These files are often a fertile source of discovery when Internet access and use are relevant to your case. For example, in a hostile work environment employment case, cookies, cache files or history logs may show visits by an employer to sexually offensive websites.

[a]   Reported Cases

• *United States v. Triumph Capital Group, Inc.,* 211 F.R.D. 31 n.12 (D. Conn. 2002). The Court described an Internet cache file: "Internet cache files hold the contents of Web sites that the computer has visited. These files are usually saved with a '.jpeg' or '.jpg' extension to the file name. They can contain images as well as text. They are not susceptible to keyword searches."

• *Commonwealth v. Simone*, No. CR.03-0986, 2003 WL 22994245, at *1, *3 (Cir.Ct. Virg. Nov. 12, 2003). Child pornography images were found on the "temporary Internet file of the defendant's computer cache." The expert described the process of how these images are saved in the cache file.

• *Charles E. Hill & Assocs. v. Compuserve, Inc.*, 2003 WL 22327827 (S.D. Ind. Sept. 26, 2003). The Court describes the process of the how the "cache" section of a hard drive works.

• *State v. Guthrie*, 627 N.W.2d 401, 408 (S.Dak. 2001). After the defendant's wife was found drowned in a bathtub "accident" the state's computer expert found that the defendant's computer "had been used to conduct numerous Internet searches on subjects uncannily related . . . to the drowning. [The computer had been used to] conduct specific Internet searches using an online search engine--the repeated queries were for 'household accidents' and 'bathtub accidents.'"

[4]   Firewalls

When you connect your computer to the Internet, you are exposing your data to unauthorized outside access. To avoid unauthorized access, while at the same time permitting access to employees, customers or suppliers, a firewall in usually installed. A firewall is like a funnel through which all Internet information flows and precludes access to unauthorized users. *Cobell v. Norton,* 394 F. Supp. 2d 164, n1 (D.D.C. 2005) ("The main purpose of a firewall system is to control access to or from a protected network (i.e. a site). It implements a network access policy by forcing connections to pass through the firewall, where they can be evaluated . . . The general reasoning behind firewall usage is that without a firewall, a subnet's systems expose themselves to inherently insecure services.").

It also monitors and records the transmission of information in firewall logs. For electronic discovery purposes, firewalls collect Internet related user log data that may be searched as a database. *See also,* §§ 2.6[G], *Audit Trails and Logs* and 3.5[H][3], *Firewalls and Security Servers.*

In addition, firewalls can be set up to control an employee's access to Internet resources. The firewall can monitor what sites are allowed to be accessed and the length of time on the site. Such audits are useful if an employee has engaged in unauthorized activities on the Internet.

[a]   Reported Case

* *Liggett v. Rumsfeld,* No. CIV.04-1363, 2005 U.S. Dist. LEXIS 34162, at *5-7 (D. Va. Aug. 29, 2005). After firewall logs had allegedly shown that the plaintiff accessed sexually explicit websites and sexually explicit materials were found stored on the computer's hard drive the plaintiff was suspended for 10 days. The plaintiff in response asserted that he had not accessed the pornographic websites, his password was not secure and the computer had been used by someone else before it was assigned to him.

* *United States v. Simons,* 206 F.3d 392 (4th Cir. 1999). A vendor contracted with a government agency for the management of the government's computer network, including monitoring for any inappropriate use of computer resources. The vendor employee entered the keyword "sex" into the firewall database and found a large number of Internet "hits" originating from the defendant's computer.

[5]   Web Logs (Blogs)

Web **logs** or blogs are a simple method of web publication - of posting one idea at a time with links to various other sites while retaining the personal voice of the writer. *McCabe v. Basham,* No. CIV.05-0073, 2006 U.S. Dist. LEXIS 8976, n.4 (D. Iowa Feb. 16, 2006) ("A 'blog' is 'an online personal journal with reflections, comments, and often hyperlinks provided by the writer.' Merriam-Webster's Collegiate Dictionary (11th ed. 2005)."

Their popularity is rapidly increasing in the business world because of the ease of publishing and the immediacy of posts. For electronic discovery purposes, the web content in blogs can easily and quickly change. For an example of a blog, visit the *Electronic Discovery and Evidence* blog at http://arkfeld.blogs.com/ede/.

[a]   Reported Cases

• *Nicholson v. City of Chattanooga,* No. CIV.04-168, 2005 U.S. Dist. LEXIS 42041 (D. Tenn. Oct. 17, 2005). The Court noted that the plaintiff "relies upon an unidentified and unauthenticated document purporting to be an internet 'web blog' written by one of the emergency medical professionals sent to the scene of the shooting."

• *United States v. Ameline,* 376 F.3d 967, 986 n.4 (9th Cir. 2004). In a criminal case the Court noted that a blog provided information on one of the issues in the case, "For a 'blog' on the internet cataloguing in detail recent developments relating to Blakely, *see,* 'Sentencing Law and Policy' at http://sentencing.typepad.com, a website of Professor Douglas A. Berman of the Moritz College of Law at The Ohio State University."

[b]   Other Authorities

• Paul S. Gutman, *Say What?: Blogging and Employment Law in Conflict,* 27 Colum. J.L. & Arts 145 (Fall 2003) (article explores the ramifications of employees' blogging regarding their jobs and other matters).

[6]   Spyware

Spyware is any software that covertly obtains user information, with or without an Internet connection, and without the user's knowledge. *Sotelo v. DirectRevenue, LLC,* 384 F. Supp. 2d 1219 (D. Ill. 2005). Though usually installed to gather advertising information, they have been used to monitor and record keystroke activity such as passwords or credit card numbers, scan files on the hard drive, view other programs such as chat programs or word processing documents. After gathering the information it is sent back to its developer who uses the information or sells it. This executable program is usually transmitted via freeware or shareware programs, but may also be part of regular software purchases. It has been known to lead to system crashes or general system instability.

[a] Reported Cases

- *F.T.C. v. MaxTheater, Inc.,* No. CIV.05-0069, 2005 WL 1027121, *1 (E.D. Wash. Mar. 31, 2005). "F. 'Spyware,' which includes 'adware,' is defined by the Defendants in their marketing media as including programs that 'secretly install on your computer without your permission or knowledge' and may cause 'pop ups,' banner advertisements, and other extraneous ads, send 'spam' e-mail messages, hijack search engine links or home pages, track online activity, allow others to remotely access a computer, record private information or steal passwords. It also includes 'adware, keyloggers, trojans, hijackers, dialers, viruses, spam, and general ad serving.' G. 'Anti-spyware' product' means any product, however denominated, including but not limited to 'SpywareAssassin,' that does or purports to identify, monitor, remove, block, or otherwise prevent spyware from residing on a computer."

- *O'Brien v. O'Brien,* 2005 WL 322367 (Fla. Dist. Ct. App. Feb. 11, 2005). In a divorce case, the wife was found to have illegally "intercepted" electronic communications on her husband's computer using a spyware program called "Spector." The Court found that the wife had violated the Florida Security of Communications Act and, therefore, the trial court did not abuse its discretion in ruling that this evidence was inadmissible in the divorce proceeding.

- *United States v. Ropp,* 347 F. Supp.2d 831 (C.D.Cal. 2004). The Court held that interception of keystrokes did not violate Wiretap Act. The defendant intercepted keystrokes "by installing a device, called a KeyKatcher, on the desktop computer of Karen Beck . . . Ropp placed the KeyKatcher on the cable that connects Ms. Beck's keyboard to her computer's central processing unit (CPU). As Ms. Beck composed e-mails and other messages by depressing keys on the keyboard (an act known to some of us as 'typing'), the KeyKatcher recorded and stored the electronic impulses traveling down the cable between her keyboard and the computer to which it was attached. The KeyKatcher, in this way, 'eavesdrops' on the person typing messages into the computer."

- *United States v. Scarfo,* 180 F. Supp.2d 572, 574 (D.N.J. 2001). The Court denied the defendant's motion to suppress when the FBI suspected the defendant of loansharking and illegal gambling and installed what is known as a:

  'Key Logger System' ('KLS') on the computer and/or computer keyboard in order to decipher the passphrase to the encrypted file, thereby gaining entry to the file. The KLS records the keystrokes an individual enters on a personal computer's keyboard. The government utilized the KLS in order to 'catch' Scarfo's passphrases to the encrypted file while he was entering them onto his keyboard. Scarfo's personal computer features a modem for communication over telephone lines and he possesses an America Online account. The F.B.I. obtained the passphrase to the 'Factors' file and retrieved what is alleged to be incriminating evidence.

[b]   Other Authorities

• Jason Krause, *Beware of Spyware Litigants Sometimes Resort to Computer Snooping, But it Could be a Crime,* 91 A.B.A. J. 59 (June 2005). The author noted that spyware is "[s]oftware that spies on a person's computer [and] is easy to install and very difficult to detect. One product, called Spector Pro, costs $90 and can be e-mailed to an unsuspecting target. If someone opens the e-mail and clicks on the attachment, a program will automatically download that can monitor everything done on that computer and relay the information back to the sender of the e-mail."

[7]   Wiki

Wiki is a web application which allows users to add and edit content collectively using a web browser. *English Mountain Spring Water Co. v. Chumley,* 2005 WL 2756072 (Tenn. Ct.App., October 25, 2005). ("Wikipedia . . . is a multilingual, Web-based, free-content encyclopedia. It is written collaboratively by volunteers with wiki software, meaning articles can be added or changed by nearly anyone.").

§ 3.10   DATABASE

Databases are one of the most frequently sought after and disclosed sources of electronic information. The reason is that they often hold the primary information and knowledge of a business. The Courts have held that "[e]lectronic versions of . . . databases . . . fall within the scope of FED. R. CIV. P. 26." *Super Film of America, Inc. v. UCB Films Inc.,* 219 F.R.D. 649, 661(D. Kan 2004).

An important aspect of every business is record keeping. In our information society, this has become an important aspect of business, and much of the world's computing power is dedicated to maintaining and using databases to keep track of these records. Today, most businesses keep track of their customers and manage large amounts of information about their company's business or financial records by using databases.

Databases of all kinds pervade almost every business. All kinds of data, from e-mail and contact information to financial data and records of sales, are stored in some form of a database. Databases are used to track employee information, payrolls, job classifications, retirement benefits and a host of other business related information. *Cook v. Deloitte & Touche, LLP,* No. CIV.03-3926, 2005 U.S. Dist. LEXIS 22252, at *8, 14 (D.N.Y. Sept. 30, 2005) (database contained a file for each employee "reflecting each telephone call or letter between [employer] and the employee, including notes summarizing the substance of the contact . . . [and a database] describing vacant positions."). Other databases hold information about customers, production, employee performance, internal processes, etc.

Evidentiary issues arise since "database information is constantly changing, being updated and being linked together from multiple sources. On top of that, information is constantly changing in ways that make it hard to know what's authentic." Jason Krause, *The Paperless Chase, Litigators and Courts Wrestle with Database Discovery,* 91 A.B.A. J. 49 (April 2005).

In addition, these same databases can be linked to a website for a dynamic exchange of information with the Web user.

The first basic concept to understand about databases is that they are merely a collection of data. For example, the first name of a business customer may be stored in a database field. This by itself is meaningless; however, if you combine the first name field with the last name field and customer's location, this might disclose information which may be useful to the business or to your case. A database application simply translates and organizes data into information. Databases are able to store large amounts of data and range from a simple, yet powerful, database program like Microsoft Access to large programs like Oracle.

A company's database may be located in one place, or may be distributed. A distributed database is one that is located somewhere other than where the users are. It is connected to them through communication lines. For example, sales figures for a chain of discount stores might be located in computers at the various stores, but the data would also be available to executives in regional offices or corporate headquarters. The Court in *In re Telxon Corp. Securities Litigation,* No. CIV.98-2876, 2004 WL 3192729, at *16 (N.D. Ohio Jul. 16, 2004) noted the difficulty of providing one correct version of a database for discovery and observed that, "PWC stored data on two main databases: a central archive server ('archive') and various local servers. In addition, persons working on an audit might download portions of a database onto the hard drive of their laptop computers. Proper procedure called for periodically uploading work done on a database from a laptop to the local server to the archive, thus ensuring that all work was saved eventually to the archive. That was not always done, however. For this reason, differing versions of a database might be found in a laptop, the local server, and the archive."

[A]   Description

In computer terminology, a database is simply a collection of mutually related data or information stored in computer record fields. *N.A.A.C.P. v. Acusport Corp.* 210 F.R.D., 268, 278-279 (E.D.N.Y. Sept. 18, 2002) (case provides extensive discussion of the different components of a database). A database is similar to a common address book. You enter last names in your address book. Then, when you need to locate a person by their last name, you go to the section that begins with the first letter of their last name. This is the same for a database, where you would put the last name of a person in the LAST NAME database field and then conduct an electronic search to locate the name of the person for whom you are looking.

A database management system (DBMS) is a set of features that lets you manage the data within the database. This generally includes the ability to select records, delete, add, sort and so forth. A database administrator is charged with managing the organization's data resources, a job that often includes database planning, design, operational training, user support, security and maintenance.

Computerized database management systems are the single largest repositories of electronic data desired for electronic discovery. Though there are several types of database management systems, relational, flat-file, etc., most databases used in business today are relational. This includes large systems such as Oracle, SQL Server, DB2 and the smaller systems like Access and Paradox. Relational databases are used in many kinds of application systems. A few of these are financial, personnel, engineering, project management, scheduling, contract and manufacturing management.

[B]   Components of a Database File

Tables

Databases are based on tables. Tables contain rows and columns and form the underlying foundation of all databases. These tables contain the structured information that comprises a database. There can be one or multiple tables for a single database.

Tables are broken up into rows and columns. Each row represents a database record. Each column contains the mutually related data from different records. Each item or cell in the row is called a "field." A field is a "single item" of information. The following flat file database table contains 3 rows and 5 columns. The table would contain 50 rows or records if the company had 50 employees.

First Name	Last Name	Dept.	Position	Pay Grade
Bill	Smith	Finance	Auditor	GSA 17
Mary	Ford	IT	Director	GSA 11
Frank	Gallo	IT	Technician	GSA 16

Field

A field is where specific information is entered and stored. All of us have had the task of completing paper forms that request specific information. For example, a request for your last name would be included on a driver's license application form. In a database, the location for your last name is labeled a "field." After you enter information into this field area, you can search the field for a specific last name(s) and retrieve these records for onscreen or printed reports. There can be one or many fields in a database.

Field Properties

Most software programs provide the capability to limit and define what information can be entered into a specific field in a computer form. These are called field properties, definitions, or elements, depending upon the program. They control the entry of information into the field. Some forensic specialists refer to this limiting function as database "metadata." Field properties are important because they filter or limit what data can be entered into a field.

The following are examples of field properties that define what information can be entered into a particular field on a computer form.

Data Type: One attribute that may be definable for a field is the Data Type. Some of the data types that one can define a field to accept are alpha/numeric (A1000-A0010), numeric numbers (003, 056), numeric range (34-56), dates (09/02/89, 3/13/77, 4/2/90), real numbers with a decimal point (23.09), text (Smith sold 10,000 widgets to ABC Company), notes (some programs limit the amount of text), time (defined by hours, minutes, and AM or PM) or dollar amounts ($20.00).

Data Entry Width: For each field that you create, one can also decide the data width of the field. The data width is the number of characters or lines that can be assigned for a particular field. In some programs, the maximum data width depends on the data type. For the data type DATE, the maximum length is 8 characters in some programs - so 04/10/89 as a date is permissible.

Unique Values or No Duplicates Allowed: A third field property that is generally available is the capability to provide unique values to data. This prevents duplicates from being entered into particular fields in a form. For example, if one defines a field labeled "social security number" to only accept unique values, then no duplicate Social Security number can be inserted in that specific field.

Validation Codes: Validation codes set rules, such as the spelling of a state or last names, to a field. The importance of this field property is that the data entered will be consistent for sorting and reports. For example, many databases have field validation rules for the field labeled "State." For example, if you try to enter the word "Arizzona," for the state name, it will not accept it until you spell it correctly.

Required Field: Another property of a field that one may be permitted to assign is required entry in a field. Essentially, this means that you are required to enter data into this field. Otherwise, the computer will not save the record. For example, one could require that the "last name" field always be filled in before a database form can be saved as a record.

Form

A computer form is the data entry screen that contains a collection of fields. Each name or label on the form is a field. The collection of these fields makes up a computer form. After each field name or label, information relating to that field can be entered. Once entered, the data is stored in a cell in the underlying table. The form is the interface between the table and the data entry. For example, when a database is created in Microsoft Access, a common field could be "Last Name." This field is a cell in the table. This same field could also be placed on other forms for data entry purposes. When data is entered on this form or another form, the data is actually being inserted into the underlying common table or a relational table for storage.

Record

A record is a filled-in form. Before any information is added, the screen is called a form. Once information is entered and saved into a field, the form is then called a record.

[C]   Flat-file and Relational Databases

Flat File

A flat file database (sometimes referred to as a file manager) enables you to create data files and retrieve data from those files, but only one table or file at a time. A file manager can be used to create a mailing list, a customer list, inventory list, a list of your personal friends and so on. You can later update them, delete information, or rearrange the order of the records. A file manager also allows you to search and extract information from files, display the information and generate printed reports.

Flat-file databases consist of only one table. A table is divided into rows and columns. This table cannot be "related" to other database tables.

Relational

For more complex sets of data, a database may consist of many different tables such as in a relational database. The Court in *Business Objects, S.A. v. Microstrategy, Inc.,* 393 F.3d 1366, 1367 (Fed. Cir. 2005) in an extensive discussion of relational databases explained that, "[a] relational database is a computerized compilation of data organized into tables, each table having columns (attributes), with column headings, and rows of information. Tables that share at least one attribute in common are 'related.' Tables without a common attribute may still be related via other tables with which they do share a common attribute. The pathways relating those separate tables to each other are called 'joins.' Once tables have been related by a join, a user may combine or correlate the information in the joined tables to derive new useful information."

As noted, a relational database stores information in a collection of tables, each table storing information about one subject. These tables can be "related" for business or other informational purposes. For example, if you have a race discrimination case, you may want to combine information from a personnel database table with a job database table to create a report showing which individuals, based on race, etc., have particular jobs. The two tables must share a similar field of information, such as a social security number or employee ID, but otherwise can maintain unique data. The social security number or employee ID field creates a relation between the two tables, thus forming a relational database.

In generating reports, a relational database matches information from a field in one table with information in a corresponding field of another table to produce a third table that combines requested data from both tables. For example, if one table contains the fields EMPLOYEE-ID, LAST-NAME, FIRST-NAME and HIRE-DATE, and another table contains the fields DEPT, EMPLOYEE-ID and SALARY, a relational database can match the EMPLOYEE-ID fields in the two tables to find information as to the names of all employees earning a certain salary or employees hired after a certain date within different departments. In other words, a relational database uses matching values in two or more tables to relate information from one table to the other table.

Key Fields

As noted, each table consists of a number of rows, each of which corresponds to a single database record. In a relational database, data in several tables is related through the use of a common key field. The key field is a unique field used to identify a record. Databases keep all of these records straight through the use of keys.

Every database table may have one or more columns designated as the primary key. The value this key holds is usually unique for each record in the database. The database will enforce the uniqueness of the key and if you try to insert a record into a table with a primary key that duplicates an existing record, the insert will fail.

A relational database stores information in a collection of tables - each table storing information about one subject. For example, you may want to combine information from a Pay Grade table with an Employee table to create a report showing the hire date of the clerk with the pay grade of the employee. The two tables share one type of information in this case, employee ID number, but otherwise maintain unique data. This type of requested database discovery report would show the disparity of wages for a female clerk hired during the same time period as her male co-workers, yet her pay grade for the same position is substantially lower.

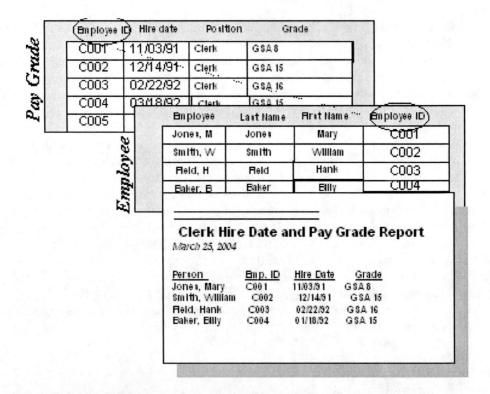

[D]   Metadata and Data Dictionary

A database generally has a data dictionary. A data dictionary stores the metadata or data definitions and descriptions of database structure. It generally will contain the names and descriptions of every data element in the database and how data elements relate to each other. The data dictionary may also contain information about the types of data or metadata, including information about application programs, business processes, data flows, business controls, computer jobs, and business procedures.

Generally, the field properties of a database are considered "metadata." To discover this metadata, request copies of operating instructions, user manuals, database design manual and any other information that will disclose the database field properties.

[1]   Reported Cases

- *Williams v. Sprint/United Mgmt. Co.,* 230 F.R.D. 640, 647 (D. Kan. 2005). "It is important to note that metadata varies with different applications. . . . At the other end of the spectrum is a database application where the database is a completely undifferentiated mass of tables of data. The metadata is the key to showing the relationships between the data; without such metadata, the tables of data would have little meaning."

- *N.A.A.C.P. v. Acusport Corp.,* 210 F.R.D. 268, 280 (E.D.N.Y. 2002). After an extensive discussion of databases, the Court affirmed the discovery of data dictionaries and discussed the metadata contained in the dictionaries. The Court stated, "BATF has produced two annotated data dictionaries that identify what data is contained in its databases and how it is arranged. *Data dictionaries are repositories of metadata, or information about data, such as its meaning, relationships to other data, origin, usage and format.* Two dictionaries were necessary because, as indicated before, the FTS and FLS are separate databases maintained on separate servers." (emphasis added).

- *In re Telxon Corp. Securities Litigation,* No. CIV.98-2876, 2004 WL 3192729 (N.D. Ohio Jul. 16, 2004). In this securities action the magistrate judge recommended that the motion for sanctions be granted and that default judgment be entered for the plaintiff primarily for discovery abuses involved with the disclosure of databases. The Court discussed the "metadata" available in the database:

> The program allows users to link documents, and the program tags each document with data about the document's history. These "metadata" include the author of the document, the dates and authors of modifications of the document, when and by whom a document was reviewed, and when the document was last accessed. A hard copy of a document might give one person as the last individual to modify a document and the date of that modification while the metadata attached to the document might give an entirely different person and date for a later modification because the later modifier did not record the later modification on the document itself. Each document is also assigned a numerical code which, inter alia, encodes what type of document it is (e.g., "control," "assets," "liabilities and capital," etc.).

[E] Searching and Reports

Many databases can be copied and produced in their entirety to the opposing party. However, a database generally contains too much information to make direct data access practical. Then a party will query and provide a report of the various relevant database portions in a format the opposing party can use.

One of the features that make database management system software (DBMS) so useful is the ability to retrieve just the information for which you are looking. This process is known as querying the database. One uses a report generator to make a query that causes the database engine to extract and condense only the information of interest, and present information in a readable report. To query a database you issue commands in a special query language.

The Court in *Business Objects, S.A. v. Microstrategy, Inc.,* 393 F.3d 1366, 1367 (Fed. Cir. 2005) discussed the querying process in a patent infringement case:

> Users' access and correlate information in relational databases only by use of a relational database management system (RDBMS), which consists of hardware and software. To access such information, a user sends queries to the RDBMS, which executes the queries and retrieves the requested information from the tables in the relational database. A RDBMS, however, only recognizes queries written in complex "query languages." The most common query language is Structured Query Language (SQL).

> A proper query in these languages consists of one or more "clauses." Common types of clauses are SELECT, WHERE, FROM, HAVING, ORDER BY, and GROUP BY clauses. Thus, to compose a proper inquiry, a user must understand the structure and content of the relational database as well as the complex syntax of the specific query language. These complexities generally prevent laypersons from drafting queries in query languages.

A query language is a set of commands for creating, updating, and accessing data from a database. Query languages allow forensic specialists and other users to ask ad hoc questions of the database interactively without the aid of programmers. One form of query language is SQL, or structured query language. Most large-scale databases use the Structured Query Language (SQL) to define all user and administrator interactions. There are a large number of graphical user interfaces (GUIs) that simplify SQL database searches and reports. Some familiar query language is less then "<," greater than ">," equal to "=" and so on. From these searches data reports are generated. *See also,* § 5.4[E][5], *Keyword Searching.*

Queries and reports must be customized for each specific data request. They do not exist unless they are "programmed." This means that a new request for specific output from a relational database may require the development of forms for queries and reports. These queries can be ordered by the Court. In *Jinks-Umstead v. England,* 227 F.R.D. 143, 148 (D.D.C. 2005), the Court held that while the defendant had "produced all existing hard copies of reports that were generated from the FIS database, that database still contains information relevant to the workload and staffing . . . the court also understands that this information can be retrieved if data queries are formulated and entered into the system . . . the [defendant] must formulate queries and recover FIS data relevant to the workload at the EFACHES field offices from January 1, 1997 through October 1, 1999, and defendant must produce this information to plaintiff."

The DBMS software lets you generate printed reports containing the results of your queries. You must generally specify the format you want the report to take -- its title, its column headings and which fields will be included. Most databases use a series of report generator screens to guide one through this process.

A data report may look like (or even be) a Web page, set of Web pages or a spreadsheet. The report might be exported to a spreadsheet to allow the user to manipulate the data so that it has more meaning. Database engines (as the applications that handle databases are called) routinely handle thousands, tens of thousands or even hundreds of thousands of records efficiently. SABRE, the widely used airline reservation system, has millions of records.

[F]   Reported Cases

Underlying System and Accessible

- *Dunn v. Midwestern Indem.*, 88 F.R.D. 191, 194 (D.C. Ohio 1980). "In many instances it will be essential for the discovering party to know the underlying theory and the procedures employed in preparing and storing machine-readable records. When this is true, litigants should be allowed to discover any materials relating to the record holder's computer hardware, the programming techniques employed in connection with the relevant data, the principles governing the structure of the stored data, and the operation of the data processing system. When statistical analyses have been developed from more traditional records with the assistance of computer techniques, the underlying data used to compose the statistical computer input, the methods used to select, categorize, and evaluate the data for analysis, and all of the computer outputs normally are proper subjects for discovery."

- In *Fautek v. Montgomery Ward & Co.*, 96 F.R.D. 141 (N.D. Ill. 1982). The defendants were ordered to produce the coding information necessary to understand the computerized information.

- *Quinby v. WestLB AG*, No. CIV.04-7406, 2005 U.S. Dist. LEXIS 35583, n.3 (D.N.Y. Dec. 15, 2005), *aff.,* 2006 U.S. Dist. LEXIS 1178 (D.N.Y. Jan. 11, 2006). The Court found that active databases are considered "accessible" and stated, "[t]he Lotus Notes Database is an active, on-line database. Such a storage device was described in *Zubulake:* On-line storage is generally provided by magnetic disk. It is used in the very active stages of an electronic records['] life -- when it is being created or received and processed, as well as when the access frequency is high and the required speed of access is very fast, i.e., milliseconds. Examples of online data include hard drives."

Discovery Requests

- *Ex Parte Wal-Mart, Inc.*, 809 So. 2d 818, 819 (Ala. 2001). The Plaintiff sought discovery of Wal-mart's database containing of "all customer incident reports and employee accident review forms." The Appellate Court limited the search to *falling merchandise incidents only* with geographic and temporal limits.

- *Cummings v. General Motors Corp.* 365 F.3d 944, 954 (10th Cir. 2004). In this personal injury action the Court held that "we find no abuse of discretion in the denial of the motion to compel access to GM's databases and the grant of a protective order to GM. As noted by the magistrate judge, 'Plaintiffs' proposed computer database searches are overly broad in scope, duplicative of prior requests and unduly burdensome."

- *Demelash v. Ross Stores, Inc.,* 20 P.3d 447 (Wash. Ct. App. 2001). In a false shoplifting arrest, the court allowed discovery of a computerized summary of the store's database files.

- *Ayers v. SGS Control Servs.,* No. CIV. 03-9078, 2006 U.S. Dist. LEXIS 17591, at *5-8 (D.N.Y. Apr. 3, 2006). The defendants objected to providing the payroll and timekeeping records in an electronic format, though available in this format, since they had already been produced in a paper format. The Court rejected defendant's argument and held that to require the plaintiff to create there own database would be "'burdensome, time consuming, and expensive' and that since '[t]his Court is charged with securing the 'just, speedy, and inexpensive determination of every action . . . ' that the defendants will produce the records in an electronic format.'"

- *Itzenson v. Hartford Life and Accident Ins. Co.*, 2000 WL 1507422 (E.D.Pa. Oct. 10, 2000). The Court noted that "[i]t is difficult to believe that in the computer era" that the defendant could not search and retrieve files based on specific claims categories.

- *In re Ford Motor Company,* 345 F.3d 1315 (11th Cir. 2003). The plaintiff alleged that the seatbelt buckle was defectively designed and sought access to Ford's database to conduct searches for other claims relating to unlatching seatbelt buckles. The Appellate Court reversed trial court's granting unlimited access to the database on the grounds that Ford must first have an opportunity to object to retrieved evidence.

- *In re Lowe's Companies Inc.*, 134 S.W.3d 876, 879-880 (Tex. App. 2004). The Appeals Court reversed the trial court's order providing the plaintiff with full access to Lowe's database concerning "falling merchandise" claims. The Court found that the discovery request was without limits as to time, place, or subject matter.

Types of Databases

- *Air Prods. & Chem., Inc. v. Inter-Chemical Ltd.,* No. CIV.03-6140, 2003 WL 22917491 (E.D.Pa. Dec. 2, 2003). The plaintiff was seeking, "[t]he names of each costumer and prospective costumer for Surfynol® 104 [that] is maintained on the following Air Products' databases (the 'Databases'): (1) Sales Account Management Database; (2) Current Pricing Database; (3) Leads Tracking Database; (4) Power Play Database; and the Contact Report Database."

- *Lyondell-Citgo Refinfing, LP. v. Petroleos De Venezuela, S.A.,* No. CIV.02-0795, 2005 WL 356808, at *1 (S.D.N.Y. Feb. 15, 2005). The Court required disclosure of "plaintiff's counsel Board of Director minutes and related Board documents, in hard copy and electronic database, for the period January 1, 1998 to December 31, 2002."

Sanctions

- *Jinks-Umstead v. England,* No. CIV.99-2691, 2005 U.S. Dist. LEXIS 22291 (D.D.C. Oct. 4, 2005). The plaintiff sought sanctions for failure to preserve workload reports produced from a database that provided justification for an employment decision that resulted in a reduction in force. The Court ruled against any sanctions and stated that even though the reports were not available that the underlying data was and the plaintiff would be provided access to query the database.

- *In re Telxon Corp. Securities Litigation,* No. CIV.98-2876, 2004 WL 3192729, at *16 (N.D. Ohio Jul. 16, 2004). After an extended discussion in a securities action the magistrate judge recommended that the motion for sanctions be granted and that default judgment be entered for the plaintiff primarily for discovery abuses involved with the disclosure of databases.

- *Tulip Computers Inter. B. V. v. Dell Computer Corp.,* 52 Fed. R. Serv. 3d 1420 (D. Del. 2002). Dell Computer stated it did not have the ability to search its own database for requested case information. The plaintiff's computer forensic database experts were then allowed access to the database and discovered that they could perform searches on the database and also learned that Dell could have performed the same searches.

Form of Disclosure

- *Procter & Gamble Co. v. Haugen,* 427 F.3d 727 (10th Cir. 2005). The plaintiff's expert obtained data from a third party marketing database for use in their opinions to establish damages. On discussing alternatives to access the marketing data the court found that providing defendants with regular online access to the information would not necessarily have satisfied defendants' discovery request because of the "rolling" nature of the marketing database, i.e., data in the database was added and deleted on a continuous basis. The defendants were interested in obtaining a concrete set of marketing related data (i.e., a set of data with established beginning and ending dates) rather than access to the rolling database. The Appellate Court discussed the dynamic nature of databases and the various alternatives to obtaining the data including using Rule 45 to subpoena information directly from the third-party data provider.

• *Adams v. Dan River Mills, Inc.,* 54 F.R.D. 220 (W.D. Va. 1972). The plaintiff filed discovery seeking the defendant's computerized master payroll file along with computer printouts for W-2 forms of the defendant's employees. The defendant objected, arguing that they had already produced hardcopy printouts of the information that the plaintiff was seeking. However, the plaintiff persuaded the Court that obtaining the computer data would be the least expensive and a more accurate method of preparing the underlying data for the statistical analysis.

• *Satchell v. FedEx Corp.,* No. CIV.03-02659, 2005 WL 646058, at *3 (N.D.Cal. Mar. 21, 2005). The Court held that "electronic data [in databases] produced for class discovery purposes is not an adequate substitute for the personnel records of comparators and other discovery sought."

• *Overseas Private Investment Corporation v. Mandelbaum,* No. CIV.97-1138, 1998 WL 647208 (D.D.C. Aug. 19, 1998). This case involved a breach of contract action between two companies. The Court required the disclosure of e-mail in a database format. The Court opinion set out a database report format, including a list of database fields, for the e-mail in dispute. Included fields were a summary of the e-mail, date, author, recipient and others copied.

• *Donaldson v. Pillsbury Co.,* 554 F.2d 825, 832 (8th Cir. 1977). The Court held that "[d]ata in computer-readable form is more easily subjected to analysis."

[G]   Other Authorities (reserved)

[H]   Discovery Pointers

• In many database programs database records that are "deleted" are not actually deleted. These database records may not be deleted until the database is "packed." In requesting information from database programs, request the "prepacked" version of the database program.

• For electronic discovery purposes it is important to recognize that data is contained in one or multiple database tables. The way to extract and view information in a comprehensive manner is to use a report generator and SQL to extract data from the different rows and columns of the different table to create a customized report. The level of complexity and difficulty will vary depending on the intricacies of the database. Remember that a database is generally only a repository of data, it may require additional third party tools to extract data for your discovery needs.

- Until an expert is able to view a database, it is difficult to predict whether the search for your data will be simple or complex. A competent database forensic expert can prove invaluable during this time.

- When discovering database information, be specific in what you are requesting. If your request is overbroad as it pertains to the facts and issues in your case the opposing party will likely be filing a burdensome objection. If you are producing a database report try to narrow the request to minimize the "programming" time to prepare the report.

- If the opposing party provides only the raw data, it will appear as a long list of undefined numbers and text. To organize the data it is necessary to have it reported to you in a structure with labels, columns and other information. These customized reports will prevent the need to discover the entire database.

- Determine if the database is a flat file or relational database.

- Determine the size of the database. How many records are contained within the database?

- Determine if a data dictionary is available. This may disclose the content of the database, fields, business procedures, query forms, report structure, and other metadata. If a data dictionary is not available, consider an onsite inspection with your expert to understand the nature of and complexity of the database.

- Determine if you wish to get a copy of the entire database. Many times databases can be outputted in a comma-delimited format and then it can be imported into Microsoft Excel or other software for analysis. However, a database may be too large and complex to import into another software program so after a properly structured query a smaller database subset can be used for analysis.

- Determine the best report format for the information you need and whether it should be a paper printout or an electronic copy or subset of the database. Paper printouts usually are too large to analyze efficiently.

- Determine whether it would be best for you and your expert to have an onsite inspection to query the database and obtain the results through the opposing party's personnel.

§ 3.11   SPREADSHEETS

[A]   Generally

Spreadsheets can be used in a variety of business functions, and oftentimes used by individuals to keep their financial and other records. Spreadsheets have long been used in business and are of interest for electronic discovery because of their content. Calculations and mathematical analyses, mailing lists, to-do lists, attendance rosters, invoices, real estate closing statement calculations, truth in lending statements and mortgage payments, loan calculations and amortization schedules are a few of the uses of spreadsheets.

In business they may be the output of a single user or many users in a work group. In addition, they may be used as a data repository or a formatted report from a financial or transactional database. Spreadsheets differ substantially from their paper version in that electronic versions reveal the formulae of their computations. Printed spreadsheets may not display certain "hidden" columns, rows or cells of data. They also may reveal links to the underlying raw data. As noted in *Public Citizen v. Carlin,* 2 F. Supp.2d 1, 14 (D.D.C. 1997), "paper print-outs of computer spreadsheets only display the results of calculations made on the spreadsheet, while the actual electronic version of the spreadsheet will show the formula used to make the calculations." In a leading decision, the Court in *Williams v. Sprint/United Mgmt. Co.,* 230 F.R.D. 640 (D. Kan. 2005) ordered an employer in an employment discrimination case to restore the metadata it had "scrubbed" or "erased" from Excel spreadsheet files and "unlock" them.

Spreadsheet application programs are able to perform simple and complex mathematical calculations automatically. The data is generally arranged in a table of numbers in rows and columns. In most spreadsheet programs, columns are designated by letters and rows are designated by numbers. The intersection of the row and column is called a cell. Each cell is identified by a unique cell address composed of the row and column designation. A value, such as a number, is inserted into a cell. Each value can have a predefined relationship to the other values. If you change one value, the other values may automatically change as well.

Different types of data can be entered into the active cell such as a *value, label, formula* or a *function.* A *value* is a number. Numbers can be entered such as "2," and the formatting for that number, such as a dollar sign, can be programmed to be inserted automatically. A *label* is any descriptive text placed in a cell. A *formula* is an expression that defines how one cell relates to other cells. A *formula* includes one or more mathematical operators to indicate the computations to be performed in the cell. It may include operators for addition, subtraction, multiplication, division and other mathematical formulas.

Spreadsheet packages have text, data formatting, and charting capabilities. For discovery purposes it is important to remember that there can be different worksheets within the same spreadsheet.

[B]   Metadata

If you receive a printed copy or image printout of a spreadsheet, hidden formulas and formatting coding are unavailable. One should always request original spreadsheet data files. The following metadata is then available:

- Calculations or formulas are not visible in a printout version (only the result of the calculation is visible);
- Hidden cells, columns, rows and post-it style comments;
- Hidden worksheets;
- Hidden formulas; and
- Display of all blank rows and columns.

In addition, other metadata about a spreadsheet that is not normally visible when the document is printed may include file editing history such as:

- Comments (text, audio or video);
- Name of the person who created the document;
- Date and time it was created;
- How many times it has been edited:
- Name of the last person to edit the document; and
- Date and time of the last revision.

Finally, this metadata may assist in explaining why changes were made, or provide critical foundation evidence to authenticate the document.

[C]   Reported Cases

- *Williams v. Sprint/United Mgmt. Co.,* 230 F.R.D. 640, 642-643 (D. Kan. 2005). The Court ordered an employer in an employment discrimination case to restore the metadata it had "scrubbed" or "erased" from Excel spreadsheet files and "unlock" them. The plaintiff argued that the "reason for requesting that the spreadsheets be produced in their electronic form was [to enable them to] perform 'statistical or manipulative things without taking the spreadsheets and going through the laborious process of keying in all that data again.'"

- *McDowell v. Gov't. of the Dist. of Columbia,* 233 F.R.D. 192, 198 (D.D.C. 2006). The plaintiff was forced to hire her own "IT consultant to reformat the spreadsheets (mainly by reformatting the date fields and omitting certain charge data so each record would be on just one line) so the spreadsheets could be sorted into chronological order."

- *In re Natural Gas Commodity Litig.,* No. CIV.03-6186, 2005 U.S. Dist. LEXIS 27470, at *64-67 (D.N.Y. Nov. 14, 2005). In this securities fraud action the Court noted that the defendants "has already produced both redacted and unredacted spreadsheets to the government in connection with criminal proceedings . . . [this shows that this information can be produced] in electronic format and still redact information . . . Moreover, . . . the parties 'learned that McGraw-Hill has an outside document management firm that would oversee this [document] production, and thus this would not impinge on the newsgathering responsibilities of [a defendant's] employees.'"

- *Simon Property Group L.P. v. mySimon, Inc.,* 194 F.R.D. 639 (S.D. Ind. 2000). Spreadsheets are discoverable. *See also, Super Film of America, Inc. v. UCB Films Inc.,* 219 F.R.D. 649, 657 (D. Kan 2004).

- *Lyondell-Citgo Refinfing, LP. v. Petroleos De Venezuela*, S.A., No. CIV.02-0795, 2005 WL 356808, at *1 (S.D.N.Y. Feb. 15, 2005). Court required disclosure of "sales summary spreadsheet(s), [and] defendants shall produce to plaintiff both a hard copy and an electronic copy of such document(s)." *See also, Pamlab, L.L.C. v. Rite Aid Corp.,* No. CIV.04-1115, 2005 WL 1400407 (E.D.La. Jun. 8, 2005) where the Court required production of both an electronic and hard copy of spreadsheets.

- *Eolas Technologies Inc. v. Microsoft Corp.*, NO. CIV.99C0626, 2002 WL 31375531 at *27 (N.D. Ill. Oct. 18, 2002). The Court granted plaintiff's discovery request for "garden-variety spreadsheet summary data regarding licenses, revenue and profitability of accused server versions of Windows 2000 and Windows NT 4.0 operating system software with Internet Explorer."

- *James v. City of Dallas,* No. CIV.98-436, 2003 WL 22342799, at *4 (N.D.Tex. Aug. 28, 2003). The Court in entering an injunction against the City of Dallas noted that when,

    a statistician testifying as an expert for the City, examined the [spreadsheet] tables summarizing the Class member demolition and notice data [he] located several instances of "plugged values", i.e., cells in the spreadsheet in which the data appears to have been manually inserted rather than resulting from a calculation pursuant to a mathematical formula. Plaintiffs' stipulated that the summary tables do contain several such plugged values; Warren located approximately one dozen such instances. The Court finds Warren's testimony credible. However, given the thousands of cells in the spreadsheets, and the likelihood of gaps in any data set of such size and complexity, the one dozen instances of demonstrated plugged values does not materially lessen the credibility or reliability of the summaries prepared by Plaintiffs. Moreover, the original source for Plaintiffs' data was the files of the City.

- *Reich v. Haemonetics Corp.,* 907 F. Supp. 512, 514 (D. Mass. 1995). The Court in discussing the spreadsheet evidence observed, "[t]he basic structure of a sales transaction is as follows: the sales representative (whose status under the FLSA is not at issue in this case) negotiates mutually-agreeable terms for a sale with a potential customer, then enters this information into a computerized spreadsheet. The sales representative then sends this spreadsheet to a Business Analyst via electronic mail ('e-mail'). When the Business Analyst opens the e-mail, he or she 'unlocks' a second page of the spreadsheet by using a password. The sales representative does not have access to the second page of the spreadsheet. Information on the second page of the spreadsheet includes the company's target gross margin for each product, the target revenue for each product, and the difference between the actual and target margins and revenues."

§ 3.12 TEXT DOCUMENTS (WORD PROCESSING)

[A] Generally

Most businesses and individuals use word processors. They are a fruitful source of discovery since they may include edit, control and version histories not found on paper copies of the same documents. They can be easily searched with full-text search software and generally can be reviewed in less time than paper copies. Along with spreadsheets, they are among the easiest formats to identify, copy and produce from desktops, disks, pen drives, servers and backup tapes.

Text documents are generally created and revised in word processing application programs. Word processors can edit documents by deleting and inserting words. Depending on the program, word processors can usually display on the computer screen how they will look in printed form. Some programs incorporate graphics created with another program, correctly align mathematical formulae, create and print form letters, perform calculations, display documents in multiple onscreen windows and enable users to record macros that simplify difficult or repetitive operations.

The two most popular word processors are Microsoft Word (www.microsoft.com) and WordPerfect (www.corel.com).

When discovering word processing document files, the following features may be important and generally do not appear on a printed version of a document:

Backup or Temporary Copies. Most word processing programs make automatic backup copies of the last revisions of a document, and in some cases, temporary copies of files from a floppy or other portable storage media. Oftentimes the user is unaware that the software is automatically saving another copy in case of power failure or something else that may corrupt the primary document. On most networks, these file copies are saved to a user's hard drive as opposed to the network server. As a result, backup copies continue to reside on the user's hard drive even after the document or file is deleted from the network server.

Revisions. The revision feature will show where text or graphics have been added, deleted or moved. The recipients of documents can comment on, change, or add to the document and you can view those alterations. Changes by various authors can be tracked to show who made the requested changes. In addition, documents routed to other parties can be protected from permanent change until final decisions are made. Reviewers can add annotations without changing the content of the documents. The history of these revisions may be available in the "metadata" of the text document. *See below*, § 3.12[B], *Metadata*.

Macro. A macro is a recorded series of commands, mouse clicks or keystrokes that "playback" within a word processor, spreadsheet or other application automating repetitive tasks. They can connect the word processor to other applications, such as a case or document management system and database program. Macros can be created to insert headings, data from a different program, signatures, formatting and a host of other repetitive tasks. For example, you may wish to discover whether letters were sent to customers and the content of these letters. These letters may have been linked with a customer database and the names automatically inserted, along with text, by using a macro.

Formatting. Within word processors, formatting text means changing the font, size, spacing and other character attributes.

Templates. A template is a blueprint for your routine documents. It can contain the fonts, formatting, AutoText entries, AutoCorrect entries, styles and macros for the specific document of your choice. It can also be linked directly to a database to retrieve data important to the document. For example, you could have a customer template document that would automatically fill out the customer's information, terms, etc. and format it onto your stationary.

Mail Merge. The "mail merge" feature enables you not only to merge names and addresses, but any other data into any document of your choice.

[B]   Metadata

Generally, word processing programs store and save a large amount of metadata that is not visible to the user. This is usually accomplished through special file saving features of the word processing software. For example, if a critical document is important, it may be important to know the creator of the document, the date and time of creation, the last person to edit the document, and the date and time of the last edits. This information may be crucial in constructing the history of the document.

One commentator noted, "[d]rafts and redrafts of electronic documents can oftentimes be discovered. Both Microsoft Word and WordPerfect have features that allow prior drafts of word processing documents to be recovered and viewed. Evidence that would have been impossible or extremely difficult to obtain can now become part of the truth-seeking process. Drafts of documents that were routinely lost or destroyed in the conventional paper-based world are now retrievable." Gregory S. Johnson, *A Practitioner's Overview of Digital Discovery,* 33 Gonz. L. Rev. 347, 360 (1998).

The following metadata may be available:

- Document summary;
- Mini-profile of the document;
- Identity of the author;
- Filename;
- Creation date and time;
- Access and modification time and date;
- Pathname;
- File size;
- Names of the persons who accessed, viewed, edited or printed the document;
- Revisions and dates - deletions, amendments and additions;
- Hidden text;
- Whether it was printed;
- When, where, and how long a user was on the system;
- Hidden codes - indentation of a paragraph, font changes, return at the end of line, etc.;
- Custom fields created by the author;
- Company or organization's name;
- Name of the computer that created the document;
- Comments and notations typed directly into the document; and
- Hidden text such as track changes (e.g., prior and redlined versions of the document).

[C]   Reported Cases

- *Williams v. Sprint/United Mgmt. Co.,* 230 F.R.D. 640, 646 (D. Kan. 2005). The Court noted "[m]etadata . . . is defined as 'information describing the history, tracking, or management of an electronic document.'. . . Some examples of metadata for electronic documents include: a file's name, a file's location (e.g., directory structure or pathname), file format or file type, file size, file dates (e.g., creation date, date of last data modification, date of last data access, and date of last metadata modification), and file permissions (e.g., who can read the data, who can write to it, who can run it). Some metadata, such as file dates and sizes, can easily be seen by users; other metadata can be hidden or embedded and unavailable to computer users who are not technically adept."

- *Fennell v. First Step Designs, Ltd.,* 83 F.3d 526, 530, 532 (1st Cir. 1996). The Court affirmed the trial court's denial of the plaintiff's request to discover the defendant's hard drive despite plaintiff computer expert's testimony that a key memo had been "modified." The plaintiff argued the document had been modified because the word processing program automatically assigned a new date to the document when it was opened and saved which was more than two years after the document was allegedly created. The court held that the plaintiff did not "articulate a plausible basis for the belief that discoverable materials exist which would raise a trial worthy issue."

- *Rodriguez v. City of Fresno,* No. CIV.05-1017, 2006 WL 903675 (E.D. Cal. April 7, 2006). In a civil rights case the Court ordered the city to produce documents and metadata if the documents are in an electronic format. The metadata should include what changes were made to the documents.

[D]   Other Authorities

- For a listing of specific metadata for Microsoft Word, WordPerfect and PDF documents visit Donna Payne, *Metadata-Are you Protected?* available at http://www.payneconsulting.com/pub_books/articles/ (last visited on Jun. 27, 2006).

[E]   Discovery Pointers

- Duplicate word processing files may be found on hard disks, floppy diskettes and other backup storage media. Sometimes changes or differences between versions of the same document may have evidentiary value. These differences can be identified through the use of redline and compare features of most word processing programs.

- Time stamps and the date and time created or modified dates for a word processing or other application file can be falsified or changed easily. For example:

    — A simple copy or move operation can reset times to the time of the copy/move.

    — Burning to a CD can set them to the time of the burn; copying them from the CD back to the hard disk can set them to the time of the copy.

    — Opening a file and NOT saving it can reset the time to the present.

    — Changing an attribute can change the time.

    — A computer clock that is not set correctly gives a false date/time stamp. You change the date, change the file by opening and closing it using the altered date and then you change the date back on the computer.

    — There are simple tools to set the creation/modification time to whatever time the user desires.

- If you're faced with a discovery issue that certain computer created documents have been erased, the computer files may still be available on the computer hard disk drive. Since electronic information is never actually "deleted" these files or remnants are available if they have not been overwritten by other electronic information. *See,* § 3.5[E], *Deletion of Electronic Information.*

- Word processing documents may be in several different formats - paper, microfiche or computer files such as DOC, TIFF or PDF.

§ 3.13 FAXES

[A] Generally

Fax stands for facsimile transmission. Fax communication is still a critical function of most businesses, even with the advent of e-mail. Traditionally, a fax machine scans a piece of paper, digitizes it to an image and then sends it as electronic signals over a wire or wireless connection to a fax machine. The receiving machine recreates the image.

Today, a business can receive, view, annotate and send faxes without ever having to print or manually feed a document into a fax machine. Before, faxes were sent by walking documents to the fax machine and executing the "send" function. They were similarly received by walking to the fax machine and retrieving printed paper documents. Once the fax was sent or received, the image file was lost. Computers are now capable of sending and receiving the faxes and each fax is typically preserved on the computer's hard drive. Those files now become a target for electronic data discovery.

There are several fax software programs and services that provide this capability. Many of these have been available for some time and include archive capabilities that let users keep many years of fax transmissions with minimal disk space requirements.

For electronic discovery purposes the faxes may be stored on the company's or third party servers or on the user's computer. If it is on a 3rd party's computer it may not be deleted and backups may store the fax. In addition, it is becoming routine to send and receive faxes by regular office e-mail so they may be stored on the user's computer. *See also,* § 2.5[K], *Facsimile Transmission (Faxes).*

[B] Reported Cases

- *United States v. Triumph Capital Group, Inc.,* 211 F.R.D. 31 n.11 (D. Conn. 2002). The Court described a fax, "[a]n 'image file' refers to the format of any file that contains basically a picture of data or text such as a fax or a scanned document. An image file is not susceptible to a keyword search and cannot be written to, but with certain software, it can be viewed and printed."

- *United States v. Sattar,* No. CR.02-395, 2003 WL 22510435 (S.D.N.Y. Nov. 5, 2003). The Court described the process of the FBI intercepting faxes from the defendant.

- *In re International Telemedia Associates, Inc.,* 245 B.R. 713, 718 (Bankr. N.D.Ga. 2000). For notification purposes one of the litigants "provide[d] the Trustee with a permanent facsimile number, in addition to an electronic mail address at ita0999@hotmail.com. . . . instructing the Trustee to use the new permanent facsimile number (815) 352-6137 for any future correspondence and stating that 'the received faxes are forwarded to me and stored on my E-mail.'"

[C]   Discovery Pointers

Fax server features to focus on for discovery:

* Fax servers send and receive faxes from a server integrated into the firm's network;
* Integration with e-mail programs and address books;
* Backup is automatic;
* Remote accessibility to send and receive faxes;
* Access faxes through the Web;
* Location of faxes;
* Broadcast fax capability;
* History of faxes to specific customers;
* May be integrated with document management systems;
* Annotation capability;
* Redelivery of faxes after annotations;
* Tracking of faxes; and
* Real-time routing of incoming faxes.

Request to Produce Faxes

* Provide all faxes from the computers of every person and every server related to this case.

* Provide the faxes in both native file format including attachments as well as a standard format such as TIFF, bitmap or JPEG formats.

§ 3.14   GRAPHICS

Generally, graphics refers to one of the components of a software application. Many software applications include a graphics component. Such programs are said to *support* graphics. For example, certain word processors support graphics because they let you draw or import graphic pictures. All CAD/CAM systems support graphics. Some database management systems and spreadsheet programs support graphics because they let you display data in the form of graphs and charts. Such applications are often referred to as business graphics.

Software programs are referred to as graphics applications when their primary function is the creation or use of graphics in the program. The following are considered graphics applications:

- Paint programs allow you to create rough freehand drawings. The images are stored as bit maps and can easily be edited. An example of a paint program is Microsoft Paint.

- Illustration/design programs supports more advanced features than paint programs, particularly for drawing curved lines. The images are usually stored in vector-based formats. Illustration/design programs are often called "draw" programs.

- Presentation graphics software allows you to create bar charts, pie charts, graphics and other types of images for slide shows and reports. The charts can be based on data imported from spreadsheet or other applications. Microsoft PowerPoint is an example of a presentation graphics program.

- Animation software enables you to chain and sequence a series of images to simulate movement. Each image is like a frame in a movie.

- CAD (computer-aided design) software enables architects and engineers to draft designs.

- Desktop publishing provides a full set of word-processing features as well as control over placement of text and graphics, so that you can create newsletters, advertisements, books, and other types of documents.

§ 3.15   MULTIMEDIA

Multimedia generally means the combination of text, sound, graphics and/or motion video. This combination may include the following:

- Text and sound;
- Text, sound and still or animated graphic images;
- Text, sound and video images; and
- Multiple display areas, images or presentations displayed concurrently.

From an evidentiary point of view, this trend in multimedia will mean that textual documents and data files will intermingle with audio-visual files. Databases that originally contained only text will now contain images, sound and video. Some common multimedia display programs are QuickTime and Microsoft Media.

§ 3.16   PRESENTATION

[A]   Generally

Presentation software enables users to create textual and graphics-based slide shows and reports. The software includes functions for creating various types of charts and graphs, for inserting text (in a variety of fonts), audio, video and pictures. Presentation graphics is often called *business graphics.*

The most common presentation graphical programs permit you to create bullet slides, bar graphs, pie charts, timelines, organization charts and a host of other graphical depictions that provides the viewer with a visual impression by pictures and data.

It may be necessary to discover presentation files, for instance, which contain sales presentations or other relevant slides. For example, one slide at a top-level Microsoft meeting, which included Chairman Bill Gates, warned that "Real [Network] competes directly with major components of the Windows OS [operating system]." Jonathan Krim, *E-Mails Show Microsoft Sought to Weaken Rival,* Washington Post, May 3, 2002, at E4.

Your discovery should also include the "author's notes," which may be part of the presentation slides.

[B]   Metadata

The following presentation software metadata may be available:

- The presenter's author and company name;
- Name of the computer and server on which the presentation was created;
- Hidden comments - on notes and handouts page of the slides; and
- Nonvisible portions of Object Linking and Embedding (OLE) links.

[C]   Reported Cases

- *Simon Property Group L.P. v. mySimon, Inc.,* 194 F.R.D. 639, 641 (S.D. Ind. 2000). The Court ordered disclosure of "powerpoint or similar presentations."

- *Williams v. Sprint/United Mgmt. Co.,* 230 F.R.D. 640, 647 (D. Kan. 2005). "The Microsoft Office Online website lists several examples of metadata that may be stored in Microsoft Excel spreadsheets, as well as other Microsoft applications such as Word or PowerPoint . . ."

- *X-IT Products, L.L.C. v. Walter Kidde Portable Equipment, Inc.,* 155 F. Supp. 2d 577 (E.D. Va. 2001). The PowerPoint slides supported proof of copyright infringement.

- *In re CV Therapeutics, Inc., Sec. Litig.,* No. CIV.03-03709, 2006 U.S. Dist. LEXIS 38909 (D. Cal. Apr. 6, 2006). "[D]atabase management system which, among other things, stores . . . Word, PowerPoint, Excel and Adobe Acrobat [files]."

§ 3.17   VIDEO

Video generally refers to recording, manipulating and displaying moving images in a format that can be presented on a television or on a computer monitor. It is a recording produced with a video recorder (camcorder) or some other device that captures full motion. *See also,* § 2.05[P], *Camera/Camcorder (Digital).*

§ 3.18   CONFERENCING – TEXT, AUDIO, DATA AND VIDEO

Conferencing or messaging is a live connection between people in separate locations for the purpose of communication, usually involving audio and often text as well as video.

Essentially any interaction that can be done in person can now be accomplished remotely by using audio, text and application conferencing. For example, you can share a word processor real-time over the Internet, which would permit you to work on a contract with a customer from a different location.

Real-time collaboration or "virtual" conferencing tools are available for businesses and individuals to work live from different physical locations. Real-time collaboration tools include text-based chat, audio and video conferencing and application and data sharing. All of these tools work over the Internet or over a local area network using standard Internet protocols.

One of the most popular forms of conferencing is "text messaging." Text messaging is sending short messages to a digital phone, pager, PDA, or other handheld device. Usually, messaging takes place between two or more mobile devices. The messages are not usually more then a couple of hundred characters in length. You simply enter the recipient's phone number, enter your name and then type your message and send it.

Some business applications for these real-time collaboration tools are:

- Customer or supplier conferences;
- Working on contracts;
- Business meetings;
- Training; and
- Interviewing prospective employees.

Video conferencing is an advanced form of teleconferencing that uses video cameras, microphones, computers and digital phone lines to allow people to meet when they cannot be at the same geographic location. Many times these video conferences are recorded on secondary storage media that can be discovered for litigation purposes.

For examples of Web-based conferencing systems see Live Meeting (http://www.microsoft.com/uc/livemeeting/default.mspx) and WebEx (www.webex.com).

[A]   Reported Case

- *Collaboration Props. v. Tandberg ASA,* No. CIV.05-01940, 2006 U.S. Dist. LEXIS 42465, at *2 (D. Cal. Jun. 22, 2006). "The asserted patents cover, generally, a multimedia communication and collaboration system. The disclosed invention combines voice and video conferencing with the ability to exchange data and other media types between geographically dispersed locations. Users of the system interact with each other via 'collaborative multimedia workstations,' . . . which facilitate the exchange of audio, video and data."

§ 3.19   AUDIO FILES

Audio has moved from analog recording with LPs (long-playing records) and tape cassettes as the playback medium to digital recording using computers with a digital sound playback.

Digital audio files are usually compressed for less storage requirements and faster transmission. For example, audio files can be sent in short stand-alone segments as files in the wave file format. A Wave file is an audio file format, created by Microsoft, which has become a standard PC audio file format. A Wave file is identified by a file name extension of WAV. It is used primarily in personal computers.

The most popular audio file format today is MP3. MP3 is a standard technology and format for compressing a sound sequence into a very small file while preserving the original level of sound quality when it is played.

In order for users to receive sound in real-time for a multimedia effect, listening to music or in order to take part in an audio or video conference, sound must be delivered as streaming sound.

The current audio delivery methods include RealAudio (Progressive Networks' RealAudio), Shockwave (Macromedia) and MP3. RealAudio and Shockwave are designed to allow a real-time playback of audio directly from a website.

Discovery of audio files will grow in importance as electronic messaging allows for text, audio and video to be part of integrated e-mail and World Wide Web content.

§ 3.20   PHOTOGRAPHS AND IMAGES

A photograph (often called a photo) is a picture that is produced by photography. Traditionally a photograph was produced by printing a film negative on paper. This has changed with the advent of digital photography. *See,* §§ 2.5[P], *Camera/Camcorder (Digital)* and 8.16, *Photographs* for admissibility issues. For a discussion of images see § 5.03[B], *Images.*

[A]   Reported Case

• *United States v. Hair,* 2006 U.S. App. LEXIS 10443, n. 2 (11th Cir. 2006) (unpublished). "'JPEG' image is a packet of compressed data sent over the internet that, when opened, displays an image or picture. JPEGs are usually photographs, and are created when the user 'compresses' the photo into a JPEG file. The user can then send that file over a network (or the internet) to another person, who can open the file and view the picture in its original form. (citation omitted)"

This page intentionally left blank.

Chapter 4

Computer Forensics, Experts and Service Bureaus

§ 4.1 COMPUTER FORENSICS

Computer forensics involves the identification, preservation, extraction, documentation and analysis of computer evidence. There are specially trained individuals to assist in the processing of computer evidence. They have many different software tools and forensic techniques available that can extract and analyze electronic information, even if it is hidden, deleted, lost or altered.

Computer forensics can be used to identify evidence when personal computers are used in the commission of crimes, violation of company policies, to recover deleted or altered computer data and other cases involved with the location or recovery of computer data. Computer evidence that is located and extracted by a forensic specialist is often created without the knowledge of the computer user. For example, you find in the cache files and Internet history logs, electronic evidence revealing the Internet browsing activities of a particular user. In addition, computer specialists can forensically copy hard drives, floppy disks and other storage media for subsequent analysis and restoration of deleted files.

There are key differences between electronic discovery and computer forensics.

Electronic discovery is primarily the request, collection, review, production and management of electronic information. This process will generally involve a computer IT professional who will isolate, collect, process and manage electronic information for review and subsequent disclosure by the production attorney. The requesting party's IT professionals will then receive and process the data for review. The chain of custody in the collection and disclosure is important during this process. An electronic discovery specialist's primary expertise is in processing electronic information in a manageable and cost-effective method.

On the other hand, computer forensics primarily involves analyzing hard drive files and residual data. This media may contain valuable electronic information that could have been deleted, corrupted or residual data that may exist in the unallocated or slack portions of the hard drive. *See,* § 2.06[F], *Residual Data - Slack Space, File Slack and Swap File.* In order to restore this data, computer forensic techniques such as creating a bit-by-bit image copy of a hard drive are utilized. A forensic copy of a hard drive means that all of the data on a hard drive, both the active data and residual data, is copied and available for forensic analysis. A bit by bit image copy can also be referred to as a "clone" or "mirror" copy of a hard drive.

Computer forensics is, in effect, a subset of the electronic discovery process and data population.

One of the key differences between electronic discovery and computer forensics is the collection of "live" data v. "dead" data. Live data normally involves the active files and other information which can be collected without using computer forensic restoration techniques.

Generally, obtaining a forensic copy of a hard drive is not permitted by the courts. The reason for this is that besides being expensive, courts are reluctant to expose the opposing party's electronic information since the data may contain privileged or other confidential information. It is generally only allowed in cases where criminal activity has taken place, allegations of stolen trade secrets or other proprietary data have been made, or in cases involving the destruction or deletion of computer files such as e-mail which may be relevant to the issues in your case. *See,* § 7.7[H], *Inspection of Opposing Party's Computer System.*

Computer forensics focuses not only on a bit by bit image copy of a hard drive, but also on the analysis and interpretation of data on the storage media. There are many cases where a computer forensic expert has been indispensable in the analysis and interpretation of data on hard drives. *See,* § 4.5, *Locating and Selecting Experts and Consultants.* They have been involved in searching file data fragments for information, restoring deleted files, identifying passwords, searching Internet temporary files and other forensic areas. They can also determine whether or not data on a computer has been recently and intentionally scrubbed or deleted. *See,* § 4.5[D], *Reported Cases.*

After a forensic examination, experts are generally requested to testify in depositions or in court regarding their findings. Because of their background and training, they are able to provide the necessary expert testimony regarding the data examination. However, their background and training and their use of forensic techniques will be closely scrutinized. For this reason, it is vitally important that you choose qualified forensic experts. Otherwise, like all experts in cases, their credibility may become a decisive issue with the court. *Gates Rubber Co. v. Bando Chemical Indus., Ltd.,* 167 F.R.D. 90 (D. Colo. 1996); *See,* § 8.08, *Testimony and Opinions by Experts and Lay Witnesses.*

Electronic discovery in a broad sense includes the forensic collection and examination of electronic data. Most companies either provide or are closely partnered with other companies to provide the services you need. However, be selective in choosing qualified assistance. There are several cases where the court has considered or imposed sanctions for the problems created by the computer forensic experts or electronic discovery service bureaus. These include the use of inappropriate computer forensic techniques by experts as well as the delay in the processing and disclosure of electronic information to the opposing side. *See,* §§ 4.5[D], *Reported Cases* and 8.08, *Testimony and Opinions by Experts and Lay Witnesses.*

§ 4.2   EXPERTS, CONSULTANTS, AND SERVICE BUREAUS

While electronic discovery is an essential part of the litigation process, most lawyers simply do not know where to begin. The reason for this is that in a paper-based world, the need to understand how electronic information is generated and stored has not been necessary. Lawyers were not trained in law school to discover, disclose and control electronic information. For this reason, many lawyers initially will hire forensic specialists to assist with electronic discovery. For example, having knowledge of your client's data storage systems will allow you to effectively negotiate discovery limitations, and if necessary, challenge unduly burdensome requests in court.

A "computer forensic" specialist is part of the new "electronic discovery" industry. The use of such a specialist is similar to hiring an accident reconstructionist, investigator or economist to assist in the preparation of a case. For example, forensic specialists can assist with the following electronic discovery tasks:

- Assessing the opposing party's computer systems and determine what data may be available;

- Harvesting and extracting electronic data and metadata from programs such as Microsoft Outlook;

- Negotiating for the exchange of electronic information;

- Making a forensic or mirror image copy of a hard disk;

- Monitoring the discovery of electronic information from the opposing party;

- Assisting with discovery cost containment;

- Providing advice on the how to search data;

- Providing education to the attorneys and the court on electronic discovery issues; and

- Providing in-court testimony on a computer forensic issue.

See, § 4.4, *Services and Scope of Work – Forensic Specialists.*

As the legal profession transitions to discovery of electronic information, the discovery protocols and extraction of electronic information will become commonplace. More and more of these functions will be provided within the law firm without the necessity of using an outside forensic specialist. This is similar to the use of litigation support systems that were initially provided by outside vendors, but today, are housed within the firm.

§ 4.3   TYPE OF EXPERTS, CONSULTANTS, AND SERVICE BUREAUS

[A]   Generally

There are a variety of experts, consultants, and service bureaus (vendors) that can assist in the discovery, extraction and presentation of your electronic information. Since the use of these experts is relatively new, there is no accepted standard for the type of forensic specialist that you need or the type of service that is offered. *Hopson v. Mayor & City Council of Baltimore*, 232 F.R.D. 228, 239, n.32 (D. Md. 2005). ("[a] cottage industry of companies assisting with the production and retrieval of electronic data and litigation has recently arisen.").

A forensic specialist will offer expert advice as well as other services in a "vendor" or "service bureau" role. They may advise you not only how to discover the electronic evidence, but also the extraction, conversion, analysis and presentation of electronic information.

An "electronic discovery" specialist should be retained to assist with the discovery and processing of electronic information. It is not advisable to utilize legal assistants (unless they have the experience and training), relatives or other "nonexperts."

[B]   Computer Forensic Experts

A computer forensic expert generally provides expertise regarding the generation, storage, recovery, location and analysis of computer evidence.

This individual expert can provide "expert" opinions in order to educate counsel and testify in court as to computer evidence. When an expert is to testify regarding computer evidence, the court will examine their experience, educational credentials and other background information closely. Such experts may review computer evidence directly using various forensic techniques and prepare expert forensic reports, affidavits, etc. They may also be called on to assist the court, as a neutral expert, in monitoring the electronic discovery process.

It is becoming more common for lawyers to retain computer forensic experts to examine and obtain electronic information from hard drives, floppy diskettes, Zip disks and even cell phones and handheld computer devices. They are also called on to clone or mirror media in order to recover deleted, lost or residual data left on computers. Experts charge between $150 and $500 per hour for their forensic services.

A forensic expert is needed if you intend to secure electronic information directly from a standalone or networked computer system. Otherwise you risk that the evidence may be damaged, destroyed or compromised in some way. For example, you will want to ensure that time and date stamps for computer files are not changed by inadvertently opening files. Depending on what files you need, booting up a computer will change the time and date stamps on certain files and will overwrite unallocated or free space on a computer system. This space may contain residual data that may have importance in your case. *Antioch Co. v. Scrapbook Borders. Inc.*, 210 F.R.D. 645, 652-54 (D. Minn. 2002) ("Simply booting a computer can possibly destroy valuable metadata . . . that could be relevant in a lawsuit").

A computer forensic expert may not be needed if you are merely exchanging computer discovery files. However, these experts can provide a host of other services as explained in the sections below.

This expert is distinguished from data processing and data recovery consultants based on their education, experience and training in the forensic area and capacity to testify in the courtroom.

[C]   Electronic Information Processing Consultants

After the electronic information has been acquired or "harvested," electronic information processing consultants can provide expertise on how to process this information through the extraction, conversion and presentation stages. *See, § 5.5, Identifying, Collecting and Producing.* These consultants are available to assist in converting data from different software applications into databases, full text and images for control and presentation purposes. They should be able to provide cost estimates for processing various types of data (i.e., e-mail, word processing documents, etc.).

[D]   Data Recovery Consultants

Data recovery consultants provide data recovery services for information that has been deleted or lost as the result of mishap or intentional deletion of such data. A data recovery consultant should be distinguished from a computer forensic expert based on comparatively less training, education or experience in the acquisition and authentication of computer evidence. They often provide their services to the general public, and not to the law enforcement or legal community. They may hold themselves out as experts to recover deleted, lost or residual data; but they may not be qualified to testify to authenticate electronic data, establish a chain of custody or on other computer forensic issues.

[E]   Neutral and Partisan Experts

A computer forensic expert can be neutral or partisan. A neutral expert may be appointed by the court or selected by both parties to assist in the discovery and disclosure of electronic information. Generally, they possess significant forensic experience and educational credentials as well as a legal background. A partisan expert is one who is generally hired by one of the parties to the litigation. They will provide expertise and consultation, as well as testify in court on behalf of one of the parties.

[F] Court Appointed Experts

Federal courts, under FED. R. CIV. P. 53 and FED. R. EVID. 706, have the authority to appoint experts to assist the parties in arriving at a reasonable discovery plan, forensically image hard drives, monitor discovery plans for compliance and for other purposes. These appointees can range from an accredited computer forensics expert to an individual who has a substantial legal background as well as an information technology background. *See also,* § 7.11, *Special Masters and Court-Appointed Experts.*

[G] Electronic Evidence Preparation Consultants

There are many information technology consultants who are changing from providing law office and litigation management consultation services to providing services pertaining to the discovery and production of electronic evidence. These individuals' skills and credentials will vary depending on their background, education and experience. They may assist the attorney in discovering or disclosing electronic information, but generally do not possess sufficient expertise to testify in court.

These consultants are marketing their services under a variety of titles. These include electronic discovery management consultants, electronic evidence preparation consultants, litigation electronic discovery monitors and other titles usually containing the words "electronic," "discovery" and/or "evidence."

[H] Service Bureaus

There are numerous service bureaus that advertise their ability to assist in the acquisition, conversion, extraction and presentation of electronic evidence. Some of the service bureaus have been in business for many years and possess the necessary staff and expertise to assist you in the different discovery processing stages. However, many service bureaus have sprung up overnight and hold themselves out as "experts" in the electronic discovery area, even though they do not possess the necessary credentials. Legal professionals will be well advised to check out references and other credentials prior to retaining a service bureau. In addition, these service bureaus may have developed or are tied in with specific electronic discovery hardware and software that may or may not be suitable for your needs.

Service bureaus and the processing of electronic information will become standardized over the next several years. During the early stages of this transition, vendors providing these services and processing costs may change frequently.

[I]   Operating System and Other Information Technology Experts

Since there are so many types of storage media, devices, locations, operating systems, database structures, network systems, etc., it may be necessary to hire more than one expert or consultant to assist you with discovery. This is especially true if the electronic information is contained in enterprise-based databases, multiple operating systems and so on.

§ 4.4   SERVICES AND SCOPE OF WORK – FORENSIC SPECIALISTS

Because of the specialties and complexities that can often be found in discovery or disclosure of electronic information, it is important to focus on the type of services needed. There is a range of services that a forensic computer specialist can provide - from assistance in the preparation of interrogatories to expert testimony in the courtroom. Cases can involve employees who sent sensitive documents outside the company using e-mail and cases involving financial records of a drug enterprise. The type of electronic information sought is one of the factors that will determine the type of "electronic discovery" service needed.

One commentator has noted,

> [B]oth parties engaged in computer-based discovery will need the assistance of computer experts. This is costly, but in the long run may save costs and time. Once the experts have had an opportunity to assess their respective parties' computer systems and capabilities, they will be in a much better position than the attorneys to negotiate the technical aspects of conducting discovery, including search protocols, privilege and relevance screening and production. Often the lawyers can be taken out of the picture entirely. In many cases, the experts on opposing sides have met and worked out agreements on the exchange of computer system information, the procedures for inspection, the search terms each side will use and other details best left to those with technical knowledge and experience.

Kenneth J. Withers, *Computer Based Discovery in Civil Litigation,* 2000 Fed. Cts. L. Rev. 2 (2000).

Outlined below are the different types of services available from a forensic specialist.

[A]   Case Strategy and Monitoring

Initially, a forensic specialist should be retained to assist with planning and monitoring the discovery process. Your initial efforts should focus on your overall electronic discovery case strategy. Some considerations:

• Determine how the opposing party used computers and other storage devices during the events in question. The forensic specialist will assist in determining what type of information may be available on storage media and devices and where it may be located.

- The discovery of electronic documents is especially important where relevant information is unavailable in traditional printed form. This might be the case if there are gaps in the production of paper-based documents, or if electronic communications (such as e-mail and Internet usage) played a role in the disputed events.

- Costs should always be considered in concert with decisions to pursue electronic evidence. For that reason it is cost-effective to narrow your document request, in order to limit the review and processing time of electronic information.

- Discuss with the expert the necessity of targeting computers that may have been replaced during the time in question. Because of the upgrade cycle for new releases of software, computers and software programs are changed and upgraded often.

- Discussions should be held as to how the other side will react to your demands for production of electronic information. If they react in a negative manner, what additional strategies should be used to ensure the disclosure of the computer evidence?

- A specialist can assist with formulating a litigation discovery response plan with your clients in order to assure the orderly and timely disclosure of electronic information.

- Discuss with your expert the necessity of hiring additional consultants and experts to provide technology advice. Other experts may be needed to consult regarding a specific computer platform or hardware setup from which you need to obtain electronic information.

Properly utilized, a forensic specialist can make easier the discovery of electronic information as well as save time and cost.

[1]   Other Authorities

- Lisa M. Arent et al., *EDiscovery: Preserving, Requesting & Producing Electronic Information,* 19 Santa Clara Computer & High Tech. L.J. 131, 176 (2002). The author urges the use of experts to assist in "streamlin[ing] the process and plan[ning] a strategy for discovery and production of electronic information" and assisting with issues concerning cost allocation of data production.

[B]   Court Testimony

One of the most frequent uses of a computer forensic expert is having them testify in court regarding discovery or production issues. This is especially important when there is a need to establish technology facts and opinions relating to the acquisition or production of electronic data. Since these experts may have to provide testimony and lay a foundation for electronic information, ensure that your expert has the necessary credentials. There are several cases where the court has commented directly on the lack of experience and expertise of expert witnesses that have testified on electronic information discovery issues. *See,* § 8.08, *Testimony and Opinions by Experts and Lay Witnesses.*

In one case, a representative from a data recovery company "appeared as a technical expert" in the notorious "Filegate" case, in which the FBI was claimed to have improperly given the White House hundreds of files on former political appointees. *Alexander v. FBI,* Civil No. 96-2123, 97-1288 (RCL). To educate U.S. District Judge Royce Lamberth on how long it took to cull all relevant e-mail messages from Justice Department computers . . . [the representative] brought their equipment into the judge's chambers for a live demo. [The judge] came away with a better understanding of the technology because we made it tangible . . . He interacted with the data management engineer . . . He felt after the demo that he had his arms around the technology." Kate Marquess, *Technical Difficulties,* A.B.A. J. (Jan. 2001), at 55.

[C]   Cost of Discovery

One critical factor to discuss with the forensic specialist at the outset is the cost of discovery or production of electronic information. The cost can be significant depending on the volume, location and format of the electronic information. Depending on the value of the case and resources available, narrowing of the data request parameters and using search and retrieval technology may be employed to reduce discovery costs. *See also,* §§ 5.5[C], *Ways to Limit Your Cost Exposure* and 5.7[E], *Electronic Discovery Cost Estimates.* Not only will the assistance of a computer specialist be needed, but also attorneys and their legal staff will need to review and redact any privileged material. The cost should be monitored and meetings should be held as certain financial limits are reached.

[D]   Identify Data Types

In all discovery cases, one of the first things to do is to identify what type of electronic information you are seeking to discover. There are many different types of business or personal data that may be relevant to the claims and defenses of your case. These may include e-mail communications, spreadsheet calculations, business databases, accounting records, fax transmissions and Internet usage logs. A forensic specialist can assist as to what data types are available and what type of information they will hold.

For example, a word processing document, as well as the "metadata" (which includes prior versions of the document), may need to be discovered. A forensic specialist can advise how to frame interrogatories, requests for production and deposition questions to obtain this information.

For an extensive listing of different data types that may be relevant to your case *see* § 3.6, *Data Types*.

[E]   Identify Storage Media

A forensic specialist can assist in identifying different storage media where the electronic information may be stored such as hard drives, floppy disks, CD-ROMs, DVDs, magnetic tapes and other media. They also can assist in explaining the features of the different types of storage media. This will include identification of whether the media is temporary, semipermanent or permanent. This may affect the timeliness of your request for disclosure and preservation issues. For further information on different storage media and their characteristics *see* § 2.4, *Storage Media*.

[F]   Identify Storage Devices

There are many different types of storage devices where electronic information may be stored, and more are being developed. A forensic specialist can assist in identifying which storage devices may contain the electronic information you are requesting. The information may be stored on a network server, a peer-to-peer network, a desktop computer, PDA, wireless telephone, an Intranet storage device such as a Web server or on a variety of other storage devices. For an extensive list of possible storage devices *see* § 2.5, *Storage Devices*.

[G]   Identify Storage Location

Because electronic information can be so easily generated and transmitted, data can be stored in many different locations. The information can be located at various service providers, such as Internet, telephone or satellite service providers. In addition, consider whether the information is stored on backup files, branch or home office computers and in other storage locations. The location of electronic information will vary depending on the needs of your case. For a more complete listing of possible storage locations *see* § 2.6, *Storage Locations*.

[H]   Assist with Preservation Efforts

If you have been requested to disclose information, preservation of the data is vitally important. Electronic information can be easily destroyed. Once the duty to preserve is found, immediate steps have to be taken with your client to ensure the preservation of electronic information. Failure to do so can result in severe sanctions from the court. *See,* §§ 7.09[D], *Duty to Preserve* and 7.9, *Sanctions*. A forensic specialist can assist with ensuring that the relevant data is preserved for future disclosure.

[I]   Assist with Scope of Production and Format of Disclosure

Scope of Production

One key area in which a forensic specialist may assist is the scope of production of electronic information. The expert should be able to assist the court and attorneys as to how the electronic information may be filtered and culled for review purposes. They can assist with how to handle obsolete hardware and software conversion and search efforts, how to eliminate redundant documents, provide a sample of data to be evaluated and provide suggestions on how to protect confidential information during the discovery process.

The expert may also provide assistance on what searches to conduct. The expert should not operate the opposing party's computer to avoid claims of erasing data, exceeding the scope of discovery requests or causing damage to the opposing party's hardware or software.

Disclosure Formats

Once the electronic information has been identified and collected, the issue of what format electronic information should be disclosed in needs to be addressed. For example, would it be sufficient if the electronic data is converted into an image, such as a TIFF and then disclosed? Under some circumstances this may be sufficient. However, disclosure in his format will not allow for searching of the data by electronic means and will not provide any "metadata" contained in the document. A forensic specialist can assist with ensuring that the electronic information is disclosed in a file format that will be most beneficial to the parties. *See,* § 5.3, *Electronic Data Formats.*

[J]   Ensure Chain of Custody

During the discovery process, one must always be vigilant about the chain of custody of evidence, especially in criminal cases. A forensic expert should be able to testify as to the chain of custody and help establish authenticity as needed. Chain of custody documentation should include a report of when the electronic evidence was received, handling logs, serial numbers of hard drives and from which computer the information was obtained.

Be aware that electronic data discovery is being used at an accelerating pace and numerous evidentiary objections are available to exclude the evidence. Care and guidance must be taken in the acquisition, extraction, preservation and presentation of electronic data to overcome these objections. For a further discussion of evidentiary issues *see* Chapter 8, *Admissibility of Electronic Evidence* and § 8.10[C], *Chain of Custody.*

[K]   Assist with the Collecting, Processing and Conversion of Electronic Information

After the acquisition of the data, a forensic specialist can assist with how to process and convert the data for review and presentation in the courtroom. Since this is a developing area, the software tools for extracting, converting and presenting the data are constantly changing. Some of the "new" electronic discovery software tools may not be as reliable as you need, so exercise caution in your selection.

Unfortunately, some computer forensics specialists, not only provide expert services, but also sell, as a vendor, processing and conversion services and/or software. The best solution is to select an independent forensic computer expert/consultant who is not tied to a specific software conversion package or data depository, but who can advise you as to the different electronic discovery services and software available in the marketplace to best meet your needs. For further discussion on the processing of electronic information *see* Chapter 5, *Collecting, Processing and Searching Electronic Information.*

[L]   Assist with Recovering Lost or Deleted Data and Cloning Hard Drives

There are two areas where an expert is required: one, recovering loss or deleted electronic information; and two, making a forensic copy of a hard drive or other storage media. If data has been deleted or lost, a computer expert may be able to "restore" the data or determine whether the specified data has ever existed on storage media and if it did, whether its disappearance was inadvertent or deliberate.

Computers do not delete data, but merely delete the address where the data resides. The data "deleted" may be e-mail, word processing documents, spreadsheets, database and other electronic information. If new data is written over this vacant address, then the deleted information is generally not recoverable, but until that time, deleted files can be restored.

If electronic information was deleted, lost or altered, the forensic expert should be able to provide the necessary factual and technical foundation to persuade the court to allow for restoration of the deleted files. For example, if the opposing party deletes e-mail after thirty days and has not implemented a preservation policy, then a forensic expert should be able to provide the court with the necessary testimony to allow the court to order that certain hard drives or other storage media be cloned in an attempt to recover deleted or lost files.

They may also be able to recover residual or ambient data from storage media. Such data is partial data that is still available on a hard drive after a file has been "deleted," and that has not been overridden by new data. Some other "hidden" storage areas where data may be found on a hard drive are in the swap files used by a Windows operating system or on unallocated space on a hard drive. This data may be in the form of e-mail fragments, word processing fragments and other data types that have been generated by the computer. *See also,* § 2.6[F], *Residual Data - Unallocated or Slack Space, File Slack and Swap File.*

In order to restore this lost or deleted data, it is generally necessary to make a forensic copy (sometimes referred to as a "clone" or "mirror") of the storage media or device. Cloning a hard drive or other storage media means performing a bit stream backup, which involves the copying of every bit of data on a storage device. This is different than just copying "active files" to a storage media. After cloning, the actual restoration, processing and searching of electronic data should be performed on copies of these clones.

For a discussion of court-mandated procedures for making a forensic copy of a hard drive see § 7.7[H][5], *Procedure - Forensic Copy of Storage Media (Hard Drive, etc.).*

[1]   Discovery Pointer

• If you need to clone the storage media, the ideal situation is to have a forensic computer expert make a clone of the storage media, such as a hard drive, and then analyze it in their computer lab. Also, this will ensure that the data is collected in a forensically sound fashion in the event that chain of custody or authentication becomes an issue later on. However, if the cloned hard drive is provided to you, it will decrease the costs involved of sending an expert to the location of the computers and waiting while hard drives are cloned.

[M]   Assist with Preparation and Compliance with Court Discovery Tools

The specialist can assist with a preservation letter, initial disclosure, drafting of interrogatory questions, request for production and questions for a deposition of the opposing party's information technology personnel.

For further discussion of court discovery procedural rules *see* Chapter 7, *Court Procedural Rules and Case Law.*

[N]   Working with Opposing Party's Computer Expert

A forensic specialist can assess the opposing party's computer system and be in a position to assist in negotiating with the opposing party's expert, an acceptable discovery agreement including search protocols, privilege, relevance screening and production of electronic data. Discovery logistics of this type can streamline the discovery process, and save time and cost.

[O]   Assist as a Court Appointed Expert

In some cases a computer forensic expert can assist the court in monitoring to ensure compliance with an electronic discovery court order. They can serve as a special master, mediator or a neutral third party to help the litigants develop reasonable discovery plans. *See als,o* § 7.11, *Special Masters and Court-Appointed Experts.*

[P]   Provide Risk Retention Advice for Electronic Information

A computer forensic specialist can provide expertise regarding retention policies for your clients. Often electronic information, though it is outdated, may have to be reviewed to determine whether it is relevant to the litigation. This can be costly. In a paper-based environment, retention policies are enforced and ensure the orderly destruction of outdated material. However, electronic information can be easily copied and preserved which creates disclosure and review problems. A computer forensics specialist should be able to provide an audit of the company's electronic information and its retention policies to reduce the risk of keeping outdated data and then having to review and produce it if litigation arises.

§ 4.5   LOCATING AND SELECTING EXPERTS AND CONSULTANTS

A computer forensic specialist will specialize in different litigation areas. Depending on your forensic needs, it is critical that the right specialist is selected for your electronic discovery or production needs. These specialists have expertise in various areas such as forensics, law, strategy planning, litigation support and so on.

[A]   Selecting Forensic Specialists

There are several considerations in the evaluation and selection of experts, consultants or service bureaus. Since electronic discovery is relatively new, the selection and retention of a forensic specialist(s) can be challenging and confusing. Set out below are some considerations in the selection of a specialist.

Identification of Experts

*   To identify an expert, review articles or publications written by the expert and testimony in cases in which they have testified. Are the articles or reports understandable? Request a copy of any written reports they have prepared and signed as an expert witness. Sometimes, one expert may be appropriate to address a complex data issue, such as encryption, while another expert may be suited to evaluate certain logic errors in the source code of a specific programming language.

Expert's Background

*   Does the expert/consultant understand the technology as well as the legal discovery process? If the specialist you intend to hire has familiarity with not only the technology

aspects of the electronic information, but is also aware of discovery and trial procedures, then they will be able to assist in both disciplines.

- Three important criteria are whether the expert has the appropriate training, experience and educational credentials. The expert may be required to give an expert opinion in front of a judge or jury. If they testify are they able to articulate the technical issues in an understandable fashion to a jury?

- Does the expert/consultant have an investigative background that can assist when they are viewing computer evidence? Often, the expert/consultant will be viewing residual data or metadata. If the specialist understands the claims or defenses of the case, they will be able to spot evidence that may be of value to your case.

- Do the expert's skills, experience and educational background fit the particular project?

Forensic Background

- Does the expert have the necessary background in dealing with various formats of electronic media? Are they able to investigate data from backup tapes, floppy disks, hard drives, and other permanent and removable media? Do they have the expertise with the special operating system(s)?

- Is the expert/consultant familiar with the use of the latest software and hardware tools to recover and extract electronic evidence? They should have at their disposal the latest forensic literature and tools for the discovery process.

- Does the expert have the background to maintain the chain of custody and understand the proper handling of electronic media for forensic purposes?

- Does the expert have the necessary tools and equipment to make a forensic image copy of the media in question since the image may be examined by third parties? Do they have the tools to restore deleted data or search through residual or slack space on the storage media?

- Does the expert have the necessary processing equipment to handle large data collections?

- Is the expert able to process the data to provide it in a format acceptable to you and/or the opposing party?

- Does the expert have qualified references? Ask for the contact person for the consultant's last five jobs, not just the references the consultant provides you.

Relationship with Firm

- Does the expert/consultant understand the need to control costs? Generally, the costs of processing and reviewing electronic information can be substantial and get out of hand quickly.

- Does the expert have the personality, temperament and people skills to get along with firm members?

- Does the expert bring knowledge gained from other legal discovery related jobs to enhance your discovery efforts?

- Does the expert have excellent communication skills? Are they able to use simple language to communicate about electronic discovery issues so that you understand the concepts?

- Does the specialist have a responsive and professional reputation?

- What are their fees for forensic services? Forensic specialists charge generally from $125 to $500 an hour, depending on their skills and expertise.

Expert's Company

- Is the expert/consultant tied to specific hardware, software vendors or online data depositories? "Independent" consultants should not recommend the value or utility of specific software packages and receive a commission or some other form of remuneration from a software company to sell their products. They should be able to independently recommend the best and most cost efficient software, hardware and other services for your electronic discovery needs.

- Does the expert subcontract the work or have the necessary employees to handle your needs?

- Does the expert have secure office space?

- Does the specialist have enough employees to do the job in a timely fashion?

    There are many litigation support and trial service bureaus that will assist in handling the conversion of electronic information. If you decide to engage an outside service to assist, keep the following in mind:

- Has the vendor provided an estimate of the cost of processing the anticipated discovery? They should be able to estimate the cost if you provide approximately how many megabytes of electronic information will be discovered or produced. This cost estimate should include how much it will cost to acquire, extract, deduplicate and convert to a presentation format.

- Make sure there is no conflict of interest by the service bureau.

[B]   Locating Forensic Specialists

Below is a partial list of consultants and service providers that provide forensic services.

- Applied Discovery (www.applieddiscovery.com).

- Cataphora (www.cataphora.com).

- Computer Forensics, Inc. (www.forensics.com).

- Cricket Technologies, Inc. (www.crickettechnologies.com).

- Electronic Evidence Discovery, Inc. (www.eedinc.com).

- Evidence Exchange (www.evidenceexchange.com).

- Encore Legal Solutions (www.encorelegal.com).

- Ibis Consulting (www.ibisconsulting.com).

- inData (www.indatacorp.com).

- Kroll (www.krollontrack.com).

- NTI (www.forensics-intl.com).

- SPI Litigation Direct (http://www.spitech.com).

- Speros, William, forensic specialist (e -mail: SperosBill@cs.com).

[C]   Agreement with Forensic Specialist

Consider using the following methods and contractual clauses to ensure a favorable result:

- Disclose and discuss the firm's electronic discovery goals.

- Set forth in writing the responsibilities and duties that the consultant will assume. Set forth the proposed services and deliverables (reports, deadlines and benchmarks). Incorporate proposals into the contract.

- Set forth in writing the project's anticipated cost. Does the consultant bill by the project or by the hour? When is payment due and how should it be made? Withhold a final payment until the project is completed and accepted. Consider dividing the project into pieces so the cost will be based on the individual subprojects completed. Provide an early notification method if the consultant feels that there will be a cost or time overrun on the project. Request a written explanation of why such an overrun may occur.

- Reserve the right to terminate at any time, paying for services received. Set forth the name, if you want a particular consultant. Do not permit the consultant to enter into contracts on your behalf.

- Delineate the lines of authority in writing. Do not allow the consultant to obtain approval from another member of the firm on a project or extension of a project without your approval.

- The costs should be monitored closely. Updated reports at regular intervals should be the norm in order to ensure compliance with costs and budget estimates.

- Discuss the methodology of how price quotes will be obtained. Be sure to compare apples to apples.

- Discuss strategies on quality of products, lowest prices, staff training, implementation strategies, installation of products and testing.

- Determine if the consultant will receive any remuneration from any service bureau or vendor for services or software purchased.

Confidentiality Agreement

Confidentiality clauses should be included in any agreement. Terms should include the following:

During the course of the case and while providing consultation, equipment and technical support, employees of _____ will be exposed to exhibits and other information which _____ deems to be attorney work product, privileged information, proprietary information or some other kind of information which is deemed to be confidential by the law firm of _____.

No employee shall divulge any information related to this case to any person or entity in any manner whatsoever, whether or not this information has been identified as confidential. Each employee agrees to be bound by any and all stipulations of counsel, orders of the court and any other agreement of the parties regarding confidentiality and nondisclosure of information.

Consultants can provide tremendous value for the money and can guide you through the electronic discovery process. Take time in your selection process.

[D]   Reported Cases

Expert as an Officer of the Court

- *Simon Property Group L.P. v. mySimon, Inc.*, 194 F.R.D. 639, 641 (S.D. Ind. 2000). The plaintiff permitted "to attempt (at its own expense) the task of recovering deleted computer files from computers used by the four named individuals, whether at home or at work." The expert the plaintiff was to hire was to be designated as a neutral officer of the court.

- *Playboy Enterprises, Inc. v. Welles*, 60 F. Supp. 2d 1050 (S.D. Cal. 1999). The plaintiff paid the cost for a computer expert to make a forensic copy of the defendant's hard drive. The expert the plaintiff was to hire was to be designated as a neutral officer of the court.

Share Cost

- *Ranta v. Ranta*, 2004 WL 504588 (Conn. Super. Feb. 25, 2004). The Court ordered the parties in a divorce proceeding to share equally all costs associated with hiring a computer forensics expert to inspect the wife's laptop.

Forensic Expert Credentials and Qualifications

- *See*, §§ 7.11, *Special Masters and Court-Appointed Experts* and 8.8, *Testimony and Opinions by Experts and Lay Witnesses.*

Chain of Custody

- *See*, §§ 8.10[C], *Chain of Custody* and 5.05[G], *Chain of Custody, Audit Reports and Hash Values.*

Need for Forensic Expert or Forensic Company

- *Balboa Threadworks, Inc. v. Stucky,* No. CIV.05-1157, 2006 U.S. Dist. LEXIS 29265, at *15-16 (D. Kan. Mar. 24, 2006). The Court ruled, "[a]s to the formulation of a search protocol, whether one using key word searches and/or other search procedures, the parties are directed to meet and confer in an attempt to agree on an appropriate protocol, and should lean heavily on their respective computer experts in designing such a protocol."

- *Hopson v. Mayor & City Council of Baltimore*, 232 F.R.D. 228, 245 (D. Md. 2005). The Court commented upon pending Rule 16 and the "meet and confer" mandate and ordered the parties and their "IT representative to consult in good faith in an effort to informally discover sufficient information about the Defendants' IT systems and electronic records to agree upon a proposed discovery plan to submit to the court for review and approval."

- *In re Priceline.com Inc. Sec. Litig.*, 233 F.R.D. 88, 89 (D. Conn. 2005). The Court noted that both sides' experts had submitted affidavits regarding the computer storage and other issues of the case and then set forth a production procedure, including sampling, to guide the parties to reduce the costly process of restoring and disclosing electronic information.

- *Tulip Computers Inter. B. V. v. Dell Computer Corp.*, 52 Fed. R. Serv. 3d 1420 (D. Del. 2002). Dell Computer stated it did not have the ability to search its own database for the requested case information. The plaintiff's forensic database experts were then allowed access to the database and discovered that they could perform searches on the database and also learned that Dell could have performed the same searches.

- *Keir v. UnumProvident*, 2003 WL 21997747 (S.D.N.Y. Aug. 22, 2003). The Court admonished the defendant for failure to confer with IT experts on how to preserve electronic evidence and would consider sanctions depending upon further discovery.

- *New York National Organization for Women v. Cuomo*, No. CIV.93-7146, 1998 WL 395320, at *3 (S.D.N.Y. Jul. 14, 1998). The plaintiff failed to provide expert testimony as to how, if they had learned of the destruction of the computer information earlier, that they could have restored the deleted information.

- *Concord Boat Corp. v. Brunswick Corp.*, No. CIV.95-781, 1996 WL 33347247 at *2, *3 (E.D. Ark. Dec. 23, 1996). The Court ordered the parties, counsel and computer experts to meet and make a good faith attempt to resolve electronic discovery issues.

- *In re Lorazepam and Clorazepate Antitrust Litigation*, 300 F. Supp. 2d 43, 47(D.D.C. 2004). The Court ruled that the plaintiff had to take the discovery that was provided on "23 CD-ROM's . . . to a company that specializes in computer forensics or electronic discovery to ascertain whether the information on the 23 CD-ROM's can be either read and searched by a commercially available software or whether it can be converted to a format that will render it capable of being read and searched by commercially available software."

- *Murphy Oil USA, Inc. v. Fluor Daniel, Inc.*, 52 Fed.R. Serv.3d 168 (E.D.La. 2002). The Court discussed experts' estimate of costs to process electronic discovery.

- *Liafail, Inc., v. Learning 2000*, No. CIV.01-599, 2002 WL 31954396 (D. Del. 2002). The Court reviewed the handling of electronic information and depending on further discovery may impose an adverse instruction sanction for the party's failure to preserve evidence on its laptop computers.

- *See also, § 7.11, Special Masters and Court-Appointed Experts.*

Vendor Delay

- *Residential Funding Corp. v. DeGeorge Fin. Corp.,* 306 F.3d 99, 108 (2d Cir. 2002). Appellate court vacated the trial court's imposition of an adverse instruction sanction against the nonproducing party, who was deemed to have engaged in "purposeful sluggishness" behavior and remanded with instructions to allow discovery on the reasons for delaying its decision to retain an outside vendor to retrieve e-mails from backup tapes. Court also wanted more discovery on why the party continued to rely on the vendor "throughout months of apparently fruitless attempts to retrieve the critical e-mails," in refusing to provide technical information regarding the e-mails to the adverse party's expert, and other things.

- *In re Worldcom,* No.CIV.02-3288, 2004 WL 768573 (S.D.N.Y. April 12, 2004). Defendants ordered to provide electronic discovery by a certain date and failure to do so may relieve the plaintiffs from a prior order requiring them to share in the cost of providing electronic discovery.

Credentials and Criticism of Forensic Experts

- *See, § 8.8, Testimony and Opinions by Experts and Lay Witnesses.*

Types of Forensic Analysis

   Internet and e-mail use

- *In re Wagner,* No. CIV.02-95231, 2004 WL 1469780 (N.Y.A.D. July 1, 2004). A forensic expert discovered from an employee's hard drive that the employee deliberately accessed and transmitted offensive material obtained from the Web. The Appellate Court affirmed the state employee's termination for using the Internet and e-mail for personal purposes to access and send offensive content.

- *People v. Smith,* 2001 WL 1264553 (Cal. App. 6 Dist. Oct. 23, 2001) (unpublished). The computer expert testified that on the defendant's computer were Internet searches showing that he was tracking down the victim.

- *Giardina v. Lockheed Martin Corp.,* 2003 WL 1338826 (E.D.L.A. 2003). The Court ordered a company to search for all incidents of employees accessing other websites.

- *In re Pharmatrak, Inc. Privacy Litigation,* 220 F. Supp. 2d 4 (D. Mass. 2002), *rev'd on other grounds,* 329 F.3d 9 (1st Cir. 2003). The computer forensic expert analyzed the defendant's website tracking logs and was able to determine that defendant's "cookies" had captured and possessed detailed private information about the plaintiffs, including their names, addresses, telephone numbers, dates of birth, sex, insurance status, medical conditions, education levels, occupations and e-mail content.

- *Paramount Pictures Corp. v. Davis,* 234 F.R.D. 102 (D. Pa. 2005). Through the use of forensics, the plaintiff was able to trace infringement activity through the defendant's IP address.

- *State v. Guthrie,* 627 N.W.2d 401, 408 (S.D. 2001). After the defendant's wife was found drowned in a bathtub "accident" the state's computer expert found that the defendant's computer "had been used to conduct numerous Internet searches on subjects uncannily related . . . to the drowning. [The computer had been used to] conduct specific Internet searches using an online search engine - the repeated queries were for 'household' accidents' and 'bathtub accidents.'" *See also, State v. Guthrie,* 654 N.W.2d 201(S.D. 2002) where the same computer expert was able to show that the victim's purported computerized suicide note had been written after her death and on a computer that did not belong to her.

Delivery of e-mail

- *Am. Boat Co. v. Unknown Sunken Barge,* 418 F.3d 910, 913 (8th Cir. 2005). A computer forensic expert (Internet service provider network administrator) testified that an attorney did not receive an e-mail court order sent by the district court.

- *United States v. Ray,* 428 F.3d 1172, 1173-1175 (8th Cir. 2005). The Court affirmed defendant's extortion conviction finding that "[the defendant] admitted that he used his computer and logged onto the Internet several times a day, and that three of the emails sent to Best Buy traced back to the Internet address he was using on the given day and time the extortion emails were sent. Further, an FBI computer forensic expert found three of the emails and other incriminating documents on the hard drive of Ray's computer. The expert testified the emails and documents were created by someone typing on that computer, and that someone had logged onto the Internet from that computer using the screen name and password used to send the emails. The expert also stated there was no evidence of any type of remote access or hacking found on Ray's computer."

Deleted files

- *Kucala Enterprises, Ltd. v. Auto Wax Co., Inc.,* 56 Fed. R. Serv. 3d 487 (N.D. Ill. 2003); *adopted as modified, Kucala Enterprises, Ltd. v. Auto Wax Co., Inc.,* 57 Fed. R. Serv. 3d 501 (N.D. Ill. 2003). The magistrate ordered dismissal of case, later modified by the district court, after a computer forensic expert found that a computer program called "Evidence Eliminator" was used to delete 12,000 files from its owner's desktop computer a few hours before the defendant's computer specialist was to inspect the computer pursuant to court order.

• *Kemper Mortg., Inc. v. Russell,* No. CIV.06-042, 2006 U.S. Dist. LEXIS 20729, at *5-7 (D. Ohio Apr. 6, 2006). The Court ruled plaintiff was entitled to an adverse inference when it was discovered by forensics that the defendant "caused to be installed on his laptop computer a program called 'Window Washer' . . . which prevents the forensic recovery of deleted electronic files by overwriting them."

• *Advantacare Health Partners v. Access IV,* No. CIV.03-04496, 2004 WL 1837997, at *2 (N.D.Cal. Aug. 17, 2004), *aff'd,* 2005 WL 1398641 (N.D.Cal. Jun. 14, 2005). The Court granted a default judgment and stated:

> [Plaintiffs obtained a TRO] . . . to produce 'any and all compact disks containing information obtained from [defendant's] computers, computer systems and/or computer network.' . . . [and] forensic copies of 'the hard drive and/or network server for any computer' . . . [a]fter service of the TRO, Defendants . . . sought to destroy evidence . . . [evidence was produced showing that the defendant] visited numerous websites, searching for computer data deletion software. . . . [defendant] deleted more than thirteen thousand files from his home computer using BC Wipe. He also deleted files from the office computer and server . . . deleted more than one hundred files from his home computer, just hours before presenting the hard drive . . . for copying pursuant to the TRO. . . [plaintiff's] computer forensic expert. . . . found thousands of AdvantaCare files stored on Dangerfield's office computers, home computer, and the hard drive that functioned as Access IV's server. He also discovered that Defendants continued to access and delete AdvantaCare files located on Dangerfield's office computer, the server, and Dangerfield's home computer after the cease and desist letter was sent and after the TRO was issued. Alcock could not recover files deleted with BC Wipe.

• *United States v. Triumph Capital Group,* 211 F.R.D. 31 (D. Conn. 2002). So that the data would not be altered, the government made mirror images of the hard drive and then proceeded with the computer forensic investigation. The Court discussed the law and technical issues relating to detecting deleted files and protecting electronic evidence against spoliation claims.

• *RKI Inc. v. Grimes,* 200 F. Supp. 2d 916 (N.D. Ill. 2002). The Court found that evidence of defragmentation of a computer several times provided evidence of spoliation.

• *Anderson v. Crossroads Capital Partners, L.L.C.,* No. CIV.01-2000, 2004 WL 256512 (D. Minn. Feb. 10 2004). In a sexual harassment and whistleblower case, the defendants' computer forensic expert examined the plaintiff's hard drive and discovered that a data wiping software application had been installed after the plaintiff had agreed not to "delete any existing documents" in a deposition, in particular, an October 2001 document. The computer forensic expert also found that the hard drive installed in the machine was manufactured in August 2002 and installed after the deposition.

- *Lexis-Nexis v. Beer,* 41 F. Supp. 2d 950, 953 (D. Minn. 1999). The employer sued a former employee for misappropriation of trade secrets and observed that, "[a]fter obtaining the laptop, Beer's counsel attempted to make an image copy of the laptop's hard drive. Beer's counsel now concedes that, during this process, they inadvertently overwrote the remnants of some previously deleted data. . . . Lexis-Nexis's expert [also] determined that Beer had deleted a number of important Lexis-Nexis documents that he had not earlier acknowledged possessing, including detailed customer reports called Ultimate Reports."

Discovering date computer data entered

- *Laurin v. Pokoik,* No. CIV.02-1938, 2004 WL 2724767, at *2 (S.D.N.Y. Nov. 30, 2004). In an employment case the plaintiff sought documents concerning the date of an entry she made in a computerized ledger kept on the defendant's computer system. The Court held that the plaintiff could retain a forensic expert at her own expense to determine if there is evidence of "the true date when the entry was actually entered into the computer system."

- *Wild v. Alster,* 377 F. Supp. 2d 186, 193-195 (D.D.C. 2005). The Court denied plaintiff's motion for a new trial where she argued that she was entitled have an expert examine the hard drive of the defendants' computer to explore whether it contained the dates that photographs of the plaintiff were taken. She had alleged a doctor had altered the photographs after her malpractice claim was filed.

- *Davison v. Eldorado Resorts LLC,* No. CIV. 05-0021, 2006 U.S. Dist. LEXIS 12598, at *26, 27 (D. Nev. Mar. 10, 2006). The plaintiff filed an ERISA complaint alleging that the defendants failed to provide her medical coverage. Defendants filed a motion to deny admission, on authenticity grounds, of nine appeal letters never received by the defendants. Forensic testimony showed that they were allegedly typed by the plaintiff on a computer but the "saved" dates of the files on a CD were more than 180 days after the appeal deadline.

Discovering fraudulent computer data

- *Munshani v. Signal Lake Venture Fund II,* LP, 13 Mass. L.Rptr. 732, 2001 WL 1526954, at *3-4 (Mass. Super. Ct. Oct. 9, 2001). The Court found that the plaintiff had fabricated documents based upon testimony of a court-appointed forensic consultant who revealed fraud in the creation of e-mail evidence. *See also Munshani v. Signal Lake Venture Fund II*, 2004 WL 584588 (Mass. App. Mar. 26, 2004) where on appeal, the plaintiff admitted that he fabricated the e-mail and submitted a false affidavit, after an expert in a 147-page report arrived at this same conclusion. The plaintiff argued that the judge erred in finding that the e-mail was material to the case and that dismissal sanctions were too severe under the circumstances. The appellate court rejected the plaintiff's argument and declared that the judge was justified in "imposing the ultimate sanction of dismissal."

• *Premier Homes and Land Corp. v. Cheswell, Inc.,* 240 F. Supp. 2d 97 (D. Mass. 2002). Party admitted to fabricating e-mail and lease addendum as opposing party's expert was obtaining a mirror copy of the hard drive. Court, for fraud, dismissed the case and reduced the computer expert fees from $200 to $100 per hour.

Discovering computer virus

• *United States v. Lloyd*, 269 F.3d 228, 234 (3rd Cir. 2001). Computer experts were able to determine that a company's former employee had "purged" the company's files by using a "time bomb." The expert "characterized a string of commands entitled 'FUSE.EXE' as a 'time bomb' because anyone who attempted to log onto the server on any date after July 30, 1996 would detonate the program and cause a massive deletion of data."

Discovering, accessing and copying computer files

• *YCA v. Berry,* No. CIV.03-3116, 2004 WL 1093385 (N.D. Ill. May 7, 2004). A computer forensic expert discovered e-mail that were later used to contradict the defendant's testimony which led to sanctions for the dishonest testimony. In addition, the Court noted, "Berry's posture [evaded telling plaintiffs that computer may contain relevant evidence] with respect to Mandall's [computer forensic expert] testimony brings to mind the tale of the criminal who murders his parents and then begs the Court's mercy because he is an orphan."

• *Sonista, Inc. v. Hsieh,* No. CIV.04-04080, 2005 U.S. Dist. LEXIS 31397 (N.D. Cal. Nov. 21, 2005). The Court granted summary judgment after several e-mail were discovered by a forensic expert showing that the defendant had performed numerous tasks in setting up and incorporating a competing company before resigning from his employment.

• *Tilberg v. Next Mgmt. Co.,* No. CIV.04-7373, 2005 U.S. Dist. LEXIS 24892, at *2-4 (D.N.Y. Oct. 24, 2005). The Court allowed the employee full access to search the employer's e-mail server, central server, and individual workstations after her computer forensic expert had searched and found numerous references to important documents on the "active space" and in deleted files of the employer's computers.

- *LeJeune v. Coin Acceptors, Inc.,* 849 A.2d 451 (Md. 2004). The computer forensic experts were able to show that the defendant copied numerous trade secret files from his former employer's work computer as well as evidence of his attempt to cover up evidence of the downloads.

- *Creative Sci. Sys. v. Forex Capital Mkts., LLC,* No. CIV.04-03746, 2006 U.S. Dist. LEXIS 20116, at *12-13 (D. Cal. Apr. 4, 2006). The Court issued a preservation order that a forensic expert was to copy "the configuration file of any load balancing servers and [run] . . . a utility program that generates a specific digital signature (a 'MD5 hash value') for each file . . . and then [the expert] . . . shall be permitted to compare the MD5 hash values for the files on the . . . servers with the MD5 hash values for file unique to the NetZyme software . . ." to determine if the software was improperly used by the defendant.

- *United States v. Hilton,* No. 97-78, 2000 WL 894679 (D. Maine 2000). The Court reviewed the computer expert's testimony regarding the possessing and handling of electronic data to show criminal intent in a child pornography case.

- *Four Seasons Hotels and Resorts v. Consorcio Barr,* 267 F. Supp. 2d 1268 (S.D. Fla. 2003). The Court reviewed and discussed the extensive forensic investigation of the various computer systems and that the defendant improperly accessed the plaintiff's computer system, downloaded confidential files, deleted files and tried to cover up his actions.

[E]   Other Authorities

- Joan E. Feldman, *The Expert's Role In Computer-based Discovery,* 71 ALI-ABA 121 (May 2005).

- Lisa M. Arent et al., *EDiscovery: Preserving, Requesting & Producing Electronic Information,* 19 Santa Clara Computer & High Tech. L.J. 131, 176 (2002).

- Gene J. Koprowski, *Picking the Right Consultant to Help You with E-discovery, Digital Discovery & e-Evidence,* (Feb. 2001) at 12-13.

- Andy Johnson-Laird, *Smoking Guns and Spinning Disks,* 11 Computer Law 1 (1994). This article discusses the typical state of computer files subject to discovery and the role of the computer forensics expert.

- Johnette Hassell & Susan Steen, *Demystifying Computer Forensics,* 50 L.A.B.J. 278 (Dec./Jan. 2002/2003).

This page intentionally left blank.

Chapter 5

Collecting, Processing and Searching Electronic Information

§ 5.1   GENERALLY

The discovery and disclosure process of electronic information involves collecting, searching, extracting, reviewing and then converting the data to a presentation format for use in depositions, and later, at trial. There are "electronic discovery" software tools to assist in processing e-mail, attachments, and other electronic discovery. These tools can process the information to a format that is more familiar and useful to attorneys: a database record for each document, the full-text of that document and a TIFF or PDF image of how the original electronic document appeared. After processing, the materials can be searched by word, date or phrase using standard litigation support software. In addition, TIFF and PDF images of electronic documents are usable by any of the popular trial presentation packages for use in depositions or the courtroom.

During the collecting and processing stages, be alert to authentication and other evidentiary issues regarding the electronic information. Electronic information is not automatically admissible. The rules of evidence apply to this information, just like traditional paper-based information. *See,* Chapter 8, *Admissibility of Electronic Evidence.*

Below are several of the steps involved in the discovery and production of electronic information:

Requesting Party:

- Determine types and locations of electronic information relevant to your case;

- Determine scope and estimated cost of the relevant information targeted; and

- File appropriate discovery pleadings such as a request for production (unless mandatory disclosure is available) of the information desired from the disclosing party.

Disclosing Party:

- Confer with client regarding the locations and type of relevant electronic data;

- Search, locate and preserve data;

- Negotiate compliance with the requesting party;

- Review for relevance and the presence of privileged information;

- Produce data to the opposing party in an agreeable format.

Requesting Party:

- Determine whether data disclosed is in compliance with request;

- Search for "smoking guns" and other relevant data;

- Organize and classify the data according to categories, issues, witnesses, etc.; and

- Convert it to an acceptable deposition or trial presentation format.

       For an extensive discussion regarding the steps in the discovery and production of electronic information *see* Chapter 6, *Discovery and Production Process*.

§ 5.2   VALUE OF COLLECTING INFORMATION IN AN ELECTRONIC FORMAT

       The transition from conventional paper to information in an electronic format should lower the cost and time of conducting pretrial discovery, analysis of case information as well as the presentation of evidence in trial. Kenneth J. Withers, *Computer-Based Discovery in Federal Civil Litigation*, Practical Litigator (November 2001); MANUAL FOR COMPLEX LITIGATION (FOURTH) § 11.446. Discovery of information in an electronic format provides many benefits not found in traditional paper-based discovery. These include the capability to:

- Search, retrieve and organize large amounts of data quickly;

- Perform computer-sophisticated analysis on the case information;

- Store, duplicate and transmit information quickly and inexpensively;

- Preserve electronic information links and attachments; and

- Present electronic evidence in the courtroom that results in timesaving and focuses the jury on critical evidence.

       Electronic data discovery will not eliminate paper discovery, but can reduce the roles that paper plays in litigation. There will be a shift away from the conventional page-by-page review of printed documents, to computer searches by names, dates, etc., and then onscreen review of case information. However, in certain cases, it may still be important to discover the printed copy since it may contain marginalia and other handwritten notations.

[A]   Searching and Managing Data

The time involved in reviewing and managing evidence can be substantially reduced by using computer-based word-searching, sorting and other forms of electronic organization. Electronic information that is outputted to either a database or full text can be searched by word, phrases, dates, etc. The cost of using a standard litigation support system is reduced dramatically if the documents are in electronic form from the start and do not need to be scanned and coded. J. Roger Tamer, *Preparing for Electronic Discovery*, N.Y.L.J., Jan. 25, 1999, at S5.

For example, in the Fen-Phen litigation "much of the evidence presented against American Home Products . . . was based on e-mail." *The Cost of Unmanaged E-mail*, Corporate Counsellor (May 2001). The plaintiff's cost of filtering through 33 million e-mail was minimal because they used full text software to search through the e-mail. The searching process would have been costly if the opposing party had produced the e-mail in an image or printed format as opposed to a full text electronic format.

Contrast this with paper discovery. Where one generally will receive, categorize and review each document manually for keywords, names, type, etc., and then record the information in a computer. One can then search the computer notes for specific case information. However, if you want to search for individual words in a paper document, it would be necessary to scan the document, use optical character recognition software to convert it to a searchable full text format, clean up the errors of the conversion process and then computer search the material. This is time-consuming and costly. If you obtain the evidentiary material in an electronic format, you can eliminate the costly conversion steps that are commonplace with paper-based discovery.

Duplicating Data

If you obtain discovery in an electronic format, it will make it easier to store, transmit, produce and duplicate case material. "The costs of photocopying and transport can be reduced dramatically or eliminated altogether. In the nationwide breast implant litigation, MDL-926, conversion of just one-third of the discovery documents and court papers to computer form resulted in an estimated savings of $1,146,500 in copying costs per party requesting a complete set of the documents." Kenneth J. Withers, *Computer-Based Discovery in Federal Civil Litigation*, Practical Litigator (November 2001).

Electronic information in an electronic format can be inexpensively duplicated using storage media such as CD-ROM or DVD.

Transmitting and Collaborating

Electronic evidence can be instantly transmitted and shared with co-counsel, either through duplication of the electronic information onto storage media or by transmitting the data using the Internet. One innovative technique is to transmit and store the data to an online data depository, where the information can be viewed, analyzed and comments saved for collaboration among a geographically dispersed litigation team.

Preservation of Links and Attachments of the Core Document

Proper handling of electronic information will preserve the attachments, links and web pointers within the data. For example, if there are file attachments linked to e-mail messages, then these will remain intact if properly converted and can be searched. In addition, a web pointer contained within an e-mail can be preserved for analysis.

[B]   Analyzing Computer Data

Discovery of electronic information in the appropriate data format provides the capability of importing the data and analyzing it in a variety of litigation support, financial or other application software packages. "Electronic format is easy to search and lends itself readily to financial analysis, using spreadsheets and other methods." *In re Keyspan Corp. Securities Litigation,* No. CIV.01-5852, 2003 WL 1702279, at *13 n.5 (E.D.N.Y. Mar. 21, 2003).

As an example, consider the benefit that you would receive from obtaining financial statements in an electronic format, as opposed to traditional paper-based discovery. In order to analyze the data prior to electronic discovery, one would have received the financial documents and then attempted to convert them into an electronic format through scanning and optical character recognition (which can be very costly). Assuming the conversion was accurate, one would be able to search the data, but would not be able to use financial formulas to perform your own analysis, since the data is not linked with a specific application program. For example, it would be difficult to correlate financial statements with other financial documents, such as a general ledger or receivables, in order to verify their mathematical accuracy. However, if you discover electronic data, as well as the application program, or use an available financial analysis program to import the data, then an attorney could both search the individual financial information, and perform financial analysis on the data.

In the Microsoft antitrust litigation, the Court granted the Department of Justice direct access to Microsoft's computerized sales and pricing data that simplified the task of quantifying potential damages. Kim S. Nash & Patrick Thibodeau, *What's in a Database? Microsoft Sales Evidence: Court Allows DOJ to Check Files in Redmond,* Computerworld, Oct. 19, 1998.

[1]   Reported Cases

• *For a list of cases discussing databases see § 3.10[F], Reported Cases.*

[C]   Electronic Courtroom Presentations

Once in electronic format, e-mail and other electronic information can easily be converted to an image format that can be presented in depositions or in the courtroom. This saves time in presenting evidence to the court and juries, since paper is not passed around the courtroom, and the factfinder easily focuses on critical information.

[D]   Automated Litigation Support System (ALS)

Automated litigation support generally refers to operations that support legal functions in litigation. Legal services functions such as docketing, document or transcript management can be supported using automated support software systems such as Amicus Attorney (docketing), Summation and Concordance (document management) and Summation and TextMap (transcript management). These computer-assisted systems are capable of acquiring, searching, sorting, classifying, indexing, storing, retrieving, and analyzing information needed to conduct litigation. ALS can manage a large volume of documents, electronic data, transcripts and other data in a secure environment for quick retrieval and analysis during litigation. From simple to complex cases these systems are essential for managing paper and electronic evidence.

It is important to determine whether an ALS system you are considering using in a case is a standalone or integrated litigation software program. Fifteen years ago litigation support programs were generally standalone applications. They consisted of a standalone database or a full text search and retrieval system and were not integrated with other programs. It was difficult to manage your case because of the different command structures and functionality of these unrelated software programs. However, in the last several years we have seen new modules added to existing litigation support packages or different vendor application packages "integrating" with each other to assist in the electronic management and analysis of your cases.

The integration of different software applications - word processing, databases, imaging, spreadsheets, full text and so on - that enables one to link and share case information is vitally important. There are many tasks that have to be performed as you prepare your case. These tasks include an overall plan, document indexes, witness depositions and indexes, correspondence and deposition management, electronic information control, interrogatory control, production document control, admissions, pretrial orders, substantive motion preparation, opening statements, closing arguments, and so on. If you are "integrating" different software applications be sure they can handle these tasks seamlessly and easily.

For example, Summation (www.summation.com) is an integrated searchable ALS system and includes the following components: database, full text, real time, imaging, and OCR.

• A database is simply a collection of mutually related data or information stored in computer record fields. They are organized collections of information similar to index cards, phone books, manual trial notebooks or file cabinets of documents. They are generally used to control document data such as an author, recipient, document type, connected legal issues, etc.

• Full text documents are those documents that have the "complete text" or "full text" of a document stored in a computer file. These documents can be word or phrase searched and you can instantly access the exact location of the words in the full text documents. Examples of full text documents include depositions and trial transcripts. Essentially, any document produced in a word processor is a "full text" document.

• Imaging is a technology that stores documents as electronic photographs in a computer system. These digitized computer files of documents are known as images. Images cannot be searched. They are generally linked to a database to assist in the retrieval process.

• Optical Character Recognition (OCR) is software that can convert the letters or numbers that appear on a page to a bit mapped image and then into a computer readable text known as ASCII. These words can then be searched using full text software.

• Real-time transcription is the capability of the court reporter to use a computer-assisted stenograph machine to have the testimony of a witness appear on a computer monitor within seconds from the time the words are spoken.

Many firms today have internally implemented ALS systems as opposed to having the system managed by outside service bureaus. However, the management of electronic and paper information can be difficult unless one has a working knowledge of these systems. Initially, firms may hire ALS "consultants" to assist in the implementation of these systems.

[1]   Reported Cases

• *United States v. Wecht,* No. CR.06-0026, 2006 U.S. Dist. LEXIS 39266, at *28, 64 (D. Pa. Jun. 14, 2006). The Court, at the defendant's request, ordered the parties to share in the expense of creating an electronic database and images of the trial exhibits reasoning that otherwise it "would continue the use of outdated pretrial methodology. Further the taxpayers have heavily invested in court technology and courtroom technology. To not implement the above procedure, including the creation of a searchable database, would deny the taxpayers the cost savings and efficiencies that should result from such investment." The Court later ordered a contempt hearing following trial "to adjudicate whether defense counsel's conduct," in moving for disclosure of exhibits in a paper format, asserting it was unable to work with the electronic database among other issues, constituted contempt.

- *Pueblo of Laguna v. United States,* 60 Fed. Cl. 133, 142-143 (Fed.Cl. 2004). The Court ordered, "(a) The parties shall meet and confer . . . to develop a plan for indexing documents, data and tangible things reasonably anticipated to be subject to discovery in this case. The resulting plan shall be submitted to this court as a proposed order under RCFC 16(e). . . . (b) The parties should attempt to reach agreement on all issues regarding the indexation of documents, data, and tangible things." The Court then set out in detail what was expected from the ALS system included what data will be indexed, anticipated costs, etc.

- *See also,* § 7.3[E], *Discovery and Preservation Orders - Rule 16(c).*

§ 5.3 ELECTRONIC DATA FORMATS

During the early stages of electronic discovery you must make the critical decision as to the type of format you want the electronic information to be reviewed, produced or received. This decision will impact, from that point forward, every aspect of the electronic discovery production and disclosure process. For example, it will determine whether the data is searchable, whether metadata is retained and will impact the cost of managing your litigation information. Failure to request or to produce the proper data format can have severe consequences. *See,* § 7.7[G], *Form of Production of Computer-based Data.*

Whatever format is chosen should be one that allows the parties to verify the genuineness and authenticity of the electronic data for evidentiary purposes.

There are several electronic data formats that you need to be conversant: native file, images, database and full text.

[A] Native File Format

A native file is the *file format* used by a specific software application. *See,* §3.4[C], *File Formats.*. The native file format of an application is usually proprietary and is not transferable to other applications unless conversation software is used. For example, a native file created in Microsoft Excel is saved in a proprietary file format with a file extension of XLS. Within Excel you can open, modify and save any changes to the file. If you want to use the same file in Lotus 123 then a conversion process would need to be performed on the XLS file. However, the conversion process may not accurately convert the Excel file into the new Lotus 123 file format.

Generally, the producing party will provide electronic discovery in its native file format. *Treppel v. Biovail Corp.,* 233 F.R.D. 363, 369-370 (D.N.Y. 2006)("proposed order would require the parties to produce in native file format all relevant information currently maintained in 'accessible' form . . . ").

For example, a Microsoft Outlook calendaring and e-mail file would be provided in its native PST file. After obtaining the native file, it can be outputted to a database file, full text search and retrieval format and/or a graphical or printed format representing its original document appearance. The native file can be searched using a program such as dtSearch (www.dtSearch.com) or converted to other searchable formats. There are several software programs that can convert the native file format data without the necessity of acquiring the underlying application software. These programs will convert the native file into a common program interchange format that then can be imported into other computer software programs.

One issue is whether the native file should be produced. Producing electronic information in native file format allows a party to view the original document including any metadata and tracked changes. *See,* §§ 3.07, *Metadata, Hidden or Embedded Information* and 7.07[B][2], *Metadata.* However, a party may pose objections to this form of disclosure since with native files it is presently difficult to redact privileged information, the inability to Bates stamp the documents and raises authenticity concerns. The solution often utilized is a combination of native file and TIFF image disclosure.

[1]   Reported Cases

- *In re Priceline.com Inc. Sec. Litig.,* 233 F.R.D. 88, 89 (D. Conn. 2005). "In order to be viewed, a file must be restored [from a backup tape] to its 'native format.' 'Native format' is the default format of a file, and access to this file is typically provided through the software program on which it was created or through which it was viewed. For example, if the file was created in Microsoft Word and has been saved as a Microsoft Word file, it can be viewed or modified through Microsoft Word."

- *See also,* § 7.07[G], *Form of Production of Computer-based Data.*

[B]   Images

Imaging is a process whereby documents are scanned into a system and stored electronically as a "picture" in a non-searchable format. These digitized computer files of documents are known as images.

Generally, imaging refers to converting paper documents into electronic pictures. However, electronic information can also be converted to images for disclosure purposes, redaction or presentation in the courtroom.

An imaging system consists of a computer, scanner, document management software, storage device and a printer. A document page is sent through a scanner and "scanned." Since the image cannot be searched, key information of the document is indexed into a database to identify the document for later retrieval. However, if the image is processed using OCR software, this will convert the words on a document into text that can be subsequently edited or searched.

The producing party may offer to provide you a copy of the electronic documents or e-mail in an image format such as TIFF or PDF or in paper. They are able to provide disclosure in this format by converting the electronic data into essentially "electronic paper." This type of disclosure does NOT contain the metadata nor allows for electronic searching of the data (unless it is in a searchable PDF format). A paper document or a TIFF or PDF file is not "equivalent" to a copy of the data file in its native electronic format.

The two primary imaging formats used in the legal profession are TIFF and PDF.

TIFF (Tagged Image File Format)

A TIFF is a standard file format for storing images as bit maps. It is used especially for scanning documents because it can support any size, resolution and color depth. *Williams v. Sprint/United Mgmt. Co.,* 230 F.R.D. 640, 643, n8 (D. Kan. 2005) ("TIFF (Tagged Image File Format) is one of the most widely used and supported graphic file formats for storing bit-mapped images, with many different compression formats and resolutions. A TIFF file is characterized by its '.tif' file name extension. (citation omitted)").

If a company wishes to print out hard copies of restored e-mails and attachments, and search the documents manually for responsiveness and privilege, this can be facilitated by initially converting e-mails and attachments to TIFF.

PDF (Portable Document Format)

PDF stands for Portable Document Format and is a universal file format that preserves the fonts, images, graphics and layouts of any source document, such as a Microsoft Word document, regardless of the application and platform used to create it. After converting the file to a PDF format anyone with (a free) Adobe Reader software can view the document as it originally appeared in the application program. This precludes the necessity of having to obtain a licensed copy of the application program to view the document. Documents, spreadsheets, e-mail and graphics can all be converted to PDF.

PDF is one of the most widely used "document" formats in the world of technology and in the courts. Many courts are using it as the standard format for the filing of court documents in jurisdictions that permit electronic filing. It is also being used as the document format for filing CD-ROM briefs and to prevent alterations of electronic documents.

However, metadata from the original document is lost if you convert and print a file to a PDF format.

There are two different types of PDF files:

- The IMAGE ONLY format is an exact electronic picture of the paper document. Generally, this is the type of PDF format that is created when you scan paper into PDF. It cannot be word searched, unless the image is subsequently OCR'ed.

- The IMAGE FORMAT with SEARCHABLE TEXT FORMAT is an electronic picture or image of the document that also contains background "hidden" text that can be word searched using Adobe Reader software. This type of PDF format is created by "printing" a word processing document to a PDF format using Adobe PDF Distiller or a similar product.

Some of the features of the PDF format are as follows:

- PDF can import TIFF, GIF or BMP document images, which then can be converted into searchable PDF files using Acrobat Capture or other OCR software;

- Since one can download Adobe Acrobat Reader free of charge, PDF files are universally accessible without necessitating financial commitment to the software, unless you wish to author PDF documents;

- Since the original documents are converted into a PDF format, it does not make a difference which version of word processing or other application software was used to create the document; and

- Acrobat offers annotation and markup tools if you wish to add comments and other information to the image. Highlighting, strike through, circling, underlining, and comment boxes are available. It can be used effectively for trial team collaboration and trial presentation. In addition, electronic stamps such as confidential, draft, final and other user created messages are available to place on documents.

If you decide to present an e-mail message or other electronic document in court in its original document format appearance, it can be directly converted, using specialized software, to an image (TIFF or PDF format) or printed on paper. If it is converted to an image format, it can be imported into standard electronic trial presentation programs for courtroom use.

[1]   Reported Case

- *J.C. Assocs. v. Fid. & Guar. Ins. Co.*, No. CIV.01-2437, 2006 U.S. Dist. LEXIS 32919 (D.D.C. May 25, 2006). The Court ordered the plaintiff to make available to the defendant an OCR-scan program (OmniPage Pro) to permit the defendant to convert and search these files for specific keywords, check for privilege and then disclose to the plaintiff.

[C]   Database

The first basic concept to understand about databases is that they are merely a collection of mutually related data or information stored in computer record fields. *See also,* § 3.10, *Database.* Databases can control, in a structured manner, litigation and electronic discovery information. Once stored, the information can be retrieved, organized, placed in report or chart format, and used and reused in any manner that is important to you.

Organization and retrieval of facts, documents and their relation to the issues and witnesses of a case can become a major headache for trial attorneys especially because of electronic information. This can take valuable time away from developing proper strategies for trial preparation and presentation. Many attorneys voice their concerns over their factual material and repeatedly say that "we need a system to index evidence . . . to produce a chronological report of the important evidence in this case . . . to list the trial exhibits in an upcoming case . . . to determine which documents witness Smith is connected."

One widely used solution relating to their concerns is creating databases to control and organize electronic discovery, persons connected with this data and the legal issues that pertain to this information. The purpose of litigation discovery databases is to establish a computerized and controlled central collection of evidence and documents relevant to the case. Having this information available in this format will enable you to quickly locate, update, categorize and cross-reference the electronic information in your case.

Database programs offer litigation management for e-mail and other electronic information evidence, business databases, word processing documents, privilege logs, witness lists, brief banks, exhibit lists and work product information.

The primary components of a database are the table(s) where the information is kept, the form where information is entered and the report that summarizes the data entered into the records.

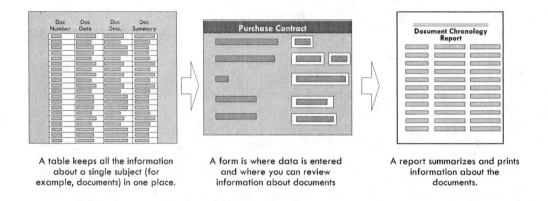

A table keeps all the information about a single subject (for example, documents) in one place.

A form is where data is entered and where you can review information about documents

A report summarizes and prints information about the documents.

Electronic discovery software can extract and convert data and metadata from computer files, such as e-mail messages, into separate fields of information for importation into a database program. The extracted data is saved to a common format, such as a comma-delimited format, which can be subsequently imported into a database program. For example, an e-mail message may have fields such as author, recipient, a date, subject and the body. These separate database fields can be extracted and then imported into a database program such as Summation.

These database records can also be linked to attachments, such as a word processing file attached to an e-mail. Duplicated e-mail can also be linked to the "original" e-mail message for later viewing, if needed. This database, attachments and duplicates, could then be uploaded to an Internet data depository for instant viewing by lawyers located in different parts of the country. They could quickly examine the data for privilege and confidential information.

Simultaneously, TIFF images of the "document" can be generated and linked to the database record. These TIFF images are an electronic print copy of the electronic information, and can be redacted or used as exhibits for depositions and for presentation in the courtroom.

[D]   Full Text

Along with a searchable database file, you may choose to export electronic discovery into a full text format. Full text output is not separated into specific fields like a database, but instead a "complete" file containing all the text is produced for searching. It is nonstructured. Full text search and retrieval systems enable you to search for any word in a "full text" format stored on a computer disk and then go to that exact location. For example, if a lawyer was searching for the term "fired" in an e-mail message, the software would immediately find the term every time it was used in the electronic data file. You can then view the word in each part of the file where the word is found.

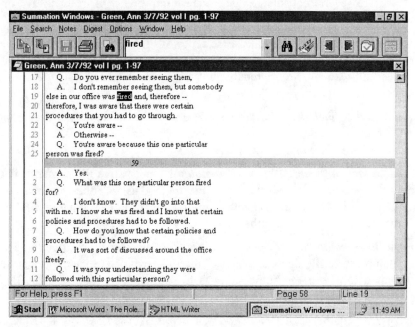

ASCII is a format that most computer programs recognize for transferring data between programs. Essentially any document produced is in a full text format if it is in an ASCII format. Once in an ASCII format, it can be imported and searched in a full text program. The most noteworthy example is the deposition of a witness. Other examples of full text documents include databases, business documents, trial transcripts, witness interviews and expert reports.

There are many full text search engines. For example, if a brief is in your word processor, the program's "FIND" feature will search and locate any word in that brief.

Generally, full text search and retrieve programs are used to "cull" or "winnow" electronic discovery to a manageable level. For example, you may use full text to search a large e-mail file, containing the e-mail of more than 50 employees, and locate relevant e-mail for specific individuals involved in the case. After this filtering and conducting a privilege review, you would disclose the information to the requesting party.

[E]   Summary of Format Types

There are several considerations in determining what form to receive or disclose electronic discovery.

- *Is the data searchable?* TIFF and some types of PDF files are not searchable, and, of course paper would have to be converted using OCR technology to search. Native files, databases, full text, etc. are searchable but may have to be translated to convert it to a useful searchable format.

- *Will metadata be included with the form?* Unless the metadata are also printed, TIFF and PDF file formats do not generally include metadata. *See,* §§ 3.07, *Metadata, Hidden or Embedded Information* and 7.07[B][2], *Metadata.*

- *Can one redact confidential or privileged data?* In a native file format it is generally difficult to redact privileged material. One method is to either place a code where privileged data has been electronically removed or to process a native file to a TIF or PDF image or paper and redact the data.

- *Can you Bates stamp the documents disclosed?* Generally, it is difficult to sequentially Bates stamp native file documents, other then its own native page numbering system. One method to assure file authenticity is to use hashing. *See,* § 5.05[G], *Chain of Custody, Audit Reports and Hash Values.*

See also, §§ 7.07[G], *Form of Production of Computer-based Data,* 7.07[E], *Kept in the Usual Course of Business,* and 7.07[D], *Translated Into Reasonably Useful Form.*

Below is a table of general characteristics of the different file formats:

Table 1: File Format Characteristics

Formats	Searchable	Metadata	Redaction	Bates Numbering
Native File[a]	Yes	Yes	No	No
TIFF	No	No	Yes	Yes
PDF	Depends[b]	Yes	Yes	Yes
Paper	No	No	Yes	Yes
Database	Yes	Yes	No	No
Full Text	Yes	Yes	No	No

a. Generally, the producing party will collect the electronic data in its native file format. Once in this format a party can convert the native file into various formats including database, full text, image (TIFF and PDF) or paper. However, metadata from the original electronic data or native file may be lost if you convert and print a file to a paper or PDF format or other formats unless the metadata is also converted or printed.

b. There are two different types of PDF files: •The IMAGE ONLY format is an exact electronic picture of the paper document. Generally, this is the type of PDF format that is created when you scan paper into PDF. It cannot be word searched, unless the image is subsequently OCR'ed (optical character recognition). •The IMAGE FORMAT PDF with SEARCHABLE TEXT FORMAT is an electronic picture or image of the document that also contains background "hidden" text that can be word searched using Adobe Reader software.

[F]   Reported Cases (reserved)

[G]   Other Authorities

- MANUAL FOR COMPLEX LITIGATION (FOURTH) § 11.446:

Evolving procedures use document-management technologies to minimize cost and exposure and, with time, parties and technology will likely continue to become more and more sophisticated. The judge should encourage the parties to discuss the issues of production forms early in litigation, preferably prior to any production, to avoid the waste and duplication of producing the same data in different formats. The relatively inexpensive production of computer-readable images may suffice for the vast majority of requested data. Dynamic data may need to be produced in native format, or in a modified format in which the integrity of the data can be maintained while the data can be manipulated for analysis. If raw data are produced, appropriate applications, file structures, manuals, and other tools necessary for the proper translation and use of the data must be provided. Files (such as E-mail) for which metadata is essential to the understanding of the primary data should be identified and produced in an appropriate format. There may even be rare instances in which paper printouts (hard copy) are appropriate. No one form of production will be appropriate for all types of data in all cases.

§ 5.4   SEARCHING ELECTRONIC INFORMATION

[A]   Generally

Searching electronic information is a critical component of your cases. Today, all organizations, businesses and individuals generate large amounts of data in an electronic format. Since important business and personal records may be in an electronic format, and may not be printed out, electronic searching becomes all the more critical. Searching can assist in all aspects of electronic discovery. For example, e-mail between key witnesses may establish consistent and frequent contact on important dates in your case. Locating and documenting these findings will strengthen the admissibility of the evidence and ensure a consistent and precise illustration of the alleged conduct.

Whether you are reviewing information from your client for production or receiving data, it has to be searched and analyzed. Searching electronic information may determine the outcome of your case.

One of the significant advantages of collecting and discovering information in an electronic format is the ability to search for individual words, names, phrases or dates and obtain the results instantly. Similar to a Westlaw or Lexis search, software is available to allow you to index and immediately search electronic evidentiary material. For example, you could obtain the e-mail files containing thousands or tens of thousands of e-mail messages and using search software, import the information and then search it immediately. This is low cost compared to organizing and searching for information in a paper-based system.

There are many techniques for searching data to find relevant admissible evidence. These include searching by keyword, file type, time stamps and other file attributes. More advanced data search techniques include text and numeric pattern recognition, as well as searching for audio, graphics and video files. In addition to locating an evidence file of factual importance, searching electronic information is useful in recreating a timeline of events at issue in litigation.

Another important point is that if you retain information in its electronic format, attachments and links can be preserved and converted for searching. For example, e-mail may have an attachment to a word processing document. When properly converted, both the e-mail and attachment can be searched simultaneously.

However, developing exact search protocols are difficult to fashion. Because of a lack of standardization of language, misspellings, abbreviations, etc. locating specific data can be quite challenging. In addition, files can be encrypted that preclude access to critical information. Sometimes these files can be broken into but the cost may be prohibitive.

[B]   Advantages

There are several advantages to searching electronic information by keyword or other methods.

• Keyword searching can assist in meeting your obligation to preserve relevant evidence and avoid spoliation claims, as opposed to conducting paper review for this information. By deciding upon key terms such as witness names, relevant dates, subject matter such as products or events, addresses and other relevant keywords potentially responsive records can be immediately retrieved and preserved.

• After the initial filtering, keyword searching can help to identify privileged or confidential documents (trade secret or other proprietary data). Obviously, if documents are marked "privileged" or "confidential" they will be isolated and kept in a confidential folder. Keyword searches would also locate attorneys' names, legal advice references and so on. Also, this would assist, depending on the jurisdiction, in establishing your reasonable efforts to prevent the inadvertent disclosure of privileged material. *See also,* § 7.4[H], *Work Product Doctrine, Attorney Client Privilege and Trade Secrets.*

• The Court in *Zubulake v. UBS Warburg LLC*, 216 F.R.D. 280, 290 (S.D.N.Y. 2003) suggested a "series of targeted keyword searches" as a means to reduce the cost and burden of privilege review. Otherwise, it would be a significant burden, which may still have to be done, to manually review this electronic data. It is suggested that if there might be privileged data inadvertently disclosed, that you enter into a privilege or confidential nonwaiver agreement with the opposing party as well as obtain a court order to that effect.

• Electronic searching will also uncover "metadata" contained in native files which is not available from hardcopy printouts.

• After the documents are electronically retrieved, disclosure in an electronic format would be significantly less costly than printing the documents. *See, Zubulake v. UBS Warburg LLC,* 217 F.R.D. 309, 317 (S.D.N.Y. 2003) ("[e]lectronic evidence is frequently cheaper and easier to produce than paper evidence because it can be searched automatically, key words can be run for privilege checks, and the production can be made in electronic form, obviating the need for mass photocopying").

• Finally, and most important, keyword searching can assist the requesting or producing party to possibly locate the "smoking gun" or other valuable evidence for use in summary judgments, witness preparation, cross-examination of witnesses or any other aspect of your case.

[C]   Search Limitations

Though keyword searching has been labeled a solution to handle the large volume of electronic data in cases, there are certain limitations when conducting keyword searches.

First, because of the lack of standardized terms used in conversations and documents, it is doubtful that you will retrieve all relevant documents to your search terms. For example, if information is sought about a particular automobile in a case, and the word "car" or "automobile" is searched, then references to a "Corvette" or "Bronco" will not be located. Electronic searching is simply looking to match the word, without regard to the meaning of the keyword.

The formulation of a query or keywords is difficult if the keywords have numerous synonyms, can be described in several different ways or ideas can be expressed in numerous methods. Often, the meaning of a certain keyword is dependant upon the context of when it is spoken or how the speaker or author uses the term figuratively.

Second, the search query may locate ambiguous uses of the search words. It may retrieve "hits" of the words that are not relevant to your inquiry. For example, if you search for the word "legal" or "copyright" it may retrieve operating system files that have no connection with your case.

Third, these limitations have resulted in what is commonly termed "false confidence syndrome." Carol M. Bast & Ransford C. Pyle, *Legal Research in the Computer Age: A Paradigm Shift?*, 93 Law Library Journal 285, 292-293 (2001).

> The most obvious difference between print indexing and CALR [computer assisted legal research] indexing is that the latter is constructed by the researcher rather than by the publisher. The success of a CALR search depends on recall, precision, and fallout. The recall percentage is the number of relevant documents retrieved compared to the total number of relevant documents in the database. The precision percentage is the number of relevant documents retrieved compared to the total number of documents retrieved. The fallout percentage is the number of irrelevant documents retrieved compared to the total number of irrelevant documents in the database.

> To increase recall, the researcher broadens the scope of the search. With a broader search, recall increases but precision decreases, since such a search retrieves more documents, many of them irrelevant. Many CALR databases contain a large number of documents and the fallout problem can be significant. To increase precision, the researcher might limit the number of documents retrieved by adding keywords to the search query. Of course, with a narrower search, precision increases but recall decreases, possibly omitting a number of highly relevant documents.

> Precision is an easy percentage to measure but recall is not, since the researcher would have to know the total number of relevant documents in the database and compare the number of relevant documents found using a particular search query against that total. A curious phenomenon is that researcher perception of the thoroughness of CALR varies greatly from the recall actually achieved. A researcher, happy with retrieving a number of relevant documents, may overestimate recall and be falsely confident that the research results are satisfactory. "A relatively high precision will give high user satisfaction as long as alternative methods do not disclose to the lawyer that the recall is low. The lawyer is satisfied and the providers of the system get positive feedback from their users." Several studies have documented this "false confidence syndrome." An often-referenced study indicates that the average recall may be as low as 20%.

This often-referenced study revealed that a keyword search failed to retrieve a significant number of electronic documents that were relevant to a case. The study, commonly referred to as the Blair and Maron Report, is actually named David C. Blair & M. E. Maron, *An Evaluation of Retrieval Effectiveness for a Full-Text Document-Retrieval System,* 28 Com. ACM 289 (1985). The study was based on the massive Bay Area Rapid Transit (BART) accident case where a computerized train failed to stop at the end of a line and crashed through the wall and into the parking lot. Forty thousand documents were converted to a full text format. One of the law firms reasoned that with the right search you could find anything. The startling conclusion was when the documents were searched the software retrieved only 20% of the relevant forty thousand on-line documents.

Fourth, one of the most important things to remember is that the keyword will only retrieve those documents containing the keyword. A keyword search will not retrieve documents containing a keyword if the keyword is misspelled in the query. In addition, if the keyword is already misspelled in the data population it will not retrieve any material containing the misspelled word.

[D]   Technological Difficulties and Data Depository

[1]   Diverse Computer Systems

Most companies' computer systems and data collections are diverse and fragmented. Many companies have built up their computer systems over years and have different databases, platforms, file formats, multiple storage devices and so on. IT departments rarely have a system that provides for a single keyword search over the entire data population. Instead, business units often have separate IT staff, business managers and computer requirements. They retrieve data based on specific projects, not in anticipation of possible litigation.

If you are the requesting party, questions must be asked of the producing party whether all formats and locations of relevant data have been considered and properly searched. Separate searches should be required for all standalone data sources, either on servers or on desktop computers, PDA's or other storage media depending on backup and document retention polices.

[2]   Online Data Depository

The "online" or "virtual" document depository is best described as an online litigation support system where documents and other materials can be searched, retrieved and then viewed and/or printed. These depositories can be set up on a secure Internet website and accessed through broadband or dial up and be available to attorneys at different physical locations. By using this type of system geographically dispersed attorneys can access the data and make notes, coding and other comments to the data that can be preserved for all the attorneys to share.

Many firms today routinely use computerized litigation support systems for storage and retrieval of documentary evidence. As a result attorneys should consider, in appropriate cases, establishing shared computer-based depositories. These shared depositories may have common indexes, abstracts, transcripts and other data. Appropriate protocols or data segregation would need to be developed to protect privileged data such as "work product."

See, MANUAL FOR COMPLEX LITIGATION (FOURTH) § 111.444:

> Central document depositories can promote efficient and economical management of voluminous documents in multiparty litigation. Requiring the production of all discovery materials in common, computer-readable formats and insisting that these materials be made available on centrally generated computer-readable media (such as CD-ROM or DVD) or through a secure Internet Web site or a dial-in computer network may reduce substantially the expense and burden of document production and inspection.

See, In re Bridgestone/Firestone, Inc., 129 F. Supp. 2d 1207, 1213 (S.D. Ind. 2001) (Case Management Order dated Jan. 30, 2001).

These systems have many advantages since they are available 24/7. Users can be easily trained and anyone with a laptop and modem can access the documents. Extra attention should be given to ensure these systems are secure.

This online or offline data depository is created to ensure an archive of litigation data. This will ensure that responsive data is indexed and privileged data is tagged to assist with the analysis of your case. Leaving responsive litigation data on the company's computer system may interrupt the company's business operations when conducting keyword searches and will be problematic trying to segregate and retain the privileged status of data. For this reason, consideration should be given to creating a separate database to house all of the client's data. This also will permit universal searching of the data.

Many outside companies now specialize in creating these single source databases and provide assistance in not only creating the database, but also serving as an independent expert verifying the collection and procedures in accumulating the data in case of a court challenge. However, the costs of retaining such a vendor and "control" of a database housed on a vendor's computer system have to be considered especially if costs or other aspects of the management of the database are issues. In addition, your IT staffs' cooperation with these outside vendors is critical for success of these projects.

If you are considering setting up a keyword searchable data depository to house the data the following issues should be considered.

•   Obtain cost estimates for the project. This would include the cost of the database setup, collecting and populating the database and the search platform.

* Other cost considerations include computer processing time and searches of the data. Generally, cost overages will occur in the form of unanticipated events leading to additional work by the outside vendor.

    Some online data depository service bureaus include:

* CaseVault (www.casevault.com), part of the Summation (www.summation.com) family of litigation support products;

* CaseCentral (www.casecentral.com); and

* Lextranet (www.lextranet.com).

[E]   Search Engines

[1]   Generally

A search engine is a tool that helps you locate key information in your electronic data, whether in a structured or unstructured format. When you enter a keyword or phrase into a search engine, the computer will return a list of documents, e-mail or other data "hits" related to the keywords entered.

There are several types of search engines that use various search technologies. The most prevalent search engine is the "keyword" search engine. Others include natural search, adaptive pattern recognition and others. However, there has been very little academic research involving the comparative accuracy of these different search methodologies. Jason R. Baron, *Toward A Federal Benchmarking Standard for Evaluating Information,* 6 Sedona Conf. J. 237 (Fall, 2005).

Search engines generally search "indexed" databases. These are databases that have already indexed the words in documents, e-mail and other data along with the location of the words in the various data sources. When you conduct a keyword search, you are conducting a search of this index. This process greatly increases the search speed of the system and will return a list of results with location pointers to the electronic data that you are searching.

Full-text indexing systems generally pick up every word in the text except commonly occurring stop words such as "a," "an," "the," "is," "and," "or" and "www." Some of the search engines discriminate uppercase from lowercase; others store all words without reference to capitalization.

[2]   Using Original Application Software to Search

There are several reasons why you may choose not to use the original application software to search and review the data files discovered.

- Application data may be provided to you in one of thousands of different computer file formats and on many different types of storage media. Even if you had the native application software to open a computer file, it would be a tedious and inconsistent process to allow human operators to follow complex instructions and manually try to open computer files and extract the information. This approach of opening and printing electronic information may take hundreds of staff hours. Also, if you use this "open and print" approach to viewing electronic information, it may not provide the "metadata" that could be important to your case.

- You will be handling several different data types from several different software programs. You will want to have the electronic data integrated into a single litigation support system that can be searched simultaneously.

- The information you are seeking is in the application data files. The opposition's application software does not contain the data files. After receiving data files, they can be processed with electronic discovery software, without needing the original application software.

- If you choose to perform further analysis such as financial calculations on the data, then you may need to import and analyze it in a different software package such as a spreadsheet.

- The opposition's software may require different, and possibly more expensive, hardware as well as a different operating system in order to function.

- One may have to purchase the application software so as not to violate any licensing restrictions.

- If you open a computer file in the application software program that created the data, cosmetic updating or macro features may change the contents of the document or e-mail.

However, the application software may be needed if the other side is relying on specific software for computerized computations that will be used in court. This would include engineering computations, accident reconstruction computations, etc. This raises several issues regarding the availability of the software, and maybe hardware, to run the software, licensing agreements and other issues. Hon. Shira A. Scheindlin & Jeffrey Rabkin, *Electronic Discovery in Federal Civil Litigation: Is Rule 34 Up to the Task?* 41 B.C. L. Rev. 327 (Mar. 2000). Under these circumstances, it is important to not only obtain the software, but also the instructions, source code and other related documentation.

[3]   Recall and Precision

The goal of keyword searching is to retrieve the information that is relevant. In searching parlance, this is referred to as recall and precision. Recall means to retrieve all information that is connected that could be useful. Precision relates only to those documents that are useful.

These two concepts are inversely related. As the precision of your search increases, the recall of the number of documents decreases. If your request is too precise, then only one or two documents will be recalled. For example, if I search for "car" then I would "recall" all references to "car" regardless of which witness discusses a car. However, if I search for "corvette" then the search is more precise and the number of occurrences would be significantly lower. The problem with too precise a search is that if the "corvette" is referred to as a "car" by a witness, then you will not locate that particular reference if you only search for "corvette."

One can "program" a computer for these cross-reference checks, but this would have to be programmed for every type of word or concept to be searched. Some software programs, however, are preprogrammed with cross-references to certain words.

Every search feature supports recall or precision. For example, how close key words are grouped in a document would increase precision but decrease recall. Wildcard searches would increase recall but decrease precision. The importance of this concept is that if your search is too broad, then the number of documents recalled will take a long time to review, whereas if your precision is reasonable, then the number of "relevant hits" will be manageable. Recall and cross-referencing the text with keywords can strengthen precision. For example, some full text software offers you the ability to add synonyms. When you are conducting a search, the synonyms would automatically be included in the search.

The following are advanced search engines and features available with some search engine software programs. As you will discover, the emphasis is on a sort of "artificial intelligence" built into the program. These full text search advances are important to the location of electronic information, but the sharp persevering inquisitive mind of a researcher cannot be overstated. An individual familiar with the vocabulary of a case can increase the retrieval of key information tenfold

[4]   Advanced Search Engines and Features.

Full text search programs are a valuable tool if used with a clear understanding of their strengths and weaknesses. It is strongly suggested that whatever search software you consider that you perform a test to determine its accuracy using data with which you are familiar in order to judge the search results. The following are some of the software search enhancements that are part of some search engines.

- Soundalikes - A method whereby the computer will take a word and produce a list of words that "sound" similar. For example, searching soundalikes for the word "confident" would yield confidential, confidence, etc. It will use the consonants of the main word and will retrieve soundalike words.

- Synonym Search - Many programs allow you to search for synonyms. For example, if "car" and "automobile" were used in the document, then when you search for "car," all occurrences of car and automobile would be retrieved.

- Similar Document Searching - This enhancement finds all documents that are similar to the primary document. For example, if you locate a particularly important document, then the computer would analyze the document for keywords, location of words and concepts within the document, the number of times they appear and so on to compare with the other documents. Then other similar documents would be retrieved for your viewing.

- Fuzzy Searching - This technique locates words that closely match the spelling of the primary word. Many of the popular word processor packages have this capability when you do a spell check. It will retrieve similarly spelled words and suggest possible replacements. For example, if the primary word is "liability" then the location of the words "libility," "liable," and "lability" should be brought to the reader's attention. The use of fuzzy searching can be valuable when locating materials that have been OCR'ed (Optical Character Recognition). When converting documents to full text using OCR software, the errors that occur include leaving out letters or misspelling words. Fuzzy searching will retrieve close spellings of those words for review. The sophistication of fuzzy searching varies from product to product.

- Statistical Searching - This search tool retrieves words that are statistically related to your primary word. Statistical association of words to other words is accomplished at the time the document is "indexed." When a document is imported into the full text software, the program produces an index of all the words and their relationship to other words. When you "expand" your search of the primary word, it will retrieve all documents where "other" words are statistically related to the primary word, even though the primary word is not in the document. When the primary search term is not in the document, then documents that you would have not been able to locate because they do not contain the primary word will be retrieved.

- Conceptual, Thesaurus, or Related Searching - This search tool will provide words that are similar or close in meaning to the primary word. There can be shades of different meanings to the similar words. For example, if you search for the word "car" then the "hits" returned would include "auto" or "vehicle" automatically. Some full text software includes a thesaurus. Others permit you to purchase or create a thesaurus for your case. However, this can be quite time consuming.

- Content-Based Searching - Unlike keyword search systems, content-based search systems try to determine what you mean, not just what you say. In the best circumstances, a content-based search returns hits on documents that are "about" the subject/theme you're exploring, even if the words in the document don't precisely match the words you enter into the query. This type of search would present the documents, witnesses and other communications for a specific event, i.e., contract negotiations, financial dealings, etc. This would provide the context of the electronic communications about events and correlating them to specific individuals. See Cataphora (www.cataphora.com) for an example of a content-based search system.

- Topical Searching - This tool enables you to search documents by topics and subtopics relevant to your case. You can provide weighted relevance to the different topic outlines to retrieve only those documents that pertain to the topics and the precision will be determined by the weight given to the topic. This can be especially useful if you know and can define the various topic outlines - implying that you know the contents of your document set - in order to retrieve the documents based upon the weight you give to the various topics and subtopics. Topical searching offers an advantage if you specialize in a particular area of law and the terms as applied to a group of documents remains the same.

- Weighted Relevance Searching - This will allow you to sort and retrieve documents according to the "weight" given to the documents. The weight will depend on the weighted criteria of the software program. Some programs will give statistical weight to the number of times the primary search terms are found in a given document and their proximity to each other. The purpose is to retrieve first the most "relevant" documents for your review. In comparison, a topical search would return the documents where you provide the emphasis given to a topic - whereas the weighted relevance would return the documents where the terms are located most frequently and in proximity to each other. Natural language programs are using weighted relevance as they group words and return the relevance of the terms in close proximity.

- Adaptive Pattern Recognition - This system indexes every letter on every page. It learns and remembers binary patterns found in the text. When you conduct a search, it conducts the search based on discreet patterns in the text. For example, if you search for "asbestos," then even if the word is spelled as "asbest~~" or "asbstos," the algorithm will find enough patterns to locate these hits. This technology has proven especially useful with documents that have been OCR'ed and have not been cleaned up after conversion.

- Associative Retrieval - Where certain terms appear frequently near the terms you are searching, these may provide clues for further searching using the new associative words.

- Natural Language or Non-Boolean Retrieval - Instead of using "and/or" connectors, you prepare your search request in ordinary language and the computer automatically converts it into algorithms. Depending on the software, it can be extremely beneficial and enable you to retrieve exact information quickly and accurately.

- Clusters of Related Phrases - One technique that may provide assistance to your case is to find all documents that contain clusters of related phrases. This tool deconstructs sentences linguistically, indexing relevant phrases. It builds a table of terms occurring together and finds statistical clusters of these co-occurrences. Then the results are delivered in a series of navigable concept maps. One can discover patterns in vast bodies of text. This is especially useful for the search and retrieval of all kinds of digital data - e-mails, word processing documents, etc.

[5]   Keyword Searching

Keyword searching is looking in a database or other data depository for specific words or combination of words relevant to your case. These keywords would be chosen based on the subject matter of the litigation, witnesses and other information connected to the case. The most effective way to "cull" or "winnow" down a large population of electronic information would include keyword searches, time range(s), file types and/or key individuals who created or modified electronic information.

Unfortunately, there is no standard full text engine or command structure followed by all keyword search engines. However, many use the standard Boolean search format. There are generally software proprietary differences on how to formulate search requests. For example, some developers require that combinations of words, such as General Motors, be in parentheses or quotes, while others do not require this. The software manual for a particular software product needs to be consulted for the appropriate search syntax to use.

[a]   Types of Keyword Searches

Boolean Searches. A Boolean search is a search for information using "AND," "OR" and "NOT" commands.

— AND Command - If you want to search a number of different documents for keywords "driving" and "beer," then the search phrase would be "driving AND beer." If a document contained these two terms, then it would be a "hit" and it would retrieve the document and the location where the document and terms can be found. The more terms you include in the search with AND such as "driving AND beer AND night AND juvenile," the narrower the search.

— OR Command - If you wish to include more documents, then use the OR command. If you search for "driving OR beer" then any documents containing "beer" or "driving" would be returned. This obviously enlarges the number of documents that will be located.

— NOT Command - If you wish to exclude documents, then you need to use the word NOT. For example, if the important information involves driving and beer but it will return unneeded documents involving a prior boat accident involving beer and driving, then the search phrase "beer AND driving NOT 'prior boat accident'" would return only the relevant documents. A quote around the phrase "prior boat accident" generally directs the computer to locate these three words together.

• Single Word Search - This search will retrieve documents containing the single word for which you are searching. For example, if you type in the word "fired," all occurrences of this word in the full text will be located.

• Wildcard Search - This search will retrieve different conjugations of the same word. You would use symbols such as * or ? that would be added to your words. Using an asterisk means that any word ending or beginning with the specified letters will be retrieved. For example, use the search request *tion to retrieve all words ending in "tion" or *auto* to retrieve all words containing the letters "auto." If you type in the search phrase *process*, it would locate the words process, reprocess, processor, processing, etc.

• Lowercase Letter Search - This is more effective than using uppercase text because the search engine usually finds both upper and lowercase matches. If you use uppercase, you may restrict your matches to only uppercase.

• Proximity Search - Key word proximity refers to the distance in space, as measured in words, between two words or two key phrases. For instance, to retrieve all instances in which the word "car" occurs within 3 lines of the word "accident," type in the appropriate search command (depends upon the search engine rules) such as "car /3 accident."

• Phrase Search - Use double quotes around words that are a part of a phrase. This will locate data where your keywords appear in the exact same order (e.g., "great barrier reef" or "General Motors").

• Combined Word Searching - Combined word searches are used to combine synonym, proximity, and/or Boolean searches. For example, you can search and locate all words beginning with "auto," but not the word "automatic," and also get hits for the word "car."

[b]   Developing Keyword Search Strings

Before conducting searches on your electronic evidence, work with your forensic specialist, client and others to create a list of keyword search strings related to names, dates and terms that relate to the claims or defenses of your case. As you perform the searches, you will locate e-mail messages, URLs, word processing documents and other data files relevant to your keyword. The results of your searches will show fact patterns that may require additional investigation and discovery. Below are various considerations in developing your keyword searches.

Preliminary Considerations

- Who originates the keyword list - producing party, requesting party or both?

- How many keyword searches to conduct (usually 30 - 50 searches)?

- Determine possible data sources from depositions of IT personnel, witnesses, etc.

- Determine what search method will be used and keyword search rules for particular data sources.

- Determine whether to search by file type, time stamps and other file attributes.

- Determine the type of data that you wish to retrieve (documents, e-mail, spreadsheets, presentations, graphics, audio or video).

- Determine the data sources (human resources' database, privilege logs, e-mail "inbox" and "outbox" folders for selected individuals, etc.).

- Determine whether the database(s) allows searches by subject as well as by keywords (*See,* § 5.4[F], *Subject Search*).

- Determine the location of data, database files or document management systems (corporate headquarters network, standalone computers, etc.).

- Determine whether the network logs and other auditing files are wanted (provides date and time and who opened certain files, who accessed the network system, etc.).

Formulating the Keyword List

- Keyword list creators (attorney, client, expert in subject matter, expert in building keyword search strings and others).

- Brainstorm the possible names, events, dates and phrases that may be connected with the case.

- Compile a list of last names, first names, surnames, nicknames, positions and other titles of individuals connected with the case.

- Determine the acronyms and abbreviations, buzzwords and/or euphemisms related to the keywords or factual issues.

- List date ranges that correspond with the critical time period of the case (date documents created, modified, etc.).

- Determine key event terms (cardiac, heart, operations, nurse orders, etc.).

- Determine what phrases to search ("General Motors," "merger agreement" "employment agreement" etc.).

- Use a thesaurus to locate similar keywords ("fracture," "broken," etc.).

- Avoid words such as common names, adjectives and adverbs that increase the number of documents retrieved ("went," "and," "Mary," etc.).

- Consider name variations, possible misspellings and using all lowercase lettering.

- Consider using wildcard symbols to enlarge or decrease the number of relevant hits.

- Avoid retrieving operating system and application software files (avoid keywords such as computer, system and legal).

Methods of Hiding Data

- Changing spelling of words (Monday to Munday, Smith to Smit).

- Changing file extensions (ABCmergeragreement.doc to ABCmergeragreement.jpg).

- Odd file sizes (word processing is 2 megabytes).

- Unusual dates (date on e-mail is in the future, battery failed thus resetting dates automatically or old file was opened for viewing and then saved to a later date).

Conducting Your Searches

- Run a sample of your search strings. (Try to run a test of your keywords by using one individual's name whose role in the case you are familiar with and electronic information that you know is connected to that person).

- After obtaining the sampling refine your searches.

- Try the same approach on documents that are retrieved pursuant to dates that you are searching.

- Modify your searches based on the results, databases, software applications, hardware configurations and other factors as they occur.

- Continue the process until the records retrieved from additional searching are marginal.

Keyword List - Slip and Fall Case Example

• Data to be searched (e-mail database and the store accident database).

• Date of the event (4-6-02, 04/06/02, April 6, 2002, date range 3-23-02 to 5-1-02).

• Injured party's name ("Frank Perkins" "Perkins" "Perkans" "Perkens" "customer" "husband" "patient" "mechanic" etc.)

• Prior experiences shopping at the store - dates, times, events, etc. ("July 4th sale" "with my daughters").

• Witness names and statements ("witness" "security officer" "captain" "Frank Boros" "Boros" "eyewitness" "statement" etc.).

• Address or location of the accident ("store" "4500 North 34th Street" "ABC Store" "office supply store" etc.).

• Names of doctor and other health professionals and/or hospitals ("Dr. Markham" "Markham" "doctor" "EMT" "paramedic" "injury report" "Good Samaritan Hospital," etc.).

[F]   Subject Search

Besides keyword searching you may want to consider conducting a subject search. A subject search, or a controlled language search, searches predefined subject headings for each database. An item like a document, report or article is abstracted and subject headings are assigned to indicate the main content of the item. Each item may be assigned anywhere from two to eight subject headings depending on the database. A search can then be conducted on these subject headings. For this strategy to be effective the abstractor must have used the appropriate heading or subject term. Usually the list of subject headings is found in the database's online thesaurus or data dictionary. The subject matter headings are database specific.

[G]   Reports

Generating reports that condense and simplify huge volumes of data will prove invaluable in your case preparation and trial. Depending on the search engine and report writer that are available, various reports can be generated from your keyword search results. Report options should enable the viewer to view, print or export custom reports and data to other litigation support software applications. Some report formats to consider:

• Digest - This report allows you to manually capture a portion of text from within a document and send it to a computer file or print it out on a report. This is useful for digesting large documents by copying only the necessary and important information to the report.

- Vocabulary Listing - This report will provide a complete or partial list of any words contained within a database file. This report can provide the number and location of each occurrence of a word. Words such as "asbestos," "earnings," and "speed" can be printed out with source, document, page, and line locations for retrieval and reference to the underlying data. Such reports will increase your understanding of what the key terms are in the database. With this knowledge, one can then prepare search phrases that are more precise.

- Surrounding Text Report - This report is similar to the above report, except the report writer will automatically print the text surrounding a keyword. The number of lines before and after the word is generally defined by the user.

- Occurrences - A feature useful in some report writers is a display of all the occurrences of a search request. The occurrence display will show all occurrences of the master word by data source, page and line number.

[H] Searching Audio, Video and Graphics

There are new developments in searching for audio, video and graphical information. Audio software packages are available to assist if you are searching for a particular voice in a large set of audiotapes. The audiotapes would be converted into a digital format and the audio search software would locate the voice of the particular person. This same development is occurring both in video and graphical formats such as photographs. In a video, a certain face or scene would be identified and then electronic software would search throughout digitized videotapes for a similar face or scene. *See also,* § 2.5[H], *Voice Mail and Answering Machine.*

§ 5.5 IDENTIFYING, COLLECTING AND PRODUCING

[A] Generally

During the identifying, collecting and producing phase a party's objective is to assemble electronic information (including the metadata) which pertains to the claims or defenses of the litigation. The accumulation of electronic information may include e-mail, documents, databases, Internet history files, calendars and schedules.

The producing party is confronted with common problems associated with production of any evidence, limited time and costs. For that reason, it is well worth the time to devise an efficient and thorough collection plan designed to accomplish the following:

- Determine the likely location of all relevant data;

- Determine how to identify relevant data;

- Organize, review and catalogue the data once it is identified; and

- Coordinate the systematic and uniform collection and production of data from all locations.

The identification phase, in conjunction with the preservation stage, is the time that the types, source and location of all documents must be identified for preservation. Outside counsel should immediately meet with their client and key IT personnel to determine where responsive data might be found. Identify any and all types of data that would be relevant and responsive to a document request. These would include e-mail, databases, word processing documents, spreadsheets and other materials. These documents should be categorized according to their responsiveness and whether they may be privileged or not privileged. Determine from the legal or regulatory proceeding the individuals or business entity that is the focus of the discovery or compliance request. It is also advisable to conduct interviews of key witnesses to determine electronic data subject to discovery and whether they possess any of this evidence on their business or personal computing systems.

During the accumulation phase of electronic discovery, it is suggested that you initially retain the services of a forensic specialist. They are best equipped to advise you of the formats and media to accumulate electronic discovery. Since data comes in many formats and on many different storage media, advice on the appropriate format and media are essential to ensure the successful processing of electronic information.

During this acquisition phase one should be familiar with:

- How electronic information is generated (§ 2.2, *Creating Electronic Information*);

- How storage and retrieval operate (§ 2.3, *Storage and Retrieval of Electronic Information*);

- The different storage media and devices (§§ 2.4-2.5, *Storage Media and Devices*);

- Recovering deleted data and/or deleted e-mail; (§ 3.5[E], *Deletion of Electronic Information*);

- The various storage locations (§ 2.6, *Storage Locations*); and

- Possible data types of electronic information (§ 3.6 *Data Types - Generally*).

You will encounter problems if, after identification, the data is improperly collected. Many clients and their IT staff may not employ the proper forensic procedures for collecting the data and may begin opening and closing without realizing that it changes the data by altering the dates, metadata, and file attributes. After preservation, it is best to bring in qualified forensic experts to prevent spoliation and other problems.

[B]   Voluntary and Involuntary Production

The voluntary production of electronic information (mandatory disclosure rules) by the opposing party generally results in low acquisition costs for the requesting party. Information can be provided on a CD-ROM or DVD or other electronic media by merely copying the data.

Involuntary disclosure through discovery requests (such as interrogatories and requests for production, or requests for inspection of the opposing party's information technology systems) is more expensive, especially if discovery disputes arise.

[C]   Ways to Limit Your Cost Exposure

The cost of electronic discovery can increase quickly so it is important to communicate your cost constraints to your litigation team, outside vendors and forensic specialists. There are many stories of unexpected and substantial cost overruns in electronic discovery.

There are several cost categories to consider when discovering or producing electronic information. They are the cost of:

- Retention and use of a forensic specialist(s);

- Identifying, locating and collecting electronic information;

- Reviewing for attorney/client privilege information, trade secrets, etc.;

- Replicating of data for the opposing party; and

- Extracting and converting to a database or full text for use in standard litigation software.

There are several techniques to limit the cost of electronic discovery and production:

- Limit your discovery to specific individuals or organizations. If you attempt to discover electronic information of all employees of a specific company or organization, the resulting production could be overwhelming. It is better to limit your discovery to individuals within the organization who have information pertaining to your claims for defenses. In addition, limiting your discovery requests will prevent challenges that you are on a "fishing expedition" or other objections.

- Narrow the subject matter of your request. Limit your request to the specific claims or defenses in your case. Requesting information that does not pertain to the case will result in the filing of protective orders with the court.

- Set forth a timeframe for the information that you are requesting. The search for information should be limited to specific time periods in question.

- Obtain a nonwaiver agreement and court order regarding confidential information. Costs increase significantly when you have to review electronic information prior to disclosure for work product, trade secrets and other privileges. For example, you could perform a broad-based computer word or name search for privileged material, but you may miss some of the confidential material. If you obtain a nonwaiver agreement and court order, then, if you inadvertently miss and disclose this information to the opposing side, it may not waive the privilege.

- If it comports with statutory and regulatory mandates and there is no anticipated litigation, advise clients to enforce retention policies. One of the costliest aspects of disclosing information is to review outdated e-mail and other electronic information. If your client does not consistently enforce retention policies, then more information than necessary may have to be reviewed. In addition, even though your client may have been forthright and appropriate in their business dealings, disgruntled employees might make inappropriate remarks that may be subject to discovery.

- Generally, it is not necessary to obtain the application and operating software that create the data. The actual operating system or application software may not be relevant to your case. Usually obtaining the native data file is sufficient since "electronic discovery" software is available to extract the important data. *See,* § 5.4[E][2], *Using Original Application Software to Search.*

- Collect discovery in an electronic format. It is far less costly to obtain information in an electronic format, than to scan paper, code and/or use optical character recognition software to convert the information to an electronic format.

- Consider an on-site inspection. If the electronic information is so voluminous that it would be a significant burden to duplicate and process, then the opposing side may allow you to conduct specialized searches on their computer system. The producing party may prefer this method, so that the amount of information is limited and is available for review for confidential information prior to disclosure.

[D]   Collection and Review - File Format

Generally, if you request your client to preserve relevant electronic information, they will conduct a search of their electronic data for the information you request. For the different methods of searching for data see § 5.4, *Searching Electronic Information*. This electronic data generally will be e-mail, word processing documents, spreadsheets and business databases. After they collect this information — which is usually in native file format — there are several options available for reviewing the documents in an electronic format for privilege or other confidential information. *See,* § 5.3, *Electronic Data Formats*.

[E]   Storage Media Used for Production

Generally, the producing party will provide this electronic information on the media storage device of your choice - DVD, CD-ROM, etc. It is suggested for both parties that the data be provided in "non-rewriteable, non-erasable" format. This traditionally has meant using the "write once, read many" (WORM) optical media. Data in this type of format will reduce chain of custody and authentication evidentiary problems.

[F]   Forensic Copy of Storage Media

Under some circumstances (improper deletion of files, Internet usage, etc.) you might need to forensically copy (also referred to as "clone" or "mirror") an image of the storage media that contains the electronic information that you are requesting.

However, obtaining a clone or mirror of storage medium, such as a hard drive, may be difficult to obtain through discovery requests. The reason for this is that the producing party may be aware that a bit for bit forensic image contains deleted material subject to restoration. They generally will argue that all data that are relevant to the claims or defenses have been produced, and that deleted files may contain trade secrets, attorney client privilege material, etc. However, if you can show that the other side deleted, lost or altered files relevant to the case you may be able to obtain a mirror clone of the storage media. *See also,* § 7.7[H], *Inspection of Opposing Party's Computer System.*

A forensic copy of storage media is different from a backup copy. Backup copies, obtained by using a copy command, will copy active files from one disk to another. It will not copy deleted files or other residual data from one disk to another.

There are many forensic issues that have to be addressed if you are obtaining a forensic copy of the storage media. For example, a copy must be obtained without booting up the computer. The starting or normal operation of a computer can destroy electronic information that is present in unallocated storage space, Windows swap files and in other areas. Because of these and other forensic issues, it is best to retain the services of a forensic specialist if you are going to obtain a forensic copy of storage media.

There is specific software available to forensically copy evidence from computers. Forensic software such as Encase (www.encase.com) can create a bit for bit copy from storage media like a hard drive.

After obtaining forensic copy and before making any analysis of the computer evidence, make an exact bit stream backup copy of the original copy in order to preserve the electronic information. "This immensely powerful capability of being able to conduct investigations on forensically sound copies of the data rather than on the data itself preserves the integrity of the original information as best evidence." J. Bates, *The Fundamentals of Computer Forensics, International Journal of Forensic Computing* (Feb. 1997). Never analyze the original electronic copy of information given to your firm. *See also, §* 7.07[H][5], *Obtaining Forensic or Mirror Image Copy of Storage Media.*

[G]   Chain of Custody, Audit Reports and Hash Values

As with any discovery process, electronic data processing should be tracked for chain of custody to protect admissibility. For a general discussion of evidentiary issues see Chapter 8, *Admissibility of Electronic Evidence.*

Depending on the circumstances of the case, a chain of custody foundation may have to be established for the admission of evidence. When there is a chance of confusion or that data may have been altered or tampered with, evidence establishing a chain of custody is important. A chain of custody is generally asking a custodian or a witness regarding the origin, storage and handling of the electronic evidence. In a computer record case this may involve the procedures for gathering the data and how it was copied and saved. In addition, it will include testimony about the storage media used to store and transfer the data.

In a case involving the forensic analysis of a hard drive, the chain of custody would involve questions as to the transporting, handling and copying process.

The forensic copying process involves the byte-for-byte copy of everything on a hard drive including active and deleted files, unallocated space, residual data, etc. A nonforensic copy would only copy the directory structure and active files.

One way to ensure the integrity of data is for examiners or others to handle the original evidence as little as possible. It is generally recommended to create a "master copy" of the device. The master copy is then used to create additional mirror images for disclosure to the opposing party for analysis and examination of evidence.

In order to prevent any allegation that produced electronic data has not been altered it is suggested that a hash value be generated for electronic discovery computer files. The objective is to be able to establish that the image copy is identical to the original. The accuracy is determined by matching the "hash" value of the original with the forensic copy. A hash value is the output when a mathematical algorithm is applied to a computer file. This "message value" is unique and serves to distinguish it from other computer files and can be used for authentication purposes. If the electronic information is altered or changed, the number will be different. One of the most commonly used hash values is the MD5 (Message Digest 5) HASH system. "MD5 is an algorithm that is used to generate a unique 128-bit fingerprint of a file of any length, (even an entire disk)." Shawn McCreight and John Patzakis, *Hash Sets and Their Proper Construction*, available at http://www.guidancesoftware.com/ support/downloads/hashsets/hashsets_wp.pdf (last visited July 21, 2006).

A hash value can be applied to a file, a section of a disk, or a whole disk and recorded. The hash value will then change if the data in a file, section or disk is changed or altered.

A hash value should be created to ensure that the additional images created from the forensic master copy are the same. After it is determined that the hash values are identical then the forensic expert or others can search the forensic copy and provide responsive data to the requesting party.

When you receive electronic files, there should be an audit or accounting of every file throughout the discovery, conversion and presentation process. The report should reflect every step of the intake and final production of the information to ensure verification. At a minimum, this report should include:

- The type of the original storage media;

- Description of the different directories or subdirectories;

- Number of megabytes and description of different computer files on the storage media;

- The number of files within each piece of storage medium;

- Number of files where data was extracted and converted to database, full text or images;

- Hash conversion value;

- By whom, from where and when the data was extracted;

- The number of images that were rendered from this conversion; and

- A listing of those files not converted with an explanation.

See also, § 8.10, *Requirement of Authentication or Identification.*

[1]   Reported Cases

- *Williams v. Sprint/United Mgmt. Co.,* 230 F.R.D. 640, 655-656 (D. Kan. 2005). In this age discrimination action the defendant employer refused to unlock the value of cells in a spreadsheet "to ensure the integrity of the data regarding RIFs, i.e., to ensure that the data could not be accidentally or intentionally altered. . . . Defendant's concerns regarding maintaining the integrity of the spreadsheet's values and data could have been addressed by the less intrusive and more efficient use of 'hash marks.' For example, Defendant could have run the data through a mathematical process to generate a shorter symbolic reference to the original file, called a 'hash mark' or 'hash value,' that is unique to that particular file. This 'digital fingerprint' akin to a tamper-evident seal on a software package would have shown if the electronic spreadsheets were altered. When an electronic file is sent with a hash mark, others can read it, but the file cannot be altered without a change also occurring in the hash mark. The producing party can be certain that the file was not altered by running the creator's hash mark algorithm to verify that the original hash mark is generated. This method allows a large amount of data to be self-authenticating with a rather small hash mark, efficiently assuring that the original image has not been manipulated."

- *Liturgical Publ'n, Inc. v. Karides,* 2006 Wisc. App. LEXIS 313, n.7 (Wis. Ct. App. 2006). The Court ordered that a former employee's computer be analyzed by comparing hash values to determine if the employee had any unauthorized files on his computer. The Court noted "[h]ash values are defined by the parties as alphanumeric identifiers of files." No similar hash values were found and the Court refused to order further analysis of the employee's computer to determine if reformatting of the computer had occurred terming further analysis a "fishing expedition."

- *V Cable Inc. v. Budnick,* 23 Fed. Appx. 64, 65-66 (2nd Cir. 2001)(unpublished). The Appellant had suggested that the computers "from which these records were obtained, cannot be authenticated due to a break in their chain of custody" and they had been corrupted by the analysis and retrieval of documents. However, the Court ruled that computer printouts of business sales records were admissible under business record hearsay exception, even though the computers had been sent to an independent software company for analysis.

- *United States v. Grimmett,* 2004 WL 3171788, at *2 (D.Kan. Aug. 10, 2004). The Court explained the search efforts by the officer in a child pornography case and noted that the "[officer] used a software program known as 'EnCase' [forensic imaging software] to examine the contents of the hard disk drive."

- *State v. Cook,* 149 Ohio App.3d 422, 428-429, 777 N.E.2d 822, 887-888 (Ohio App. 2002). The criminal defendant objected to the admissibility of a report that was generated using EnCase from the "mirror image" of his hard drive. The defendant objected on the basis that the reliability of the custodial and processing steps was flawed. The Court responded: "There is no doubt that the mirror image was an authentic copy of what was present on the computer's hard drive."

- *Taylor v. State,* 93 S.W. 3d 487, 498-508 (Tex.App 2002). The Court in reversing the criminal conviction found several errors including,

  As previously discussed at length, [the officer] testified he had copied Taylor's hard drive. He testified the portions of the target hard drive containing the copy made of Taylor's hard drive by the EnCase program were identical. He based his testimony on his observation of two hash marks on his computer screen at the time the copying process was completed--the acquisition hash and the verification hash. Marshall made no recording of this in any form, although the EnCase software provides a verification process that would have provided written documentation of the quality of the copying procedure. . . . handling of the copy of the information on Taylor's hard drive, the key physical evidence in the case, was defective, and that Taylor's hard drive was copied to a "contaminated" hard drive [officer failed to "wipe" the disk onto which the material was copied] . . . which may have already contained pornographic data . .

. [also] before copying the drive, Marshall executed a format command against Taylor's drive, when he should have formatted the target drive. By doing so, he destroyed the file allocation table for Taylor's computer and there was no structure in place for the files which were copied [and] . . . the State failed to provide the defense with a copy of Taylor's hard drive and a copy of the hard drive to which Taylor's hard drive was copied.

• *Galaxy Computer Services, Inc. v. Baker*, No. CIV.04-1036, 2005 WL 1278956 (E.D.Va. May 27, 2005). The Court denied the defendant's motion to exclude evidence because of alleged breaks in the chain of custody of the digital evidence. The defendant argued that the plaintiff's expert failed to follow their own internal chain of custody procedures and that the electronic evidence may now be tainted. The Court held that this allegation would not preclude admission but, instead, would go to the weight to be given the evidence.

[2]   Other Authorities

• *Secure Hash Standard* (SHS), FIPS PUBS 180-2, NIST (August 2002) available at http://csrc.nist.gov/publications/fips/fips180-2/fips180-2withchangenotice.pdf. This article by the National Institute of Standards and Technology (NIST) discusses different hash standards.

• Dean M. Harts, *Reel to Real: Should You Believe What You See?*, 66 Def. Couns. J. 514 (Oct. 1999). "B. **Use Hash Marks** Another option involves running a data or image file through a mathematical process to generate a shorter symbolic reference to the original file, called a 'hash mark,' that is unique to that particular file. When the same file is processed through the same algorithm, the same hash mark will result. A new hash mark necessarily results whenever the base message is altered in any manner. The hash mark is a standard size, usually much smaller than the file, so relatively large files can be verified with the addition of a relatively small amount of data. n66 n66 See Biddle, supra note 63, at 11-48-49. The ABA guidelines analogize the hash result to a fingerprint. When a file is sent with a hash mark, others can read it, but the file cannot be altered without a change also occurring in the hash mark. The recipient can be certain that the file was not altered by running the creator's hash mark algorithm to verify that the original hash mark is generated. Thus, the large amount of data involved in digital imaging could be self-authenticating with a rather small hash mark, efficiently assuring that the original image has not been manipulated."

§ 5.6   SECURITY OF ELECTRONIC INFORMATION

The security of electronic information is important, regardless if you are requesting or producing information on behalf of your client. Electronic information may include information containing sensitive personnel data, trade secrets, attorney work product, attorney client and other confidential business information. To protect this information, legal professionals must secure and control access on both the physical and electronic level. *Jones v. Goord,* 2002 U.S. Dist. LEXIS 8707, at *35-38 (D.N.Y. 2002) (Court refused defendant-inmate's request for disclosure of prison underlying code and programming information since it would endanger the system to potential hacking.)

Physical security would relate to computer rooms, access to hard drives, removable storage and backup media. Electronic security would include firewalls, passwords, encryption and access levels to stored data.

In addition, special consideration should be given to potential damage of the electronic information from computer viruses or worms. Care should be taken when opening acquired discovery files. It is suggested to run computer virus scanning software over the acquired data on a standalone computer. *See also,* § 3.5, [H], *Computer Security Protocols.*

§ 5.7   EXTRACTION AND CONVERSION

[A]   Generally

Once you have acquired electronic information (especially in its native file format), the data usually has to be extracted and converted from the produced computer files. Extraction is the process of removing user and text data and/or metadata from computer files. During the removal process it is converted into a format for importing into a database and/or full text application and eventually converted into images or paper for presentation in a deposition or in the courtroom. During the extraction and conversion of information from its native application format, the focus is on two types of computer data - the user data from the software application and the "metadata" that is hidden in the computer file.

For example, in e-mail, text data can be extracted and converted into database fields such as the author, recipient, a date, subject, a message, attachments, web pointers, etc. The metadata, such as the time and date the e-mail was received, who viewed the message, etc. can also be extracted, converted and imported into a database application. After importing into a database application, which is part of most standard litigation programs, the data can then be electronically searched, reviewed and analyzed.

For e-mail, this process also includes extracting, for viewing, attachments and web pointers or other information contained in the e-mail. For a discussion of data types *see* § 5.3, *Electronic Data Formats.*

[B]   Metadata

Metadata, also known as the embedded or hidden data, refers to data that is automatically generated and stored in computer data files. For e-mail it includes the date and time that the e-mail was received, all recipients (even those that were blind copied) and other information that may be valuable to the claims or defenses in your case. In other types of computer data files, hidden information may include hidden comments and prior revisions in word processing documents; a file's location, creator, date created and date last accessed; and in spreadsheets unseen rows, cells and worksheets. Again, if you only view the computer file in its native application, you may not be able to view metadata. For a general discussion of metadata *see* § 3.7, *Metadata, Hidden, or Embedded Information* and §§ 3.7–3.19 for metadata found in different file types.

[C]   Electronic Discovery Software

"Electronic discovery" software has been developed to extract application data and metadata from computer files. The software will not only extract user data from application files, but also the metadata for each file. The extracted data can then be imported into a standard litigation support package such as Summation. The "extraction" software one chooses should be capable of providing an audit trail and linking mechanism to the e-mail message or other computer file from where the information was obtained.

There are several vendors that provide services and software to extract data from the many different software applications into a usable database, full text format and/or image. Once converted, the data can be searched, annotated and later used in trial. For a list of software and vendors *see* § 5.10, *Types of Electronic Discovery Software.*

A word of caution is necessary. As the electronic discovery industry grows you will find many "homemade" conversion utilities. It is necessary to determine which software is best for your needs and can accurately extract both user data and metadata from different software applications, as well as keep any attachments linked.

[D]   Special Conversion Issues

Sometimes after acquiring electronic files you will find that files are protected with passwords that prohibit your access to their contents. Spreadsheet files are frequently protected by users with passwords. If the passwords are unavailable, there is password detection software available that will repetitively try different password combinations to open files. These password protection programs are relatively inexpensive and can be effective. *See,* § 3.5[H][2], *Limiting Access Rights to Approved Users.*

[E]   Electronic Discovery Cost Estimates

Conversion and Extraction

Estimating the cost for the conversion and extraction of data from electronic information is difficult because data is generally measured in gigabytes as opposed to the number of bankers' boxes of documents. The number of e-mail per megabyte can change depending on the size and the type of attachment. For example, an attached word processing document would be smaller in size compared to a graphics file.

The cost will also depend on the actual amount of relevant data that will be culled from the larger data population. Your data group will consist of information from certain individuals, projects, date ranges and other limiting factors. In addition, due to the recent development of new software tools and an increased number of vendors, the cost structure for the conversion of electronic data is undergoing a significant change.

Electronic data is produced in computer files that consist of a unit of measurement such as KB (kilobyte), MB (megabyte) or GB (gigabyte). The inquiry is how many e-mail, documents and other units of electronic information are contained within the storage unit. Once you determine the volume of data within the storage unit you can estimate the cost of extracting and converting electronic data into database abstracts, full text and images.

Below are some "rules of thumb" to estimate the number of e-mail, word processing documents and images within a unit of measurement of storage media.

Storage Size	Word Processing (# of pages)	E-Mail (# of e-mail)	Images (Group IV TIFF) (# of images)
1 Megabyte	100	21	20
Floppy disk (3-1/2" HD) (1.44 megabytes)	150	30	28
CD ROM (640 megabytes)	65,000	13,650	13,000 – 15,000
Laptop hard disk (20 gigabytes)	2,000,000	420,000	400,000 – 600,000
PC hard disk (80 gigabytes)	8,000,000	1,680,000	1,600,000 – 2,400,000
Network hard disk (400 gigabytes)	40,000,000	8,400,000	8,000,000

Word Processing. The estimated number of pages above makes the assumption that there is approximately 10 kilobytes per word processing page. A 100-page document in Microsoft Word is generally 1 megabyte, without graphics. The actual storage required per page will vary depending on the program used to create the document. Graphics-based (Windows) word processors require more storage space for documents than text-based (DOS) word processors.

The cost of extracting data from a word processing file is between 7 and 16 cents per page depending on whether the project is completed in-house or at the service bureau's facility.

E-mail. The cost estimates for extracting data from e-mail may change significantly depending on the service bureau and method of estimating the cost. The estimated cost of converting e-mail depends on whether the service bureau is charging on a per message or per page basis and whether attachments are included in the cost estimate.

Generally, e-mail can be quantified in terms of the number of pages per e-mail with or without attachments. The rule of thumb is that there are 1.8 pages per e-mail and 3.5 pages of e-mail attachments. Generally 50% of e-mail contains attachments. Therefore, for each e-mail it is estimated that there are 3.55 pages. (1.8 pages per e-mail and half of the e-mail have attachments or 1.75 pages of attachments per e-mail, which totals 3.55 pages per e-mail.)

For each megabyte of e-mail data it is estimated that there are 21 e-mail or approximately 75 pages. For each gigabyte of e-mail data there would be approximately 21,000 e-mail or 74,550 pages.

Generally, vendors will charge between 6 to 10 cents per page or 6 to 10 cents per e-mail message (without attachments) to extract data. The output is usually generally provided in a database (comma delimited), full text and image format.

Scanned Images. A scanned document page (image) file size is generally 50 kilobytes per image. Scanned images may contain metadata such as when the image was created, etc. The cost of extracting metadata from images is generally 5 cents per page.

Databases. The cost of estimating the number of database records per megabyte is difficult because of the different length of individual database records and the specific application used to create the record.

However, once the number of database pages per megabyte is established, most vendors will estimate extraction cost on a per page or database record basis.

Backup Tapes

Below are some categories and estimates for restoring the contents of backup tapes. Again, the estimates you receive may differ greatly. The restoration of backup tapes requires:

- Cataloging backup tape contents;

• Restoring backup data to hard drives;

• Capturing the contents of a hard drive for evidentiary purposes;

• Searching and analyzing data from the drive;

• Copying data to DVD, CD or other storage media; and

• Loading data into litigation support database or converting to TIFF or PDF.

The pricing for this process may be fixed or hourly depending upon the complexity and difficulty of the restoration. The price for this type of data processing range from $200 to $6,000 per backup tape or hard drive, again depending upon the level of service requested.

Questions to Ask

These services may be included in the cost of the electronic discovery collection and processing or priced separately.

• Will the company go on site to collect the data?

• Do they use hashing procedures to ensure chain of custody and other authentication issues?

• In what form will the data be collected?

• What is the company's documentation process for all phases of electronic discovery?

• Can the company provide a preliminary estimate of the amount of data on storage media by disclosing the file type and amount of data by file type and file size?

• How many different file types can the company identify with their software?

• Is the company able to determine whether files are encrypted, infected with viruses and do they have the capacity to break passwords?

• Do they provide deduplication services? If so, what is the different criteria they can use to determine whether a file is a duplicate? (metadata comparison, hashing comparison, field level identifiers, content based, etc.)

• Is the company able to process parent-child relationships and metadata for all types of files?

• Does the search software search across all known file types and metadata or only specific field types?

• Can the company convert data to PDF or TIFF?

• What is the accuracy rate for processing data?

- In what format can the data be exported? (Summation, Concordance, TIFF, etc.)

- Is a document depository available to host the data to allow for remote users to access the data? If so, how do they charge for hosting services, i.e., by seat, user, gigabytes downloaded, monthly storage fees, etc.?

- How are paper documents integrated into the system?

- How is the data secured at the vendor's facility?

[1]   Reported Cases

- *Hagemeyer North America, Inc. v. Gateway Data Sciences Corp.,* 222 F.R.D. 594, 601 (E.D.Wis. 2004).

  One of the reasons for the high cost of searching backup tapes is that they store more information than most other storage media. To illustrate, a CD-ROM's storage capacity is 650 megabytes, the equivalent of 325,000 typewritten pages; computer networks create backup data measured in terabytes-1,000,000 megabytes-which is the equivalent of 500 billion typewritten pages. MANUAL FOR COMPLEX LITIGATION (FOURTH) § 11.446. Additionally, backup tapes require more time and labor to search than other media because of the way data is organized on them; "tape drives . . . are sequential-access devices, which means that to read any particular block of data, you need to read all the preceding blocks." InternetNews.Com, supra, (quoted in Zubulake I, 217 F.R.D. at 319). This type of organization is a main reason that each backup tape may take anywhere from several minutes to five days to restore. . . . Adding to the difficulty, each must be restored separately onto a hard drive in order to be searched. Id. Accordingly, the cost to review the backup tapes can be hundreds of thousands of dollars depending on the number of tapes that are to be searched.

- *In re Priceline.com Inc. Sec. Litig.,* 233 F.R.D. 88, 89-90 (D. Conn. 2005). "The process of viewing the files stored as computer data is expensive and time-consuming. The parties have estimated that the cost of restoring a backup tape will range from $200 to $800 per tape, if it is even at all possible. The cost of restoration is in addition to the cost of searching the files, culling for duplicate files, and converting responsive files for production. These costs are exclusive of attorneys' fees associated with reviewing and producing the amount of information that could be responsive."

- *In re Instinet Group, Inc.,* 2005 Del. Ch. LEXIS 195, at *9-10 (Del. Ch. Nov. 30, 2005). In a case involving the disallowance of attorney fees and costs relating to shareholder litigation, the Court criticized the plaintiffs for converting electronic documents into paper for review.

- *Sempra Energy Trading Corp. v. Brown,* No. CIV.04-4169, 2004 WL 2714404, at *5 (N.D.Cal. Nov. 30, 2004). Though dismissed on other grounds the Court noted that the plaintiff's electronic discovery cost, "to date: (1) . . . [has been] in excess of $209,000 to restore the email from digital backup tapes in order that it could be reviewed and produced; (2) attorneys' fees to review approximately 218,000 documents resulting therefrom . . . [plaintiff] alleges that it has spent approximately $1,600,000 in attorneys' fees and costs to date and will continue to incur attorneys' fees and costs in excess of $500,000 per month until the process is completed sometime in early 2005."

- *Medtronic Sofamore Danek, Inc. v. Michelson,* No. CIV.01-2373, 2003 WL 21468573, at * 7 (W.D. Tenn. May 13, 2003). The plaintiff informed the court that, "its preferred vendor, Kroll Ontrack, will restore, search, and de-duplicate the data on 124 sample tapes for a flat fee of $605,300" or approximately $4,881 per tape."

- *Zubulake v. UBS Warburg LLC,* 216 F.R.D. 280, 282-83 (S.D.N.Y. 2003). The consultant estimated that it would cost $166,000 for restoring and searching 77 backup tapes or $2,304.92 per backup tape.

- *Wiginton v. Ellis,* No. CIV.02-6832, 2003 WL 22439865, *3 n.3 (N.D. Ill. Oct. 27, 2003). The Court discusses the cost of preserving data in a large corporation. The court noted, "[t]herefore, he estimates that to restore just the tapes for the last day of each month for all 125 local servers for one year would take between 9,000 and 18,000 hours. Each backup tape costs approximately $50, so it would cost $12,500 a day to not overwrite daily backup tapes. Defendant states that besides the e-mail backup tapes, the only other way to retrieve e-mails is to look one by one at each employee's computer which would take thousands of hours."

[2]   Other Authorities

- Greg McPolin, *E-Discovery: A Common Term That Is Little Understood,* 7 N.Y.L.J. 1(Jan. 27, 2003). This article discusses various e-discovery costs.

- *See also,* § 7.4[G][6], *Cost Allocation.*

[F]   Electronic Numbering and Other Designations

Litigation support programs offer the capability of electronically numbering or "Bates stamping" an image of the electronic image record. Such a number can be imbedded as a footer on the electronic image that can be seen when printed. Additional designations such as "confidential" or "privileged" can also be added.

[G]   Parent-Child Relationships

An e-mail message or other electronic file that has a file attached is referred to as a compound document. An e-mail message that has an attachment is called the parent document and the attachment is called the child document. It is important to maintain the parent/child relationship of electronic data when reviewing and converting electronic information.

[H]   Redaction - Privileged Material

When disclosing discovery documents it is important to "redact" or block out privileged information. This may include private personal information such as social security numbers, etc. With paper it is not difficult to use a black marker and cross out privileged or private information.

However, with electronic data, there is no effective way to redact an electronic document while it is in its native file format. At the present time, a native file cannot be redacted and then disclosed as an electronic file without changing the file contents. For that reason a computer file such as an electronic document or an e-mail message and their attachments must first be converted from a native format to a TIFF or PDF image, redacted, and then the redacted image would be disclosed to the opposing party.

§ 5.8   FILTERING AND DEDUPLICATION

To minimize the costs associated with not only the conversion of electronic information, but also the subsequent viewing and analysis, it is extremely beneficial to filter and deduplicate electronic information.

[A]   Filtering

Filtering (culling or winnowing) electronic information is reducing the size of the electronic file population by limiting computer files to specific criteria like keywords, names, dates, etc. Filtering can occur before or after the collection of electronic file information. You may decide to stipulate to search terms to run on the opposing party's computer system in order to locate specific computer files for production. This will limit or filter the amount of electronic information and computer files that the other side will disclose to you. You may also decide to filter the data that was provided by the opposing party, to limit your data population.

When possible, reduce the amount of electronic material to review. Don't process the whole population of computer files. For example, if a particular individual is the subject of the lawsuit, run a keyword search on his first name, last name, title, nicknames, other names or titles used, e-mail addresses and any other information that may identify him in any e-mail, word processing document, spreadsheet or other computer files. Then separate this person's e-mail from the other employees' e-mail. This will filter the data, and result in lower staff time to review information as well as conversion costs.

[B]   Deduplication

Deduplication means the process of separating duplicate e-mail messages, word processing documents and other computer files from the electronic file collection. To reduce the volume of electronic information, eliminating duplicates is essential. For example, people often send the same e-mail message too more than one recipient or a word-processing document to multiple recipients. These should be separated and not reviewed several times.

The deduplication process operates by setting specific matching criteria regarding data files and their content. The matching criteria are determined by the user and may include matches for the author, recipient, subject line, date, time of creation of the e-mail and other criteria. If the criteria match between two e-mail or files, then one will be deemed a duplicate. However, deduplicating does not necessarily mean destroying or deleting duplicates from your electronic file information. It may mean that this information is labeled as duplicate, and then tied to the original message or a word processing document. Then, if necessary, you can move back and forth between the original and duplicates.

[1]   Reported Case

•   *Wiginton v. CB Richard Ellis, Inc.*, No. CIV.02-6832, 2004 WL 1895122, at *2 (N.D.Ill. Aug. 10, 2004). The service bureau "was also instructed to use the process of de-duplication, the process whereby documents which appear in a user's mailbox on multiple days are not counted as multiple hits. For example, if the same e-mail appeared in an inbox over a period of several months, only one copy of the document would be produced."

•   *Medtronic Sofamor Danek, Inc. v. Michelson,* 56 Fed. R. Serv. 3d 1159, 1160 (W.D. Tenn. 2003). "The de-duplication and conversion are required so that large volumes of data in different formats may be searched in a reasonable time."

§ 5.9   CATEGORIZING AND REVIEWING

Even though the motives of the requesting and producing party are adversarial, both can benefit by using a computer to categorize, review and search electronic information.

[A]   Categorizing

An important function when reviewing electronic or paper-based discovery is to categorize the information by type, issue ,or other terms as they pertain to the factual or legal claims or defenses. When working with large amounts of information, separating this information into categories makes it more manageable, such as privileged material, work product, document types, legal issues and witnesses. For example, if you receive e-mail folders from a number of different individuals you will discover that often they will categorize the information in certain subfolders or subdirectories. However, some of these subfolders may not be relevant to your case. Criteria should be developed as to how to categorize these types of e-mail folders in a case.

[B]   Reviewing

The cost of reviewing electronic information by legal professionals can be monumental. Just think about the daunting task of reviewing 5, 10 or 15 years of company correspondence or e-mail messaging, assuming it is all relevant. The real, substantial cost of electronic discovery is generally not in the request or acquisition of the data, but in the human cost of reviewing the information to support your contentions or to locate confidential information.

There are electronic search tools that may be useful in reviewing confidential electronic information, but they are not panaceas. It is well documented that because of the lack of standardization of terms in the human language, full text or database searching does not find all occurrences of concepts for which you are searching. *See,* § 5.4, *Searching Electronic Information.* Human review is often necessary.

When using database or full text software you can search voluminous amounts of electronic information in seconds for specific words, phrases, names, dates, etc. In some instances, you will be successful in locating relevant information or the "smoking gun." Once located, if you use litigation support software, you can easily code the information by name, issue or other criteria for subsequent use.

§ 5.10   TYPES OF ELECTRONIC DISCOVERY SOFTWARE

There are several different types of software that can be used to process and search electronic information. The list set out below is a sampling of available software and is by no means an exhaustive listing. For a description of electronic format types see § 5.3, *Electronic Data Formats.*

[A]   Collecting Data

- EnCase (www.encase.com) is software that provides previewing, basic analysis and the capability of creating a forensic copy of storage media.

[B]   Harvesting or Extracting Data

- Cricket Box (Cricket Technologies - http://www.crickettechnologies.com/) is an e-discovery appliance designed for the litigation support market. This device and software process hundreds of file types by dragging and dropping the desired files with the use of a graphic interface. Processing options allow you to retain original folder and sub-folder relationships, perform deduplication using industry standard SHA-1 checksums, and export data to common litigation support applications.

- Discovery Cracker (Doculex - http://www.doculex.com/). Discovery Cracker is an in-house application that captures different forms of electronic files, then converts them to industry standard image files, and then generates an associated index including full text and field specific data.

- Discovery OnDemand (Daticon - www.daticon.com) is a standalone hardware and software electronic discovery-processing center. Discovery OnDemand provides tools to convert e-mail, attachments to e-mail and other standalone electronic files. It converts the electronic information to a database record for each document, the full-text of that document and a TIFF image of what that document would look like if printed at the time it was sent, received or last modified. It can optionally assign Bates numbers to the electronic documents for control purposes. It captures metadata, maintains file threads and file attachments and eliminates duplicate files.

- Hard Copy Pro Plus (Mobious Solutions - www.mobiousinc.com) converts e-mail (along with all attachments and attachments within attachments) and electronic documents to TIFFs. It also extracts text and metadata to import and populate litigation support software like Summation and Concordance.

[C]   Searching Electronic Discovery

[1]   Database

For a discussion and description of databases *see* § 3.10, *Database*. Some database products to consider are:

- Summation (www.summation.com);
- Microsoft Access (www.microsoft.com);

- Paradox (www.corel.com);
- Concordance (www.dataflight.com); and
- FileMaker Pro (www.filemaker.com).

[2] Full Text Search

Text retrieval software can be either generic (a horizontal consumer market) or legal specific (a vertical legal market). Generic software is usually less expensive and will perform full text searches very well. Legal specific full text packages are generally more expensive and are customized for use in the legal profession. For example, customized features may include maintaining the name, volume, page and line number integrity for a deposition in the full text program itself. What this means is that if you "digest" specific passages of text into a file, it will format the text with accurate name, volume, page and line numbers. This is extremely useful and efficient for attaching testimony to motions for summary judgments, etc. Other "legal specific" features include inserting enhancements such as notes, legal issue coding, dates, image attachments and cross-referencing. Subsequent searches can include the text, notes, cross-references and other enhancements. Reports are also generally customized for legal specific needs.

Legal specific full text "electronic discovery" software includes Summation (www.summation.com), which includes an integrated full text, database, outliner and imaging program.

The following "smart" search engines use a variety of advanced search techniques.

- Engenium (www.engenium.com);
- Cataphora (www.cataphora.com);
- Attenex (www.attenex.com);
- RetrievalWare (www.convera.com);
- Autonomy (www.autonomy.com); and
- DolphinSearch (www.dolphinsearch.com).

Some generic full text packages are:

- dtSearch (www.dtSearch.com);
- ZyIndex (www.zylab.com);
- ConText by Oracle (www.oracle.com);
- ISYS (www.isysdev.com);
- Excalibur/EFS (www.excalib.com); and
- askSam (www.asksam.com).

[3]   Conversion to Image (TIFF, PDF, etc.)

*   Zprint (www.imagecap.com)(can convert and print more than 250 different file formats.)
*   The Quick View Plus (http://www.avantstar.com/Products/Quick_View_Plus/QuickViewPlusOverview).

[4]   Metadata Viewer

*   Metadata viewer (www.esqinc.com/).

[5]   Software for Wiping and Deleting Files

*   Eraser (www.tolvanen.com);
*   Disk Wiper (www.acronis.com/products/powerutilities/);
*   Evidence Eliminator (www.evidence-eliminator.com); and

[D]   Criteria for Choosing Software

Many firms are beginning the process of selecting "electronic discovery" software to handle the conversion and extraction of electronic information in-house. Two commentators noted, "EDD [Electronic Data Discovery] does not necessarily mean you have to outsource. A third service also has been launched: 'Do-it-yourself' EDD conversion tools, to help law firms and corporate law departments control their electronic data. These tools offer the ability to do in-house what the service providers can do on a larger scale: convert electronic data into TIFF images with database records, cross-reference files, and the full text of electronic data. It may not make sense in all cases, but it can be a viable option in those instances involving manageable amounts of data." Cliff Shnier & Daryl Teshima, *Do It Yourself EDD*, Law Technology News, Aug. 2002 at 25.

Below are some criteria suggested by Cliff Shnier, Esq, to assist in the selection of appropriate electronic discovery software.

General Company Information

*   Year company founded, company headquarters and company website.

*   Year first version released, release date of current version, expected release date of next major upgrade or version and cost to existing customers for update to new version.

Customer Base

*   Number of installs for this product (# of different sites), number of installs in prior fiscal year and percentage of law firm clients with product installed.

System Information

- Name of product, product description, database supported and hardware provided.

- Hardware specifications, processor, hard drive space and memory.

- Telephone support hours.

Implementation/Training

- Training necessary, typical number of days of training required for system implementation and training performed by vendor or reseller/partner.

Pricing

- Software sold as stand-alone with hardware or as a networked client server application, base unit price (hardware), per click charge and additional costs.

- Reseller or the vendor sells the system and backs the warranty terms.

- Pricing for software or software/hardware solution, "per page" processing charge and cost of additional "per pages" purchased.

General Functions

- Output Formats: Summation, Concordance, IPRO, JFS, DocuLex and/or ASCII Delimiter.

- Deduplication of e-mail function, output to full text and conversion capability to TIFF or PDF.

- Process with generic viewer or native applications, if native applications, applications that are preinstalled.

- Case files handled: Word, WordPerfect, Excel, PowerPoint, MS Project, Visio, Outlook, Outlook Express, Lotus Notes, Zip files and others.

Specific Features

- Bates numbering system available, password-protected documents, unknown file types and file types identified by the extension or metadata.

- Option to produce a database record without processing, application includes a search engine to identify relevant documents prior to conversion and documents eliminated for image conversion upfront.

Reports

- File inventory report for CD investigation, total pages produced by project and total pages produced by source/custodian.

Help

- Available online for each screen, manuals provided, context sensitive for each field and online user documentation available.

[E]   Other Authorities

- Chris Santella, *Working with Electronic Evidence with Summation,* available at www.llrx.com/features/summation.htm.

- *What's on that hard drive?* Available at http://www.u1.net/u1.netcast/issue15.asp and view the Tech Tips section.

Chapter 6

Discovery and Production Process

§ 6.1   DISCOVERY PROCESS

[A]   Generally

Discovery is changing in response to the pervasive use of computers. This change affects the way we discover and manage case information today and in the future.

Historically limited to depositions, interrogatories, interviews, and the paper records of the opposing party, effective discovery now includes vast amounts of electronic evidence. In fact, experts estimate that within five to seven years electronic evidence will replace paper as the primary source of discovery in commercial litigation.

Elizabeth Bacon Ehlers, et al., *E-Discovery*, Chapter 2, Business, Law, and the Internet: Essential Guidance for You, Your Clients, and Your Firm (2002).

Discovery in more and more cases involves e-mail, word-processing documents, spreadsheets and records of Internet activity. In most cases, computer-based discovery will be routine and uneventful. The parties may agree simply to exchange computer disks, instead of paper. In many cases, however, computer-based discovery generates disputes, some of which raise novel technical and legal issues.

Electronic discovery can raise unique issues that generally do not occur in conventional paper-based discovery. Among the most common difficulties with discovery are the location and volume of electronic information, preservation of data subject to discovery, scope of discovery, production format, privileged data, deleted information, backup tapes (including archives and legacy data), procedures for an on-site inspection and the need for expert assistance.

There are different costs associated with discovery of electronic information. For a discovering party these costs include the acquisition, conversion and subsequent review of electronic information. For the producing party, it requires you to understand your client's computer systems, storage locations and retention policies and properly review the information prior to disclosure in order to assert privileges (attorney-client, work product, trade secrets, etc.).

Early identification of the computer system configurations, location and volume of electronic information and reasonable discovery negotiations with the requesting party will often be the key to reducing costs and delay.

From the onset, you need to have a plan and strategy for the acquisition, conversion and searching of electronic information. This will assist in limiting disputes and costs and ensuring discovery of the important electronic information relevant to your cases.

[B]   Understanding Electronic Discovery

The process of discovering electronic information from the opposing party in an average case is a relatively recent phenomenon and is not understood by many practitioners. It is essential that you understand the basics of electronic information not only for discovering, but also for producing computer data.

For the discovering party you must be able to respond to objections relating to privacy issues, fishing expedition claims, burdensome arguments, etc. You will also need to understand where important information may be "hidden" within modern information systems, the likelihood that such information can be recovered and the cost of acquiring this electronic information.

For the producing party, you must understand computer-based discovery in order to comply with the discovery requests and/or effectively oppose objectionable requests. If you determine that a request is objectionable on the grounds that it is overly broad or unduly burdensome, than it is essential that you persuade the court as to the legal and technology aspects of your objections. For a producing party, this can have a monumental effect on your case because of the costs associated with locating, reviewing and producing electronic information. To argue that a request is overly broad or unduly burdensome, you'll need to be familiar with active and archived computer files, capability of searching and retrieving the requested information and the total costs associated with production.

Once objections have been lodged, then the requesting party must be able to persuade the court of the likelihood that the information can be discovered and that it can be obtained with relative ease. In court, the astute practitioner can gain an advantage by educating the court as to the realities of the proposed request for electronic discovery.

In most cases the parties will have a mutual interest in conducting discovery in an efficient and cost-effective manner. However, this is not always the case. In *Danis v. USN Communications,* No. CIV.98-7482, 2000 WL 1694325, at * 4-5 (N.D. Ill. Oct. 20, 2000) the Court noted that, "neither side to this motion has demonstrated to this Court a complete mastery of what types of documents were generated by USN in the ordinary course of business, how they were used or their significance . . . [A]s a result, both sides were the losers. They lavished huge sums of time and money on an issue that did not remotely justify the expenditure, and which would have been more profitable spent focusing on the merits of this case."

Thus, it would be advantageous for both parties to exchange information about their computer systems informally or pursuant to court procedural rules such as FED. R. CIV. P. 26(j), the "meet and confer" section of the federal rules. *See,* § 7.4[K], *Meet and Confer - Rule 26(f).* In addition, the presence of a computer expert(s) would assist the parties in understanding their respective computer systems. *See,* Chapter 4, *Computer Forensics, Experts and Service Bureaus* and § 7.3[D], *Electronic Discovery Checklist - Pretrial Agenda.*

[C]   Discovery Steps

[1]   Overview and Strategy

The formulation and execution of a discovery plan and strategy unique to the claims or defenses of your case are essential. Cases are more often won or lost during discovery, rather than at trial. The use of trials in disposing of cases has been steadily declining. One study noted that 11.5 percent of federal civil cases were disposed of by trial in 1962, 40 years later in 2002 only 1.8 percent of cases were disposed of by trial. Marc Galanter, *The Vanishing Trial: An Examination of Trials and Related Matters in Federal and State Courts* at http://www.abanet.org/litigation/vanishingtrial/vanishingtrial.pdf (last visited July 22, 2006). For this reason, pretrial electronic and paper-based discovery in support of your claim or defense often determines the outcome of your case.

Once you are retained on a case, a discovery and production strategy for electronic information needs to be developed. The plan should include the type and location of electronic information, client and expert assistance, discovery cost, preservation issues, scheduling for interrogatories, depositions and request for production, etc. This plan can be refined and improved as your circumstances change, but it is critical that it is in place to ensure the proper focus of your litigation team and resources.

The discovery of information will include all relevant electronic data stored on various media and devices. This may include e-mail messages, word-processing files, databases, Internet history files, calendars and schedules. In addition, you need to focus on the storage devices, storage media and the storage locations of the electronic information. This data can reside on desktops, laptops or on a floppy disk – locally or globally.

Your client may be able to assist you in identifying the opposing party's hardware, software and system configurations.

A forensic specialist can provide assistance on the estimated cost, system configurations, recovering deleted information and ensuring that the chain of custody and authentication of electronic information is preserved. In addition, this same information will assist you if the opposing party makes an electronic discovery request on your client.

Discovery court rules such as interrogatories and request for production may need to be used to obtain electronic information, if voluntary disclosure is unsuccessful or unavailable. In addition, if a preservation letter does not result in the retention of electronic information, then a preservation protective order from the court may be necessary. Specific interrogatory questions may need to be asked regarding information technology positions and the computer infrastructure of the opposing party. Depositions may need to be conducted to question parties, employees and other witnesses about electronic information. If the rules permit, you should propound follow-up interrogatories and other discovery requests. If necessary, reopen depositions to clarify information technology questions. Also, submit request for admissions to lay evidentiary foundations for electronic information.

A well-thought out strategy will include a written discovery log of the discovery issues, responses and scheduling concerns during the litigation. There have been several court decisions that have criticized lawyers who have failed to properly advise and follow up with their clients regarding the preservation and production of discoverable electronic information. *See,* § 7.9, *Sanctions.* For your own protection, it is important to be specific and methodical in the manner which you discover or produce electronic information.

Your plan should factor in the opposing party's request for electronic information from your client. You can be assured that the opposing party will "mirror" your electronic discovery requests to your own client. Think ahead when aggressively asserting or defending your rights with electronic discovery, since you may very well be on the reverse side of your argument very quickly.

A comprehensive plan and strategy will contribute to the success of the discovery and/or production of electronic information. It will also assist in controlling the associated costs which can be substantial. Implementation of the plan will involve input from your litigation team, clients and from forensic specialists. The plan can be refined and changed as a case continues, but it will provide the needed focus to effectively discover or produce electronic information.

[2]   Nature of Case and Type of Information Sought

Nature of Case

With any case, your first step is to focus on the specific relevant case information you desire from the opposing side. The nature of the case will define the type and sources of electronic information sought. In interviewing the client make sure you understand the factual issues of the case and the basis for the factual assertions by your client. For example, a case involving Internet usage will focus on Internet logs, usage patterns, browser history, downloaded Internet files, etc. On the other hand a case involving a domestic relations dispute may focus on the family's personal accounting records, electronic messaging and Internet chat rooms. A case involving a business dispute about anticompetitive matters will focus on electronic messaging, customer database, memos and letters, sales figures and marketing messages.

Type of Electronic Information Sought

The type of electronic information you are seeking will depend on the factual issues in your lawsuit. This information may parallel information that is already available in a printed format. However, there is often additional case information in an electronic format, which is not available in a printed format, such as metadata.

Your electronic information objectives should focus on how the opposing side used computers to generate data or documents during the events in question. You will need to know what business functions were involved and the software supporting those functions. For example, if financial forecasting is important, then you will want to know what financial and accounting software was used. If it was important as to who was present at a series of meetings, then scheduling and calendaring software would be directly related to the events. If health information was requested from a hospital then you have to determine whether or not their information systems captured the different steps in treating and providing care to the patient. Finally, if you wanted to determine if a person was blind copied on an electronic message, then electronic messaging data would be requested thus allowing you to view the e-mail and metadata.

For example, in a copyright and trademark infringement case against the operator of a computer bulletin board, the Court's ex parte order authorizing seizure of the defendant's computer and memory led to evidence that the defendant tracked (or could track) user uploads and downloads of the plaintiff's copyrighted video games. This proof aided the plaintiff's case of contributory copyright infringement and direct trademark infringement. *Sega Enters. Ltd. v. MAPHIA,* 948 F. Supp. 923 (N.D. Cal. 1996).

For most cases, the focus of your discovery will be on electronic communications (e-mail, voice mail and instant or text messaging), electronic documents (word processing, spreadsheets, and company policies and procedures), personal information systems (calendaring, scheduling and rolodex systems), databases (financial, human resources and project databases) and computer system information (system logs and audit trail as to the use of the computer and by whom).

Before any document or computer-based discovery is initiated the parties may choose to exchange information about their clients' respective computer systems. The information would include identifying which computer systems are in place at the moment, which computer systems were in place during the period of time relevant to anticipated discovery, the volume of the computerized information (including backups and archives) that will be searched in the course of discovery, the capabilities of each party to perform searches and produce material in a usable format and the measures being taken to secure and preserve potential computer evidence.

Information about the opposing party's computer system can originate from different sources. If necessary, retain a forensic specialist who is familiar with the industry's hardware and software configurations or who have specific knowledge of the opposing party's computer system. Knowledge may exist with experts who have been involved in prior lawsuits against the same party. Disgruntled former employees can provide a wealth of information and insight into the use and type of information technology by the opposing party. Also, consult with your client to discuss what type of information may be available, as well as the location of the information.

Don't forget that video and voice mail are also potential repositories for important data. Increasingly, computer systems are used for video, audio or text conferencing. Often, text, audio or video messages are saved, forwarded or both. It is important to make sure that your litigation team understands that information kept in this format is also discoverable.

[3] Type of Storage Media, Devices and Locations

Understanding the possible storage media, devices and locations of electronic information will assist with not only the discovery, but also the production of electronic information. Electronic information is classified as to storage media (hard drive, floppy, etc.), storage devices (a desktop computer, etc.) and storage locations (home, office, etc.). For an extensive review of the different types of storage media, devices and locations see §§ 2.4–2.6.

Computer data can be found on many different types of storage media and devices, and located in many places. A specific file can be located on the original computer storage media and backed up or archived on other media. The same computer file can be found on many devices including desktop computers, laptops, PDAs and other newly developed computer devices. The location of the file can be at the office, home or in remote computer storage facilities. *See,* § 2.6, *Storage Locations.*

[4] Scope and Specificity of Request

The scope of your request should be no different from when you are seeking paper-based discovery. A discovery request should be broad, but not so broad as to be construed as a fishing expedition. Your request will generally be denied, if the information sought is not relevant to your claims or defenses. For example, if you are seeking information relating to an anticompetitive action and request employee benefit data, your request will probably be denied. However, if there is evidence of destruction of relevant information, by the failure of the opposing party to preserve information, then discovery requests seeking "all hard drives" may be found to be reasonable by the courts.

In addition, requesting excessive data would increase the burden on the requesting party to conduct a meaningful review of the data.

Formulate discovery requests that ensure you will receive all relevant forms of the computer-based evidence. Failure to set forth the different types of computer data may result in the opposing party being unaware of the computer data types and, thus, may fail to preserve the computer information. For example, if your document request fails to designate off-site backups or deleted files, then it is unlikely that the opposing party will preserve and produce this information. Be prepared that even if your request is specific and unambiguous, the court may require technical education before they will grant discovery of some types of computer information, especially when you are seeking deleted information.

If electronic information is not kept in a systematic way, a broader request for information may be necessary. If information has been "deleted," you may need to insist on inspecting the opposing party's computer storage system since copies made with commercial backup programs will not preserve deleted information.

Be prepared for the opposing party to limit your request by:

- Narrowing your request arguing the information sought is not relevant to the claims or defenses;

- Offering an alternative procedure for locating and producing records that you are seeking, such as proposing a list of keywords to be used in conducting searches on the opposing party's computer or a list of directories or servers to be searched;

- Limiting your searches of electronic messages or other electronic information to specific personnel or date ranges; and

- Submitting a substantial cost estimate and extended schedule for screening and production of electronic information.

For cases construing the burden and cost of discovery requests see § 7.4[G], *Limiting Discovery - Rule 26(b)(2)*.

[5]   Client Assistance

Litigators should meet and get to know the information managers at their client's organization (and their own law firms) and spend time learning systems and vernacular to better understand and prepare for discovery. This is also beneficial since it is likely that the opposing party will depose your client's information manager(s) regarding their computer information system and data policies.

The client interview may be an important source of information about the opposing party's computer hardware, software and electronic information. Employees at your client's business may be some of the most knowledgeable about the opposing party's computer system and its capabilities. In fact, after interviewing your client and other witnesses in the case, you should review the electronic evidence to see how well your client's arguments hold up, as well as any to discover any potential gaps or inconsistencies in your case.

After interviewing clients, you may learn of additional electronic records (regulatory agency files, Internet data, prior data records of related cases, etc.), witnesses and even other attorneys who may have experience against the opposing party. For example, a disgruntled ex-employee may possess significant electronic financial records of the opposing party that may be used for impeachment.

[6]   Computer and Forensic Expert Assistance

Determine at the outset whether you need the services of computer and forensic specialists to assist you in discovering electronic information. Initially, technical assistance from your client or in-house information technology employees can be invaluable. Once you learn about the opposing party's information technology system, then you are in a position to decide whether to retain forensic specialists for discovery of electronic information. *See,* § 4.4, *Services and Scope of Work – Forensic Specialists.*

Generally, it is necessary to retain at least one forensic specialist and maybe multiple specialists, depending on the complexity of the targeted electronic information. For example, many computer experts specialize in certain platforms (Microsoft operating system, UNIX, etc.) and are unable to give expert opinions about other platforms. Other specialists may be experts in recovering deleted files, rebuilding fragmented files, cloning the opposing party's hard drives and other storage media or identifying documents that may have had the date altered.

Experts can be expensive. The cost of a computer specialist/expert is between $75 and $500 per hour depending on their skill, experience and background. Though costly, in the end, it will save money and time. Retaining a computer expert by both sides, or a neutral expert, early in the process may facilitate the negotiation and exchange of electronic information.

After the experts, for both sides, have had the opportunity to discuss their respective client's computer systems and capabilities, then they can advise the attorneys how to negotiate the technical aspects of conducting discovery and production. They can provide advice about the structure, types, devices and storage media housing the information. They can also advise about search terms (if you are searching the opposing party's computer system) cloning a hard drive, viewing privileged data, relevance screening and the form of production. Often, the experts can propose agreements on the exchange of information.

You may also want to consider the use of a court appointed neutral expert who can assist both sides. For example, if the opposition objects to your expert cloning hard drives because of the possibility of damaging the information system or viewing privileged data, then you might suggest that the court appoint a neutral computer forensic expert to assist in the cloning of hard drives. For further discussions see Chapter 4, *Computer Forensics, Experts and Service Bureaus* and § 7.11, *Special Masters and Court-Appointed Experts.*

[7]   Preservation Request

[a]   Generally

A "preservation notice or request" usually takes the form of a letter notifying the opposing party to preserve all responsive data to the subject matter of litigation. A preservation letter should be sent to the opposing party outlining the claims, persons connected with the claims and possible sources of electronic evidence. Unlike traditional paper-based discovery, failure to immediately request preservation of electronic information can result in its loss. Electronic data can easily be inadvertently or intentionally deleted or altered. Loss of electronic information can occur during daily operation of a computer, rotating backup tapes, editing database records and deleting user files. Data on computer systems can be overwritten in seconds or may remain for months or years. For this reason, it is important that if the relevant information is stored electronically one act quickly to preserve the data by sending a preservation request and/or seeking court assistance by a protective order.

A forensic specialist can assist in determining whether immediate preservation of computer data is needed. Also, if the discovering party is unsure of the identification of all electronic data that may be material, the request should ask what steps have been taken to ensure electronic information will not be destroyed or changed before the identification process is completed.

At the outset, it is important to determine what steps the opposing counsel has taken or is taking to ensure that likely discovery material in his client's or a third party's possession will be preserved until the discovery process is complete. *See,* § 7.9[F], *Affirmative Continual Obligation to Preserve and Disclose.* Consideration should be given to seeking a discovery, preservation or injunction order from the court. *See,* §§ 7.3[E], *Discovery and Preservation Orders - Rule 16(c)* and 7.14, *Injunctions.* If a preservation notice is sent, then opposing counsel must ensure that there is no inadvertent or intentional destruction of computer data. Failure to preserve evidence can lead to a default judgment or other court-imposed sanctions. *See,* § 7.9[K], *Spoliation.*

[b]   Notice to Opposing Party and Your Client

The opposing party has a duty to preserve electronic information. Depending on your jurisdiction, this duty may arise on the likelihood of litigation, on notice of a claim, preservation letter, filing of a complaint or the reception of a discovery request. In addition, there may be a statutory duty to preserve records. *See,* § 7.9[D], *Duty to Preserve.* The scope of the obligation to preserve is not dictated by the preservation letter, but by rules of procedure and applicable case law. *Wiginton v. Ellis,* No. CIV.02-6832, 2003 WL 22439865, at *1-5 (N.D. Ill. Oct. 27, 2003). (discussing scope of duty to preserve and plaintiff's preservation letter).

[c]   Notice – Terms

It is helpful to have some idea of the types of computer-based documents being pursued before sending the opposing party a preservation letter.

The notice should list the specific type of information, where it might be located, and their duty (with relevant case cites) to preserve the information.

The letter should advise your opposing counsel (or party) that electronic information will be material to the litigation, request preservation and warn that failure to preserve the evidence will be addressed under the law of spoliation. For an example of an all-inclusive preservation letter see the Form Spoliation Letter to Opposing Counsel at http://www.discoveryresources.org/docs/Formspoliationletter.doc (last visited on July 22, 2006).

Listed below are other preservation considerations that may be relevant to your case.

*   In general and specific terms, describe the electronic information that you want to preserve and its location;

    — The notice should identify the types of data to preserve. This data may include word processing files, calendaring program data, e-mails, computer logs, etc.

    — The notice may also set forth the specific hardware that should be preserved including desktop, laptop and personal computers, local hard drives, personal digital assistants, and mobile phones.

*   Advise the party that even if paper copies are available that the electronic data needs to be preserved;

*   Ask the company to refrain from operating PCs (desktop or laptop) and network workstations until an exact readable image is made of all the relevant electronic information without altering, in any way, the original files;

*   Request the party to disable or suspend any automatic or routine deletion procedures pursuant to a document retention policy or other procedure;

*   Request the opposing party to preserve backup tapes or other archival data;

*   Request documents that have been logically deleted, but not physically erased;

*   Request the actual media (whether magnetic, optical or other type) that has been used to store documents, including backup or archive media;

- If there is a statute or regulation requiring preservation of specific data types, cite the source;

- Request preservation of any hard copy or electronic materials necessary to understand or interpret the electronic data you are seeking;

- Review §§ 2.04-2.06 for a list of storage media, devices and storage locations that may be relevant to your case;

- Review §§ 3.3-3.19 for specific data file types to request;

- Request preservation of electronic information created after delivery of the preservation letter;

- Cite to case law, statutes or other legal authorities referencing "spoliation," "adverse inferences" or other sanctions for failure to preserve and disclose.

[d]   Reported Cases

- *Wiginton v. Ellis,* No. CIV.02-6832, 2003 WL 22439865, at *1, 4, 5 (N.D. Ill. Oct. 27, 2003). In a class action sexual harassment suit, the Court found that the defendant acted in bad faith by continuing its normal document retention and destruction policies despite the plaintiff's earlier notice of preservation. The Court observed that the preservation letter was sent to:

  CBRE's general counsel, asking that CBRE: not destroy, conceal or alter any paper or electronic files and other data generated by and/or stored on CBRE's computers and storage media . . . or any other electronic data, such as voice mail that relates in any way to the subject matter of this litigation, or any information which is likely to lead to the discovery of admissible evidence. . . . This issue is especially important here because CBRE controls virtually all of the documents that will be at issue. (emphasis added). The September 27 Letter described electronic data and storage media which would be subject to the discovery requests including: 1) types of files; 2) on-line data storage; 3) off-line data storage; 4) data storage devices that were replaced; 5) fixed drives on personal computers and workstations; 6) programs and utilities; 7) system modification logs; 8) personal computers; and 9) evidence created subsequent to the letter. Specifically, Plaintiff instructed CBRE: to preserve all e-mails, both sent and received, whether internally or externally; all word-processed files, including drafts and revisions; all spreadsheets, including drafts and revisions; all databases; all presentation data or slide shows produced by presentation software . . . all Internet and Web-browser-generated history files, caches and "cookies" files generated at the work station of each employee and/or agent in CBRE's employ and on any and all backup storage media. . . . Further, you are to preserve any log or logs of network use by employees or otherwise . . . and to preserve all copies of your backup tapes and the software necessary to reconstruct the data on those tapes, so that there can be made a complete, bit-by-bit "mirror" evidentiary image copy of the storage media of each and every personal computer (and/or workstation) and network server in CBRE's control and custody, as well as image copies of all hard drives retained and no longer in service, but in use at any time from January 1, 1990 to the present.

In response, the defendant requested its employees to retain any records of any type that pertained to *Wiginton*. The court found that the notice of preservation was "significant because it alerted CBRE to the types of electronic information (within the realm of all relevant documents) that were likely to be requested during discovery." The court held that the defendant had a duty to preserve "e-mails, videos, internet downloads which contain or relate to any sexually inappropriate or otherwise offensive material . . . [and] the computer hard drives, e-mail accounts and internet records of anyone who left the company who had been accused of sexual harassment or misconduct."

[e]   Retention Policy of Opposing Party

After providing notice to the opposing party, discovery should be conducted to determine whether the adversary retained the relevant computer data. Defendants usually make a diligent effort to preserve paper versions of documents, but because of a lack of technical expertise may be lackadaisical in preserving computer data. Usually, the requesting party will fail to compel the complete production of the computer data and the defendant will fail to preserve it in its entirety.

The starting point for determining whether the party preserves the evidence is the producing party's retention policy. Understanding how the opposing party retains data will enable you to determine whether relevant data has been retained or improperly destroyed. Also, even if a retention policy is in effect, the company and its employees may largely ignore it. Remember that even if data has been improperly destroyed or deleted, it may be possible to recover this deleted data.

Also, check the various record acts for your state or for the agency. Some statutes or regulations may require the retention of documents relevant to certain claims. See, e.g., 29 C.F.R. § 1602.14 (EEOC record-keeping requirements).

[f]   Parties to Whom Notice Should Be Sent

The preservation letter should be sent to the opposing party as well as to third parties who may have data that is relevant to the claims or defenses of the action. *See,* § 7.10, *Obtaining Data From Third Parties.*

[g]   Form of Preservation

It is advisable to set forth the form of preservation of the computer data. For example, you may wish to instruct the opposing party to:

- Segregate and secure backup and archival media;

- Create "mirror" copies of all active network servers, desktop hard drives, laptops and similar hardware. This is the only sure preservative method of retaining computer data. Issues about the relevance and whether the data is privileged can be decided later, after the computer data has been preserved.

[h]   Court Orders

If you do not obtain cooperation from the opposing or a 3rd party regarding preservation of computer data, then it may be necessary to obtain a protective or preservation order from the courts.

It is suggested that you obtain a FED. R. CIV. P. 16 (or similar state procedural rule) order in order to prevent any party or third party from destroying evidence and preserving the status quo. In some cases, parties have combined a preservation letter along with a Rule 16 order. Obtaining a Rule 16 order may require retaining a forensic specialist to educate the court as to why a preservation order should be issued. For further discussions and cases involving issuance of protective orders see § 7.3[E], *Discovery and Preservation Orders - Rule 16(c).*

For nonparties, FED. R. CIV. P. 45(a)(1)(C) allows for issuance of a deposition subpoena requiring witnesses to produce and permit inspection and copying of "designated . . . tangible things . . ." For further discussion see § 7.10, *Obtaining Data From Third Parties.*

[i]   Failure to Preserve Electronic Information

If you determine that the opposing side has failed to implement a preservation policy, and is routinely deleting and destroying computer data, then it may be necessary to request access to the "deleted" data. Though deleted, data files can be recovered, if they have not been overwritten by new data. In addition, failing to preserve information, though requested, may give rise to an inference of spoliation if the data cannot be recovered.

Even though it is possible to recover deleted information, the courts may not permit it. To justify access to the opposing party's computer to recover deleted information, you have to provide at least threshold reasons why the court should permit inspection. Failure to do so will result in allegations of "fishing expedition" or unjustified access to privileged or irrelevant data prohibited by the court rules. If you're intending to target deleted information, then you should put your opponent on notice immediately and document reasons why this information is relevant to claims or defenses of the case. The court will require you to show why the recovery of this information is necessary and justifiable. For example, in a trade secret case, recovery of a deleted computer file may be central to your claims. However, there may not be any justification in a standard employment dispute to access the opposing party's computer to recover deleted information. *See,* § 7.7[H], *Inspection of Opposing Party's Computer System.*

[8]   Waiver of Privileges - Attorney Work Product, etc.

Whether you are seeking or defending against a request for electronic information, both sides should consider the use of a protective order and/or confidentiality agreement to ensure nonwaiver of privileged material. Disclosure of confidential material can often waive its privileged protection. *See,* § 7.4[H], *Work Product Doctrine, Attorney Client Privilege and Trade Secrets.*

There may be a significant amount of electronic information that needs to be disclosed and may contain confidential case material. It may require many, many hours for the producing party to sift through e-mail and other data to ensure no confidential material is inadvertently disclosed. The producing party may use search software to locate some of the privileged material, but may not retrieve all the material. In that case, if the parties entered into a nonwaiver agreement then case information could be disclosed without the risk (depending on your jurisdiction) of the privileged material being introduced as evidence. *See,* § 7.4[H], *Work Product Doctrine, Attorney Client Privilege and Trade Secrets.* This could lower the cost of discovery compliance by the producing party and protect privileged material. For a further discussion of protective orders see § 7.3[E], *Discovery and Preservation Orders - Rule 16(c)* and § 7.4[I], *Protective Orders - Rule 26(c).*

[9]   Search Efforts - Production from Opposing Party

How can you be sure that your opponent has made a good-faith effort to search for electronic or paper documents that you requested? This is a difficult question because the opposing counsel may not have an information technology background and will have to rely on certifications from their clients or others. Usually the requesting party will not contest the search results because of the immense volume of information to be searched, different techniques used to search the information, lack of standards by the courts and the likelihood that the courts will not question the producing party's methods. However, the courts have recently taken a more active role in validating the search efforts of the producing party. *See,* §§ 5.4, *Searching Electronic Information* and 7.7[C], *Search Protocol and Certification.*

To attempt to verify the search results from the opposing party the following questions can be propounded either through FED. R. CIV. P. 33 interrogatories or through FED. R. CIV. P. 30(b)(6) depositions.

- Document Retention Policy

    — Describe your document or record retention policy for the electronic information sought.

    — After receiving the request for discovery, please describe the actions taken and instructions given to the staff to preserve electronic evidence.

    — When were you advised to preserve the data?

    — What steps did you take to implement a preservation policy?

    — Have you contacted users to determine if they made backups of the data?

- Storage Locations

    — What electronic information locations were searched? For a list of possible locations see § 2.6, *Storage Locations.*

    — Did you have the assistance of a forensic specialist in the location, search and acquisition of electronic data?

- Storage Devices

    — What storage devices were searched? Do employees have computers at home? For a list of storage devices see § 2.5, *Storage Devices.*

- Storage Media

    — Describe the various storage media that are used to store the data that was located.

    — For a list of storage media see § 2.4, *Storage Media.*

- Preservation of Data

    — Did you clone or mirror the storage media? Did you make the clone without booting up the computer?

- Search Efforts

    — Describe the methodology of the search.

    — Describe the date ranges and times for the information search that was conducted.

— Name the individuals and/or experts who were involved in the search.

— Describe exactly what these individuals did to search for electronic data.

— Describe the software applications that were searched.

— List the keywords, combination of keywords and other search commands that were applied to the database.

— List the synonyms, alternate spellings and the specific terms for the issues involved in the case.

— List the names, position titles, alternate means and other search terms for the individuals whose electronic data was searched.

• Collection of Data

— Describe the collection method of the data that was responsive to the search request.

— Did you provide all duplicates and attachments of electronic messages?

— Describe the chain of custody of the information that was provided.

— If copies were made of the hard drives, please describe the methodology.

[a]   Reported Case

• *Zubulake v. UBS Warburg, LLC,* 217 F.R.D. 309, 317 (S.D.N.Y. 2003). Court found producing party had not completed a thorough search. The Court stated:

Nonetheless, UBS argues that Zubulake is not entitled to any further discovery because it already produced all responsive documents, to wit, the 100 pages of e-mails. This argument is unpersuasive for two reasons. First, because of the way that UBS backs up its e-mail files, it clearly could not have searched all of its e-mails without restoring the ninety-four backup tapes (which UBS admits that it has not done). UBS therefore cannot represent that it has produced all responsive e-mails. Second, Zubulake herself has produced more than 450 pages of relevant e-mails, including e-mails that would have been responsive to her discovery requests but were never produced by UBS. These two facts strongly suggest that there are e-mails that Zubulake has not received that reside on UBS's backup media.

[10]   Sampling

One emerging cost containment trend favored by the courts is to determine whether it is worthwhile to proceed with discovery of data by obtaining a sampling of the electronic data. Data sampling involves taking data samples of databases files, electronic messaging files, etc. and then performing a statistical analysis of how much relevant information is available and what it would cost to review and produce the data.

Sampling may provide a solution since discovery must be conducted in a limited period of time from many different sources. *See,* § 7.4[G][5], *Sampling.*

[11]   Form of Discovery

Should you request that electronic information be produced in a print or electronic format, or both? This question will arise as you begin obtaining discovery of electronic information. There are several factors to consider when deciding which format(s) to request.

For an extensive discussion of the electronic file format and legal issues surrounding the form of discovery see §§ 5.3, *Electronic Data Formats,* 7.07[D], *Translated Into Reasonably Useful Form,* 7.07[E], *Kept in the Usual Course of Business,* and 7.7[G], *Form of Production of Computer-based Data.*

[12]   Production File Format

Understanding data formats and conversion helps in the discovery of electronic information, and later in the management and analysis of data. A critical element of electronic discovery is having the data delivered in a usable format. The data must be delivered in a format that allows you to extract, convert, import and search it. *See,* § 5.3, *Electronic Data Formats.*

[13]   Data Virus Check

Prior to importing and viewing the produced data, scan the data for possible viruses using an up-to-date anti-virus program. It may be necessary to disconnect your reviewing computer from your network to ensure its security. *See,* § 3.5[I], *Computer Viruses.*

[14]   Timing of Exchange

In *In re Carbon Dioxide Industry Antitrust Litigation,* 155 F.R.D. 209 (M.D. FL. 1993) the court ruled that there was no reason to order that the parties exchange their computer data simultaneously.

[15]   Evidentiary Issues

Always consider the evidentiary issues connected with the exchange of data. In order to minimize evidentiary issues, consider discovery exchanges that will reduce or eliminate questions of authenticity. Some suggested methods are to have the discovery supervised by a neutral party, create a neutral, secure electronic document repository, exchange read-only storage media such as CD-ROMs and request a chain-of-custody certification. *See,* Chapter 8, *Admissibility of Electronic Evidence* for further discussion on evidentiary considerations.

[16]   Data Security

An important issue in electronic discovery is the requirement to secure data to protect your client's or the opposing party's confidential information. In a paper-based discovery, locked storage areas are able to secure papers and files. However, electronic data may contain confidential client data, trade secrets, attorney client communication and other sensitive data that must be protected. One needs to focus on physical security by providing for physical security of the premises, limiting access to computers and storage media. In addition, electronic security should be enhanced by using firewalls, encryption, passwords and standalone systems to prevent access to case data. Your data also needs to be protected against power surges, static electricity, fire, and water damage. All these things can cause the loss of data, and in some cases can permanently damage the computer itself.

§ 6.2   PRODUCTION PROCESS

[A]   Generally

Producing electronic information involves many of the same legal principles, strategies and understanding as in requesting electronic information. It will require you to understand how computers work as well as how information technologies are used in your client's personal or business life. During this process you need to provide proactive advice to your client as to the preservation, cost and scope of production, as well as current document retention policies.

You will discover that even though your clients feel that they have conducted their business in an open, honest and ethical manner that it can be difficult to defend against electronic evidence. Since e-mail and other forms of electronic information are often created in an informal manner, many times this information can contain derogatory information. Whether it is taken out of context or is the result of a disgruntled employee, it can be extremely damaging to your case when it is shown in the courtroom.

Many clients are unaware of their electronic discovery retention obligations. An attorney survey conducted by the American Bar Association's Litigation Section revealed that:

- Eighty-three percent said that their clients had no established protocol for responding to discovery requests, and only 5.8 percent said that protocols were being developed;

- Sixty-eight percent said that their clients rarely, if ever, took steps to prevent automatic overwriting processes for relevant electronic data; and

- Seventy-six percent said that 30 percent or more of their clients were unaware that electronic information could later become evidence.

PricewaterhouseCoopers/Section of Litigation of the American Bar Association, *Pulse Survey, Digital Discovery and its Importance on the Practice of Litigation* (May 15, 2000).

[1]   Reported Case

- *In re Priceline.com Inc. Sec. Litig.,* 233 F.R.D. 88, 90-91 (D. Conn. 2005). The Court set forth the following production order,

    1. Defendants shall retain possession of the original data through the restoration, data management, and document review stages. . . . 2. Restoration of backup tapes shall proceed on a measured basis, with cost-shifting determinations made at each step of the process. . . . 3. No party shall waive any claim that information contained on a computer file is privileged because that party produced an inventory, spreadsheet, or other survey of the contents of an item upon which data is stored. . . . 4. Defendants shall produce responsive information contained in stored data files to plaintiffs in TIFF or PDF form with Bates numbering and appropriate confidentiality designations, shall produce searchable metadata databases, and shall maintain the original data itself in native format for the duration of the litigation. . . . 5. Defendants shall begin to produce responsive information from the e-mail files of the 113 individuals and the remainder of the snapshot in the manner consistent with the preceding directive. . . . 6. If one party seeks relief from the court concerning the scope of information searched or produced, the party producing the information shall not delay working toward the production of information that is not in dispute. . . . 7. Beginning in January of 2006, defendants shall file a status report on the production of electronic information. . . . 8. Cost-shifting shall be applied for in the method set forth in the proposed revisions to Rule 26(b)(2) . . .

- *Medtronic v. Michelson,* No. CIV.01-2373, 2003 WL 21212601, at *1 (W.D. Tenn. May 13, 2003). The Court stated:

Producing electronic data requires, at minimum, several steps: (1) designing and applying a search program to identify potentially relevant electronic files, (2) reviewing the resulting documents for relevance, (3) reviewing the resulting documents for privilege; (4) deciding whether the documents should be produced in electronic or printed form, and (5) actual production.

[B]   Experienced Counsel

The courts are requiring that business organizations retain outside counsel who are experienced, knowledgeable and skilled to assist in the production of electronic discovery. *See*, § 7.9[G][1], *Outside Counsel Duties.* Sanctions can result in the failure to retain or consult with outside counsel who is experienced and capable in electronic data disclosure.

This line of cases illustrates that either through a lack of communication or miscommunication, failure to disclose can lead to expensive and damaging results. In fact, courts can impose severe consequences for electronic discovery problems, including adverse jury instructions, preclusion of evidence and even default. *See*, § 7.9, *Sanctions.*

[C]   Production Response Plan

A production response plan will assist in focusing on the legal, technical, and factual issues involved in the production of electronic information. Ideally this "rapid response" plan will be in place prior to or in anticipation of litigation. It should be a key component of the documentary retention policy for any organization. The plan will act as a blueprint for a litigation response team. The plan should address the following areas:

- Account for archived and nonarchived information, storage locations, file saving backup protocols and application and operating system information;

- Ensure adequate computer resources for ongoing discovery and production efforts;

- Method for capturing data, file format explanations and access to the raw data;

- Designation of specific members of your firm and of your client's organization who are familiar with documentary retention policy and your client's information technology infrastructure and applications. This team will be responsible for ensuring the proper preservation and location of electronic information to be produced;

- Protocol for the possible interruption of the day-to-day business in order to isolate and preserve electronic information; and

- Collecting and reviewing the data to ensure that it does not contain privileged information that may be waived on inadvertent disclosure.

[1]   Client's Electronic Information

To avoid sanctions that could affect the outcome of the case, you have a duty to diligently and thoroughly seek out and monitor the collection and preservation of electronic information in your client's possession. *See,* § 7.9[F], *Affirmative Continual Obligation to Preserve and Disclose.* This will involve discussions about storage locations, devices and media containing electronic data. Failure to do so will place you in a position of having to respond to accusations of spoliation of data when witnesses testify that additional electronic information was available, but is now destroyed. To avoid this, when responding to a discovery request, indicate the scope and extent of the search that was done to comply with the request. This will avoid any accusations of deliberately hiding evidence since a company may not be aware of the full extent of retrievable electronic information that it has stored on its systems.

Below is some of the technology information you will need to discover about your client's computer systems:

- Operating systems and application programs;

- Backup and archival procedures;

- The location of computer data files, both active and archived; (This may include computer files on an employee's computer or other device, whether at home or at the office. See, §§ 2.4–2.6 for a list of Storage Media, Devices and Locations.)

- Location of databases, e-mail, word processing documents and other relevant data;

- Cost of locating, reviewing and producing relevant information; (This would include the cost to convert or extract data into a usable format for analysis and production.)

- Structure of the present and past e-mail system (Since electronic mail is one of the most sought-after forms of electronic information one must have a clear understanding of your client's e-mail systems.);

- Document and other computer data file retention policies in place, and whether there is an immediate necessity of stopping the deletion or purging of data files that may be relevant to the case;

- Accessibility issues for each computer location, device or media such as passwords, security and encryption keys;

- Segregate responsive electronic data on a dedicated computer for review;

- Document retention policies for the automatic recycling of backup tapes;

- Installation of new hardware and location of replacements; and

- Capability to search and retrieve data requested by the opposing party.

Develop a strategy for locating electronic information focusing on the likely costs and benefits of collecting and producing this electronic data. Most courts dislike discovery that can be characterized as a fishing expedition. An open and reasonable approach to discovery, outlining the potential costs and benefits of gathering and disclosing information will assist your position with the court. Limitations on the scope of production of electronic data can be accomplished by suggesting data searches of key words, date range limitations and other methods limiting the population of computer data.

Fostering a cooperative and open relationship with your client's technology staff can assist in your disclosure efforts. Discussions with your client's technology personnel will provide you a working familiarity with how data is created, managed and stored within their organization. It will also provide information as to technology management personnel, backup and archival procedures, electronic messaging and Internet services.

In addition, you will be better prepared for future depositions since many of these technology people may be deposed under FED. R. CIV. P. 30(b)(6). They also can assist in advising you of what to search for on the opposing party's computer systems such as application programs and backup archival media.

As noted above, the courts have not been reluctant to impose sanctions against the producing attorney or his client when a party fails to adequately search, locate and preserve electronic data. For this reason, one should maintain a discovery log that documents the scope and extent of the search for computer data. Often, the company may not be aware of data stored on its own systems that may be responsive to a discovery request. This discovery log may have to be disclosed when responding to a document request in order to avoid any accusations of intentionally or inadvertently hiding evidence.

Practice Pointer:

- One alternative (that may be available in your jurisdiction) to reviewing the massive amount of e-mail is to enter into an agreement with opposing counsel that you will not waive any privileges if you inadvertently disclose confidential information. *See,* §§ 7.4[I], *Protective Orders - Rule 26(c)* and 7.4[H], *Work Product Doctrine, Attorney Client Privilege and Trade Secrets.*

[2]   Preservation of Evidence

There is no consensus among the courts as to when the obligation to preserve electronic data arises. Depending on your jurisdiction, the obligation may arise on awareness of the potential claim, likelihood of litigation, receipt of a demand or preservation letter, the actual filing of the complaint or a discovery request. *See,* § 7.9[D], *Duty to Preserve.*

Once the preservation obligation is triggered, you and your clients will be questioned as to what steps were taken to ensure that likely discovery material would be preserved until the discovery process was completed. This may include proving the steps you took to preserve the data in question. To ensure that you have identified the relevant data types, locations, devices and media, review the list set out in Chapter 2, Creation and Storage of Electronic Information and Chapter 3, Structure and Type of Electronic Information. After locating the data, it may be necessary to preserve data by creating a clone of the media, halting the client's data and e-mail purging or deletion policies and stopping the rotation of backup tapes. Time is of the essence in initiating preservation efforts when you have been put on notice or are aware of a potential claim being filed against your client. *See*, § 7.9[K], *Spoliation.*

[a]   Discovery Pointers

- After the client has been put on notice to preserve electronic data, advise them not to erase or reuse backup tapes that may contain relevant data, even though it is part of their normal backup procedure.

[3]   Raise Appropriate Objections

The same defenses or objections against discovery of your paper files, applies against discovery of your electronic files. The disclosing party may object on the basis that the production is an undue burden, violation of the attorney client privilege, protected work product or an overbroad request. *See*, § 7.4, *Production and Protection of Case Information.*

[4]   Negotiate Compliance

The stated purpose of discovery underlying FED. R. CIV. P. 1 is "to secure the just, speedy, and inexpensive determination of every action." If the opposing party engages in stonewalling and other delaying tactics, then discovery is inconsistent with the underlying principle of Rule 1. The purpose of discovery is not to obtain all the data you can, but also to focus on the relevant, critical information that will assist in resolving the dispute. The parties should keep their attention focused on, not the universe of relevant information, but instead the relevant information that pertains to the claims of defenses in their case.

[5]   Scope of Production - Limiting Disclosure

With this purpose in mind, the parties should focus on reasonable limits on the scope of production. The sheer volume of potentially responsive data can be overwhelming. *Rowe Entm't, Inc. v. William Morris Agency, Inc.,* 205 F.R.D. 421, 429 (S.D.N.Y. 2002) (explaining that electronic data is so voluminous because, unlike paper documents, "the costs of storage are virtually nil. Information is retained not because it is expected to be used, but because there is no compelling reason to discard it"), *aff'd,* 2002 WL 975713 (S.D.N.Y. May 9, 2002). Generally, the disclosing party, on learning of the voluminous amounts of electronic data, will object on the grounds of an undue burden or an overbroad request. A more effective approach may be to develop limiting data search protocols. They can be developed with the input and agreement of the opposing party and/or assistance of a partisan or neutral forensic specialist. The search protocol can greatly narrow the data file population that has to be reviewed and produced.

The following data search protocols should be considered:

- Date/time range limits. One search parameter would be to limit the date or time range for e-mail, word processing documents or other electronic information.

- Author, recipient or other key personnel. Consider limiting searches to individuals by name, title or other references relating to the subject matter of the litigation. Key search terms would include e-mail addresses of certain individuals or names of individuals in the subject line.

- Key terms. A list of key terms can be developed that are common to the claims and/or defenses. A key term such as "asbestos" can then be searched through a voluminous amount of information.

- Certain data file types. One can search by data files types in order to limit the electronic data population. For example, if presentation files are at issue in a trademark infringement case, then one can search for Microsoft PowerPoint files or similar presentation files. Microsoft PowerPoint and other application data files have specific file extensions that allow for searching by these extensions. Chapter 3, Structure and Type of Electronic Information discuss the various data types that may be available.

These different search techniques can reduce the population of electronic information to be reviewed, thus resulting in time and cost savings. *See also,* § 5.5[C], *Ways to Limit Your Cost Exposure.*

[6]   Screen for Privilege and Relevance

After identifying and collecting electronic information, the normal document review policies and practices still apply. One must still review the documents for confidential information. *See,* § 7.4[H], *Work Product Doctrine, Attorney Client Privilege and Trade Secrets.* One of the difficulties with electronic information is that because of the volume, it is difficult to ensure that all protected information has been removed from the electronic data to be produced. Search software is available to search the data using key terms and other methods to locate privileged data. However, one cannot rely on keyword searches alone to filter out the appropriate computer data for production. *See,* § 5.4, *Searching Electronic Information.* There is no substitute for visual review. In addition, you may want to consider entering into a nonwaiver of confidential information agreement with opposing counsel to lessen the burden of reviewing the data, as well as protection against inadvertent disclosure of this data.

[7]   Securing Data

An important issue in electronic discovery is how to secure production data to protect your client's confidential information. In a paper-based discovery, locked storage areas are able to secure papers and files. However, electronic information may contain confidential client information such as trade secrets, attorney-client communications and other sensitive data. These can easily be copied and transmitted. You must focus on electronic security using passwords and limiting access by other means, and controlling physical security of computer rooms, computers and storage media. To accomplish this you can use firewalls, encryption, passwords and standalone systems to prevent access to important data. Also, be aware that viruses may be included in the produced data which can harm and damage computer systems and data. A virus-scanning program should be used to ensure data is viruses free.

[8]   Form and Choice of Media for Production

Though it is more efficient to produce and disclose data in an electronic format, some requesting parties may want the data to be printed and disclosed. In order to review the different electronic data formats see § 5.3, *Electronic Data Formats*. In addition, the form of production may be contested because of cost and other issues. *See,* §§ 7.07[D], *Translated Into Reasonably Useful Form,* 7.07[E], *Kept in the Usual Course of Business,* and 7.7[G], *Form of Production of Computer-based Data.*

[D]   Document Retention Policy Before Litigation

Organizations for a variety of reasons create and store records. Primarily, it enables an organization to retrieve information that is supportive of the goals and mission of the entity. In addition, organizations will maintain records to comply with existing regulatory and other legal mandates. As a result most companies have informal and formal document retention systems to ensure that records are available for the organization's purposes and to comply with legal obligations.

A document retention program involves the systematic review, classification, retention and, ultimately, the destruction of electronic and paper records. To manage data effectively a company needs a reasonable document retention policy. It will provide benefits by ensuring that data is not inadvertently destroyed, which could lead to sanctions. An ill-conceived and unreasonable document retention program will subject a company to severe legal exposure if responsive data to anticipated litigation is destroyed or if needed for compliance mandates.

The primary problem with document retention systems is that computer data is often stored in a disorganized manner, difficult to retrieve and rarely deleted. Users treat inexpensive hard drives and other storage media as bottomless receptacles into which data is saved and rarely purged. The problem occurs when you have to sort through this data for litigation or compliance purposes, much of which may be irrelevant to the dispute. The true cost of processing and filtering electronic information is not the technology involved, but the costs of having humans review the information. The human costs associated with electronic discovery can be substantial and defeat the purposes of a fair, just and speedy resolution of the dispute. For this reason, if the company manages its data in an effective way, it will substantially reduce future litigation costs.

An effective data retention policy is one that is adopted before a dispute arises. It will not only assist the corporation in regaining control over its information, but provide for less costly compliance with data requests. Such policy must be in compliance with regulatory and governmental requirements and for valid business purposes. An effective policy will prevent fishing expeditions into a company's data, as well as provide a framework and storage location for dealing with confidential company information. As one commentator noted, "[i]f a company waits until it is embroiled in litigation before it closely analyzes exactly what is stored in its files, it will be too late. Any review needs to be conducted by both technical and legal personnel to sensitize the company to the risks involved in its conduct." James Pooley & David Shaw, *The Emerging Law of Computer Networks: Finding Out What's There -Technical and Legal Aspects of Discovery*, 4 Tex. Intell. Prop. L.J. 57, 65 (Fall 1995).

The core of the retention policy will define the method for determining the record retention period, procedure and the person in charge of the records.

A document retention policy should be clearly defined, reasonable and address various items such as:

• What is the retention period for specific document types such as e-mail?

• What is the life cycle for the different record types?

• Are backup tapes recycled weekly, monthly or for some other time period?

• Is archived data retained on a monthly, yearly or other time period?

• Where are the storage locations for the data?

• What is the data collection and disclosure protocol if production is necessary?

• When should audits be performed to ensure compliance with the policy?

As long as document retention policies are consistent with federal, state and local legislation and regulations, companies are free to develop retention policies that are reasonably tailored to their own needs. However, the courts have been reviewing document retention policies as they pertain to discovery. *In Lewy v. Remington Arms Co.*, 836 F.2d 1104, 1112 (8th Cir. 1988) the Court provided various factors for guidance to determine whether the retention program was reasonable. The Court stated, "[a] three year retention policy may be sufficient for documents such as appointment books or telephone messages, but inadequate for documents such as customer complaints." *See also,* §§ 7.9[D], *Duty to Preserve* and 7.09[H], *Document Retention Policy - Prior to Litigation*.

It is important that the company implements a document retention policy in good faith and that it follows its official policy at all times, and not when litigation is anticipated. The arbitrary enforcement and use of a document retention policy will cast suspicion on the motives of an organization by the courts or a regulatory agency. In a seminal case the United States Supreme Court in *Arthur Andersen, L.L.P. v. United States,* 2005 WL 1262915, at *5 (U.S. May 31, 2005) reversed the defendant's criminal conviction for shredding records immediately before receiving a SEC subpoena. The Court reversed the case based on erroneous jury instructions which failed to require a "consciousness of wrongdoing" and a "nexus" between the "persuasion" to enforce the document retention policy and any particular legal proceeding. The court noted that, "[i]t is, of course, not wrongful for a manager to instruct his employees to comply with a valid document retention policy under ordinary circumstances."

Always consider that the implementation of a document retention system may benefit the organization by enabling the reconstruction of events that may support the claims of defenses in your case. The formulation of a comprehensive document retention program can assist a company in minimizing the cost and potential liability in future litigation.

[1]   Reported Cases

- *See,* §§ 7.9[D], *Duty to Preserve* and 7.09[H], *Document Retention Policy - Prior to Litigation.*

[2]   Other Authorities

- Christopher V. Cotton, *Document Retention Programs for Electronic Records: Applying a Reasonableness Standard to the Electronic Era*, 24 Iowa J. Corp. L. 417 (1999).

- Christopher R. Chase, *To Shred or Not to Shred: Document Retention Policies and Federal Obstruction of Justice Statutes,* 8 Ford. J. Corp. & Fin. L. 721 (2003).

- Nancy Flynn, I*nstant Messaging Rules, A Business Guide to Managing Policies, Security, and Legal Issues for Safe IM Communication,* AMACON, (2004).

Chapter 7

Court Procedural Rules and Case Law

§ 7.1   FEDERAL COURT PROCEDURAL RULES

Over the past several years, courts have become aware of the widespread use of electronic data and have provided rules that support the discovery of electronic information. The Federal Rules of Civil Procedure, local rules of practice, and similar state court rules provide the judicial procedural framework for the discovery of electronic data.

Since computer-based discovery is relatively new to most practitioners, many do not understand the computer issues involved in requesting and disclosing electronic information. To be effective, both sides must have an understanding of their clients' computer systems during the pretrial stage of litigation or it can result in a frustrating and wasteful experience for the parties. For assistance during the pretrial discovery process the court can appoint, or the parties can retain, forensic specialists. The specialists can help in educating, negotiating and ensuring compliance regarding discovery requests and production issues. If the parties, in good faith, exchange information about their clients' respective computer systems at the outset of litigation, then the pretrial process will be beneficial for both sides. If the parties or specialists cannot resolve issues, the court has the tools to assist in the process. In addition, overstating cost estimates on the retrieval or restoration of electronic information or on other issues will endanger counsel's credibility and could impede the resolution of the dispute.

[A]   Pending FRCP Amendments

On April 12, 2006, the United States Supreme Court, without comment, approved the pending "e-discovery" amendments to the Federal Rules of Civil Procedure. These rules concern the discovery of "electronically stored information" (ESI) and affect Rules 16, 26, 33, 34, 37, 45 and Form 35. The rules have been sent to Congress and will become effective on December 1, 2006 unless Congress acts to change or defer the amendments. The pending amendments are available on the United States Supreme Court's website at: http://www.supremecourtus.gov/orders/courtorders/frcv06p.pdf (last visited on July 27, 2006). A copy of the pending amendments, and the Committee Notes, can be found at the United States Court website located at http://www.uscourts.gov/rules/newrules6.html (last visited on July 27, 2006).

These pending amendments and committee notes are included in the following sections under the applicable procedural rule.

These amendments are based on the premise that since electronic information is different from paper that different procedural rules are necessary. These differences which include the volume of data, complexity of computer systems, inaccessibility and a waiver of confidential information, among other issues, have led to the pending amendments. These amendments will have a significant impact on the discovery of evidence.

[B]   State Rules - Electronic Discovery

Though it is beyond the scope of this treatise to discuss the specific electronic discovery procedural rules for each state, it is important to note that some states, including Texas, Virginia, Mississippi, Illinois and California have adopted special rules pertaining to electronic discovery.

For example, Texas Rules of Civil Procedure, Rule 196.4 *Electronic or Magnetic Data,* provides, "[t]o obtain discovery of data or information that exists in electronic or magnetic form, the requesting party must specifically request production of electronic or magnetic data and specify the form in which the requesting party wants it produced. The responding party must produce the electronic or magnetic data that is responsive to the request and is reasonably available to the responding party in its ordinary course of business. . . ."; *see also,* State of Virginia Supreme Court Rule 3A:12 (Among other limitations this restrictive provision provides that information stored in electronic format need only be produced in electronic form if a hard copy is unavailable.); Mississippi Rules of Civil Procedure Rule 26(b)(5) (the party must specifically request production of electronic data, is limited to that reasonably available in the ordinary course of business, and if extraordinary steps are required to retrieve such information, the requesting party may have to pay the expense.); Illinois Supreme Court Rule 201(b)(1) (the word "documents" for purposes of the scope of discovery includes "all reasonable information in computer storage."); California Code of Civil Procedure 2017 (provides for the use of technology in conducting discovery).

§ 7.2   PROMOTE EFFICIENCY AND REASONABLE INQUIRY

[A]   FED. R. CIV. P. 1

Rule 1. Scope and Purpose of Rules

These rules govern the procedure in the United States district courts in all suits of a civil nature whether cognizable as cases at law or in equity or in admiralty, with the exceptions stated in Rule 81. They shall be construed and administered to secure the just, speedy and inexpensive determination of every action.

[1]   Purpose

The purpose of the Federal Rules of Civil Procedure is "to secure the just, speedy, and inexpensive determination of every action." FED. R. CIV. P. 1. These rules can assist in minimizing delays, provide cost savings and result in resolution of electronic discovery disputes.

[2]   Reported Cases

- *Ayers v. SGS Control Servs.,* No. CIV. 03-9078, 2006 U.S. Dist. LEXIS 17591, at *5-8 (D.N.Y. Apr. 3, 2006). The defendants objected to providing the payroll and timekeeping records in an electronic format, though available in this format, since they had already been produced in a paper format. The Court rejected the defendant's argument and held that to require the plaintiff to create their own database would be "burdensome, time consuming, and expensive" and that since "[t]his Court is charged with securing the 'just, speedy, and inexpensive determination of every action . . . '" that the defendants will produce the records in an electronic format.

- *Illinois Tool Works, Inc. v. Metro Mark Products, Ltd.,* 43 F. Supp. 2d 951, 952 (N.D. Ill. 1999).

  The Rules of Civil Procedure - including those governing discovery - seek to promote 'the just, speedy, and inexpensive determination of every action.' FED. R. CIV. P. 1. However, it is painfully obvious to litigants and courts that disputes over discovery can render this goal illusory. Whether through over-reaching by the party seeking discovery or recalcitrance by the party responding to discovery requests (or sometimes both), needless discovery disputes all too often disrupt the progress of a lawsuit, inflict additional expense on the parties, and require judicial attention that would be far better spent on addressing the merits of parties' disputes.

- *National Union Elec. Corp. v. Matsushita Elec. Indus. Co.,* 494 F. Supp. 1257, 1262-1263 (E.D. Pa. 1980). The Court stated:

  It may well be that Judge Charles E. Clark and the framers of the Federal Rules of Civil Procedure could not foresee the computer age. However, we know we now live in an era when much of the data which our society desires to retain is stored in computer discs. This process will escalate in years to come; we suspect that by the year 2000 virtually all data will be stored in some form of computer memory. To interpret the Federal Rules which, after all, are to be construed to "secure the just, speedy, and inexpensive determination of every action," F.R.Civ.P. 1, . . . in a manner which would preclude the production of material such as is requested here, would eventually defeat their purpose.

- *Hickman v. Taylor,* 329 U.S. 495, 501 (1947). "The various instruments of discovery now serve (1) as a device, along with the pre-trial hearing under Rule 16, to narrow and clarify the basic issues between the parties and (2) as a device for ascertaining the facts, or information as to the existence or whereabouts of facts, relative to those issues. Thus, civil trials in the federal courts no longer need be carried on in the dark. The way is now clear, consistent with recognized privileges, for the parties to obtain the fullest possible knowledge of the issues and facts before trial."

[B]   FED. R. CIV. P. 11

FED. R. CIV. P. 11 provides:

(a) Signature. Every pleading, written motion, and other paper shall be signed by at least one attorney of record. . . .

(b) Representations to Court. By presenting to the court (whether by signing, filing, submitting, or later advocating) a pleading, written motion, or other paper, an attorney or unrepresented party is certifying that to the best of the person's knowledge, information, and belief, formed after an inquiry reasonable under the circumstances. . . .

(1) it is not being presented for any improper purpose, such as to harass or to cause unnecessary delay or needless increase in the cost of litigation;

(2) the claims, defenses, and other legal contentions therein are warranted by existing law or by a nonfrivolous argument for the extension, modification, or reversal of existing law or the establishment of new law;

(3) the allegations and other factual contentions have evidentiary support or, if specifically so identified, are likely to have evidentiary support after a reasonable opportunity for further investigation or discovery; and

(4) the denials of factual contentions are warranted on the evidence or, if specifically so identified, are reasonably based on a lack of information or belief.

(c) Sanctions. If, after notice and a reasonable opportunity to respond, the court determines that subdivision (b) has been violated, the court may, subject to the conditions stated below, impose an appropriate sanction upon the attorneys, law firms, or parties that have violated subdivision (b) or are responsible for the violation. . . .

(d) Inapplicability to Discovery. Subdivisions (a) through (c) of this rule do not apply to disclosures and discovery requests, responses, objections, and motions that are subject to the provisions of Rules 26 through 37.

[1]   Purpose

The language of Rule 11 "stresses the need for some prefiling inquiry into both the facts and the law to satisfy the affirmative duty imposed by the rule. The standard is one of reasonableness under the circumstances." Advisory Committee Note to 1983 amendment to

Rule 11. Rule 11 "continues to require litigants to 'stop-and-think' before initially making legal or factual contentions." Advisory Committee Note to 1993 amendment to Rule 11(b) and (c). A failure to produce documents or otherwise respond to a discovery request does not come within Rule 11's proscriptions.

[2]   Reported Cases

- *Jiminez v. Madison Area Technical College*, 321 F.3d 652 (7th Cir. 2003). The Court of Appeals imposed Rule 11 sanctions on the plaintiff and her attorney. The plaintiff had produced "a number of inflammatory letters and e-mails allegedly written by various colleagues and supervisors" and made reference to these in her racial discrimination complaint. The district court concluded in a Rule 11 hearing that the letters and e-mail were "obviously fraudulent."

- *In re Bailey*, 321 B.R. 169 (Bankr. E.D.Pa. 2005). The Court awarded sanctions against the attorney for failing to make a reasonable inquiry of the debtor's bankruptcy background using PACER, an electronic docketing service.

- *The Carlton Group v. Tobin*, No. CIV.02-5065, 2003 WL 21782650 (S.D.N.Y. July 31, 2003). The Court refused Rule 11 sanctions and held that plaintiffs had made a substantial prefiling inquiry that gave them a reasonable basis that defendants had been wrongfully deleting data, stole data and used it to unlawfully to compete against the plaintiff. The parties all shared a common communication switch and data line.

- *National Assoc. of Radiation Survivors v. Turnage*, 115 F.R.D. 543, 558 n.4 (N.D.Cal. 1987). The Court held that destruction of documents "specifically responsive to outstanding discovery requests" could be sanctioned under Rule 11, "insofar as the destroyed documents contradicted the facts asserted in applicable pleadings, papers, or motions," and under Rule 26(g), "insofar as particular discovery responses failed to include the documents."

§ 7.3   COURT MANAGEMENT TOOLS

[A]   FED. R. CIV. P. 16(a)-(c), (f)

Pretrial Conferences; Scheduling; Management

(a) Pretrial Conferences; Objectives. In any action, the court may in its discretion direct the attorneys for the parties and any unrepresented parties to appear before it for a conference or conferences before trial for such purposes as (1) expediting the disposition of the action; (2) establishing early and continuing control so that the case will not be protracted because of lack of management; (3) discouraging wasteful pretrial activities; (4) improving the quality of the trial through more thorough preparation, and; (5) facilitating the settlement of the case.

(b) Scheduling and Planning. Except in categories of actions exempted by district court rule as inappropriate, the district judge, or a magistrate judge when authorized by district court rule, shall, after receiving the report from the parties under Rule 26(f) or after consulting with the attorneys for the parties and any unrepresented parties by a scheduling conference, telephone, mail, or other suitable means, enter a scheduling order that limits the time (1) to join other parties and to amend the pleadings; (2) to file motions; and (3) to complete discovery. The scheduling order may also include (4) modifications of the times for disclosures under Rules 26(a) and 26(e)(1) and of the extent of discovery to be permitted; (5) the date or dates for conferences before trial, a final pretrial conference, and trial; and (6) any other matters appropriate in the circumstances of the case. The order shall issue as soon as practicable but in any event within 90 days after the appearance of a defendant and within 120 days after the complaint has been served on a defendant. A schedule shall not be modified except upon a showing of good cause and by leave of the district judge or, when authorized by local rule, by a magistrate judge.

(c) Subjects for Consideration at Pretrial Conferences. At any conference under this rule consideration may be given, and the court may take appropriate action, with respect to . . . (3) the possibility of obtaining admissions of fact and of documents which will avoid unnecessary proof, stipulations regarding the authenticity of documents, and advance rulings from the court on the admissibility of evidence . . . (6) the control and scheduling of discovery, including orders affecting disclosures and discovery pursuant to Rule 26 and Rules 29 through 37; (7) the identification of witnesses and documents, the need and schedule for filing and exchanging pretrial briefs, and the date or dates for further conferences and for trial; (8) the advisability of referring matters to a magistrate judge or master; (9) settlement and the use of special procedures to assist in resolving the dispute when authorized by statute or local rule; (10) the form and substance of the pretrial order; . . . (12) the need for adopting special procedures for managing potentially difficult or protracted actions that may involve complex issues, multiple parties, difficult legal questions, or unusual proof problems; . . . and (16) such other matters as may facilitate the just, speedy, and inexpensive disposition of the action. At least one of the attorneys for each party participating in any conference before trial shall have authority to enter into stipulations and to make admissions regarding all matters that the participants may reasonably anticipate may be discussed. If appropriate, the court may require that a party or its representative be present or reasonably available by telephone in order to consider possible settlement of the dispute.

* * *

(f) Sanctions. If a party or party's attorney fails to obey a scheduling or pretrial order, or if no appearance is made on behalf of a party at a scheduling or pretrial conference, or if a party or party's attorney is substantially unprepared to participate in the conference, or if a party or party's attorney fails to participate in good faith, the judge, upon motion or the judge's own initiative, may make such orders with regard thereto as are just, and among others any of the orders provided in Rule 37(b)(2)(B), (C), (D). In lieu of or in addition to any other sanction, the judge shall require the party or the attorney representing the party or both to pay the reasonable expenses incurred because of any noncompliance with this rule, including attorney's fees, unless the judge finds that the noncompliance was substantially justified or that other circumstances make an award of expenses unjust.

[B]   Pending FED. R. CIV. P. 16 Amendment

Rule 16. Pretrial Conferences; Scheduling; Management

* * * * *

(b) Scheduling and Planning. Except in categories of actions exempted by district court rule as inappropriate, the district judge, or a magistrate judge when authorized by district court rule, shall, after receiving the report from the parties under Rule 26(f) or after consulting with the attorneys for the parties and any unrepresented parties by a scheduling conference, telephone, mail, or other suitable means, enter a scheduling order that limits the time

(1) to join other parties and to amend the pleadings;

(2) to file motions; and

(3) to complete discovery. The scheduling order also may include

(4) modifications of the times for disclosures under Rules 26(a) and 26(e)(1) and of the extent of discovery to be permitted;

(5) provisions for disclosure or discovery of electronically stored information;

(6) any agreements the parties reach for asserting claims of privilege or of protection as trial-preparation material after production; (emphasis added)

(7) the date or dates for conferences before trial, a final pretrial conference, and trial; and

(8) any other matters appropriate in the circumstances of the case.

The order shall issue as soon as practicable but in any event within 90 days after the appearance of a defendant and within 120 days after the complaint has been served on a defendant. A schedule shall not be modified except upon a showing of good cause and by leave of the district judge or, when authorized by local rule, by a magistrate judge. (emphasis added).

* * * * *

Committee Note

The amendment to Rule 16(b) is designed to alert the court to the possible need to address the handling of discovery of electronically stored information early in the litigation if such discovery is expected to occur. Rule 26(f) is amended to direct the parties to discuss discovery of electronically stored information if such discovery is contemplated in the action. Form 35 is amended to call for a report to the court about the results of this discussion. In many instances, the court's involvement early in the litigation will help avoid difficulties that might otherwise arise.

Rule 16(b) is also amended to include among the topics that may be addressed in the scheduling order any agreements that the parties reach to facilitate discovery by minimizing the risk of waiver of privilege or work-product protection. Rule 26(f) is amended to add to the discovery plan the parties' proposal for the court to enter a case-management or other order adopting such an agreement. The parties may agree to various arrangements. For example, they may agree to initial provision of requested materials without waiver of privilege or protection to enable the party seeking production to designate the materials desired or protection for actual production, with the privilege review of only those materials to follow. Alternatively, they may agree that if privileged or protected information is inadvertently produced, the producing party may by timely notice assert the privilege or protection and obtain return of the materials without waiver. Other arrangements are possible. In most circumstances, a party who receives information under such an arrangement cannot assert that production of the information waived a claim of privilege or of protection as trial-preparation material.

An order that includes the parties' agreement may be helpful in avoiding delay and excessive cost in discovery. *See* MANUAL FOR COMPLEX LITIGATION (FOURTH) § 11.446. Rule 16(b)(6) recognizes the propriety of including such agreements in the court's order. The rule does not provide the court with authority to enter such a case-management or other order without party agreement, or limit the court's authority to act on motion.

[C]   Purpose

Rule 16 is an effective pretrial judicial management tool that provides for pretrial conferences, scheduling and management of a case. Rule 16 enables judges to manage computer-based discovery and assist in ensuring that the parties communicate and negotiate solutions to their discovery issues. Rule 16(c) lists several areas that may be addressed during the pretrial conference, and provides a judge the authority to supplement that list with additional rulings for computer-based discovery.

Pending FED. R. CIV. P. 16 Amendment

The pending "e-discovery" amendment expands Rule 16 and permits the Court, after consulting with counsel, to enter a scheduling order regarding the "disclosure or discovery of electronically stored information [ESI]" and any agreement regarding "claims of privilege or of protection as trial-preparation material after production" for ESI. One purpose of this amendment is to allow the Court to involve itself "early in the litigation [which] will help avoid difficulties that might otherwise arise."

The scheduling order will be partially based upon amended Form 35 which includes a section on how the parties jointly propose, following a meet and confer, that the disclosure or discovery of electronically stored information should be handled. *See,* § 7.04[K][2], *Pending Rule 26(f) and Form 35 Amendments.* It also covers whether the parties have reached agreement regarding protections against inadvertent forfeiture or a waiver of privilege. If properly followed, implementation of the Rule 26(f) meet and confer provision followed by a Rule 16 scheduling order should substantially reduce extensive depositions and other discovery procedural tools.

The Committee's Note provides that "[t]he rule does not provide the court with authority to enter such a case-management or other order [regarding a waiver of privilege] without party agreement, or limit the court's authority to act on motion."

In *Hopson v. Mayor & City Council of Baltimore,* 232 F.R.D. 228, 245 (D. Md. 2005) the Court commented upon pending Rule 16 and the "meet and confer" mandate and stated, "the proposed changes to Rule 16(f) make clear, counsel have a duty to take the initiative in meeting and conferring to plan for appropriate discovery of electronically stored information at the commencement of any case in which electronic records will be sought." The Court then discussed in detail the issues the parties should discuss.

[D]   Electronic Discovery Checklist - Pretrial Agenda

The following checklist regarding computer-based discovery is designed for a Rule 16 pre-trial conference with the opposing party. It provides a useful mode of organization. Kenneth J. Withers, *Computer-Based Discovery in Federal Civil Litigation,* Federal Courts Law Review (October 2000) (Appendix A).

A Rule 16(c) Pretrial Conference Agenda for Computer-Based Discovery

The following checklist represents a maximalist approach. It should be scaled to fit the needs of the particular case, the resources of the parties, and the litigating styles of the attorneys involved.

I. When is a Detailed Rule 16 Notice Most Appropriate?

- When the substantive allegations involve computer-generated records, e.g., software development, e-commerce, unlawful Internet trafficking, etc.

- When the authenticity or completeness of computer records is likely to be contested

- When a substantial amount of disclosure or discovery will involve information or records in electronic form, e.g., e-mail, word processing, spreadsheets, and databases

- When one or both parties is an organization that routinely used computers in its day-to-day business operations during the period relevant to the facts of the case

- When one or both parties has converted substantial numbers of potentially relevant records to digital form for management or archival purposes

- When expert witnesses will develop testimony based in large part on computer data and/or modeling, or when either party plans to present a substantial amount of evidence in digital form at trial

- In any potential "big document" case in which cost associated with managing paper discovery could be avoided by encouraging exchange of digital or imaged documents (especially if multiple parties are involved)

The purpose of a detailed Rule 16 notice is to save the parties time and expense by anticipating the most common issues of computer-based discovery, developing a reasonable discovery plan, and avoiding unnecessary conflict. A detailed Rule 16 notice would not be appropriate if, in the opinion of the judge, the notice might serve to alarm the parties needlessly, raise unreasonable expectations or demands, or encourage the parties to engage in wasteful discovery.

II. Preservation of Evidence

A. What steps have counsel taken to ensure that likely discovery material in their clients' possession (or in the possession of third parties) will be preserved until the discovery process is complete? If counsel have not yet identified all material that should be disclosed or may be discoverable, what steps have been taken to ensure that material will not be destroyed or changed before counsels' investigations are complete?

If more specific direction is needed:

B. Have counsel identified computer records relevant to the subject matter of the action, e.g.,

- Word processing documents, including drafts or versions not necessarily in paper form

- Databases or spreadsheets containing relevant information
- E-mail, voicemail, or other computer-mediated communications
- Relevant system records, such as logs, Internet use history files, and access records

C. Have counsel located the following computer records:
  - Active computer files on network servers
  - Computer files on desktop or local hard drives
  - Backup tapes or disks, wherever located
  - Archival tapes or disks, wherever located
  - Laptop computers, home computers, and other satellite locations
  - Media or hardware on which relevant records may have been "deleted" but are recoverable using reasonable efforts

D. Have counsel made sure all relevant computer records at all relevant locations are secure, e.g.,
  - Suspended all routine electronic document deletion and media recycling
  - Segregated and secured backup and archival media
  - Created "mirror" copies of all active network servers, desktop hard drives, laptops, and similar hardware

E. Have counsel considered entering into an agreement to preserve evidence?

F. Does either party plan to seek a preservation order from the court?

III. Disclosure and Preliminary Discovery

A. Have counsel designated technical point-persons who know about their clients' computer systems to assist in managing computer records and answering discovery requests?

B. Have counsel prepared a description of their respective parties' computer systems for exchange? Does either party need to know more before discovery can proceed?

If, after considering whether the hints in the following list may do more harm than good, the judge determines that the parties are unclear as to what they need to know at this stage and should get further guidance, the judge may suggest that they exchange information on the following points:

- Number, types, and locations of computers currently in use

- Number, types, and locations of computers no longer in use, but relevant to the facts of the case
- Operating system and application software currently in use
- Operating system and application software no longer in use, but relevant to the facts of the case
- Name and version of network operating system currently in use
- Names and versions of network operating systems no longer in use, but relevant to the facts of the case
- File-naming and location-saving conventions
- Disk or tape labeling conventions
- Backup and archival disk or tape inventories or schedules
- Most likely locations of records relevant to the subject matter of the action
- Backup rotation schedules and archiving procedures, including any backup programs in use at any relevant time
- Electronic records management policies and procedures
- Corporate policies regarding employee use of company computers and data
- Identities of all current and former personnel who had access to network administration, backup, archiving, or other system operations during any relevant time

C. Do counsel anticipate the need to notice any depositions or propound any interrogatories to obtain further information about the opposing party's computer systems or electronic records management procedures?

D. Have counsel explored with their clients (in appropriate situations) the procedures and costs involved to:
- Locate and isolate relevant files from e-mail, word processing, and other collections
- Recover relevant files generated on outdated or dormant computer systems (so-called "legacy data")
- Recover deleted relevant files from hard drives, backup media, and other sources

E. Do counsel anticipate the need to conduct an on-site inspection of the opposing party's computer system?
- Consideration of an agreed-upon protocol

- Permission to use outside experts
- Agreement on neutral expert

IV. Electronic Document Production

A. Will counsel use computerized litigation support databases to organize and store documents and other discovery material?

B. Have counsel considered common formats for all electronic document exchange, e.g., TIFF images with OCR-generated text, e-mail in ASCII format, etc.?

C. Have counsel (particularly in multi-party cases) considered a central electronic document repository?

D. Have counsel considered an attorney-client privilege non-waiver agreement, to avoid the costs associated with intensive privilege screening before production?

E. Do counsel anticipate requesting data in non-routine format, e.g.,
  - Printing by respondent of electronic documents not normally in print form
  - Creation by respondent of customized database reports
  - Performance by respondent of customized searches or data mining

F. Have counsel agreed upon cost allocation outside the usual rule that parties absorb their own disclosure costs, e.g.,
  - Requesting parties will pay non-routine data retrieval and production costs
  - Parties will negotiate data recovery and legacy data restoration costs

G. Does either party anticipate objecting to the production of computer records or software necessary to manipulate the records based on:
  - Trade secret
  - Licensing restrictions
  - Copyright restrictions
  - Statutory or regulatory privacy restrictions

V. Testifying Experts

A. Will any testifying expert(s) rely on computer data provided by either party, or rely on his or her own data?

B. Will any testifying expert(s) use custom, proprietary, or publicly available software to process data, generate a report, or make a presentation?

C. Do counsel anticipate requesting discovery of either the underlying data or the software used by any testifying expert?

VI. Anticipating Evidentiary Disputes

Have counsel considered discovery procedures designed to reduce or eliminate questions of authenticity, e.g.,

- Computer discovery supervised by neutral party
- Neutral, secure electronic document repository
- Exchange of read-only disks or CD-ROMs
- Chain-of-custody certifications

[E]   Discovery and Preservation Orders - Rule 16(c)

Because of the fragile nature of electronic evidence, rendering electronic data inaccessible and the possible destruction through the normal use of computers, it may become necessary to ensure that the evidence is preserved immediately. Organizations have a duty, without being so ordered by a court, to preserve documents that they reasonably anticipate may be discoverable in anticipated litigation. *See,* § 7.9[D], *Duty to Preserve.* However, if a party believes that their opponent may not halt data purging policies, or has other information that evidence may be tampered with or destroyed, a protective order may be appropriate. An order of preservation is a temporary or permanent court order requiring a party to preserve evidence, including electronic information.

The Federal Rules of Civil Procedure do not address the obligation to preserve electronic information nor the standards for issuing an order. Sources of judicial authority to request preservation of electronic data is through the use of a protective order based on Rule 16 or through the court's inherent authority. Rule 16 empowers the court to issue orders "control[ling] and scheduling discovery, including orders affecting disclosures and discovery," orders "adopting special procedures for managing potentially difficult or protracted actions that may involve complex issues . . . or unusual proof problems" and orders relating to "such other matters as may facilitate the just, speedy, and inexpensive disposition of the action." FED. R. CIV. P. 16(c)(6), (12) and (16). In *Pueblo of Laguna v. United States*, 60 Fed. Cl. 133, 136, 138 (2004) the Court ruled that "the court will neither lightly exercise its inherent power to protect evidence nor indulge in an exercise in futility."

Because of the speed with which potentially relevant documents may be destroyed or made inaccessible when they are in electronic form, a court must be actively involved in preservation issues from the earliest stages of litigation. This active involvement must be tempered with an understanding of the potential harm that an overbroad preservation order may cause. It will often be impossible to construct an appropriate and precise preservation order until there have been some discovery and significant interaction with counsel.

Rule 16 is generally used in the early stages of litigation. However, a party may not have adequate information about their opponent's computer system and storage practices to request a protective order. A party should immediately take steps to understand the opponent's computer system in order to request the court for expedited disclosure of specific computer information so that the preservation issue can be decided.

During initial pretrial proceedings, the court can fashion a variety of discovery orders including issuing preservation orders, mandating the parties meet and resolve technology discovery issues, ordering the creation of joint document databases and deciding on the need for any protective orders. *See also, § 7.4[I], Protective Orders - Rule 26(c).* However, the first approach is always to send a preservation letter, as soon as the discovery party is contemplating litigation, in order to put the opposing party on notice to preserve data. *See, § 6.1[C][7], Preservation Request.*

Since all parties are already required to preserve all relevant data in their possession, custody or control, the courts in deciding whether to issue a preservation order, have focused on various factors. These factors include the level of concern for the continued existence of evidence in question, any likely irreparable harm absent an order, and nonmovant's capability to maintain evidence that is sought to be preserved. *Treppel v. Biovail Corp.,* 233 F.R.D. 363, 369-370 (D.N.Y. 2006); *Capricorn Power Co., Inc. v. Siemens Westinghouse Power Corp.,* 220 F.R.D. 429 (W.D. Pa. 2004); *Cf. Pueblo of Laguna v. United States,* 2004 WL 542633, 60 Fed. Cl. 133 (Fed. Cl. 2004); *United States ex rel. Smith v. Boeing Co.,* No. CIV.05-1073, 2005 U.S. Dist. LEXIS 36890, at *5-7 (D. Kan. Aug. 31, 2005).

Another approach for obtaining a preservation order is to enter into an agreement pursuant to FED. R. CIV. P. 29. This empowers the parties to enter into a written stipulation that involves procedures governing discovery. The parties can then have the court enter such a stipulation as a court order. For example, in *In re Infant Formula Antitrust Litigation,* No. MDL-878, 1991 WL 214162 (N.D. Fla. Aug. 15, 1991) the parties entered into a document request stipulation that was subsequently ordered by the court.

For immediate action, it may be necessary to pursue a temporary restraining order (TRO) to preserve electronic data pursuant to FED. R. CIV. P. 65. In *Armstrong v. Bush,* 807 F. Supp. 816, 823 (D.D.C. 1992), the court entered a temporary restraining order requiring the preservation of current and existing computer backup tapes. *See, § 7.14, Injunctions.*

Pending Rule 26(f) Amendment

Pending Rule 26(f) Committee Note provides specific guidance for counsel in conferring on data preservation issues. It provides that counsel should discuss preserving data and agree upon reasonable steps to do so. The Committee noted that "[t]he requirement that the parties discuss preservation does not imply that courts should routinely enter preservation orders. A preservation order entered over objections should be narrowly tailored. Ex parte preservation orders should issue only in exceptional circumstances." *See,* § 7.04[K], *Meet and Confer - Rule 26(f).*

[1] Reported Cases - Electronic Discovery Format Order

- *In Re: Propulsid Products Liability,* MDL No. 1355, Pretrial Order No. 8, *Defendants' Production of Hard Copy Docs,* Jan. 18, 2001 available at http://propulsid.laed.uscourts.gov/Orders/order8.pdf (last visited on July 27, 2006). The Court issued an extensive discovery order listing the specifics of providing discovery in an electronic format for the parties. The discovery details included, among others, that all documents are produced in an electronic image form with a unique identifier, database coding, and OCR text files for documents without redactions.

- *Order Concerning Electronic Discovery, from Prempro Products Liability MDL,* 03-CV-1507 (E.D. Ark. Nov. 17, 2003) at http://www.fjc.gov/public/pdf.nsf/lookup/ElecDi13.pdf/$file/ElecDi13.pdf (last visited on July 27, 2006). The Court issued an extensive electronic discovery order focusing on the underlying computer setup, preservation and disclosure of electronic data.

- *In re Diet Drugs,* No. 1203, 1999 WL 124414, at *5 (E.D. Pa. Feb. 10, 1999). The court ordered the sharing of work product including "CD-ROMs reflecting searchable images of the key documents," "a bibliographic database providing a 'coded' index of such key documents," "abstracts and subjective analyses of the depositions," "timelines, 'casts of characters,' issues outlines, and other work product" and "reports of 'generic experts.'"

- *Bell v. Automobile Club of Michigan,* 80 F.R.D. 228, 233 (E.D. Mich. 1978), *app. dism'd without op.,* 601 F.2d 587 (6th Cir. 1979), *cert. denied,* 99 S.Ct. 2839 (1979). The Court ordered the parties to set up a computer data bank. The Court's order of April 23, 1975 stated: "The use of computerized data requires the Co-operation of all parties. The parties are directed to meet: (1) to resolve technological problems, (2) to determine what information, if any, contained on the tapes and in the cardex file will not be required by plaintiffs, (3) to establish what protective conditions, if any, are to be attached to the disclosure and use of this information, and (4) to determine appropriate costs."

[2] Reported Cases - Preservation Order

Burden of Proof

- *Treppel v. Biovail Corp.,* 233 F.R.D. 363, 372 (D.N.Y. 2006). The Court denied the plaintiff's request for a preservation order since the plaintiff had failed to establish that any "evidence has in fact been lost, that it was likely relevant to claims or defenses in this action, and that an order will not impose undue hardship on [the defendant]."

- *Capricorn Power Co., Inc. v. Siemens Westinghouse Power Corp.*, 220 F.R.D. 429 (W.D.Pa. 2004). In a detailed analysis of both parties' request for a preservation order the Court utilized a three-pronged test that the appropriateness of preservation order depends on court's level of concern for continuing existence of evidence in question, any likely irreparable harm absent a preservation order, and the party's capability to maintain evidence sought to be preserved. Since the parties had failed to demonstrate that evidence in question would be lost or destroyed and failed to develop the irreparable harm argument, the motion was denied. *See also, United States ex rel. Smith v. Boeing Co.*, No. CIV.05-1073, 2005 U.S. Dist. LEXIS 36890 (D. Kan. Aug. 31, 2005) (court refused to grant preservation order finding that the three-prong test was not met).

- *Pueblo of Laguna v. United States*, 60 Fed. Cl. 133 (Ct.Cl. 2004). In an accounting action, the plaintiff tribe sought a preservation order arguing that in a prior case involving a different tribe that electronic and other data had been destroyed. Under RCFC 16(c), the court partially granted the plaintiff's request including ordering procedures for inspection and retention of available electronic data.

- *Williams v. Massachusetts Mut. Life Ins. Co.*, 226 F.R.D. 144, 146-147 (D. Mass. 2005). "The court, however, will order Defendants to preserve all documents, hard drives and e-mail boxes which were searched by their forensic expert . . . Such an order, in the court's estimation, is not unduly burdensome and is necessary, at a minimum, to preserve Plaintiff's appellate rights."

- *Antioch v. Scrapbook Borders, Inc.*, 210 F.R.D. 645, 651-652 (D. Minn. 2002). The Court in a copyright infringement action granted the plaintiff's request for a preservation order and stated, "we conclude that the Defendants may have relevant information, on their computer equipment, which is being lost through normal use of the computer, and which might be relevant to the Plaintiff's claims, or the Defendants' defenses. This information may be in the form of stored or deleted computer files, programs, or e-mails, on the Defendants' computer equipment."

- *In re Merrill Lynch & Co., Inc. Research Reports Sec. Litig.*, No. MDL.02-1484 14842004 WL 305601, at *1 (S.D.N.Y Feb. 18, 2004). In a SEC action, the plaintiff requested discovery in order to preserve and restore e-mails deleted by the defendant. The Court denied the request since the plaintiff failed to establish an "imminent risk" of data being deleted and rendered irretrievable. *But see, In re Pacific Gateway Exchange, Inc.*, No. CIV.00-1211, 2001 WL 1334747 (N.D. Cal. Oct. 17, 2001) where the Court granted discovery since the data may become irretrievably lost.

- *In re Tyco International, Ltd., Securities Litigation*, No. 00-MD-1335-B, 2000 WL 33654141 (D.N.H. Jul. 27, 2000). Court refused to adopt the parties' written agreement concerning preservation of defendants' documents and data, finding that it would unnecessarily duplicate or alter the obligations already imposed by the preservation provision in the Private Securities Litigation Reform Act of 1995, 15 U.S.C. § 78u-4(b)(3)(C)(I)1.

- *Procter & Gamble Co. v. Haugen*, 179 F.R.D. 622 (D. Utah 1998), *aff'd in part and rev'd in part,* 222 F.3d 1262 (10th Cir. 2000). The Court noted that it is a better practice for a party seeking discovery to request an immediate order from the Court that all computer files are to be retained and not destroyed pending preliminary discovery. This would furnish a standard for the adequacy of the disclosure efforts.

- *Abdallah v. The Coca-Cola Co.*, 1999 WL 527835, at *2 (N.D.Ga. July 16, 1999). The Court denied plaintiffs request for a document preservation order, "[finding] no basis for concern regarding [defendant's] efforts to preserve all documents relevant to this lawsuit. . . ."

- *In re Potash Antitrust Litigation,* 1994 WL 1108312, at *8 (D. Minn. Dec. 5, 1994). The Court denied the request for a preservation order even though the plaintiffs argued they "may suffer irreparable harm." In response the defendants argued "there has been no persuasive showing that the Plaintiffs are likely to suffer any harm, particularly when the Defendants have 'taken appropriate steps to preserve documents and records.'"

Preservation Orders

- *Creative Sci. Sys. v. Forex Capital Mkts., LLC,* No. CIV.04-03746, 2006 U.S. Dist. LEXIS 20116, at *4-5 (D. Cal. Apr. 4, 2006). Sanctions were issued after the defendant failed to preserve electronic information pursuant to the following Order of the Court,

    FXCM and Refco shall preserve all relevant documents as defined under Federal Rule of Civil Procedure 34(a), including but not limited to all electronic evidence or evidence stored on computers regardless of the medium on which it is stored. This Order applies to and includes, but is not limited to: (1) all copies of NetZyme(R) Enterprise or portions thereof; (2) any configuration file on any load balancing server used by FXCM, including but not limited to the "Big IP" server used by FXCM; and (3) all evidence of distribution of FXCM and/or Refco client software, including but not limited [*5] to any FXCM customer database.

    For purposes of this Order, "preserve" is to be interpreted broadly to accomplish the goal of maintaining the integrity of all documents, data, and tangible things including all documents as defined above and those that are reasonably anticipated to be subject to discovery under Federal Rules of Civil Procedure 26 or 34 in this action. To preserve includes taking steps to prevent the partial or full destruction, alteration, testing, deletion, shredding, incineration, erasing, wiping, relocation, migration, theft or mutation of such material, as well as negligent or intentional handling that would make material incomplete or inaccessible.

- *In re Vioxx Products Liability Litigation,* No. MDL 1657, 2005 WL 756742 (E.D.La. Feb. 18, 2005). In a pretrial order the Court stated:

  13. PRESERVATION OF EVIDENCE --- All parties and their counsel are reminded of their duty to preserve evidence that may be relevant to this action. The duty extends to documents, data, and tangible things in possession, custody and control of the parties to this action, and any employees, agents, contractors, carriers, bailees, or other nonparties who possess materials reasonably anticipated to be subject to discovery in this action. "Documents, data, and tangible things" is to be interpreted broadly to include writings, records, files, correspondence, reports, memoranda, calendars, diaries, minutes, electronic messages, voice mail, E-mail, telephone message records or logs, computer and network activity logs, hard drives, backup data, removable computer storage media such as tapes, discs and cards, printouts, document image files, Web pages, databases, spreadsheets, software, books, ledgers, journals, orders, invoices, bills, vouchers, checks statements, worksheets, summaries, compilations, computations, charts, diagrams, graphic presentations, drawings, films, charts, digital or chemical process photographs, video, phonographic, tape or digital recordings or transcripts thereof, drafts, jottings and notes, studies or drafts of studies or other similar such material. Information that serves to identify, locate, or link such material, such as file inventories, file folders, indices, and metadata, is also included in this definition. Until the parties reach an agreement on a preservation plan or the Court orders otherwise, each party shall take reasonable steps to preserve all documents, data and tangible things containing information potentially relevant to the subject matter of this litigation. Counsel is under an obligation to the Court to exercise all reasonable efforts to identify and notify parties and nonparties, including employees of corporate or institutional parties.

- *F.T.C. v. MaxTheater, Inc.,* No. CIV.05-006, 2005 WL 1027121 (E.D. Wash. Mar. 31, 2005). The Court issued a preservation order and stated,

  IT IS FURTHER ORDERED that the defendants, and those persons in active concert or participation with them who receive actual notice of this Order by personal service or otherwise, are hereby restrained and enjoined from destroying, erasing, mutilating, concealing, altering, transferring, writing over, or otherwise disposing of, in any manner, directly or indirectly, any documents or records of any kind . . . including but not limited to, computerized files, storage media (including but not limited to floppy disks, hard drives, CD-ROMS, zip disks, punch cards, magnetic tape, backup tapes, and computer chips) on which information has been saved, any and all equipment needed to read any such material, contracts, accounting data, correspondence, advertisements (including, but not limited to, advertisements placed on the World Wide Web or the Internet), FTP logs, Service Access Logs, USENET Newsgroups postings, World Wide Web pages, books, written or printed records, handwritten notes, telephone logs, telephone scripts, receipt books, ledgers, personal and business canceled checks and check registers, bank statements, appointment books, copies of federal, state or local business or personal income or property tax returns, and other documents or records of any kind that relate to the business practices or business or personal finances of the defendants.

- *In Re: Propulsid Products Liability,* MDL No. 1355, Pretrial Order No. 10, Production and Preservation of Defendants' Electronic Data, April 19, 2001 at http://propulsid.laed.uscourts.gov/Orders/order10.pdf (last visited on July 27, 2006). The Court issued an extensive protocol for the "production and preservation of electronic data . . . including e-mail, electronic peer-to-peer messages, word processing documents, spreadsheets, electronic slide presentations, databases, and other electronic data items, now existing or hereafter created, containing information relating to facts at issue in the litigation ('discoverable electronic information')." *See also, Order for Preservation of Records, from Baycol Products Litigation,* MDL 1431 (D. Minn. March 4, 2002) available at http://www.fjc.gov/public/pdf.nsf/lookup/ElecDi21.pdf/$file/ElecDi21.pdf (last visited on July 22, 2006).

- *Linnen v. A.H. Robins Co.,* No. 97-2307, 1999 WL 462015, at *8 (Mass. Super. Ct. Jun. 16, 1999). In this wrongful death action against the makers of Phen-Fen, the plaintiffs, after filing the complaint, obtained an *ex parte* order from the court requiring the defendant to preserve all documents and other information relevant to this action including e-mail. The Court order stated in part:

  All defendants must take all necessary steps to assure that their employees, agents, accountants and attorneys refrain from discarding, destroying, erasing, purging or deleting any such documents including, but not limited to, computer memory, computer disks, data compilations, e-mail messages sent and received and all back-up computer files or devices, including but not limited to electronic, optical or magnetic storage media until such time as this court enters a superseding Order regarding the preservation of documents and potential evidence relevant to the above-captioned litigation.

[3] Other Authorities

- MANUAL FOR COMPLEX LITIGATION (FOURTH) § 21.446: "Digital or electronic information can be stored in any of the following: mainframe computers, network servers, personal computers, hand-held devices, automobiles, or household appliances; or it can be accessible via the Internet, from private networks, or from third parties. Any discovery plan must address issues relating to such information, including the search for it and its location, retrieval, form of production, inspection, preservation, and use at trial."

- MANUAL FOR COMPLEX LITIGATION (FOURTH) § 21.442: "Before discovery starts, and perhaps before the initial conference, the court should consider whether to enter an order requiring the parties to preserve and retain documents, files, data, and records that may be relevant to the litigation. Because such an order may interfere with the normal operations of the parties and impose unforeseen burdens, it is advisable to discuss with counsel at the first opportunity the need for a preservation order and, if one is needed, the scope, duration, method of data preservation, and other terms that will best preserve relevant matter without imposing undue burdens."

- MANUAL FOR COMPLEX LITIGATION (FOURTH) § 40.25: This section sets forth a suggested "meet and confer" process regarding preservation issues including an interim preservation order to a final detailed preservation agreement or Court order.

- John L. Carroll, *Preservation of Documents in the Electronic Age - What Should Courts Do?,* 2005 Fed. Cts. L. Rev. 5 (2005).

- Mark D. Robbins, *Computers and the Discovery of New Evidence - A New Dimension to Civil Procedure,* 17 J. Marshall J. Computer & Info. L. 411, 500 (1999).

[F]   Sanctions - Rule 16(f)

[1]   Purpose

FED. R. CIV. P. 16(f) and 37, along with their inherent authority, provides the court with the discretion to impose sanctions for noncompliance with discovery rules. *See also,* § 7.9, *Sanctions.*

[2]   Reported Cases

- *In re Prudential Ins. Co. of America Sales Practices Litigation,* 169 F.R.D. 598, 614 (D.N.J. 1997). The Court stated:

    The Federal Rules of Civil Procedure provide for sanctions when a party to a litigation fails to obey a pre-trial order. FED. R. CIV. P. 16(f). Beyond the formal rules and legislative dictates, the Court possesses the inherent authority to punish those who abuse the judicial process. *Republic of the Philippines v. Westinghouse Electric Corporation, 43* F.3d 65, 73 (3d Cir. 1995). The reason for the rule and the warrant for its existence lies in the fact that a court, in order to achieve the orderly and expeditious disposition of cases, must have the control necessary to manage its own affairs. *Chambers v. NASCO*, 501 U.S. 32, 43, 111 S.Ct. 2123, 2132, 115 L.Ed.2d 27 (1991).

• *Shepherd v. American Broadcasting Cos.*, 62 F.3d 1469, 1474 (D.C. Cir. 1995). The Court stated: "When rules alone do not provide courts with sufficient authority to protect their integrity and prevent abuses of the judicial process, the inherent power fills the gap."

• *Smith ex rel. El Ali v. Altegra Credit Co.*, No. CIV.02-8221, 2004 WL 2399773, *4 (E.D.Pa. Sept. 22, 2004). "The purpose of sanctions authorized by Rule 16(f) is to prevent the undue delay in disposing of cases. *See* David L. Shapiro, *Federal Rule 16: A Look at the Theory and Practice of Rulemaking*, 137 U. PA. L.REV. 1969, 1987 (1989) ('A final purpose of [the 1983 amendments to Rule 16] . . . is reflected in the inclusion in the rule itself of a provision for sanctions against parties and attorneys who violate orders or who fail to participate at all or with sufficient enthusiasm in a pretrial conference.'").

[G]   Discovery Pointers

• Send a preservation letter, as soon as the discovery party is contemplating litigation, in order to put the opposing party on notice to preserve data. *See*, § 6.1[C][7], *Preservation Request.*

• Consider asking the court for a protective order requiring preservation of e-mail and other computer files in order to protect against routine or deliberate deletions or overwriting of data. *See*, § 7.3[E], *Discovery and Preservation Orders - Rule 16(c).*

• Follow up with a request for production asking for identification and production of all e-mail and computer files.

• Finally, consider sending interrogatories or immediately conducting a FED. R. CIV. P. 30(b)(6) deposition to determine whether any computer files have been deleted, and whether any software has been utilized that wipes files or reformats a computer's hard drive.

§ 7.4   PRODUCTION AND PROTECTION OF CASE INFORMATION

[A]   FED. R. CIV. P. 26

See the individual sections below.

[1]   Purpose

FED. R. CIV. P. 26 requires a party to inform opposing counsel, without receiving any discovery request, as to which witnesses, documents and other materials will be used in support of the claims or defenses contained in the pleadings. The courts have consistently ruled that information in electronic form is to be considered the same as information in paper form. "Rules 26(b) and 34 of the Federal Rules of Civil Procedure instruct that computer-stored information is discoverable under the same rules that pertain to tangible, written materials." *In re Brand Name Prescription Drugs Antitrust Litigation,* No. CIV.94-897, 1995 WL 360526, at *1 (N.D. Ill. Jun. 15, 1995). *See also,* § 7.7[B], *"Document" - Definition;* § 7.9[D], *Duty to Preserve,* and § 7.9[E], *Scope of Duty to Preserve.*

Generally, the disclosure must be made within 14 days of the Rule 26(f) meet and confer conference unless a different time period is agreed to by the parties or by court order. FED. R. CIV. P. 26(a)(1)(E).

Since these disclosures are often made soon after the case commences, and before any other discovery takes place, it is unlikely that either party will have a comprehensive understanding of their client's electronic data collection. For this reason, it is important to continue with other formalized discovery to ensure that you receive all the responsive data pertaining to the claims or defenses in the case.

Rule 26(c) can be an important tool for discovery dispute resolution. After disclosure statements have been filed, a judge may be called upon to expand or limit the discovery, protect particular data, balance the benefits and burdens of discovery and/or shift discovery costs.

Pending FED. R. CIV. P. 26 Amendment

The pending Rule 26 "e-discovery" amendments, specifically, 26(a) and Rule 26(f), require the parties to initially disclose "electronically stored information" (ESI) and generally "meet and confer" regarding ESI, and in particular, data preservation, form of production and privilege waiver. After the initial disclosures and "meet and confer" counsel are required to report to the Court and engage in a pretrial scheduling conference with the judge regarding ESI. *See,* § § 7.03[B], *Pending Rule 16 Amendment and* 7.04[K][2], *Pending Rule 26(f) and Form 35 Amendments.*

[2]   Local Rules of Practice

Several federal jurisdictions have promulgated local rules of practice and other guidelines that impose obligations on parties concerning electronic discovery. For example, in *Mosaid Technologies Inc. v. Samsung Electronics Co., Ltd.,* 2004 WL 2797536, at *6 (D. N.J. 2004) the Court noted that "Local Civil Rule 26.1 was amended to include a section concerning discovery of digital information. . . . Among other things, that rule requires counsel to investigate how a client's computers store digital information, to review with the client potentially discoverable evidence, and to raise the topic of e-discovery at the Rule 26(f) conference, including preservation and production of digital information. Unless and until parties agree not to pursue e-discovery, the parties have an obligation to preserve potentially relevant digital information."

Some federal district courts with local rules regarding electronic discovery include:

- Eastern and Western District of Arkansas Local Rule 26.1;

- District of Wyoming Local Rule 26.1;

- Middle District of Pennsylvania Local Rule 26.1;

- District of New Jersey Local Rule 26.1(d);

- Mississippi Court Order 13 (May 29, 2003) amending Mississippi Rule of Civil Procedure 26;

- District of Kansas, Electronic Discovery Guidelines;

- District of Delaware, Default Standards for Discovery of Electronic Documents; and

- Proposed Model Local Rule on Electronic Discovery, Ninth Circuit Advisory Board (May 2004).

[3]   Reported Cases

- *Danis v. USN Communications, Inc.,* No. CIV.98-7482, 2000 WL 1694325, at *1 (N.D. Ill. Oct. 20, 2000). The Court stated:

  Day in and day out, in countless courts throughout this country, courts resolve disputes of every kind imaginable. Even when disappointed (or outraged) by the outcome, the parties to these disputes do not engage in lawlessness or self-help. Having had their day in court, the parties accept judgment and move on with their lives. They would not do so unless they had faith in the integrity of our judicial system. Not a faith that the system is perfect and will never err, but rather a faith that the system will give the parties a fair opportunity to be heard. This fair opportunity to be heard is achieved through lawyers for each side, having obtained and marshaled the relevant evidence, presenting their clients' respective positions vigorously. Our system is premised on the view that through this clash of competing stories, judges and juries will have the information they need to make a fair decision. In our system of civil litigation, the discovery process is the principal means by which lawyers and parties assemble the facts, and decide what information to present at trial. Federal Rule of Civil Procedure 26 requires a party to produce non-privileged documents which are "relevant to the subject matter involved in the pending action." That requirement embraces not only documents admissible at trial but also documents and information that are "reasonably calculated to lead to the discovery of admissible evidence." This broad duty of disclosure extends to all documents that fit the definition of relevance for the purposes of discovery - whether the documents are good, bad, or indifferent. While it may seem contrary to the adversarial process to require such "self-reporting," it is in fact a central tenet of our discovery process.

- *Bills v. Kennecott Corp.,* 108 F.R.D. 459, 462 (D. Utah 1985). "Computers have become so commonplace that most court battles now involve discovery of some type of computer-stored information."

[4]   Other Authorities

- David J. Waxse, *"Do I Really Have to Do That?" Rule 26(a)(1) Disclosures and Electronic Information,* 10 RICH. J.L. & TECH. 50 (2004), at http://law.richmond.edu/jolt/v10i5/article50.pdf.
- Lisa M. Arent, Robert D. Brownstone & William A. Fenwick, *EDiscovery: Preserving, Requesting & Producing Electronic Information,* 19 Santa Clara Computer & High Tech. L.J. 131 (2002).
- The Sedona Conference, *The Sedona Principles: Best Practices, Recommendations & Principles for Addressing Electronic Document Production* (2004*).* This set of principles has been developed from the corporate defense perspective.

[B]   Disclosure of Witnesses – Rule 26(a)(1)(A)

Rule 26. General Provisions Governing Discovery; Duty of Disclosure

(a) Required Disclosures; Methods to Discover Additional Matter.

(1) Initial Disclosures. Except in categories of proceedings specified in Rule 26(a)(1)(E), or to the extent otherwise stipulated or directed by order, a party must, without awaiting a discovery request, provide to other parties:

(A) the name and, if known, the address and telephone number of each individual likely to have discoverable information that the disclosing party may use to support its claims or defenses, unless solely for impeachment, identifying the subjects of the information . . .

[1] Purpose

Under Rule 26(a)(1)(A) a party is required to disclose the name, address and telephone number of "each individual likely to have discoverable information that the disclosing party may use to support its claims or defenses, unless solely for impeachment."

This disclosure should contain the identification of the party's management information systems (MIS) managers as persons with discoverable information of their client's electronic information systems.

[2] Reported Cases

- *Clark Const. Group, Inc. v. City of Memphis,* No. CIV.01-2780, 2005 WL 1618767, at *3 (W.D. Tenn. Mar. 14, 2005). In this breach of contract case, the Court ruled that the city's project manager, who destroyed more than 2,000 paper and electronic documents, was under a duty to preserve documents since this duty extends to "any document made by an individual 'likely to have discoverable information that the disclosing party may use to support its claim or defenses.' FED.R.CIV.P. 26(a)(1)(A)."

- *Zubulake v. UBS Warburg LLC,* No. CIV.02-1243, 2004 WL 1620866, at *9 (S.D.N.Y. July 20, 2004). The Court in this discrimination case stated "counsel should communicate directly with the 'key players' in the litigation, i.e., the people identified in a party's initial disclosure and any subsequent supplementation thereto. [FN82 *See* FED.R.CIV.P. 26(a)(1)(A)] Because these 'key players' are the 'employees likely to have relevant information,' it is particularly important that the preservation duty be communicated clearly to them. As with the litigation hold, the key players should be periodically reminded that the preservation duty is still in place."

[C] Initial Disclosures - Rule 26(a)(1)(B)

[1] Rule 26(a)(1)(B)

Rule 26(a)(1)(B)

[A] party must without awaiting a discovery request, provide to other parties: . . . (B) a copy of or a description by category or location of, all *documents, data compilations,* and tangible things that are in the possession, custody or control of the party and that the disclosing party may use to support its claims or defenses unless solely for impeachment . . . (emphasis added).

[2] Advisory Notes

FED. R. CIV. P. 26 advisory committee notes (1993 amendments) state:

(B) is included as a substitute for the inquiries routinely made about the existence and location of documents and other tangible things in the possession, custody, or control of the disclosing party. Although, unlike subdivision (a)(3)(C), an itemized listing of each exhibit is not required, the disclosure should describe and categorize, to the extent identified during the initial investigation, the nature and location of potentially relevant documents and records, including computerized data and other electronically-recorded information, sufficiently to enable opposing parties (1) to make an informed decision concerning which documents might need to be examined, at least initially, and (2) to frame their document requests in a manner likely to avoid squabbles resulting from the wording of the requests. As with potential witnesses, the requirement for disclosure of documents applies to all potentially relevant items then known to the party, whether or not supportive of its contentions in the case.

For a discussion of what data is included in the definition of the word "document" *see* § 7.7[B], *"Document" - Definition*.

[3]   Pending Rule 26(a)(1)(B) Amendment

(B) a copy of, or a description by category and location of, all documents, <u>electronically stored information,</u> and tangible things that are in the possession, custody, or control of the party and that the disclosing party may use to support its claims or defenses, unless solely for impeachment; (emphasis added).

* * * * *

Committee Note

Subdivision (a). Rule 26(a)(1)(B) is amended to parallel Rule 34(a) by recognizing that a party must disclose electronically stored information as well as documents that it may use to support its claims or defenses. The term "electronically stored information" has the same broad meaning in Rule 26(a)(1) as in Rule 34(a). This amendment is consistent with the 1993 addition of Rule 26(a)(1)(B). The term "data compilations" is deleted as unnecessary because it is a subset of both documents and electronically stored information.

[4]   Purpose

The party making the disclosure must provide a list of "all documents, data compilations, and tangible things" that are in the possession, custody, or control of the disclosing party. In addition, either the disclosing party must provide a copy of such documents or a description by category and location of the documents listed. Thus, information is generally discoverable unless it falls within a privilege (such as the attorney-client privilege or work product doctrine).

A party's initial disclosures pursuant to FED. R. CIV. P. 26(a)(1) must include electronic information. To determine what information must be disclosed pursuant to this rule, counsel should communicate with their clients to determine what electronic information is available including not only active current files, but also back-up, archival and legacy computer files. Determine and disclose what electronic information may be used to support claims or defenses, unless it will be used "solely for impeachment." "Once a party and her counsel have identified all of the sources of potentially relevant information, they are under a duty to retain that information . . . and to produce information responsive to the opposing party's requests." *Zubulake v. UBS Warburg LLC,* No. CIV.02-1243, 2004 WL 1620866, at *8 (S.D.N.Y. July 20, 2004).

Rule 26(a)(1)(B) does not require the production of "data compilations." It provides the disclosing party the option of providing a description by category and location or a copy of the data compilations. Generally, it will be necessary to acquire the electronic data through a Rule 34 discovery motion.

FED. R. CIV. P. 26(e) imposes a duty to supplement these disclosures.

The proper electronic format for initial disclosures is covered in §§ 5.3, *Electronic Data Formats,* 7.07[D], *Translated Into Reasonably Useful Form,* 7.07[E], *Kept in the Usual Course of Business,* and 7.7[G], *Form of Production of Computer-based Data.*

Pending Rule 26(a)(1)(B) Amendment

This pending rule amendment recognizes that a party has an obligation to initially disclose "electronically stored information" as well as documents that it may use to support its claims or defenses. According to the Committee Note "electronically stored information" (ESI) is to have the same broad meaning in Rule 26(a)(1) as in Rule 34(a).

[5] Reported Cases

- *Kleiner v. Burns,* No. CIV.00-2160, 2000 WL 1909470, at *9-10 (D. Kan. Dec. 15, 2000). In this copyright infringement suit the Court found Rule 26(a)(1)(B) disclosure obligations require a party to describe and categorize the nature and location of electronic information. The Court found that Yahoo! should have disclosed all relevant "e-mails, voice mails, web sites, web pages, and all other forms of electronic data in its possession, custody or control" in its initial disclosures.

- *Phoenix Four, Inc. v. Strategic Resources Corp.,* No. CIV. 05-4837, 2006 WL 1409413 (S.D.N.Y. May 23, 2006). In this investment action for fraud the defendant failed to determine that one of its servers contained a substantial amount of discoverable data until a few months before trial. The Court, citing to pending rules 26(a) and (b)(2), imposed monetary sanctions and found that the defendant's counsel deficiencies constituted "gross negligence."

- *In re Lorazepam and Clorazepate Antitrust Litigation,* 300 F. Supp. 2d 43, 47(D.D.C. 2004). The plaintiff objected to the electronic discovery production arguing that an "index" should have been provided. The Court ruled that, "[t]he glory of electronic information is not merely that it saves space but that it permits the computer to search for words or 'strings' of text in seconds. The Blues can, for example, look for the White Paper they insist exists by searching for the word 'white' within a certain number of words from the word 'paper,' thus replicating for themselves the search done several years ago by a computer forensic scientist. In this sense, the presence of the information on the CD-ROM's is an opportunity for the Blues rather than a problem."

- *In re Bristol-Myers Squibb Securities Litigation,* 205 F.R.D. 437, 439, 441 (D.N.J. 2002). The Court stated, "[t]he Court, mindful of Rule 26(a)(1)(B) finds that where a party already possesses relevant information in electronic form, it is obligated, by way of mandatory disclosure, to so advise the adversary. Once advised of the existence of electronic data, a party may then make an informed decision as to the manner by which discovery could be produced."

- *Gary Price Studios, Inc. v. Randolph Rose Collection, Inc.,* No. CIV.03-969, 2006 U.S. Dist. LEXIS 30197, at *3-7 (D.N.Y. May 12, 2006). The Court found it to be harmless error and not sanctionable under Rule 37 for failure of the defendant to disclose web pages. In dicta, the Court noted that since the web pages were not in the defendant's "possession, control or custody" that there was no violation of Rule 26(a)(1)(B) and Rule 34.

- *Super Film of America, Inc. v. UCB Films Inc.,* 219 F.R.D. 649, 657 (D. Kan. 2004). Citing to FED.R.CIV.P. 26(a)(1)(B) the court rejected the producing party's attempt to fulfill its production obligation by "simply turning over its two computers to [the requesting party] for inspection." The Court denied the producing party's unduly burdensome argument and noted, "this would unfairly shift the burden and expense of discovery to [the requesting party] and could potentially result in relevant and otherwise discoverable information being shielded from UCB."

[6]   Discovery Pointer

- Since document retention policies can affect the preservation of data, it may be advisable to include the document retention policies of your client under FED. R. CIV. P. 26 (a) involving initial disclosures. In this way, the policies can be discussed and brought to light in a Rule 16(b) or 26(f) conference. This would place the parties on notice of the document retention policies and provide for resolution as to the continuation of policies, as long as no relevant data would be destroyed.

- When you receive Rule 26 disclosures from an adversary that describes and categorizes electronic documents, request the specific location of the electronic versions (the particular PC, and/or network drives, directory paths, etc.).

[D]   Expert Witness Reports - FED. R. CIV. P. 26(a)(2)(A), Rule 26(a)(2)(B) and Rule 26(b)(4)

[1]   RULE 26(a)(2)(A)

Under FED. R. CIV. P. 26(a)(2)(A), parties must disclose "the identity of any person who may be used at trial to present evidence on Rules 702, 703, or 705 of the Federal Rules of Evidence."

[2]   Rule 26(a)(2)(B)

(B) Except as otherwise stipulated or directed by the court, this disclosure shall, with respect to a witness who is retained or specially employed to provide expert testimony in the case or whose duties as an employee of the party regularly involve giving expert testimony, be accompanied by a written report prepared and signed by the witness. The report shall contain a complete statement of all opinions to be expressed and the basis and reasons therefor; the data or other information considered by the witness in forming the opinions; any exhibits to be used as a summary of or support for the opinions; the qualifications of the witness, including a list of all publications authored by the witness within the preceding ten years; the compensation to be paid for the study and testimony; and a listing of any other cases in which the witness has testified as an expert at trial or by deposition within the preceding four years.

[3]   Rule 26(b)(4)

(4) Trial Preparation: Experts.

(A) A party may depose any person who has been identified as an expert whose opinions may be presented at trial. If a report from the expert is required under subdivision (a)(2)(B), the deposition shall not be conducted until after the report is provided.

(B) A party may, through interrogatories or by deposition, discover facts known or opinions held by an expert who has been retained or specially employed by another party in anticipation of litigation or preparation for trial and who is not expected to be called as a witness at trial, only as provided in Rule 35(b) or upon a showing of exceptional circumstances under which it is impracticable for the party seeking discovery to obtain facts or opinions on the same subject by other means.

(C) Unless manifest injustice would result, (i) the court shall require that the party seeking discovery pay the expert a reasonable fee for time spent in responding to discovery under this subdivision; and (ii) with respect to discovery obtained under subdivision (b)(4)(B) of this rule the court shall require the party seeking discovery to pay the other party a fair portion of the fees and expenses reasonably incurred by the latter party in obtaining facts and opinions from the expert.

[4]   Purpose

After disclosing the identity of experts pursuant to FED. R. CIV. P. 26(a)(2)(A), FED. R. CIV. P. 26(a)(2)(B) and 26(b)(4)(A) allow for the discovery of the subject matter on which the expert is expected to testify, the substance of facts and opinions to which an expert is expected to testify, "*the data or other information considered by the witness in forming the opinions,*" and the summary of the grounds for each opinion. FED. R. CIV. P. 26(b)(4)(A) & (B) distinguishes between testifying and nontestifying (consultant) experts.

Since a danger exists that computer generated information might be hearsay, erroneous, inaccurate or misleading, parties have been given access to computer inputs and outputs, underlying data and the computer program methodology relied on by expert witnesses who are providing opinions on computerized records. Because the computer-generated evidence can be persuasive, one of the only methods of attacking or challenging the credibility of that evidence is to test the underlying program and data. For example, access to the data will allow a party to test the evidence for reliability, and thus be positioned to challenge the authenticity and business records exception to the hearsay rule, if the data is proven to be unreliable.

For example, in *Perma Research & Dev. Co. v. Singer Co.,* 542 F.2d 111, 125 (2d Cir. 1976), *cert. denied,* 975 S. Ct. 507 (1976), Van Graafeiland, J., dissenting, stated:

Although the computer has tremendous potential for improving our system of justice by generating more meaningful evidence than was previously available, it presents a real danger of being the vehicle of introducing erroneous, misleading, or unreliable evidence. The possibility of an undetected error in computer-generated evidence is a function of many factors: the underlying data may be hearsay; errors may be introduced in any one of several stages of processing; the computer might be erroneously programmed, programmed to permit an error to go undetected, or programmed to introduce error into the data; and the computer may inaccurately display the data or display it in a biased manner. Because of the complexities of examining the creation of computer-generated evidence and the deceptively neat package in which the computer can display its work product, courts and practitioners must exercise more care with computer-generated evidence than with evidence generated by more traditional means. Roberts, *A Practitioner's Primer on Computer-Generated Evidence,* 41 U.Chi.L.Rev. 254, 255-56 (1974).

[5]   Reported Cases - Discovery of Expert Data

- *Fidelity Nat. Title Ins. Co. of New York v. Intercounty Nat. Title Ins. Co.,* No. CIV.04-2335, 2005 WL 1413902 (7th Cir. Jun. 17, 2005). The Appellate Court reversed the jury verdict and the trial judge's ruling excluding the plaintiff's expert from testifying since other alternative means could have been used to remedy the circumstances surrounding the destruction of the interview notes considered by the expert. However, the Court noted,

  A litigant is required to disclose to his opponent any information "considered" by the litigant's testifying expert . . . [the plaintiff's] further argument that because the notes were discarded pursuant to [its expert witness's] "document retention" (i.e., document destruction) policy, there was no violation of Rule 26, is also frivolous. There is nothing wrong with a policy of destroying documents after the point is reached at which there is no good business reason to retain them. *Cf. Arthur Andersen LLP v. United States* . . . 2005 WL 1262915, at *5 (U.S. May 31, 2005). Without such a policy a firm or an individual could drown in paper. There is no legal duty to be a pack rat. But a firm's document-retention policy cannot trump Rule 26(a)(2)(B). The rule does not require merely that the party disclose data that it happens to have retained; it must disclose all the data that an expert that it retained to testify at trial "considered," implying that it must retain those data, as otherwise it could not disclose them. *Trigon Ins. Co. v. United States,* 204 F.R.D. 277, 288-89 (E.D.Va. 2001). A testifying expert must disclose and therefore retain whatever materials are given him to review in preparing his testimony, even if in the end he does not rely on them in formulating his expert opinion, because such materials often contain effective ammunition for cross-examination.

- *Synthes Spine Co., L.P. v. Walden,* 232 F.R.D. 460, 464 (D. Pa. 2005). The Court found that the expert had to disclose all materials, regardless of privilege, that he had used to formulate his opinions including, "e-mails, summaries of lost sales, summary spreadsheets, pleadings, corporate information, sales charts and breakdowns, time analyses, retainer letters and invoices, and draft expert reports."

- *MasterCard International Inc. v. First National Bank of Omaha,* No. CIV.02-3691, 2004 WL 326708, at *1, *6 (S.D. N.Y. Feb. 23, 2004). The defendant moved for an order in limine precluding the testimony of the plaintiff's expert at trial on the ground that "he destroyed relevant electronic correspondence with MasterCard's counsel and with a litigation consulting firm, as well as draft versions of his expert report, in violation of Rule 26(a)(2)(B), FED.R.CIV.P. . . . Rule 26(a)(2)(B) requires disclosure of 'the data and other information' considered by the [expert] in forming [the expert's] opinion. Rule 26(a)(2)(B), FED.R.CIV.P." The Court found no destruction and denied the defendant's motion. Also, since both experts updated drafts of expert opinions electronically and did not save the drafts, preclusion of testimony would be denied.

- *Brill-Edwards v. Ryder Truck Rental, Inc.,* No. CIV.01-1768, 2003 WL 23511733, at *1 (D. Conn. Jan. 24, 2003). In an automobile accident case the Court refused to allow the deposition of a non testifying expert who "retrieved a sensing diagnostic module (data recorder) installed in the Aurora and generated a printout of the data contained in the recorder ['Vetronic' and 'Crash Data Retrieval System (CDR)'] . . . It thus does not appear that the document is more than the presentation of raw data taken from the recorder."

- *United States Fidelity & Guaranty Co. v. Braspetro Oil Servs. Co.,* No. CIV.98-3099, 2002 WL 15652, at *9 (S.D.N.Y. Jan. 7, 2002). The Court in ruling on a discovery dispute concerning the waiver of alleged privileged material provided to an expert, ordered the defendants to produce "everything on Defendants' privilege logs, and includes all documents, privileged or unprivileged, furnished in hard-copy or electronic form, as well as all indexes and search tools (such as OCR) furnished therewith."

- *Williams v. E.I. du Pont de Nemours & Co.,* 119 F.R.D. 648 (W.D. Ky. 1987). Court ordered disclosure of computer information (database, code books and a user's manual) that was being used by the EEOC's expert to prepare a statistical analysis.

- *Trigon Ins. Co. v. United States,* 204 F.R.D. 277, 282 (E.D. Va. 2001). The plaintiff hired a computer forensic expert to try and recover draft documents from the defendant's consulting expert's hard drive. The Court awarded sanctions in the form of an adverse inference instruction, preclusion of consultants working with experts and costs against the government for failure to take timely measures to ensure the preservation of the draft reports.

- *Shu-Tao Lin v. McDonnell Douglas Corp.,* 574 F. Supp. 1407 (S.D.N.Y. 1983), *judgment affirmed in part, reversed in part,* 742 F.2d 45 (2d Cir. 1984). Court ruled the defendant had the right to discover the expert's computer methodology and data on the issue of damages.

- *City of Cleveland v. Cleveland Electric Illuminating Co.,* 538 F. Supp. 1257, 1267 (N.D. Ohio 1980). The Court stated, "[i]t is essential that the underlying data used in the analyses, programs and programming method and all relevant computer inputs and outputs be made available to the opposing party far in advance of trial. This procedure is required in the interest of fairness and should facilitate the introduction of admissible computer evidence. Such procedure provides the adverse party and the court with an opportunity to test and examine the inputs, the program and all outputs prior to trial."

- *Pearl Brewing Co. v. Joseph Schlitz Brewing Co.*, 415 F. Supp. 1122, 1138 (S.D. Tex. 1976). The Court granted a discovery request regarding *nontestifying* experts, under the exceptional circumstances test within the meaning of Rule 26(b)(4)(B), to justify disclosure of "mechanical methods, tests, procedures, assumptions and comparisons which will support the conclusions of . . . the trial expert."

- *United States v. Dioguardi*, 428 F.2d 1033 (2d Cir.), *cert. denied,* 400 U.S. 825 (1970). The Court granted discovery request for the complete software program used to generate an expert's report.

- *Bartley v. Isuzu Motors Limited*, 151 F.R.D. 659, 660 (D. Colo. 1993). Court allowed broad discovery of an expert's study regarding a simulation of an automobile accident. The defendant obtained disclosure of all simulations run before arriving at the final simulation to be used at trial.

- *United States v. Liebert*, 519 F.2d 542, 547 (3d Cir.) *cert. denied*, 423 U.S. 985 (1975). The defendant was given access to the IRS's list of who did not file returns and the manner in how the lists were prepared. The Court stated, "A party seeking to impeach the reliability of computer evidence should have sufficient opportunity to ascertain by pre-trial discovery whether both the machine and those who supply it with data input and information have performed their tasks accurately."

[E]   Identification of Exhibits - Rule 26(a)(3)(C)

[1]   Rule 26(a)(3)(C)

Under Rule 26(a)(3)(C) "a party must provide to other parties and promptly file with the court the following information regarding the evidence that it may present at trial other than solely for impeachment: . . . (C) an appropriate identification of each document or other exhibit, including summaries of other evidence, separately identifying those which the party expects to offer and those which the party may offer if the need arises."

[2]   Purpose

A party who without substantial justification fails to disclose information pursuant to Rule 26(a)(3)(C) is not permitted to use the evidence at trial, unless it is harmless or unless it is used solely for impeachment.

[F]   Relevancy and Overbroad Concerns - Rule 26(b)(1)

[1]   Rule 26(b)(1)

(b) Discovery Scope and Limits. Unless otherwise limited by order of the court in accordance with these rules, the scope of discovery is as follows:

(1) In General. Parties may obtain discovery regarding any matter, not privileged, that is relevant to the claim or defense of any party, including the existence, description, nature, custody, condition, and location of any books, documents, or other tangible things and the identity and location of persons having knowledge of any discoverable matter. For good cause, the court may order discovery of any matter relevant to the subject matter involved in the action. Relevant information need not be admissible at the trial if the discovery appears reasonably calculated to lead to the discovery of admissible evidence. All discovery is subject to the limitations imposed by Rule 26(b)(2)(i), (ii), and (iii).

[2]   Purpose

FED. R. CIV. P. 26(b)(1) permits discovery of matters that are not privileged and "relevant to the claim or defense" as long as "the discovery appears reasonably calculated to lead to the discovery of admissible evidence . . . For good cause, the court may order discovery of any matter relevant to the subject matter involved in the action." "Rules 26(b) and 34 . . . that computer-stored information is discoverable under the same rules that pertain to tangible, written materials." *Rowe Entertainment, Inc. v. William Morris Agency, Inc.,* 205 F.R.D. 421, 433 (S.D.N.Y. 2002), *aff'd,* 2002 WL 975713 (S.D.N.Y. May 9, 2002).

Even though court rules allow for discovery of electronic information, it does not mean that electronic information is discoverable. Information is only discoverable if it is "relevant to the claim or defense of any party" or if it "appears reasonably calculated to lead to the discovery of admissible evidence." FED. R. CIV. P. 26(b)(1); *Medtronic v. Michelson,* CIV.01-2373, 2003 WL 21212601 (W.D. Tenn. May 13, 2003). The test for relevant material under Rule 26 is extremely broad. *See, Oppenheimer Fund, Inc. v. Sanders,* 437 U.S. 340, 351 n.12 (1978); *Allen v. Howmedica Leibinger, Inc.,* 190 F.R.D. 518, 521 (W.D. Tenn. 1999); *Behnia v. Shapiro,* 176 F.R.D. 277, 280 (N.D. Ill. 1997); *But cf. BG Real Estate Services v. American Equity Ins. Co.,* No. CIV.04-3408, 2005 WL 1309048, at *3-5 (E.D.La. May 18, 2005) (court refused to extend discovery to the "good cause" broad subject matter mandate contained within Rule 26 noting that the request for the entire "computer hard drive" was overly broad.).

One of the threshold discovery showings is whether or not the information sought is relevant to the dispute. Generally, requests for computer information will be denied, if they are irrelevant or overbroad to the claims or defenses of the case. *Rowlin v. Alabama Dept. of Public Safety,* 200 F.R.D. 459 (D.C. Ala. 2001); *Thompson v. Dept. of Housing and Urban Devel.,* 199 F.R.D. 168 (D. Md. 2001). "When the discovery sought appears relevant, the party resisting the discovery has the burden to establish the lack of relevance by demonstrating that the requested discovery either does not come within the broad scope of relevance as defined under FED. R. CIV. P. 26(b)(1) or is of such marginal relevance that the potential harm occasioned by discovery would outweigh the ordinary presumption in favor of broad disclosure." *Moore v. Chertoff,* No. CIV.00-953, 2006 U.S. Dist. LEXIS 31391, at *7-8 (D.D.C. May 22, 2006).

[3]   Reported Cases - Objection on the Ground of Relevance

- *Williams v. Sprint/United Mgmt. Co.,* 230 F.R.D. 640, 652-653 (D. Kan. 2005). The Court ordered an employer in an employment discrimination case to restore the metadata it had "scrubbed" or "erased" from Excel spreadsheet files and "unlock" them. In denying a relevancy objection to the metadata, the Court found "metadata associated with any changes to the spreadsheets, the dates of any changes, the identification of the individuals making any changes, and other metadata from which Plaintiffs could determine the final versus draft version of the spreadsheets appear relevant."

- *Fischer v. United Parcel Serv. Co.,* 2006 WL 1046973 (E.D. Mich. Apr. 19, 2006). The defendant was unable to find an attachment to a responsive e-mail during the discovery process. The Court granted the plaintiff's request to discuss with the defendant's employee their search efforts to locate the attachment. The Court granted the discovery request ruling that even though the attachment may not be admissible and irrelevant, it could reasonably lead to the discovery of admissible evidence.

- *Floeter v. City of Orlando,* 2006 WL 1000306 (M.D. Fla. Apr. 14, 2006). In this employment discrimination case, the plaintiff requested the opportunity to inspect two computers and also wanted a computer printout of all e-mails from a specific police lieutenant. The Court citing Rule 34 stated that a party does not have the right "to conduct the actual search." In addition, the Court ruled that there was no showing that any inspection of the computers or production of printouts of e-mail would lead to discoverable evidence.

- *Wright v. AmSouth Bancorp,* 320 F.3d 1198, 1205 (11th Cir. 2003). In this employment discrimination action, the Court denied the plaintiff's motion to compel because his request was overbroad, unduly burdensome and made no "reasonable showing of relevance" for electronic data. The plaintiff sought discovery of computer disks and tapes containing "computer diskette or tape copy of all word processing files created, modified and/or accessed" by five of the defendant's employees for a two and a half year period.

- *Clark Const. Group, Inc. v. City of Memphis,* No. CIV.01-2780, 2005 WL 1618767, at *3 (W.D. Tenn. Mar. 14, 2005). In this breach of contract case, the Court ruled that the city's project manager who destroyed more than 2,000 paper and electronic documents was under a duty to preserve documents. The Court noted, "[i]n his deposition [project manager] stated that he destroyed those documents which a reasonable person would not view as relevant. However, the decision as to what was potentially relevant should not have been left to Webber's sole discretion. Webber is not a lawyer, and counsel for the City admitted during the hearing that he was not necessarily qualified to ascertain whether a document or handwritten notation was potentially relevant to Clark. While the Court does not doubt that Webber believes that any reasonable person should be able to make a determination as to relevance, Webber fails to recognize that what is reasonable to one person might not be reasonable to another. Likewise, what might be potentially relevant to a person trained in law might not be relevant to a lay person."

- *Strausser v. Yalamachi,* 669 So. 2d 1142, 1144-45 (Fla. Ct. App. 1996). The Court denied access to a computer because party seeking the information did not show that it was likely that relevant information would be retrieved.

- *Bashir v. National R.R. Passenger Corporation,* 929 F. Supp. 404 (S.D. Fla. 1996). Finding that speed tapes, which defendant had destroyed, were irrelevant where the train's engineer, assistant engineer and conductor had testified consistently to the train's speed.

- *Marker v. Union Fidelity Life Insurance Co.,* 125 F.R.D. 121, 122-23 (M.D.N.C. 1989). Even though the party seeking discovery showed that production of data could be done inexpensively due to computer storage, the Court still found that the seeking party failed to show a particularized need for past litigation and claims' history of insurance company, when the case involved only coverage and not bad faith.

- *Boone v. Federal Express Corp.,* 59 F.3d 84 (8th Cir. 1995). The Court allowed the plaintiff in an employment discrimination action to offer as evidence e-mail messages exchanged between coworkers regarding his employment to support his contention that employees conspired to deprive him of his civil rights. However, the Court found the e-mail messages were not supportive of his claims.

- *Allan Pen Co. v. Springfield Photo Mount Co.,* 653 F.2d 17, 23-24 (1st Cir. 1984). Although computer-generated evidence of sales was destroyed after its identification in interrogatory answers, the Court found that the lost evidence would not itself have established a relevant fact, so the Court refused to draw an inference of the fact from the destruction of the computer-generated evidence.

- *Lexis-Nexis v. Beer,* 41 F. Supp. 2d 950 (D. Minn. 1999). The defendant had not preserved electronic data, but the plaintiff could not demonstrate that any of the lost data would have contained evidence relevant to the litigation. The Court decided to enter only monetary sanctions, which it deferred to a later date.

- *New York National Organization for Women v. Cuomo*, No. CIV.93-7146, 1998 WL 395320 (S.D.N.Y. Jul. 14, 1998). The plaintiff failed to show that the destruction of any evidence was prejudicial, i.e., that the destroyed information had some relevance to the litigation. The Court held that a fishing expedition would not be permitted.

- *Alexander v. F.B.I.*, 194 F.R.D. 316 (D.D.C. 2000). The Court held that the terms "HRC," "Hillary," and "FBI" would be excluded as search terms in the search of the White House e-mail system by plaintiffs who brought suit alleging misuse of their FBI files by White House personnel. The Court ruled that such terms would call for a search for all e-mail that made any reference to the First Lady or the FBI, without regard to context, and would yield a large number of irrelevant e-mail.

[4]   Reported Cases - Objection on the Ground of Overbroad

The courts are not permitting unbridled access or fishing expeditions into the producing party's computer storage devices or software applications.

- *Quinby v. WestLB AG*, No. CIV.04-7406, 2006 U.S. Dist. LEXIS 1178 (D.N.Y. Jan. 11, 2006). The Court ruled that the defendant's request was overbroad because the subpoenas would yield a vast amount of irrelevant material from the employee's entire personal e-mail accounts for the requested period.

- *Pendlebury v. Starbucks Coffee Co.*, No. CIV.04-80521, 2005 U.S. Dist. LEXIS 36748 (D. Fla. Aug. 29, 2005). In this Fair Labor Standards Act (FLSA) collective action the employer sought invoices, statements, or call logs that reflected calls, text messages or other communications to or from certain communications devices and descriptors used by the employees when sending electronic mail or posting communications on internet media. The Court denied the request finding the request overbroad and invaded the privacy of the employees.

- *Wright v. AmSouth Bancorp*, 320 F.3d 1198, 1205 (11th Cir. 2003). The Court denied the plaintiff's motion to compel because his request was overbroad, unduly burdensome and made no "reasonable showing of relevance" for these items. In this employment case plaintiff sought discovery of computer disks and tapes containing "computer diskette or tape copy of all word processing files created, modified and/or accessed" by five of the defendant's employees for a two and a half year period.

- *Positive Software Solutions v. New Century Mortgage Corp.*, 259 F. Supp. 2d 561 (N.D. Tex. 2003). The Court denied as overbroad the plaintiff's motion to compel imaging "of all of Defendants' media potentially containing any of the software and electronic evidence relevant to the claims in this suit" and "all images of [the defendants'] computer storage facilities, drives, and servers taken to date."

- *Dikeman v. Stearns,* 560 S.E.2d 115, 117 (Ga. Ct. App. 2002). The trial court found the defendant's request for a full and complete copy of the law firm's computer hard drive which was used to generate the defendant's documents "overbroad, oppressive, and annoying."

- *Koch v. Koch,* 203 F.3d 1202, 1238 (10th Cir. 2000). In the words of the Court, "[w]hen a plaintiff first pleads its allegations in entirely indefinite terms, without in fact knowing of any specific wrongdoing by the defendant, and then bases massive discovery requests upon those nebulous allegations in the hope of finding particular evidence of wrongdoing, that plaintiff abuses the judicial process. That is what occurred here. The limits which Rule 26(b)(2)(iii) place upon discovery are aimed at just such a tactic."

- *Sabouri v. Ohio Bureau of Employment Servs.,* No. CIV.97-715, 2000 WL 1620915 (S.D. Oh. Oct. 24, 2000). In this employment discrimination case, the plaintiff made a broad request for a printout of the file directories of the computers used by various employees. The Court rejected the broader request, noting, "Although plaintiff is entitled to view files that relate to him or to the claims or defenses asserted in this action, he has no right to rummage through the computer files of the defendants."

- *Sabouri v. Ohio Bureau of Employment Servs.,* No. CIV.97-715, 2000 WL 1620915 (S.D. Ohio Oct. 24, 2000). The plaintiff in an age discrimination action sought an order compelling the defendant employer to produce complete printouts of the file directories of several employees' computers over a several month period, and the court denied the motion on the grounds that it was overbroad.

- *Strasser v. Yalamanchi,* 669 So.2d 1142 (Fla. Dist. Ct. App. 1996). The plaintiff sought unrestricted access to the defendant's computer system arguing that defendant had purged relevant computer records. The appellate court quashed the order stating that the unrestricted access was overly broad and could pose a threat to medical patients' confidential records and the records of the defendant's business, and that there was little evidence that the purged documents could, in fact, be retrieved.

- *Alexander v. F.B.I.,* 188 F.R.D. 111, 116 (D.C. Cir. 1998). The court refused to require Defendants to restore all deleted files and e-mail where Plaintiff did not propose "targeted and appropriately worded searches of backed-up and archived email and deleted hard drives for a limited number of individuals."

- *Murlas Living Trust v. Mobil Oil Co.,* No. 93-C-6956, 1995 W.L. 124186 (N.D. Ill. Mar. 20, 1995). The Court refused to allow unlimited access to company databases.

- *In re Grand Jury Subpoena Duces Tecum Dated Nov. 15, 1993,* 846 F. Supp. 11 (S.D.N.Y. 1994). Discovery requests seeking electronic data was denied as overbroad because they sought "all hard drives, all archival tapes" rather than specific information.

- *Procter & Gamble Co. v. Haugen*, 179 F.R.D. 622 (D. Utah 1998), *aff'd in part and rev'd in part,* 222 F.3d 1262 (10th Cir. 2000). Court limited search terms to be used on the defendant's computer system.

- *Fennell v. First Step Designs Limited*, 83 F.3d 526 (1st Cir. 1996). Though not on overbroad grounds, the appellate court affirmed the district court's decision denying plaintiff's request for additional discovery of word processing files on a computer hard drive. The plaintiff argued that a particular document might have been fabricated and backdated. Both courts found that creating a mirror of the hard drive involved risks and costs, and was nothing more than a "fishing expedition."

- *New York National Organization for Women v. Cuomo*, No. CIV.93-7146, 1998 WL 395320, at *3 (S.D.N.Y. Jul. 14, 1998). As to some of the requested records, the Court refused to find prejudice for destroying documents, and stated, "[b]ut they fail to identify with any specificity what information they would have been reasonably likely to find. In essence, they argue that the defendants' conduct deprived them of a pond in which they would like to have gone on a fishing expedition. That is not a showing of prejudice."

- *Lawyers Title Ins. Corp. v. U.S. Fidelity & Guar. Co.,* 122 F.R.D. 567, 570 (N.D. Cal. 1988). The plaintiffs sought discovery of information about the defendant's computer system as a means of evaluating the adequacy of the defendant's production of documents and to help frame more effective discovery requests. The Court in denying the overbroad request stated, "[t]he mere possibility that a party might not produce all relevant, unprotected documents, is not a sufficient basis for ordering such a party to disclose its entire computerized system of information management."

- *Williams v. E.I. du Pont de Nemours & Co.,* 119 F.R.D. 648, 651 (W.D. Ky. 1987). The Court allowed E.I. du Pont to discover EEOC database, code books and a user manual. However, "du Pont's request for 'documents relating to the program(s) used to create the database' and 'all print-outs generated through the use of the database' is overbroad and may introduce into the discovery documents that are not relevant and which reveal to the defendant alternative methods of analysis or programs outside the scope of the expert's report. FED. R. CIV. P. 26(c)."

[G]   Limiting Discovery - Rule 26(b)(2)

[1]   Rule 26(b)(2)

Limitations . . . use of the discovery methods otherwise permitted under these rules and by any local rule shall be limited by the court if it determines that: (i) the discovery sought is unreasonably cumulative or duplicative, or is obtainable from some other source that is more convenient, less burdensome, or less expensive; (ii) the party seeking discovery has had ample opportunity by discovery in the action to obtain the information sought; or (iii) the burden or expense of the proposed discovery outweighs its likely benefit, taking into account the needs of the case, the amount in controversy, the parties' resources, the importance of the issues at stake in the litigation, and the importance of the proposed discovery in resolving the issues. The court may act upon its own initiative after reasonable notice or pursuant to a motion under Rule 26(c).

[2]   Pending Rule 26(b)(2) Amendment

Rule 26. General Provisions Governing Discovery; Duty of Disclosure

* * * * *

(b) Discovery Scope and Limits. Unless otherwise limited by order of the court in accordance with these rules, the scope of discovery is as follows: * * * * *

(2) Limitations.
(A) By order, the court may alter the limits in these rules on the number of depositions and interrogatories or the length of depositions under Rule 30. By order or local rule, the court may also limit the number of requests under Rule 36.
(B) A party need not provide discovery of electronically stored information from sources that the party identifies as not reasonably accessible because of undue burden or cost. On motion to compel discovery or for a protective order, the party from whom discovery is sought must show that the information is not reasonably accessible because of undue burden or cost. If that showing is made, the court may nonetheless order discovery from such sources if the requesting party shows good cause, considering the limitations of Rule 26(b)(2)(C). The court may specify conditions for the discovery. (emphasis added).
(C) The frequency or extent of use of the discovery methods otherwise permitted under these rules and by any local rule shall be limited by the court if it determines that: (i) the discovery sought is unreasonably cumulative or duplicative, or is obtainable from some other source that is more convenient, less burdensome, or less expensive; (ii) the party seeking discovery has had ample opportunity by discovery in the action to obtain the information sought; or (iii) the burden or expense of the proposed discovery outweighs its likely benefit, taking into account the needs of the case, the amount in controversy, the parties' resources, the importance of the issues at stake in the litigation, and the importance of the proposed discovery in resolving the issues. The court may act upon its own initiative after reasonable notice or pursuant to a motion under Rule 26(c). * * * * *

Committee Note

Subdivision (b)(2). The amendment to Rule 26(b)(2) is designed to address issues raised by difficulties in locating, retrieving, and providing discovery of some electronically stored information. Electronic storage systems often make it easier to locate and retrieve information. These advantages are properly taken into account in determining the reasonable scope of discovery in a particular case. But some sources of electronically stored information can be accessed only with substantial burden and cost. In a particular case, these burdens and costs may make the information on such sources not reasonably accessible.

It is not possible to define in a rule the different types of technological features that may affect the burdens and costs of accessing electronically stored information. Information systems are designed to provide ready access to information used in regular ongoing activities. They also may be designed so as to provide ready access to information that is not regularly used. But a system may retain information on sources that are accessible only by incurring substantial burdens or costs. Subparagraph (B) is added to regulate discovery from such sources.

Under this rule, a responding party should produce electronically stored information that is relevant, not privileged, and reasonably accessible, subject to the (b)(2)(C) limitations that apply to all discovery. The responding party must also identify, by category or type, the sources containing potentially responsive information that it is neither searching nor producing. The identification should, to the extent possible, provide enough detail to enable the requesting party to evaluate the burdens and costs of providing the discovery and the likelihood of finding responsive information on the identified sources.

A party's identification of sources of electronically stored information as not reasonably accessible does not relieve the party of its common-law or statutory duties to preserve evidence. Whether a responding party is required to preserve unsearched sources of potentially responsive information that it believes are not reasonably accessible depends on the circumstances of each case. It is often useful for the parties to discuss this issue early in discovery.

The volume of — and the ability to search — much electronically stored information means that in many cases the responding party will be able to produce information from reasonably accessible sources that will fully satisfy the parties' discovery needs. In many circumstances the requesting party should obtain and evaluate the information from such sources before insisting that the responding party search and produce information contained on sources that are not reasonably accessible. If the requesting party continues to seek discovery of information from sources identified as not reasonably accessible, the parties should discuss the burdens and costs of accessing and retrieving the information, the needs that may establish good cause for requiring all or part of the requested discovery even if the information sought is not reasonably accessible, and conditions on obtaining and producing the information that may be appropriate.

If the parties cannot agree whether, or on what terms, sources identified as not reasonably accessible should be searched and discoverable information produced, the issue may be raised either by a motion to compel discovery or by a motion for a protective order. The parties must confer before bringing either motion. If the parties do not resolve the issue and the court must decide, the responding party must show that the identified sources of information are not reasonably accessible because of undue burden or cost. The requesting party may need discovery to test this assertion. Such discovery might take the form of requiring the responding party to conduct a sampling of information contained on the sources identified as not reasonably accessible; allowing some form of inspection of such sources; or taking depositions of witnesses knowledgeable about the responding party's information systems.

     Once it is shown that a source of electronically stored information is not reasonably accessible, the requesting party may still obtain discovery by showing good cause, considering the limitations of Rule 26(b)(2)(C) that balance the costs and potential benefits of discovery. The decision whether to require a responding party to search for and produce information that is not reasonably accessible depends not only on the burdens and costs of doing so, but also on whether those burdens and costs can be justified in the circumstances of the case. Appropriate considerations may include: (1) the specificity of the discovery request; (2) the quantity of information available from other and more easily -accessed sources; (3) the failure to produce relevant information that seems likely to have existed but is no longer available on more easily accessed sources; (4) the likelihood of finding relevant, responsive information that cannot be obtained from other, more easily accessed sources; (5) predictions as to the importance and usefulness of the further information; (6) the importance of the issues at stake in the litigation; and (7) the parties' resources.

     The responding party has the burden as to one aspect of the inquiry — whether the identified sources are not reasonably accessible in light of the burdens and costs required to search for, retrieve, and produce whatever responsive information may be found. The requesting party has the burden of showing that its need for the discovery outweighs the burdens and costs of locating, retrieving, and producing the information. In some cases, the court will be able to determine whether the identified sources are not reasonably accessible and whether the requesting party has shown good cause for some or all of the discovery, consistent with the limitations of Rule 26(b)(2)(C), through a single proceeding or presentation. The good-cause determination, however, may be complicated because the court and parties may know little about what information the sources identified as not reasonably accessible might contain, whether it is relevant, or how valuable it may be to the litigation. In such cases, the parties may need some focused discovery, which may include sampling of the sources, to learn more about what burdens and costs are involved in accessing the information, what the information consists of, and how valuable it is for the litigation in light of information that can be obtained by exhausting other opportunities for discovery.

     The good-cause inquiry and consideration of the Rule 26(b)(2)(C) limitations are coupled with the authority to set conditions for discovery. The conditions may take the form of limits on the amount, type, or sources of information required to be accessed and produced.

The conditions may also include payment by the requesting party of part or all of the reasonable costs of obtaining information from sources that are not reasonably accessible. A requesting party's willingness to share or bear the access costs may be weighed by the court in determining whether there is good cause. But the producing party's burdens in reviewing the information for relevance and privilege may weigh against permitting the requested discovery.

The limitations of Rule 26(b)(2)(C) continue to apply to all discovery of electronically stored information, including that stored on reasonably accessible electronic sources.

[3]   Purpose

Essentially, the court will limit discovery if:

a. The discovery sought is unreasonably cumulative or duplicative or the discovery is obtainable from some other source that is more convenient, less burdensome or less expensive;

b. Where the requesting party has had ample opportunity in discovery to obtain the information;

c. The burden or expense of the discovery outweighs its likely benefit.

Under FED. R. CIV. P. 26, the trial court has the power to limit discovery "if the burden or expense of the proposed discovery outweighs its likely benefit." This language was added in 1983 to combat "excessively costly and time-consuming activities that are disproportionate to the nature of the case, the amount involved, or the issues or values at stake . . . [by] giving the court authority to reduce the amount of discovery that may be directed to matters that are otherwise proper subjects of inquiry." FED. R. CIV. P. 26 advisory committee notes.

In 1993 the current Rule 26(b)(2)(i), (ii), and (iii) was created citing the "information explosion of recent decades [which] has greatly increased both the potential cost of wide-ranging discovery and the potential for discovery to be used as an instrument of delay or oppression." FED. R. CIV. P. 26 advisory committee notes.

Although there is no specific cost-bearing provision in the present Federal Rules of Civil Procedure, courts in cases involving a range of issues from products liability to employment discrimination has recognized that Rule 26(b)(2)(iii) provides the inherent authority to shift the costs of discovery to the requesting party or apply the concept of proportionality. 8 Wright, Miller & Marcus, *Federal Practice and Procedure,* § 2008.1, *Proportionality.* In *Sanders v. Levy,* 558 F.2d 636 (2d Cir. 1976), *rev'd on other grounds sub nom., Oppenheimer Fund, Inc. v. Sanders,* 437 U.S. 340 (1978) the Court ruled that Rule 26(c) and Rule 34 allows the court to shift the expense of computer programming to the discovering party if the request poses an undue burden or expense. *See also,* § 7.4[G][6], *Cost Allocation.*

While discussing the cost/benefit analysis, the court in *Thompson v. US Dept. of Housing and Urban Development,* 219 F.R.D 93, 99 (D.Md. Dec. 12, 2003) noted "[u]nder Rules 26(b)(2) and 26(c), a court is provided abundant resources to tailor discovery requests to avoid unfair burden or expense and yet assure fair disclosure of important information. The options available are limited only by the court's own imagination and the quality and quantity of the factual information provided by the parties to be used by the court in evaluating the Rule 26(b)(2) factors."

Pending Rule 26(b)(2) Amendment

This pending amendment has been labeled a "two-tiered" system for discovery of ESI - "accessible vs. inaccessible." This distinction was noted in the decision of *Zubulake v. UBS Warburg, LLC,* 217 F.R.D. 309 (S.D.N.Y. 2003) which categorized accessibility based on the different types of storage media; *See,* §§ 7.04 [G][6][d], *Rowe/Zubulake Factors* and 3.06[B], *Classification of Data.*

The first tier is "accessible" electronic information which is discoverable. As the Committee Note states, "a responding party should produce electronically stored information that is relevant, not privileged, and reasonably accessible, subject to the (b)(2)(C) limitations that apply to all discovery."

The second tier pertains to "inaccessible" electronic information. Under the pending Rule 26(b)(2) amendment a "party need not provide discovery of electronically stored information" (ESI) if the party identifies the ESI as "not reasonably accessible because of undue burden or cost." The Committee Note in providing guidance stated, "[t]he responding party must also identify, by category or type, the sources containing potentially responsive information that it is neither searching nor producing. The identification should, to the extent possible, provide enough detail to enable the requesting party to evaluate the burdens and costs of providing the discovery and the likelihood of finding responsive information on the identified sources." *See, Phoenix Four, Inc. v. Strategic Resources Corp.,* No. CIV. 05-4837, 2006 WL 1409413, n.7 (S.D.N.Y. May 23, 2006) (court found under pending amendment Rule 26(b)(2) that "a difficult-to-access source 'legacy data that remains from obsolete systems and is unintelligible on the successor systems.' . . . which is in a partitioned section of the [server's] hard drive and not accessible from [the defendant's] newly configured computer system, fits squarely within this description.").

According to the Committee Note, identification of "not reasonably accessible data" does not relieve the party of the duty to preserve evidence.

After such identification, the requesting party is obligated to file a "motion to compel discovery or for a protective order" if it still seeks the discovery. Once filed, the burden shifts to the producing party who must establish that the "information is not reasonably accessible because of undue burden or cost." The requesting party may need to take a sampling of the data or conduct Rule 30(b)(6) depositions of parties knowledgeable about the producing party's information system to contest the claim that the ESI is inaccessible.

Even if the producing party can show that the ESI is not "reasonably accessible" the Court can still order discovery if "good cause" is found after taking into consideration the limitations imposed by Rule 26(b)(2)(C).

[4]   Objection on the Ground of Undue Burden or Expense

[a]   Generally

A party seeking to limit its production or access to electronic materials may defend against discovery requests by asserting objections contained within FED. R. CIV. P. 26(b)(2)(iii) such as the request being burdensome. The court has broad discretion in deciding what is an undue burden. *Fennell v. First Step Designs Ltd.,* 83 F.3d 526 (1st Cir. 1996). Discovery requests objections for electronic information usually fall under the category of undue burden or expense. As one Court noted,

> [R]equests to discover electronically stored information do not have the same impact on the receiving party as do those requests for "hard copy" records. For example, the scope of what is included in the phrase "electronic records" can be enormous, encompassing voice mail, e-mail, deleted e-mail, data files, program files, back-up files, archival tapes, temporary files, system history files, web site information in textual, graphical or audio format, web site files, cache files, "cookies" and other electronically stored information.

Thompson v. U.S. Dept. of Housing and Urban Development, 219 F.R.D. 93, 96 (D.Md. 2003).

In ruling on a "burdensome" objection, the court will examine the relative costs and burdens to the parties, the need for the information and whether the party requesting the discovery will benefit from the information. A party raising an objection against burdensome or oppressive electronic discovery requests must educate the court as to the costs and burdens of the requests, argue that these costs and burdens outweigh the value and be ready to offer reasonable alternatives. *Gen. Elec. Capital Corp. v. Lear Corp.,* 215 F.R.D. 637, 640-641 (D. Kan. 2003) (obligation on objecting party to "provide sufficient detail and explanation about the nature of the burden in terms of time, money and procedure required to produce the requested documents.); *Hopson v. Mayor & City Council of Baltimore,* 232 F.R.D. 228, 231, 238 (D. Md. 2005). ("affidavit . . . fell short of what would be necessary for a proper application of the cost-benefit analysis required by Rule 26(b)(2) to enable the court fairly to tailor the discovery allowed in this particular case."*; Thompson v. Jiffy Lube Int'l,* No. CIV.05-1203, 2006 U.S. Dist. LEXIS 27837, at *1-4 (D. Kan. May 1, 2006) ("With respect to the issues of cost and electronic discovery, the limited explanations provided by the parties do not provide sufficient information for the court to determine whether production of the electronic data is unduly burdensome. Unquestionably, producing 100 million vehicle reports dating back to 1997 entails a significant cost; however, the court questions whether defendant considered the most efficient method for producing such information when estimating the cost of generating readable 'TIFF' images of vehicle history reports at $10,000,000. Similarly, plaintiffs' conclusory assertion that the information can be produced in 'native PST format' and then printed 'without any additional costs' is equally unpersuasive. The court is simply unable to determine the reasonable costs of electronic production based on the current record.")

Burdensome arguments

Generally, a party arguing that disclosures of electronic information is burdensome points to:
- The cost of locating and retrieving what can be a massive amount of data;
- The cost of computer programming changes needed to compile and extract the data;
- The cost of human review of the data for privileges or other confidential material; and
- The business interruption caused by shutting down computer systems to clone storage media or conduct system wide searches.

Counterpoints to the burdensome argument

In response, arguments can be made that:
- Locating and retrieving electronic information is less costly than retrieving paper;
- Since the opposing party decided to use computers for business use, this is the cost of conducting business;
- Narrowing the time frame and the scope of the request of the electronic information desired can reduce production cost. (You can limit searches of data by requesting information for a specific time period, specific department or people, files by extensions and program and system files).
- The document population can be reduced by not requesting duplicative data (based on preset criteria);
- Sampling of data should be performed to determine statistically how much relevant material may be present. (This will narrow the scope of the document population. *See,* § 7.4[G][5], *Sampling*);
- The electronic copy contains more information (metadata) than their paper counterparts;

- Conducting discovery of the opposing party's computer system on weekends or at night will minimize disruptions to their operation;

- Computers can quickly search, retrieve and sort relevant and privileged e-mail and other documents, thus decreasing the time necessary to review e-mail for privileges or confidential business information; and

- Finally, if the concern is that privileged communications may be inadvertently disclosed, a nonwaiver agreement can be executed.

One commentator noted, "[d]iscovery that otherwise might be impermissibly burdensome, such as requiring detailed identification of all known documents referring to relevant issues, may not be burdensome if the computerized system is able to generate the identifications. Similarly, the existence of a computerized litigation support system will affect a party's obligation to identify business records produced in lieu of answering interrogatories." William W Schwarzer et al., *Civil Discovery and Mandatory Disclosure: A Guide to Efficient Practice* 1-23 (2d Ed. 1994).

[b]   Reported Cases - Burdensome Objection Upheld

Courts have generally found that a request is burdensome in response to a request for unrestricted access to a party's hard drive, for unrestricted on-site access or where a party has already produced similar responsive information.

Hard Drive

- *BG Real Estate Services v. American Equity Ins. Co.,* No. CIV.04-3408, 2005 WL 1309048, at *3-5 (E.D.La. May 18, 2005). In this insurance discovery dispute case the Court refused to extend discovery to the "good cause" broad subject matter mandate contained within Rule 26. The Court noted that, "Rule 26(b) is not a discovery blank check. It requires balancing and imposes on the court the obligation to rein in overly broad, potentially abusive discovery like some of plaintiffs' requests in this case. . . . The request for the entire 'computer hard drive' referenced in this request is overly broad . . . The entire 'computer hard drive' need not be produced. . . . However, a computer hard drive is one of the 'other data compilations' referenced in FED.R.CIV.P. 34(a). If particular non-privileged items on the referenced computer hard drive are responsive . . . those items must be 'translated, if necessary, by the respondent through detection devices into reasonably usable form,' FED.R.CIV.P. 34(a) (for example, by printing out the items on paper) . . ."

- *Symantec Corporation v. McAfee Assoc. Inc.,* No. CIV.97-20367, 1998 WL 740807 (N.D. Cal. Aug. 14, 1998). The Court held that production of copies of all hard drives that had access to a specific server was unduly burdensome.

E-mail

- *Thompson v. Jiffy Lube Int'l,* No. CIV.05-1203, 2006 U.S. Dist. LEXIS 27837, at *1-4 (D. Kan. May 1, 2006). The Court rejected the plaintiff's production request based on mere suspicion for "any and all information related to email dating back to 1997 as overly broad. The Court noted that Rule 34(a) requires that 'the request shall set forth, either by individual item or by category, the items to be inspected and describe each with reasonable particularity.'"

Timeliness

- *Medtronic Sofamor Danek, Inc. v. Michelson,* No. CIV.01-2373, 2004 WL 2905399, at *3 (W.D. Tenn. May 3, 2004). "The defendants' request for the production of deleted electronic files and e-mails is untimely as filed nearly five months after the close of discovery and unduly burdensome in light of the quickly approaching trial date."

On-site access

- *Strasser v. Yalamanchi,* 669 So. 2d 1142 (Fla. Dist. Ct. App. 1996). The trial court granted the plaintiff's request allowing unrestricted on-site access to the defendant's computer system. On appeal the court reversed and remanded with instructions that inspection of the computer system should only be allowed if the plaintiff could show a likelihood of recovering the requested data that the inspection was to be limited in time and scope and measures were taken to protect confidential information.

- *Van Westrienen v. Americontinental Collection Corp.,* 189 F.R.D. 440, 441 (D. Or. 1999). The Court in responding to "plaintiffs' desire to obtain cart blanche access to defendants' computer systems and/or files" held that "plaintiffs are not entitled to unbridled access [of] Defendant's computer system . . . Plaintiffs should pursue other less burdensome alternatives, such as identifying the number of letters and their content."

Likelihood of discovery

- *Fennell v. First Step Designs,* 83 F.3d 526, 532 (1st Cir. 1996). The plaintiff in an attempt to prove that a letter had been backdated requested the opportunity to examine the hard drive of the defendant's computer. The Court denied the request because the plaintiff failed to show "a particularized likelihood of discovering . . . [the] information [sought]."

Database

- *Murlas Living Trust v. Mobil Oil Company,* No. CIV.93-6956, 1995 W.L. 124186 (N.D. Ill. Mar. 20, 1995). The Court denied discovery of an entire database as burdensome.

Overall burden

- *Convolve, Inc. v. Compaq Computer Corp.*, 223 F.R.D. 162 (S.D.N.Y. 2004) In a patent infringement and trade secrets action, the Court found the plaintiff's discovery request "would require an expenditure of time and resources far out of proportion to the marginal value of the materials to this litigation." The Court found this even assuming the data was pertinent since the plaintiff had failed to show that this information would go beyond that already provided by defendant.

- *PamLab, L.L.C. v. Rite Aid Corporation,* No. CIV.04-1115, 2004 WL 2358106 (E.D.La. 2004). The Court found unduly burdensome an interrogatory request seeking manual retrieval of information for each time one of its pharmacists dispensed a certain product. However, the Court ordered if the defendant could produce such information from its computer system it should do so, and to coordinate with the plaintiff to identify a sampling process regarding manual retrieval.

- *Concord Boat Corp. v. Brunswick Corp.,* No. LR-C-95-781, 1996 WL 33347247, at *1, *4 (E.D. Ark. 1996). The Court denied the plaintiff's motion to compel, noting that among the other electronic discovery requests, "[a]n all-encompassing search of all files . . . deleted in the last five years would clearly be extremely burdensome," and therefore, the plaintiff must narrow request to specific documents or make additional showing as why the benefit would outweigh the burden in producing the documents requested.

- *Alexander v. F.B.I.,* 188 F.R.D. 111 (D.D.C. 1998). The White House persuaded the Court that the time and money involved in complying with electronic discovery for e-mail, documents and other computer files would be burdensome and oppressive.

[c]   Cases - Burdensome Objection Denied

Overall burden

- *Oppenheimer Fund, Inc. v. Sanders*, 437 U.S. 340, 362 (1978). The Supreme Court in addressing the use of computerized information to identify members of a class in a class action stated, "although it may be expensive to retrieve information stored in computers when no program yet exists for the particular job, there is no reason to think that the same information could be extracted any less expensively if the records were kept in less modern forms. Indeed, one might expect the reverse to be true, for otherwise computers would not have gained such widespread use in the storing and handling of information."

- *Zubulake v. UBS Warburg, LLC,* 217 F.R.D. 309, 318 (S.D.N.Y. 2003). The Court stated, "[m]any courts have automatically assumed that an undue burden or expense may arise simply because electronic evidence is involved. This makes no sense. Electronic evidence is frequently cheaper and easier to produce than paper evidence because it can be searched automatically, key words can be run for privilege checks, and the production can be made in electronic form obviating the need for mass photocopying."

- *In re Brand Name Prescription Drugs Antitrust Litigation,* No. CIV.94-897, 1995 WL 360526, at *2 (N.D. Ill. Jun. 15, 1995). The Court found that where a party chooses to store data in a certain manner, even if the cost is significant, that "[t]he normal and reasonable translation of electronic data into a form usable by the discovering party should be the ordinary and foreseeable burden of a respondent."

- *Dunn v. Midwestern Indemnity,* 88 F.R.D. 191, 198 (S.D. Ohio 1980). The plaintiff sought the application software and data concerning homeowner policyholders. The Court stated, "[m]erely because compliance . . . would be costly or time-consuming is not ordinarily sufficient reason to grant a protective order where the requested material is relevant and necessary to the discovery of evidence."

Burdensome to requesting party

- *Super Film of America, Inc. v. UCB Films Inc.,* 219 F.R.D. 649, 657 (D. Kan 2004). The producing party's attempt to fulfill its production obligation by "simply turning over its two computers to [the requesting party] for inspection would unfairly shift the burden and expense of discovery to [the requesting party] and could potentially result in relevant and otherwise discoverable information being shielded from UCB."

Internet data

- *Giardina v. Lockheed Martin Corp.,* No. CIV.02-1030, 2003 WL 1338826 (E.D. La. March 14, 2003). In this employment discrimination, the Court held that requiring the defendant to provide a list of nonwork related internet sites accessed on sixteen computers in three areas over the course of twenty months was not burdensome. The Court rejected the defendant's argument that the burden, estimated at more than fifty hours of work, was excessive.

Database

- *PHE, Inc. v. Department of Justice,* 139 F.R.D. 249, 257 (D.D.C. 1991). The Court rejected a burdensome objection stating, "[t]he plaintiffs admit that their distribution operations are computerized. Although no program may presently exist to obtain the information requested, the Court is satisfied that with little effort the plaintiffs can retrieve the necessary and appropriate information."
- *Mackey v. IBP, Inc.,* 167 F.R.D. 186, 198 (D. Kan. 1996). The defendant conceded that the data compilations needed to answer an interrogatory would cost $1500. The Court ruled that the cost of $1500 required for the computer technician's time to compile the data was not unduly burdensome.
- *National Union Electric Corp. v. Matsuhita Electric Industrial Co.,* 494 F. Supp. 1257, 1262-63 (E.D. Pa. 1980). "Although there may be some difference between requiring the production of existing tapes and requiring a party to program the computer as to produce data in computer-readable as opposed to printout form, we find it to be distinction without a difference, at least in the circumstances of this case."
- *In re Air Crash Disaster at Detroit Metropolitan Airport on Aug. 16,* 130 F.R.D. 634, 636 (E.D. Mich. 1989). In ruling against a burdensome objection, the Court adopted "the reasoning of the court in *National Union* and orders MDC to duplicate the flight director program and data on a nine-track tape as requested by Northwest."
- *State of Missouri ex rel. Stolfa v. Ely,* 875 S.W.2d 579, 582 (Mo. Ct. App. 1994). In this negligence claim the Court rejected an argument that a discovery request seeking claims files over a three-year period was unduly burdensome where the producing party had a database of the claims covering most of the time periods, even though actual location of the physical files may present a burden.
- *Bills v. Kennecott Corp.,* 108 F.R.D. 459, 461 (D. Utah 1985). "[S]ome courts have required the responding parties to develop programs to extract the requested information and to assist the requesting party in reading and interpreting information stored on computer tape."

Particular facts

- *Zapata v. IBP, Inc.,* No. CIV.93-2366, 1994 WL 649322, at *3 (D. Kan. Nov. 10, 1994). Class action plaintiffs sought historical information regarding employees from a defendant employer to demonstrate discrimination claims. The Court stated, "The court also overrules the objection that production of the computer data for employee histories is unduly burdensome. As the party resisting the discovery, defendant has the burden to show facts to justify the objection. It has not carried that burden . . . It has not demonstrated by affidavit or anything else of record that the discovery will be unduly burdensome. All discovery, of course, is to some extent burdensome."

[5]   Sampling

One of the emerging trends by the courts is to order a party to perform a sampling search on a limited number of backup tapes and other storage media to determine if and how much relevant evidence exists. *Rowe Entertainment, Inc. v. William Morris Agency, Inc.,* 205 F.R.D. 421, 433 (S.D.N.Y. 2002), *aff'd,* 2002 WL 975713 (S.D.N.Y. May 9, 2002); *Zubulake v. UBS Warburg LLC,* 217 F.R.D. 309, 323-324 (S.D.N.Y. 2003). Sampling involves conducting test runs of data to determine statistically the volume of relevant data available in computer files. This will provide proof of the cost and burden necessary to restore backup tapes or legacy data. *See also,* § 2.6[C][3][d], *Sampling and Restoration.*

After performing the sampling, parties are required to present their findings to the Court for determination of whether production should be ordered, and if so, whether a cost-shifting analysis should be applied.

[a]   Reported Cases

- *Thompson v. Jiffy Lube Int'l,* No. CIV.05-1203, 2006 U.S. Dist. LEXIS 27837, at *10-11 (D. Kan. May 1, 2006). The Court ordered the parties to meet and confer on alternatives, such as random sampling and reasonable methods and formats for producing electronic information.

- *In re Priceline.com Inc. Sec. Litig.,* 233 F.R.D. 88, 89-90 (D. Conn. 2005). In a motion to compel production of electronic discovery, the Court in a securities case set forth a production procedure, including sampling, to guide the parties to reduce the costly process of restoring and disclosing electronic information.

- *Hagemeyer North America, Inc. v. Gateway Data Sciences Corp.,* 222 F.R.D. 594, 601 (E.D.Wis. 2004). The Court required the parties to engage in sampling of backup tapes since one of the parties would have to acquire additional hardware and software to perform the complete restoration/search. After sampling, the parties were to report back to the Court regarding whether to shift costs of production.

- *Wiginton v. CB Richard Ellis, Inc.,* No. CIV.02-6832, 2004 WL 1895122 (N.D.Ill. Aug. 10, 2004). The plaintiffs alleged a nationwide pattern and practice of sexual harassment and argued that the defendants should pay for the cost of discovery after a sampling of backup data was performed. The Court in a detailed discussion of the sampling process ordered the discovery to go forward, however, shifted some of the costs to the plaintiffs.

- *McPeek v. Ashcroft,* 202 F.R.D. 31, 34 (D.D.C. 2001). The Court required the defendant, Department of Justice, to restore, at its own expense, e-mail "attributable to [one supervisor's] computer" as a "test run" to decide how to approach further discovery of any computer evidence of retaliation.

• *Linnen v. A.H. Robins Co.,* No. 97-2307, 1999 WL 462015 (Mass. Super. Ct. Jun. 16, 1999). The Court ordered compliance with the protocol established in a related MDL proceeding, which enabled samples to be produced from the various categories of computer tapes.

[b] Other Authorities

• MANUAL FOR COMPLEX LITIGATION (FOURTH) § 423: "Parties may have vast collections of computerized data, such as stored E-mail messages or backup files containing routine business information kept for disaster recovery purposes. Unlike collections of paper documents, these data are not normally organized for retrieval by date, author, addressee, or subject matter, and may be very costly and time-consuming to investigate thoroughly. Under such circumstances, judges have ordered that random samples of data storage media be restored and analyzed to determine if further discovery is warranted under the benefit versus burden considerations of Rule 26(b)(2)(iii)."

[6] Cost Allocation

[a] Generally

A recurring issue is who pays for the cost of production of electronic information. Traditionally, parties have had to pay for their own discovery costs. The presumption is that the producing party bears the cost of gathering, reviewing and disclosing responsive documents. *Oppenheimer Fund, Inc. v. Sanders,* 437 U.S. 340 (1978). The requesting party pays for the photocopying charges. *Cardenas v. Dorel Juvenile Group, Inc.,* 230 F.R.D. 611, 633 (D. Kan. 2005). The producing party has the burden of the cost of *preserving data,* especially in the absence of a demand for a litigation hold. *Kemper Mortg., Inc. v. Russell,* No. CIV.06-042, 2006 U.S. Dist. LEXIS 20729, at *5-7 (D. Ohio Apr. 6, 2006). The producing party must pay "for any costs incurred in reviewing . . . documents for privilege." *Zubulake v. UBS Warburg LLC,* 216 F.R.D. 280, 290. (S.D.N.Y. 2003); *Rowe Entm't, Inc. v. William Morris Agency, Inc.,* 205 F.R.D. 421, 432 (D.N.Y. 2002); *Computer Assocs. Int'l, Inc. v. Quest Software, Inc.,* No. CIV.02-4721, 2003 U.S. Dist. LEXIS 9198 (D. Ill. Jun. 3, 2003).

Even though "the presumption is that the responding party must bear the expense of complying with discovery requests . . . he may invoke the district court's discretion under Rule 26(c) to grant orders protecting him from 'undue burden or expense' . . . including orders conditioning discovery on the requesting party's payment of the costs of discovery." *Rowe Entertainment, Inc. v. William Morris Agency, Inc.,* 205 F.R.D. 421, 429 (S.D.N.Y. 2002), *aff'd,* 2002 WL 975713 (S.D.N.Y. May 9, 2002); *Southern Ute Indian Tribe v. Amoco Prod. Co.,* 2 F.3d 1023, 1029-30 (10th Cir. 1993).

The court has the inherent authority to revisit cost allocation decisions. In *In re Two Appeals Arising Out of San Juan Dupont Plaza Hotel Fire,* 994 F.2d 956, 965 (1st Cir. 1993), the Court held that the trial court had the implied power under FED. R. CIV. P. 26 to revisit the allocations of case management expenses. The Court stated, "a trial judge's power to promulgate cost-sharing orders must carry with it the power to readjust such orders as changed circumstances require . . . we acknowledged the district court's power to 'reshape and refashion its cost-sharing orders as new information comes to light, or as information already known takes on added significance.'"

As noted, FED. R. CIV. P. 26(c) permits the disclosing party to challenge the discovery request as unduly burdensome or costly. The FED. R. CIV. P. 34 advisory committee notes provide that the producing party should pay the costs of producing computer data so long as it is not an undue burden or expense, "when data can as a practical matter be made usable by the discovering party only through respondent's devices, respondent may be required to use his devices to translate the data into usable form." In *Sanders v. Levy,* 558 F.2d 636 (2d Cir. 1977), *rev'd on other grounds sub nom., Oppenheimer Fund, Inc. v. Sanders,* 437 U.S. 340 (1978) the Court ruled that Rule 26(c) and Rule 34 allows the court to shift the expense of computer programming to the discovering party where the request poses an undue burden or expense.

In making this cost allocation determination, courts will weigh the benefits and burdens of the discovery and "consider the needs of the case . . . the importance of the issues at stake, the potential for finding relevant material and the importance of the proposed discovery in resolving the issues." FED. R. CIV. P. 26(b)(2). The court is required to find some balance between allowing pretrial discovery that could possibly enable a plaintiff to satisfy his pleading burden, and protecting a defendant from expensive and time-consuming discovery.

Under these circumstances the federal rules explicitly allow courts to modify discovery requests based on a cost-benefit ratio or proportionality basis. This "proportionality" test "imposes general limitations on the scope of discovery." *Zubulake v. UBS Warburg, LLC,* 217 F.R.D. 309, 316 (S.D.N.Y. 2003).

Generally, it still holds true that a producing party bears the costs and burden of responding to discovery requests, even electronic discovery. Cost shifting is not required to be considered in every case involving discovery of electronic data. Furthermore, it is incorrect to assume that the production of electronic data is more expensive than production in paper format. After the documents are electronically retrieved, disclosure in an electronic format would be significantly less costly than printing the documents. *See, Zubulake v. UBS Warburg LLC,* 217 F.R.D. 309, 317 (S.D.N.Y. 2003) ("[e]lectronic evidence is frequently cheaper and easier to produce than paper evidence because it can be searched automatically, key words can be run for privilege checks, and the production can be made in electronic form, obviating the need for mass photocopying").

However, limiting factors such as statutory proscriptions, undue burden, relevancy, redundant data, privileged data and privacy issues may preclude or shift part of the cost burden to the requesting party.

Courts have applied several different approaches in determining cost shifting when discovery of electronic information is involved; traditional, marginal utility, and the Rowe/Zubulake factors test.

[b] Traditional Cost Allocation Approach

Some courts have utilized the general provisions of Rule 26(b)(2) in determining whether to shift costs.

Requesting Party to Pay Costs

- *Playboy Enterprises, Inc. v. Welles,* 60 F. Supp. 2d 1050 (S.D. Cal. 1999). Citing to FED.R.CIV.P. 26(b)(2) the Court ordered the plaintiff to pay for the cost of a computer expert to make a forensic copy of the defendant's hard drive.

- *Simon Property Group L.P. v. mySimon, Inc.,* 194 F.R.D. 639, 641 (S.D. Ind. 2000). Citing to FED.R.CIV.P. 26(b)(2)(iii) the plaintiff was permitted "to attempt (at its own expense) the task of recovering deleted computer files from computers used by the four named individuals, whether at home or at work."

- *Kormendi v. Computer Associates Int'l., Inc.,* No. CIV.02-2996, 2002 WL 31385832 (S.D.N.Y. Oct. 21, 2002). Without citing to any legal authority, the Court ordered the plaintiff to pay for searches of e-mail, regardless if located on the defendant's network system or on individual computers.

- *Anti-Monopoly, Inc. v. Hasbro, Inc.,* No. CIV.94-2120, 1995 W.L. 649934 (S.D.N.Y. Nov. 3, 1995). Citing to prior case precedent, the Court suggested that the requesting party should pay the defendant's costs in creating a special computer program required to retrieve data from the defendant's computers.

- *Pearl Brewing Co. v. Jos. Schlitz Brewing Co.,* 415 F. Supp. 1122, 1136 (S.D. Tex. 1976). Without citing to any specific legal authority as to cost, the defendant, at its own expense, would be permitted to copy "(1) the documentation of each program as to code and contents; (2) the documentation as to 'alternative' program code and contents rejected for trial usage; and (3) an explanation of present and prior computer testing runs."

- *National Union Electric Corp. v. Matsushita Electric Industrial Co.,* 494 F. Supp. 1257, 1262 (E.D. Pa. 1980). The Court stated, "[a]s we have noted, the defendants have expressed their willingness to pay the costs of whatever operations are necessary to manufacture a computer-readable tape. As a result, the problem of allocating the burden of discovery expense, which might be significant in otherwise similar situations . . . is non-existent here."

Responding Party to Pay Costs

- *United States v. Davey,* 543 F.2d 996 (2d Cir. 1976). Without citing to any legal authority, the Court ruled that the cost of $1,305 to the taxpayer of duplicating its own computer tapes constituted a reasonable cost of doing business.

Parties Split the Cost

- *Penk v. Oregon State Bd. of Higher Education,* 816 F.2d 458 (9th Cir. 1987), *cert. denied,* 108 S. Ct. 158, *reh. denied,* 108 S. Ct. 473 (1987). Citing to FED.R.CIV.P. 26(c)(2), the Court ordered the plaintiff to share in the $100,000 cost of updating the defendant's database for a proper statistical analysis in a sex discrimination case.

- *Sattar v. Motorola,* 138 F.3d 1164, 1171 (7th Cir. 1998). Without citing to any legal precedent or procedural rule, the Court held that if the defendant were unable to provide the computerized information in a usable electronic format, parties would each bear half of the cost of printing 210,000 pages of e-mail.

- *Commissioners of the State Ins. Fund ex rel. State Ins. Fund v. Polito,* No. CIV.95-10239, 1997 WL 281930 (S.D.N.Y. May 27, 1997). Without citing to any legal authority, the Court ordered defendants to pay for locating and compiling accounting information. The plaintiffs were ordered to pay for cost of a copy of computerized data compilations containing financial information.

Business Choice of Electronic Data Systems

These courts that take the traditionalist approach have opined that companies using computer technology to generate data must assume the risk of the discovery costs when required to produce that data. These courts have been unwilling to award companies for choosing electronic data systems that preclude access to relevant data.

- *Oppenheimer Fund, Inc. v. Sanders,* 437 U.S. 340, 362 (1978). The Supreme Court ordered the producing party to pay the cost "[t]o compile a list of the class members' names and addresses . . . to sort manually through many records, keypunch 150,000 to 300,000 computer cards, and create several new computer programs." The Court noted, "although it may be expensive to retrieve information stored in computers when no program yet exists for the particular job, there is no reason to think that the same information could be extracted any less expensively if the records were kept in less modern forms. Indeed, one might expect the reverse to be true, for otherwise computers would not have gained such widespread use in the storing and handling of information."

- *Zubulake v. UBS Warburg LLC,* 217 F.R.D. 309, 317 (S.D. N.Y. 2003). "The Supreme Court [*Oppenheimer Fund, Inc. v. Sanders,* 437 U.S. 340 (1978)] has instructed that the presumption is that the responding party must bear the expense of complying with discovery requests [and] . . . [a]ny principled approach to electronic evidence must respect this presumption."

- *Kemper Mortg., Inc. v. Russell,* No. CIV.06-042, 2006 U.S. Dist. LEXIS 20729, at *5-7 (D. Ohio Apr. 6, 2006). The Court ruled that the producing party has the burden of the cost of *preserving data,* especially in the absence of a demand for a litigation hold. The Court stated, "Computers have become a standard tool of doing business, with many associated benefits and costs. One of the benefits but also burdens is that it is easier to preserve a great deal of information than it was with paper systems."

- *Toledo Fair Hous. Ctr. v. Nationwide Mut. Ins. Co.,* 703 N.E.2d 340, 354 (Ohio C.P. 1996). "Furthermore, a party cannot avoid discovery when its own recordkeeping system makes discovery burdensome. If a party chooses to store information in a manner that tends to conceal rather than reveal, that party bears the burden of putting the information in a format useable by others."

- *Linnen v. A.H. Robins Co., Inc.,* 10 Mass. L. Rptr. 189, 1999 WL 462015, at *6 (Mass. Super. Ct. 1999). In this state court action, the plaintiff sought e-mail records in the form of computer tapes, which the Court ordered the defendant to produce. The cost of restoration was approximately $1,200,000. However, the Court first ordered that the parties perform a sampling of the tapes and then the parties could reopen the restoration of all the tapes' issue. The Court stated, "[w]hile the court certainly recognizes the significant cost associated with restoring and producing responsive communication from these tapes . . . that this is one of the risks taken on by companies which have made the decision to avail themselves of the computer technology now available to the business world. To permit a corporation such as [the defendant] to reap the benefits of such technology and simultaneously use that technology as a shield in litigation would lead to incongruous and unfair results."

- *In re Brand Name Prescription Drugs Antitrust Litigation,* 1995 WL 360526, at *2, 3 (N.D. Ill. 1995). The Court stated, "if a party chooses an electronic storage method, the necessity for a retrieval program or method is an ordinary and foreseeable risk. . . . The normal and reasonable translation of electronic data into a form usable by the discovering party should be the ordinary and foreseeable burden of a respondent in the absence of a showing of extraordinary hardship." The Court held that the defendant to pay the costs (estimated between $50,000 and $70,000) for the preparation and disclosure of the company's e-mail data tapes and the plaintiff to pay $0.21 per page for copies of documents selected from the defendant's productions.

• *Daewoo Electronics Co., Ltd. v. U.S.*, 10 Ct. Int'l. Trade 754, 650 F. Supp. 1003, 1006-1007 (1986).

In concluding, the court notes that the government's attitude towards its obligation to transmit information and the characterization of that duty as an interference with, or unwarranted burden on normal administrative operation, has the potential to create very serious problems. It raises the specter of a society in which decisions may be unexaminable because they are accomplished by electronic means too complex and unique to be transmitted in a comprehensible way even to those citizens sufficiently knowledgeable to analyze the relevant data. In this cybernetic new world the effort needed to transmit and explain the basis for the decisions would interfere with the making of other decisions, so that all functioning comes to depend on insulation from critical examination.

The normal and reasonable translation of electronic data into a form useable by the discovering party should be the ordinary and foreseeable burden of a respondent in the absence of a showing of extraordinary hardship.

[c]   Marginal Utility Test

The marginal utility approach is based on economic principles. *In McPeek v. Ashcroft,* 202 F.R.D. 31, 34 (D.D.C. 2001) the Court adopted a "marginal utility" analysis to determine which party was required to pay the cost of discovery of electronic records. The Court stated, "[a] fairer approach borrows, by analogy, from the economic principle of 'marginal utility.' The more likely it is that the backup tape contains information that is relevant to a claim or defense, the fairer it is that the government agency search at its own expense. The less likely it is, the more unjust it would be to make the agency search at its own expense. The difference is 'at the margin.'" *See also, J.C. Assocs. v. Fid. & Guar. Ins. Co.,* No. CIV.01-2437, 2006 U.S. Dist. LEXIS 32919 (D.D.C. May 25, 2006) (where the court ordered the defendant to use an optical character recognition program to convert and then search for specific keywords, check for privilege and then disclose to the plaintiff. The Court ordered the defendant to report the time and costs for conversion which he would use to determine cost allocation pursuant to *McPeek.*).

[d]   Rowe/Zubulake Factors

Rowe factors

The case of *Rowe Entertainment, Inc. v. William Morris Agency, Inc.,* 205 F.R.D. 421, 429 (S.D.N.Y. 2002), *aff'd,* 2002 WL 975713 (S.D.N.Y. May 9, 2002) is one of the seminal cases providing the initial groundwork for determining cost allocation issues for electronic discovery. In *Rowe,* the Court set the standard for cost shifting and affirmed the traditional view that the normal and reasonable costs incurred in producing electronic data into a usable form are normally borne by the producing party. As the Court noted, "[i]f the total cost of the requested discovery is not substantial, then there is no cause to deviate from the presumption that the responding party will bear the expense." *Id.* at 431. However, if the costs are extraordinary, the Court ruled that a cost allocation analysis should be conducted.

The Court considered several factors in determining the cost allocation for electronic discovery:

> Because of the shortcomings of either bright-line rule, courts have adopted a balancing approach taking into consideration such factors as: (1) the specificity of the discovery requests; (2) the likelihood of discovering critical information; (3) the availability of such information from other sources; (4) the purposes for which the responding party maintains the requested data (5) the relative benefit to the parties of obtaining the information; (6) the total cost associated with production; (7) the relative ability of each party to control costs and its incentive to do so; and (8) the resources available to each party. Each of these factors is relevant in determining whether discovery costs should be shifted in this case.

Id. at 429. In *Rowe*, the court allocated costs in proportion to the benefit and needs of the electronic discovery requested by the party.

Zubulake factors

The *Zubulake* decisions retain the traditional presumption that the producing party pays for discovery (assuming it is "accessible" electronic discovery), while formulating a fact-specific cost-shifting analysis for determining cost allocation for "inaccessible" electronic data. *See*, § 3.06[B], *Classification of Data*. This case built upon earlier seminal cost allocation court decisions of *Rowe Entertainment, Inc. v. William Morris Agency, Inc.,* 205 F.R.D. 421, 429 (S.D.N.Y. 2002), *aff'd,* 2002 WL 975713 (S.D.N.Y. May 9, 2002) and *McPeek v. Ashcroft,* 202 F.R.D. 31, 34 (D.D.C. 2001).

In a series of reported decisions arising from the same case, the Court extensively discussed discovery of electronic data as well as the application of a seven-point test to determine cost allocation for inaccessible electronic information. *Zubulake v. UBS Warburg, LLC,* 217 F.R.D. 309 (S.D.N.Y. 2003) ("Zubulake I") (setting forth cost allocation factors for determining cost allocation); *Zubulake v. UBS Warburg LLC,* 216 F.R.D. 280 (S.D.N.Y. 2003) ("Zubulake III") (applying the allocation factors and splitting the costs between the parties); *Zubulake v. UBS Warburg LLC,* 220 F.R.D. 212 (S.D.N.Y. 2003) ("Zubulake IV") (denying a request for an adverse inference instruction request for failure to preserve data); and *Zubulake v. UBS Warburg LLC,* No. CIV.02-12432004, WL 1620866, at *8 (S.D.N.Y. July 20, 2004) ("Zubulake V") (granting a request for an adverse inference instruction for failure to preserve relevant data).

In *Zubulake I* a former female employee brought a gender discrimination and retaliation claim against her former employer. At issue was the discovery of electronic information - specifically electronic mail - in the control and possession of the employer.

The court addressed the specific issues as to whether the employee was entitled to discovery of relevant e-mails that had been deleted and were stored on backup tapes and whether cost shifting was appropriate for the court to consider. The plaintiff contended that key e-mail exchanged among the defendants' employees existed only on backup tapes and other archived media. Defendants contended that it would cost approximately $175,000 (down from an earlier estimate of $300,000 dollars), in addition to attorney time in reviewing the e-mail, to disclose the electronic information from the backup and archived media. The Court held that the employee was entitled to discovery of deleted relevant e-mail that resided on backup storage media. Of special significance was the court's analysis regarding the discovery and cost allocation of electronic information. The court phrased the issue as "[t]o what extent is inaccessible electronic data discoverable, and who should pay for its production?" *Id.* at 311.

After the Court analyzed in detail the restoration processes of electronic information from backup tape and optical storage, the Court discussed the application of the federal discovery rules to electronic evidence and costs allocation (proportionality test) issues regarding the restoration and production of electronic information.

However, the Court ruled that the cost shifting did not have to be considered in every case because the Supreme Court has instructed that "the presumption is that the responding party must bear the expense of complying with discovery requests. . . ." (citing from *Oppenheimer Fund, Inc. v. Sanders,* 437 U.S. 340, 358 (1978). *Id.* at *316.

The Court when considering the cost shifting request classified data as "accessible" versus "inaccessible," and ruled that cost allocation *only applied* to inaccessible data. The court noted that e-mail that was available on active computer files was easily accessible and, therefore, the cost shifting analysis would not apply. However, data stored on the optical and tape backup systems was less accessible and more expensive to produce and, therefore, the cost allocation test would be applied. In its decision the Court set forth a three-step analysis in resolving the scope and cost of discovery when electronic information is involved.

First, it is necessary to thoroughly understand the responding party's computer system, both with respect to active and stored data. For data that is kept in an accessible format, the usual rules of discovery apply: the responding party should pay the costs of producing responsive data. A court should consider cost-shifting only when electronic data is relatively inaccessible, such as in backup tapes.

Second, because the cost-shifting analysis is so fact-intensive, it is necessary to determine what data may be found on the inaccessible media. Requiring the responding party to restore and produce responsive documents from a small sample of the requested backup tapes is a sensible approach in most cases.

Third, and finally, in conducting the cost-shifting analysis, the following factors should be considered, weighted more-or-less in the following order: 1. The extent to which the request is specifically tailored to discover relevant information; 2. The availability of such information from other sources; 3. The total cost of production, compared to the amount in controversy; 4. The total cost of production, compared to the resources available to each party; 5. The relative ability of each party to control costs and its incentive to do so; 6. The importance of the issues at stake in the litigation; and 7. The relative benefits to the parties of obtaining the information.

Just over two months later in *Zubulake III* the Court applied the cost shifting principles set forth in *Zubulake I*. As requested by the court in *Zubulake I* the defendants had performed a sampling of the backup tapes to determine their relevancy as well as the cost of restoring the e-mail backup tapes. After performing the sample restoration of backup e-mails, the defendants argued that the cost of production of the remaining e-mail backup tapes should be shifted to the plaintiff. The court ruled that the plaintiff was to share in the cost of restoration, although the defendant was to bear the major part of the expense - defendants to pay 75% and the plaintiff to pay 25% of the cost of restoration. The court also ruled that the defendant must pay "for any costs incurred in reviewing the restored documents for privilege." *Id.* at 290.

[i]   Reported Cases - Zubulake/Rowe Factors

Requesting Party to Pay the Cost

*   *Quinby v. WestLB AG,* No. CIV.04-7406, 2005 U.S. Dist. LEXIS 35583 (D.N.Y. Dec. 15, 2005). The Court refused to issue sanctions for failure of the defendant and their attorneys to disclose that some of the sought after data was located on a separate database and some data was already with their electronic discovery vendor, Kroll. The Court held that even though it had ordered the parties to respond to the *Zubulake* standards specifically "2. The availability of such information from other sources; 3. The total cost of production, compared to the amount in controversy" that the defendant was not subject to sanctions for failing to disclose the information was available from other sources. Also, the data collected for other non-related projects had been in a readily accessible format, but, after the projects ended, Kroll archived the data onto Kroll's own back-up tapes, making the data inaccessible. *But see, Treppel v. Biovail Corp.,* 233 F.R.D. 363, n.4 (D.N.Y. 2006) ("One of my colleagues recently declined to sanction a party for converting data to an inaccessible format [Quinby case], taking the position that there is no obligation to preserve electronic data in an accessible form, even when litigation is anticipated. (citation omitted) I respectfully disagree."

- *OpenTV v. Liberate Technologies,* 219 F.R.D. 474 (N.D.Cal. 2003). In this software patent infringement action the Court in applying the *Zubulake* factors held that electronic data in the form of source code was stored in an inaccessible format for the purposes of discovery, and, therefore, it was appropriate for parties to split equally the cost of extraction of the source code from the defendant's database, but the defendant would bear the cost of copying the source code for plaintiff once it was extracted.

- *Hagemeyer North America, Inc. v. Gateway Data Sciences Corp.,* 222 F.R.D. 594, 601 (E.D.Wis. 2004). After reviewing the different approaches to cost shifting the Court adopted the *Zubulake* test and held that the defendant was required to adopt a sample of backup tapes and then the parties needed to make additional submissions addressing the cost allocation issue.

- *Murphy Oil USA, Inc. v. Fluor Daniel, Inc.,* 52 Fed.R.Serv.3d 168 (E.D.La. 2002). The defendant's e-mail retention policy provided that backup tapes were recycled after 45 days. The court noted, "If Fluor had followed this policy, the e-mail issue would be moot. Fluor does not explain why, but it maintained its backup tapes for the entire fourteen month period. As a consequence it has 93 e-mail backup tapes." Applying the *Rowe* factors the court shifted the cost of production, estimated to be $6 million, to the plaintiff; however, it required the defendant to bear the expense of reviewing the material for privilege.

Responding Party to Pay the Cost

- *Xpedior Creditor Trust v. Credit Suisse First Boston (USA), Inc.* 309 F. Supp. 2d 459 (S.D.N.Y. 2003). The Honorable Shira A. Scheindlin, who authored this opinion, applied the cost shifting test that she originated in *Zubulake I*. The Court applied the *Zubulake* seven factor cost shifting test and found that since the data resided on optical disks and DLT tapes and was accessible, cost shifting was inappropriate.

- *Computer Assocs. Int'l., Inc. v. Quest Software, Inc.,* No. CIV.02- 4721, 2003 WL 21277129, at *2 (N.D. Ill. Jun. 3, 2003). The Court in applying the *Rowe* test ruled that cost of reviewing forensically imaged hard drive for possible confidential data would not to be shifted to the requesting party. The Court stated, "[d]efendants here seek to recover the costs of their preventive measures undertaken before the actual disclosure of the information to the plaintiff. These costs are analogous to the review of documents for privileged information and should not be shifted to the requesting party."

- *Wachtel v. Guardian Life Ins. Co.,* No. CIV.01-4183, 2006 WL 1286189 (D.N.J. May 8, 2006)(unpublished). The Court affirmed the magistrate's imposition of a spoliation inference and refused to consider cost allocation because of discovery mismanagement.

- *Bills v. Kennecott,* 108 F.R.D. 459, 464 (D. Utah 1985). In a case prior to the *Rowe* and *Zubulake* decisions, the defendants were ordered to pay the cost (approximately $5,400) of producing detailed employee information stored on the defendant's computer. The Court set forth the following factors in making their decision: "In the instant action, this Court has been persuaded by the following additional factors in exercising its discretion to deny the defendant's motion to shift the costs of discovery: (1) The amount of money involved is not excessive or inordinate; (2) The relative expense and burden in obtaining the data would be substantially greater to the requesting party as compared with the responding party; (3) The amount of money required to obtain the data as set forth by defendant would be a substantial burden to plaintiffs; (4) The responding party is benefited in its case to some degree by producing the data in question."

Parties to Share the Cost

- *Multitechnology Services, L.P. v. Verizon Southwest f/k/a GTE Southwest Inc.,* No. CIV.02-702, 2004 WL 1553480 (N.D.Tex. Jul. 12, 2004). The Court acknowledged that the data was in an "accessible" format, and, therefore, the production costs should have been borne by the producing party according to *Zubulake*. However, the Court decided against following that part of the *Zubulake* case and after applying the *Zubulake* factors held that the parties should share the $60,000 cost of discovery.

- *Medtronic Sofamor Danek, Inc. v. Michelson,* 229 F.R.D. 550, 552 (D. Tenn. 2003). The defendant filed a motion to compel requesting "approximately 996 computer network backup tapes containing, among other things, electronic mail, plus an estimated 300 gigabytes of other electronic data [from employee files on Medtronic computers] that is not in a backed-up format . . . " The plaintiff opposed the motion arguing that it was unduly burdensome. The Court applied the *Rowe* cost-shifting test and imposed some of the costs on the discovering party.

- *Wiginton v. CB Richard Ellis, Inc.,* No. CIV.02-6832, 2004 WL 1895122, at *4 (N.D.Ill. Aug. 10, 2004). The plaintiffs alleged a nationwide pattern and practice of sexual harassment and argued that the defendants should pay for the cost of discovery after a sampling of backup data was performed. The Court in a detailed discussion of the sampling process and using the *Zubulake* test with the addition of another factor ordered the discovery to go forward, however, shifted some of the costs to the plaintiffs. The additional factor was "consider[ing] the importance of the requested discovery in resolving the issues of the litigation."

- *Byers v. Illinois State Police,* No. CIV.99-8105, 2002 WL 1264004 (N.D. Ill. Jun. 3, 2002). The Court citing to the *Rowe* decision and ordered the parties to split the cost of recovering archived e-mail in an employment discrimination suit. The defendants would still be required to assume the cost of reviewing the discovery prior to production.

[e]   Particularization of Facts Needed

- *Thompson v. U.S. Dept. of Housing and Urban Dev.,* 219 F.R.D. 93, 98 (D. Md. 2003). In considering discovery sanctions for defendants' failure to produce 80,000 e-mails until after the discovery cutoff, the Court found that the balancing factors of Rule 26(b)(2) may be used to determine burdens in electronic discovery, and that the key is a particularized showing of the burden of producing electronic information. The Court stated, "[r]egardless of which test is used, the most important ingredient for the analytical process to produce a fair result is a particularization of the facts to support any challenge to discovery of electronic records. Conclusory or factually unsupported assertions by counsel that the discovery of electronic materials should be denied because of burden or expense can be expected to fail. *See, e.g., St. Paul Reinsurance Co., Ltd. v. Commercial Financial Corp.,* 198 F.R.D. 508, 511-12 (N.D. Iowa 2000) (citing numerous cases that hold that a party resisting discovery bears the burden of demonstrating lack of relevance, burden or excessive expense, and that generalized or conclusory allegations are insufficient. Instead, a particularized showing, by affidavit or similar submission is required to present facts supporting the challenge) . . . failing to do so waives the objection."

- *St. Paul Reinsurance Co., Ltd. v. Commercial Financial Corp.,* 198 F.R.D. 508, 511-12 (N.D. Iowa 2000). The Court cited to several cases holding that a party who opposes discovery bears the burden of proof (by affidavit or otherwise) of lack of relevance, burden or excessive expense. The Court went on to say that generalized or conclusory allegations are insufficient. *See also, Super Film of America, Inc. v. UCB Films Inc.,* 219 F.R.D. 649, 657 (D. Kan 2004); *Marens v. Carrabba's Italian Grill, Inc.,* 196 F.R.D. 35, 38 (D.Md. 2000).

[f]   Other Authorities

- Mohammad Iqbal, *The New Paradigms of E-discovery and Cost-shifting,* 72 Def. Couns. J. 283 (July, 2005).

- Jessica Lynn Repa, Comment, *Adjudicating Beyond the Scope of Ordinary Business: Why the Inaccessibility Test in Zubulake Unduly Stifles Cost-shifting During Electronic Discovery,* 54 Am. U. L. Rev. 257 (2004).

- Marnie H. Pulver, Note, *Electronic Media Discovery: The Economic Benefit of Pay-Per-View,* 21 Cardozo L.Rev. 1379 (2000).

- ABA Civil Discovery Standards, § 29(b)(3), *Discovery of Electronic Information* (August 2004). The new ABA Civil Discovery Standards suggest a list of sixteen factors that the court should consider in deciding whether to allow requested discovery and to allocate the costs of that discovery.

- Corinne L. Giacobbe, Note, *Allocating Discovery Costs in the Computer Age: Deciding Who Should Bear the Costs of Discovery of Electronically Stored Data*, 57 Wash. & Lee L. Rev. 257, 260-61 (Winter 2000).

[H] Work Product Doctrine, Attorney Client Privilege and Trade Secrets

[1] Work Product

[a] Rule 26(b)(3)

Trial Preparation: Materials. Subject to the provisions of subdivision (b)(4) of this rule, a party may obtain discovery of documents and tangible things otherwise discoverable under subdivision (b)(1) of this rule and prepared in anticipation of litigation or for trial by or for another party or by or for that other party's representative (including the other party's attorney, consultant, surety, indemnitor, insurer, or agent) only upon a showing that the party seeking discovery has substantial need of the materials in the preparation of the party's case and that the party is unable without undue hardship to obtain the substantial equivalent of the materials by other means. In ordering discovery of such materials when the required showing has been made, the court shall protect against disclosure of the mental impressions, conclusions, opinions, or legal theories of an attorney or other representative of a party concerning the litigation.

[2] Pending Rule 26(b)(5)(A) & (B) Amendment

Rule 26. General Provisions Governing Discovery; Duty of Disclosure

(b) Discovery Scope and Limits. Unless otherwise limited by order of the court in accordance with these rules, the scope of discovery is as follows:

* * * * *

(5) Claims of Privilege or Protection of Trial-Preparation Materials.

(A) Information Withheld. When a party withholds information otherwise discoverable under these rules by claiming that it is privileged or subject to protection as trial-preparation material, the party shall make the claim expressly and shall describe the nature of the documents, communications, or things not produced or disclosed in a manner that, without revealing information itself privileged or protected, will enable other parties to assess the applicability of the privilege or protection. (emphasis added).

(B) Information Produced. If information is produced in discovery that is subject to a claim of privilege or of protection as trial-preparation material, the party making the claim may notify any party that received the information of the claim and the basis for it. After being notified, a party must promptly return, sequester, or destroy the specified information and any copies it has and may not use or disclose the information until the claim is resolved. A receiving party may promptly present the information to the court under seal for a determination of the claim. If the receiving party disclosed the information before being notified, it must take reasonable steps to retrieve it. The producing party must preserve the information until the claim is resolved. (emphasis added).

* * * * *

Committee Note

Subdivision (b)(5). The Committee has repeatedly been advised that the risk of privilege waiver, and the work necessary to avoid it, add to the costs and delay of discovery. When the review is of electronically stored information, the risk of waiver, and the time and effort required to avoid it, can increase substantially because of the volume of electronically stored information and the difficulty in ensuring that all information to be produced has in fact been reviewed. Rule 26(b)(5)(A) provides a procedure for a party that has withheld information on the basis of privilege or protection as trial-preparation material to make the claim so that the requesting party can decide whether to contest the claim and the court can resolve the dispute. Rule 26(b)(5)(B) is added to provide a procedure for a party to assert a claim of privilege or trial-preparation material protection after information is produced in discovery in the action and, if the claim is contested, permit any party that received the information to present the matter to the court for resolution.

Rule 26(b)(5)(B) does not address whether the privilege or protection that is asserted after production was waived by the production. The courts have developed principles to determine whether, and under what circumstances, waiver results from inadvertent production of privileged or protected information. Rule 26(b)(5)(B) provides a procedure for presenting and addressing these issues. Rule 26(b)(5)(B) works in tandem with Rule 26(f), which is amended to direct the parties to discuss privilege issues in preparing their discovery plan, and which, with amended Rule 16(b), allows the parties to ask the court to include in an order any agreements the parties reach regarding issues of privilege or trial-preparation material protection. Agreements reached under Rule 26(f)(4) and orders including such agreements entered under Rule 16(b)(6) may be considered when a court determines whether a waiver has occurred. Such agreements and orders ordinarily control if they adopt procedures different from those in Rule 26(b)(5)(B).

A party asserting a claim of privilege or protection after production must give notice to the receiving party. That notice should be in writing unless the circumstances preclude it. Such circumstances could include the assertion of the claim during a deposition. The notice should be as specific as possible in identifying the information and stating the basis for the claim. Because the receiving party must decide whether to challenge the claim and may sequester the information and submit it to the court for a ruling on whether the claimed privilege or protection applies and whether it has been waived, the notice should be sufficiently detailed so as to enable the receiving party and the court to understand the basis for the claim and to determine whether waiver has occurred. Courts will continue to examine whether a claim of privilege or protection was made at a reasonable time when delay is part of the waiver determination under the governing law.

After receiving notice, each party that received the information must promptly return, sequester, or destroy the information and any copies it has. The option of sequestering or destroying the information is included in part because the receiving party may have incorporated the information in protected trial preparation materials. No receiving party may use or disclose the information pending resolution of the privilege claim. The receiving party may present to the court the questions whether the information is privileged or protected as trial-preparation material, and whether the privilege or protection has been waived. If it does so, it must provide the court with the grounds for the privilege or protection specified in the producing party's notice, and serve all parties. In presenting the question, the party may use the content of the information only to the extent permitted by the applicable law of privilege, protection for trial preparation material, and professional responsibility.

If a party disclosed the information to nonparties before receiving notice of a claim of privilege or protection as trial-preparation material, it must take reasonable steps to retrieve the information and to return it, sequester it until the claim is resolved, or destroy it.

Whether the information is returned or not, the producing party must preserve the information pending the court's ruling on whether the claim of privilege or of protection is properly asserted and whether it was waived. As with claims made under Rule 26(b)(5)(A), there may be no ruling if the other parties do not contest the claim.

[a]   Purpose

This rule essentially provides that documents and tangible things prepared in anticipation of litigation are discoverable upon a showing of:

* Substantial need; and

* Inability (without undue hardship) to obtain the material elsewhere.

* However, mental impressions, conclusions, opinions and legal theories are always protected.

The Supreme Court initially recognized the work product doctrine or "privilege" in *Hickman v. Taylor,* 329 U.S. 495 (1947). It is based on the premise that "it is essential that a lawyer work with a certain degree of privacy, free from unnecessary intrusion by opposing parties and their counsel." *Id.* at 510. The Court noted that if attorney work product was freely discoverable, "[t]he effect on the legal profession would be demoralizing [and] the interests of the clients and the cause of justice would be poorly served." *Id.* at 511. The work product doctrine protects not only materials that are prepared by attorneys themselves, but also by their investigators or other agents. *See, United States v. Nobles,* 422 U.S. 225, 238-39 (1975).

However, work product protection "is not absolute. Like other qualified privileges, it may be waived." *Nobles,* 422 U.S. at 239. For example, "an intentional disclosure of opinion work-product to a testifying expert effectively waives the work-product privilege." *Simon Prop. Group L.P. v. mySimon, Inc.,* 194 F.R.D. 644, 647 (S.D. Ind. 2000); *In re Chrysler Motors Corp. Overnight Evaluation Program Litig.,* 860 F.2d 844 (8th Cir. 1988) (party waived work product privilege to a database by disclosing to counsel in different litigation.). Also, work product may be discoverable if the opposing party can show a substantial need and is unable without undue hardship to obtain the materials elsewhere. FED. R. CIV. P. 26(b)(3).

Work product generally refers to documents, materials and tangible things that are prepared in anticipation of litigation or trial. *Hickman v. Taylor,* 329 U.S. 495 (1947). It protects "mental impressions, conclusions, opinions, or legal theories of an attorney or other representative of a party concerning the litigation." Rule 26(b)(3) involves the legal theories and strategy of the attorney. Preparation of the case requires the attorney to sift through and choose relevant from the irrelevant facts. This work is often reflected in interviews, statements, memoranda, document databases, correspondence and other work product. These materials are generally protected.

An attorney may assert a work product claim even though the client has waived the privilege. *Carte Blanche (Singapore) PTE, Ltd. v. Diners Club Int'l., Inc.,* 130 F.R.D. 28, 32 (S.D.N.Y. 1990).

The work product doctrine distinguishes between fact work product and opinion work product. The courts afford greater protection to opinion work product as opposed to factual work product. *Upjohn Co. v. United States,* 449 U.S. 383, 401-02 (1981); *Kintera, Inc. v. Convio, Inc.,* 219 F.R.D. 503, 507 (S.D.Cal. 2003). The Court in *Kintera* described "fact work product" as consisting of factual material that is prepared in anticipation of litigation or trial. As the *Kintera* court noted,

> Where the selection, organization, and characterization of facts reveals the theories, opinions, or mental impressions of a party or the party's representative, that material qualifies as opinion work product. (citation omitted) In ordering discovery of such materials, the court shall protect against disclosure of the mental impressions, conclusions, opinions, or legal theories of an attorney or other representative of a party concerning the litigation. . . . Opinion work product receives "nearly absolute protection." . . . Therefore, materials containing mental impressions, conclusions, opinions, and legal theories of an attorney are discoverable only in rare and extraordinary circumstances. . . . Opinion work product includes such items as an attorney's legal strategy, intended lines of proof, evaluation of the strengths and weaknesses of the case, and the inferences drawn from interviews of witnesses. . .

Id at 507.

As the name suggests fact work product generally pertains to documents composed of factual information as opposed to the mental impressions of an attorney. A party seeking fact work product must meet the substantial need/undue hardship test required under Rule 26(b)(3).

"Opinion work product" is material which reveals the mental processes or opinions of counsel. Opinion work product can consist of the "mental impressions, subjective evaluations, strategy, opinions, legal theories and conclusions of counsel, and the subjective evaluations and mental impressions of counsel's agents." *Hickman v. Taylor,* 329 U.S. 495 (1947); 4 James Wm. Moore et al., *Moore's Federal Practice* § 26.64[1] at 26-349-50 (1989) ("Opinion work product relates to the litigation preparation, strategy and appraisal of the strengths and weaknesses of an action or of the activities of the attorneys involved, rather than to the underlying evidence.").

The fact work product doctrine can be overcome, however, by a showing of sufficient need for the documents. Where the party seeking disclosure demonstrates a substantial need for the information and establishes that they cannot obtain the information (or its equivalent) by alternative means without undue hardship, disclosure of the documents may be ordered.

The work product privilege, unlike the attorney-client privilege, does not depend on an expectation or intent that the communication will remain confidential. *See,* 8 Charles A. Wright, et al., *Federal Practice & Procedure: Civil 2d* § 2024 (2d Ed. 1994). A waiver will occur when the information is voluntarily disclosed to an adversary. *United States v. Nobles,* 422 U.S. at 239. The courts have held that there is no waiver when there has not been a disclosure that has "substantially increased the opportunities for potential adversaries to obtain information." 8 Charles A. Wright, et al., *Federal Practice & Procedure: Civil 2d* § 2024 (2d Ed. 1994).

In the context of electronic discovery, producing parties in turning over large amounts of data expose themselves to the risk of inadvertently disclosing protected work product or other privileged materials. Another problem that the practitioner should be aware of is the metadata that is part of every computer file. Metadata is hidden data that may disclose work product, attorney client material or other confidential material. *See,* § 3.7, *Metadata, Hidden, or Embedded Information;* Campbell C. Steele, *Attorneys Beware: Metadata's Impact on Privilege, Work Product, and the Ethical Rules,* 35 U. Mem. L. Rev. 911(Summer 2005).

Pending Rule 26(b)(5)(A) & (B) Amendment

As a result of the substantial volume of ESI, delaying discovery and the risk of producing privileged information, Rule 26(b)(5)(B) was added to provide a procedure, in the absence of an agreement, for a party to assert a claim of privilege or trial-preparation material protection after privileged information is produced during discovery. If the claim is then contested by the receiving party, a procedure is set forth to have the Court resolve the dispute.

As a procedural rule, "Rule 26(b)(5)(B) does not address whether the privilege or protection that is asserted after production was waived by the production. The courts have developed principles to determine whether, and under what circumstances, waiver results from inadvertent production of privileged or protected information." Rule 26(b)(5)(A) & (B) Amendment, Committee Note; *See,* §§ 7.04[H], *Work Product and Attorney Client Privilege - Rule 26(b)(3)* (discussion of the substantive law regarding privilege waiver) and 7.4[I][3], *Nonwaiver - Clawback and Quick-Peek Agreements.* However, one Court has held that given the nature of electronic discovery, and pursuant to FED. R. EVID. (Proposed Rule) 512 and FED. R. EVID. 501, the defendants would not waive privilege based on the erroneous production of privileged materials if reasonable steps were taken to protect against a waiver of privilege and work product protection. *Hopson v. Mayor & City Council of Baltimore,* 232 F.R.D. 228 (D. Md. 2005), *but see, In re Qwest Communications Int'l., Inc.,* No. CIV.06-1070, 2006 WL 1668246 (10th Cir. Jun. 19, 2006) (Appellate Court affirmed lower court decision holding that the plaintiff waived the attorney client and work product privileges, as to third parties, by voluntarily disclosing privileged documents to government investigators. Even though the plaintiff and government agencies had entered into a confidentiality agreement, the Court declined to adopt a "selective or limited waiver" that would limit production of confidential materials only to the government agencies).

If the parties desire, they can enter into an agreement regarding nonwaiver of privileged information that can differ from the procedure set out in Rule 26(b)(5)(B). *See,* §7.4[I][3], *Nonwaiver - Clawback and Quick-Peek Agreements.* Rule 26(b)(5)(B) and amended Rule 26(f) direct the parties to discuss privilege issues in preparing their discovery plan. Amended Rule 16(b), permits the Court to enter a scheduling order, if an agreement is reached, regarding "claims of privilege or of protection as trial-preparation material after production" for ESI. Further, the Court can consider privilege agreements entered into under Rule 16 . . . [in determining whether] a waiver has occurred. Pending Rule 26(b)(5)(A) & (B) Amendment, Committee Note. Thus, the parties may mutually agree that any disclosure of privileged data is not subject to a waiver and have the Court enter such an order.

This privilege procedure applies to both electronic and paper documents and is not limited to the inadvertent production of electronic discovery. Rule 26(b)(5)(B) requires the return of the privileged information to the producing party or to the Court subject to subsequent resolution by the Court of any waiver claim made by the receiving party. Further, there is no time limitation as to when a "demand" for return of the privileged information can be made. The issue still remains as to whether the "non-waiver" protection applies to third parties.

Finally, Rule 26(b)(5)(B) requires that the receiving party take "reasonable steps" to retrieve information if it is sent onto third parties before notice of its privileged status.

[b]   Reported Cases - Work Product

Waiver

- *In re Qwest Communications Int'l., Inc.,* No. CIV.06-1070, 2006 WL 1668246 (10th Cir. Jun. 19, 2006). The Appellate Court affirmed lower court decision holding that the plaintiff waived the attorney client and work product privileges, as to third parties, by voluntarily disclosing privileged documents to government investigators. Even though the plaintiff and government agencies had entered into a confidentiality agreement, the Court declined to adopt a "selective or limited waiver" that would limit production of confidential materials only to the government agencies.

- *In re OM Group Sec. Litig.,* 226 F.R.D. 579 (N.D. Ohio 2005). In a detailed discussion, the Court found that e-mail sent among company audit committee, counsel, and counsel's accounting consultant were not protected by the work product privilege because they were produced for a business purpose. However, they would be protected by the attorney client privilege except for the content disclosed in PowerPoint presentations to the Board which constituted a privilege waiver.

- *In re Grand Jury Subpoena,* 220 F.R.D. 130 (D. Mass. 2004). In this grand jury investigation, the Court provided a detailed discussion between fact and opinion work product and the protections afforded to each. The Court held that attorney's notes were not protected based on the crime fraud exception and that the notes were not prepared in anticipation of litigation.

- *Communications Benton v. Brookfield Properties Corp.,* No. CIV.02-6892, 2003 WL 21749602 (S.D.N.Y July 29, 2003). The Court held that e-mail sent prior to representation was not protected by work product protection.

Nonwaiver

- *Hopson v. Mayor & City Council of Baltimore,* 232 F.R.D. 228 (D. Md. 2005). In this employment discrimination claim the defendants objected to the extensive electronic discovery request on the grounds of it being burdensome and expensive primarily on the grounds of the preproduction privilege review of the information. After a detailed review of the privilege waiver issues in disclosing a voluminous amount of electronic data, the Court explained that given the nature of electronic discovery, and pursuant to FED. R. EVID. (Proposed Rule) 512 and FED. R. EVID. 501, the defendants would not waive privilege based on the erroneous production of privileged materials if reasonable steps were taken to protect against a waiver of privilege and work product protection.

- *United States v. Martha Stewart,* 287 F. Supp. 2d 461, 468 (S.D.N.Y. 2003). The Court held that the client's action in forwarding attorney client e-mail to her daughter did waive the attorney client privilege, however, it did not waive the work product privilege and, therefore, the e-mail was to remain confidential. The court found that the e-mail was created in preparation for litigation and its disclosure did not substantially increase the opportunities for potential adversaries to obtain the information.

- *Tilberg v. Next Mgmt. Co.,* No. CIV.04-7373, 2005 U.S. Dist. LEXIS 36336 (D.N.Y. Dec. 28, 2005). A forensic search of the defendant's computer uncovered e-mail which the defendant asserted were privileged. The Court found that these e-mails with nonparties, employees of the defendant, would be protected under the work product protection as long as defendant's counsel would submit an affidavit confirming that the information was requested in anticipation of litigation.

- *Banks v. United States,* No. CIV.03-5533, 2005 WL 958399, at *1 (W.D. Wash. Apr. 7, 2005). The plaintiff's filed a motion to reconsider the Court's order finding nonwaiver in the disclosure of e-mail. In denying the motion the Court listed the five factor test used to determine if the work product privilege was waived. "The factors are: (1) the reasonableness of the precautions to prevent inadvertent disclosure; (2) the time taken to rectify the error; (3) the scope of the discovery; (4) the extent of the disclosure; and (5) the overriding issue of fairness." (citations omitted).

- *In re Natural Gas Commodity Litigation,* No. CIV.03-6186, 2005 WL 1457666 (S.D.N.Y. Jun. 21, 2005). The Court upheld the work product doctrine and stated: "because defendants had explicit written confidentiality and non-waiver agreements with the governmental agencies, and because plaintiffs have not shown a substantial need for defendants' experts' and counsels' analyses, having been provided the underlying documents and data on which the analyses were based . . . the Court finds that defendants did not waive the work product privilege."

- *In re Cendant Corp. Securities Litigation*, 343 F.3d 658 (3d Cir. 2003). The Court held that the work product of a litigation consultant reflecting the private communications between client, counsel, and counsel's litigation consultant was protected as *opinion work product*.

- *Conticommodity Services, Inc. Securities Litigation*, 123 F.R.D. 574, 578 (N.D. Ill. 1988). Computer run showing various tax calculations regarding amended returns, prepared for a discussion of litigation strategy among attorneys, were protected from discovery by work product immunity.

- *Indiana State Board of Public Welfare v. Tioga Pines Living Ctr.*, 592 N.E.2d 1274 (Ind. Ct. App. 1992). Computer simulations reflecting possible Medicaid reimbursement methodologies, prepared after commencement of the lawsuit, would be protected as work product.

Form of disclosure

- *National Union Elec. Corp. v. Matsushita Elec. Indus. Co. Ltd.*, 494 F. Supp. 1257, 1262 (E.D. Pa. 1980). In this leading case, the Court ordered the plaintiff to produce computer tape of certain data (television sales and production data, etc.) that plaintiff previously supplied in printed form. Court held that work product privilege did not preclude defendants from obtaining the requested relief since defendants decided what data plaintiff was to gather and how it would be arranged by virtue of framing of their interrogatories.

Substantial need

- *Holmgren v. State Farm Mut. Auto. Ins. Co.*, 976 F.2d 573, 577 (9th Cir. 1992). In a bad faith insurance claim, the Court held that settlement ranges are opinion work product, but are discoverable and admissible "when mental impressions are at issue in a case and the need for the material is compelling."

- *Maloney v. Sisters of Charity Hospital*, 165 F.R.D. 26, 30-31 (W.D.N.Y. 1995). The Court held that computer printouts containing statistical information pertaining to a proposed reduction in force that were prepared in anticipation of litigation were *fact work product*. The discovering party could not show substantial need and the inability to obtain a substantial equivalent from alternative sources.

Additional evidence needed

- *In re Asia Global Crossing, Ltd.,* 322 B.R. 247 (Bankr. S.D.N.Y. 2005). The trustee in a bankruptcy proceeding moved to compel production of e-mail and other documents that the "insiders" alleged were protected by the attorney client and work product privilege. The Court could not determine, without further evidence, whether e-mails were fact or opinion work product and, thus, whether insiders had waived any work-product privilege attached to unencrypted e-mail communications.

[c]   Reported Cases - Litigation Support Databases

Recently, with the advent of computer databases, there have been several cases questioning whether or not litigation databases, images or full text data are discoverable, and not protected under the work product immunity. The litigation support system is ordinarily protected as work product under FED. R. CIV. P. 26(b)(3). *In re IBM Peripherals EDP Devices Antitrust Litig.,* 5 Computer Law Serv. 878 (N.D. Cal. 1975); *Montrose Chemical Corp. of California v. Train*, 491 F.2d 63 (D.C. Cir. 1974). Though it may be designated as work product by the courts if they determine it to be "factual" work product as opposed to "opinion" work product then the court can require disclosure if a party can demonstrate substantial need for the materials and cannot obtain the materials in the same or a similar form without extreme hardship. *See, § 7.4[H][1], Work Product.*

However, "as the process of selection and inputting of material becomes more mechanical, it may be possible to urge that such systems disclose little or no fact or opinion work product, or that the fields or segments that really include such information can be blocked out while the remainder is subject to discovery." Wright & Miller, *Federal Practice & Procedure*, § 2218.

In order to protect litigation databases, more thought should be given to ensure these databases reflect the fact and opinion work product of the attorney, and not just a mechanical insertion of data into a computer database. In an article addressing this issue, the authors stated:

> The designers of computer-based litigation support systems have been quick to appreciate that immunity from discovery may be obtained by incorporating opinion work product into the system. Their actions, aimed at establishing that the support system is designed and controlled by attorneys, do not necessarily convert it into opinion work product. Whether the creator or possessor of information is an attorney is not in itself determinative. The fact that an attorney has designed the system or shaped the data is relevant to whether the system might disclose the kind of 'mental impressions, conclusions, opinions or legal theories' that are protected by the rule. The crucial question then, is not whether a lawyer has control over or helped shape the system, but whether discovery

would actually reveal the subjective mental impressions of the party or its representatives as to its strategy in the law suit.

Sherman & Kinnard, *The Development, Discovery, and Use of Computer Support Systems in Achieving Efficiency in Litigation*, 79 Colum. L. Rev. 267, 285-286 (1979).

Not Discoverable

- *Shipes v. BIC Corp.*, 154 F.R.D. 301, 309 (M.D. Ga. 1994). The defendant's in-house counsel's computer insurance claims database, was work product and not subject to discovery.

- *Sporck v. Ped*, 759 F.2d 312, 315 (3d Cir.), *cert. denied*, 474 U.S. 903 (1985). "The threshold issue in this case is whether the selection process of defense counsel in grouping certain documents together out of the thousands produced in this litigation is work product entitled to protection under Federal Rule of Civil Procedure 26(b)(3) and the principles of *Hickman v. Taylor*, 329 U.S. 495, 67 S.Ct. 385, 91 L.Ed. 451 (1947)." The materials were found to be protected work product.

- *United States v. American Telephone & Telegraph Company*, 642 F.2d 1285, 1298-99 (D.C. Cir. 1980). In this leading case, the Court held that a database of documents that had been furnished to the *United States* by MCI was protected as work product because they were prepared in anticipation of MCI's case against AT&T. The privilege had not been waived, even though provided to a third party by MCI, due to the common interest between transferor and transferee.

- *In re IBM Peripherals EDP Devices Antitrust Litig.*, 5 Computer Law Serv. 878 (N.D. Cal. 1975). The Court stated, "[t]he trial support system created by IBM's counsel reflects their mental impressions, theories and thought processes, and the Court is not satisfied that information contained in that system can be segregated from such lawyers' mental impressions and theories."

- *Santiago v. Miles*, 121 F.R.D. 636 (W.D.N.Y. 1988). In a civil rights action against prison officials claiming discrimination in work assignments, computer reports, generated using a program prepared at request of counsel in anticipation of trial, were found to contain counsel's thoughts and impressions, and were protected under Rule 26(b)(3). A second category of computer printouts, used by prison official to prepare reports regarding ethnic distribution of job assignments, was not protected by the work product doctrine because they were not prepared in anticipation of litigation.

- *Sporck v. Peil*, 759 F.2d 312, 315 (3d Cir. 1985). In preparation for a deposition counsel selected certain documents for review for his client. The Court protected the selection and held that "[i]n selecting and ordering a few documents out of thousands counsel could not help but reveal important aspects of his understanding of the case. Indeed, in a case such as this . . . the process of selection and distillation is often more critical than pure legal research."

Discoverable, Pay Portion

- *Portis v. City of Chicago,* No. CIV.02-3139, 2005 U.S. Dist. LEXIS 18241 (D. Ill. Aug. 24, 2005). After holding that the defendant had to pay its fair share of a litigation support database, the court also held that the consultant who created the database had to answer deposition questions pertaining to the data, methods, tests, procedures, and assumptions underlying the database. However, the consultant could not be questioned about data that could have been included but was rejected, for whatever reason.

- *Portis v. City of Chicago,* No. CIV.02-3139, 2004 WL 1535854 (N.D.Ill. Apr. 15, 2004). Plaintiffs had compiled a database of selected data from other computer databases and arrest reports provided by defendant. Defendants sought access to the database and the plaintiffs asserted attorney work product protection against disclosure of the database. The Court found that the database constituted factual work product, but the city had shown a substantial need for access to the database and recreating the $90,000 database would be duplicative and costly. The Court required disclosure of the database and required defendants to pay half of its costs, less $5,000 they had incurred through special programming costs.

- *Williams v. E.I. du Pont de Nemours & Co.,* 119 F.R.D. 648, 650 (W.D. Ky. 1987). E.I. du Pont was allowed to discover the EEOC database, code books and a user manual coded from du Pont's paper disclosure. The EEOC was using the database to establish statistical evidence of the employer's discrimination violation. The employer was entitled to the database, after paying a "fair portion of [the] cost to create [the] database" to allow effective cross-examination of Commission's expert who created the database.

- *Fauteck v. Montgomery Ward & Co.,* 91 F.R.D. 393 (N.D. Ill. 1980). The Court required production of a computerized database contingent on the plaintiff's willingness to reimburse defendant for half the cost of creating it.

Discoverable, Did Not Pay

- *Hambarian v. C.I.R.,* 118 T.C. No. 35 (U.S. Tax Ct. Jun. 13, 2002). The defendant attorney's database containing documents turned over by the prosecutor during discovery were subject to discovery. The Court stated, "[a]s the Petitioner failed to make the requisite showing of how the disclosure of the documents selected would reveal the defense attorney's mental impressions of the case, the requested documents and computerized electronic media are not protected by the work product doctrine."

- *Hines v. Widnall*, 183 F.R.D. 596, 601 (N.D. Fla. 1998). In this racial discrimination case, the plaintiffs sought discovery of images and the word-searchable database that had been prepared by defendant for "geographically dispersed attorneys." Even though the cost to convert the paper to computer images was $250,000, the Court ordered disclosure citing the lack of work product involved and did not order the plaintiff to pay a share of the conversion cost. The Court noted that: "The defendant is the United States of America, an entity with virtually unlimited assets."

- *State ex rel. Humphrey v. Philip Morris Inc.*, 606 N.W.2d 676 (Minn. App. 2000). The Court ordered production of a litigation database under the "substantial need" test, even though it constituted attorney work product.

- *Minnesota v. Philip Morris, Inc.*, No. CX-95-2536, 1995 WL 862582, at *1 (Minn. App. Dec. 26, 1995). The Court refused to protect a client's litigation database from discovery, in part, finding that "the computerized databases include fields containing objective information."

- *Scovish v. Upjohn Co.*, No. 526520, 1995 WL 731755, at *4 (Conn. Super. Nov. 22, 1995). Though work product, the Court ruled that there was a substantial need for a litigation database and stated:

  Relying on this court's broad discretion in fashioning discovery orders, the court orders that the defendant supply the plaintiff with a copy of its bates-stamp index and accompanying database after the defendant has redacted those portions of the material which may contain the subjective thoughts, opinions, strategies, or legal theories of its attorneys. To the extent that this material is contained in a computerized format or stored on magnetic tape(s) or other like electronic storage devise(s), the defendant can supply the plaintiff, at her request, with said material in lieu of a printed hard copy.

- *State of Colorado v. Schmidt-Tiago Construction Co.*, 108 F.R.D. 731, 734-35 (D. Colo. 1985). The Court held computer printouts were prepared before a lawsuit and not in anticipation of litigation, but rather in the ordinary course of business, so there was no work product protection.

[d] Other Authorities

- Proposed FED. R. EVID. 502. On May 15, 2006, the Advisory Committee on Evidence Rules approved for publication proposed new evidence Rule 502 on work product and attorney client privilege waiver. The status of the proposed rule is available at http://www.uscourts.gov/rules/.

[3]   Attorney-Client Privilege

The attorney-client privilege protects "confidential communications by a client to an attorney made in order to obtain legal assistance" from the attorney in his capacity as a legal advisor. *Fisher v. United States*, 425 U.S. 391 (1976). The general principles of the attorney-client privilege as outlined by the court in *United States v. Evans*, 113 F.3d 1457, 1461 (7th Cir. 1997) (Citing to Professor Wigmore) are: "(1) Where legal advice of any kind is sought (2) from a professional legal advisor in his capacity as such, (3) the communications relating to that purpose, (4) made in confidence (5) by the client, (6) are at his instance permanently protected (7) from disclosure by himself or by the legal advisor, (8) except the protection be waived." *See also,* 24 Charles Alan Wright & Kenneth W. Graham, Jr., *Federal Practice & Procedure* § 5472 (1986).

The attorney-client privilege applies to electronic communications and other materials. *City of Reno v. Reno Police Protective Assoc.,* 59 P.3d 1212 (Nev. 2002). "Although e-mail communication, like any other form of communication, carries the risk of unauthorized disclosure, the prevailing view is that lawyers and clients may communicate confidential information through unencrypted e-mail with a reasonable expectation of confidentiality and privacy." *In re Asia Global Crossing, Ltd.,* 322 B.R. 247, 256 (Bankr. S.D.N.Y. 2005). E-mail and other computer files contain metadata or "hidden data" that may disclose work product, attorney client material or other confidential material. *See,* §§ § 3.7, *Metadata, Hidden, or Embedded Information* , 7.04[K][2], *Pending Rule 26(f)* and *Form 35 Amendments* (Committee Note explaining metadata privilege issues).

The attorney client privilege may be waived if found to be in furtherance of a crime or fraud or for failure to provide sufficient detail in privilege logs. *Rambus, Inc. v. Infineon Technologies AG,* 220 F.R.D. 264 (E.D. Va. 2004) (retaining and consulting a lawyer to develop a document retention policy, if done in anticipation of litigation, may invoke the crime/fraud exception to the attorney client privilege); *In re Grand Jury Investigation,* 445 F.3d 266 (3d Cir. 2006) (appellate court held that the "crime fraud" exception to the attorney client privilege applied when the client used the attorney's communication about the scope of grand jury subpoenas as the basis for deleting company e-mails*); In re Universal Serv. Fund Tel. Billing Practices Litig.,* 232 F.R.D. 669 (D. Kan. 2005) (Court found that a party had not waived its attorney client privilege under Rule 26(b)(5) by failing to list each separate e-mail in an e-mail strand in the privilege logs); *Williams v. Sprint/United Mgmt. Co.,* 230 F.R.D. 640 (D. Kan. 2005) (Court found that since the employer had failed to provide a privilege log for the electronic documents it claimed contained metadata that would reveal privileged communications, it waived any privilege).

[a]   Court Approaches to Inadvertent Disclosure

A problem associated with the production of electronic materials is the inadvertent disclosure of privileged information. A party waives the privilege, work product and/or attorney client, if the person voluntarily discloses or consents to the disclosure of any significant part of the matter or communication, or fails to take reasonable precautions against inadvertent disclosure. *Alldread v. City of Grenada*, 988 F.2d 1425, 1434 (5th Cir. 1993); *In re Lernout & Hauspie Sec. Litig.*, 2004 WL 1196189 (D. Mass. May 27, 2004) (subject matter waiver found where production of e-mail was not inadvertent but voluntary); *In re Qwest Communications Int'l., Inc.*, No. CIV.06-1070, 2006 WL 1668246 (10th Cir. Jun. 19, 2006) (Appellate Court affirmed lower court decision holding that the plaintiff waived the attorney client and work product privileges, as to third parties, by voluntarily disclosing privileged documents to government investigators even though the plaintiff and government agencies had entered into a confidentiality agreement).

The waiver problem in electronic discovery arises because of inadvertent disclosure when reviewing, generally, a large amount of data. "The inadvertent production of a privileged document is a specter that haunts every document intensive case." *Federal Deposit Ins. Co. v. Marine Midland Realty Credit Corp.*, 138 F.R.D. 479, 480 (E.D. Va. 1991). The general rule is "[a]ny voluntary disclosure by the holder of the attorney-client privilege is inconsistent with the attorney-client confidential relationship and thus waives the privilege." *Powers v. Chicago Transit Authority*, 890 F.2d 1355, 1359 (7th Cir. 1989). *See also,* § 7.4[I][3], *Nonwaiver or Claw-back Agreements.* Theft of an e-mail and subsequent disclosure does not waive the privilege. *Baptiste v. Cushman & Wakefield, Inc.*, No. CIV.03-2102, 2004 WL 330235 (S.D.N.Y. Feb. 20, 2004).

The pending Rule 26(b)(5) amendment provides for a procedural protocol for asserting a claim of the inadvertent disclosure of protected material. Though the pending rule does not suggest a substantive solution one Court has taken the approach that because of the unique characteristics of electronic information that a party does not waive privilege on the erroneous production of privileged materials if reasonable steps were taken to protect against a waiver of privilege and work product protection. *Hopson v. Mayor & City Council of Baltimore*, 232 F.R.D. 228 (D. Md. 2005).

In cases involving the adjudication of federal questions, privileges asserted in response to discovery requests are determined under federal law, not the law of the forum state. FED. R. EVID. 501; *United States v. Zolin*, 491 U.S. 554, 562, 109 S. Ct. 2619, 105 L. Ed. 2d 469 (1989). Substantively, the courts have addressed the inadvertent waiver issue by using one of three tests to determine if the privilege has been waived. These approaches include: (1) the strict liability test; (2) the client intent test; and (3) the case-specific test. 8 Charles Wright et al., *Federal Practice and Procedure* § 20.16.2 at 241 (1994).

[i]   The "Strict Liability" Approach

One line of cases holds that the inadvertent disclosure of a privileged document constitutes a waiver.

- *Ares-Serono, Inc. v. Organon Int'l., B.V.,* 160 F.R.D. 1 (D. Mass. 1994). Patent application was inadvertently disclosed. The Court applied a strict accountability rule to inadvertent disclosures and held that the privilege had been waived.

- *Underwater Storage, Inc. v. United States Rubber Co.,* 314 F. Supp. 546, 548-49 (D.D.C. 1970). The Court held that if a party's attorney inadvertently produces a document for inspection, the client is held to have waived its attorney-client privilege.

- *Christman v. Brauvin Realty Advisors, Inc.,* 185 F.R.D. 251, 257 (N.D. Ill. 1999). This case found that the attorney-client privilege was waived when a party to the lawsuit communicated with someone outside of the attorney-client relationship. Once a letter was "cc'd" or "copied to" a person outside of the attorney-client relationship, the privilege had been waived.

- *Genentech, Inc. v. U.S. Intern. Trade Com'n.,* 122 F.3d 1409 (Fed. Cir. 1997). Generally, inadvertent disclosure of a confidential communication or attorney work product to a third party, such as an adversary in litigation, constitutes a waiver of privilege as to those items.

- *Carter v. Gibbs,* 909 F.2d 1450, 1451 (Fed. Cir. 1990). Inadvertent disclosure of work product or attorney client information waives the privilege.

- *In re Sealed Case,* 877 F.2d 976, 980 (D.C. Cir. 1989). The Court found, "[a]lthough the attorney-client privilege is of ancient lineage and continuing importance, the confidentiality of communications covered by the privilege must be jealously guarded by the holder of the privilege lest it be waived. The courts will grant no greater protection to those who assert the privilege than their own precautions warrant. We therefore agree with those courts which have held that the privilege is lost 'even if the disclosure is inadvertent.'"

[ii]   Client Intent Test

This rule provides that an attorney's negligence cannot waive the privilege because the client, and not the attorney, is the holder of the privilege.

- *Georgetown Manor, Inc. v. Ethan Allen, Inc.,* 753 F. Supp. 936, 938 (S.D. Fla. 1991). Court ruled, "that mere inadvertent production by the attorney does not waive the client's privilege." *See also, Mendenhall v. Barber-Green Co.,* 531 F. Supp. 951, 954 (N.D. Ill. 1982).

- *Hollingsworth v. Time Warner Cable,* No. C-030663, 2004 WL 1363847 (Ohio Ct. App. Jun. 18, 2004). In this discrimination case, the Appellate Court reversed the trial court and held that the "inadvertent" waiver of one e-mail by the employer relating to the employee's termination waived the "attorney-client" privilege for all other e-mail relating to the same subject matter. *But see, In re Spring Ford Industries, Inc.,* No. CIV.02-15015, 2004 WL 1291223 (E.D. Pa. May 20, 2004) (where the Court held that the voluntary disclosure of an "educational" e-mail by the client did not waive the privilege for other e-mail relating to the same subject matter.

- *Corey v. Norman, Hanson & DeTroy,* 742 A.2d 933, 941 (Me. 1999). Even though an attorney inadvertently disclosed a memorandum marked "Confidential and Legally Privileged," the Court stated, "[a] truly inadvertent disclosure cannot and does not constitute a waiver of the attorney-client privilege."

- *Alldread v. City of Grenada,* 988 F.2d 1425, 1434-35 (5th Cir. 1993). Inadvertent disclosure of audiotapes and transcripts of executive sessions by the city containing privileged communications, did not waive the privilege.

[iii]   The Case Specific Test

The third approach takes the middle of the road, and focuses on the reasonableness of the steps taken to preserve the confidentiality of privileged documents. *In re Copper Market Antitrust Litigation,* 200 F.R.D. 213, 222 (S.D.N.Y. 2001); *Parkway Gallery Furniture, Inc. v. Kittinger/Pennsylvania House Group, Inc.,* 116 F.R.D. 46, 50-52 (M.D.N.C. 1987); *Lois Sportswear, U.S.A., Inc. v. Levi Strauss Co.,* 104 F.R.D. 103, 105-07 (S.D.N.Y. 1985); and *Hartford Fire Ins. Co. v. Garvey,* 109 F.R.D. 323, 328-32 (N.D. Cal. 1985) (waiver of work product privileged material). This approach considers inadvertent disclosure to be a form of waiver. *Briggs & Stratton Corp. v. Concrete Sales and Services, Inc.,* 176 F.R.D. 695, 699 (M.D. Ga. 1997).

In determining whether an inadvertent disclosure waives the attorney-client privilege, the court must "consider the circumstances surrounding a disclosure on a case-by-case basis." *Alldread v. City of Grenada,* 988 F.2d 1425, 1433-1434 (5th Cir. 1993). Factors to be considered include:

- The reasonableness of precautions to prevent disclosure;
- The amount of time taken to remedy the error;
- The scope of discovery;
- The extent of the disclosure; and
- The overriding issue of fairness.

Id. at 1433 (citing *Hartford Fire Ins. Co. v. Garvey,* 109 F.R.D. 323 (N.D. Cal. 1985).

- *Crossroads Sys. (Tex.), Inc. v. DOT Hill Sys. Corp.,* No. CIV.03-754, 2006 U.S. Dist. LEXIS 36181, at *6-7 (D. Tex. May 31, 2006). The Court ruled that the inadvertent disclosure of an e-mail waived the attorney client privilege because of counsel's delay (seven months) in attempting to remedy the disclosure.

- *Atronic Int'l, GmbH v. SAI Semispecialists of Am., Inc.,* 232 F.R.D. 160 (D.N.Y. 2005). Court affirmed the magistrates order that the plaintiff's inadvertent disclosure of two e-mails waived the attorney client privilege because plaintiff's precautions in preserving privilege were inexcusably careless and the privileged information went to the heart of the dispute.

- *In re Asia Global Crossing, Ltd.,* 322 B.R. 247 (Bankr. S.D.N.Y. 2005). The trustee in a bankruptcy proceeding moved to compel production of e-mail and other documents that the "insiders" alleged were protected by the attorney client and work product privilege. The Court held that further evidence was needed to determine if the "insiders" had waived any attorney-client privilege by sending communications, without any encryption, over debtor-employer's e-mail system without information as to whether debtor had policy against personal use of its e-mail system or had policy of monitoring employee e-mail. The Court further ruled that the attorney-client privilege was waived with respect to e-mail copied to counsel for debtor-corporation or that were subsequently forwarded to the corporation's consultant. Finally, the Court could not determine without further evidence as to whether e-mails were fact or opinion work product and, thus, whether insiders had waived any work-product privilege attaching to unencrypted e-mail communications.

- *Kaufman v. Sungard Invest. Sys.,* No. CIV. 05-1236, 2006 WL 1307882 (D.N.J. May 10, 2006)(unpublished). The Court affirmed the magistrate's ruling that privileged e-mails between the plaintiff and her lawyer were discoverable because the plaintiff had voluntarily waived the privilege as to certain e-mail and based on the company's notice to employees there was no reasonable expectation of privacy for e-mails sent on the company's network computer system. *But see, Curto v. Medical World Communs., Inc.,* No. CIV.03-6327, 2006 U.S. Dist. LEXIS 29387 (D.N.Y. May 15, 2006). The Court ruled that the plaintiff did not waive the attorney client privilege regarding specific e-mails residing on the employee's laptop computer.

- *United States v. Rigas,* 281 F. Supp. 2d 733 (S.D. N.Y. 2003). After the United States Attorney's office received 23 hard drives through a discovery request, they were placed on the agency's network system. A paralegal inadvertently copied privileged government information onto the same area where the hard drives were stored. These "hard drives" were subsequently disclosed to the defendants who moved the court to retain the privileged material. The court held the disclosure of the privileged material did not waive the privilege.

- *United States v. Martha Stewart,* 287 F. Supp. 2d 461 (S.D.N.Y. 2003). The Court held that the client's action in forwarding attorney client e-mail to her daughter did waive the attorney client privilege, however, it did not waive the work product privilege and, therefore, the e-mail was to remain confidential.

- *In re Spring Ford Industries, Inc.,* NO. 02-15015, 2004 WL 1291223 (E.D. Pa. May 20, 2004). The Court held that the voluntary disclosure of an "educational" e-mail by the client did not waive the privilege for other e-mail relating to the same subject matter.

- *Amgen, Inc. v. Hoechst Marion Roussel, Inc.,* 190 F.R.D. 287 (D. Mass. 2000). Defendants, after reviewing more than 200,000 document pages, during which they set aside privileged documents, inadvertently sent them to the plaintiffs. The Court looked at various factors, and held that because of the gross negligence, the privilege was waived.

- *United States v. Keystone Sanitation Co., Inc.,* 885 F. Supp. 672 (M.D. Pa. 1994). In this environmental case the defendants inadvertently disclosed e-mail messages, which contained attorney client privilege material. The Court ruled that disclosure of the e-mail messages containing attorney-client privilege material was waived.

- *S.E.C. v. Cassano,* 189 F.R.D. 83, 86 (S.D.N.Y. 1999). SEC's inadvertent disclosure of a 100-page legal strategy memo resulted in the waiver of the work product privilege. The Court reviewed several factors and found that SEC was careless in including the memo in a disclosure that contained more than 50 boxes of documents.

- *Wichita Land & Cattle Co. v. American Federal Bank, F.S.B.,* 148 F.R.D. 456 (D.D.C. 1992). The defendant reviewed forty boxes of documents, and requested that a certain number be copied. The plaintiff then informed the defendant that certain documents were privileged and inadvertently disclosed. The defendant's motion to compel was granted, and disclosure of the documents waived the attorney client and work product privilege.

- *Transamerica Computer Company, Inc. v. International Business Machines Corporation,* 573 F.2d 646, 651 (9th Cir. 1978). In reversing the lower court's decision, the Court held that the privilege was not waived when a party produced more than 17 million pages within 3 months, and inadvertently disclosed 5,800 pages of privileged material. The Court found that because of "the extraordinary circumstances of the accelerated discovery proceedings" that the privilege was not waived.

[b]   Reported Cases

- *S.E.C. v. Beacon Hill Asset Management LLC,* No. CIV.02-8855, 2004 WL 1746790, at *9 (S.D.N.Y. Aug. 3, 2004). In this securities action the SEC sought to compel production of documents withheld on the basis of the attorney-client privilege and work-product protection. The Court stated,

> [t]he spreadsheets, however, are another matter. . . . To the extent that BH relies on the attorney-client privilege to protect the spreadsheets, its index and affidavit are woefully inadequate. The index does not identify who prepared the spreadsheets or the attorney to whom each was sent. Thus, the index fails to identify an essential element of the attorney-client privilege, namely the existence of an attorney-client communication. . . . ("The standard for testing the adequacy of the privilege log is whether, as to each document, it sets forth specific facts that, if credited, would suffice to establish each element of the privilege or immunity that is claimed."). The affirmation submitted in opposition to the SEC's motion does nothing to fill this evidentiary void.

- *Quaciari v. Allstate Ins. Co.,* No. CIV.97-2028, 1997 WL 570921 (E.D.Pa. Sept. 3, 1997). The Court denied the the plaintiff's motion to compel production of an electronic claims diary holding that it was protected by the attorney-client privilege.

- *United States v. Mathias,* 96 F.3d 1577, 1583 (11th Cir. 1996). The Court held that a cordless telephone conversation with an attorney was not protected because the caller had no reasonable expectation of privacy.

- *In re Avantel, S.A.,* 343 F.3d 311 (5th Cir. 2003). The Appellate Court agreed with the district court that copying an attorney on a corporate e-mail is not, by itself, sufficient to invoke attorney client privilege.

- *Barton v. U.S. Dist. Court for Central Dist. of Cal.,* 410 F.3d 1104 (9th Cir. 2005). The Appellate Court held that a law firm's questionnaires regarding an antidepressant drug which were completed and submitted to the law firm on the internet were submitted in the course of an attorney-client relationship. The Court also ruled that the disclaimer at bottom of the law firm's online questionnaire regarding an antidepressant drug did not act as a waiver of confidentiality.

- *eSpeed, Inc. v. Chicago Board of Trade,* No. M8-85, 2002 WL 827099 (S.D.N.Y. May 1, 2002). The Court found that a series of e-mails and attachments did not contain client confidences and, therefore, were not privileged.

- *Renda Marine, Inc. v. United States,* 62 Fed.Cl. 371 (Fed.Cl. 2004). In a contractual dispute the plaintiff moved to compel production of e-mail arguing that the attorney client privilege had been waived. The Court held that redacted e-mail sent by a senior attorney to two subordinate attorneys and a paralegal in the same office were protected by the attorney-client privilege, e-mail in which the message appeared solely to concern the agency's internal management of the FOIA process was not privileged and e-mails discussing whether or not the government should consult an independent geotechnical expert in conjunction with suit were privileged.

[c]   Other Authorities

- Douglas R. Richmond, *The Attorney-client Privilege and Associated Confidentiality Concerns in The Post-Enron Era,* 110 Penn St. L. Rev. 381(Fall 2005).

- ABA Section of Litigation Electronic Discovery Standard 32, suggests in a detailed outline that parties, "[t]o ameliorate attorney-client privilege and work product concerns attendant to the production of electronic data, stipulate to a court order that would cover several areas applicable to ensure that extraction and review of privileged/protected data does not result in waiver of privilege or protection."

- Proposed FED. R. EVID. 502. On May 15, 2006, the Advisory Committee on Evidence Rules approved for publication proposed new evidence Rule 502 on work product and attorney client privilege waiver. The status of the proposed rule is available at http://www.uscourts.gov/rules/.

[4]   Trade Secrets

[a]   Purpose

Trade secrets may consist of information, formulas, pattern, compilations, programs, devices, techniques or processes which when used in one's business gives the owner an economic advantage over its competitor because it s not known or others do not use it. *Restatement of Torts,* § 757, comment (b); *Burten v. Milton Bradley Co.,* 763 F.2d 461, 463 (1st Cir. 1985). Its economic value depends on making reasonable efforts to keep it secret.

The two most prevalent trade secrets are customer lists and special knowledge or information that relates to business or manufacturing operations. Due to their nature, trade secrets such as customer lists, are often stored on computers. The protections afforded trade secrets are more important as business has evolved into a service based and information oriented economy. The growth of the computer and communications industries increase the risk of a mobile work force misappropriating trade secrets as they move to competitors.

"Trade secret law, unlike copyright and patent law, is governed exclusively by state law." Mary Brandt Jensen, *Softright: A Legislative Solution to The Problem of Users' and Producers' Rights in Computer Software,* 44 La L Rev 1413, 1426 (May 1984). "The states have taken two basic approaches to the law of trade secrets. Approximately forty states have adopted versions of the Uniform Trade Secrets Act ('UTSA'), which was first proposed in 1979. Another ten states, including New York, New Jersey and Pennsylvania, have not adopted the UTSA and continue to rely upon common law principles . . ." Steven J. Fram and Joseph A. Martin, *Trade Secret Litigation,* 798 PLI/Pat 655, 662-663 (2004); Jager, *Trade Secrets Law* (2001); R. Milgrim, *Milgrim on Trade Secrets* (2001).

Though dependent on state law it is generally acknowledged that "[f]or a trade secret to be afforded protection by the courts, the owner must make 'reasonable efforts to maintain its secrecy.'" *Catalyst & Chemical Services, Inc. v. Global Ground Support,* 350 F. Supp.2d 1, 8 (D.D.C. 2004). "Courts consider several factors in examining [whether reasonable efforts have been made], including: 1) the existence or absence of a CDA, 2) the nature and extent of precautions taken, 3) the circumstances under which the information was disclosed and 4) the degree to which the information has been placed in the public domain or rendered readily ascertainable." *TouchPoint Solutions, Inc. v. Eastman Kodak Co.,* 345 F. Supp.2d 23, 29 (D. Mass. 2004).

Trade secrets are usually commingled with other business information and present problems during electronic discovery to protect trade secrets from disclosure. However, there is no absolute privilege for trade secrets or confidential information in litigation. *Federal Open Market Comm. v. Merrill,* 443 U.S. 340, 362 (1979). Problems relating to trade secrets are often addressed through an appropriate confidentiality agreement and/or protective order. Therefore, if you reach the discovery stage of the litigation, a protective order is essential.

The Federal Rules of Civil Procedure specifically provide that: "for good cause shown . . . the court . . . may make any order which justice requires to protect a party or person from annoyance, embarrassment, oppression, or undue burden . . . including . . . that a trade secret . . . not be revealed or be revealed only in a designated way." The courts have discretion in how to fashion a protective order limiting access to trade secrets. Such limitations may include disclosure to only counsel or only counsel and parties, imposition of protocols to protect trade secrets stored on computer equipment, or may deny access to computer equipment all together.

[b]   Reported Cases

- *Medtronic v. Michelson*, No. CIV.01-2373, 2003 WL 21212601 (W.D. Tenn. May 13, 2003). The Court entered a protective order and set forth a detailed discovery protocol to search and segregate privileged data pursuant to the discovery order. The Court also imposed the protective order regarding confidentiality on the vendors.

- *Strasser v. Yalamanchi*, 669 So. 2d 1144-1145 (D.C. App. Fla. 1996). The defendant objected to the inspection of his computer system by the plaintiff alleging that it would be a "wholesale intrusion into all of its proprietary business files and statutorily protected patient information." The Court remanded and instructed the lower court that the plaintiff would have to establish that there was reasonable likelihood of retrieving purged electronic data and, if so, that an appropriate protocol be set up to protect the proprietary data.

- *Dodge, Warren & Peters Ins. Servs. v. Riley,* 105 Cal. App. 4th 1414, 130 Cal. Rptr. 2d 385 (2003). After the plaintiff alleged misappropriation of trade secrets, unfair business practices, breach of fiduciary duty and breach of contract, they filed an ex parte application seeking to "freeze" defendants' electronically stored data. The Appellate Court affirmed the trial court's decision to issue a preliminary injunction against defendants, requiring preservation of electronic evidence and ordering them to allow a court-appointed expert to copy the data, recover lost or deleted files, and perform automated searches of the evidence under guidelines agreed to by the parties or established by the court.

[c]   Other Authorities (reserved)

[I]   Protective Orders - Rule 26(c)

[1]   Rule 26(c)

(c) Protective Orders. Upon motion by a party or by the person from whom discovery is sought, accompanied by a certification that the movant has in good faith conferred or attempted to confer with other affected parties in an effort to resolve the dispute without court action, and for good cause shown, the court in which the action is pending or alternatively, on matters relating to a deposition, the court in the district where the deposition is to be taken may make any order which justice requires to protect a party or person from annoyance, embarrassment, oppression, or undue burden or expense, including one or more of the following:

(1) that the disclosure or discovery not be had;

(2) that the disclosure or discovery may be had only on specified terms and conditions, including a designation of the time or place;

(3) that the discovery may be had only by a method of discovery other than that selected by the party seeking discovery;

(4) that certain matters not be inquired into, or that the scope of the disclosure or discovery be limited to certain matters;

(5) that discovery be conducted with no one present except persons designated by the court;

(6) that a deposition, after being sealed, be opened only by order of the court;

(7) that a trade secret or other confidential research, development, or commercial information not be revealed or be revealed only in a designated way; and

(8) that the parties simultaneously file specified documents or information enclosed in sealed envelopes to be opened as directed by the court.

[2]   Purpose

Upon a motion by a person responding to a discovery request, and for good cause shown, the court "may make any order which *justice requires* to protect a party or person from *annoyance, embarrassment, oppression, undue burden or expense.*" (emphasis added). FED. R. CIV. P. 26(c).

Protective orders provide a safeguard or protection for parties and other persons in light of the broad reach of discovery. FED. R. CIV. P. 26(c), Advisory comm. notes (1970); FED. R. CIV. P. 34, Advisory comm. notes (1970); *United States v. CBS, Inc.*, 666 F.2d 364, 368-369 (9th Cir. 1982). The court in *G-I Holdings, Inc. v. Baron & Budd*, 199 F.R.D. 529, 532, 533 (S.D.N.Y. 2001) stated:

> [A] party seeking the issuance of a protective order relating to discovery must show good cause that such an order is needed to protect it from annoyance, embarrassment, oppression, or undue burden or expense. Where a party seeks a protective order on the grounds that the information sought is protected by the attorney-client privilege, that party has the burden of establishing the essential elements of the privilege. In determining whether to issue a protective order, and the form any such order should take, the court must "compare the potential hardship to the party against whom discovery is sought, if discovery is granted, with that to the party seeking discovery if it is denied." (citations omitted).

Protective orders are often sought in electronic discovery cases on the basis that retrieval of computer data is unreasonably burdensome or costly and to protect privacy, trade secrets, confidentiality and other privileges. These orders limit the use and dissemination of disclosed materials and generally require that the materials be destroyed at the end of litigation. Some orders provide that the information can only be viewed by the opposing party's attorney, staff and experts and precludes access of the material to in-house counsel and the opposing party.

In addition, the Court has the authority to grant protective orders limiting discovery for being overbroad or not relevant and directing the party seeking discovery to pay some portion of the cost involved. *See also, § 7.4[F], Relevancy and Overbroad Concerns - Rule 26(b)(1), § 7.4[G][4], Objection on the Ground of Undue Burden or Expense*, and § 7.4[G][6], *Cost Allocation.*

[3]   Nonwaiver - Clawback and Quick-Peek Agreements

To limit the cost of reviewing the significant volumes of electronic information and try to prevent the waiver of inadvertent disclosure of privileged information parties have entered into nonwaiver agreements commonly termed "clawback" or "quick-peek."

In a clawback arrangement, both parties to a dispute agree in writing that inadvertent production of privileged materials will not automatically constitute a waiver of privilege. If the producing party realizes the disclosure in a reasonable time, he can request the document's return, or "claw it back," and the other party must comply. The requesting party is presumptively barred from using the privileged document to further his client's case.

Instead of authorizing a less thorough review, a quick-peek agreement altogether eliminates the need for an initial privilege review. In this type of arrangement, the requesting party is allowed to see his opponent's entire data set before production. The requester identifies relevant information from his opponent's mass of information. The producing party then extracts privileged information from the now smaller set and turns over his responsive documents and a privilege log. As in a clawback agreement, a quick-peek agreement includes a provision stipulating that production of privileged documents does not waive any privileges.

Laura Catherine Daniel, *The Dubious Origins and Dangers of Clawback and Quick-Peek Agreements: An Argument Against Their Codification in the Federal Rules of Civil Procedure,* 47 Wm. & Mary L. Rev. 663, 667 (Nov. 2005).

The Courts have acknowledged the use of this type of nonwaiver agreements. *Zubulake v. UBS Warburg LLC,* 216 F.R.D. 280, 290 (S.D.N.Y. 2003) ("[w]hen reviewing electronic data, that review may range from reading every word of every document to conducting a series of targeted key word searches. Indeed, many parties to document-intensive litigation enter into so-called 'claw-back' agreements that allow the parties to forego privilege review altogether in favor of an agreement to return inadvertently produced privileged documents."). *Medtronic v. Michelson,* 56 Fed. R. Serv. 3d 1159 (W.D. Tenn. 2003) (nonwaiver protective order entered by the Court in electronic discovery case); *In re Bridgestone/Firestone, Inc.,* 129 F. Supp. 2d 1207, 1219 (S.D. Ind. 2001) (Case Management Order dated Jan. 30, 2001, allowing for nonwaiver agreement); *Cardiac Pacemakers, Inc. v. St. Jude Medical, Inc.,* No. IP96-1718, 2001 WL 699850, at *3 (S.D. Ind. 2001) (upholding the protective order the Court noted, "[t]he protective order was the product of negotiations among able counsel who deliberately chose to modify the otherwise applicable law concerning inadvertent disclosure of privileged documents.").

These agreements, however, may not be upheld by the courts. *See, In re Chrysler Motors Corp. Overnight Evaluation Program Litig.,* 860 F.2d 844, 846–47 (8th Cir. 1988); *Khandji v. Keystone Resorts Mgmt., Inc.,* 140 F.R.D. 697, 700 (D. Colo. 1992); *Chubb Integrated Sys. v. Nat'l. Bank,* 103 F.R.D. 52, 67–68 (D.D.C. 1984); *Ciba-Geigy Corp. v. Sandoz, Ltd.,* 916 F. Supp. 404 (D.N.J. 1995) (production of documents from litigation database without first conducting privilege review constituted inexcusable neglect and waived attorney-client privilege even though an inadvertent disclosure clause was contained in protective order).

Other issues in entering into these types of agreements are the status of privileged materials that are subsequently disclosed to third parties and the ethical implications of revealing attorney client confidences. *See*, § 1.05, *Ethical Obligations*.

One remedy may be to complete the traditional privilege review but have the Court issue an order that an inadvertent disclosure will not affect a waiver of privilege. In *In re Bridgestone/Firestone, Inc., ATX, ATX II, & Wilderness Tires Prods. Liab. Litig.*, 129 F. Supp. 2d 1207 (D. Ind. 2001) the Court entered the following privilege waiver provision:

> In the event that a privileged document is inadvertently produced by any party to this proceeding, the party may request that the document be returned. In the event that such a request is made, all parties to the litigation and their counsel shall promptly return all copies of the document in their possession, custody, or control to the producing party and shall not retain or make any [copies]. Such inadvertent disclosure of a privileged document shall not be deemed a waiver with respect to that document or other documents involving similar subject matter.

In this situation the party does not voluntarily give up the attorney-client privilege to the documents and inadvertent disclosure is protected.

[4]   Reported Cases

* *Westlake Vinyls, Inc. v. Goodrich Corp.*, No. CIV.03-00240, 2005 U.S. Dist. LEXIS 16339 (D. Ky. Aug. 8, 2005). The Court denied a third party's motion to compel disclosure of privileged documents since the plaintiff had taken reasonable steps to protect the privileged documents and that the third party had acknowledged that a tacit clawback agreement was in place.

* *J.C. Associates v. Fidelity & Guar. Ins. Co.*, No. CIV.01-2437, 2005 WL 1570140, at *2 (D.D.C. Jul. 1, 2005). The Court stated, "[t]he solution that has emerged within certain segments of the bar is the creative use of protective orders, whereby the parties agree that disclosure of the documents pursuant to the order is not and cannot be construed as a waiver of any privilege. Under this regimen, the defendant is relieved of any obligation to review the files prior to production and its doing so cannot be deemed a waiver of any privilege that could be claimed. Thus, the first question presented is whether the defendant will agree to this procedure." The Court ordered the defendant to advise the Court whether it was "willing to surrender the 428 files to the plaintiff pursuant to a protective order in which it would be agreed that the surrender of the files to [the] plaintiff is not a waiver of either the attorney-client or work-product privileges?"

- *Murphy Oil USA, Inc. v. Fluor Daniel, Inc.,* 52 Fed.R.Serv.3d 168 (E.D.La. 2002). The Court discussed two alternative nonwaiver protocols regarding e-mails containing privileged data.

- *Jicarilla Apache Nation v. United States,* 60 Fed. Cl. 413, 414 (Fed. Cl. 2004). Pursuant to Rule 16 and Rule 26(c) the Court for "good cause" set forth a detailed Confidentiality Agreement and Protective Order to "facilitate efficient discovery and authorize production of confidential and proprietary materials while protecting them from disclosure . . ." The Order applied to electronic and printed evidence.

- *Medtronic v. Michelson,* No. CIV.01-2373, 2003 WL 21212601 (W.D. Tenn. May 13, 2003). The Court entered a protective order for the nonwaiver of privileged electronic information produced pursuant to the discovery order. The Court imposed the protective order regarding confidentiality on the vendors also.

- *Holland v. GMAC Mortgage Corp.,* No. 03-2666-CM, 2004 WL 1534179, at *1 (D. Kan. Jun. 30, 2004). The Court granted a stipulated request to keep certain documents relating to trade secrets confidential, but refused to grant a protective order shielding "computer records or other confidential computer record" because "the mere fact that a document is a computer record or an electronic document does not warrant protection from disclosure."

- *Multitechnology Services, L.P. v. Verizon Southwest f/k/a GTE Southwest Inc.,* No. CIV.02-70, 22004 WL 1553480, at *1 (N.D. Tex. 2004). "Complaints of undue burden and expense [regarding electronic discovery] are properly addressed by motion for protective order under Federal Rule of Civil Procedure 26(c), including an order conditioning discovery on the requesting party's payment of the costs of discovery."

- *Rowe Entertainment, Inc. v. William Morris Agency, Inc.,* 205 F.R.D. 421, 429 (S.D.N.Y. 2002), *aff'd,* 2002 WL 975713 (S.D.N.Y. May 9, 2002). "To the extent that the corporate defendants' own privacy interests are at issue, they are adequately protected by the confidentiality order in this case. . . . Thus, there is no justification for a blanket order precluding discovery of the defendants' e-mail on the ground that such discovery is unlikely to provide relevant information or will invade the privacy of non-parties."

- *Bills v. Kennecott Corp.,* 108 F.R.D. 459, 462 (D.C. Utah 1985). A protective order under FED. R. CIV. P. 26(c) is available "for undue expense or burden in order to shift the financial burden to the requesting party or to limit discovery."

- *Playboy Enterprises, Inc. v. Welles,* 60 F. Supp. 2d 1050, 1055 (S.D. Cal. 1999). Court ordered the defendants to produce its computer files to a computer specialist appointed by the court. It issued a protective order to preserve the defendant's attorney-client privilege and privacy concerns. The Court stated: "To the extent the computer specialist has direct or indirect access to information protected by the attorney-client privilege, such 'disclosure' will not result in a waiver of the attorney-client privilege. Plaintiff herein, by requesting this discovery, is barred from asserting in this litigation that any such disclosure to the Court designated expert constitutes any waiver by Defendant of any attorney-client privilege."

• *United States v. Sungard Data Systems,* 173 F. Supp. 2d 20 (D.D.C. 2001). The Court pursuant to Rule 26(c) set forth specific confidentiality requirements, including a method for designating confidential electronic documents and to whom the documents could be disclosed.

• *Dynamic Microprocessor Associates v. EKD Computer Sales*, 919 F. Supp. 101, 106 (E.D.N.Y. 1996). "The source code constitutes a trade secret . . . As such, the source codes are clearly subject to the terms and conditions of a protective order issued pursuant to Rule 26(c), FED. R. CIV. P. . . . The conditions under which discovery may take place and the protective conditions imposed depend on the facts of the particular case." (citations omitted).

[5]   Other Authorities

• MANUAL FOR COMPLEX LITIGATION (FOURTH) § 11.431. Notwithstanding a nonwaiver order or similar agreement, confidential document disclosure in earlier litigation may waive the attorney-client privilege or work product protection for the same documents in subsequent litigation.

• The Sedona Conference, *The Sedona Principles: Best Practices Recommendations & Principles for Addressing Electronic Document Production*, 37 (2004) available at http://www.thesedonaconference.org/content/miscFiles/publications_html?grp=wgs110 (last visited on July 26, 2006). "Despite the apparent advantage of reducing the costs of pre-production reviews for privilege and confidentiality (and maybe even responsiveness), there are a host of risks and problems that make 'clawback' productions impracticable and, for most cases, ill-advised."

• Whitney Adams & Mark Touchy, *Clawback Agreements Help Protect Privileged Documents,* 7 N.T.L.J. 5 (Feb. 2004).

• Mark D. Robins, *Computers and the Discovery of Evidence-A New Dimension to Civil Procedure,* 17 J. Marshall J. Computer & Info. L. 411 (Winter 1999).

• The Sedona Guidelines: *Best Practices Addressing Protective Orders, Confidentiality and Public Access in Civil Cases* (Revised April 2005).

[J]   Expedited Discovery and Supplementation - Rule 26(d) and (e)

[1]   Rule 26(d) and (e)

FED. R. CIV. P. 26(d) and (e) provides:

(d) Timing and Sequence of Discovery. Except in categories of proceedings exempted from initial disclosure under Rule 26(a)(1)(E), or when authorized under these rules or by order or agreement of the parties, a party may not seek discovery from any source before the parties have conferred as required by Rule 26(f). Unless the court upon motion, for the convenience of parties and witnesses and in the interests of justice, orders otherwise, methods of discovery may be used in any sequence, and the fact that a party is conducting discovery, whether by deposition or otherwise, does not operate to delay any other party's discovery.

(e) Supplementation of Disclosures and Responses. A party who has made a disclosure under subdivision (a) or responded to a request for discovery with a disclosure or response is under a duty to supplement or correct the disclosure or response to include information thereafter acquired if ordered by the court or in the following circumstances:

(1) A party is under a duty to supplement at appropriate intervals its disclosures under subdivision (a) if the party learns that in some material respect the information disclosed is incomplete or incorrect and if the additional or corrective information has not otherwise been made known to the other parties during the discovery process or in writing. With respect to testimony of an expert from whom a report is required under subdivision (a)(2)(B) the duty extends both to information contained in the report and to information provided through a deposition of the expert, and any additions or other changes to this information shall be disclosed by the time the party's disclosures under Rule 26(a)(3) are due. (2) A party is under a duty seasonally to amend a prior response to an interrogatory, request for production, or request for admission if the party learns that the response is in some material respect incomplete or incorrect and if the additional or corrective information has not otherwise been made known to the other parties during the discovery process or in writing.

[2]   Purpose

Rule 26(d)

Rule 26(d) proscribes "discovery from any source before the parties have conferred as required by Rule 26(f)." Under Rule 26(d) a party may not "serve" discovery nor "seek" discovery from any source until after the Rule 26(f) conference. The drafters of the rule believed that "it is desirable that the parties' proposals regarding discovery be developed through a process where they meet in person, informally explore the nature and basis of the issues, and discuss how discovery can be conducted most efficiently and economically." *See,*

FED.R.CIV.P. 26(f) 1993 advisory committee note. The goal of the rule is to facilitate orderly, efficient, and economical discovery by creating an incentive to meet and devise a joint discovery plan at an early stage of the litigation.

Specific standards for evaluating expedited discovery motions are not set out in the Federal Rules of Civil Procedure. However, the Rules provide the court with authority to direct expedited discovery in limited circumstances. Rule 26(b) provides the court with broad discretion in structuring discovery, stating "for good cause, the court may order discovery of any matter relevant to the subject matter involved in the action." FED. R. CIV. P. 26(b)(1). In commenting upon Rule 26(d) the Court in *Physician Interactive v. Lathian Systems, Inc.,* No. CIV.03-1193, 2003 WL 23018270, at *4 (E.D. Va. Dec. 5, 2003) stated that the Court has:

> wide latitude in controlling discovery and ⋯ its rulings will not be overturned absent a showing of clear abuse of discretion. (citations omitted) Specifically, Federal Rules of Civil Procedure 26(d), 30(a), 33(b), 34(b) and 36 give this Court the power to adjust the timing requirements imposed under Rule 26(d) and if warranted, to expedite the time for responding to the discovery sought. Courts have held that expedited discovery is warranted when some unusual circumstances or conditions exist that would likely prejudice the party if they were required to wait the normal time.

In determining the appropriateness of expedited discovery Courts have generally employed one of two standards. The first is very similar to a preliminary injunction analysis and looks closely at the merits of the requests. The second is the reasonableness standard, which requires the party to prove that the requests are reasonable under the circumstances. *Better Packages, Inc. v. Zheng,* No. CIV.05-4477, 2006 U.S. Dist. LEXIS 30119 (D.N.J. May 17, 2006); *Entertainment Technology Corp. v. Walt Disney Imagineering,* No. CIV.03-3546, 2003 WL 22519440 (E.D.Pa. Oct. 2, 2003); and *see also,* § 7.14, *Injunctions.*

Consideration should be given toward requesting expedited discovery to ensure preservation of electronic evidence. Generally, a party may not seek discovery until after the Rule 26(f) conference, which is held twenty-one days before the scheduling conference or twenty-one days before an order is due pursuant to Rule 16(b). Rule 16(b) orders are due within 120 days of the filing of the complaint. Therefore, discovery generally does not commence until approximately three months after the filing of the complaint. Depending on the circumstances of a case, electronic information may be destroyed during this period of time from overwriting of backup tapes, etc.

A motion for expedited discovery should include particular facts supporting the grounds for the motion. For example, if there is evidence that a party has not suspended its document retention policy and that backup tapes are being overwritten the court would view favorably a request for expedited discovery. The motion should also reserve the right to conduct ordinary discovery during the litigation so as not to waive or limit your rights.

In addition to expedited discovery you may want to consider obtaining a preservation order and/or seeking an ex parte seizure order. *See,* § 7.3[E], *Discovery and Preservation Orders - Rule 16(c)* and § 7.14, *Injunctions.*

Rule 26(e)

A party has a duty to supplement or correct a Rule 26(a) disclosure to include information thereafter acquired if "the party learns that in some material respect the information disclosed is incomplete or incorrect and if the additional or corrective information has not otherwise been made known to the other parties during the discovery process or in writing." FED.R.CIV.P. 26(e).

A party is under "a duty seasonably" to amend prior discovery responses. FED.R.CIV.P. 26(e)(2). However, the rule does not define "seasonably." The Advisory Committee Notes explain that "[s]upplementations need not be made as each new item of information is learned but should be made at appropriate intervals during the discovery period, and with special promptness as the trial date approaches." FED.R.CIV.P. 26(e) advisory committee notes, 1993 amendment.

Rule 37(c)(1) provides sanctions if a party fails to comply with Rule 26(a) and Rule 26(e) by providing that a party who "without substantial justification fails to disclose information required by Rule 26(a) or 26(e)(1) . . . is not, unless such failure is harmless, permitted to use as evidence at a trial, at a hearing, or on a motion any witness or information not so disclosed." FED.R.CIV.P. 37(c)(1). "In addition to or in lieu of this sanction, the court, on motion and after affording an opportunity to be heard, may impose other appropriate sanctions. In addition to requiring payment of reasonable expenses, including and may include informing the jury of the failure to make the disclosure." *In re Telxon Corp. Securities Litigation,* No. CIV.98-2876, 2004 WL 3192729, at *20 (N.D. Ohio Jul. 16, 2004).

In *Allen v. Bake-Line Products, Inc.,* No. CIV.98-1119, 2001 WL 883693, at *1 (N.D.Ill. Aug. 6, 2001) the Court noted the difference between regular discovery and Rule 26(e):

> It is important in this context to distinguish between "discovery" and "investigation." Discovery is the process whereby one party learns the evidentiary basis of the opposing party's case and involves an exchange of information. That is the process that ceases at the date discovery is ordered closed. We know of no rule that requires a party to cease the investigation of its own case at the close of discovery. Indeed, Rule 26(e)(2) of the Federal Rules of Civil Procedure is designed, at least in part, to deal with the problem of later-discovered evidence and requires that a party be under a continuing duty to supplement or correct previous responses to certain discovery requests, including a request for production, whenever the party learns that the [previous] response is in some material way incomplete or incorrect.

[3]   **Reported Cases**

- *Physician Interactive v. Lathian Systems, Inc.,* No. CIV.03-1193, 2003 WL 23018270, at *11 (E.D. Va. Dec. 5, 2003). In this trade secret case the plaintiff alleged that the defendants secretly hacked the plaintiff's website and stole their confidential customer lists and computer software code. The Court granted the plaintiff's request for expedited discovery and an injunction "to enter the [the] Defendants computer server, Mr. Martinez's work and home desktop and notebook computers, and any sites where the computers used in the alleged attacks are located, in order to obtain a 'mirror image' of the computer equipment containing electronic data relating to Defendants' alleged attacks on Plaintiff's server. This discovery is limited only to information on Defendants' computers related to the alleged attacks, and must be done with the assistance of a computer forensic expert."

- *Antioch Co. v. Scrapbook Borders, Inc.,* 210 F.R.D. 645 (D. Minn. 2002). In this infringement case, the plaintiff's motion to expedite discovery and for appointment of a forensic expert were granted to ensure preservation and examination of records on the computer hard drives.

- *In re Telxon Corp. Securities Litigation,* No. CIV.98-2876, 2004 WL 3192729, at *20 (N.D. Ohio Jul. 16, 2004). In this securities action, the magistrate judge recommended that the motion for sanctions be granted and that default judgment be entered for the plaintiff primarily for discovery abuses involved with the disclosure of databases. The Court discussed the continuing obligation the defendant was under pursuant to Rule 26(e).

[K]   **Meet and Confer - Rule 26(f)**

[1]   **Rule 26(f)**

FED. R. CIV. P. 26(f) provides:

(f) Conference of Parties; Planning for Discovery. Except in categories of proceedings exempted from initial disclosure under Rule 26(a)(1)(E) or when otherwise ordered, the parties must, as soon as practicable and in any event at least 21 days before a scheduling conference is held or a scheduling order is due under Rule 16(b), confer to consider the nature and basis of their claims and defenses and the possibilities for a prompt settlement or resolution of the case, to make or arrange for the disclosures required by Rule 26(a)(1), and to develop a proposed discovery plan that indicates the parties' views and proposals concerning:

(1) what changes should be made in the timing, form, or requirement for disclosures under Rule 26(a), including a statement as to when disclosures under Rule 26(a)(1) were made or will be made:

(2) the subjects on which discovery may be needed, when discovery should be completed, and whether discovery should be conducted in phases or be limited to or focused upon particular issues;

(3) what changes should be made in the limitations on discovery imposed under these rules or by local rule, and what other limitations should be imposed; and

(4) any other orders that should be entered by the court under Rule 26(c) or under Rule 16(b) and (c).

[2]   Pending Rule 26(f) and Form 35 Amendments

(f) Conference of Parties; Planning for Discovery.

Except in categories of proceedings exempted from initial disclosure under Rule 26(a)(1)(E) or when otherwise ordered, the parties must, as soon as practicable and in any event at least 21 days before a scheduling conference is held or a scheduling order is due under Rule 16(b), confer to consider the nature and basis of their claims and defenses and the possibilities for a prompt settlement or resolution of the case, to make or arrange for the disclosures required by Rule 26(a)(1), to discuss any issues relating to preserving discoverable information, and to develop a proposed discovery plan that indicates the parties' views and proposals concerning: (emphasis added)

(1) what changes should be made in the timing, form, or requirement for disclosures under Rule 26(a), including a statement as to when disclosures under Rule 26(a)(1) were made or will be made;

(2) the subjects on which discovery may be needed, when discovery should be completed, and whether discovery should be conducted in phases or be limited to or focused upon particular issues;

(3) any issues relating to disclosure or discovery of electronically stored information, including the form or forms in which it should be produced; (emphasis added)

(4) any issues relating to claims of privilege or of protection as trial-preparation material, including — if the parties agree on a procedure to assert such claims after production — whether to ask the court to include their agreement in an order; (emphasis added)

(5) what changes should be made in the limitations on discovery imposed under these rules or by local rule, and what other limitations should be imposed; and

(6) any other orders that should be entered by the court under Rule 26(c) or under Rule 16(b) and (c) (emphasis added).

* * * * *

Form 35. Report of Parties' Planning Meeting

* * * * *

3. Discovery Plan. The parties jointly propose to the court the following discovery plan: [Use separate paragraphs or subparagraphs as necessary if parties disagree.]

Discovery will be needed on the following subjects: _____ (brief description of subjects on which discovery will be needed)_____

Disclosure or discovery of electronically stored information should be handled as follows:_____(brief description of parties' proposals) (Emphasis added)

The parties have agreed to an order regarding claims of privilege or protection as trial-preparation material asserted after production, as follows: (brief description of provisions of proposed order) (emphasis added)

All discovery commenced in time to be completed by _____(date)_____.
[Discovery on _____(issue for early discovery)_____to be completed by _____(date)_____.]

Committee Note

Subdivision (f). Rule 26(f) is amended to direct the parties to discuss discovery of electronically stored information during their discovery-planning conference. The rule focuses on "issues relating to disclosure or discovery of electronically stored information"; the discussion is not required in cases not involving electronic discovery, and the amendment imposes no additional requirements in those cases. When the parties do anticipate disclosure or discovery of electronically stored information, discussion at the outset may avoid later difficulties or ease their resolution.

When a case involves discovery of electronically stored information, the issues to be addressed during the Rule 26(f) conference depend on the nature and extent of the contemplated discovery and of the parties' information systems. It may be important for the parties to discuss those systems, and accordingly, important for counsel to become familiar with those systems before the conference. With that information, the parties can develop a discovery plan that takes into account the capabilities of their computer systems. In appropriate cases identification of, and early discovery from, individuals with special knowledge of a party's computer systems may be helpful.

The particular issues regarding electronically stored information that deserve attention during the discovery planning stage depend on the specifics of the given case. *See,* MANUAL FOR COMPLEX LITIGATION (FOURTH) § 40.25(2) (listing topics for discussion in a proposed order regarding meet-and-confer sessions). For example, the parties may specify the topics for such discovery and the time period for which discovery will be sought. They may identify the various sources of such information within a party's control that should be searched for electronically stored information. They may discuss whether the information is reasonably accessible to the party that has it, including the burden or cost of retrieving and reviewing the information. *See,* Rule 26(b)(2)(B). Rule 26(f)(3) explicitly directs the parties to discuss the form or forms in which electronically stored information might be produced. The parties may be able to reach agreement on the forms of production, making discovery more efficient. Rule 34(b) is amended to permit a requesting party to specify the form or forms in which it wants electronically stored information produced. If the requesting party does not specify a form, Rule 34(b) directs the responding party to state the forms it intends to use in the production. Early discussion of the forms of production may facilitate the application of Rule 34(b) by allowing the parties to determine what forms of production will meet both parties' needs. Early identification of disputes over the forms of production may help avoid the expense and delay of searches or productions using inappropriate forms.

Rule 26(f) is also amended to direct the parties to discuss any issues regarding preservation of discoverable information during their conference as they develop a discovery plan. This provision applies to all sorts of discoverable information, but can be particularly important with regard to electronically stored information. The volume and dynamic nature of electronically stored information may complicate preservation obligations. The ordinary operation of computers involves both the automatic creation and the automatic deletion or overwriting of certain information. Failure to address preservation issues early in the litigation increases uncertainty and raises a risk of disputes.

The parties' discussion should pay particular attention to the balance between the competing needs to preserve relevant evidence and to continue routine operations critical to ongoing activities. Complete or broad cessation of a party's routine computer operations could paralyze the party's activities. *Cf.* MANUAL FOR COMPLEX LITIGATION (FOURTH) § 11.422 ("A blanket preservation order may be prohibitively expensive and unduly burdensome for parties dependent on computer systems for their day-to-day operations.") The parties should take account of these considerations in their discussions, with the goal of agreeing on reasonable preservation steps.

The requirement that the parties discuss preservation does not imply that courts should routinely enter preservation orders. A preservation order entered over objections should be narrowly tailored. Ex parte preservation orders should issue only in exceptional circumstances.

Rule 26(f) is also amended to provide that the parties should discuss any issues relating to assertions of privilege or of protection as trial preparation materials, including whether the parties can facilitate discovery by agreeing on procedures for asserting claims of privilege or protection after production and whether to ask the court to enter an order that includes any agreement the parties reach. The Committee has repeatedly been advised about the discovery difficulties that can result from efforts to guard against waiver of privilege and work-product protection. Frequently parties find it necessary to spend large amounts of time reviewing materials requested through discovery to avoid waiving privilege. These efforts are necessary because materials subject to a claim of privilege or protection are often difficult to identify. A failure to withhold even one such item may result in an argument that there has been a waiver of privilege as to all other privileged materials on that subject matter. Efforts to avoid the risk of waiver can impose substantial costs on the party producing the material and the time required for the privilege review can substantially delay access for the party seeking discovery.

These problems often become more acute when discovery of electronically stored information is sought. The volume of such data, and the informality that attends use of e-mail and some other types of electronically stored information, may make privilege determinations more difficult, and privilege review correspondingly more expensive and time consuming. Other aspects of electronically stored information pose particular difficulties for privilege review. For example, production may be sought of information automatically included in electronic files but not apparent to the creator or to readers. Computer programs may retain draft language, editorial comments, and other deleted matter (sometimes referred to as "embedded data" or "embedded edits") in an electronic file but not make them apparent to the reader. Information describing the history, tracking, or management of an electronic file (sometimes called "metadata") is usually not apparent to the reader viewing a hard copy or a screen image. Whether this information should be produced may be among the topics discussed in the Rule 26(f) conference. If it is, it may need to be reviewed to ensure that no privileged information is included, further complicating the task of privilege review.

Parties may attempt to minimize these costs and delays by agreeing to protocols that minimize the risk of waiver. They may agree that the responding party will provide certain requested materials for initial examination without waiving any privilege or protection — sometimes known as a "quick peek." The requesting party then designates the documents it wishes to have actually produced. This designation is the Rule 34 request. The responding party then responds in the usual course, screening only those documents actually requested for formal production and asserting privilege claims as provided in Rule 26(b)(5)(A). On other occasions, parties enter agreements — sometimes called "clawback agreements"— that production without intent to waive privilege or protection should not be a waiver so long as the responding party identifies the documents mistakenly produced, and that the documents should be returned under those circumstances. Other voluntary arrangements may be appropriate depending on the circumstances of each litigation. In most circumstances, a party who receives information under such an arrangement cannot assert that production of the information waived a claim of privilege or of protection as trial-preparation material.

Although these agreements may not be appropriate for all cases, in certain cases they can facilitate prompt and economical discovery by reducing delay before the discovering party obtains access to documents, and by reducing the cost and burden of review by the producing party. A case-management or other order including such agreements may further facilitate the discovery process. Form 35 is amended to include a report to the court about any agreement regarding protections against inadvertent forfeiture or waiver of privilege or protection that the parties have reached, and Rule 16(b) is amended to recognize that the court may include such an agreement in a case management or other order. If the parties agree to entry of such an order, their proposal should be included in the report to the court.

Rule 26(b)(5)(B) is added to establish a parallel procedure to assert privilege or protection as trial-preparation material after production, leaving the question of waiver to later determination by the court.

[3] Purpose

The Rule 26(f) conference is an opportunity to discuss the "claims or defenses" of a case and disclosure of electronic information with the opposing party. Rule 26(f) requires the parties confer with each other at least 21 days before the Rule 16(b) scheduling conference and file a written report of their proposed discovery plan within 14 days after their Rule 26(f) conference. Rule 26(a)(1) requires (unless they agree otherwise) that the parties make their initial disclosures to each other within 14 days after their Rule 26(f) conference.

Some district courts, through their local rules of practice, also require the parties to discuss the handling of electronic information. *Mosaid Technologies Inc. v. Samsung Electronics Co., Ltd.*, 2004 WL 2797536 (D. N.J. 2004) For example, "[t]he FED. R. CIV. P. 26(f) report filed with the court must contain the parties' views and proposals regarding . . . [w]hether any party will likely be requested to disclose or produce information from electronic or computer-based media. If so, the report must also include a variety of details on electronic discovery as specified by the rule." U.S. Dist. Ct. Ark. L. R. 26.1. *See also,* § 7.4[A][2], *Local Rules of Practice.*

Such a conference can assist the parties in disclosing their client's type of computer systems and a number of other electronic discovery issues. *See,* § 7.3[D], *Electronic Discovery Checklist - Pretrial Agenda* and § 5.3, *Electronic Data Formats.*

Pending Rule 26(f) and Form 35 Amendments

The framers of the "e-discovery" amendments sought to ensure collaborative communication about electronic discovery issues at the beginning of the case. To effectuate this goal a "Conference of Parties" is mandated by Rule 26(f); "Required Disclosures" are governed by Rule 26(a); and the "Scheduling" and "Planning" aspects of Rule 16(b) were drafted to ensure the active and timely discussion of e-discovery issues.

Pending Rule 26(f) directs the parties to discuss during a "meet and confer" conference:

- "any issues relating to preserving discoverable information, and to develop a proposed discovery plan that indicates the parties' views and proposals concerning"
- "any issues relating to disclosure or discovery of electronically stored information, including the form or forms in which it should be produced;"
- "any issues relating to claims of privilege or of protection as trial-preparation material, including — if the parties agree on a procedure to assert such claims after production — whether to ask the court to include their agreement in an order . . . "

To effectively represent your clients at this meet and confer conference it is necessary for counsel to understand and then discuss their client's respective computer systems. For an extensive checklist regarding "meet and confer" issues to discuss see § 7.03[D], *Electronic Discovery Checklist - Pretrial Agenda*.

Preservation Issues

The Committee Note suggests reviewing "MANUAL FOR COMPLEX LITIGATION (4th) § 40.25(2)" for a listing of preservation topics to consider during the "meet and confer" session. *See also,* § 7.3[E], *Discovery and Preservation Orders - Rule 16(c)*. This Manual section provides:

2. Subjects for Consideration

The parties should attempt to reach agreement on all issues regarding the preservation of documents, data, and tangible things. These issues include, but are not necessarily limited to:

(a) the extent of the preservation obligation, identifying the types of material to be preserved, the subject matter, time frame, the authors and addressees, and key words to be used in identifying responsive materials;

(b) the identification of persons responsible for carrying out preservation obligations on behalf of each party;

(c) the form and method of providing notice of the duty to preserve to persons

identified as custodians of documents, data, and tangible things;
(d) mechanisms for monitoring, certifying, or auditing custodian compliance with preservation obligations;
(e) whether preservation will require suspending or modifying any routine business processes or procedures, with special attention to document management programs and the recycling of computer data storage media;
(f) the methods to preserve any volatile but potentially discoverable material, such as voicemail, active data in databases, or electronic messages;
(g) the anticipated costs of preservation and ways to reduce or share these costs; and
(h) a mechanism to review and modify the preservation obligation as discovery proceeds, eliminating or adding particular categories of documents, data, and tangible things.

* * * * *

General Disclosure or Discovery Issues and Form of Production

Other topics the Committee Note suggests discussing include:

- The "topics for electronic discovery" and "the time period for which discovery will be sought"
- The "various sources of such information within a party's control that should be searched for electronically stored information."
- "[W]hether the information is reasonably accessible to the party that has it, including the burden or cost of retrieving and reviewing the information. *See* Rule 26(b)(2)(B)."
- "Rule 26(f)(3) explicitly directs the parties to discuss the form or forms in which electronically stored information might be produced. . . . Rule 34(b) is amended to permit a requesting party to specify the form or forms in which it wants electronically stored information produced. If the requesting party does not specify a form, Rule 34(b) directs the responding party to state the forms it intends to use in the production. . . ."
- "[T]he parties should discuss any issues relating to assertions of privilege or of protection as trial preparation materials, including whether the parties can facilitate discovery by agreeing on procedures for asserting claims of privilege or protection after production and whether to ask the court to enter an order that includes any agreement the parties reach." This would include discussion of the disclosure and waiver issues concerning metadata. Also, discussion should include whether a "quick peek" or "clawback agreement" should be entered into by the parties.

In *Hopson v. Mayor & City Council of Baltimore,* 232 F.R.D. 228, 245 (D. Md. 2005) the Court commented upon pending Rule 16 and the "meet and confer" mandate and stated, "the proposed changes to Rule 16(f) make clear, counsel have a duty to take the initiative in meeting and conferring to plan for appropriate discovery of electronically stored information at the commencement of any case in which electronic records will be sought." The Court then discussed in detail the issues the parties should discuss.

[4]   Reported Cases

*   *In re Bristol-Myers Squibb Sec. Litig.,* 205 F.R.D. 437, 443-444 (D.N.J. 2002) the Court stated,

    FED. R. CIV. P. 26(f) provides that before a Rule 16 Conference, the parties "confer . . . to develop a proposed discovery plan. . . ." In the electronic age, this meet and confer should include a discussion on whether each side possesses information in electronic form, whether they intend to produce such material, whether each other's software is compatible, whether there exists any privilege issue requiring redaction, and how to allocate costs involved with each of the foregoing . . . Although there may be room for clearer direction in existing rules and orders that explicitly address cost allocation in production of paper and electronic information, counsel should take advantage of the required Rule 26(f) meeting to discuss issues associated with electronic discovery. As the eve of electronic case filing (ECF) is upon us, in this and most other Districts, the production of electronic information should be at the forefront of any discussion of issues involving discovery and trial, including the fair and economical allocation of costs. Of course, in some instances, paper, rather than electronic, production may still be the preferable method of discovery.

*   *Thompson v. Jiffy Lube Int'l,* No. CIV.05-1203, 2006 U.S. Dist. LEXIS 27837, at *10-11 (D. Kan. May 1, 2006). The Court ordered the parties to meet and confer on alternatives, such as random sampling and reasonable methods and formats for producing electronic information.

*   *Kemper Mortg., Inc. v. Russell,* No. CIV.06-042, 2006 U.S. Dist. LEXIS 20729, at *5-7 (D. Ohio Apr. 6, 2006). "The parties shall file their report under FED. R. CIV. P. 26(f) [and] . . . are encouraged to include plans for electronic discovery in that report."

*   *United States ex rel. Smith v. Boeing Co.,* No. CIV.05-1073, 2005 U.S. Dist. LEXIS 36890, at *7 (D. Kan. Aug. 31, 2005). The Court stated "the parties have a duty under Rule 26(f) to meet and develop a discovery plan, including arrangements for electronic discovery in accordance with this court's Electronic Discovery Guidelines."

*   *In re Livent, Inc. Noteholders Sec. Litig.,* No. CIV.98-176, 2003 WL 23254 (S.D.N.Y. Jan. 2, 2003). In a securities case the defendant, who had produced 39 e-mails, opposed

the plaintiff's motion for an order compelling it to search "all computer systems, servers and other storage devices, backup tapes, and . . . individual hard drives" for documents responsive to outstanding requests. In denying the plaintiffs' motion, the judge ordered the parties to meet and confer, and if unable to reach resolution, to submit a joint letter outlining the areas of disagreement.

[5]   Other Authority

- *Joint Stipulation and Order Regarding Meet and Confer Discussions*, contributed by Ken Withers, Federal Judicial Center. Available at http://www.fjc.gov/public/home.nsf/ autoframe?openform&url_l=/public/home.nsf/inavgeneral?openpage&url_r=/public/ home.nsf/pages/196 (last visited on July 22, 2006).

[L]   Certification - Rule 26(g)

[1]   Rule 26(g)

(g) Signing of Disclosures, Discovery Requests, Responses, and Objections.

(1) Every disclosure made pursuant to subdivision (a)(1) or subdivision (a)(3) shall be signed by at least one attorney of record in the attorney's individual name, whose address shall be stated. An unrepresented party shall sign the disclosure and state the party's address. The signature of the attorney or party constitutes a certification that to the best of the signer's knowledge, information, and belief, formed after a reasonable inquiry, the disclosure is complete and correct as of the time it is made.

(2) Every discovery request, response, or objection made by a party represented by an attorney shall be signed by at least one attorney of record in the attorney's individual name, whose address shall be stated. An unrepresented party shall sign the request, response, or objection and state the party's address. The signature of the attorney or party constitutes a certification that to the best of the signer's knowledge, information, and belief, formed after a reasonable inquiry, the request, response, or objection is:

(A) consistent with these rules and warranted by existing law or a good faith argument for the extension, modification, or reversal of existing law;

(B) not interposed for any improper purpose, such as to harass or to cause unnecessary delay or needless increase in the cost of litigation; and

(C) not unreasonable or unduly burdensome or expensive, given the needs of the case, the discovery already had in the case, the amount in controversy, and the importance of the issues at stake in the litigation.

If a request, response, or objection is not signed, it shall be stricken unless it is signed promptly after the omission is called to the attention of the party making the request, response, or objection, and a party shall not be obligated to take any action with respect to it until it is signed.

(3) If without substantial justification a certification is made in violation of the rule, the court, upon motion or upon its own initiative, shall impose upon the person who made the certification, the party on whose behalf the disclosure, request, response, or objection is made, or both, an appropriate sanction, which may include an order to pay the amount of the reasonable expenses incurred because of the violation, including a reasonable attorney's fee.

[2]   Purpose

Rule 26(g)(2) requires an attorney to sign all discovery requests, responses and objections. By signing an attorney is certifying that to the "best of the signer's knowledge, information, and belief, formed after a reasonable inquiry, the request, response, or objection is: . . . (B) not interposed for any improper purpose, such as to harass or to cause unnecessary delay or needless increase in the cost of litigation. . . . (C) not unreasonable or unduly burdensome or expensive, given the needs of the case, the discovery already had in the case, the amount in controversy, and the importance of the issues at stake in the litigation." Rule 26(g)(3) provides for an "appropriate sanction, which may include an order to pay the amount of the reasonable expenses incurred because of the violation, including a reasonable attorney's fee."

The purpose of Rule 26(g) is to create "an affirmative duty to engage in pretrial discovery in a responsible manner." FED. R. CIV. P. 26(g) Advisory Committee Notes to 1983 Amendments. The attorney's signature is not a certification of the truthfulness of the client's responses. "Rather, the signature certifies that the lawyer has made a reasonable effort to assure that the client has provided all the information and documents available to him that are responsive to the discovery demand." FED. R. CIV. P. 26(g) Advisory Committee Notes to 1983 Amendments. What is reasonable is a matter for the court to decide on the totality of the circumstances. FED. R. CIV. P. 26(g) Advisory Committee Notes to 1983 Amendments. If a certification is made in violation of Rule 26(g)(3) is without "substantial justification then sanctions may be imposed."

[3] Reported Cases

- *Quinby v. WestLB AG,* No. CIV.04-7406, 2006 U.S. Dist. LEXIS 1178 (D.N.Y. Jan. 11, 2006). The Court denied the plaintiff's motion for sanctions for violating FED. R. CIV. P. 26(g)(3) based on two affidavits executed by the employer's chief information officer and an electronic evidence consultant. The plaintiff argued that the affidavits and subsequent testimony failed to reveal the extent of e-mails the employer possessed and how they were stored.

- *E*Trade Secs. LLC v. Deutsche Bank AG,* 230 F.R.D. 582 (D. Minn. 2005) *aff.* 230 F.R.D. 582 (D. Minn. 2005). The court imposed fines for the defendant's counsel's failure to provide "substantial justification" for its discovery certifications under FED. R. CIV. P. 26(g). In particular the defendant's counsel failed to make a reasonable inquiry into the existence of monthly compliance reports and broker audio recordings of phone conversations.

- *MMI Prods. v. Long,* 231 F.R.D. 215 (D. Md. 2005). The Court reversed the magistrate's proposed ruling to sanction the defendant and its counsel pursuant to FED. R. CIV. P. 26(g)(3) for failure to make reasonable inquiries into the reliability of their own expert's report.

§ 7.5 DEPOSITIONS

[A] FED. R. CIV. P. 30

Rule 30. Depositions Upon Oral Examination

(a) When Depositions May Be Taken; When Leave Required.

(1) A Party may take the testimony of any person, including a party, by deposition upon oral examination without leave of court except as provided in paragraph (2). The attendance of witnesses may be compelled by subpoena as provided in Rule 45.

* * *

(b) Notice of Examination: General Requirements; Method of Recording; Production of Documents and Things; Deposition of Organization; Deposition by Telephone.

* * *

(5) The notice to a party deponent may be accompanied by a request made in compliance with Rule 34 for the production of documents and tangible things at the taking of the deposition. The procedure of Rule 34 shall apply to the request.

(6) A party may in the party's notice and in a subpoena name as the deponent a public or private corporation or a partnership or association or governmental agency and describe with reasonable particularity the matters on which examination is requested. In that event, the organization so named shall designate one or more officers, directors, or managing agents, or other persons who consent to testify on its behalf, and may set forth, for each person designated, the matters on which the person will testify. A subpoena shall advise a non-party organization of its duty to make such a designation. The persons so designated shall testify as to matters known or reasonably available to the organization. This subdivision (b)(6) does not preclude taking a deposition by any other procedure authorized in these rules.

[B]   Purpose

Rule 30 provides that a party may generally take the testimony of any person without leave of court and may compel the attendance of witnesses by subpoena. This broad discovery rule permits a deponent to be examined regarding any matter, not privileged, which is relevant to the subject matter involved in the pending action so long as it appears reasonably calculated to lead to the discovery of admissible evidence. *See,* § 7.4[F], *Relevancy and Overbroad Concerns - Rule 26(b)(1).*

The requesting party must "describe with reasonable particularity the matters on which examination is requested."

Such description of the deposition topics triggers several duties on the part of the responding entity. First, the responding entity must designate a deponent who is knowledgeable on the subject matter identified as the area of inquiry. . . . Second, the responding entity must designate more than one deponent if multiple deponents are necessary to respond to all of the relevant areas of inquiry. . . . Third, the responding entity must prepare the deponent so that he or she can testify on matters not only within his or her personal knowledge, but also on matters reasonably known by the responding entity. . . . Fourth, if it becomes apparent during the deposition that the designated deponent is unable to respond to the relevant areas of inquiry, then the responding entity has the duty to substitute the designated deponent with a knowledgeable deponent.

United States ex rel. Fago v. M & T Mortg. Corp., 235 F.R.D. 11, 33 (D.D.C. 2006)

With nontechnical witnesses it is important to depose individuals regarding their use of storage media, devices and locations. The area of questioning should include how they individually organize and store data, the different electronic devices used within the organization and by themselves, e-mail addresses for the relevant time period, whether data is stored on home computers and the organization's directives to the employees regarding the identification and preservation of responsive data.

The multitude of possible storage medium, devices and locations, combined with the significant volume of data, can provide a significant challenge in the discovery of electronic information. If voluntary disclosure and cooperation with opposing counsel are ineffective, then it may be advisable to take a Rule 30 (b)(6) deposition of the person(s) most knowledgeable about a company's computer system.

Under Rule 30(b)(6), a party may depose a representative of an organization for the purpose of obtaining testimony on the topics set forth within the notice of deposition. The testimony sought may be about data storage, backup and archival policies, retention procedures and underlying computer setup and computer platforms.

Conducting a 30(b)(6) deposition can be an effective method of obtaining computer systems' information that can later be used for interrogatories, request to produce or for other depositions. In addition, information obtained in these depositions can be used as admissions against the opposing party. Organizations can designate an officer, director, managing agent or others to testify on the organization's behalf "as to matters known or reasonably available to the organization" including testimony regarding computer networks and electronic information storage.

Such notice should also require that the person(s) describe in detail the identification and location of computer-based information. A request for production should accompany the deposition notice requesting computer documentation such as user manuals, computer data policies, document retention policies, disaster recovery plans, backup procedures or other documents relevant to the data you are seeking.

[C]   Reported Cases

- *In re Carbon Dioxide Industry Antitrust Litigation*, 155 F.R.D. 209, 214 (M.D. Fla. 1993). The Court granted the plaintiff's request for a Rule 30(b)(6) deposition to identify data that the defendants maintained on their computers and the hardware and software necessary to access the information. The Court stated that such "depositions to identify how data is maintained and to determine what hardware and software is necessary to access the information are preliminary depositions necessary to proceed with merits discovery."

- *Pamlab, L.L.C. v. Rite Aid Corp.*, No. CIV.04-1115, 2005 WL 589573 (E.D.La. Mar. 3, 2005). In a detailed opinion, the Court modified the plaintiff's Rule 30(b)(6) notice of deposition regarding the defendant's computer system and other matters.

- *Alexander v. F.B.I.*, 188 F.R.D. 111 (D.D.C. 1998). The defendant sought a protective order quashing Plaintiffs' Notice of Deposition and Request for Documents Pursuant to Rule 30(b)(6) & (b)(5) for persons knowledgeable about the defendant's computer system and data. The Court granted in part and denied in part the order and addressed the details and feasibility of recovery of files, as well as costs, delays and other burdens associated with such an effort in the Executive Office of the President.

- *Fischer v. United Parcel Serv. Co.,* 2006 WL 1046973 (E.D. Mich. Apr. 19, 2006). The defendant was unable to find an attachment to a responsive e-mail during the discovery process. The plaintiff requested the opportunity to depose an employee of the defendant to determine their search efforts to locate the attachment. The Court denied the request but allowed for an interview of the employee and also, that even though the attachment may not be admissible and irrelevant, it could reasonably lead to the discovery of admissible evidence.

- *York v. Hartford Underwriters Ins. Co.,* No. CIV.01-590, 2002 WL 31465306 (N.D. Okla. Nov. 4, 2002). The Court granted the plaintiff's request to conduct a 30(b)(6) deposition on the defendant's use of a claim adjusting software program called "Colossus" used on her claim.

- *Tulip Computers Inter. B. V. v. Dell Computer Corp.,* 52 Fed. R. Serv. 3d 1420 (D. Del. 2002). Though Dell failed to produce an adequately prepared 30(b)(6) witness the Court did not impose sanctions.

- *Smith v. Texaco, Inc.,* 951 F. Supp. 109 (E.D. Tex. 1997). The Court ordered the defendant to produce an employee familiar with the computer system and data retrieval for a Rule 30(b)(6) deposition.

- *Patterson v. Avery Dennison Corp.,* 281 F.3d 676, 681-82 (7th Cir. 2002). The Appellate Court affirmed the trial court's refusal to compel the deposition of a high-ranking company officer based on one e-mail the corporate officer had sent asking the HR officer to look into the case.

[D]   Discovery Pointers

- For a list of possible IT personnel to depose see § 3.2[B], *Information Technology Staff Positions.*

- Many IT employees participate in online listservs, newsgroups or chatrooms. During a 30(b)(6) deposition you may decide to ask them about their participation so you can later discover any comments they have made about the case to the group. It may be beneficial to request production of the computer documents, procedures and other materials before the date of the deposition. However, it may be more economical and time efficient to depose the opposing party's computer information specialist(s) to tell you specifically what storage media, devices and/or locations (computers, servers, hard disks, floppy disks or CDs) are available.

- To assist in pretrial discovery, consider a Rule 30(b)(6) deposition of technology personnel prior to the Rule 16(c) pretrial conference or for purposes of Rule 26 disclosures. *See,* § 7.4[J], *Expedited Discovery and Supplementation - Rule 26(d) and (e).*

[E]   Sample Deposition Notice and Request for Production

A sample notice and request for production could read:

TO: PLAINTIFF:
You are hereby notified that the Defendant(s) will take the deposition of _____, pursuant to Rule 30(b)(6) of the Federal Rules of Civil Procedure, at _____ a.m., before a court reporter or other person duly authorized to administer oaths, at the offices of _____located at _____This deposition shall continue from day to day thereafter until completed.

RULE 30(b)(6) DESIGNATION

Pursuant to Rule 30(b)(6) of the Federal Rules of Civil Procedure, the [Plaintiff/Defendant] shall designate one or more of its officials, employees, agents or consultants who have knowledge of and will testify upon oral examination on behalf of the [Plaintiff/Defendant] regarding:
1. E-mail Systems. The system or systems used since _____ to create, transmit, store, retrieve and delete so-called 'electronic mail' (said representative(s) to have knowledge of the maintenance and operation of all electronic mail systems, including, but not limited to, the construction of so-called 'user id tables' used in connection with such electronic mail systems).
2. Personal Computers. Systems for recording the acquisition, location, and/or disposition of personal electronic computers used by any official, employee, detailee, resident, volunteer, intern, visitor or others who have a business relationship with the [Plaintiff/Defendant].
3. Overview of Systems and Users Involved. System Configuration. This includes the types of computers and other hardware used by the company's system; network and desktop operating systems; and the types of network and communications software and hardware used.
4. Application Software and Utilities. This includes the names and versions of all application software, and all utilities used. These applications may be of the commercial variety, or they may be custom-made to suit a company's particular needs.

5. Back-up Procedures. This will include the name and version of the back-up software used; the medium for storage of backup information; the retention of back-up data, information as to how such data is stored and where they store the backup tapes.
6. Accessibility. Information about user names, logons, passwords, and information about any encryption programs used.
7. Documents. This will include information about:
    •how documents are indexed;
    •how documents are maintained;
    •the locations of documents;
    •whether documents are in an electronic form;
    •whether documents are regularly electronically archived;
    •how electronic documents are maintained;
    •the electronic document retention policy; and
    •how often electronic document files are purged.
8. Retention Policies. What is the company's retention policy regarding electronic information? Whether the [plaintiff/defendant] purged any responsive documents since the inception of this lawsuit?

REQUEST FOR PRODUCTION OF DOCUMENTS

The designated witness (or witnesses) shall produce in advance of the deposition, at least 7 days, for inspection and copying or, if previously produced, shall identify by name or title and by document number, the following documents:

REQUEST NO. 1: All documents that refer or relate to the items noted above as the subject matter of the Rule 30(b)(6) deposition. (additional language if needed, "including but not limited to:").

REQUEST NO. 2: All "technical manuals, instructions, booklets and memoranda to employees concerning the operation of the system."

§ 7.6   INTERROGATORIES TO PARTY

[A]   FED. R. CIV. P. 33

Rule 33. Interrogatories to Parties

(a) Availability. Without leave of court or written stipulation, any party may serve upon any other party written interrogatories, not exceeding 25 in number including all discrete subparts, to be answered by the party served or, if the party served is a public or private corporation or a partnership or association or governmental agency, by any officer or agent, who shall furnish such information as is available to the party. Leave to serve additional interrogatories shall be granted to the extent consistent with the principles of Rule 26(b)(2).

Without leave of court or written stipulation, interrogatories may not be served before the time specified in Rule 26(d).

* * *

(c) Scope; Use at Trial. Interrogatories may relate to any matters which can be inquired into under Rule 26(b)(1), and the answers may be used to the extent permitted by the rules of evidence.

(d) Option to Produce Business Records. Where the answer to an interrogatory may be derived or ascertained from the business records of the party upon whom the interrogatory has been served or from an examination, audit or inspection of such business records, including a compilation, abstract or summary thereof, and the burden of deriving or ascertaining the answer is substantially the same for the party serving the interrogatory as for the party served, it is a sufficient answer to such interrogatory to specify the records from which the answer may be derived or ascertained and to afford to the party serving the interrogatory reasonable opportunity to examine, audit or inspect such records and to make copies, compilations, abstracts or summaries. A specification shall be in sufficient detail to permit the interrogating party to locate and to identify, as readily as can the party served, the records from which the answer may be ascertained.

[B]   Pending Rule 33 Amendment

Rule 33. Interrogatories to Parties

* * * * *

(d) Option to Produce Business Records. Where the answer to an interrogatory may be derived or ascertained from the business records, <u>including electronically stored information,</u> of the party upon whom the interrogatory has been served or from an examination, audit or inspection of such business records, including a compilation, abstract or summary thereof, and the burden of deriving or ascertaining the answer is substantially the same for the party serving the interrogatory as for the party served, it is a sufficient answer to such interrogatory to specify the records from which the answer may be derived or ascertained and to afford to the party serving the interrogatory reasonable opportunity to examine, audit or inspect such records and to make copies, compilations, abstracts, or summaries. A specification shall be in sufficient detail to permit the interrogating party to locate and to identify, as readily as can the party served, the records from which the answer may be ascertained. (emphasis added).

Committee Note

Rule 33(d) is amended to parallel Rule 34(a) by recognizing the importance of electronically stored information. The term "electronically stored information" has the same broad meaning in Rule 33(d) as in Rule 34(a). Much business information is stored only in electronic form; the Rule 33(d) option should be available with respect to such records as well.

Special difficulties may arise in using electronically stored information, either due to its form or because it is dependent on a particular computer system. Rule 33(d) allows a responding party to substitute access to documents or electronically stored information for an answer only if the burden of deriving the answer will be substantially the same for either party. Rule 33(d) states that a party electing to respond to an interrogatory by providing electronically stored information must ensure that the interrogating party can locate and identify it "as readily as can the party served," and that the responding party must give the interrogating party a "reasonable opportunity to examine, audit, or inspect" the information. Depending on the circumstances, satisfying these provisions with regard to electronically stored information may require the responding party to provide some combination of technical support, information on application software, or other assistance. The key question is whether such support enables the interrogating party to derive or ascertain the answer from the electronically stored information as readily as the responding party. A party that wishes to invoke Rule 33(d) by specifying electronically stored information may be required to provide direct access to its electronic information system, but only if that is necessary to afford the requesting party an adequate opportunity to derive or ascertain the answer to the interrogatory. In that situation, the responding party's need to protect sensitive interests of confidentiality or privacy may mean that it must derive or ascertain and provide the answer itself rather than invoke Rule 33(d).

[C]   Purpose

Interrogatories are written questions regarding any matter, not privileged, addressed and served on other parties to a lawsuit. Interrogatories, along with depositions and requests for production of documents, are standard discovery tools. Interrogatories can be served early in the lawsuit, and thereby provide a party with initial information about the claims or defenses in the case. Interrogatories are also well suited to identify witnesses (especially computer personnel) known to have knowledge about the case. This would include the names and addresses of computer personnel, computer job duties, employment dates and other information.

The initial disclosure requirements of FED. R. CIV. P. 26(a)(1) does away with the need for many standard interrogatories. *Williams v. Sprint/United Mgmt. Co.,* No. CIV.03-2200, 2006 U.S. Dist. LEXIS 11832, at *26 (D. Kan. Mar. 21, 2006).

There is a limit on the number of interrogatories that can be propounded, so it is important that the initial disclosure be in compliance so that you do not have to use interrogatories to obtain the information. Also, under Rule 26(a)(1)(A), a party is required to disclose the name, address and telephone number of "each individual likely to have discoverable information that the disclosing party may use to support its claims or defenses, unless solely for impeachment." Such a disclosure should contain the identification of a party's management information systems (MIS) managers as persons with discoverable information.

In electronic discovery cases propounding interrogatories may assist in later framing specific requests for Rule 34 production of document requests as well as Rule 30(b)(6) depositions. If properly framed in a specific, straightforward manner valuable information can be obtained regarding sources of electronic information, document retention policies and identification of key IT personnel such as network administrators.

One alternative to obtaining computer discovery information, other than by interrogatories, is by conducting a Rule 30(b)(6) deposition. Unlike interrogatories, depositions allow you to ask detailed questions and then follow-up on initial answers that may be evasive or not responsive. Also, since some computer terminology is susceptible to more than one meaning, the deposition would allow you to clarify the opposing party's answers.

Rule 33(d) permits parties to answer interrogatories by making available for inspection and copying business records, including "compilations," where "the burden of deriving or ascertaining the answer is substantially the same for the party serving the interrogatory as for the party served." If the opposing party chooses this option, there are several issues that have to be resolved. Some of these issues are:

• Whether the discovery will be in electronic or paper format;

• Whether additional information, such as a user manual, will need to be provided to permit usable access to the data;

• Whether a standard disclosure format is required; and

• Whether the cost will be allocated.

Pending Rule 33 Amendment

Rule 33(d) has always allowed a party to answer an interrogatory by specifying business records where the answer is located. The amendment to Rule 33(d) now allows a party to point to electronically stored information to answer the interrogatory.

[D]   Reported Cases

- *Treppel v. Biovail Corp.*, 233 F.R.D. 363, 373-374 (D.N.Y. 2006). A document retention questionnaire appended to a proposed e-discovery stipulation would be treated as interrogatories and allowed in the interest of justice since the plaintiff had already exceeded the twenty-five permitted by FED. R. CIV. P. 33.

- *Powerhouse Marks, L.L.C. v. Chi Hsin Impex, Inc.*, No. CIV. 04-73923, 2006 U.S. Dist. LEXIS 2767, at *9-11 (D. Mich. Jan. 12, 2006). In response to interrogatories, the defendant ordered "to compute and provide in summary fashion annual sales figures and expenditures for specific products."

- *United States ex rel. Fago v. M & T Mortg. Corp.*, 235 F.R.D. 11 (D.D.C. 2006). The Court ruled that pursuant to Rule 33(d) the answer to the interrogatory could be derived from electronically stored records and should be produced from this data. However, the Court ordered the responding party to submit a brief to explain if it felt accessing this "archived" data would be burdensome.

- *Jackson v. City of San Antonio*, No. CIV.03-0049, 2006 U.S. Dist. LEXIS 8091 (W.D. Tex., Jan. 31, 2006). The plaintiff objected to the defendants' production of computerized pay and time records in response to discovery as being an unauthorized "data dump." They also argued the computerized records failed to include field descriptors which made the records "unhelpful, unuseable, and nonresponsive." The Court ruled that "because the burden of culling out the requested information is no greater for plaintiffs than it would be for defendants, the rules permit defendants the option to respond by producing their business records. F.R.Civ.P. 33(d)." Also, the defendant supplied the field descriptors at a later date.

- *Sonnino v. Univ. of Kansas Hosp. Auth.*, 220 F.R.D. 633, 655 (D.Kan. 2004). In this employment case the defendant was ordered to provide a complete and full response to interrogatory seeking information about computer and e-mail systems since the defendant's "very brief and general response" was insufficient.

- *Simon Property Group LP v. mySimon, Inc.*, 194 F.R.D. 639 (S.D. Ind. 2000). In order to recover deleted files in a trademark infringement case, the Court required the defendant to answer an interrogatory to identify each office and home computer, computer server and electronic recording devices used by four corporate employees since the development of the alleged infringing product.

- *PHE, Inc. v. Department of Justice*, 139 F.R.D. 249, 257 (D.D.C. 1991). In this federal prosecution of federal obscenity statutes, plaintiffs objected to interrogatories submitted by the Department of Justice on the basis of burdensome. Court denied the objections and found that the plaintiffs would only have to incur "modest additional expenditures," since plaintiffs' operations were computerized and they could retrieve necessary and appropriate information with little effort.

- *Donaldson v. Pillsbury Co.*, 554 F.2d 825, 832 (8th Cir. 1977). Court refused to require party to respond to interrogatories seeking information in computer-readable form since the data existed in "500 to 2,000 different file and report formats," and the data had already been produced in other previous discovery.

- *State Farm Mut. Auto. Ins. Co. v. Engleke,* 824 S.W.2d 747, 750-51 (Tex. Ct. App. 1992). Interrogatory seeking information relating to 500,000 other lawsuits against an insurer was found not to be unduly burdensome insofar as responsive information could be generated from the insurer's computer system, and the response was limited to the state in question.

- *Layfman v. Oakley Bldg. & Loan Co.,* 72 F.R.D. 116 (S.D. Ohio 1976). The Court ordered the defendants to answer an interrogatory requesting the type of data, which was entered into the computers and electronic data processing equipment used by the defendant.

- *International Asso. of Machinists v. United Aircraft Corp.,* 220 F. Supp. 19 (D. Conn. 1963), *aff'd on other grounds*, 337 F.2d 5 (2d Cir. 1964). The plaintiffs had promulgated interrogatories that required the analysis of detailed personnel records. The defendant attempted to comply with the interrogatory by delivering 120,000 pages of individual personnel records weighing more than 450 lbs. The plaintiff's counsel complained and the Court ordered the defendant to analyze the records electronically, at its own expense, and answer the interrogatories.

- *Greyhound Computer Corp., Inc. v. IBM*, 3 Comp. L. Serv. Rep. 138 (D. Minn. 1971). *Greyhound* sent interrogatories to *IBM* and in response received a recitation of source materials and locations where the information could be found. After *Greyhound's* counsel found rooms full of thousands of documents, the Court ordered that where information was on computer tapes it should be produced. Also, the defendant was to provide someone familiar with the material and assist the plaintiff's counsel and to furnish printouts of any taped information.

[E]   Sample Interrogatories

- Description of Back-up Policies

    Describe policies and procedures followed by [plaintiff/defendant] for backing-up files and data on the computer system(s) [utilized by plaintiff/defendant], including, but not limited to, the frequency of backups, the type of backup (full, differential or incremental), the software used during [period of time], the number of sets of tapes or other media and the rotation of such media and whether such policies are in writing.

- Description of Retention and Destruction Policies

    Describe all record retention and destruction policies and procedures followed by [plaintiff/defendant] during [period of time] including, but not limited to, the date the policy was adopted, the types of documents covered and the respective retention periods, the frequency of document destruction, whether any record is kept of what documents are destroyed, the manner the policy is communicated to [plaintiff's/defendant's] employees and the identity of all employees with responsibility for implementing and executing the policy.

§ 7.7   REQUEST TO PRODUCE AND INSPECT

[A]   FED. R. CIV. P. 34

FED. R. CIV. P. 34(a) states:

(a) Scope. Any party may serve on any other party a request (1) to produce and permit the party making the request, or someone acting on the requestor's behalf, to inspect and copy, any designated *documents* (including writings, drawings, graphs, charts, photographs, phonorecords, *and other data compilations* from which information can be obtained, *translated, if necessary, by the respondent through detection devices into reasonably usable form*), *or to inspect and copy, test, or sample* any tangible things which constitute or contain matters within the scope of Rule 26(b) and which are in the possession, custody or control of the party upon whom the request is served; or (2) to permit entry upon designated land or other property in the possession or control of the party upon whom the request is served for the purpose of inspection and measuring, surveying, photographing, testing, or sampling the property or any designated object or operation thereon, within the scope of Rule 26(b). (emphasis added).

(b) Procedure. The request shall set forth, either by individual item or by category, the items to be inspected and describe each with reasonable particularity. . . . The party upon whom the request is served shall serve a written response within 30 days after the service of the request. . . . The response shall state, with respect to each item or category, that inspection and related activities will be permitted as requested, unless the request is objected to, in which event the reasons for the objection shall be stated. If objection is made to part of an item or category, the part shall be specified and inspection permitted of the remaining parts. The party submitting the request may move for an order under

Rule 37(a) with respect to any objection to or other failure to respond to the request or any part thereof, or any failure to permit inspection as requested.

A party who produces documents for inspection shall produce them as they are kept in the usual course of business or shall organize and label them to correspond with the categories in the request. (emphasis added).

(c) Persons Not Parties. A person not a party to the action may be compelled to produce documents and things or to submit to an inspection as provided in Rule 45.

[1] Pending Rule 34 Amendment

Rule 34. Production of Documents, <u>Electronically Stored Information,</u> and Things and Entry Upon Land for Inspection and Other Purposes (emphasis added)

(a) Scope. Any party may serve on any other party a request (1) to produce and permit the party making the request, or someone acting on the requestor's behalf, to inspect, copy, <u>test, or sample</u> any designated documents <u>or electronically stored information</u> — including writings, drawings, graphs, charts, photographs, <u>sound recordings, images,</u> and other <u>data or</u> data compilations <u>stored in any medium</u> from which information can be obtained — translated, if necessary, by the respondent into reasonably usable form, or to inspect, copy, test, or sample any designated tangible things which constitute or contain matters within the scope of Rule 26(b) and which are in the possession, custody or control of the party upon whom the request is served; or (2) to permit entry upon designated land or other property in the possession or control of the party upon whom the request is served for the purpose of inspection and measuring, surveying, photographing, testing, or sampling the property or any designated object or operation thereon, within the scope of Rule 26(b). (emphasis added).

(b) Procedure. The request shall set forth, either by individual item or by category, the items to be inspected, and describe each with reasonable particularity. The request shall specify a reasonable time, place, and manner of making the inspection and performing the related acts. <u>The request may specify the form or forms in which electronically stored information is to be produced.</u> Without leave of court or written stipulation, a request may not be served before the time specified in Rule 26(d). The party upon whom the request is served shall serve a written response within 30 days after the service of the request. A shorter or longer time may be directed by the court or, in the absence of such an order, agreed to in writing by the parties, subject to Rule 29. The response shall state, with respect to each item or category, that inspection and related activities will be permitted as requested, unless the request is objected to, <u>including an objection to the requested form or forms for producing electronically stored information, stating</u> the reasons for the objection. If objection is made to part of an item or category, the part shall be specified and inspection permitted of the remaining parts. <u>If objection is made to the requested form or forms for producing electronically stored information — or if no form was specified in the request — the responding party must state the form or forms it intends to use.</u> The party submitting the request may move for an order under Rule 37(a) with respect to any objection to or other failure to respond to the request or any part thereof, or any failure to permit inspection as requested. (emphasis added).

<u>Unless the parties otherwise agree, or the court otherwise orders:</u>

(i) a party who produces documents for inspection shall produce them as they are kept in the usual course of business or shall organize and label them to correspond with the categories in the request;

<u>(ii) if a request does not specify the form or forms for producing electronically stored information, a responding party must produce the information in a form or forms in which it is ordinarily maintained or in a form or forms that are reasonably usable; and</u>

<u>(iii) a party need not produce the same electronically stored information in more than one form.</u> (emphasis added).

Committee Note

Subdivision (a). As originally adopted, Rule 34 focused on discovery of "documents" and "things." In 1970, Rule 34(a) was amended to include discovery of data compilations, anticipating that the use of computerized information would increase. Since then, the growth in electronically stored information and in the variety of systems for creating and storing such information has been dramatic. Lawyers and judges interpreted the term "documents" to include electronically stored information because it was obviously improper to allow a party to evade discovery obligations on the basis that the label had not kept pace with changes in information technology. But it has become increasingly difficult to say that all forms of electronically stored information, many dynamic in nature, fit within the traditional concept of a "document." Electronically stored information may exist in dynamic databases and other forms far different from fixed expression on paper. Rule 34(a) is amended to confirm that discovery of electronically stored information stands on equal footing with discovery of paper documents. The change clarifies that Rule 34 applies to information that is fixed in a tangible form and to information that is stored in a medium from which it can be retrieved and examined. At the same time, a Rule 34 request for production of "documents" should be understood to encompass, and the response should include, electronically stored information unless discovery in the action has clearly distinguished between electronically stored information and "documents."

Discoverable information often exists in both paper and electronic form, and the same or similar information might exist in both. The items listed in Rule 34(a) show different ways in which information may be recorded or stored. Images, for example, might be hard-copy documents or electronically stored information. The wide variety of computer systems currently in use, and the rapidity of technological change, counsel against a limiting or precise definition of electronically stored information. Rule 34(a)(1) is expansive and includes any type of information that is stored electronically. A common example often sought in discovery is electronic communications, such as email. The rule covers — either as documents or as electronically stored information — information "stored in any medium," to encompass future developments in computer technology. Rule 34(a)(1) is intended to be broad enough to cover all current types of computer-based information, and flexible enough to encompass future changes and developments.

References elsewhere in the rules to "electronically stored information" should be understood to invoke this expansive approach. A companion change is made to Rule 33(d), making it explicit that parties choosing to respond to an interrogatory by permitting access to responsive records may do so by providing access to electronically stored information. More generally, the term used in Rule 34(a)(1) appears in a number of other amendments, such as those to Rules 26(a)(1), 26(b)(2), 26(b)(5)(B), 26(f), 34(b), 37(f), and 45. In each of these rules, electronically stored information has the same broad meaning it has under Rule 34(a)(1). References to "documents" appear in discovery rules that are not amended, including Rules 30(f), 36(a), and 37(c)(2). These references should be interpreted to include electronically stored information as circumstances warrant.

The term "electronically stored information" is broad, but whether material that falls within this term should be produced, and in what form, are separate questions that must be addressed under Rules 26(b), 26(c), and 34(b).

The Rule 34(a) requirement that, if necessary, a party producing electronically stored information translate it into reasonably usable form does not address the issue of translating from one human language to another. *See, In re Puerto Rico Elect. Power Auth.,* 687 F.2d 501, 504-510 (1st Cir. 1989).

Rule 34(a)(1) is also amended to make clear that parties may request an opportunity to test or sample materials sought under the rule in addition to inspecting and copying them. That opportunity may be important for both electronically stored information and hard-copy materials. The current rule is not clear that such testing or sampling is authorized; the amendment expressly permits it. As with any other form of discovery, issues of burden and intrusiveness raised by requests to test or sample can be addressed under Rules 26(b)(2) and 26(c). Inspection or testing of certain types of electronically stored information or of a responding party's electronic information system may raise issues of confidentiality or privacy. The addition of testing and sampling to Rule 34(a) with regard to documents and electronically stored information is not meant to create a routine right of direct access to a party's electronic information system, although such access might be justified in some circumstances. Courts should guard against undue intrusiveness resulting from inspecting or testing such systems.

Rule 34(a)(1) is further amended to make clear that tangible things must — like documents and land sought to be examined — be designated in the request.

Subdivision (b). Rule 34(b) provides that a party must produce documents as they are kept in the usual course of business or must organize and label them to correspond with the categories in the discovery request. The production of electronically stored information should be subject to comparable requirements to protect against deliberate or inadvertent production in ways that raise unnecessary obstacles for the requesting party. Rule 34(b) is amended to ensure similar protection for electronically stored information.

The amendment to Rule 34(b) permits the requesting party to designate the form or forms in which it wants electronically stored information produced. The form of production is more important to the exchange of electronically stored information than of hard-copy materials, although a party might specify hard copy as the requested form. Specification of the desired form or forms may facilitate the orderly, efficient, and cost-effective discovery of electronically stored information. The rule recognizes that different forms of production may be appropriate for different types of electronically stored information. Using current technology, for example, a party might be called upon to produce word processing documents, email messages, electronic spreadsheets, different image or sound files, and material from databases. Requiring that such diverse types of electronically stored information all be produced in the same form could prove impossible, and even if possible could increase the cost and burdens of producing and using the information. The rule therefore provides that the requesting party may ask for different forms of production for different types of electronically stored information.

The rule does not require that the requesting party choose a form or forms of production. The requesting party may not have a preference. In some cases, the requesting party may not know what form the producing party uses to maintain its electronically stored information, although Rule 26(f)(3) is amended to call for discussion of the form of production in the parties' prediscovery conference.

The responding party also is involved in determining the form of production. In the written response to the production request that Rule 34 requires, the responding party must state the form it intends to use for producing electronically stored information if the requesting party does not specify a form or if the responding party objects to a form that the requesting party specifies. Stating the intended form before the production occurs may permit the parties to identify and seek to resolve disputes before the expense and work of the production occurs. A party that responds to a discovery request by simply producing electronically stored information in a form of its choice, without identifying that form in advance of the production in the response required by Rule 34(b), runs a risk that the requesting party can show that the produced form is not reasonably usable and that it is entitled to production of some or all of the information in an additional form. Additional time might be required to permit a responding party to assess the appropriate form or forms of production.

If the requesting party is not satisfied with the form stated by the responding party, or if the responding party has objected to the form specified by the requesting party, the parties must meet and confer under Rule 37(a)(2)(B) in an effort to resolve the matter before the requesting party can file a motion to compel. If they cannot agree and the court resolves the dispute, the court is not limited to the forms initially chosen by the requesting party, stated by the responding party, or specified in this rule for situations in which there is no court order or party agreement.

If the form of production is not specified by party agreement or court order, the responding party must produce electronically stored information either in a form or forms in which it is ordinarily maintained or in a form or forms that are reasonably usable. Rule 34(a) requires that, if necessary, a responding party "translate" information it produces into a "reasonably usable" form. Under some circumstances, the responding party may need to provide some reasonable amount of technical support, information on application software, or other reasonable assistance to enable the requesting party to use the information. The rule does not require a party to produce electronically stored information in the form it which it is ordinarily maintained, as long as it is produced in a reasonably usable form. But the option to produce in a reasonably usable form does not mean that a responding party is free to convert electronically stored information from the form in which it is ordinarily maintained to a different form that makes it more difficult or burdensome for the requesting party to use the information efficiently in the litigation. If the responding party ordinarily maintains the information it is producing in a way that makes it searchable by electronic means, the information should not be produced in a form that removes or significantly degrades this feature.

Some electronically stored information may be ordinarily maintained in a form that is not reasonably usable by any party. One example is "legacy" data that can be used only by superseded systems. The questions whether a producing party should be required to convert such information to a more usable form, or should be required to produce it at all, should be addressed under Rule 26(b)(2)(B).

Whether or not the requesting party specified the form of production, Rule 34(b) provides that the same electronically stored information ordinarily need be produced in only one form.

[2]   Purpose

FED. R. CIV. P. 34 addresses the production of documents and other information from opposing parties. The text of Rule 34 permits the discovery of any "documents" and "data compilations from which information can be obtained, translated, if necessary, by the respondent through detection devices into reasonably useful form." The 1970 Advisory Committee Notes to Rule 34 further provide that Rule 34 "applies to electronic data compilations from which information can be obtained only with the use of detection devices." Rule 34(a) allows the responding party to search his records to produce the required, relevant data. A discovery request may not be served until after the time specified in Rule 26(b) unless discovery is expedited by the court pursuant to Rule 26(d) or the parties enter into a written stipulation. Late requests for ESI may preclude its production. *Wild v. Alster,* 377 F. Supp. 2d 186, 195 (D.D.C. 2005).

Depending on the request, the Rule 34 response and/or objections should set forth what steps have been taken to produce responsive electronic data and documents. This will deter a motion to compel if a production protocol is provided along with the disclosure of the documents. Also, appropriate objections based on relevancy, overbroad, burdensome, cost and other reasons should be set forth in the response.

The rationale for disclosing documents in a computerized format was recognized by the United States Supreme Court more than 25 years ago. In *Oppenheimer Fund, Inc. v. Sanders,* 437 U.S. 340, 362 (1978) the Supreme Court ordered the producing party to pay the cost "[t]o compile a list of the class members' names and addresses . . . to sort manually through many records, keypunch 150,000 to 300,000 computer cards, and create several new computer programs." The Court noted, "although it may be expensive to retrieve information stored in computers when no program yet exists for the particular job, there is no reason to think that the same information could be extracted any less expensively if the records were kept in less modern forms. Indeed, one might expect the reverse to be true, for otherwise computers would not have gained such widespread use in the storing and handling of information."

There are several ways to obtain computer data in a case. FED. R. CIV. P. 34 provides for the identification, copying and production of data or under Rule 33(d) the data can be made available for inspection. In addition, individuals noticed for a deposition can be required to produce data by a subpoena duces tecum. Finally, third parties can be compelled to disclose data pursuant to Rule 45.

The party that is served with a request to produce electronic data may object based on relevancy, overbroad, etc. If this is not acceptable to the requesting party then the party needs to file a motion to compel pursuant to Rule 37. *See, e.g., GFI Computer Indus., Inc. v. Fry,* 476 F.2d 1, 3 (5th Cir. 1973).

Pending Rule 34 Amendment

Pending Rule 34 has fundamentally changed production nomenclature by introducing "electronically stored information" (ESI) into discovery. The Courts have begun citing to the new e-discovery amendments in their decisions. *Williams v. Sprint/United Mgmt. Co.,* 230 F.R.D. 640 (D. Kan. 2005) (court discussed pending e-discovery Rule 34 regarding "electronically stored information" (ESI), metadata and form of production); *Hopson v. Mayor & City Council of Baltimore,* 232 F.R.D. 228, 245 (D. Md. 2005) (court commented upon pending Rule 16 and the "meet and confer" mandate and stated, "the proposed changes to Rule 16(f) make clear, counsel have a duty to take the initiative in meeting and conferring to plan for appropriate discovery of electronically stored information at the commencement of any case in which electronic records will be sought.").

The pending Rule 34(a) Amendment Committee Note recognizes:

- That the drafters are viewing ESI in the context of systems that create and store this information.
- That "Rule 34 applies to information that is fixed in a tangible form and to information that is stored in a medium from which it can be retrieved and examined."

- That "a Rule 34 request for production of 'documents' should be understood to encompass, and the response should include, electronically stored information . . ."

- "Discoverable information often exists in both paper and electronic form, and the same or similar information might exist in both."

- "The items listed in Rule 34(a) show different ways in which information may be recorded or stored."

- "Rule 34(a)(1) is expansive and includes any type of information that is stored electronically. . . . Rule 34(a)(1) is intended to be broad enough to cover all current types of computer-based information, and flexible enough to encompass future changes and developments."

- "References elsewhere in the rules to 'electronically stored information' should be understood to invoke this expansive approach . . . More generally, the term used in Rule 34(a)(1) appears in a number of other amendments, such as those to Rules 26(a)(1), 26(b)(2), 26(b)(5)(B), 26(f), 34(b), 37(f), and 45. In each of these rules, electronically stored information has the same broad meaning it has under Rule 34(a)(1)."

- "Rule 34(a)(1) is also amended to make clear that parties may request an opportunity to test or sample materials sought under the rule in addition to inspecting and copying them. "

- "Inspection or testing of certain types of electronically stored information or of a responding party's electronic information system may raise issues of confidentiality or privacy."

[3]   Reported Cases

- *Anti-Monopoly, Inc. v. Hasbro, Inc.*, No. CIV.94-2120, 1995 W.L. 649934, at *2 (S.D.N.Y. Nov. 3, 1995). "[T]oday it is blackletter law that computerized data is discoverable if relevant."

- *PHE, Inc. v. Department of Justice*, 139 F.R.D. 249, 257 (D.D.C. 1991). The Court ordered the plaintiffs to produce computerized tax records even though they had no program capable of collecting and displaying the data. The Court stated, "[a]lthough no program may presently exist to obtain the information requested, the Court is satisfied that with little effort the plaintiffs can retrieve the necessary and appropriate information. . . . It would not be unreasonable to require the plaintiffs to incur modest additional expenditures so as to provide the defendants with the discovery necessary to establish that they are not acting in bad faith and vindictively."

- *Cardenas v. Dorel Juvenile Group, Inc.*, 230 F.R.D. 611, 619-620 (D. Kan. 2005). "While there is a general presumption 'that the responding party must bear the expense of complying with discovery requests,' [n30 *Oppenheimer Fund, Inc. v. Sanders*, 437

U.S. 340, 98 S.Ct. 2380, 2393, 57 L.Ed.2d 253 (1978)] that presumption is trumped by Rule 34. Courts have held that under Rule 34, a responding party need only make requested documents available for inspection and copying; it need not pay the copying costs. Consequently, DJG is not required to pay for any photocopying of the requested documents."

- *See*, § 7.4[G][6], *Cost Allocation* for additional cases holding that where companies use computer technology to generate data they must assume the risk of the discovery costs when required to produce that data.

[B]   "Document" - Definition

[1]   Generally

The basic building block of federal civil discovery, as far as electronic discovery is concerned, is the "document." In order to make initial disclosures under FED. R. CIV. P. 26, to answer an interrogatory under Rule 33 or to respond to requests for production under Rule 34 or Rule 45, you must understand what constitutes a "document."

Rule 34(a) defines documents as "including writings, drawings, graphs, charts, photographs, phonorecords, and other data compilations from which information can be obtained, translated, if necessary, by the respondent through detection devices, into reasonably usable form." The FED. R. CIV. P. 34 advisory committee notes (1970 amendment) states, "[t]he inclusive description of 'documents' is revised to accord with changing technology."

The Courts have held that the definition of "documents" under Rule 34 includes all types of computer data, as well as "deleted" data. *Bills v. Kennecott Corp.,* 108 F.R.D. 459, 462 (D. Utah 1985); *Kleiner v. Burns,* No. 00-2160, 2000 WL 1909470, at *4 (D. Kan. Dec. 15, 2000); *Zubulake v. UBS Warburg, LLC,* 217 F.R.D. 309, 313 n.19 (S.D.N.Y. 2003); *Antioch Co. v. Scrapbook Borders, Inc.,* 210 F.R.D. 645, 652 (D. Minn. 2002); and *Williams v. Sprint/United Mgmt. Co.,* 230 F.R.D. 640 (D. Kan. 2005) (court discussed pending definition of "document" and the pending e-discovery Rule 34 regarding "electronically stored information" (ESI), metadata and form of production).

One of the difficulties with the present definition and concept of the term "document" is that it connotes a singular data or final paper "record." However, "compound" documents and "drafts" of documents are common in the world of electronic information. For example, if a common e-mail message includes a "hyperlink" to a website or some other computer data, do you have a disclosure obligation under Rule 34 to produce the web data along with the e-mail? In another example, do you have the obligation to produce all drafts of a word processing document pursuant to your preservation obligation?

Pending Rule 34 Amendment - "electronically stored information" (ESI)

The Committee Note explains that "[e]lectronically stored information may exist in dynamic databases and other forms far different from fixed expression on paper. Rule 34(a) is amended to confirm that discovery of electronically stored information stands on equal footing with discovery of paper documents. The change clarifies that Rule 34 applies to information that is fixed in a tangible form and to information that is stored in a medium from which it can be retrieved and examined."

[a]   Reported Cases

* *Kleiner v. Burns,* No. 00-2160, 2000 WL 1909470, at *4 (D. Kan. Dec. 15, 2000). In a copyright infringement the Court held "computerized data and other electronically-recorded information" will include but not be limited to "voice mail messages and files, backup voice mail files, e-mail messages and files, backup e-mail files, deleted e-mail, data files, program files, backup and archival tapes, temporary files, system history files, web site information stored in textual, graphical or audio format, web site log files, cache files, cookies and other electronically recorded information." The Court did not intend for the list to be exhaustive and noted "the disclosing party shall take reasonable steps to ensure that it discloses any backup copies of files or archival tapes that will provide information about any 'deleted' electronic data." The Court addressed the Rule 26(a)(1)(B) disclosure obligations to include an obligation to describe and categorize the nature and location of electronic information.

* *McGuire v. Acufex Microsurgical, Inc.,* 175 F.R.D. 149, 155-156 (D. Mass. 1997). The Court ruled on the issue of whether prior drafts of a "document" had to be retained for preservation purposes in a claim for sexual harassment. One of the defendant's supervisors [not the harasser] had deleted a portion of a draft of an internal memorandum prior to including it in the plaintiff's personnel file because the human resources' staff had decided that the paragraph in question was "inappropriate." The court held that employers can edit drafts of memos in the sexual harassment context when those edits concern "obvious errors made by someone other than the accused harasser." The court explained that "to hold otherwise would be to create a new set of affirmative obligations for employers, unheard of in the law - to preserve all drafts of internal memos."

* *Mosaid Technologies Inc. v. Samsung Electronics Co., Ltd.,* 348 F. Supp.2d 332, 336-337 (D.N.J. 2004). In a commercial litigation case the defendant failed to preserve e-mail and argued that the plaintiff failed to use the word "e-mail" in its discovery request. The Court rejected the argument and said it was implied when it asked for correspondence and other communications.

- *Rowe Entertainment, Inc. v. The William Morris Agency, Inc.,* 205 F.R.D. 421, 428 (S.D.N.Y. 2002), *aff'd,* 2002 WL 975713 (S.D.N.Y. May 9, 2002). The Court stated, "[e]lectronic documents are no less subject to disclosure than paper records."

- *Simon Property Group v. mySimon, Inc.,* 194 F.R.D. 639, 640 (S.D. Ind. 2000). The Court held that computer records, including records that have been deleted, are discoverable documents subject to Rule 34. These included "all available word processing documents, electronic mail messages, powerpoint or similar presentations, spreadsheets and similar files." *See also, Antioch Co. v. Scrapbook Borders, Inc.,* 210 F.R.D. 645, 652 (D. Minn. 2002); *Playboy Enterprises v. Welles,* 60 F. Supp. 2d 1050, 1052-53 (S.D. Cal. 1999).

- *In re Vioxx Products Liability Litigation,* No. MDL1657, 2005 WL 756742 (E.D.La. Feb. 18, 2005). The Court in their preservation order stated that the terms "Documents, data and tangible things is to be broadly interpreted to include . . . metadata. . . ."

- *Momah v. Albert Einstein Medical Center,* 164 F.R.D. 412 (E.D. Pa. 1996). The Court allowed discovery of one computer record, specifically, the computer "list files" screen. The "list files" screen would display different information about documents created on the computer including the dates on which each document was created and last edited.

- *Crown Life Ins. Co. v. Craig,* 995 F.2d 1376 (7th Cir. 1993). Raw data is a "document" for purposes of Rule 34 even if the data has not been put in "hard copy" form. Party alleged that it was inaccessible and failed to produce the data, which resulted in a default judgment.

- *Armstrong v. Executive Office of the President, Office of Admin,* 1 F.3d 1274, 1285 (D.C. Cir. 1993). "Our discussion assumes that directories, distribution lists, etc. become part of an electronic record when they are incorporated in that record to specify senders and receivers of documents. We believe such an assumption is warranted as the most natural way of understanding the relation between the substance of a message and its origin and destination."

- *United States v. Hutson,* 821 F.2d 1015, 1019-1020 (5th Cir. 1987). "Data compilation" encompasses computerized records.

[b]   Other Authorities

- Shannon M. Curreri, *Defining "Document" in the Digital Landscape of Electronic Discovery,* 38 Loy. L.A. L. Rev. 1541, *1541 (2005).

- For specific issues related to databases see § 3.10 *Databases.*

- Hon. Shira A. Scheindlin & Jeffrey Rabkin, *Electronic Discovery in Federal Civil Litigation: Is Rule 34 Up to the Task?* 41 B.C. L. Rev. 327 (Mar. 2000).

[2]   **Metadata**

The Courts have generally allowed the discovery of metadata associated with computer files. For a general discussion of metadata see § 3.7, *Metadata, Hidden, or Embedded Information.*

[a]   **Reported Cases**

- *Williams v. Sprint/United Mgmt. Co.,* 230 F.R.D. 640 (D. Kan. 2005). The Court ordered an employer in an employment discrimination case to restore the metadata it had "scrubbed" or "erased" from Excel spreadsheet files and "unlock" them. The Court ordered the employer to produce the spreadsheets in the manner in which they are maintained and considered sanctions for the improper disclosure.

- *In re Priceline.com Inc. Sec. Litig.,* 233 F.R.D. 88, 91 (D. Conn. 2005). The Court ordered that "[d]efendants shall produce responsive information contained in stored data files to plaintiffs in TIFF or PDF form with Bates numbering and appropriate confidentiality designations, shall produce searchable metadata databases, and shall maintain the original data itself in native format for the duration of the litigation."

- *Hagenbuch v. 3B6 Sistemi Elettronici Industriali S.R.L.,* 2006 W.L. 665005 (N.D. Ill. Mar. 8, 2006). The Court ordered the defendant to produce electronic information in native file format instead of the TIFF format that the defendant desired. The defendant argued that production in a TIFF format would allow it to produce the data with bates labeling and to protect confidential or privileged information. The Court rejected the position observing that TIFF production does not contain "the creation and modification dates of a document, e-mail attachments and recipients, and metadata" which was possibly relevant to plaintiff's case as it could relate to the chronology of events and "who received what information and when."

- *Zenith Electronics Corp. v. WH-TV Broadcasting Corp.,* No. CIV.01-4366, 2004 WL 1631676, at *7 (N.D.Ill. Jul. 19, 2004). In a dispute over taxable costs the Court observed, "[o]n April 25, 2003, WH-TV moved to compel Motorola to produce the files in electronic form. WH-TV stated that it was necessary to have the files in electronic form, because the electronic files contained 'metadata' that are not printed on the hard copies. WH-TV also noted that having the files in electronic form would allow it to search them more easily."

- *Krumwiede v. Brighton Associates,* L.L.C., No. CIV.05-3003, 2006 WL 1308629 (N.D. Ill. May 8, 2006). The Court entered a default judgment against the plaintiff for activity evidencing the intent to destroy or hide evidence by deleting files, creating ZIP files (nesting data), moving data and multiple use of defragmentation. The Court also held that "even if the thousands of altered and modified documents located on Brighton's laptop are not actually deleted, the changes to the file metadata call the authenticity of the files and their content into question and make it impossible for [the defendant] to rely on them."

[b]   Other Authorities

- ABA Civil Discovery Standards, § 29(b)(ii)(B) contains this description of metadata: "A party requesting information in electronic form should also consider . . . [a]sking for the production of metadata associated with the responsive data - i.e., ancillary electronic information that relates to responsive electronic data, such as information that would indicate whether and when the responsive electronic data was created, edited, sent, received and/or opened."

- The MANUAL FOR COMPLEX LITIGATION (FOURTH) § 21.446 recognizes the following potential data subject to discovery, "Metadata, or 'information about information.' . . . System data, or information generated and maintained by the computer itself. . . . Backup data, generally stored off-line on tapes or disks. . . . Files purposely deleted by a computer user. . . . Residual data that exist in bits and pieces throughout a computer hard drive."

- J. Brian Beckham, *Production, Preservation, And Disclosure Of Metadata*, 7 Colum. Sci. & Tech. L. Rev. 1 (2005-2006).

- Campbell C. Steele, *Attorneys Beware: Metadata's Impact on Privilege, Work Product, and the Ethical Rules,* 35 U. Mem. L. Rev. 911 (Summer 2005).

[C]   Search Protocol and Certification

[1]   Generally

Searching electronic information is a critical component of your cases. Whether you are reviewing information from your client for production or receiving data, it has to be searched and analyzed.

Today, all organizations, businesses, and individuals generate large amounts of data in an electronic format. Since important business and personal records may be in an electronic format, and may not be printed out, electronic searching for discoverable evidence becomes all the more critical. Searching can assist in all aspects of electronic discovery. For example, e-mail between key witnesses may establish consistent and frequent contact on important dates in your case. Locating and documenting these findings will strengthen the admissibility of the evidence and ensure a consistent and precise illustration of the alleged conduct. Searching electronic information may determine the outcome of your case.

One of the significant advantages of collecting and discovering information in an electronic format is the ability to search for individual words, names, phrases or dates and obtain the results instantly. Similar to a Westlaw or Lexis search, software is available to allow you to index and immediately search electronic evidentiary material. For example, you could obtain the e-mail files containing thousands or tens of thousands of e-mail messages and using search software, import the information and then search it immediately. In addition, e-mail may have an attachment to a word processing document. When properly converted, both the e-mail and attachment can be searched simultaneously. This is low cost compared to organizing and searching for information in a paper-based system.

There are many techniques for searching data to find relevant admissible evidence. *See, § 5.04, Searching Electronic Information.* These include searching by keyword, file type, time stamps and other file attributes. More advanced data search techniques include text and numeric pattern recognition, as well as searching for audio, graphics and video files. In addition to locating an evidence file of factual importance, searching electronic information is useful in recreating a timeline of events at issue in litigation.

For a discussion of the creation of search terms see § 5.4[E][5], *Keyword Searching.*

[2]   Search Protocol

One of the most critical processes in the production of electronic evidence is the search protocol that is adopted by the disclosing party. Issues such as which computer devices and media were accessed in acquiring the data, what search terms were utilized to gather the evidence and what filtering rules were in effect all can have a profound effect upon the resulting data population that is disclosed. Also, special attention should be given to the producing party's search software capabilities and limitations since it may unreasonably limit the data population. As discussed in § 5.04, *Searching Electronic Information* there are many different types of searches that can be used on a data population including keyword, Boolean, conceptual, clustering and other types that determine what information is retrieved and how it is organized.

The Courts are beginning to recognize these different search technologies and protocols in reported decisions. Over the next several years this will become one of the hotly contested areas of electronic discovery.

The Honorable James C. Francis IV, who authored one of the seminal cost allocation decisions, *Rowe Entertainment, Inc. v. William Morris Agency, Inc.,* 205 F.R.D. 421, 429 (S.D.N.Y. 2002), *aff'd,* 2002 WL 975713 (S.D.N.Y. May 9, 2002), recently discussed the necessity of a search protocol and certification in *Treppel v. Biovail Corp.,* 233 F.R.D. 363, 373-374 (D.N.Y. 2006). Judge Francis stated:

1. Search Protocol   [The defendant] . . . has yet to produce any documents in response to the plaintiff's document request. When [the defendant] . . . received the [production] request, [the defendant] . . . suggested defining the scope of any review of electronic records by stipulating which files would be searched and what search terms would be utilized. The plaintiff declined, apparently believing that 'the use of search terms has no application to the standard discovery process of locating and producing accessible hard copy and electronic documents.' . . . The plaintiff's assumption is flawed. Even in a case involving exclusively hard copy documents, there is no obligation on the part of a responding party to examine every scrap of paper in its potentially voluminous files in order to comply with its discovery obligations. Rather, it must conduct a diligent search, which involves developing a reasonably comprehensive search strategy. Such a strategy might, for example, include identifying key employees and reviewing any of their files that are likely to be relevant to the claims in the litigation. *See, e.g., General Electric Corp. v. Lear Corp.,* 215 F.R.D. 637, 640 (D. Kan. 2003); *McPeek v. Ashcroft,* 202 F.R.D. 31, 32-33 (D.D.C. 2001) ("In a traditional 'paper' case, the producing party searches where she thinks appropriate for the documents requested under FED. R. CIV. P. 34. She is aided by the fact that files are traditionally organized by subject or chronology ("chron" files), such as all the files of a   particular person, independent of subject."). Defined search strategies are even more appropriate in cases involving electronic data, where the number of documents may be exponentially greater. . . . (citations omitted) Thus, the plaintiff's refusal to stipulate to a search methodology in this case was apparently based on a misconception of the scope of the responding party's obligation. At the same time, it was a missed opportunity; the plaintiff might have convinced [the defendant] to broaden its search in ways that would uncover more responsive documents and avoid subsequent disputes. . . . In addition, [the defendant] . . . shall provide the plaintiff with a detailed explanation of the search protocol it implements. . . . This ruling is not an endorsement of the methodology that [the defendant] . . . has suggested, either in relation to the choice of files to be   searched or the terms to be applied. It is, instead, an interim step that is subject to revision once [the defendant] . . . has responded to the interrogatories relating to its electronic data and the plaintiff has articulated any specific concerns about the scope of the search.

[a]   **Reported Cases**

Meet and Confer

- *Balboa Threadworks, Inc. v. Stucky,* No. CIV.05-1157, 2006 U.S. Dist. LEXIS 29265, at *15-16 (D. Kan. Mar. 24, 2006). The Court ruled, "As to the formulation of a search protocol, whether one using key word searches and/or other search procedures, the parties are directed to meet and confer in an attempt to agree on an appropriate protocol, and should lean heavily on their respective computer experts in designing such a protocol. Numerous types and varieties of search protocols have been discussed and adopted by courts and these may guide the parties in designing a search protocol to be used in this case. (citations omitted)."

- *J.C. Associates v. Fidelity & Guar. Ins. Co.,* No. CIV.01-2437, 2005 WL 1570140 (D.D.C. Jul. 1, 2005). The defendant described their search methodology for electronic data,

  The defendant's [manager] has determined that there are 1,363,000 active and inactive claims files that might contain information pertaining to the interpretation of the pollution exclusion. . . . Defendant's counsel caused a search to be conducted of all the claims files from 1986 to the present [and defendant] explains that the claims made by the insureds, those captured in the files, are not indexed or organized based on a particular coverage issue (e.g. "pollution exclusion" or "failure to notify carrier timely") or the specific claim presented. . . . According to defendant's counsel, the coding used describes "general category types" such as asbestos or hazardous waste. Use of that code in an electronic search yielded 454 files (including the six at issue here) that are, in defendant's counsel's view, most likely to contain information pertaining the interpretation of the pollution exclusion. Nineteen of those filed involved claims made in Maryland, Virginia or the District of Columbia. The defendant proposes that it be permitted to fulfill its discovery obligations by providing those nineteen files subject to its claiming pertinent privileges as to documents that are in the files.

- *J.C. Assocs. v. Fid. & Guar. Ins. Co.,* No. CIV.01-2437, 2006 U.S. Dist. LEXIS 32919, at *3-5 (D.D.C. May 25, 2006). The Court issued a protocol order which included sampling, conversion and search protocols. In processing the data, the Court ordered the defendant to use an optical character recognition program to convert and then search for specific keywords, check for privilege, and then disclose to plaintiff.

Search Capability

- *In re Cheyenne Software, Inc.*, No. CIV.94-2771, 1997 WL 714891 (E.D.N.Y. Aug. 18, 1997). In response to word searches, the Court ordered the production of 44,000 pages of e-mail.

Type of Data

- *Procter & Gamble Co. v. Haugen*, 427 F.3d 727 (10th Cir. 2005). The plaintiff's expert obtained data from a third party marketing database for use in their opinions to establish damages. On discussing alternatives to access the marketing data the court found that providing the defendants with regular online access to the information would not necessarily have satisfied the defendants' discovery request because of the "rolling" nature of the marketing database, i.e., data in the database was added and deleted on a continuous basis. The defendants were interested in obtaining a concrete set of marketing related data (i.e., a set of data with established beginning and ending dates) rather than access to the rolling database.

Search Terms

- *In re Search of 3817 W. West End, First Floor, Chicago, Ill.*, 2004 WL 1380272 (N.D. Ill. May 27, 2004). The Court raised possible ways with the government of focusing the search of subject computers, including, limiting the search to specific time periods, using key word searches, and/or limiting the search to text files and excluding graphics files.

- *Wiginton v. CB Richard Ellis, Inc.*, No. CIV.02-6832, 2003 WL 22439865, at *6 (N.D. Ill. Oct. 27, 2003). The Court criticized one of the parties for failing to conduct searches of e-mails, when such searches could have identified responsive documents that should have been preserved. In a later decision the Court in *Wiginton v. CB Richard Ellis, Inc.*, No. CIV.02-6832, 2004 WL 1895122, at *2 (N.D.Ill. Aug. 10, 2004) reviewed the searching process for electronic documents and ordered that "the parties to each choose four [additional] terms from the list of search terms developed by Plaintiffs. Plaintiffs instructed [a service bureau] to search for the eight terms and produce all of the documents containing search terms."

- *Tulip Computers Inter. B. V. v. Dell Computer Corp.*, No. CIV.00-981, 2002 WL 818061, at *4 (D. Del. Apr. 30, 2002). The Court stated, "Tulip's consultant will search the CD ROM on certain mutually agreed-upon search terms that relate to the infringing products or to this case. Such terms may involve 'Tulip' or code words for the allegedly infringing models such as 'STINGER,' 'MASH,' or 'HONEYCUT.' If the search terms generate hits, Dell will review the documents and produce them to Tulip subject to the privilege and confidentiality designations provided under the protective order."

- *Procter & Gamble Co. v. Haugen,* 179 F.R.D. 622 (D. Utah 1998), *aff'd in part and rev'd in part,* 222 F.3d 1262 (10th Cir. 2000). The Court discussed the keywords submitted by the requesting party and their relevance to the case. The magistrate's order, which was sustained in part, authorized keyword searches of 25 terms in the electronic databases.

- *Rowe Entertainment, Inc. v. Wm. Morris Agency, Inc.,* 2002 WL 975713, at *5 (S.D.N.Y. May 9, 2002), *aff'd,* 2002 WL 975713 (S.D.N.Y. May 9, 2002). The requesting party attempted to demonstrate that search of backup tapes could be narrowed by sampling through automated searching using agreed list of search terms.

- *Medtronic Sofamor Danek, Inc. v. Michelson,* No. CIV.01-2373, 2003 WL 21468573, at *3-4 (W.D. Tenn. May 13, 2003). The requesting party was required to pay a portion of the cost of restoring backup tapes based partially on the fact that the party did not limit requests by date and suggested search terms which were claimed to be too broad.

- *United States v. Welch,* 401 F. Supp. 2d 1172, 1180-1181 (D. Kan. 2005). The Court noted that "[c]omputer storage devices . . . can store the equivalent of thousands of pages of information . . . when the user wants to conceal criminal evidence, he often stores it in random order with deceptive file names. This requires searching authorities to examine all the stored data to determine whether it is included in the warrant."

- *Alexander v. Federal Bureau of Investigation,* 188 F.R.D. 111, 117 (D.D.C. 1998). The Court allowed discovery of "targeted and appropriately worded searches of backed-up and archived e-mail and deleted hard-drives for a limited number of individuals." Subsequently, the Court in *Alexander v. Federal Bureau of Investigation,* 194 F.R.D. 316, 323 (D.D.C. 2000) noted that the parties agreed to search the e-mail for 40 individuals utilizing 36 search terms.

- *United States v. Triumph Capital Group, Inc.,* 211 F.R.D. 31, 47 (D. Conn. 2002). The Court ruled that a search warrant could not be limited to specific keyword terms and stated, "[c]omputer searches, especially those seeking evidence of deletion, are technical and complex and cannot be limited to precise, specific steps or only one permissible method. Directories and files can be encrypted, hidden or misleadingly titled, stored in unusual formats, and commingled with unrelated and innocuous files that have no relation to the crimes under investigation. Descriptive file names or file extensions such as '.jpg' cannot be relied on to determine the type of file because a computer user can save a file with any name or extension he chooses."

- *In Re: Propulsid Products Liability,* MDL No. 1355, Pretrial Order No. 10, Production and Preservation of Defendants' Electronic Data, Apr. 19, 2001 available at http://

propulsid.laed.uscourts.gov/Orders/order10.pdf. The Court in a pretrial order ruled, "data will be prescreened for responsiveness utilizing search terms agreed upon by the parties. The parties shall cooperate to identify query terms designed to retrieve discoverable electronic data. The parties will then meet and confer or otherwise cooperate as to resolving any dispute."

Multiple Searches

- *Zubulake v. UBS Warburg LLC,* No. CIV.02-1243, 2004 WL 1620866, *8 (S.D.N.Y. July 20, 2004). The Court stated, "[f]or example, counsel could create a broad list of search terms, run a search for a limited time frame, and then segregate responsive documents. It might be advisable to solicit a list of search terms from the opposing party for this purpose, so that it could not later complain about which terms were used.] When the opposing party propounds its document requests, the parties could negotiate a list of search terms to be used in identifying responsive documents, and counsel would only be obliged to review documents that came up as 'hits' on the second, more restrictive search. The initial broad cut merely guarantees that relevant documents are not lost."

- *Cumis Ins. Co. v. Diebold, Inc.,* No. CIV.02-7346, 2004 WL 1126173, at *1 n.1 (E.D.Pa. May 20, 2004). The Court ordered additional searches since the responding party was shown not to have produced all of the electronic information based on the fact that responsive documents regarding Diebold were found in the possession of third parties.

- *Commonwealth v. Ellis,* 1999 WL 815818 (Mass. Super. Aug. 27, 1999). The Court ruled that "keyword searches are likely the most efficient types of searches, but unless the computer analyst knows how the data was organized and stored, there will necessarily be trial and error to determine key phrases, words, and places."

- *In re Amsted Industries, Inc. "Erisa" Litigation,* No. CIV.01-2963, 2002 WL 31844956, at *2 (N.D. Ill. Dec. 18, 2002). Court granted additional keyword search request because of enlargement of the subject matter of litigation and also ruled producing party, who had already searched the backup tapes, must search "the in-box, saved, and sent folders of any relevant individual's e-mail in the same manner."

- *McPeek v. Ashcroft*, No. CIV.00-201, 2003 WL 75780 (D.D.C. Jan. 9, 2003). The Court refused to allow additional keyword searches of backup tapes based upon the undue burden and the limited likelihood that relevant information could be retrieved.

[b] Other Authorities

- *See also,* § 7.7[H], *Inspection of Opposing Party's Computer System.*
- Eastern and Western Districts of Arkansas Local Civil Rule 26.1:

5. Search methodology. If the parties intend to employ an electronic search to locate relevant electronic documents, the parties shall disclose any restrictions as to scope and method which might affect their ability to conduct a complete electronic search of the electronic documents. The parties shall reach agreement as to the method of searching, and the words, terms, and phrases to be searched with the assistance of the respective e-discovery liaisons, who are charged with familiarity with the parties' respective systems. The parties also shall reach agreement as to the timing and conditions of any additional searches which may become necessary in the normal course of discovery. To minimize the expense, the parties may consider limiting the scope of the electronic search (e.g., time frames, fields, document types).

- Jason R. Baron, *Toward a Federal Benchmarking Standard for Evaluating Information Retrieval Products Used in E-Discovery,* 6 Sedona Conf. J. 237 (2005).

- Steven C. Bennett, *E-Discovery by Keyword Search*, 15 No. 3 Prac. Litigator 7 (May 2004).

- Michael Ravnitzky & Jeanne Weigum, *Filtered or Unfiltered Information: Choices in How to Make the Minnesota Tobacco Document Depository Records More Accessible to the Public*, 25 WMLR 715 (1999).

[3]   Certification

To prevent spoliation and admissibility issues, you should always have a certification prepared of the identification, collection and production process. Such a certification, preferably from an independent third-party, will be a strong defense against spoliation claims because of delay in preserving relevant data, improper data collection and a host of other issues. The chain of custody certification needs to document how the data was identified, what computer systems were searched, from where the data originated, who took possession, who had access to it, and so forth.

[a]   Reported Cases

Search protocol certification required

- *Convolve, Inc. v. Compaq Computer Corp.,* 223 F.R.D. 162, 168 (S.D.N.Y. 2004) "Because this document is plainly relevant and because Compaq previously provided incorrect information about its RFPs and RFQs, it is important to ensure that its search has been comprehensive. Therefore, Compaq shall submit an affidavit setting forth in detail the steps taken to identify RFPs and RFQs, including those stored in electronic databases, which refer to the capability of switching between quiet mode and performance mode."

- *Lava Trading, Inc., Hartford Fire Ins. Co.,* No. CIV.03-7037, 2005 WL 459267, at *16 (S.D.N.Y. Feb. 24, 2005). "Finally, to clear up any ambiguity about the completeness of plaintiff's production at this late date, plaintiff will be required to provide an affidavit by one or more Lava officials with knowledge of the facts detailing the scope of the document searches undertaken in response to defendant's three Rule 34 notices and the completeness of the production of all responsive documents. This is to be done by March 4, 2005, and defendant will be permitted to depose the affiants, if desired, to inquire into the details of all searches."

- *Innovative Piledriving Prods., LLC v. Unisto Oy,* No. CIV.04-453, 2005 U.S. Dist. LEXIS 23652, at *4-7 (D. Ind. Oct. 14, 2005). Plaintiff ordered to "execute an affidavit . . . stating that after diligent search there are no responsive documents in its 'possession, custody or control,' . . . Specifically, the affidavit must articulate the efforts [plaintiff] has taken to locate, retrieve, and restore the responsive electronic data that apparently was automatically deleted from [the plaintiff's] computer systems."

- *Judicial Watch, Inc. v. United States Department of Justice,* 185 F. Supp. 2d 54, 64-65 (D.D.C. 2002). The Court ruled that the agency was required to file supplemental affidavits explaining precisely how keyword searches were conducted and stated, "[d]efendant, however, provides no description of how the electronic index is organized or how the search was conducted . . . [t]he Pustay declaration fails to explain whether key words were used and if so which key words were used to search for responsive documents. Without knowing these details regarding the defendant's search, the Court cannot determine whether defendant's efforts were 'reasonably calculated' to recover the responsive records."

Search protocol certification not required

- *Benson v. St. Joseph Reg'l Health Ctr.,* No. CIV.04-04323, 2006 U.S. Dist. LEXIS 28795, at *12-14 (D. Tex. May 1, 2006). The Court denied plaintiff's request for a search protocol certification since defendants "have certified and represented to the Court that they have complied fully with Plaintiffs' requests and made reasonable efforts to find and disclose all responsive documents and emails." In addition, plaintiffs were unable point to any missing electronic evidence and defendant's witnesses had all testified that they had conducted searches and found no responsive data.

- *Harbuck v. Teets,* 152 Fed. Appx. 846, 847-849 (11th Cir. 2005)(unpublished). In this employment discrimination case, the Court used its IT personnel to evaluate electronic data out of the presence of both parties. The plaintiff objected arguing it did not have a chance to examine the person "as to the person's methodology and retrieval methods." The Appellate Court found that the district court did not abuse its discretion in having its personnel evaluate the data.

Search protocol disregarded

• *Rowe Entertainment, Inc. v. William Morris Agency, Inc.,* No. CIV.98-827, 2005 WL 22833, at *53 n.143 (S.D.N.Y. Jan. 5, 2005). The Court agreed to the search terms for certain employees proposed by the plaintiff who was to "(1) notify Defendants' counsel of the search procedure to be used by Plaintiffs in identifying responsive e-mails, including specific word searches; (2) identify any e-mails they considered 'material' to this litigation; and (3) produce them to Defendants in 'hard copy with Bates Stamp.'" The plaintiff failed to abide by the order and as a result the plaintiff's exhibit for summary judgment purposes was disregarded by the Court.

Search protocol description

• *United States v. Maali,* 346 F. Supp.2d 1226, 1264 (M.D.Fla. 2004). The defendants challenged:

> the manner in which the computer hard drives were seized, copied, and searched. They contend that the seizure was overbroad and that steps were not taken to keep track of what files the searchers viewed on the master hard drive . . . 83 computer hard drives were seized from the search sites. These hard drives were then copied . . . A total of approximately three million computer files were seized . . . agent then "culled down" these three million computer files to 270,000 files by eliminating "program" files and other non-data type files. In reducing the number of potentially-responsive files the CART agent did not open the files to examine them for responsiveness to the warrant but instead removed files based only on type, attempting to leave all data-type files on the resulting "master" hard drive. This master hard drive was then turned over . . . [to agents] to be searched through the use of text strings for computer documents responsive to the search warrants. . . . The Defendants criticize the searchers' failure to attempt to search the computers onsite and the compilation of a master hard drive with deletion of only non-data type files. They also assert that the failure of the searchers to keep records of the text-string searches that were run on the "master hard drive" requires suppression. However, the Defendants' arguments are without merit and the Court finds no constitutional infirmity in the execution of the search as it pertains to computers.

- *Defenders of Wildlife v. U.S. Department of Interior,* 314 F. Supp.2d 1, 13 n.16 (D.D.C. 2004). The Court found that the government had properly conducted an FOIA electronic search supported by "OGE's declarations properly explained manual search of conflict of interest files, automated search of electronic files, consultation with OGE attorneys working on matters pertaining to deputy secretary, and why certain files were not searched . . . Ms. Newton's supplemental declaration described the adequacy of the search by explaining that many of these files were in fact searched, others were not searched for valid reasons, and alternative methods were undertaken to update the computerized search."

Challeging Search Protocol

- *Williams v. Massachusetts Mut. Life Ins.* Co. 226 F.R.D. 144, 146 (D. Mass. 2005). The Court ruled that it was "similarly disinclined to allow Plaintiff to conduct the forensic study at his own expense. Before permitting such an intrusion into an opposing party's information system--particularly where, as here, that party has undertaken its own search and forensic analysis and has sworn to its accuracy--the inquiring party must present at least some reliable information that the opposing party's representations are misleading or substantively inaccurate."

Discovery of Search Protocol

- *Fischer v. United Parcel Serv. Co.,* 2006 WL 1046973 (E.D. Mich. Apr. 19, 2006). The defendant was unable to find an attachment to a responsive e-mail during the discovery process. The plaintiff requested the opportunity to discuss the with an employee of the defendant their search efforts to locate the attachment. The Court granted the request ruling that even though the attachment may not be admissible and irrelevant, it could reasonably lead to the discovery of admissible evidence.

[D]   Translated Into Reasonably Useful Form

Rule 34 permits the discovery of any "documents" and "data compilations from which information can be obtained, translated, if necessary, by the respondent through detection devices into reasonably useful form." *See also,* § § 7.07[G], *Form of Production of Computer-based Data* and 7.07[E], *Kept in the Usual Course of Business.*

Pending Rule 34 Amendment

The pending Rule 34(b) Amendment Committee Note recognizes that:

- "Rule 34(b) provides that a party must produce documents as they are kept in the usual course of business or must organize and label them to correspond with the categories in the discovery request."

- "If the form of production is not specified by party agreement or court order, the responding party must produce electronically stored information either in a form or forms in which it is ordinarily maintained or in a form or forms that are reasonably usable."

- "Rule 34(a) requires that, if necessary, a responding party "translate" information it produces into a "reasonably usable" form."

For the complete text of the pending Rule 34 amendment and the Committee Note see § 7.7[A][1], *Pending Rule 34 Amendment.*

[1]   Reported Cases

- *Powerhouse Marks, L.L.C. v. Chi Hsin Impex, Inc.,* No. CIV.04-73923, 2006 U.S. Dist. LEXIS 2767, at *9-11 (D. Mich. Jan. 12, 2006). In response to interrogatories, the defendant was ordered "to compute and provide in summary fashion annual sales figures and expenditures for specific products. Under the Federal Rules, a party may be ordered to produce such information even when the electronic information does not exist in the format requested. *See generally* FED. R. CIV. P. 34, Advisory Committee's notes specifying that a 'respondent may be required to use his devices to translate the data into usable form.'"

- *Jackson v. City of San Antonio,* No. CIV.03-0049, 2006 U.S. Dist. LEXIS 8091 (W.D. Tex., Jan. 31, 2006). The plaintiff objected to defendants' form of production of computerized pay and time records in response to discovery as being an unauthorized "data dump." They also argued the computerized records failed to include field descriptors which made the records "unhelpful, unuseable, and nonresponsive." The Court ruled that "because the burden of culling out the requested information is no greater for plaintiffs than it would be for defendants, the rules permit defendants the option to respond by producing their business records. F.R.Civ.P. 33(d)." Also, the defendant supplied the field descriptors at a later date.

- *Evolution, Inc. v. Suntrust Bank,* No. CIV.01-2409, 2004 WL 2278559 (D.Kan. Sept. 29, 2004). In this software infringement action the Court found that defendant had been uncooperative in refusing to provide instructions on how to restore and load software and to allow copying of the third party software controls.

- *Sattar v. Motorola, Inc.,* 138 F.3d 1164, 1171 (7th Cir. 1998). The Court ordered a party that produced e-mail on tapes to provide additional assistance to enable the adversary to read e-mail, including either downloading the e-mail onto a hard-drive, loaning adversary a copy of necessary software, or offering adversary access to computer system.

- *Daewoo Electronic Co., Ltd. v. United States,* 650 F. Supp. 1003, 1007 (Ct. Int'l. Trade 1986). The Court ordered production of computerized data with computerized instructions.

- *Fautek v. Montgomery Ward & Co.,* 96 F.R.D. 141, 144-46 (N.D. Ill. 1982). The Court sanctioned party for not producing codes necessary to understand electronic data.

- *Williams v. E.I. du Pont de Nemours & Co.,* 119 F.R.D. 648, 651 (W.D. Ky. 1987). The Court ordered production of a computer database with related information such as "codebooks" and user manuals.

[2]   Other Authorities

7-37A Moore's Federal Practice - Civil § 37A.30

A party's failure to produce relevant evidence is not excused because the volume of computer-based records to be searched is enormous and prevents a full understanding of its contents. The difficulties in retrieving pertinent information are ordinarily assumed by the responding party because it has selected its own computerized record-keeping system. *Translating computer data into a reasonably understandable form is a necessary and foreseeable burden.* Accordingly, the requesting party should not be forced to pay discovery costs incurred in retrieving evidence as a result of the responding party's decision to choose a particular recording system (*see, e.g.,* § 37A.33[4][b]). (emphasis added).

[E]   Kept in the Usual Course of Business

[1]   Rule 34 (b)

Rule 34(b) has directed that "[a] party who produces documents for inspection shall produce them as they are kept in the usual course of business or shall organize and label them to correspond with the categories in the request." The Advisory Committee Note to the 1980 amendment stated the purpose was to prevent a respondent from "deliberately . . . mix(ing) critical documents with others in the hope of obscuring significance" and to provide the requesting party with documents in usable form.

The producing party has the burden pursuant to Rule 34(b) of establishing that the documents were produced "as they are kept in the ordinary course of business. . . . A mere assertion that they were so produced is not sufficient to carry that burden. In addition, merely categorizing the documents produced does not, without some further explanation, satisfy the requirement that they be produced as kept in the usual course of business." *Cardenas v. Dorel Juvenile Group, Inc.,* 230 F.R.D. 611, 618-619 (D. Kan. 2005); *Bergersen v. Shelter Mut. Ins. Co.,* 2006 WL 334675 (D. Kan. Feb. 14, 2006). Some jurisdictions require a timely motion challenging the form of production. *Bergersen v. Shelter Mutual Ins. Co.,* 2006 WL 334675 (D. Kan. Feb. 14, 2006) (Court denied plaintiff's motion to compel the defendant to produce the documents "as they are kept in the usual course of business" because it was not filed within 30 days after receipt of defendants' discovery responses); *Wild v. Alster,* 377 F. Supp. 2d 186, 193-195 (D.D.C. 2005) (court partially denied plaintiff's request to examine the defendant's hard drive filed 18 months after the close of discovery).

For specific issues related to databases see §§ 3.10 *Databases* and 7.9[J][5], *Database.*

[2]   Pending Rule 34 Amendment

Rule 34. Production of Documents, <u>Electronically Stored Information,</u> and Things and Entry Upon Land for Inspection and Other Purposes (emphasis added) . . .

(b) Procedure. . . .

<u>Unless the parties otherwise agree, or the court otherwise orders:</u>

(i) a party who produces documents for inspection shall produce them as they are kept in the usual course of business or shall organize and label them to correspond with the categories in the request;

<u>(ii) if a request does not specify the form or forms for producing electronically stored information, a responding party must produce the information in a form or forms in which it is ordinarily maintained or in a form or forms that are reasonably usable; and</u>

<u>(iii) a party need not produce the same electronically stored information in more than one form.</u> (emphasis added).

Committee Note

Subdivision (b). Rule 34(b) provides that a party must produce documents as they are kept in the usual course of business or must organize and label them to correspond with the categories in the discovery request. The production of electronically stored information should be subject to comparable requirements to protect against deliberate or inadvertent production in ways that raise unnecessary obstacles for the requesting party. Rule 34(b) is amended to ensure similar protection for electronically stored information.

[3] Purpose

Pending Rule 34 Amendment

The pending Rule 34(b) Amendment Committee Note recognizes that:

- "Rule 34(b) provides that a party must produce documents as they are kept in the usual course of business or must organize and label them to correspond with the categories in the discovery request."

- *See also,* § § 7.07[D], *Translated Into Reasonably Useful Form* and 7.07[G], *Form of Production of Computer-based Data.*

For the complete text of the pending Rule 34 amendment and the Committee Note see § 7.7[A][1], *Pending Rule 34 Amendment.*

[4] Reported Cases

- *Bergersen v. Shelter Mutual Ins. Co.,* 2006 WL 334675 (D. Kan. Feb. 14, 2006). The Court stated, "[i]t is clear that the documents produced by Defendants were not produced 'as they are kept in the usual course of business'. . . . Parties producing documents electronically often enter into agreed orders concerning the protocol to be followed. . . . Those agreements may contain provisions for (1) keying which documents were produced from electronic files and which were scanned from hard-copy files, (2) keeping multi-page documents as a unit, (3) providing source information which identifies, where possible, the custodian of a particular document or set of documents, etc."

- *Williams v. Sprint/United Mgmt. Co.,* 230 F.R.D. 640, 656-657 (D. Kan. 2005). The Court ordered an employer in an employment discrimination case to restore the metadata it had "scrubbed" or "erased" from Excel spreadsheet files and "unlock" them. The Court stated, "[t]he Court, however, wants to clarify the law regarding the production of metadata. . . . *When the Court orders a party to produce an electronic document in the form in which it is regularly maintained, i.e., in its native format or as an active file, that production must include all metadata* unless that party timely objects to production of the metadata, the parties agree that the metadata should not be produced, or the producing party requests a protective order." (emphasis added).

- *Residential Constructors, LLC v. Ace Prop. & Cas. Ins. Co.,* No. CIV.05-01318, 2006 WL 1582122, *1-2 (D. Nev. Jun. 5, 2006). Defendant filed a motion to compel the plaintiff to provide an index or table of contents for documents that had been imaged and produced on CD-ROM. Plaintiff argued that the documents were searchable by keyword and they were produced as kept in the usual course of business. The Court ruled, "[p]laintiff has gathered these documents together from different entities and locations and has assembled the documents together in the boxes, which have now been imaged onto a computer data base. Clearly some form of table of contents or index of the materials produced should be provided."

- *Fenster Family Patent Holdings, Inc. v. Siemens Medical Solutions USA, Inc.,* No. CIV.04-0038, 2005 U.S. Dist. LEXIS 20788, at *12-14 (D. Del. Sept. 20, 2005). After the plaintiff filed a motion to compel, the defendant agreed to produce specific documents in a searchable format. However, defendant provided information that some older documents were only available on microfilm and that it fulfilled its obligations under the Federal Rules by producing them in the format in which they were maintained.

- *CP Solutions PTE, Ltd. v. GE,* No. CIV.04-2150, 2006 U.S. Dist. LEXIS 27053, at *1-15 (D. Conn. Feb. 6, 2006). In a decision contrary to the pending "e-discovery" rules, the Court refused to order disclosure of the "native files" instead allowing the defendants to disclose TIFF images that were not searchable. Plaintiffs had requested the electronic data "as they are kept in the normal course of business." The Court ruled that the TIFF images complied with this mandate and ignored the fact that the metadata was not produced with the TIFF images and the e-mail had been separated from the attachments. However, the Court did rule that the TIFF attachments would have to be "reattached" to the appropriate e-mail.

- *In re Adelphia Communications Corp.* 317 B.R. 612, 623 (Bankr. S.D.N.Y. 2004). "The Rigas Defendants are entitled to the production of documents in a way by which they can work with them. Though the Rigas Defendants have millions of pages of documents in electronic form, they do not have the documents in a way that segregates them by subject matter or the file from which they came, nor do they have the ability to search them."

- *Zakre v. Norddeutsche Landesbank Girozentrale,* No. CIV.03-0257, 2004 WL 764895 (S.D.N.Y. Apr. 9 2004). The Court ruled that the defendant had satisfied its obligation under FED. R. CIV. P. 34 to disclose information "as they are kept in the usual course of business" by providing text searchable access to more than 200,000 e-mail.

- *In re Lorazepam and Clorazepate Antitrust Litigation,* 300 F. Supp. 2d 43, 47 (D.D.C. 2004). The plaintiff objected to the electronic discovery production arguing that an "index" should have been provided. The Court ruled that, "[t]he glory of electronic information is not merely that it saves space but that it permits the computer to search for words or 'strings' of text in seconds. The Blues can, for example, look for the White Paper they insist exists by searching for the word 'white' within a certain number of words from the word 'paper,' thus replicating for themselves the search done several years ago by a computer forensic scientist. In this sense, the presence of the information on the CD-ROM's is an opportunity for the Blues rather than a problem."

- *Hagemeyer North America, Inc. v. Gateway Data Sciences Corp.*, 222 F.R.D. 594, 601 (E.D.Wis. 2004). The Court held that, "[a] party responding to a document request under Rule 34 has a choice of producing the documents 'as they are kept in the usual course of business' or of 'organiz[ing] and label[ing] them to correspond with the categories in the request.' FED.R.CIV.P. 34(b). When producing documents, the responding party cannot attempt to hide a needle in a haystack by mingling responsive documents with large numbers of nonresponsive documents. (citation omitted) However, according to the plain language of Rule 34, a responding party has no duty to organize and label the documents if it has produced them as they are kept in the usual course of business."

[F]   Possession, Custody or Control

A request under FED. R. CIV. P. 34 must be directed to matters which are in the possession, custody, or control of the party upon whom the request is served. In determining matters which must be produced under Rule 34, the focus is on the party's legal right to custody or control of the documents in question. *United States v. International Union of Petroleum and Industrial Workers, AFL-CIO,* 870 F.2d 1450, 1452 (9th Cir. 1989). Thus, a party need not have actual possession of documents to be deemed in control of them if the party has the legal right to control or obtain them. The legal ownership of a document is not determinative, however, possession or control is sufficient to permit a request for production.

[1]   Reported Cases

- *Super Film of America, Inc. v. UCB Films Inc.,* 219 F.R.D. 649, 657 (D. Kan. 2004). In a contractual dispute the Court held that under "FED.R.CIV.P. 34(a), a party may be required to produce relevant documents and tangible things that are within its 'possession, custody or control.' . . . '[C]ontrol comprehends not only possession but also the right, authority, or ability to obtain the documents.' Therefore, Rule 34(a) enables a party seeking discovery to require production of documents beyond the actual possession of the opposing party if such party has retained 'any right or ability to influence the person in whose possession the documents lie.'"

- *In re Bankers Trust Co.,* 61 F.3d 465, 469 (6th Cir. 1995), *cert. dismissed,* 517 U.S. 1205 (1996). On a bank's petition to vacate a discovery order requiring the bank to produce Federal Reserve examination reports and documents prepared by the Federal Reserve and the bank during the examination process, the Court of Appeals held that the discovery order was consistent with FED. R. CIV. P. 34. "Documents are deemed in the possession, custody, or control of a party for purposes of FRCP 34 if the party has actual possession, custody, or control, or has the right to obtain the documents on demand; legal ownership is not determinative. Thus, the bank, in possession of documents forwarded to it by the Federal Reserve, had possession, custody, or control within the meaning of FRCP 34."

- *In re ATM Fee Antitrust Litig.,* 233 F.R.D. 542 (D. Cal. 2005). The Court ruled that a holding company who controlled a wholly-owned subsidiary must produce relevant documents pursuant to a Rule 34 request for production.

- *Alexander v. F.B.I.,* 194 F.R.D. 299, 301 (D.D.C. 2000). In this case, a defendant stated in her responses to requests for production that she would produce only those documents in her possession. A supplemental response was ordered from the defendant as to whether all documents, including those not in her possession but still within her control, had been produced. The term "control" is defined not as possession, but as the legal right to obtain documents on demand.

- *Rosie D. v. Romney,* 256 F. Supp. 2d 115, 119 (D. Mass. 2003). "As used in rule providing procedures for requesting documents which were within scope of discovery and were in possession, custody or control of the party upon whom the request was served, concept of 'control' exists where party has a legal right to obtain documents, and such control may be established by existence of principal-agent relationship or pursuant to contractual provision."

- *Hagemeyer North America, Inc. v. Gateway Data Sciences Corp.,* 222 F.R.D. 594, 598-599 (E.D.Wis. 2004). Pursuant to Rule 34 the Court denied plaintiff's motion to compel the production of the defendant's e-mail which the defendant asserted that it did not "possess" the documents. The Court held that "[a] party need not produce documents or tangible things that are not in existence or within its control. . . . In the face of a denial by a party that it has possession, custody or control of documents, the [requesting] party must make an adequate showing to overcome this assertion."

[G]   Form of Production of Computer-based Data

[1]   Rule 34

FED. R. CIV. P. 34(a) requires that information from computer-based data compilations be translated, if necessary, into a "reasonably usable form." FED. R. CIV. P. 34 advisory committee notes (1970 amendments) provides:

> *[W]hen the data can as a practical matter be made usable by the discovering party only through respondent's devices, respondent may be required to use his devices to translate the data into usable form.* In many instances, this means that respondent will have to supply a print-out of computer data. The burden thus placed on respondent will vary from case to case, and the courts have ample power under Rule 26(c) to protect respondent against undue burden or expense, either by restricting discovery or requiring that the discovering party pay costs.

Similarly, if the discovering party needs to check the electronic source itself, the court may protect respondent with respect to preservation of his records, confidentiality of nondiscoverable matters, and costs. (emphasis added.).

[2]   Pending Rule 34 Amendment

(b) Procedure. . . . <u>The request may specify the form or forms in which electronically stored information is to be produced.</u> . . . The response shall state, with respect to each item or category, that inspection and related activities will be permitted as requested, unless the request is objected to,<u> including an objection to the requested form or forms for producing electronically stored information, stating</u> the reasons for the objection. . . . <u>If objection is made to the requested form or forms for producing electronically stored information — or if no form was specified in the request — the responding party must state the form or forms it intends to use.</u> . . . (emphasis added)

* * * * *

<u>Unless the parties otherwise agree, or the court otherwise orders:</u>

(i) a party who produces documents for inspection shall produce them as they are kept in the usual course of business or shall organize and label them to correspond with the categories in the request;

<u>(ii) if a request does not specify the form or forms for producing electronically stored information, a responding party must produce the information in a form or forms in which it is ordinarily maintained or in a form or forms that are reasonably usable; and</u> (emphasis added)

<u>(iii) a party need not produce the same electronically stored information in more than one form.</u> (emphasis added).

Committee Note

The pending Rule 34(b) Amendment Committee Note recognizes that:

- "Rule 34(b) provides that a party must produce documents as they are kept in the usual course of business or must organize and label them to correspond with the categories in the discovery request."
- "Rule 34(b) permits the requesting party to designate the form or forms in which it wants electronically stored information produced."
- "The rule therefore provides that the requesting party may ask for different forms of production for different types of electronically stored information."

- "The rule does not require that the requesting party choose a form or forms of production."

- "In the written response to the production request that Rule 34 requires, the responding party must state the form it intends to use for producing electronically stored information if the requesting party does not specify a form or if the responding party objects to a form that the requesting party specifies."

- "If the requesting party is not satisfied with the form stated by the responding party, or if the responding party has objected to the form specified by the requesting party, the parties must meet and confer under Rule 37(a)(2)(B) in an effort to resolve the matter before the requesting party can file a motion to compel."

- "If the form of production is not specified by party agreement or court order, the responding party must produce electronically stored information either in a form or forms in which it is ordinarily maintained or in a form or forms that are reasonably usable."

- "Rule 34(a) requires that, if necessary, a responding party "translate" information it produces into a 'reasonably usable' form."

For the complete text of the pending Rule 34 amendment and the Committee Note see § 7.7[A][1], *Pending Rule 34 Amendment.*

[3]   Purpose

Traditionally, documents were only produced in a printed format. However, different format options, along with metadata, have become available with the widespread use of electronic information. *See,* § 5.3, *Electronic Data Formats.* Counsel should communicate what production format they desire at the commencement of the case, or otherwise seek court assistance if a disagreement arises. *Northern Crossarm Co. v. Chemical Specialities,* No. CIV.03-415, 2004 WL 635606 (W.D. Wis. Mar. 3, 2004).

Often, case information requested will be both in an electronic and paper or printed format. The issue will be whether to request information in either an electronic or printed format, or both. It may be prudent to discover the information in both formats for the following reasons.

If you obtain the printed or paper format, handwritten notes and other marginalia may be present on the paper copies. Also, paper discovery will often provide validation as to whether or not electronic information has been accurately and comprehensively disclosed.

Obtaining information in an electronic format will allow you to discover metadata, as well as the capability to manage and perform analysis of case information. *See,* § 5.2, *Value of Collecting Information in an Electronic Format* and § 5.3, *Electronic Data Formats.* Metadata provides additional information that is not contained in the paper or printed format. Such metadata may prove invaluable depending upon the factual allegations in your claims or defenses. Also, analysis of relational databases and spreadsheets, meaningless in a paper form, can be conducted after the data has been imported into the computer using the appropriate software. Paper copies are not an acceptable substitute under these circumstances.

Pending Rule 34 Amendment

Pending Rule 34(b) has now elevated the "form" of production into a major issue in litigation. The "form" of production will determine whether the ESI can be searched, privileged information redacted, Bates numbered, and if the metadata are available for review. Also, it may determine the genuineness and authenticity of the data. For a review of characteristics of the different file formats see § 5.3, *Electronic Data Formats.*

Rule 34 (b) has added a new procedure to resolve the issue of what "form" "electronically stored information" (ESI) should be disclosed. ESI is subject to processing and conversion to different types of electronic "forms" which may be pivotal in searching or analyzing the data for use in your case.

For this reason, the requesting party pursuant to Rule 34(b) "may specify the form or forms in which electronically stored information is to be produced." However, the producing party can object to the "form(s)" request and provide reasons for the objection. If no type of form(s) are requested the responding party must disclose in its answer what form(s) the data will be disclosed. Also, if no specific form is requested the responding party must "produce the information in a form or forms in which it is ordinarily maintained or in a form or forms that are reasonably usable . . . [and] a party need not produce the same electronically stored information in more than one form."

The pending Rule 26(f) amendment requires the parties to discuss "any issues relating to disclosure or discovery of electronically stored information, including the form or forms in which it should be produced . . ."

[4]   Reported Cases

Hard copy produced, subsequently required to produce electronic copy

*   *National Union Elec. Corp. v. Matsushita Elec. Indus. Co. Ltd.,* 494 F. Supp. 1257, 1262 (E.D. Pa. 1980). In this seminal case, the Court ordered plaintiff to produce computer tape of certain data (television sales and production data, etc.) that plaintiff previously supplied in printed form. Court noted the relative cost for plaintiff to produce the tape by reprogramming the computer, which defendant was to pay, was far less than reentering the data into a computer. The defendant agreed to pay the costs for the reprogramming, and the Court stated, "[a]lthough there may be some difference between requiring the production of existing tapes and requiring a party to so program

the computer as to produce data in computer-readable as opposed to printout form, we find it to be a distinction without a difference. . . . the manufacture of a machine-readable copy of a computer disc is in principle no different from the manufacture of a photocopy of a written document, a common enough method of responding to a request for document production."

- *In re Bristol-Myers Squibb Securities Litigation,* 205 F.R.D. 437, 439, 441 (D.N.J. 2002). The defendant in responding to discovery, delivered paper copies 'blown back' from electronic images. The plaintiff was unaware that the discovery was available in a digital format, later objected and sought the electronic copies, and also refused to pay for either the paper or electronic copies. The Court stated: "[t]he Court, mindful of Rule 26(a)(1)(B) finds that where a party already possesses relevant information in electronic form, it is obligated, by way of mandatory disclosure, to so advise the adversary. Once advised of the existence of electronic data, a party may then make an informed decision as to the manner by which discovery could be produced." The plaintiff ordered to pay for paper copies, but not electronic copies.

- *Cornell Research Found. v. Hewlett Packard Co.,* 223 F.R.D. 55, 74 (D.N.Y. 2003). After the defendant disclosed schematic drawings in a paper format at a substantial expense, the Court ordered the documents to be produced in an electronic format and stated, "[t]he mere fact that information which as a matter of ordinary course of one's business is electronically stored has been produced in functional equivalent, such as through hard copy, does not in and of itself excuse a party from producing the requested information in electronic form. (citations omitted)."

- *Zhou v. Pittsburgh State University,* No. CIV.01-2493, 2003 WL 1905988 (D. Kan. Feb. 5, 2003). In this employment discrimination case, the Court required the defendant to produce the discovery information in an electronic format even though typed copies of the discovery had already been provided.

- *In re Dow Corning Corp.,* 250 B.R. 298 (Bankr. E.D. Mich. 2000). The Court ruled that the federal government was required to make medical records stored in computer databases available to the debtor, even though government had offered worldwide warehouse locations where the data could be found in a printed format.

- *In re Honeywell Intern., Inc. Securities Litigation,* No. M8-85, 2003 WL 22722961, at *2 (S.D.N.Y. 2003). The Court ruled that a nonparty had to produce the data in electronic format, after disclosing it in printed form, since it had not complied with Rule 34 that required the documents be disclosed "as kept in the usual course of business."

- *Hines v. Windall,* 183 F.R.D. 596 (N.D. Fla. 1998). The Court ordered defendant to produce computerized images of records, after paper copies had been produced.

- *Storch v. IPCO Safety Prods. Co.,* No. CIV.96-7592, 1997 WL 401589, at *2 (E.D. Pa. July 16, 1997). In a Medical Leave Act case defendant offered the discovery in a printed format and the Court ruled, "that in this age of high-technology where much of our information is transmitted by computer and computer disks, it is not unreasonable for the defendant to produce the information on computer disk for the plaintiff."

- *In re Air Crash Disaster at Detroit Metro. Airport*, 130 F.R.D. 634, 635-636 (E.D. Mich. 1989). Court directed McDonnell Douglas Corp. to produce computer tape of a flight director simulation program and data, even though it had previously produced a hard copy since it would be extremely difficult and costly to manually load "95 pages of single-spaced printout of the program and underlying data onto a nine-track tape."

- *Anti-Monopoly, Inc. v. Hasbro,* Inc., No. CIV.94-2120, 1995 W.L. 649934, at *2 (S.D.N.Y. Nov. 3, 1995). The Court required the defendant to provide the information in an electronic format, after producing it in a hard copy format. Court noted that "the rule is clear: production of information in 'hard copy' documentary form does not preclude a party from receiving that same information in computerized/electronic form." Further, the producing party may be required to design a computer program to extract the data from its computerized business records subject to the court's discretion as to the allocation of the cost of designing such a computer program.

- *In re Bristol-Myers Squibb Securities Litigation,* 205 F.R.D. 437, 439, 441 (D.N.J. 2002). The defendant in responding to discovery, delivered paper copies 'blown back' from electronic images. The plaintiff was unaware that the discovery was available in a digital format, later objected and sought the electronic copies, and also refused to pay for either the paper or electronic copies. The Court stated: "[t]he Court, mindful of Rule 26(a)(1)(B) finds that where a party already possesses relevant information in electronic form, it is obligated, by way of mandatory disclosure, to so advise the adversary. Once advised of the existence of electronic data, a party may then make an informed decision as to the manner by which discovery could be produced." The plaintiff was ordered to pay for paper copies, but not electronic copies.

- *United States v. Davey*, 543 F.2d 996, 999 (2d Cir. 1976). The Court ordered the taxpayer to produce certain computer tapes containing transactions and records relating to general expenses and losses to the IRS, after it had already provided a printout of the information. The Court held that, "inspection of the requested tapes . . . would incidentally insure greater accuracy and a substantial saving in auditing time by enabling the IRS, through use of the taxpayer's own record medium, to trace transactions from the original documents to the tax return."

- *American Brass v. United States,* 699 F. Supp. 934 (Ct. Int'l. Trade 1988). Court ordered production of computer tapes, subject to a protective order, after the requesting party had already received a certified copy of the records in the form of microfilm and printouts. The Court held that "data released in an unusable form are . . . the equivalent of no data at all." (citing *Timken Co. v. United States*, 659 F. Supp. 239, 240 n.3 (Ct. Int'l. Trade 1987).

- *Adams v. Dan River Mills, Inc.*, 54 F.R.D. 220, 222 (W.D. Va. 1972). After producing the requested information in a paper format, the Court ordered the defendant to produce the date in an electronic format. After reviewing the Advisory Committee Note to Rule 34, the Court stated, "While it appears to this court that the above language only directly covers the situation where the respondent can be required to prepare the information in a usable form, such as a print-out, it does not appear to preclude the production of computer input information such as computer cards or tapes. Likewise, this court is aware of no reason why documents of this nature should not be subject to discovery. Because of the accuracy and inexpensiveness of producing the requested documents in the case at bar, this court sees no reason why defendant should not be required to produce the computer cards or tapes and the W-2 print-outs to the plaintiffs."

- *Donaldson v. Pillsbury Co.*, 554 F.2d 825, 832 (8th Cir.), *cert. denied*, 434 U.S. 856 (1977). Case remanded to reconsider different issues including whether the plaintiffs should be allowed their request for a machine-readable version of data that had already been produced in hard copy form.

- *Fautek v. Montgomery Ward & Co.*, 96 F.R.D. 141 (N.D. Ill. 1982). The defendant was sanctioned for failure to inform the plaintiff that personnel records were available in computer readable form. Defendants also ordered to produce the coding information necessary to understand the computerized information.

- *Timken Co. v. United States*, 659 F. Supp. 239, 267-268 (Ct. Int'l. Trade 1987). Court ordered production of computer tapes, though information had been previously provided to the plaintiff in roughly fifteen thousand pages of computer printout. The plaintiff contended that "the sheer volume of data submitted in the questionnaire responses preclude[d] it from realistic participation in the investigation unless it [was] provided with access to the computer tapes containing the data."

- *Greyhound Computer Corp., Inc. v. IBM*, 3 Comp. L. Serv. Rep. 138 (D. Minn. 1971). *Greyhound* sent interrogatories to *IBM* and in response received a recitation of source materials and locations where the information could be found. After *Greyhound's* counsel found rooms full of thousands of documents, the Court ordered that where information was on computer tapes it should be produced. Also, Defendant was to provide someone familiar with the material to assist the plaintiff's counsel and furnish printouts of any taped information.

Court required printout after electronic copy produced

- *Satchell v. FedEx Corp.*, No. CIV.03-02659, 2005 WL 646058, at *3 (N.D.Cal. Mar. 21, 2005). The Court held that "electronic data [in databases] produced for class discovery purposes is not an adequate substitute for the personnel records of comparators and other discovery sought."

Court not requiring printout, if electronic copy provided

- *Jicarilla Apache Nation v. United States,* 60 Fed. Cl. 413 (Fed. Cl. 2004). The Court ordered the production of electronic records in the form routinely used or stored (electronic or paper) along with available technical information necessary to access or use the information.

- *Sattar v. Motorola, Inc.,* 138 F.3d 1164, 1171 (7th Cir. 1998). Court refused to require printout of 210,000 pages of e-mail at producing party's expense, if producing party would provide usable computer data and software or access to computer system.

Court not requiring electronic copy, if printout produced

- *Phoenix Four, Inc. v. Strategic Resources Corp.,* No. CIV. 05-4837, 2006 WL 1409413 (S.D.N.Y. May 23, 2006). In this investment action for fraud the Court refused to impose reimbursement costs on the defendants to convert nonsearchable documents into a searchable format since plaintiffs had earlier decided to receive the documents in hard copy over the searchable "Case Vault" format.

- *Northern Crossarm Co. v. Chemical Specialities,* No. CIV.03-415, 2004 WL 635606 (W.D. Wis. Mar. 3, 2004). After the defendant had produced 65,000 e-mails in hard copy, the plaintiff requested an electronic version of the e-mail. The Court noted the parties "failure to communicate" and ruled under Rule 34 that since there had already been costs incurred in a good faith production by the producing party that it would not order the electronic version to be produced nor would it order a copy of a CD of the e-mails made for the defendant's use to be produced since it was protected work product.

- *Jones v. Goord,* No. CIV.95-8026, 2002 WL 1007614, at *6 (S.D.N.Y. May 16, 2002). The Court refused to require prison officials to disclose six different electronic databases since they had already produced the data in printed form. The Court noted the late request from the plaintiffs and stated "[a]s electronic mechanisms for storing and retrieving data have become more common, it has increasingly behooved courts and counsel to become familiar with such methods, and to develop expertise and procedures for incorporating 'electronic discovery' into the familiar rituals of litigation."

- *McNally Tunneling v. City of Evanston,* No. CIV.00-6979, 2001 WL 1568879 (N.D. Ill. Dec. 10, 2001). In a contractor dispute case the Court ruled that the city was not entitled to two complete copies - electronic and printed - of the discovery materials. Instead, the city was entitled to a printed copy to be supplemented by electronic data if the printed copies were unavailable.

- *Donaldson v. Pillsbury Co.,* 554 F.2d 825, 832 (8th Cir. 1977). Court allowed the lower court to reconsider not requiring party to respond to interrogatories seeking information in computer-readable form even though data existed in "500 to 2,000 different file and report formats." Data had already been produced in previous hard copy discovery.

Producing party required to pay for cost of computer printout of data.

- *Bills v. Kennecott Corporation,* 108 F.R.D. 459 (D.C. Utah 1985). The defendant moved for an order requiring plaintiffs to pay the cost of producing a computer printout or compiling a computer tape of the information, which the plaintiffs had requested through discovery. The plaintiffs preferred the disclosure in a paper format, which cost was approximately $5000. Court ordered defendants to pay the cost of the printout.

Court requiring paper printouts and not computer readable data

- *Williams v. Owens-Illinois, Inc.,* 665 F.2d 918, 932-33 (9th Cir. 1982). In an employment discrimination case the Court allowed defendant to provide to plaintiffs only hard-copy wage cards and not computer tapes with that data, while also requiring the defendant to process whatever computer runs the plaintiffs requested.
- *E.E.O.C. v. General Dynamics, Inc.,* 999 F.2d 113, 115-16 (5th Cir. 1993). The Court reversed lower court's ruling excluding the testimony of plaintiff's expert because he failed to produce computer tapes. Court found that paper printouts were a reasonable production in light of the vagueness of the district court's order.

Database format set out by court

- *Overseas Private Inv. Corp. v. Mandelbaum,* No. CIV.97-1138, 1998 WL 647208 (D.D.C. Aug. 19, 1998). Case involved a breach of contract action between two companies. The opinion set out a database report format to be used in disclosure of the e-mail in dispute. The format included the date, author, recipient, others copied and the substance of the e-mail.

Use of Opposing Party's Computer Personnel Denied

- *In re Plastics Additives Antitrust Litigation,* No. CIV.03-2038, 2004 WL 2743591 (E.D.Pa. 2004). The plaintiff sought the defendant's information in an electronic format, its documentation and computer personnel to assist in understanding and using the data. The Court ordered both parties to disclose the case information in an electronic format but based upon the adversarial nature of the case denied the request to have the defendant's personnel assist with the use of the data.

Native files ordered - TIFF Not adequate

- *Hagenbuch v. 3B6 Sistemi Elettronici Industriali S.R.L.,* 2006 WL 665005 (N.D. Ill. Mar. 8, 2006). The Court rejected defendant's argument that TIFF images were adequate production and ruled that,

    TIFF images were not the equivalent of the original electronic data with its metadata, etc. even though TIFF images, were easier to bate stamp. The Court in discussing TIFF documents noted, *2 Plaintiff now asks this Court to find that 3B6 USA's production of the TIFF documents is insufficient under Rule 34 Plaintiff argues that, under Rule 34, (1) he is entitled to copies of the designated electronic data, and (2) the TIFF documents created by 3B6 USA are fundamentally different from the original documents and are not documents produced as they are kept in the usual course of business. Plaintiff claims that the TIFF documents are inadequate reproductions that (1) lack clarity and color, (2) lack metadata that track when a document was created or modified and whether e-mails contained attachments and to whom they were sent, (3) lack clear indications as to where each document starts and stops (i.e., the TIFF pages all run together and make it difficult to determine which pages are part of one document), (4) lack clear indications as to which documents are stored together on the original compact discs and DVDs (i.e., over sixty original compact discs and DVDs were reduced to four compact discs containing TIFF documents), and (5) make it impossible for Plaintiff to use search terms to quickly and efficiently search through the documents electronically. (Pl.'s Reply at 6-9.) 3B6 USA acknowledges that there are real differences between the original documents and the TIFF documents but claims that the TIFF documents are reasonably usable forms of the designated electronic media that satisfy Rule 34 's requirements.

- *In re Verisign Sec. Litig.,* No. CIV.02-02270, 2004 U.S. Dist. LEXIS 22467, at *13-15 (D. Cal. Mar. 10, 2004)(unpublished). The Court affirmed the magistrate's ruling requiring defendant to disclose documents in their "native" file format, and not the TIFF format prepared by defendant. Though it may be difficult to incorporate bates numbers and redactions defendant was "solely at fault for their now inconvenient predicament."

[5]   Other Authorities

- 7 James Wm. Moore, *Moore's Federal Practice* § 34.12[3][b], 34-39 (3d ed. 1999). "Generally, a party seeking discovery of computer records may select the form of the data to be produced. A party may seek, in initial stages of discovery, information that will permit a follow-up request for material in computer readable form. Ultimately, the cost and burden of supplying the data may determine what form the requested information will take."

- MANUAL FOR COMPLEX LITIGATION (FOURTH) § 11.446. "The judge should encourage the parties to discuss the issues of production forms early in litigation, preferably prior to any production, to avoid the waste and duplication of producing the same data in different formats. The relatively inexpensive production of computer-readable images may suffice for the vast majority of requested data. Dynamic data may need to be produced in native format, or in a modified format in which the integrity of the data can be maintained while the data can be manipulated for analysis. If raw data are produced, appropriate applications, file structures, manuals, and other tools necessary for the proper translation and use of the data must be provided. Files (such as E-mail) for which metadata is essential to the understanding of the primary data should be identified and produced in an appropriate format. There may even be rare instances in which paper printouts (hard copy) are appropriate. No one form of production will be appropriate for all types of data in all cases."

- ABA Section of Litigation Civil Discovery Standard 29. "b. Discovery of Electronic Information. i. A party may ask for the production of electronic information in hard copy, in electronic form or in both forms. A party may also ask for the production of ancillary electronic information that relates to relevant electronic documents, such as information that would indicate (a) whether and when electronic mail was sent or opened by its recipient(s) or (b) whether and when information was created and/or edited. A party also may request the software necessary to retrieve, read or interpret electronic information."

- For specific issues related to databases see § 3.10 *Databases*.

[H]   Inspection of Opposing Party's Computer System

[1]   Pending Rule 34 Amendment

Rule 34. Production of Documents, <u>Electronically Stored Information,</u> and Things and Entry Upon Land for Inspection and Other Purposes (emphasis added)

(a) Scope. Any party may serve on any other party a request (1) to produce and permit the party making the request, or someone acting on the requestor's behalf, to inspect, copy, <u>test, or sample</u> any designated documents <u>or electronically stored information</u> — including writings, drawings, graphs, charts, photographs, <u>sound recordings, images,</u> and other <u>data or</u> data compilations <u>stored in any medium</u> from which information can be obtained . . . (emphasis added).

* * * * *

Committee Note

Subdivision (a). . . . Rule 34(a)(1) is also amended to make clear that parties may request an opportunity to test or sample materials sought under the rule in addition to inspecting and copying them. That opportunity may be important for both electronically stored information and hard-copy materials. The current rule is not clear that such testing or sampling is authorized; the amendment expressly permits it. As with any other form of discovery, issues of burden and intrusiveness raised by requests to test or sample can be addressed under Rules 26(b)(2) and 26(c). Inspection or testing of certain types of electronically stored information or of a responding party's electronic information system may raise issues of confidentiality or privacy. The addition of testing and sampling to Rule 34(a) with regard to documents and electronically stored information is not meant to create a routine right of direct access to a party's electronic information system, although such access might be justified in some circumstances. Courts should guard against undue intrusiveness resulting from inspecting or testing such systems.

[2]   Generally

Generally, the producing party will provide disclosure of responsive data to the requesting party's production request by physically transferring the data by CD-ROM, DVD, etc. However, FED. R. CIV. P. 34 allows for entry onto the property of an adverse party for the purpose of inspecting the property. Depending on the circumstances, Rule 34 has been interpreted to permit an inspection of an individual or corporate computer system by performing searches on computer data or by creating a forensic or "mirror" image copy of the storage media for later analysis. *See,* § 7.7[H][3], *Direct Access to Computer System.* Under certain circumstances direct seizure of a computer is permitted. *See,* § 7.14, *Injunctions.*

Careful consideration should be given to demanding direct access to a party's electronic information system for purposes of "inspecting" the system. Generally, if you serve the opposing party with a production request they will have control of what type and how the searches are performed on their system. Unless the opposing party provides a certification of which computers were searched, search terms utilized, etc. you will not have any idea if their efforts were adequate. If the court denies your request for your expert to have direct access, one alternative would be to request the court to appoint a neutral expert to perform the searches.

One of the issues when the requesting party searches the producing party's computer system is the protection of confidential or privileged information stored on the computer. To solve this problem, the data retrieved from the search is generally provided to the producing party for a privilege review prior to disclosure. Another solution is FED. R. CIV. P. 26(c), which provides for the issuance of a nonwaiver protective order so that privileged information or "trade secret or other confidential research, development, or commercial information [would] not be revealed or be revealed only in a designated way." FED. R. CIV. P. 26(c)(7). *Playboy Enters., Inc. v. Welles,* 60 F. Supp. 2d 1050 (S.D. Cal. 1999); *See,* § 7.4[I], *Protective Orders - Rule 26(c)* and § 7.4[H], *Work Product Doctrine, Attorney Client Privilege and Trade Secrets.*

Also, an onsite inspection may disrupt the business. Inspecting the conventional file room or document storage warehouse usually does not affect the ongoing business operations. However, if a comprehensive search of all data is conducted or cloning of the storage media is performed, this may require the business operations to be stopped. It would be best to conduct the searches or other computer tasks on the weekend or at night so as not to disturb the ongoing business.

FED. R. CIV. P. 45 authorizes similar options on the premises of a nonparty.

Pending Rule 34 Amendment

Pending Rule 34 provides that the requesting party can "inspect, copy, test, or sample any designated documents or electronically stored information . . . and other data or data compilations stored in any medium from which information can be obtained . . ." Under certain circumstances, "[direct access] might be justified . . ." The Committee Note provides support for direct access, "[t]he addition of testing and sampling to Rule 34(a) with regard to documents and electronically stored information is not meant to create a routine right of direct access to a party's electronic information system, although such access might be justified in some circumstances."

For the text of the pending Rule 34 Committee Note see § 7.7[A][1], *Pending Rule 34 Amendment.*

[3]   Direct Access to Computer System

The parties may agree to allow for an "inspection" of a computer system for "searching and copying" of any relevant data that is discovered. If the parties do not agree, then the requesting party must provide sufficient justification to a Court that the inspection will produce responsive evidence and no harm or interruption will be caused to the system. The opposing party may argue that allowing access to its computer systems may expose privileged data, proprietary business information or trade secrets and the privacy of its employees or customers. *See also,* § 3.5[E], *Deletion of Electronic Information.*

Generally, courts hesitate to grant the requesting party on-site access to conduct the actual search because of the risk that data may be inadvertently altered. If access is permitted to the computer system, the producing party's IT staff or a neutral third party such as a forensic expert is usually retained to perform the necessary computer tasks. The reason is that there's always a risk if the data is jeopardized that the disclosing party may hold you responsible. *Gates Rubber Co. v. Bando Chemical Indus., Ltd.,* 167 F.R.D. 90 (D. Colo. 1996). This neutral expert can perform the necessary searches on the computer, log the data for chain of custody and then provide it to the producing party to review for responsiveness and privilege before disclosing.

[a] Reported Cases - Allowing Direct Access

Computer is included in "entry upon designated land or other property"

* *Strasser v. Yalamanchi,* 669 So. 2d 1142, 1143 (D.C. App. Fla. 1996). Information contained in a computer system is not only considered a document that is subject to production, but the drive on which it is contained has been considered property that could be searched. The plaintiff's discovery request to search the defendant's computer systems for financial information fell into state discovery rule permitting "entry upon designated land or other property."

After Obstruction and Delay of Discovery

* *Tilberg v. Next Mgmt. Co.,* No. CIV.04-7373, 2005 U.S. Dist. LEXIS 24892, at *2-4 (D.N.Y. Oct. 24, 2005). The Court allowed the employee full access to search the employer's e-mail server, central server, and individual work stations after the employer had denied the existence of any documents and her computer forensic expert had searched and found numerous references to important documents on the "active space" and in deleted files of the employer's computers.

* *Cumis Ins. Co. v. Diebold, Inc.,* No. CIV.02-7346, 2004 WL 1126173, at *1 n.1 (E.D.Pa. May 20, 2004). The Court ordered additional searches since the responding party was shown not to have produced all of the electronic information based on the fact that other responsive documents regarding Diebold were found in the possession of third parties.

* *Tulip Computers Inter. B. V. v. Dell Computer Corp.,* 52 Fed. R. Serv. 3d 1420 (D. Del. 2002). After Dell had deliberately delayed and obstructed the discovery process the Court ruled that, "[t]he procedure that Tulip has suggested for the discovery of e-mail documents seems fair, efficient, and reasonable. Dell shall provide the e-mails from the hard disks of the identified executives in electronic form to the plaintiff's [forensic

specialist, who] will search the e-mails based on an agreed upon list of search terms. Tulip will give Dell a list of the e-mails that contain those search terms. Dell will then produce the e-mails to Tulip, subject to its own review for privilege and confidentiality designations."

- *GFTM, Inc. v. Wal-Mart Stores, Inc.,* No. CIV.98-7724, 2000 WL 335558 (S.D.N.Y. Mar. 30, 2000). The plaintiff was allowed on site access to the defendant's computer records as a sanction for failing to make accurate disclosure of its computer capabilities and records.

- *Illinois Tool Works, Inc. v. Metro Mark Prod. Ltd.,* 43 F. Supp. 2d 951, 959 (N.D. Ill. 1999). The Court ruled in an unfair competition case that because the defendant's conduct was "calculated to frustrate legitimate discovery" that the plaintiff would be allowed to inspect the defendant's computer system.

Recover Deleted Data

- *Physicians Interactive v. Lathian Systems, Inc.,* No. CA.03-1193, 2003 WL 23018270, at *10 (E.D. Va. Dec. 5, 2003). The Court granted an injunction for the plaintiff where defendants allegedly hacked into the plaintiff's website and stole their confidential customer lists and computer software code. The Court enjoined the defendant from using any of the information obtained and on any future attacks on the system. The Court also granted the plaintiff limited "expedited discovery to enter the sites where the computers used in the alleged attacks are located and to obtain a 'mirror image'" of the computer equipment used in the attacks. *See also,* § 7.14, *Injunctions.*

- *Strasser v. Yalamanchi,* 669 So. 2d 1142 (Fla. Dist. Ct. App. 1996). The plaintiff requested an on-site inspection of the defendant's computer system alleging that relevant documents had been deleted. The Court found that unrestricted access to the hard drive would risk disclosure of protected proprietary information and remanded with instructions that the inspection should take place only if the plaintiff showed a likelihood of discovering the purged data. Additionally, if the inspection did occur, measures had to be put into place to protect the proprietary information and the defendant's computer and databases.

- *Playboy Enters., Inc. v. Welles,* 60 F. Supp. 2d 1050 (S.D. Cal. 1999). The plaintiff requested access to the defendant's hard drive in an attempt to recover deleted e-mail. The Court found that relevant information was likely to be on the hard drive and ordered the defendant to give the plaintiff access to the hard drive by way of a court-appointed specialist trained in the area of data recovery.

- *In re Tyco International, Ltd., Securities Litigation,* No. 00-MD-1335-B, 2000 WL 33654141, at *3 (D.N.H. Jul. 27, 2000). The Court found that "large corporations typically overwrite and thereby destroy electronic data in the course of performing routine backup procedures." The Court ruled it would consider preservation requests for specific identifiable data types.

- *Simon Property Group L.P. v. mySimon, Inc.,* 194 F.R.D. 639 (D.C. Ind. 2000). The plaintiff would be granted access to the computers of certain employees of the defendant so that it could attempt to retrieve deleted files and documents in computer storage. The Court required that a protective order be signed by a neutral computer expert regarding confidential data.

Run Searches

- *Jinks-Umstead v. England,* No. CIV.99-2691, 2005 U.S. Dist. LEXIS 22291 (D.D.C. Oct. 4, 2005). The plaintiff sought sanctions for failure to preserve workload reports produced from a database that provided justification for an employment decision that resulted in a reduction in force. The Court ruled against any sanctions and stated that even though the reports were not available that the underlying data was and the plaintiff would be provided access to query the database.
- *Mary Imogene Bassett Hospital v. Sullivan,* 136 F.R.D. 42, 48 (N.D.N.Y. 1991). The Court allowed appropriately framed search requests to search a voluminous amount of electronic information.
- *In re Ford Motor Company,* 345 F.3d 1315 (11th Cir. 2003). The plaintiff alleged that the seatbelt buckle was defectively designed and sought access to Ford's database to conduct searches for other claims relating to unlatching seatbelt buckles. Appellate court reversed trial court's granting unlimited access to the database on the grounds that Ford must first have an opportunity to object to retrieved evidence.

Check for Unauthorized Software

- *Lauren Corp. v. Century Geophysical Corp.,* 953 P.2d 200 (Colo. App. 1998). The plaintiff sought an inspection of the defendants' computers to determine whether its software had been used on unauthorized computers. After granting the inspection order, the defendant destroyed some of the computers, and the Court sanctioned the defendant by issuing a spoliation order.

Obtain Raw Data

- *Crown Life Ins. v. Craig,* 995 F.2d 1376 (7th Cir. 1993). The plaintiff failed to provide access to its computers for the defendant to obtain "inaccessible raw data." The Court found that even if a company is unable to access data, it must make that data available by giving access to its hard drive. The plaintiff's failure to provide access resulted in a default judgment.

Determine Inaccuracies in Data

- *Cerruti 1881 S.A. v. Cerruti, Inc.,* 169 F.R.D. 573 (S.D.N.Y. 1996). The plaintiff was given access to the defendant's computer to determine the reason for inaccuracies on printouts of sales records. A court appointed computer expert was provided access to the hard drive and found that the records were fabricated.

Additional Searches Allowed After Relevancy Established

- *McPeek v. Ashcroft,* 212 F.R.D. 33 (D.D.C. 2003). After examining the likelihood of relevant data being found on the backup tapes, the Court allowed additional searches.

[b]   Reported Cases – Not Allowing Direct Access

Data may be manipulated or destroyed (inadvertently or intentionally)

- *Gates Rubber Co. v. Bando Chemical Industries, Ltd.,* 167 F.R.D. 90 (D. Colo. 1996). In a trade secret case, the plaintiff botched an on site inspection of the defendant's computer system. The plaintiff's expert mishandled the opposing party's computer system, which resulted in the loss of potentially critical data.

Overbroad

- *Mazur v. Wal-Mart Stores, Inc.,* No. CIV.05-85, 2006 U.S. Dist. LEXIS 20985, at *4-6 (D. Mich. 2006). The Court denied Wal-Mart's motion to compel production since it "has raised no credible reason . . . 'to produce their computer and its storage devices for inspection.' . . . Defendant's request . . . [is] for the sole purpose of allowing Wal-Mart to engage in an invasive forensic inspection of it to obtain a copy of the summary, is an unwarranted, unnecessary and indeed, heavy handed litigation tactic."

- *In re Ford Motor Company,* 345 F.3d 1315 (11th Cir. 2003). The plaintiff alleged that the seatbelt buckle was defectively designed and sought access to Ford's database to conduct searches for other claims relating to unlatching seatbelt buckles. The Appellate court reversed trial court's granting unlimited access to the database on the grounds that Ford must first have an opportunity to object to retrieved evidence.

- *Van Westrienen v. Americontinental Collection Corp.,* 189 F.R.D. 440 (D. Or. 1999). Court held that "[p]laintiffs are not entitled to unbridled access [of] Defendant's computer system. . . . Plaintiffs should pursue other less burdensome alternatives, such as identifying the number of letters and their content."

- *Stallings-Daniel v. Northern Trust Co.,* No. CIV.01-2290, 2002 WL 385566, at *1 (N.D. Ill. Mar. 12, 2002). In an employment discrimination case the Court denied the plaintiff's motion for additional electronic discovery and held that, "[n]othing in the documents produced justifies an intrusive and wholly speculative electronic investigation into defendant's e-mail files. Thus, plaintiff's motion for reconsideration is denied."

Protect Privileged or Trade Secret Information

- *Strasser v. Yalamanchi,* 669 So. 2d 1142 (Fla. Dist. Ct. App. 1996). The plaintiff sought unrestricted access to the defendant's computer system arguing that defendant had purged relevant computer records. The Appellate court quashed the order stating that the unrestricted access was overly broad and could pose a threat to medical patients' confidential records and the records of the defendant's business, and that there was little evidence that the purged documents could, in fact, be retrieved.

Fishing Expedition or Speculation

- *Williams v. Massachusetts Mut. Life Ins. Co.,* 226 F.R.D. 144 (D. Mass. 2005). The plaintiff in an employment discrimination suit would not be allowed to conduct a forensic study of the employer's electronically stored information in an attempt to locate e-mail between company officials allegedly reflecting discriminatory practice and policy, where the employer had already undertaken its own search and forensic analysis and had sworn to its accuracy. In addition, the employee provided no reliable or competent information to show that the employer's representations regarding e-mail were misleading or substantively inaccurate.

- *Floeter v. City of Orlando,* 2006 WL 1000306 (M.D. Fla. Apr. 14, 2006). In this employment discrimination case the plaintiff requested the opportunity to inspect two computers and a computer printout of all e-mails from a specific police lieutenant. The Court citing Rule 34 stated that a party does not have the right "to conduct the actual search." In addition, the Court ruled that there was no showing that any inspection or production of printouts of e-mail would lead to discoverable evidence.

- *Medical Billing Consultants, Inc. v. Intelligent Medical Objects, Inc.,* No. CIV.01-9148, 2003 WL 1809465, at *2 (N.D. Ill. Apr. 4, 2003). The plaintiff sought an order "to allow experts to perform a physical inspection of defendants' computer equipment." The plaintiff claimed that e-mail had not been disclosed and that defendant had failed to perform an adequate search of its computer files. Defendants argued that all e-mail had been turned over and any inspection would be burdensome. Court denied request and stated that, "[w]e have no reason to believe that there are additional records on the computer that will be relevant to this case."

- *Bethea v. Comcast,* 218 F.R.D. 328, 329-330 (D.D.C. 2003). The Court denied plaintiff motion to inspect the defendant's computer systems and related programs and copy any information relevant to her employment discrimination. The plaintiff's allegation of deletions of data and skepticism regarding complete disclosure was unsupported. The court stated, "[i]n the context of computer systems and computer records, inspection or seizure is not permitted unless the moving party can 'demonstrate that the documents they seek to compel do, in fact, exist and are being unlawfully withheld.'"

- *Stallings-Daniel v. N. Trust Co.,* No. CIV.01-2290, 2002 WL 385566 (N.D. Ill. Mar. 12, 2002). The plaintiff filed a motion to reconsider an order denying plaintiff's use of an expert to conduct discovery of the defendant's e-mail system. The court denied the motion, finding that plaintiff's request was based entirely on speculation and that plaintiff had presented no new information to justify such an investigation.

- *Fennell v. First Step Designs Limited,* 83 F.3d 526 (1st Cir. 1996). The appellate court affirmed the district court's decision denying plaintiff's request for additional discovery of word processing files on a computer hard drive. The plaintiff argued that a particular document might have been fabricated and backdated. Both courts found that creating a mirror of the hard drive involved risks and costs, and was nothing more than a "fishing expedition."

- *McCurdy Group v. American Biomedical Group, Inc.,* No. 00-6183, 2001 WL 536974 (10th Cir. May 21, 2001). Court denied request by party seeking all of the disk drives including backup disk drives for a five-year period of time. The Court found that it was not a sufficient reason that the requesting party was "skeptical" that the responding party had produced copies of all relevant and nonprivileged documents from the hard drives.

- *New York National Organization for Women v. Cuomo,* No. CIV.93-7146, 1998 WL 395320 (S.D.N.Y. Jul. 14, 1998). Plaintiff failed to show that the destruction of any evidence was prejudicial, i.e., that the destroyed information had some relevance to the litigation. Fishing expeditions would not be permitted.

Undue Delay

- *Medtronic Sofamor Danek, Inc. v. Michelson,* No. CIV.01-2373, 2004 WL 2905399, at *3 (W.D. Tenn. May 3, 2004). "The defendants' request for the production of deleted electronic files and e-mails is untimely as filed nearly five months after the close of discovery and unduly burdensome in light of the quickly approaching trial date."

[4]   Obtaining Forensic or Mirror Image Copy of Storage Media

A forensic or "mirror" image of a hard drive or other storage media may be sought in order to restore deleted or altered files, search for unauthorized copies of software or other confidential data.

A "mirror image" is generally described as "a forensic duplicate, which replicates bit for bit, sector for sector, all allocated and unallocated space, including slack space, on a computer hard drive." . . . Thus, in similar cases where trade secrets and electronic evidence are both involved, the Courts have granted permission to obtain mirror images of the computer equipment which may contain electronic data related to the alleged violation. (citations omitted). This is one method of assuring the preservation of evidence since electronic evidence can easily be erased and manipulated, either intentionally or unintentionally (by overwriting through continued use of the computer).

Balboa Threadworks, Inc. v. Stucky, No. CIV.05-1157, 2006 U.S. Dist. LEXIS 29265, at *7-8 (D. Kan. Mar. 24, 2006). The purpose of creating a "mirror image" is to preserve the data for later searching and analysis.

A forensic "mirror image" is different then a "backup" copy of a hard drive. A "mirror" image replicates a bit for bit copy of storage media, while a "backup" copy only copies the directory structure and "active files." A mirror image is sometimes referred to as a "bitstream copy . . . [it is] a duplicate copy of 'every bit and byte on the target drive including all files, the slack space, Master File Table, and metadata in exactly the order they appear on the original. . . . '" *United States v. Shinderman,* No. CR.05-67, 2006 U.S. Dist. LEXIS 8254, n.8 (D. Me. Mar. 2, 2006).

A forensic image of a hard drive should be identical to the original. To establish that the "mirror" image is an exact replicate of the original media a hash algorithm is generated. A hash value is unique for each computer file and distinguishes it from other computer files and is often used for authentication purposes. *See,* § 5.05[G], *Chain of Custody, Audit Reports and Hash Values.* The accuracy for the "mirror" image is determined by matching the "hash" value of the original with the hash value of the "mirror" copy.

Generally, a request for a forensic copy of a hard drive will be granted if a party can show a reasonable basis supported by specific, concrete evidence of the alteration or destruction of electronic information or for other reasons. *Balboa Threadworks, Inc. v. Stucky,* No. CIV.05-1157, 2006 U.S. Dist. LEXIS 29265 (D. Kan. Mar. 24, 2006)*; Communications Ctr., Inc. v. Hewitt,* No. CIV.03-1968, 2005 U.S. Dist. LEXIS 10891 (E.D. Cal. Apr. 5, 2005). However, "[c]ourts have been cautious in requiring the mirror imaging of computers where the request is extremely broad in nature and the connection between the computers and the claims in the lawsuit are unduly vague or unsubstantiated in nature." *Balboa Threadworks, Inc. v. Stucky,* 2006 U.S. Dist. LEXIS 29265, at *8-9 (D. Kan. Mar. 24, 2006)

In addition, evidence should be supplied to establish a basis for believing that this deleted or altered information may be recovered through this forensic analysis and is unavailable from any other source. For example, even though files have been deleted from a computer they may be found on backups of the hard drive which would not allow for the forensic analysis of a hard drive.

Generally, a party responding to a request for electronic discovery does not have a duty to restore computer files deleted from their computers during the normal course of business. However, a requesting party may demand that they be allowed to forensically image copy and analyze a hard drive or other storage media to recover deleted or altered files or for other forensic purposes. If proof is provided establishing deletion of relevant data or another basis for inspecting the hard drive, the Courts have been granting requests for such discovery. These orders can apply to network servers as well as the hard drives of individual employees' desktops and other computer devices. Depending on the circumstances, the courts may impose the cost on the requesting party or allocate the expense between the parties.

[5]   Procedure - Forensic Copy of Storage Media (Hard Drive, etc.)

[a]   Generally

The federal courts have established a set of computer inspection procedures if a forensic image copy (also referred to as a clone or mirror image) of a hard drive is ordered. *Simon Property Group L.P. v. MySimon, Inc.,* 194 F.R.D. 639, 641-42 (S.D. Ind. 2000); *Playboy Enter., Inc. v. Welles,* 60 F. Supp. 2d 1050, 1054-55 (S.D. Cal. 1999). The inspection procedure provides that: (1) parties agree on a neutral third party expert who will carry out the inspection as an officer of the court; (2) parties agree on the scope of the inspection; (3) the expert creates a mirror image of the computer data to preserve the integrity of the original evidence; (4) the expert executes the search on the mirror image of the file; (5) expert turns over the responsive data to the respondent's counsel, (6) respondents' counsel reviews the responsive data for relevance and privilege; and (7) respondents' counsel produces relevant, non privileged data to the requesting party in the agreed form. *See also,* Kenneth J. Withers, *Computer-Based Discovery in Federal Civil Litigation,* 2000 Fed. Cts. L. Rev. 2. It is normal to allow a party whose computer is being imaged to be present during the imaging process. *See, e.g., Fox Industries, Inc. v. Gurovich,* 2004 WL 2348365, *3 (E.D.N.Y., August 25, 2004) (allowing a computer expert to mirror image defendant's computer and specifically allowing both plaintiff's counsel and defendant's counsel to be present if they so desired.)

If these procedures are followed, the requesting party receives assurance that the system has been inspected and an appropriate copy has been made, while the producing party receives the necessary protection for its privileged and confidential information.

[b]   Reported Cases

- *Simon Property Group L.P. v. MySimon, Inc.*, 194 F.R.D. 639, 641-42 (S.D. Ind. 2000); *Playboy Enter., Inc. v. Welles*, 60 F. Supp. 2d 1050, 1054-55 (S.D. Cal. 1999). These are two of the seminal cases setting forth the protocol for making a forensic copy of a hard drive.

- *Northwest Airlines v. Local 2000*, No. CIV.00-08 (D. Minn. Feb. 2, 2000). The Court set forth a disclosure protocol where the plaintiff's expert was to act as a neutral 3rd party expert on behalf of the court, collect and image the defendants' hard drives and provide the parties with a complete report of all data "deemed responsive."

- *First USA Bank v. PayPal, Inc.*, 76 Fed. Appx. 935 (Fed. Cir. 2003). In a patent infringement action, the Court ordered that a corporate officer's laptop be forensically copied by forensic specialist and a search protocol be followed that would identify any potentially relevant data and allow for creation of a privilege log.

- *Warner Bros. Records, Inc. v. Souther*, No. CIV.05-279, 2006 WL 1549689, *3, 5 (W.D.N.C. Jun. 1, 2006). Court allowed plaintiffs to obtain a forensic copy of defendant's computer hard drive in the court's chambers during the hearing. After doing so, the Court issued a protective order "directing that the plaintiffs not disclose or use any electronic contents of the computer that are unrelated to this case."

- *United States v. Moussaoui*, 2003 WL 548699 (E.D.Va. Jan. 7, 2003). The Court ruled that the government did not have to provide the defendant with information retrieved from various computers. The Court found that the defendant has in its possession the computer systems and could conduct any further investigation he desired.

- *United States v. Hill*, No. CR.02-01289, 2004 WL 1376369 (C.D. Cal. Jun. 17, 2004). The Court ordered the government to produce mirror image copies of the defendant's computer storage media seized by the government in a child pornography case.

- *Rates Technology., Inc. v. Elcotel, Inc.*, 118 F.R.D. 133, 135 (M.D. Fla. 1987). The producing party agreed that the requesting party could conduct a preliminary review of a computer program whose production was requested. After reviewing, the requesting party could select specific portions of the program for production.

- *United States v. Alexander*, No. CR.04-20005, 2004 WL 2095701 (E.D. Mich. Sept. 14, 2004). The Court granted the defendant's motion for discovery and the FBI was to furnish a forensic copy of the hard drive to the defendant's expert who was to follow court mandated possession instructions.

[c]   Other Authorities

• Joseph Kashi, *How to Conduct On-site Discovery of Computer Records*, 24 Law Prac. Mgmt. 26 (Mar. 1998).

[d]   Discovery Pointers

• Use FED. R. CIV. P. 45, to obtain computer information from third parties.
• Sample request,

> Plaintiff requests that defendant permit plaintiff to enter the defendant's premises at [address] and to inspect, search, test, sample and copy the data, records and files (including e-mail sent or received by defendant and files located on remote computer systems that may be accessed by defendant's computer system(s)), on the hard drive(s), other storage devices, backup tapes and in the memory of the following computer system(s) and any other computer systems located on said premises: [List computer systems].

§ 7.8   REQUESTS FOR ADMISSIONS

[A]   FED. R. CIV. P. 36

Requests for Admission

(a) Request for Admission. A party may serve upon any other party a written request for the admission, for purposes of the pending action only, of the truth of any matters within the scope of Rule 26(b)(1) set forth in the request that relate to statements or opinions of fact or of the application of law to fact, including the genuineness of any documents described in the request. Copies of documents shall be served with the request unless they have been or are otherwise furnished or made available for inspection and copying.

[B]   Purpose

Essentially, Rule 36 provides that a party may serve upon any other party a written request for the admission of the truth that relates to:

• Statements of fact;
• Opinions about facts;
• Application of the law to the facts of your case; and
• Genuineness of documents.

The purpose of FED. R. CIV. P. 36 is to reduce trial time, facilitate proof and eliminate issues. *Moosman v. Joseph P. Blitz, Inc.,* 358 F.2d 686 (2nd Cir. 1966). If a party fails to admit the genuineness of any document or the truth of any matter as requested, and if the requesting party proves these facts, the court can order the responding party to pay reasonable attorneys' fees incurred to prove such facts. FED. R. CIV. P. 37(c)(2). Unfortunately, many lawyers do not understand the rule and fail to use it to their advantage. *United States ex rel. Englund v. Los Angeles,* No. CIV.04-0282, 2006 U.S. Dist. LEXIS 31683 (D. Cal. May 11, 2006).

Requests for admission are useful for establishing the genuineness of documents to be introduced into evidence at trial. *See, e.g., Republic Sec. Corp. v. Puerto Rico Aqueduct & Sewer Auth.,* 674 F.2d 952, 957 (1st Cir. 1982). When serving requests concerning the genuineness of documents, you must serve copies of the documents along with the requests, unless your adversary already has the documents. Otherwise, provide the documents to your adversary or make the documents available for inspection and copying. An admission of any matter under this rule conclusively establishes that matter. FED. R. CIV. P. 36(b).

Request for admissions can be effectively used to establish the genuineness of computer data such as e-mail, word processing documents and other electronic information.

[C]   Reported Cases (reserved)

[D]   Other Authorities

- MANUAL FOR COMPLEX LITIGATION (FOURTH) § 11.472.

[E]   Discovery Pointers

[1]   Sample Request for Admission

PLAINTIFF'S FIRST REQUEST FOR ADMISSION OF FACTS AND GENUINENESS OF DOCUMENTS

Plaintiff, _____, requests defendant, _____, pursuant to Rule 36 of the Federal Rules of Civil Procedure, to admit the facts and genuineness of documents as set forth below:

[Definitions if appropriate.]

1. Plaintiff is an Arizona corporation having its principal place of business in Arizona.

2. Plaintiff is a duly licensed real estate agent.

3. On or about June 6, 2003 plaintiff and defendant entered into an exclusive listing agreement bearing that date and concerning real property known as 4334 South Broadway, Phoenix, Arizona.

4. Each of the following marked documents, exhibited with this request, is a true and accurate copy and is authentic as contemplated by FED. R. EVID. 901:

Exhibit No.   Description

1.   E-mail from plaintiff to defendant dated 5-3-03. (attached)

2.   E-mail from plaintiff to seller (ABC Corporation) dated July 7, 2003, listing the sale terms. (attached).

3.   Real estate contract dated June 6, 2003 between plaintiff and defendant. (attached)

§ 7.9   SANCTIONS

[A]   FED. R. CIV. P. 37

Rule 37. Failure to Make Disclosure or Cooperate in Discovery; Sanctions

(a) Motion For Order Compelling Disclosure or Discovery. A party, upon reasonable notice to other parties and all persons affected thereby, may apply for an order compelling disclosure or discovery as follows:

* * *

(2) Motion.

(A) If a party fails to make a disclosure required by Rule 26(a), any other party may move to compel disclosure and for appropriate sanctions. The motion must include a certification that the movant has in good faith conferred or attempted to confer with the party not making the disclosure in an effort to secure the disclosure without court action.

(B) If a deponent fails to answer a question propounded or submitted under Rules 30 or 31, or a corporation or other entity fails to make a designation under Rule 30(b)(6) or 31(a), or a party fails to answer an interrogatory submitted under Rule 33, or if a party, in response to a request for inspection submitted under Rule 34, fails to respond that inspection will be permitted as requested or fails to permit inspection as requested, the discovering party may move for an order compelling an answer, or a designation, or an order compelling inspection in accordance with the request. . . .

* * *

(3) Evasive or Incomplete Disclosure, Answer, or Response. For purposes of this subdivision an evasive or incomplete disclosure, answer, or response is to be treated as a failure to disclose, answer, or respond.

(4) Expenses and Sanctions.

(A) If the motion is granted or if the disclosure or requested discovery is provided after the motion was filed, the court shall, after affording an opportunity to be heard, require the party or deponent whose conduct necessitated the motion or the party or attorney advising such conduct or both of them to pay to the moving party the reasonable expenses incurred in making the motion, including attorney's fees, unless the court finds that the motion was filed without the movant's first making a good faith effort to obtain the disclosure or discovery without court action, or that the opposing party's nondisclosure, response, or objection was substantially justified, or that other circumstances make an award of expenses unjust.

(B) If the motion is denied, the court may enter any protective order authorized under Rule 26(c) and shall, after affording an opportunity to be heard, require the moving party or the attorney filing the motion or both of them to pay to the party or deponent who opposed the motion the reasonable expenses incurred in opposing the motion, including attorney's fees, unless the court finds that the making of the motion was substantially justified or that other circumstances make an award of expenses unjust.

(C) If the motion is granted in part and denied in part, the court may enter any protective order authorized under Rule 26(c) and may, after affording an opportunity to be heard, apportion the reasonable expenses incurred in relation to the motion among the parties and persons in a just manner.

(b) Failure to Comply With Order.

* * *

(2) Sanctions by Court in Which Action is Pending. If a party or an officer, director, or managing agent of a party or a person designated under Rule 30(b)(6) or 31(a) to testify on behalf of a party fails to obey an order to provide or permit discovery, including an order made under subdivision (a) of this rule or Rule 35, or if a party fails to obey an order entered under Rule 26(f), the court in which the action is pending may make such orders in regard to the failure as are just, and among others the following:

(A) An order that the matters regarding which the order was made or any other designated facts shall be taken to be established for the purposes of the action in accordance with the claim of the party obtaining the order;

(B) An order refusing to allow the disobedient party to support or oppose designated claims or defenses, or prohibiting that party from introducing designated matters in evidence;

(C) An order striking out pleadings or parts thereof, or staying further proceedings until the order is obeyed, or dismissing the action or proceeding or any part thereof, or rendering a judgment by default against the disobedient party;

(D) In lieu of any of the foregoing orders or in addition thereto, an order treating as a contempt of court the failure to obey any orders except an order to submit to a physical or mental examination;

* * *

In lieu of any of the foregoing orders or in addition thereto, the court shall require the party failing to obey the order or the attorney advising that party or both to pay the reasonable expenses, including attorney's fees, caused by the failure, unless the court finds that the failure was substantially justified or that other circumstances make an award of expenses unjust.

(c) Failure to Disclose; False or Misleading Disclosure; Refusal to Admit.

(1) A party that without substantial justification fails to disclose information required by Rule 26(a) or 26(e)(1), or to amend a prior response to discovery as required by Rule 26(e)(2), is not, unless such failure is harmless, permitted to use as evidence at a trial, at a hearing, or on a motion any witness or information not so disclosed. In addition to or in lieu of this sanction, the court, on motion and after affording an opportunity to be heard, may impose other appropriate sanctions. In addition to requiring payment of reasonable expenses, including attorney's fees, caused by the failure, these sanctions may include any of the actions authorized under Rule 37(b)(2)(A), (B), and (C) and may include informing the jury of the failure to make the disclosure.

[B]   Pending Rule 37 Amendment

Rule 37. Failure to Make Disclosures or Cooperate in Discovery; Sanctions

* * * * *

(f) Electronically Stored Information. Absent exceptional circumstances, a court may not impose sanctions under these rules on a party for failing to provide electronically stored information lost as a result of the routine, good-faith operation of an electronic information system. (emphasis added).

* * * * *

Committee Note

Subdivision (f). Subdivision (f) is new. It focuses on a distinctive feature of computer operations, the routine alteration and deletion of information that attends ordinary use. Many steps essential to computer operation may alter or destroy information, for reasons that have nothing to do with how that information might relate to litigation. As a result, the ordinary operation of computer systems creates a risk that a party may lose potentially discoverable information without culpable conduct on its part. Under Rule 37(f), absent exceptional circumstances, sanctions cannot be imposed for loss of electronically stored information resulting from the routine, good-faith operation of an electronic information system.

Rule 37(f) applies only to information lost due to the "routine operation of an electronic information system" — the ways in which such systems are generally designed, programmed, and implemented to meet the party's technical and business needs. The "routine operation" of computer systems includes the alteration and overwriting of information, often without the operator's specific direction or awareness, a feature with no direct counterpart in hard-copy documents. Such features are essential to the operation of electronic information systems.

Rule 37(f) applies to information lost due to the routine operation of an information system only if the operation was in good faith. Good faith in the routine operation of an information system may involve a party's intervention to modify or suspend certain features of that routine operation to prevent the loss of information, if that information is subject to a preservation obligation. A preservation obligation may arise from many sources, including common law, statutes, regulations, or a court order in the case. The good faith requirement of Rule 37(f) means that a party is not permitted to exploit the routine operation of an information system to thwart discovery obligations by allowing that operation to continue in order to destroy specific stored information that it is required to preserve. When a party is under a duty to preserve information because of pending or reasonably anticipated litigation, intervention in the routine operation of an information system is one aspect of what is often called a "litigation hold." Among the factors that bear on a party's good faith in the routine operation of an information system are the steps the party took to comply with a court order in the case or party agreement requiring preservation of specific electronically stored information.

Whether good faith would call for steps to prevent the loss of information on sources that the party believes are not reasonably accessible under Rule 26(b)(2) depends on the circumstances of each case. One factor is whether the party reasonably believes that the information on such sources is likely to be discoverable and not available from reasonably accessible sources.

The protection provided by Rule 37(f) applies only to sanctions "under these rules." It does not affect other sources of authority to impose sanctions or rules of professional responsibility.

This rule restricts the imposition of "sanctions." It does not prevent a court from making the kinds of adjustments frequently used in managing discovery if a party is unable to provide relevant responsive information. For example, a court could order the responding party to produce an additional witness for deposition, respond to additional interrogatories, or make similar attempts to provide substitutes or alternatives for some or all of the lost information.

[C]   Purpose

When faced with computer-based discovery, attorneys on both sides have a responsibility to inform their clients of the duty to preserve and disclose potential evidence. The Supreme Court in noting the importance of open and complete discovery stated, "[t]he need to develop all relevant facts in the adversary system is both fundamental and comprehensive. . . . The very integrity of the judicial system and public confidence in the system depend on full disclosure of all the facts, within the framework of the rules of evidence." *Taylor v. Illinois,* 108 S.Ct. 646, 652 (1988).

FED.R.CIV.P. 37(b)(2) authorizes a court to impose various sanctions when a party "fails to obey an order to provide or permit discovery." It is clear that sanctions may be imposed upon a party or counsel who deliberately fails to "make a disclosure required by Rule 26(a), FED.R.CIV.P. 37(a)(2)(A)," or who provides an "evasive or incomplete disclosure, answer or response." FED.R.CIV.P. 37(a)(3). "The sanctions imposed should serve the threefold purposes of deterring parties from engaging in spoliation, placing the risk of an erroneous judgment on the party who wrongfully created the risk, and restoring the prejudiced party to the position it would have been in had the misconduct not occurred." *Phoenix Four, Inc. v. Strategic Resources Corp.,* No. CIV. 05-4837, 2006 WL 1409413, * 3 (S.D.N.Y. May 23, 2006).

However, "[e]ven in the absence of a discovery order, a court may impose sanctions on a party for misconduct in discovery under its inherent power to manage its own affairs." *Residential Funding Corp. v. DeGeorge Financial Corp.*, 306 F.3d 99, 106-07 (2d Cir. 2002); *Metro. Opera Ass'n, Inc. v. Local 100, Hotel Employees & Rest. Employees Int'l Union*, 212 F.R.D. 178, 219 (S.D.N.Y. 2003) (citing *Nat'l Hockey League v. Metro. Hockey Club, Inc.*, 427 U.S. 639, 640 (1976)). "[A] district court's decision to invoke Rule 37 sanctions is reviewed . . . for an abuse of discretion." *Beil v. Lakewood Eng'g & Mfg. Co.*, 15 F.3d 546, 551 (6th Cir. 1994).

The lower court's decision will be reviewed to determine if certain factors were addressed before imposing sanctions. *Procter & Gamble Co. v. Haugen*, 427 F.3d 727 (10th Cir. 2005); *Koken v. Black & Veatch Constr., Inc.*, 426 F.3d 39, 53 (1st Cir. 2005) (noting that a party "bears a formidable burden" when contesting the trial court's order relating to sanctions, the Appellate Court found that defendant had not made a sufficient record that plaintiff had not in fact made the electronic versions of damage calculations available for review.)

Courts rely on Rule 37 (b) and (c) to impose sanctions. Rule 37(b) sanctions are applied whenever any type of court order relating to discovery is disobeyed and 37(c) sanctions are imposed if a party is unable to comply with their obligations under Rule 26.

The failure of a client to preserve evidence can lead to severe sanctions from the court. Shira A. Scheindlin and Kanchana Wangkeo, *Electronic Discovery Sanctions in the Twenty-First Century,* 11 Mich. Telecomm. Tech. L. Rev. 71 (2004), available at http://www.mttlr.org/voleleven/scheindlin.pdf (last visited on July 22, 2006). Even though the alteration or destruction of the data may be unintentional, the courts are not reluctant to impose sanctions.

In conventional paper-based discovery, sources of information are generally physically stable. Unless the documentary information is damaged or destroyed by fire, flood or the lack of retention policies, paper-based discovery seldom results in loss of the evidence. However, with computer-based discovery, the information can be easily and permanently lost or changed unless a party acts immediately. In the business environment this loss can occur by recycling backup tapes, booting up a computer, opening a file or installing new computer applications or data onto a hard disk. Couple this with the increased volume, different locations and automatic purging systems for electronic evidence and it can easily lead to unfortunate consequences and spoliation of evidence.

Pending Rule 37 Amendment

Commonly termed the "safe harbor" provision pending Rule 37(f) provides that "[a]bsent exceptional circumstances, a court may not impose sanctions under these rules on a party for failing to provide electronically stored information [ESI] lost as a result of the routine, good-faith operation of an electronic information system." It protects against sanctions if ESI is lost due to the routine operation of computers and that operation was in "good faith." The rule is meant to resolve the issue of a "distinctive feature of computer operations, the routine alteration and deletion of information that attends ordinary use." Pending Rule 37 amendment, Committee Note.

However, the duty to preserve evidence, upon notice of anticipated litigation, will not be affected by this change, unless it falls within the narrow limitation set forth in Rule 37. It is still an obligation for counsel to immediately preserve electronic evidence when litigation is anticipated. *See,* § 7.09[C], *Duty to Preserve.*

This procedural rule chose a state of mind entitled "good faith" occurring during the "operation of an electronic system." The Committee avoided case law precedent that discussed culpability concepts such as negligence, recklessness and intentional when deciding whether to issue sanctions.

This standard provides substantial discretion to the judge and will entail sophisticated testimony regarding computer systems to determine if the loss was due to the "routine, good faith operation" of the computer system.

The pending amended rule allows for sanctions even in the good faith lost of data in the routine operation of a computer system if "exceptional circumstances" exist. Such exceptional circumstances may include the loss of important ESI that prejudices a party's case.

[D]   Duty to Preserve

[1]   When Duty to Preserve Arises

Unless there is a statutory duty to preserve, the courts are divided on the issue of when the duty to preserve electronic information arises. Depending on your jurisdiction, the obligation to preserve evidence may arise when:

- Litigation is pending, imminent, might occur or reasonably foreseeable;
- Litigation is anticipated or there is a likelihood of litigation;
- A complaint has been filed; or
- Discovery request received.

To avoid sanctions, electronic evidence should be preserved as soon as a party is put on notice that potential litigation may arise.

Oftentimes, attorneys are under the impression that the duty to preserve arises when they receive a preservation letter from the opposing party, a preservation order from the court or a discovery request from the opposing party. *See,* § 6.1[C][7], *Preservation Request.* This is simply not the case. The majority rule is that a preservation duty arises once a party has notice that potential litigation is likely. The law is clear that litigants have a duty to preserve evidence that may be relevant to anticipated litigation. The key issues that courts consider in determining whether or not a duty to preserve exists centers on when the party had notice of the relevance of the evidence in question in relationship to anticipated or pending litigation. This notice can arise from many different sources including the threat of a lawsuit, administrative proceedings such as an EEOC complaint, prior lawsuits, the filing of a complaint, discovery requests or discovery orders.

Determining when the obligation to preserve arises involves a specific factual inquiry with the persons involved in the case.

[a] Reported Cases

- *Zubulake v. UBS Warburg LLC,* 220 F.R.D. 212, 217 (S.D.N.Y. 2003). The Court held that a duty to preserve arose before the complaint was filed based on an e-mail labeled attorney-client privilege, where no lawyer was named on the e-mail, and a supervisor's deposition testimony that he feared the plaintiff would sue. However, the Court noted "[m]erely because one or two employees contemplate the possibility that a fellow employee might sue does not generally impose a firm-wide duty to preserve."

- *Cook Assocs., Inc. v. PCS Sales (USA), Inc.,* 271 F. Supp. 2d 1343, 1357 (D. Utah 2003). The Court found no spoliation where the defendant destroyed documents as part of routine housecleaning operation well before filing of complaint and where prelitigation communication was too general to place the defendant on notice to preserve.

- *Silvestri v. GMC,* 271 F.3d 583, 591 (4th Cir. 2001). The plaintiff, an accident victim, brought an action against the car manufacturer for failure of the airbag to deploy. The court dismissed the action for failure to preserve the auto for inspection by the defendant though the plaintiff knew "the evidence may be relevant to anticipated litigation."

- *Shamis v. Ambassador Factors Corp.,* 34 F. Supp. 2d 879, 888-89 (S.D.N.Y. 1999). The defendant sought dismissal of the case due to the producing party's destruction of "3,000 cartons of Wishbone's business and financial documents." The court, instead, allowed for a spoliation instruction to be given to the jury. The Court held that "[a] condition precedent to the imposition of sanctions is whether *Shamis* knew or should have known that the destroyed evidence was relevant to pending, imminent or reasonably foreseeable litigation."

Pending or impending litigation

- *Danis v. USN Communications,* No. CIV.98-7482, 2000 WL 1694325 (N.D. Ill. Oct. 20, 2000). The Court found that a party to pending litigation has a duty to preserve and produce discoverable evidence that a party knows or reasonably should know may be relevant to the pending or impending litigation.

- *In Century ML-Cable Corp. v. Conjugal Partnership,* 43 F. Supp. 2d 176, 181 (D.P.R. 1998). The Court stated, in determining when the duty to preserve commenced for spoliation purposes, that there was evidence that the defendants knew even before the lawsuit was commenced that plaintiffs were investigating their descrambler business.

Anticipates litigation

- *Zubulake v. UBS Warburg, LLC,* 220 F.R.D. 212, 217 (S.D.N.Y. 2003). "Thus, the relevant people at UBS anticipated litigation in April 2001. The duty to preserve attached at the time that litigation was reasonably anticipated."

- *Mathias v. Jacobs,* 197 F.R.D. 29, 37 (S.D.N.Y. 2000), vacated on other grounds, 167 F. Supp. 2d 606 (2001). Court ruled that a party is obligated to retain evidence that it knows or reasonably should know may be relevant depending on future litigation. The duty to preserve arises "whenever a party has been served with a complaint or anticipates litigation," and that service of the discovery places a party on notice to preserve the materials explicitly requested. Discovering party had served, in this noncompete case, a broad request for diaries, appointment books, calendars, schedules, electronic organizers, telephone directories, rolodex cards, diaries and documents reflecting names, addresses and phone numbers of any persons contacted by the other party. Producing party had destroyed evidence after inputting the data into a Palm Pilot.

Might occur

- *Renda Marine, Inc. v. United States,* 58 Fed. Cl. 57, 61 (Fed. Cl. 2003). In a government contract suit, the court after reviewing the different cases addressing the issue of when the duty to preserve arises, held that, "upon notice that litigation might occur," defendant had a legal obligation to preserve evidence related to the plaintiff's claim. The Court rejected the government's reliance on a record retention policy that was inconsistent with its legal duty to preserve evidence.

- *Kronisch v. United States,* 150 F.3d 112, 126 (2d Cir. 1998). A party's obligation to preserve evidence that may be relevant to litigation is triggered once the party has notice that litigation might occur.

Likelihood of claim

- *Hirsch v. General Motors Corp.,* 266 N.J. Super. 222, 628 A.2d 1108, 1122 (1993). The Court stated, "a duty to preserve evidence, independent from a court order to preserve evidence, arises where there is: (1) pending or probable litigation involving the defendants; (2) knowledge by plaintiff of the existence or likelihood of litigation; (3)

foreseeability of harm to the defendants, in other words, discarding the evidence would be prejudicial to defendants; and (4) evidence relevant to the litigation."

Prelitigation discussions

- *Computer Assocs. Int'l. v. American Fundware, Inc.,* 133 F.R.D. 166, 169 (D. Colo. 1990). The Court found, "[s]anctions may be imposed against a litigant who is on notice that documents and information in its possession are relevant to litigation, or potential litigation, or are reasonably calculated to lead to the discovery of admissible evidence, and destroys such documents and information." The Court ordered default judgment since the defendant destroyed computer source code that was the central issue in the dispute.

Had notice of claim to be filed

- *Wm. T. Thompson Co. v. General Nutrition Corp.,* 593 F. Supp. 1443, 1450 (C.D. Cal. 1984). Court ordered a default judgment against party for failure to preserve records when it had notice to preserve records prior to claim being filed, and continued to destroy records after preservation order. Some of the records were electronic, and pertained to purchases, sales and inventory. The Court held that even without a specific request for the documents, when a party knows or reasonably should know that a document will become important to a lawsuit, that party has a duty not to destroy that document.

Once complaint filed

- *Heng Chan v. Triple 8 Palace,* No. CIV. 03-6048, 2005 U.S. Dist. LEXIS 16520, at *11-13 (D.N.Y. Aug. 11, 2005). The "obligation to preserve evidence arises when the party has notice that the evidence is relevant to litigation - most commonly when suit has already been filed, providing the party responsible for the destruction with express notice, but also on occasion in other circumstances, as for example when a party should have known that the evidence may be relevant to future litigation."
- *New York National Organization for Women v. Cuomo,* No. CIV.93-7146, 1998 WL 395320 (S.D.N.Y. Jul. 14, 1998). The Court held defendant put on notice to preserve evidence once complaint was filed.
- *Turner v. Hudson Transit Lines, Inc.,* 142 F.R.D. 68, 72-73 (S.D.N.Y. 1991). Court found at a minimum that service of complaint was sufficient to put an employer on notice of litigation and its obligation to preserve all electronic information.
- *Computer Associates International, Inc. v. American Fundware, Inc., 133* F.R.D. 166, 169 (D. Colo. 1990). At a minimum, defendant under a duty "to preserve the source

code . . . twenty days . . . [after] it was served with the complaint, because, in the normal course of proceedings, it had a duty by then to investigate the matter and file an answer, or otherwise respond, to the complaint."

Obligation on requesting party to take additional steps

• *Chidichimo v. University of Chicago Press*, 681 N.E.2d 107, 110-111 (Ill. 1997). Even though the party, on notice to preserve electronic evidence, purged computer data, the Court denied sanction request since the plaintiff failed to take additional steps to ensure the preservation and protect against routine destruction.

Statutory obligation

• *In re Tyco International, Ltd., Securities Litigation*, No. 00-MD-1335-B, 2000 WL 33654141 (D.N.H. Jul. 27, 2000). Court refused to adopt the parties' written agreement concerning preservation of defendants' documents and data, finding that it would unnecessarily duplicate or alter the obligations already imposed by the preservation provision in the Private Securities Litigation Reform Act of 1995, 15 U.S.C. § 78u-4(b)(3)(C)(I)(1).

[2]   Other Authorities

Statutory Obligation to Preserve

• EEOC regulations require preservation of evidence once notice of a charge is filed. 29 C.F.R. § 1602.14.

• Regulations being revised by the National Archives and Records Administration regarding disposition of very short-term e-mail by allowing management of such records within the e-mail system. *Disposition of Electronic Mail Records with Short Retention Periods,* Final Rule, 71 Fed. Reg. 8806-8808 (Feb. 21, 2006) (to be codified at 36 C.F.R. pt. 1234). The effective date for changes is March 23, 2006.

• Sarbanes-Oxley Act of 2002, 116 Stat. 745 (2002) contains a number of document preservation requirements applicable to many publicly traded companies.

• There are many state statutes that require preservation of records. *See, e.g.*, Ala. Code § 8-1A-12 (1975).

Local Rules of Practice

• The District of Wyoming has adopted a local rule providing that counsel "shall [in their Rule 26(f) conference] attempt to agree on steps the parties will take to segregate and preserve computer-based information in order to avoid accusations of spoliation."

[3]   Discovery Pointers

• If you are requesting discovery consider sending a preservation letter and/or asking the Court for a preservation order. *See,* § 6.1[C][7], *Preservation Request* and § 7.3[E], *Discovery and Preservation Orders - Rule 16(c).*

[E]   Scope of Duty to Preserve

Once a duty to preserve arises, a party is faced with the challenging task of determining exactly what electronic information to preserve. It would be a monumental task, and expensive, to preserve every byte of electronic information the party has accumulated in active files, databases, backup tapes, etc. A company need not preserve "every scrap of paper" in its files. *Danis v. USN Comm., Inc.,* 2000 WL 1694325, at *32 (N.D. Ill. Oct. 23, 2000). On the other hand a party cannot ignore the duty to preserve and must take immediate and effective steps to preserve relevant data.

The obligations contained within Rule 26 generally determine the scope of your duty to preserve. *See,* § 7.4, *Production and Protection of Case Information.* At a minimum, a party is obligated under Rule 26(a)(1)(A) to disclose the name, address and telephone number of "each individual likely to have discoverable information that the disclosing party may use to support its claims or defenses, unless solely for impeachment." The party is also obligated to identify and preserve "a copy of or a description by category or location of, all *documents, data compilations,* and tangible things that are in the possession, custody or control of the party and that the disclosing party may use to support its claims or defenses unless solely for impeachment . . ." (emphasis added). Rule 26(a)(1)(B). Furthermore, a party must preserve "any matter, not privileged, that is relevant to the claim or defense of any party, including the existence, description, nature, custody, condition, and location of any books, documents, or other tangible things and the identity and location of persons having knowledge of any discoverable matter. For good cause, the court may order discovery of any matter relevant to the subject matter involved in the action. Relevant information need not be admissible at the trial if the discovery appears reasonably calculated to lead to the discovery of admissible evidence." Rule 26(b)(1); *Kleiner v. Burns,* 2000 WL 1909470 (D. Kan. Dec. 15, 2000); *Danis v. USN Communications,* No. CIV.98-7482, 2000 WL 1694325 (N.D. Ill. Oct. 20, 2000). In *Zubulake v. UBS Warburg LLC,* 220 F.R.D. 212, 217 (S.D.N.Y. 2003) the court stated:

At the same time, anyone who anticipates being a party or is a party to a lawsuit must not destroy unique, relevant evidence that might be useful to an adversary. "While a litigant is under no duty to keep or retain every document in its possession . . . it is under a duty to preserve what it knows, or reasonably should know, is relevant in the action, is reasonably calculated to lead to the discovery of admissible evidence, is reasonably likely to be requested during discovery and/or is the subject of a pending discovery request."

[1]   Reported Cases

- *Wm. T. Thompson Co. v. General Nutrition Corp.*, 593 F. Supp. 1443, 1555 (C.D. Cal. 1984). The Court stated, "[w]hile a litigant is under no duty to keep or retain every document in its possession once a complaint is filed, it is under a duty to preserve what it knows, or reasonably should know, is relevant in the action, is reasonably calculated to lead to the discovery of admissible evidence, is reasonably likely to be requested during discovery, and/or is the subject of a pending discovery request."

- *Wiginton v. Ellis,* No. CIV.02-6832, 2003 WL 22439865, at *4, *5 (N.D. Ill. Oct. 27, 2003). The plaintiffs sent an initial preservation letter and later stipulated to a more inclusive preservation letter. The Court held that the preservation letter did not define the scope nor duty on the producing party as to their preservation obligation. Instead, it put them on notice as to the claim and possible individuals connected with the case.

- *Illinois Tool Works, Inc. v. Metro Mark Products, LTD, et al*, 43 F. Supp. 2d 951, 952 (N.D. Ill. 1999). The Court sanctioned the defendant for failure "to preserve the integrity of all computers that are issue here without spoliation or any information contained therein." The computer in the defendant's possession failed to operate six days after the preservation order, despite functioning properly a few days earlier.

- *Turner v. Hudson Transit Lines, Inc.,* 142 F.R.D. 68, 72 (S.D.N.Y. 1991). Court held that statutory record retention period, after which documents are destroyed, was insufficient because party was on notice that litigation was likely to commence.

[F]   Affirmative Continual Obligation to Preserve and Disclose

The courts have imposed affirmative obligations on parties to preserve and not destroy responsive electronic data. These are commonly referred to as a "litigation hold." The key questions, after determining that a duty to preserve has arisen, are what affirmative actions need to be taken by counsel and his client to ensure that the data is preserved and not destroyed. Failure to take those actions may result in sanctions from the court.

Also, the courts in considering sanctions have examined closely the actions taken by a party after the late discovery of responsive data.

[1] Reported Cases

Affirmative Obligation

- *Tantivy Communs., Inc. v. Lucent Techs., Inc.,* No. CIV.04-79, 2005 U.S. Dist. LEXIS 29981, at *7-8 (D. Tex. Nov. 1, 2005). The Court in commenting upon counsel's obligation to preserve data stated, "[defendant] and its counsel are well aware that a party in litigation must suspend its routine document retention/destruction policy and establish a 'litigation hold' to ensure the preservation of relevant documents."

- *Zubulake v. UBS Warburg LLC,* 220 F.R.D. 212, 218 (S.D.N.Y. 2003). The party and its counsel should ensure that "(1) all sources of relevant information are discovered, (2) relevant information is retained on a continuing basis, and (3) relevant non-privileged material is produced to the opposing party. *Id.* . . . this Court is aware that in certain cases, some documents will 'slip through the cracks' . . ."

- *Mosaid Technologies Inc. v. Samsung Electronics Co., Ltd.,* 2004 WL 2797536, at *6 (D. N.J. 2004). In a commercial litigation case the defendant failed to preserve e-mail and a spoliation inference would be given to jury. The Court noted that, "The duty to preserve potentially relevant evidence is an affirmative obligation that a party may not shirk. When the duty to preserve is triggered, it cannot be a defense to a spoliation claim that the party inadvertently failed to place a 'litigation hold' or 'off switch' on its document retention policy to stop the destruction of that evidence."

- *Heng Chan v. Triple 8 Palace,* No. CIV. 03-6048, 2005 U.S. Dist. LEXIS 16520 (D.N.Y. Aug. 11, 2005). The defendants failed to implement a litigation hold and relevant documents were destroyed. Apparently, counsel failed to inform their client to preserve documents. The Court ordered an adverse inference instruction and awarded costs in connection with the sanction motion.

- *Convolve, Inc. v. Compaq Computer Corp.,* 223 F.R.D. 162, 175 (S.D.N.Y. 2004). The Court ruled that, "[t]he obligation to preserve evidence arises when the party has notice that the evidence is relevant to litigation or when a party should have known that the evidence may be relevant to future litigation. (citations omitted). Moreover, in the world of electronic data, the preservation obligation is not limited simply to avoiding affirmative acts of destruction. Since computer systems generally have automatic deletion features that periodically purge electronic documents such as e-mail, it is necessary for a party facing litigation to take active steps to halt that process."

- *United States v. Philip Morris, USA, Inc.,* No. CIV.99-2496, 2004 WL 1627252 (D.D.C. July 21, 2004). The company failed to follow the preservation order and destroyed e-mail for more than two years. A number of high-ranking officers who were to be called as witnesses failed to retain their e-mail under a "print and retain" policy. The defendant was barred from presenting any fact witness who had failed to preserve relevant records and was ordered to pay *$2.75 million* in fines for its spoliation of e-mail.

- *Prudential Ins. Co. of Am. Sales Practices Lit., 169 F.R.D. 598, 615 (D.N.J. 1997).* The Court fined Prudential $1 million for *"its haphazard and uncoordinated approach to document retention"* and not acting quickly to prevent the destruction of electronic data. After court ordered Prudential to preserve all relevant documents, Prudential employees continued destruction of relevant documents.

- *Kingsway Fin. Servs., Inc. v. Pricewaterhouse-Coopers LLP,* No. CIV.03-5560, 2006 WL 1520227, *1 (S.D.N.Y. Jun. 1, 2006) and *Kingsway Fin. Servs., Inc. v. Pricewaterhouse-Coopers LLP,* No. CIV.03-5560, 2006 WL 1295409 (S.D.N.Y. May 10, 2006). The defendant filed a motion for production of the document retention notices sent by plaintiff's counsel to his client. The Court ruled the "litigation hold" notices were relevant but were privileged and noted, "[l]ike a party's destruction of relevant documents, if plaintiff's document retention notices are patently deficient or inadequate in some other respect, they might support a negative inference concerning the merits of plaintiff's claims."

Continual Preservation and Disclosure Obligation

- *Williams v. Saint-Gobain Corp.,* No. CIV.00-0502, 2002 WL 1477618 (W.D.N.Y. Jun. 28, 2002). In this employment case the Court rejected a request for evidence preclusion and adverse inference instruction when it was discovered five days before trial (it was postponed) 1998 e-mails obtained from the personal computer of a former vice president. The vice-president thought the corporation already had the e-mail. After learning of their existence defendant's counsel *immediately* produced the e-mail.

- *Coleman (Parent) Holdings, Inc. v. Morgan Stanley & Co., Inc.,* 2005 WL 67071 (Fla. Cir. Ct. Mar. 1, 2005). The Court granted the plaintiff's motion for an adverse inference due to e-mail destruction and failure to comply with the judge's discovery order. Because of deleted e-mail and failure to immediately disclose discovered backup tapes in a timely manner the Court permitted the plaintiff to argue an adverse inference regarding the concealment of evidence and shifted the burden of proof to the defendant as to certain elements of the cause of action. The jury awarded 1.4 billion in damages.

- *Residential Funding Corp. v. DeGeorge Financial Corp.,* 306 F.3d 99, 108 (2d Cir. 2002). The defendant appealed the trial court's denial of their motion for an adverse instruction as a sanction for plaintiff's failure to produce certain e-mails in time for trial. The trial court denied the motion because there was no bad faith and the defendant had not shown that the e-mails would be favorable to its case. The Appellate Court found that mere negligence would support an adverse inference instruction, after it found no willful conduct in failing to produce certain e-mail in time for trial and remanded for a hearing to evaluate the impact of the "sluggish" production.

- *Wilson v. Sundstrand Corp.,* No. CIV.99-6944, 2003 WL 21961359 (N.D.Ill. Aug. 18, 2003). The Court as a sanction for discovery abuse and tardy production of "smoking gun" e-mail precluded the defendant from opposing the admission in evidence of various e-mails and records.

[G] Persons Involved in Data Preservation

[1] Outside Counsel Duties

The Courts have imposed significant responsibilities on outside counsel to continually ensure document retention compliance and to make reasonable inquires into the factual basis of its discovery responses. *Metropolitan Opera Ass'n., Inc. v. Local 100,* 212 F.R.D. 178 (S.D.N.Y. 2003), *adhered to on reconsideration,* 2004 WL 1943099 (S.D.N.Y. Aug. 27, 2004); *Turner v. Hudson Transit Lines, Inc.,* 142 F.R.D. 68, 73 (S.D.N.Y. 1991); *Zubulake v. UBS Warburg LLC,* No. CIV.02-1243, 2004 WL 1620866 (S.D. N.Y. July 20, 2004); *Danis v. USN Communications,* No. CIV.98-7482, 2000 WL 1694325 (N.D. Ill. Oct. 20, 2000); *Kier v. UnumProvident Corp.,* No. CIV.02-8781, 2003 WL 21997747, at *13 (S.D.N.Y. Aug. 22, 2003).

[a] Reported Cases

- *Heng Chan v. Triple 8 Palace,* No. CIV. 03-6048, 2005 U.S. Dist. LEXIS 16520, at *16-17 (D.N.Y. Aug. 11, 2005). "The preservation obligation runs first to counsel, who has 'a duty to advise his client of the type of information potentially relevant to the lawsuit and of the necessity of preventing its destruction.' (citations omitted) . . . Where the client is a business, its managers, in turn, are responsible for conveying to the employees the requirements for preserving evidence.(citation omitted) Thus, 'once a party reasonably anticipates litigation, it must suspend its routine document retention/ destruction policy and put in place a 'litigation hold' to ensure the preservation of relevant documents.'"

- In *Metropolitan Opera Ass'n., Inc. v. Local 100,* 212 F.R.D. 178, 222-223 (S.D.N.Y. 2003), *adhered to on reconsideration,* 2004 WL 1943099 (S.D.N.Y. Aug. 27, 2004) the Court criticized outside counsel and stated that he:

  (1) never gave adequate instructions to their clients about the clients' overall discovery obligations, what constitutes a "document" . . . (2) . . . never implemented a systematic procedure for document production or for retention of documents, including electronic documents; (3) delegated document production

to a layperson who . . . did not even understand . . . that a document included a draft or other non-identical copy, a computer file and an e-mail; (4) never went back to the layperson designated to assure that he had establish[ed] a coherent and effective system . . . and (5) . . . failed to take any action to remedy the situation or supplement the demonstrably false responses . . . The court concludes that . . . its counsel failed in a variety of instances to conduct any reasonable inquiry into the factual basis of its discovery responses . . . Such an inquiry would have required, at a minimum, a reasonable procedure to distribute discovery requests to all employees and agents of the defendant potentially possessing responsive information, and to account for the collection and subsequent production of the information to plaintiffs.

• *Zubulake v. UBS Warburg LLC,* No. CIV.02-1243, 2004 WL 1620866, at *30-31 (S.D. N.Y. July 20, 2004).

There are thus a number of steps that counsel should take to ensure compliance with the preservation obligation. While these precautions may not be enough (or may be too much) in some cases, they are designed to promote the continued preservation of potentially relevant information in the typical case. First, counsel must issue a "litigation hold" at the outset of litigation or whenever litigation is reasonably anticipated. The litigation hold should be periodically re-issued so that new employees are aware of it, and so that it is fresh in the minds of all employees. Second, counsel should communicate directly with the "key players" in the litigation, i.e., the people identified in a party's initial disclosure and any subsequent supplementation thereto. Because these "key players" are the "employees likely to have relevant information," it is particularly important that the preservation duty be communicated clearly to them. As with the litigation hold, the key players should be periodically reminded that the preservation duty is still in place. Finally, counsel should instruct all employees to produce electronic copies of their relevant active files. Counsel must also make sure that all backup media which the party is required to retain is identified and stored in a safe place. In cases involving a small number of relevant backup tapes, counsel might be advised to take physical possession of backup tapes. In other cases, it might make sense for relevant backup tapes to be segregated and placed in storage. Regardless of what particular arrangement counsel chooses to employ, the point is to separate relevant backup tapes from others. One of the primary reasons that electronic data is lost is ineffective communication with information technology personnel. By taking possession of, or otherwise safeguarding, all potentially relevant backup tapes, counsel eliminates the possibility that such tapes will be inadvertently recycled.

A party's discovery obligations do not end with the implementation of a "litigation hold" - to the contrary, that's only the beginning. Counsel must oversee compliance with the litigation hold, monitoring the party's efforts to retain and produce the relevant documents. Proper communication between a party and her lawyer will ensure (1) that all relevant information (or at least all sources of relevant information) is discovered, (2) that relevant information is retained on a continuing basis; and (3) that relevant non-privileged material is produced to the opposing party.

- *Cardenas v. Dorel Juvenile Group, Inc.,* No. CIV.04-2478, 2006 U.S. Dist. LEXIS 37465, at *23-24 (D. Kan. Jun. 1, 2006). The Court refused to order severe sanctions against the defendant for failure to locate relevant documents but stated: "[t]rial counsel have a duty to exercise some degree of oversight over their clients' employees to ensure that they are acting competently, diligently, and ethically in order to fulfill their responsibility to the Court and opposing parties. Accordingly, trial counsel have the obligation to communicate with in-house counsel to identify the persons having responsibility for the matters that are the subject of the document requests and to identify all employees likely to have been authors, recipients or custodians of documents falling within the request. Trial counsel also have an obligation to review all documents received from the client to see whether they indicate the existence of other documents not previously retrieved or produced. The Court does not find that these duties were met here . . ."

- *Phoenix Four, Inc. v. Strategic Res. Corp.,* No. CIV.05-4837, 2006 U.S. Dist. LEXIS 32211, at *6-17 (D.N.Y. May 22, 2006). The Court in citing to *Zubulake v. UBS Warburg LLC,* 229 F.R.D. 422 (S.D.N.Y. 2004) found that "Judge Scheindlin has defined the contours of counsel's duty to locate relevant electronic information (citation omitted). Counsel has the duty to properly communicate with its client to ensure that 'all sources of relevant information [are] discovered.' . . . To identify all such sources, counsel should 'become fully familiar with [its] client's document retention policies, as well as [its] client's data retention architecture.' . . . This effort would involve communicating with information technology personnel and the key players in the litigation to understand how electronic information is stored."

- *GTFM, Inc. v. Wal-Mart Stores, Inc.,* 2000 WL 335558, at *2 (S.D.N.Y. 2000). The Court criticized Wal-Mart's counsel for representing in writing that "Wal-Mart does not have the centralized computer capability to track [the relevant transactions]." Later, in a deposition, it became known that the information did exist when it was requested, but had subsequently been deleted from the computer.

- *Danis v. USN Communications, Inc.,* No. CIV.98-7482, 2000 WL 1694325, at *14 (N.D. Ill. Oct. 20, 2000). The Court sanctioned the CEO of a defendant organization for failure to consult with its outside law firm that had "scores of experienced attorneys capable of developing and implementing a suitable document preservation program in a major securities lawsuit." Instead, the CEO entrusted the responsibility for disclosure of data to an inexperienced in-house attorney, which led to sanctions against the CEO.

*   *Linnen v. A.H. Robins Co.*, No. 97-2307, 1999 WL 462015 (Mass. Super. Ct. Jun. 16, 1999). The plaintiff sought e-mail and deposed employees who were allegedly knowledgeable about their e-mail systems. During the discovery the disclosing party maintained that the data had not been retained. Later, it was revealed that there were thousands of backup tapes that contained electronic messages. The Court ordered the company to restore these tapes at cost of approximately $1.2 million and imposed sanctions.

*   *Invision Media Communications, Inc. v. Federal Ins. Co.*, 2004 WL 396037 (S.D.N.Y. Mar. 2, 2004). In an action for breach of an insurance contract, the defendant moved to compel production of documents and requested monetary sanctions, contending that the plaintiff made false statements regarding the location and existence of its documents and destroyed evidence relevant to the lawsuit. Among the documents requested by the defendant were e-mail communications sent by the plaintiff. Specifically, the defendant sought "All electronic mail communications sent or received by the plaintiffs during August 2001, September 2001 and October 2001." The plaintiff represented to the defendant that the emails could not be produced because the plaintiff archived email on its servers for only a two week period. The court found these statements false because the plaintiff eventually disclosed the requested emails after further investigation. Accordingly, the court awarded the defendant costs and attorneys fees, noting that "[a] reasonable inquiry by the plaintiff's counsel . . . would have alerted counsel that the plaintiff possessed electronic mail that fell within the scope of Federal's document request . . . the plaintiff has disregarded its discovery obligations, made misleading statements regarding the existence and location of relevant evidence, and/or failed to make reasonable inquiries into matters pertinent to the pretrial discovery phase of this litigation."

[b]   Other Authorities

*   American Bar Association Civil Discovery Standards, August 1999, Standard No. 10, *Preservation of Documents*. "When a lawyer who has been retained to handle a matter learns that litigation is probable or has been commenced, the lawyer should inform the client of its duty to preserve potentially relevant documents and of the possible consequences for failing to do so."

[2]   In-house Counsel

In-house counsel has an affirmative obligation to ensure that senior management and employees implement an effective document preservation program.

[a]   Reported Cases

- *Danis v. USN Communications*, No. CIV.98-7482, 2000 WL 1694325 (N.D. Ill. Oct. 20, 2000). Court found that inexperienced in-house counsel failed to establish a meaningful document retention program. The Court noted that there was no general notice to all employees to preserve documents, no specific criteria regarding what should and should not be saved, no attorney review of documents being thrown away, and no review of pre-existing practices relating to document preservation, including e-mail, for terminated employees. The Court imposed a $10,000 fine and recommended an adverse jury instruction regarding gaps in document disclosure for inadvertent destruction of paper and electronic discovery.

- *Zubulake v. UBS Warburg LLC,* No. CIV.02-1243, 2004 WL 1620866, at *36 (S.D. N.Y. July 20, 2004). The Court found that in-house counsel had failed to notify one of the senior management regarding the preservation hold.

- *United States v. Arthur Andersen,* LLP, No. 02-21200, 2004 WL 1344957 (5th Cir. Jun. 16, 2004), *rev'd on other grounds, Andersen, L.L.P. v. United States,* 2005 WL 1262915, (U.S. May 31, 2005). The Court of Appeals affirmed Arthur Andersen's criminal conviction for shredding records immediately before being served with a SEC subpoena. Enron's in house counsel knowing of the imminent investigation encouraged the employees to follow the document retention policy.

[3]   Senior Management Obligation

Senior management also has specific preservation obligations and must take affirmative steps to notify and ensure retention of relevant case material. *Zubulake v. UBS Warburg LLC,* No. CIV.02-1243, 2004 WL 1620866, at *30-31 (S.D.N.Y. July 20, 2004).

[a]   Reported Cases

- *Phoenix Four, Inc. v. Strategic Res. Corp.*, No. CIV.05-4837, 2006 U.S. Dist. LEXIS 32211, at *4-15, 19-20 (D.N.Y. May 22, 2006). The Court found that management "abandoned at least ten computer workstations without bothering to make any search whatsoever in order to discover whether they contained [any case related] information . . . [and] were at the least negligent in carelessly representing to counsel that 'there were no computers . . . to search' when they knew that they still possessed, and were actually using at least one of the servers from [their prior company that was the defendant in this case]."

- *Heng Chan v. Triple 8 Palace,* No. CIV. 03-6048, 2005 U.S. Dist. LEXIS 16520, at *16-17 (D.N.Y. Aug. 11, 2005). "[T]he defendants had the obligation to inform their employees of the requirements of preservation: It is no defense to suggest . . . that particular employees were not on notice. To hold otherwise would permit an agency, corporate officer, or legal department to shield itself from discovery obligations by keeping its employees ignorant. The obligation to retain discoverable materials is an affirmative one; it requires that the agency or corporate officers having notice of discovery obligations communicate those obligations to employees in possession of discoverable materials."

- *In re Prudential Ins. Co. of Amer. Sales Practices Litig.,* 169 F.R.D. 598, 615 (D.N.J. 1997). The Court found, that after the order "to preserve documents was entered, it became the obligation of senior management to initiate a comprehensive document preservation plan and to distribute it to all employees. Moreover, it was incumbent on senior management to advise its employees of the pending multidistrict litigation venued in New Jersey, to provide them with a copy of the Court's Order, and to acquaint its employees with the potential sanctions, both civil and criminal, that the Court could issue for noncompliance with this Court's Order."

- *Danis v. USN Communications, Inc.,* No. CIV.98-7482, 2000 WL 1694325, at *14 (N.D. Ill. Oct. 20, 2000). The Court sanctioned the CEO of a defendant organization for failure to consult with its outside law firm that had "scores of experienced attorneys capable of developing and implementing a suitable document preservation program in a major securities lawsuit."

[4]   Outside Directors

If the company is a public company, it should instruct outside directors to preserve relevant documents. *In re Triton Energy Ltd. Securities Litigation*, 2002 WL 32114464 (E.D. Tex. March 7, 2002); *Danis v. USN Communications, Inc.,* No. CIV.98-7482, 2000 WL 1694325, at *49 (N.D. Ill. Oct. 20, 2000).

[5]   Employees Likely to Have Relevant Information.

After a party is placed on notice of litigation, employees who are likely to have relevant electronic data should be contacted and their evidence preserved. A reasonable inquiry from prelitigation correspondence, complaint and investigation should uncover employees connected to the case whose data should be preserved. *Gen. Elec. Capital Corp. v. Lear Corp.,* 215 F.R.D. 637, 640-641 (D. Kan. 2003) (court ordered defendant "to search for responsive documents created or received by all [defendant] . . . employees who had a business relationship . . . or who were otherwise involved in the business relationship" between the parties.)

[a]   Reported Cases

- *Wiginton v. Ellis,* No. CIV.02-6832, 2003 WL 22439865, at *5 (N.D. Ill. Oct. 27, 2003). In this case the court discussed how the defendant should have discovered employees who were connected to the case and that their data should have been preserved.

- *Danis v. USN Communications*, No. CIV.98-7482, 2000 WL 1694325 (N.D. Ill. Oct. 20, 2000). The Court noted that there was no general notice to all employees to preserve documents, no specific criteria regarding what should and should not be saved, no attorney review of documents being thrown away, and no review of pre-existing practices relating to document preservation, including e-mail, for terminated employees.

[6]   Information Custodian(s)

Some of the key individuals to include in your preservation planning are the IT personnel who will actually be collecting the relevant electronic evidence.

[7]   Consultants and Experts

See, § 7.4[D], Expert Witness Reports - FED. R. CIV. P. 26(a)(2)(A), Rule 26(a)(2)(B) and Rule 26(b)(4).

[8]   Third Parties

The discovering party should consider whether notice needs to be sent to third parties such as litigants in a related lawsuit, data contractors, suppliers or vendors who may have the company's data. FED. R. CIV. P. 34, provides that a party's obligation to produce data extends to those who have "possession, custody or control" of documents. If a third party processes data for the producing party, then it is suggested to notify the third party that the data may be relevant pursuant to Rule 26. *See also, § 7.10, Obtaining Data From Third Parties.*

[H]   Document Retention Policy - Prior to Litigation

Document retention policies are standards and procedures that determine whether electronic information or paper documents are preserved. "'Document retention policies', which are created in part to keep certain information from getting into the hands of others . . . are common in business . . . It is not wrongful for a manager or company to instruct its employees to comply with a valid document retention policy under normal circumstances." *Arthur Andersen LLP v. United States,* 125 S. Ct. 2129, 2135 (2005). However, "once a party reasonably anticipates litigation, it must suspend its routine document retention/destruction policy and put in place a 'litigation hold' to ensure the preservation of relevant documents." *Thompson v. HUD,* 219 F.R.D. 93, 100 (D.Md. 2003).

A document retention policy must be implemented in good faith and followed at all times, and not when litigation is anticipated. The arbitrary enforcement and use of a document retention policy will cast suspicion on the motives of an organization by the courts or a regulatory agency. Advise your client to suspend their document destruction policy (usually includes document destruction dates) for data discoverable under Rule 26 once litigation is anticipated.

[1]   Reported Cases

Several courts have commented on routine document retention policies in the context of litigation.

- *Arthur Andersen, L.L.P. v. United States,* 2005 WL 1262915, at *5 (U.S. May 31, 2005). In a seminal case the United States Supreme Court reversed the defendant's criminal conviction for shredding records immediately before receiving a SEC subpoena. The Court reversed the case based on erroneous jury instructions which failed to require a "consciousness of wrongdoing" and a "nexus" between the "persuasion" to enforce the document retention policy and any particular legal proceeding. The court noted that, "[i]t is, of course, not wrongful for a manager to instruct his employees to comply with a valid document retention policy under ordinary circumstances."

- *Lewy v. Remington Arms Co.,* 836 F.2d 1104, 1112 (8th Cir. 1988). In a lawsuit involving an alleged defective gun, the Appellate Court discussed the various factors for guidance to determine whether a retention program is reasonable, in light of probable or pending litigation. Based on their three-year document retention policy the defendants had destroyed complaints and gun examination reports and were unable to produce them for litigation. The higher court remanded and instructed the trial court to determine the reasonableness of the defendant's retention policy based on the following factors: 1) the reasonableness of the policy in light of the facts and circumstances surrounding the relevant documents; 2) the frequency and magnitude of similar suits against the company, such that this would put the company on notice of potential litigation; and 3) whether the policy was initiated in bad faith. If the lower court found the retention policy to be unreasonable then an adverse inference instruction could be issued. The Court noted, retention of documents should occur if "the corporation knew or should have known that the documents would become material at some point in the future . . . a corporation cannot blindly destroy documents and expect to be shielded by a seemingly innocuous document retention policy."

- *Stevenson v. Union Pacific R. Co.*, 354 F.3d 739 (8th Cir. 2004). In this personal injury accident the defendant failed to preserve a voice tape of the conversation between the train crew and dispatch at the time of the accident. In conformance with their document retention policy the voice tape was overwritten after 90 days. Though the Court failed to find any bad faith or unreasonableness in the retention policy, it imposed an adverse inference for the destruction of the tape for the reason that based on its previous litigation experience that such tapes were relevant in litigation concerning serious injury or death. In a later decision, involving similar facts, the 8th Circuit in *Morris v. Union Pacific R.R.*, 373 F.3d 896, 901 (8th Cir. 2004) held that since the trial court had not made a finding of "intentional destruction indicating a desire to suppress the truth" an adverse instruction should not have been issued. The plaintiff, a tow truck operator, was called to the scene of a collision between a Union Pacific train and a tractor-trailer truck. While inspecting the vehicles, the plaintiff was injured when the train car suddenly moved forward. Taped communications between the train crew and dispatcher were destroyed after 90 days pursuant to the defendant's document retention policy. The jury verdict of eight million dollars was reversed and a new trial was ordered.

- *Broccoli v. Echostar Communications Corp*, 229 F.R.D. 506, 510 (D. Md. 2005). The Court imposed sanctions when the defendant failed to preserve electronic evidence after the plaintiff's grievances were communicated to the defendant's supervisors. In commenting upon the defendant's document retention policies, the Court stated, "[u]nder the defendant's 'extraordinary email/document retention policy, the email system automatically sends all items in a user's 'sent items' folder over seven days old to the user's 'deleted items' folder, and all items in a user's 'deleted items' folder over 14 days old are then automatically purged from the user's 'deleted items' folder. The user's purged emails are not recorded or stored in any back up files. Thus, when 21-day-old emails are purged, they are forever unretrievable. The electronic files, including the contents of all folders, sub-folders, and all email folders, of former employees are also completely deleted 30 days after the employee leaves Echostar. Again, under normal circumstances, such a policy may be a risky but arguably defensible business practice undeserving of sanctions."

- *House of Dreams, Inc. v. Lord & Taylor*, 2004 N.Y. Misc. LEXIS 3040, at *17 (N.Y. Sup. Ct. Mar. 24, 2004). In a commercial case, the Court found no spoliation because the defendants' record retention system automatically deleted e-mails "in an individual merchant's: 'outbox' [after] . . . 7 days; emails stored in his 'in-box' [after] . . . 21 days; and emails stored in his 'personal folder' [after] two years."

- *In re Prudential Insurance Co.*, 169 F.R.D. 598, 615 (D.N.J. 1997). Court imposed $1 million sanction against Prudential Insurance Co. for "its haphazard and uncoordinated approach to [electronic] document destruction." In addition to the fine, Prudential was ordered to pay substantial attorneys' fees and to present to the court within 30 days "a written manual that embodies Prudential's document preservation policy."

• *United States v. Quattrone,* 441 F.3d 153, 165 (2d Cir. 2006). The Appellate Court reversed and remanded for a new trial the criminal convictions of the defendant based on faulty jury instructions even though they stated that the evidence was sufficient to support the convictions. The defendant was aware of agency investigations when the following e-mail was sent to him and later modified for delivery to other employees, "[w]ith the recent tumble in stock prices, and many deals now trading below issue price, I understand the securities litigation bar is mounting an all out assault on broken tech IPOs. In the spirit of the end of the year (and the slow down in corporate finance work) you may want to send around a memo to all corporate finance bankers (and their assistants) reminding them of the CSFB document retention policy and suggesting that before they leave for the holidays, they should catch up on file cleanup. Today, it's administrative housekeeping. In January, it could be improper destruction of evidence."

• *Rambus, Inc. v. Infineon Technologies AG,* 220 F.R.D. 264 (E.D. Va. 2004). The Court held that even though a company implements a document retention policy in good faith that if documents are destroyed that the party knew would be relevant in future litigation sanctions may be imposed. The Court further ruled that communications about the document retention policy, if done in anticipation of litigation, may invoke the crime/fraud exception to the attorney client privilege.

• *Carlucci v. Piper Aircraft Corp.,* 102 F.R.D. 472, 481 (S.D. Fla. 1984). The Court noted, "[t]he stated purpose of the destruction of records [under the guise of a document retention policy] was the elimination of documents that might be detrimental to [the defendant] in a law suit." The Court entered a default judgment against the corporation.

• *Southeastern Medical Supply, Inc. v. Boyles, Moak & Brickell Insurance, Inc.,* 822 So. 2d 323 (Miss. Ct. App. 2002). The Court held that the alleged destruction of computer records did not give rise to an adverse inference where the computer files that were destroyed were first copied and preserved. The destruction of the computer files was done in good faith and pursuant to a routine business procedure.

[2]   Other Authorities

• Christopher R. Chase, *To Shred or Not to Shred: Document Retention Policies and Federal Obstruction of Justice Statutes,* 8 Fordham J. Corp. & Fin. L. 721, 724 (2003).

[I]   Court Order to Destroy Data During Litigation

It would be prudent to request a court order if your client is considering destroying possible relevant evidence during the lawsuit.

- *Smith v. Texaco, Inc.,* 951 F. Supp. 109, 112 (E.D. Tex. 1997), rev'd on other grounds, 263 F.3d 394 (5th Cir. 2001). In this discrimination case, the plaintiff secured a temporary restraining order preventing the defendant from moving, altering or deleting any records. This was later modified as follows: "[t]o mitigate the high costs associated with electronic document storage, the court will permit defendants to delete electronic records in the ordinary and usual course of business; provided, however, that hard copy records be made and kept of any and all electronic records of the various Human Resources records, as well as any new data used to report various actions, and the status of employees to any governmental authority."

[J]   Types of Data to Retain

[1]   Generally

Parties are under an obligation to retain all types of computer data, as well as "deleted" data. *Bills v. Kennecott Corp.,* 108 F.R.D. 459, 462 (D. Utah 1985); *Kleiner v. Burns,* No. 00-2160, 2000 WL 1909470, at *4 (D. Kan. Dec. 15, 2000); *See also,* § 7.07[B], *"Document" - Definition.*

[2]   Preservation of "Deleted" Files

In electronic discovery the courts have discussed the duty to preserve "deleted" information in two different contexts. First, the courts have held that if relevant computer information has been deleted from a desktop computer or a network system, but is available on backup tapes, there is a duty to preserve the information. *Rowe Entertainment, Inc. v. William Morris Agency, Inc.,* 53 Fed. R. Serv.3d 296 (S.D.N.Y. 2002). However, cost allocation, if appropriate, for recovering the data is a different issue and depends on several factors. *See,* § 7.4[G][6], *Cost Allocation.*

Second, the courts have granted requests to *restore* "deleted" information off of hard drives and other storage media. *Antioch Co. v. Scrapbook Borders, Inc.,* 210 F.R.D. 645, 652 (D. Minn. 2002). "[I]t is a well accepted proposition that deleted computer files, whether they be e-mails or otherwise, are discoverable." Deleting files does not necessarily destroy the information. *See,* § 3.5[E], *Deletion of Electronic Information.* If there is evidence that relevant information will be found and evidence of deletion, then the courts are generally inclined to allow for the restoration and recovery of this data. In fact, the courts have fashioned restoration procedures for recovering deleted information. *Simon Property Group*

L.P. v. mySimon, Inc., 194 F.R.D. 639, 641-42 (S.D. Ind. 2000); *Playboy Enter., Inc. v. Welles,* 60 F. Supp. 2d 1050, 1054-55 (S.D. Cal. 1999); *See,* § 7.7[H][5], *Procedure - Forensic Copy of Storage Media (Hard Drive, etc.).*

Even if electronic data has not been preserved, if the data is not relevant no sanctions should be imposed. *See,* § 7.4[F], *Relevancy and Overbroad Concerns - Rule 26(b)(1).*

[3]   Backup Tapes

Backup tapes should be retained in your case once you anticipate that a lawsuit is likely.

- *Zubulake v. UBS Warburg LLC,* 220 F.R.D. 212, 218 (S.D.N.Y. 2003). "Once a party reasonably anticipates litigation, it must suspend its routine document retention/ destruction policy and put in place a 'litigation hold' to ensure the preservation of relevant documents. As a general rule, that litigation hold does not apply to inaccessible backup tapes (e.g., those typically maintained solely for the purpose of disaster recovery), which may continue to be recycled on the schedule set forth in the company's policy. On the other hand, if backup tapes are accessible (i.e., actively used for information retrieval), then such tapes would likely be subject to the litigation hold. However, it does make sense to create one exception to this general rule. If a company can identify where particular employee documents are stored on backup tapes, then the tapes storing the documents of 'key players' to the existing or threatened litigation should be preserved if the information contained on those tapes is not otherwise available. This exception applies to all backup tapes."

[4]   Metadata

The Courts have generally allowed the discovery of metadata associated with computer files. For a general discussion of metadata see §§ 3.7, *Metadata, Hidden, or Embedded Information* and 7.07[B][2], *Metadata.*

[5]   Database

Preserving databases presents special difficulties because of the dynamic and ever-changing nature of the data. *See also,* § 3.10, *Databases.*

- *Procter & Gamble Co. v. Haugen,* 427 F.3d 727 (10th Cir. 2005). The plaintiff's expert obtained data from a third party marketing database for use in their opinions to establish damages. The Appellate Court reversed the lower court decision to dismiss the case for failure to preserve and disclose the entire third party marketing database. The Appellate Court discussed the dynamic nature of databases and the various alternatives to obtaining the data including using Rule 45 to subpoena information directly from the third party data provider.

- *Jinks-Umstead v. England,* No. CIV.99-2691, 2005 U.S. Dist. LEXIS 22291 (D.D.C. Oct. 4, 2005). The plaintiff sought sanctions for failure to preserve workload reports produced from a database that provided justification for an employment decision that resulted in a reduction in force. The Court ruled against any sanctions and stated that even though the reports were not available that the underlying data was and the plaintiff would be provided access to query the database.

[6]   Newly Created Evidence

- *Bayer Corp. v. Roche Molecular Systems, Inc.,* 72 F. Supp. 2d 1111, 1121-22 (N.D. Cal. 1999). The Court ordered a former employee in a trade secret case to produce "all existing data, including telephone messages, and [w]ith respect to the fourth quarter [future voice mail] . . . shall transcribe or otherwise preserve all voice mails that he receives on these subjects and they too must be produced."

[K]   Spoliation

[1]   Generally

Parties have a duty to preserve evidence. *Townsend v. American Insulated Panel Co., Inc.,* 174 F.R.D. 1, 3 (D. Mass. 1997); *Vasquez-Corales v. Sea-Land Service, Inc.,* 172 F.R.D. 10 (D.P.R. 1997). Failure to preserve evidence can lead to spoliation claims. Spoliation is the negligent or intentional destruction or alteration of evidence. *Pastorello v. City of New York,* No. CIV.95-470, 2003 WL 1740606 (S.D.N.Y. Apr. 01, 2003); *Silvestri v. General Motors Corp.,* 271 F.3d 583, 590 (4th Cir. 2001); *Kippenham v. Chaulk Services, Inc.,* 428 Mass. 124, 127, 697 N.E.2d 527 (1998); *See also,* § 7.9[D], *Duty to Preserve.*

The spoliation doctrine has been held to be:

- A tort action. *Smith v. Howard Johnson Co.,* 67 Ohio St. 3d 28, 615 N.E.2d 1037, 1038 (1993);

- A defense. *Donohoe v. American Isuzu Motors, Inc.* 155 F.R.D. 515 (M.D. Pa. 1994);

- An evidentiary inference or presumption. *Nation-wide Check Corp. v. Forest Hills Distribs., Inc.,* 692 F.2d 214, 218 (1st Cir. 1982);

- A discovery sanction. *Procter & Gamble Co. v. Haugen,* 179 F.R.D. 622 (D. Utah 1998), *aff'd in part and rev'd in part,* 222 F.3d 1262 (10th Cir. 2000); and

- A default judgment sanction. *Capellupo v. FMC Corp.,* 126 F.R.D. 545 (D. Minn. 1989).

The court has a variety of sanctions available if spoliation is found. In *Capellupo v. FMC Corp.,* 126 F.R.D. 545, 551-553 (D. Minn. 1989), the Court stated:

> This Court has a broad canvas upon which to paint in determining sanctions. . . . Within the Court's grasp is a "spectrum of sanctions," from which the most appropriate may be selected. . . . The most severe sanction available to the Court is default and dismissal. . . . Courts have permitted the fact-finder to draw inferences adverse to the document-destroying party. . . . Another common remedy utilized by courts to punish and deter discovery abuse is imposition of monetary sanctions. Not surprisingly, an award of attorneys' fees and costs is frequently invoked to reimburse an aggrieved party for the price of investigating and litigating document destruction. Parties liable for document destruction have been assessed their opponents' fees and costs for investigating, researching, preparing, and arguing evidentiary motions and motions for sanctions. . . . A party which has destroyed documents may also be held accountable for the fees and costs of depositions, interrogatories, and supplemental discovery costs associated with willful concealment. A court may also impose monetary sanctions to rectify unnecessary consumption of its time and resources. (citations omitted).

Motions for sanctions for spoliation must be filed in a timely manner. *Wood v. Sempra Energy Trading Corp.,* No. CIV.03-986, 2005 U.S. Dist. LEXIS 33638 (D. Conn. Dec. 9, 2005) (court refused to grant electronic discovery sanctions due to late filing of motion and no evidence of intentional hiding of evidence); *Durst v. FedEx Express,* No. CIV.03-5186, 2006 WL 1541027 (D.N.J. Jun. 2, 2006) (plaintiff's failure to raise e-mail and other discovery issues before judge or in a discovery conference and then file a motion to compel resulted in denial of motion in limine for an adverse instruction).

On review, the appellate courts require an explanation why sanctions are imposed. *Serra Chevrolet, Inc. v. GMC,* 446 F.3d 1137 (11th Cir. 2006). (lower court reversed for failure to provide a rationale for the imposition monetary sanction and striking affirmative defenses); *Procter & Gamble Co. v. Haugen,* 427 F.3d 727 (10th Cir. 2005) (lower court's dismissal reversed for alleged failure to produce electronic data for failing to adequately explain ruling.)

The courts, depending on the jurisdiction, differ as to the necessary elements to establish a claim of spoliation.

In addition, 28 U.S.C. § 1927 Section 1927 provides that "any attorney . . . who so multiplies the proceedings in any case unreasonably and vexatiously may be required by the court to satisfy personally the excess costs, expenses, and attorney's fees reasonably incurred because of such conduct." In *Quinby v. WestLB AG,* No. CIV.04-7406, 2006 U.S. Dist. LEXIS 1178, at *33-34 (D.N.Y. Jan. 11, 2006) the Court denied plaintiff's request to impose the 1927 sanction against the defendant for "misleading statements and omissions [that] have unnecessarily delayed this litigation by prolonging [defendant's] production of relevant e-mails."

[2]   Destruction of Evidence - Elements

[a]   Generally

In *McGuire v. Acufex Microsurgical, Inc.,* 175 F.R.D. 149, 154 (D. Mass. 1997) the Court stated in regards to the issue of spoliation:

> The specific elements of the claim are outlined in Jamie S. Gorelick *et al., Destruction of Evidence:* Gorelick, the leading and possibly the only treatise on the subject of destruction of evidence, identifies four elements that a court must find before imposing sanctions for the destruction: (1) An act of destruction; (2) Discoverability of the evidence; (3) An intent to destroy the evidence; (4) Occurrence of the act at a time after suit has been filed, or, if before, at a time when the filing is fairly perceived as imminent. Gorelick at §§ 3.8-3.12. As Gorelick notes, a fifth element is in a sense always required, namely prejudice to the opposing party, since sanctions are not as a rule imposed where there has been no prejudice to a party. But since the extent of the prejudice bears more on the issue of the scope of the sanction to be imposed rather than the issue of whether any sanction should be imposed at all, discussion of that element may be deferred until the scope issue is addressed. *White v. Office of the Public Defender for the State of Maryland,* 170 F.R.D. 138, 147 (D. Md. 1997) (quoting Gorelick, *Destruction of Evidence*).

Further guidance as to the standard for failing to preserve electronic data is found in Carroll, *Developments in the Law of Electronic Discovery,* 27 Am. J. Trial Advocacy 357, 368 (2003). The author stated,

> In order to obtain sanctions for document destruction, a party must show that (1) the party having control over the evidence . . . had an obligation to preserve it at the time it was destroyed, (2) the records were destroyed with a 'culpable state of mind,' and (3) the destroyed evidence was 'relevant to the party's claim or defense' such that a reasonable trier of fact could find that the evidence would support that claim or defense [citations omitted]. . . . If the party that has destroyed documents was under a duty to preserve those documents, the court must decide whether the parties seeking sanctions has established a sufficiently culpable state of mind to warrant the imposition of those sanctions. This is the area of sanction law that appears to be the most fluid. Some circuits require a showing of intentional destruction or bad faith (i.e., that the document destruction was done for the purpose of hiding adverse information before

sanctions for document destruction can be imposed). Other circuits distinguish between the type of sanctions requiring one state of mind for one sanction and another state of mind for another. . . . Other courts permit an adverse inference instruction or the exclusion of evidence on a showing of simple negligence [citations omitted].

[b]   Reported Cases

After electronic documents have been destroyed and sanctions are requested, the court, depending on the jurisdiction, will usually examine the degree of culpability, i.e., whether the destruction or failure to produce was willful or negligent.

Willful Conduct

- *Zubulake v. UBS Warburg LLC,* 220 F.R.D. 212, 220 (S.D.N.Y. 2003). "A party seeking an adverse inference instruction (or) based on the spoliation of evidence must establish the following three elements: (1) that the party having control over the evidence had an obligation to preserve it at the time it was destroyed; (2) that the records were destroyed with a 'culpable state of mind' and (3) that the destroyed evidence was 'relevant' to the party's claim or defense such that a reasonable trier of fact could find that it would support that claim or defense. In this circuit, a 'culpable state of mind' for purposes of a spoliation inference includes ordinary negligence. When evidence is destroyed in bad faith (i.e., intentionally or willfully), that fact alone is sufficient to demonstrate relevance. By contrast, when the destruction is negligent, relevance must be proven by the party seeking the sanctions."

- *Residential Funding Corp. v. DeGeorge Financial Corp.,* 306 F.3d 99, 108 (2d Cir. 2002). The defendant appealed the trial court's denial of their motion for sanctions. The Appellate Court remanded for further proceedings finding that mere negligence would support an adverse inference instruction, after it found no willful conduct in failing to produce certain e-mail in time for trial. The Court found the delay in producing the e-mail was not caused by an act of *Residential Funding* that was taken in bad faith or with gross negligence and *DeGeorge* had not shown that the missing e-mail would be favorable to its case.

- *Akiona v. United States,* 938 F.2d 158, 160,161 (9th Cir. 1991). The Court ruled that destruction of records did not entitle the plaintiff to an adverse instruction because nothing indicated:

    [T]hat the government was on notice that the records had potential relevance to litigation. Nothing in the record indicates that the government destroyed the grenade records with the intent of covering up information. Indeed, the government may have destroyed the records pursuant to its policy of destroying documents regarding grenades two years after their disposition. . . . The evidentiary rationale does not apply here. Nothing in the record indicates that the government destroyed the records pertaining to the grenade in response to this litigation. Thus, its destruction of the records does not suggest that the records would have been threatening to the defense of the case, and it is therefore not relevant in an evidentiary sense.

- *Bashir v. Amtrak,* 119 F.3d 929 (11th Cir. 1997). Court refused to grant an adverse inference instruction after a train's speed recorder tape was inadvertently lost, since there was no evidence that the tape had been destroyed in bad faith.

- *State v. Langlet,* 283 N.W.2d 330 (Iowa 1979). Court refused to issue an adverse instruction where certain tape-recorded conversations in a DWI case had inadvertently been destroyed, since there was no evidence of bad faith or intentional destruction.

Negligent Production or Destruction

- *Heng Chan v. Triple 8 Palace,* No. CIV. 03-6048, 2005 U.S. Dist. LEXIS 16520, at *18-20 (D.N.Y. Aug. 11, 2005). "The defendants' conduct demonstrates a sufficiently culpable state of mind to warrant sanctions. 'Specific intent to thwart the litigation process is not necessary.' (citations omitted). A showing of gross negligence is plainly enough to justify sanctions at least as serious as an adverse inference. (citations omitted) And the utter failure to establish any form of litigation hold at the outset of litigation is grossly negligent. (citations omitted) That is what occurred here: the defendants systematically destroyed evidence because they had never been informed of their obligation to suspend normal document destruction policies."

- *Hous. Rights Ctr. v. Sterling,* No. CIV.03-859, 2004 U.S. Dist. LEXIS 28877, at *36-37 (D. Cal. 2004). In discussing the state of mind necessary for consideration of sanctions the Court stated, "[d]efendants also argue that they did not destroy any documents in bad faith. '[T]he culpable state of mind factor is satisfied by a showing that the evidence was destroyed knowingly, even if without intent to breach a duty to preserve it, or negligently.'. (citations omitted) 'Once the duty to preserve attaches, any destruction of documents is, at a minimum, negligent.' Zubulake IV, 220 F.R.D. at 220. Destruction of documents during ongoing litigation was, at a minimum, negligent."

- *Strasser v. Yalamanchi,* 669 So.2d 1142 (Fla. Dist. Ct. App. 1996). When defendant's expert appeared to inspect Strasser's computer, he was informed that the computer hard drive had been severely damaged by lightening and thrown out and also that other documents were systematically shredded and destroyed even after being requested. Court allowed the party to add a claim for negligent destruction of evidence and allowed to introduce evidence regarding the misconduct at trial.

- *United States v. Koch Indus., Inc.,* 197 F.R.D. 463 (N.D. Okla. 1998). Court found defendants should be sanctioned for negligent destruction of documents subject to preservation order.

- *In re Cheyenne Software, Inc.*, No. CIV.94-2771, 1997 WL 714891 (E.D.N.Y. Aug. 18, 1997). Court refused to give an adverse inference charge, where defendants had failed to preserve documents on their hard drives, despite a court order that they do so. Instead, the defendants were fined $5,000 and assessed $10,000 in attorneys' fees.

Nexus or Relevance Required

- *Hous. Rights Ctr. v. Sterling,* No. CIV.03-859, 2004 U.S. Dist. LEXIS 28877, at *37-38 (D. Cal. 2004). In discussing relevance of destroyed documents the Court stated, "[R]elevant in this context means something more than sufficiently probative to satisfy Rule 401 of the Federal Rules of Evidence. Rather, the party seeking an adverse inference must adduce sufficient evidence from which a reasonable trier of fact could infer that the destroyed or unavailable evidence would have been of the nature alleged by the party affected by its destruction. *DeGeorge Fin. Corp.,* 306 F.3d at 108-09 (internal citations and quotations omitted). Where a party destroys evidence in bad faith, that bad faith alone is sufficient circumstantial evidence from which a reasonable fact finder could conclude that the missing evidence was unfavorable to that party. *Id.* at 109."

- *Heng Chan v. Triple 8 Palace,* No. CIV. 03-6048, 2005 U.S. Dist. LEXIS 16520, at *22-24 (D.N.Y. Aug. 11, 2005). "Relevance in this context may be established in two ways. First, it may be inferred if the spoliator is shown to have a sufficiently culpable state of mind. 'Where a party destroys evidence in bad faith, that bad faith alone is sufficient circumstantial evidence from which a reasonable fact finder could conclude that the missing evidence was unfavorable to the party.' (citations omitted) Likewise, 'a showing of gross negligence in the destruction or untimely production of evidence will in some circumstances suffice, standing alone, to support a finding that the evidence was unfavorable to the grossly negligent party.' . . . Second, the moving party may submit extrinsic evidence tending to demonstrate that the missing evidence would have been favorable to it." (case examples omitted).

- *Nutrition Management v. Harborside Healthcare Corp.*, No. CIV.01-0902, 2004 WL 887401, at *2 (E.D. Pa. Mar. 19 2004). The defendant admitted to having destroyed some allegedly "junk" e-mails and the plaintiff moved for sanctions. The Court stated, "[p]laintiff has provided no evidence that the content of any destroyed e-mails was important or relevant. 'Before drawing an adverse inference, courts typically require some showing, by circumstantial evidence or otherwise, of the content of the destroyed evidence.'"

- *Concord Boat Corp. v. Brunswick Corp.,* No. CIV.95-781, 1997 WL 33352759, at *6, *7 (E.D. Ark. Aug. 29, 1997). The Court reviewed in detail the factual basis establishing that the defendant had failed to preserve e-mail. However, the Court stated that "[p]laintiffs maintain that they are not obligated to demonstrate the relevance of any of the destroyed e-mails because the e-mails have been destroyed, and they have no way to directly show their relevance. However, '[s]ome extrinsic evidence of the content of the evidence is necessary for the trier of fact to be able to determine in what respect and to what extent it would have been detrimental.' (citation omitted) Furthermore, '[b]efore an adverse inference may be drawn, there must be some showing that there is in fact a nexus between the proposed inference and the information contained in the lost evidence.'"

- *Zubulake v. UBS Warburg LLC,* No. CIV.02-1243, 2004 WL 1620866, (S.D.N.Y. July 20, 2004) where the Court subsequently ordered an adverse inference instruction after a nexus was found.

[3] Spoliation Remedies

[a] Generally

Courts will examine very closely any destruction of records after a duty to preserve has been established. Sanctions range in severity from monetary sanctions, dismissal, default judgment, adverse inference, rebuttable presumption, precluded evidence, preclusion of experts and/or lay witnesses and are only limited by the court's imagination.

[b] Court's Authority to Sanction

Courts have statutory, FED. R. CIV. P. 16(f) and 37, as well as inherent authority to sanction a party for failure to preserve documents. *Carlucci v. Piper Aircraft Corp.,* 775 F.2d 1140 (11th Cir. 1985); *Trigon Ins. Co. v. United States,* 204 F.R.D. 277, 284-85 (E.D. Va. 2001).

In *Danis v. USN Communications, Inc.,* No. CIV.98-7482, 2000 WL 1694325, at *30 (N.D. Ill. Oct. 20, 2000) the Court stated:

> The Court's authority to sanction a party for the failure to preserve and/or produce documents is both inherent and statutory. *Chambers v. NASCO, Inc.,* 501 U.S. 32, 50-51, 111 S.Ct. 2123, 115 L.Ed.2d 27 (1991) (federal courts may sanction bad faith conduct by its inherent powers or by the Federal Rules of Civil Procedure); *Barnhill v. United States,* 11 F.3d 1360, 1368 (7th Cir. 1993). . . . Whether proceeding under Rule 37 of the Federal Rules of Civil Procedure or under a court's inherent powers, the "analysis is essentially the same." *Cobell v.*

Babbit, 37 F. Supp. 2d 6, 18 (D.D.C. 1999); *Gates Rubber Co. v. Bando Chem. Indus., Ltd.,* 167 F.R.D. 90, 107 (D. Col. 1996) ("any distinctions between Rule 37 and the inherent powers of the court are distinctions without differences"). However, the power to enter a default judgment or to dismiss a case for noncompliance with an order to preserve and produce documents for discovery "depends exclusively upon Rule 37 which addresses itself with particularity to the consequences of a failure to make discovery" by "any party" and authorizes "any order which is 'just.'" *Societe Internationale Pour Participations Industrielles et Commerciales, S. v. Rogers,* 357 U.S. 197, 207, 78 S.Ct. 1087, 2 L.Ed.2d 1255 (1958).

A court is provided broad discretion to determine the appropriate sanction for the destruction of evidence given the specific facts of each case. *Residential Funding Corp. v. DeGeorge Fin. Corp.,* 306 F.3d 99, 108 (2d Cir. 2002); *Trigon Ins. Co. v. United States,* 204 F.R.D. 277, 287-88 (E.D. Va. 2001).

[c]   Adverse Inference (Spoliation) Jury Instruction

[i]   Generally

An adverse inference may be drawn from the fact that documents were destroyed. This concept has been referred to as the "spoliation inference." *United States v. Koch Industries, Inc.,* 197 F.R.D. 463 (N.D. Okla. 1998). A spoliation inference permits a jury to infer that the party who destroyed potentially relevant evidence did so "out of a realization that the [evidence was] unfavorable." *Blinzler v. Marriott International, Inc.,* 81 F.3d 1148, 1158 (1st Cir. 1996). This inference may be drawn once it is shown that the party who destroyed the evidence had notice of the claim, and of the potential relevance of the evidence at issue. *Nation-Wide Check Corp. v. Forest Hills Distribs., Inc.,* 692 F.2d 214, 218 (1st Cir. 1982).

An adverse instruction can be sought not only for destruction of evidence but also for late production of evidence. As the Court stated in *Residential Funding Corp. v. DeGeorge Financial Corp.,* 306 F.3d 99, 107 (2nd Cir. 2002):

> [A] party seeking an adverse inference instruction based on the destruction of evidence must establish (1) that the party having control over the evidence had an obligation to preserve it at the time it was destroyed; (2) that the records were destroyed "with a culpable state of mind"; and (3) that the destroyed evidence was "relevant" to the party's claim or defense such that a reasonable trier of fact could find that it would support that claim or defense. (citation omitted).

Depending on the jurisdiction, "'[r]elevance' may be inferred from a showing that a party acted in bad faith because 'bad faith alone is sufficient circumstantial evidence from which a reasonable fact finder could conclude that the missing evidence was unfavorable to that party.'" *See, Residential Funding Corp. v. DeGeorge Fin. Corp.,* 306 F.3d 99, 109 (2d Cir. 2002); *Byrnie v. Town of Cromwell,* 243 F.3d 93, 108-110 (2d Cir. 2001) (court held a culpable state of mind was shown when a defendant intentionally destroyed documents it was under a duty to preserve pursuant to a regulatory document retention policy).

"An adverse inference instruction is a severe sanction that often has the effect of ending litigation because 'it is too difficult a hurdle for the spoliator to overcome.' *Zubulake IV,* 220 F.R.D. at 219. Accordingly, this sanction 'should not be given lightly.' *Id.* at 220." *Phoenix Four, Inc. v. Strategic Resources Corp.,* No. CIV.05-4837, 2006 WL 1409413, *4 (S.D.N.Y. May 23, 2006).

Though an adverse inference instruction may be allowed, a party may be entitled to provide "a reasonable rebuttal to the inference." *Stevenson v. Union Pacific R. Co.,* 354 F.3d 739 (8th Cir. 2004).

[ii]   Reported Cases - Adverse Inference Instruction Issued

- *Kemper Mortg., Inc. v. Russell,* No. CIV.06-042, 2006 U.S. Dist. LEXIS 20729, at *5-7 (D. Ohio Apr. 6, 2006). The Court ruled plaintiff was entitled to an adverse inference when the defendant "caused to be installed on his laptop computer a program called 'Window Washer' . . . which prevents the forensic recovery of deleted electronic files by overwriting them."

- *Paramount Pictures Corp. v. Davis,* 234 F.R.D. 102 (D. Pa. 2005). After tracing infringement activity through the defendant's IP address it was discovered that the defendant intentionally wiped his computer's hard drive clean in order to avoid detection of his infringing activities. The Court would consider an adverse inference sanction at trial, but refused to apply it in the context of a summary judgment.

- *E*Trade Secs. LLC v. Deutsche Bank AG,* 230 F.R.D. 582 (D. Minn. 2005) *aff.* 230 F.R.D. 582 (D. Minn. 2005). In this securities action, the court imposed fines and an adverse inference for defendant's failure to implement a proper litigation hold and preserve hard drives, telephone recordings and e-mail backup tapes that were relevant to the litigation. The Court held there was a "reasonable probability" of prejudice from the destruction of this evidence.

- *Clark Const. Group, Inc. v. City of Memphis,* No. CIV.01-2780, 2005 WL 1618767, at *10 (W.D. Tenn. Mar. 14, 2005). In this breach of contract case, the Court ruled after the city's project manager destroyed more than 2,000 paper and electronic documents that the plaintiff was "entitled to a rebuttable adverse inference establishing that the City had documents within its possession which most likely would have been relevant to this case; however, the City failed to preserve these documents, and the documents were destroyed."

- *Mosaid Technologies Inc. v. Samsung Electronics Co.,* 348 F. Supp. 2d 332 (D. N.J. 2004). In patent litigation, the defendant failed to preserve e-mail and the judge granted the plaintiff's request for an adverse inference jury instruction and attorneys' fees for the motion. The defendant argued that culpability should only arise where the destruction of e-mails was intentional, not the consequence of inadvertence or accident. The court disagreed, finding that negligence sufficed to impose an adverse inference sanction.

- *Mastercard Intern., Inc. v. Moulton,* No. CIV.03-3613, 2004 WL 1393992 (S.D.N.Y. Jun. 22, 2004). The Court found no bad faith in the defendant's failure to preserve e-mail since defendants simply persevered in their normal document retention practices. Nonetheless, the Court ruled that plaintiff would be allowed to prove the facts reflecting the nonretention of e-mail and argue to the trier of fact that this destruction of evidence, in addition to other proof offered at trial, warranted certain inferences.

- *Stevenson v. Union Pacific R. Co.,* 354 F.3d 739 (8th Cir. 2004). The Appellate Court affirmed issuance of adverse inference instruction after the defendant destroyed voice records and track maintenance records after an accident.

- *3M v. Pribyl,* 259 F.3d 587, 606 n.5 (7th Cir. 2001). The Court affirmed the issuance of a negative inference instruction after the defendant overwrote computer files responsive to the plaintiff's demands by downloading music onto his computer the day before the computer was to be inspected.

- *DirecTV, Inc. v. Randy Borow,* No. CIV.03-2581, 2005 WL 43261(N.D.Ill. Jan. 6, 2005). In this satellite piracy case the plaintiff's computer forensics expert found that defendant had used "Evidence Eliminator" to erase evidence five weeks after the filing of the complaint. The court found that defendant deliberately destroyed evidence, entered summary judgment and noted that defendant's intentional spoliation of evidence created an inference that he destroyed evidence that would have been harmful to his defense.

- *Zubulake v. UBS Warburg LLC,* 220 F.R.D. 212 (S.D.N.Y. 2003). The defendant failed to preserve backup tapes that contained missing e-mail. The judge found that the plaintiff was unable to establish that the lost evidence would have supported her claims and, therefore, an adverse inference instruction would not be authorized. However, *see Zubulake v. UBS Warburg LLC,* No. CIV.02-1243, 2004 WL 1620866, (S.D.N.Y. July 20, 2004) where the Court subsequently ordered an adverse inference instruction after a nexus was found and set forth the proposed instruction in the opinion.

- *Trigon Ins. Co. v. United States,* 204 F.R.D. 277 (E.D. Va. 2001). The Court found that an adverse inference would be authorized regarding the expert's substantive testimony and credibility based on their purposeful destruction of e-mails and draft reports.

- *Stanton v. National R.R. Passenger Corp.,* 849 F. Supp. 1524, 1528 (M.D. Ala. 1994). The Court drew an adverse inference for summary judgment purposes for the defendant's failure to preserve a computer tape indicating the speed of the train involved in an accident.

- *Applied Telematics Inc. v. Sprint Communications Co.,* No. CIV.94-4603, 1996 WL 33405972, at *4 (E.D. Pa. Sept. 17, 1996). In this patent infringement suit, information regarding two infringing devices was maintained solely on the computer, which had partly been destroyed. The plaintiff moved for a finding of an adverse inference for spoliation, which the court granted.

- *Lauren Corp. v. Century Geophysical Corp.,* 953 P.2d 200 (Colo. App. 1998). The defendant had destroyed some of the computer hardware after the court issued an order allowing for inspection of the computers to determine if the defendant had improperly used the plaintiff's software on its computers. For sanctions, the court awarded attorneys' fees and costs and the trial court imposed a presumption that defendant had used the software on machines other on than those described in the licenses.

- *ABC Home Health Servs., Inc. v. Int'l. Bus. Machs. Corp.,* 158 F.R.D. 180, 182-83 (S.D. Ga. 1994). The Court refused to dismiss the defendant's counterclaims, however, did impose a presumption against the spoliator and stated:

  > As a lesser sanction, however, ABC [plaintiff] may be entitled to a jury instruction explaining that destroyed documents are presumed to be damaging to the party responsible for the destruction. *Telectron, Inc.,* 116 F.R.D. at 133 ("[B]ad faith destruction of a relevant document . . . gives rise to a strong inference that production of that document would have been unfavorable to the party responsible for its destruction."); *see also, Vick v. Texas Employment Comm.,* 514 F.2d 734, 737 (5th Cir. 1975) ("The adverse inference to be drawn from destruction of records is predicated on bad conduct of the defendant.").

- *Linnen v. A.H. Robins Co.,* No. 97-2307, 1999 WL 462015 (Mass. Super. Ct. Jun. 16, 1999). Court granted request for adverse inference instruction for failure to preserve e-mail evidence.

[iii] Reported Cases - No Adverse Inference Instruction Issued

- *Phoenix Four, Inc. v. Strategic Resources Corp.,* No. CIV. 05-4837, 2006 WL 1409413 (S.D.N.Y. May 23, 2006). In this investment action for fraud the defendant failed to determine that one of its servers contained a substantial amount of discoverable data until a few months before trial. The Court refused to order an adverse inference since the data was subsequently disclosed but imposed monetary sanctions and ordered that the law firm share equally with defendants the cost of the monetary sanctions of attorney's fees and re-deposition costs.

- *Jinks-Umstead v. England,* 227 F.R.D. 143 (D.D.C. 2005). The Court granted the plaintiff a new trial after the defendant provided relevant database reports after the plaintiff rested her case. However, the Court refused to issue an adverse inference instruction in the new trial because the record did not demonstrate evil intent, bad faith, or willfulness on the part of the defendant.

- *Creative Sci. Sys. v. Forex Capital Mkts., LLC,* No. CIV.04-03746, 2006 U.S. Dist. LEXIS 20116 (D. Cal. Apr. 4, 2006). The Court refused to issue an adverse inference sanction because of non-convincing evidence of bad faith, however, monetary cost sanctions were imposed to analyze the server computers at issue.

- *Zubulake v.UBS Warburg LLC,* 220 F.R.D. 212 (S.D.N.Y. 2003). The defendant failed to preserve backup tapes that contained missing e-mail. The judge found that the plaintiff was unable to establish that the lost evidence would have supported her claims and, therefore, an adverse inference instruction would not be authorized. However, *see, Zubulake v. UBS Warburg LLC,* No. CIV.02-1243, 2004 WL 1620866, (S.D.N.Y. July 20, 2004) where the Court subsequently ordered an adverse inference instruction after a nexus was found.

- *McDowell v. Gov't. of the Dist. of Columbia,* 233 F.R.D. 192 (D.D.C. 2006). Despite a three-year delay in producing documents the Court refused to enter a default judgment citing insufficient government funding and staffing levels. However, if the delays continued, the Court would consider an adverse inference instruction and attorneys' fees.

- *Chidichimo v. University of Chicago Press,* 681 N.E.2d 107, 110-111 (Ill. 1997). In workman's compensation action, the Court denied a request for an evidentiary presumption instruction that the worker was lifting heavy objects when he had a heart attack since the plaintiff failed to take reasonable steps to ensure the preservation of computer data that was routinely purged.

- *Allan Pen Co. v. Springfield Photo Mount Co.,* 653 F.2d 17, 23-24 (1st Cir. 1984). Court refused to draw adverse inference even though computer-generated evidence of sales was destroyed after the commencement of the case, and after its identification in interrogatory answers.

- *In re Cheyenne Software, Inc.,* No. CIV.94-2771, 1997 WL 714891 (E.D.N.Y. Aug. 18, 1997). Despite the fact that the defendants had failed to preserve documents on their hard drives even after a Court order, the Court refused to give an adverse inference charge, and instead, the defendants were fined $5,000 and assessed $10,000 in attorneys' fees.

- *Procter & Gamble Co. v. Haugen,* 179 F.R.D. 622 (D. Utah 1998), *aff'd in part and rev'd in part,* 222 F.3d 1262 (10th Cir. 2000). Court refused to impose an evidentiary "adverse inference" remedy, but instead sanctioned the plaintiff $2,000 for each of five individuals whose e-mail were not preserved after P&G identified these people as having relevant information.

*   *Bashir v. Amtrak*, 119 F.3d 929 (11th Cir. 1997). Court refused to grant an adverse inference instruction after the train's speed recorder tape was inadvertently lost, since there was no evidence that the tape had been destroyed in bad faith.

*   *State v. Langlet*, 283 N.W.2d 330 (Iowa 1979). Court refused to issue an adverse instruction where certain tape-recorded conversations in a DWI case had inadvertently been destroyed, since there was no evidence of bad faith or intentional destruction.

[d]   Monetary Sanctions

Attorneys' fees and/or costs

*   *Phoenix Four, Inc. v. Strategic Resources Corp.,* No. CIV. 05-4837, 2006 WL 1409413 (S.D.N.Y. May 23, 2006). In this investment action for fraud the defendant failed to determine that one of its servers contained a substantial amount of discoverable data until a few months before trial. The Court, citing to the pending rules 26(a) and (b)(2), imposed monetary sanctions and found that the defendant's counsel's deficiencies constituted "gross negligence" and ordered that the law firm share equally with defendants the cost of the monetary sanctions of attorney's fees and re-deposition costs.

*   *Green v. Baca,* No. CIV.02-04744, 225 F.R.D. 612 (C.D.Cal. Jan. 25, 2005). The Court found that even though the plaintiff's discovery request was overly broad and not narrowed in good faith, defense counsel's failure to ascertain the existence of relevant computer-based information for several months justified sanctions of an order to pay $54,375 in attorneys' fees.

*   *Trigon Ins. Co. v. United States,* 234 F. Supp. 2d 592 (E.D. Va. 2002). Court imposed spoliation sanction of $179,725.70 for attorneys' fees and expenses for erasure of computer-generated communications between litigation coordinator and the United States' expert witnesses, even though a substantial amount of erased evidence was recovered.

*   *In re Prudential Insurance Co.,* 169 F.R.D. 598, 615 (D.N.J. 1997). Court imposed $1 million sanction against Prudential Insurance Co. for "its haphazard and uncoordinated approach to [electronic] document destruction." In addition to the fine, Prudential was ordered to pay substantial attorneys' fees and to present to the court within 30 days "a written manual that embodies Prudential's document preservation policy."

*   *Illinois Tool Works v. Metro Mark Products*, 43 F. Supp. 2d 951, 961 (N.D. Ill. 1999). The Court ordered the defendant to reimburse the plaintiff for the plaintiff's computer expert reasonable fees and costs, the plaintiff's attorneys' fees and costs associated with

its motion to compel and motion for sanctions, for its "purposeful effort to prevent [the] plaintiff from obtaining the information from the . . . computer." The evidence showed that someone had physically tampered with a computer holding discoverable data.

- *Metropolitan Opera Ass'n., Inc. v. Local 100*, 212 F.R.D. 178, 230(S.D.N.Y. 2003), adhered to on reconsideration, 2004 WL 1943099 (S.D.N.Y. Aug. 27, 2004). The court found liability on the part of the defendants and imposed attorneys' fees stating that "lesser sanctions, such as an adverse inference or preclusion, would not be effective in this case." The attorneys were partially based 28 U.S.C. § 1927, "[a]ny attorney or other person admitted to conduct cases in any court of the United States . . . who so multiplies the proceedings in any case unreasonably and vexatiously may be required by the court to satisfy personally the excess costs, expenses and attorneys' fees reasonably incurred because of such conduct."

- *Wm. T. Thompson Co. v. General Nutrition Corp. Inc.*, 593 F. Supp. 1443, 1445 (C.D. Cal. 1984). Court imposed sanctions and required party to pay attorneys' fees as well as entering judgment against the party who destroyed paper and electronic records.

- *Procter & Gamble Co. v. Haugen*, 179 F.R.D. 622 (D. Utah 1998), *aff'd in part and rev'd in part,* 222 F.3d 1262 (10th Cir. 2000). Even though the plaintiff had insisted, early in the case, that the defendant save all of its e-mail, the plaintiff failed to segregate and preserve e-mail files that it knew would be subject to discovery. Though there was no specific preservation order in place, the plaintiff was sanctioned $10,000 for its breach of discovery duties.

- *Second Chance Body Armor, Inc. v. American Body Armor, Inc.*, 177 F.R.D. 633 (N.D. Ill. 1998). Court imposed attorney fee and cost sanctions against party who alleged $383,000 in sales, which in fact showed sales had been approximately $2.5 million.

- *Gates Rubber Co. v. Bando Chemical Industries*, 167 F.R.D. 90, 113 (D. Colo. 1996). The Court sanctioned the defendant for the deletion of word processing files, imposing sanctions in the amount of 10% of the plaintiff's fees and costs as damages.

- *E.E.O.C. v. Sears Roebuck & Co.*, 114 F.R.D. 615, 626-27 (N.D. Ill. 1987). The Court imposed attorney fee sanctions for the plaintiff's negligence in producing incorrect, incomplete and misleading computer printouts.

- *Linnen v. A.H. Robins Co.*, No. 97-2307, 1999 WL 462015 (Mass. Super. Ct. Jun. 16, 1999). The Court sanctioned the defendant and required the party to pay the costs and fees of the discovery motion, after e-mail were discovered that the defendant originally said were not available.

- *Lauren Corp. v. Century Geophysical Corp.*, 953 P.2d 200 (Colo. App. 1998). The defendant had destroyed some of the computer hardware after the court issued an order allowing for inspection of the computers to determine if the defendant had improperly used plaintiffs' software on its computers. As sanctions the Court awarded attorneys' fees and costs and the trial court imposed a presumption that defendant had used the software on machines other than on those described in the licenses.

- *GFTM, Inc. v. Wal-Mart Stores, Inc.,* No. CIV.98-7724, 2000 WL 335558 (S.D.N.Y. Mar. 30, 2000). The Court ordered defendant to pay attorneys' fees and costs for failure to disclose computer capabilities.

Discovery abuse monetary sanction

- *United States v. Philip Morris, USA, Inc.,* No. CIV.99-2496, 2004 WL 1627252 (D.D.C. July 21, 2004). The company failed to follow the preservation order and destroyed e-mail for more than two years. A number of high-ranking officers who were to be called as witnesses failed to retain their e-mail under a "print and retain" policy. The defendant was precluded from presenting any fact witness who had failed to preserve relevant records and was ordered to pay *$2.75 million* in fines for its spoliation of e-mail.

- *Proctor & Gamble Co. v. Haugen,* 179 F.R.D. 622 (D. Utah 1998), *aff'd in part, rev'd in part,* 222 F.3d 1262 (10th Cir. 2000). The Court refused to impose an evidentiary "adverse inference" remedy, but instead sanctioned the plaintiff $2,000 for each of five individuals whose e-mail were not preserved after P&G identified these people as having relevant information.

Pay expert fees

- *Illinois Tool Works v. Metro Mark Products,* 43 F. Supp. 2d 951, 961 (N.D. Ill. 1999). The Court ordered the defendant to reimburse the plaintiff for the plaintiff's computer expert reasonable fees and costs and the plaintiff attorneys' fees and costs associated with its motion to compel and motion for sanctions for its "purposeful effort to prevent [the] plaintiff from obtaining the information from the . . . computer."

Pay for a special master and discovery plan

- *National Association of Radiation Survivors v. Turnage,* 115 F.R.D. 543 (N.D. Cal. 1987). The Court imposed a sanction of paying for a special master and a discovery plan after court learned documents sought were in computer databases. The defendant originally said they were only in paper formant and consisted of 34 million claim folders stored in 58 different locations.

Pay for restoration cost

- *Commissioner v. Ward,* 580 S.E.2d 432 (N.C. App. 2003) (unpublished). The Appellate Court approved the sanction of requiring the defendants to pay the cost of providing backup tape data. This was the result of a number of delays and violations of discovery orders relating to the discovery of both paper and electronic documents stored off-site by the defendants.

Pay for depositions

• *Phoenix Four, Inc. v. Strategic Resources Corp.,* No. CIV.05-4837, 2006 WL 1409413 (S.D.N.Y. May 23, 2006). In this investment action for fraud the defendant failed to determine that one of its servers contained a substantial amount of discoverable data until a few months before trial. The Court refused to order an adverse inference since the data was subsequently disclosed but imposed monetary sanctions and ordered that the law firm share equally with defendants the cost of the monetary sanctions of attorneys' fees and re-deposition costs.

[e]   Attorney Sanction

• *Carlucci v. Piper Aircraft Co.,* 102 F.R.D. 472 (S.D. Fla. 1984), *aff'd,* 775 F.2d 1440, 1454 (11th Cir. 1985). The lower court entered judgment for plaintiff and imposed an attorney sanction of $10,000 because the defendant destroyed records. The Appellate Court in upholding sanctions remanded "so that the district court may create a record accounting for" the amount of the sanction.

• *Landmark Legal Foundation v. E.P.A.,* 272 F. Supp. 2d 70, 87 (D.D.C. 2003). The Court ordered defendant to pay plaintiffs' legal fees and costs in bringing spoliation motion where the defendant violated preliminary court order. The defendant failed to preserve documents by reformatting hard drives, erasing e-mail backup tapes and deleting e-mails.

[f]   Defense to Recovery

• *Crown Life Insurance Company v. Craig,* 995 F.2d 1376 (7th Cir. 1993). The Court precluded the plaintiff from using its own computer data as a sanction for nonproduction, and entered default judgment for the defendant.

• *Donohoe v. American Isuzu Motors, Inc.* 155 F.R.D. 515 (M.D. Pa. 1994). In this products liability case, the Court ruled that claimant had spoliated evidence, and, therefore, it could be used as a general defense.

[g]   Dismissal or Default Judgment

Among the factors the courts will examine to determine whether the sanction of dismissal should be imposed are whether "(1) defendant acted willfully or in bad faith, (2) plaintiffs were prejudiced by defendant's actions, and (3) alternative sanctions would fail to adequately punish defendant and deter future discovery violations." *Capellupo v. FMC Corp.,* 126 F.R.D. 545, 552 (D. Minn. 1989); *Cabinetware, Inc., v. Sullivan,* No. CIV.90-313, 1991 WL 327959 (E.D. Cal. Jul. 15, 1991); *Chapman v. Auto Owners Ins. Co., 220* Ga. App. 539, 540, 469 S.E.2d 783, 784 (1996). In addition, the authority to dismiss a case originates under Rule 37. *Danis v. USN Communications, Inc.,* No. CIV.98-7482, 2000 WL 1694325, at *30 (N.D. Ill. Oct. 20, 2000).

- *Metropolitan Opera Ass'n., Inc. v. Local 100,* 212 F.R.D. 178, 230 (S.D.N.Y. 2003), *adhered to on reconsideration,* 2004 WL 1943099 (S.D.N.Y. Aug. 27, 2004). The court found liability on the part of the defendants and imposed attorneys' fees stating that "lesser sanctions, such as an adverse inference or preclusion, would not be effective in this case."

- *Procter & Gamble Co. v. Haugen,* 427 F.3d 727 (10th Cir. 2005). The lower court's decision to dismiss the case was reversed for failure to address on the record the factors that had to be evaluated before dismissing the claims as a discovery sanction and for a lack of support for concluding that plaintiff acted willfully, in bad faith, or with culpability.

- *Krumwiede v. Brighton Associates, L.L.C.,* No. CIV.05-3003, 2006 WL 1308629 (N.D. Ill. May 8, 2006). The Court entered default judgment against the plaintiff for deletion of files on the day the defendant filed its counterclaims and a preservation letter was sent to the plaintiff's counsel. The Court found that computer activity including deleting files, creating ZIP files (nesting data), movement of data and multiple use of defragmentation evidenced the intent to destroy evidence.

- *Kucala Enterprises, Ltd. v. Auto Wax Co., Inc.,* 56 Fed. R. Serv.3d 487 (N.D. Ill. 2003), *adopted as modified, Kucala Enterprises, Ltd. v. Auto Wax Co., Inc.,* 57 Fed. R. Serv. 3d 501 (N.D. Ill. 2003). The magistrate ordered dismissal of case, later modified by the district court, after a computer forensic expert found that a computer program called "Evidence Eliminator" was used to delete 12,000 files from its owner's desktop computer a few hours before the defendant's computer specialist was to inspect the computer pursuant to court order.

- *Advantacare Health Ptnrs, LP v. Access IV, Inc.,* CIV.03-04496, 2005 U.S. Dist. LEXIS 12794 (D. Cal. Jun. 14, 2005). The Court entered default judgment against all of the defendants for failure to delete plaintiff's computer files from its computers after specifically directed to do so by the Court.

- *QZO, Inc. v. Moyer,* 2004 WL 502288 (S.C. Ct. App. Mar. 15, 2004). The Appellate Court affirmed dismissal in this trade secret case where a former corporate officer had "reformatted" his hard drive a day before delivering the computer to the plaintiff's expert pursuant to a court order.

- *Anderson v. Crossroads Capital Partners, L.L.C.*, No. CIV.01-2000, 2004 WL 256512 (D. Minn. Feb. 10, 2004). The Court refused to dismiss the case but issued an adverse instruction after the plaintiff erased her computer hard drive data using a program called CyberScrub after notice was provided to her that the opposing party was seeking it in discovery.

- *Nartron Corp. v. General Motors Corp.*, 2003 WL 1985261 at *2-5 (Mich. App. Apr. 29, 2003). The Court affirmed the lower court's decision to dismiss the case for discovery abuses after reviewing the evidence of using FoxPro and WordPro in the intentional destruction of computer records.

- *Century ML-Cable Corp. v. Carrillo.*, 43 F. Supp. 2d 176 (D.P.R. 1998). Court ordered default judgment after the defendant destroyed a laptop computer containing materials regarding the modification, distribution and sales of cable TV descrambling decoders.

- *Cabinetware, Inc., v. Sullivan,* No. CIV.90-313, 1991 WL 327959 (E.D. Cal. Jul. 15, 1991). Court entered default judgment against the defendant who intentionally destroyed electronic source code files requested in discovery.

- *American Bankers Ins. Co. v. Caruth*, 786 S.W.2d 427 (Tex. Ct. App. 1990). Court entered default judgment against a party who claimed that the requested information was stored among 30,000 boxes of materials. In fact the material was on computer files that could have easily accessed the same information.

- *Computer Assocs. Int'l., Inc. v. American Fundware, Inc.*, 133 F.R.D. 166 (D. Colo. 1990). Court entered default judgment for destruction of computer source code that was central to the copyright infringement case.

- *Carlucci v. Piper Aircraft Corp.*, 102 F.R.D. 472, 481-82, 486 (S.D. Fla. 1984). Court entered default judgment after concluding that company's document retention program was often not observed and that documents had been destroyed deliberately. The Court stated: "By deliberately destroying documents, the defendant has eliminated the plaintiffs' right to have their cases decided on the merits. Accordingly, the entry of a default is the only means of effectively sanctioning the defendant and remedying the wrong."

[h]   Evidentiary Sanctions

- *Coleman (Parent) Holdings, Inc. v. Morgan Stanley & Co., Inc.*, 2005 WL 67071 (Fla. Cir. Ct. Mar. 1, 2005). The Court granted plaintiffs' motion for an adverse inference due to e-mail destruction and failure to comply with the judge's discovery order. Because of deleted e-mail and failure to immediately disclose discovered backup tapes in a timely manner the Court permitted the plaintiff to argue an adverse inference regarding the concealment of evidence and shifted the burden of proof to the defendant as to certain elements of the cause of action.

- *AdvantaCare Health Partners, LP v. Access IV,* No. CIV.03-04496, 2004 WL 1837997 (N.D. Cal. 2004). After the defendant had tried to delete computer files using BC Wipe the plaintiff sought default judgment as a sanction against defendants. The Court found defendants' conduct egregious but it did not warrant such a harsh sanction and granted an evidentiary presumption that defendant had copied every file on the plaintiff's system and monetary sanctions of $20,000. In a later decision the Court in *Advantacare Health Ptnrs, LP v. Access IV, Inc.,* No. CIV.03-04496, 2005 U.S. Dist. LEXIS 12794 (D. Cal. Jun. 14, 2005) entered default judgment against all of the defendants for failure to delete plaintiff's computer files from its computer after specifically directed to do so by the Court.

- *Wilson v. Sundstrand Corp.,* No. CIV.99-6944, 2003 WL 21961359 (N.D.Ill. Aug. 18, 2003). The Court precluded defendant from opposing the admission in evidence of various e-mails and records and imposed monetary fines as a sanction for deposition discovery abuse and late production of "smoking gun" e-mail.

- *United States v. Philip Morris, USA, Inc.,* No. CIV.99-2496, 2004 WL 1627252 (D.D.C. July 21, 2004). The defendant was precluded from presenting any fact witness who had failed to preserve relevant records and was ordered to pay *$2.75 million* in fines for its spoliation of e-mail.

[i]   Other Sanctions

- *Jinks-Umstead v. England,* 227 F.R.D. 143 (D.D.C. 2005). The Court granted the plaintiff a new trial after the defendant provided relevant database reports after the plaintiff rested her case.

- *DeLoach v. Philip Morris Co.,* 206 F.R.D. 568 (M.D.N.C. 2002). As a sanction for late disclosure of a database the defendant's expert relied upon in formulating his report the Court allowed the plaintiffs to provide a response to a rebuttal report and provided no opportunity for the Defendant to respond.

- *Thompson v. U.S. Dept. of Housing and Urban Development,* 219 F.R.D. 93, 104-105 (D. Md. 2003). After failing to produce 80,000 e-mail the Court "(1) precluding the Local Defendants from introducing into evidence . . . any of the 80,000 e-mail . . . (2) ordering that counsel . . . were forbidden to use any of these e-mail records to prepare any of their witnesses for testimony at trial . . . [and] were forbidden from attempting to refresh the recollection of any of their witnesses . . . (3) ordering that the Plaintiffs were permitted to use any of the . . . e-mail records during their case and in cross-examining any . . . [of the defendant] witnesses, (4) ordering that . . . [the defendants to pay for] any additional expense and attorney's fees in connection with reviewing . . . and analyzing them for possible use at trial . . . and finally (5) [depending on trial testimony regarding the e-mail] that the Plaintiffs were free to make a motion to the court that the failure to produce e-mail records as ordered by this court constituted a contempt of court, under Rule 37(b)(2)(D)."

- *RKI, Inc. v. Grimes,* 177 F. Supp. 2d 859 (N.D. Ill. 2001). The Court stated, "[w]hen you play with fire, you may get burned" and ordered the defendant to pay $100,000 in compensatory damages, $150,000 in punitive damages, attorney's fees, and court costs in a trade secret misappropriation case, after the defendant defragmented his home computer to prevent the plaintiff from discovering the contents of his hard drive.

- *See also,* § 1.5, *Ethical Obligations.*

[i]   No Sanction Imposed

- *MMI Products, Inc. v. Long,* 231 F.R.D. 215 (D. Md. 2005). The Court reversed the magistrate's proposed ruling to sanction defendant and its counsel pursuant to FED. R. CIV. P. 26(g)(3) for failure to make reasonable inquiries into the reliability of their own expert's report after it was discovered that the laptop in question was apparently purchased subsequent to the time of the alleged misappropriation of company information.

- *Quinby v. WestLB AG,* No. CIV.04-7406, 2006 U.S. Dist. LEXIS 1178 (D.N.Y. Jan. 11, 2006). The Court refused to order sanctions even though the defendant failed to disclose that part of the discovery was available in an accessible format and that other data had been converted from an accessible format to an inaccessible format. *But see, Treppel v. Biovail Corp.,* 233 F.R.D. 363, n.4 (D.N.Y. 2006) ("One of my colleagues recently declined to sanction a party for converting data to an inaccessible format, taking the position that there is no obligation to preserve electronic data in an accessible form, even when litigation is anticipated. (citation omitted) I respectfully disagree."

- *Convolve, Inc. v. Compaq Computer Corp.,* 223 F.R.D. 162 (S.D.N.Y. 2004). In a patent infringement and trade secrets action, a plaintiff sought sanctions arising from defendants' failure to preserve e-mails. The court denied the sanctions because plaintiffs failed to establish that the destroyed e-mails were favorable to them or intentionally deleted. The Court also denied an award of sanctions based upon defendant's failure to preserve temporary "wave forms" generated from the disk drive tuning process. Because preservation would have required "heroic efforts" and no business purpose ever dictated that such data be retained, the court would not issue sanctions.

- *Gates Rubber Co. v. Bando Chem. Indus. Ltd.,* 167 F.R.D. 90 (D. Colo. 1996). The plaintiff was ordered to pay a substantial portion of the defendant's fees and costs of the sanction proceedings, after the plaintiff only produced minimal evidence of spoliation from massive on-site inspection of the defendant's hard drives. The Court found that the sanction proceedings had been an "enormous waste of time, energy and money."

- *Aero Products Intern., Inc. v. Intex Recreation Corp.*, No. CIV.02-2590, 2004 WL 417193 (N.D. Ill. Jan. 30, 2004). Sanctions were denied by the court for delay in seeking assistance from the Court in a timely manner. The plaintiff took no steps, even including the hiring of a computer forensic expert at the defendant's expense, to assist in the recovery of the electronic data, other then filing a motion for sanctions.

- *Lakewood Engineering and Mfg. Co. v. Lasko Products, Inc.*, No. CIV.01-7867, 2003 WL 1220254 (N.D. Ill. Mar. 14, 2003). Though the plaintiff produced e-mail after the close of discovery, the cost to the defendant was minimal and, therefore, the Court refused to issue sanctions.

- *Williams v. Saint-Gobain Corp.*, 53 Fed. R. Serv.3d 360 (W.D.N.Y. 2002). The Court refused to issue sanctions in this employment discrimination case where the defendant produced e-mails five days before trial. The Court, instead, extended the time period for discovery based on finding no evidence of bad conduct.

- *McGuire v. Acufex Microsurgical, Inc.*, 175 F.R.D. 149 (D. Mass. 1997). The Court refused to issue sanctions for the human services director who deleted a paragraph from a key memorandum concerning a meeting between one of the plaintiff's supervisors and the plaintiff regarding her charges of sexual harassment. The human services director had acted in good faith, and there was no prejudice.

- *In re Application for Water Rights of Hines Highlands LP*, 929 P.2d 718, 727 (Colo. Sup. Ct. 1996). The Appellate Court affirmed the lower court's decision in refusing to impose attorneys' fees and costs as a sanction against a party who initially refused to produce the computer disk of its expert's stream flow model, where the printout that had been produced provided sufficient information to defend against the expert's model.

- *New York National Organization for Women v. Cuomo*, No. CIV.93-7146, 1998 WL 395320 (S.D.N.Y. Jul. 14, 1998). The Court refused to preclude evidence or award attorneys' fees as a sanction against defendant for failure to preserve evidence consisting of computer database and monthly summary reports. The Court also refused to allow computer searches of defendants' computer system since the plaintiff could get the information from other places.

- *EEOC v. Gen. Dynamics Corp.*, 999 F.2d 113, 116-17 (5th Cir. 1993). The Appellate court reversed the lower court's exclusion of the plaintiff's expert testimony as a sanction for failure to produce a database relied upon by the expert. The court found that the lower court's order did not clearly require the production of computer tapes.

- *Baker v. Gen. Motors Corp.*, 86 F.3d 811, 816-17 (8th Cir. 1996), *rev'd. in part on other grounds*, 118 S. Ct. 657 (1998). The Appellate court reversed an evidentiary presumption as too severe for the defendant's late production of computer summaries.

[k]   Spoliation Tort

[i]   Generally

The doctrine of spoliation of evidence can give rise to a cause of action in tort. Several courts have recognized spoliation as an intentional tort. *Smith v. Howard Johnson Co.,* 67 Ohio St. 3d 28, 615 N.E.2d 1037, 1038 (1993); *Hirsch v. General Motors Corp.,* 266 N.J. Super. 222, 628 A.2d 1108 (1993); *Hazen v. Anchorage,* 718 P.2d 456 (Ak. 1986). Others have not been willing to create an independent tort, but it can provide a basis to impose. *Austin v. Consolidated Coal Co.,* 256 Va. 78, 82, 501 S.E.2d 161 (1998); *Chambers v. NASCO, Inc.,* 501 U.S. 32 (1991); *See also,* Terry R. Spencer, *Do Not Fold Spindle Or Mutilate: The Trend Towards Recognition of Spoliation as a Separate Tort,* 30 Idaho L. Rev. 37 (1993-1994).

The Ohio Supreme Court designated the elements of the tort as follows,

(1) A cause of action exists in tort for interference with or destruction of evidence; (2a) the elements of a claim for interference with or destruction of evidence are (1) pending or probable litigation involving the plaintiff, (2) knowledge on the part of defendant that litigation exists or is probable, (3) willful destruction of evidence by defendant designed to disrupt the plaintiff's case, (4) disruption of the plaintiff's case, and (5) damages proximately caused by the defendant's acts; (2b) such a claim should be recognized between the parties to the primary action and against third parties; and (3) such a claim may be brought at the same time as the primary action.

Smith v. Howard Johnson Co., 67 Ohio St. 3d 28, 29, 615 N.E.2d 1037, 1038 (1993).

[L]   Other Authorities

* Shira A. Scheindlin and Kanchana Wangkeo, *Electronic Discovery Sanctions in the Twenty-First Century,* 11 Mich. Telecomm. Tech. L. Rev. 71 (2004), available at http://www.mttlr.org/voleleven/scheindlin.pdf (last visited on July 22, 2006).

§ 7.10   OBTAINING DATA FROM THIRD PARTIES

[A]   Rule 45

Rule 45. Subpoena

(a) Form; Issuance.

(1) Every subpoena shall . . . (C) command each person to whom it is directed to attend and give testimony or to produce and permit inspection and copying of

designated books, documents or tangible things in the possession, custody or control of that person, or to permit inspection of premises, at a time and place therein specified; and . . . A command to produce evidence or to permit inspection may be joined with a command to appear at trial or hearing or at deposition, or may be issued separately.

* * *

(c) Protection of Persons Subject to Subpoenas.

(1) A party or an attorney responsible for the issuance and service of a subpoena shall take reasonable steps to avoid imposing undue burden or expense on a person subject to that subpoena. The court on behalf of which the subpoena was issued shall enforce this duty and impose upon the party or attorney in breach of this duty an appropriate sanction, which may include, but is not limited to, lost earnings and a reasonable attorney's fee.

(2)(A) A person commanded to produce and permit inspection and copying of designated books, papers, documents or tangible things, or inspection of premises need not appear in person at the place of production or inspection unless commanded to appear for deposition, hearing or trial.

(B) Subject to paragraph (d)(2) of this rule, a person commanded to produce and permit inspection and copying may, within 14 days after service of the subpoena or before the time specified for compliance if such time is less than 14 days after service, serve upon the party or attorney designated in the subpoena written objection to inspection or copying of any or all of the designated materials or of the premises. If objection is made, the party serving the subpoena shall not be entitled to inspect and copy the materials or inspect the premises except pursuant to an order of the court by which the subpoena was issued. If objection has been made, the party serving the subpoena may, upon notice to the person commanded to produce, move at any time for an order to compel the production. Such an order to compel production shall protect any person who is not a party or an officer of a party from significant expense resulting from the inspection and copying commanded.

(3)(A) On timely motion, the court by which a subpoena was issued shall quash or modify the subpoena if it

* * *

(iii) requires disclosure of privileged or other protected matter and no exception or waiver applies, or

(iv) subjects a person to undue burden.

(B) If a subpoena

(i) requires disclosure of a trade secret or other confidential research, development, or commercial information, or

(ii) requires disclosure of an unretained expert's opinion or information not describing specific events or occurrences in dispute and resulting from the expert's study made not at the request of any party, or

* * *

(d) Duties in Responding to Subpoena.

(1) A person responding to a subpoena to produce documents shall produce them as they are kept in the usual course of business or shall organize and label them to correspond with the categories in the demand.

(2) When information subject to a subpoena is withheld on a claim that it is privileged or subject to protection as trial preparation materials, the claim shall be made expressly and shall be supported by a description of the nature of the documents, communications, or things not produced that is sufficient to enable the demanding party to contest the claim.

(e) Contempt. Failure by any person without adequate excuse to obey a subpoena served upon that person may be deemed a contempt of the court from which the subpoena issued. An adequate cause for failure to obey exists when a subpoena purports to require a non-party to attend or produce at a place not within the limits provided by clause (ii) of subparagraph (c)(3)(A).

[1]   Pending Rule 45 Amendment

Rule 45. Subpoena

(a) Form; Issuance.

(1) Every subpoena shall

(A) state the name of the court from which it is issued; and

(B) state the title of the action, the name of the court in which it is pending, and its civil action number; and

(C) command each person to whom it is directed to attend and give testimony or to produce and permit inspection, copying, testing, or sampling of designated books, documents, electronically stored information, or tangible things in the possession, custody or control of that person, or to permit inspection of premises, at a time and place therein specified; and (emphasis added)

(D) set forth the text of subdivisions (c) and (d) of this rule. A command to produce evidence or to permit inspection, <u>copying, testing, or sampling</u> may be joined with a command to appear at trial or hearing or at deposition, or may be issued separately. <u>A subpoena may specify the form or forms in which electronically stored information is to be produced.</u> (emphasis added).

(2) A subpoena must issue as follows:

* * * * *

(C) for production, <u>inspection, copying, testing, or sampling,</u> if separate from a subpoena commanding a person's attendance, from the court for the district where the production or inspection is to be made. (emphasis added).

(3) The clerk shall issue a subpoena, signed but otherwise in blank, to a party requesting it, who shall complete it before service. An attorney as officer of the court may also issue and sign a subpoena on behalf of

(A) a court in which the attorney is authorized to practice; or

(B) a court for a district in which a deposition or production is compelled by the subpoena, if the deposition or production pertains to an action pending in a court in which the attorney is authorized to practice.

(b) Service.

(1) A subpoena may be served by any person who is not a party and is not less than 18 years of age. Service of a subpoena upon a person named therein shall be made by delivering a copy thereof to such person and, if the person's attendance is commanded, by tendering to that person the fees for one day's attendance and the mileage allowed by law. When the subpoena is issued on behalf of the United States or an officer or agency thereof, fees and mileage need not be tendered. Prior notice of any commanded production of documents and things or inspection of premises before trial shall be served on each party in the manner prescribed by Rule 5(b).

(2) Subject to the provisions of clause (ii) of subparagraph (c)(3)(A) of this rule, a subpoena may be served at any place within the district of the court by which it is issued, or at any place without the district that is within 100 miles of the place of the deposition, hearing, trial, production, inspection, <u>copying, testing, or sampling</u> specified in the subpoena or at any place within the state where a state statute or rule of court permits service of a subpoena issued by a state court of general jurisdiction sitting in the place of the deposition, hearing, trial,

production, inspection, copying, testing, or sampling specified in the subpoena. When a statute of the United States provides therefor, the court upon proper application and cause shown may authorize the service of a subpoena at any other place. A subpoena directed to a witness in a foreign country who is a national or resident of the United States shall issue under the circumstances and in the manner and be served as provided in Title 28, U.S.C. § 1783. (emphasis added).

(3) Proof of service when necessary shall be made by filing with the clerk of the court by which the subpoena is issued a statement of the date and manner of service and of the names of the persons served, certified by the person who made the service.

(c) Protection of Persons Subject to Subpoenas.

(1) A party or an attorney responsible for the issuance and service of a subpoena shall take reasonable steps to avoid imposing undue burden or expense on a person subject to that subpoena. The court on behalf of which the subpoena was issued shall enforce this duty and impose upon the party or attorney in breach of this duty an appropriate sanction, which may include, but is not limited to, lost earnings and a reasonable attorney's fee.

(2) (A) A person commanded to produce and permit inspection, <u>copying, testing, or sampling</u> of designated <u>electronically stored information,</u> books, papers, documents or tangible things, or inspection of premises need not appear in person at the place of production or inspection unless commanded to appear for deposition, hearing or trial. (emphasis added).

(B) Subject to paragraph (d)(2) of this rule, a person commanded to produce and permit inspection, copying, <u>testing, or sampling</u> may, 14 days after service of the subpoena or before the time specified for compliance if such time is less than 14 days after service, serve upon the party or attorney designated in the subpoena written objection to producing any or all of the designated materials or <u>inspection</u> of the premises — <u>or to producing electronically stored information in the form or forms requested.</u> If objection is made, the party serving the subpoena shall not be entitled to inspect, copy, test, or sample the materials or inspect the premises except pursuant to an order of the court by which the subpoena was issued. If objection has been made, the party serving the subpoena may, upon notice to the person commanded to produce, move at any time for an order to compel the production, <u>inspection, copying, testing, or sampling</u>. Such an order to compel shall protect any person who is not a party or an officer of a party from significant expense resulting from the inspection, copying, testing, or sampling commanded. (emphasis added).

(3) (A) On timely motion, the court by which a subpoena was issued shall quash or modify the subpoena if it

(i) fails to allow reasonable time for compliance;

(ii) requires a person who is not a party or an officer of a party to travel to a place more than 100 miles from the place where that person resides, is employed or regularly transacts business in person, except that, subject to the provisions of clause (c)(3)(B)(iii) of this rule, such a person may in order to attend trial be commanded to travel from any such place within the state in which the trial is held;

(iii) requires disclosure of privileged or other protected matter and no exception or waiver applies; or

(iv) subjects a person to undue burden.

(B) If a subpoena

(i) requires disclosure of a trade secret or other confidential research, development, or commercial information, or

(ii) requires disclosure of an unretained expert's opinion or information not describing specific events or occurrences in dispute and resulting from the expert's study made not at the request of any party, or

(iii) requires a person who is not a party or an officer of a party to incur substantial expense to travel more than 100 miles to attend trial, the court may, to protect a person subject to or affected by the subpoena, quash or modify the subpoena or, if the party in whose behalf the subpoena is issued shows a substantial need for the testimony or material that cannot be otherwise met without undue hardship and assures that the person to whom the subpoena is addressed will be reasonably compensated, the court may order appearance or production only upon specified conditions.

(d) Duties in Responding to Subpoena.

(1) (A) A person responding to a subpoena to produce documents shall produce them as they are kept in the usual course of business or shall organize and label them to correspond with the categories in the demand.

(B) If a subpoena does not specify the form or forms for producing electronically stored information, a person responding to a subpoena must produce the information in a form or forms in which the person ordinarily maintains it or in a form or forms that are reasonably usable. (emphasis added).

(C) A person responding to a subpoena need not produce the same electronically stored information in more than one form. (emphasis added).

(D) A person responding to a subpoena need not provide discovery of electronically stored information from sources that the person identifies as not reasonably accessible because of undue burden or cost. On motion to compel discovery or to quash, the person from whom discovery is sought must show that the information sought is not reasonably accessible because of undue burden or cost. If that showing is made, the court may nonetheless order discovery from such sources if the requesting party shows good cause, considering the limitations of Rule 26(b)(2)(C). The court may specify conditions for the discovery. (emphasis added).

(2) (A) When information subject to a subpoena is withheld on a claim that it is privileged or subject to protection as trial-preparation materials, the claim shall be made expressly and shall be supported by a description of the nature of the documents, communications, or things not produced that is sufficient to enable the demanding party to contest the claim.

(B) If information is produced in response to a subpoena that is subject to a claim of privilege or of protection as trial-preparation material, the person making the claim may notify any party that received the information of the claim and the basis for it. After being notified, a party must promptly return, sequester, or destroy the specified information and any copies it has and may not use or disclose the information until the claim is resolved. A receiving party may promptly present the information to the court under seal for a determination of the claim. If the receiving party disclosed the information before being notified, it must take reasonable steps to retrieve it. The person who produced the information must preserve the information until the claim is resolved. (emphasis added).

(e) Contempt. Failure of any person without adequate excuse to obey a subpoena served upon that person may be deemed a contempt of the court from which the subpoena issued. An adequate cause for failure to obey exists when a subpoena purports to require a nonparty to attend or produce at a place not within the limits provided by clause (ii) of subparagraph (c)(3)(A).

Committee Note

Rule 45 is amended to conform the provisions for subpoenas to changes in other discovery rules, largely related to discovery of electronically stored information. Rule 34 is amended to provide in greater detail for the production of electronically stored information. Rule 45(a)(1)(C) is amended to recognize that electronically stored information, as defined in Rule 34(a), can also be sought by subpoena. Like Rule 34(b), Rule 45(a)(1) is amended to provide that the subpoena can designate a form or forms for production of electronic data. Rule 45(c)(2) is amended, like Rule 34(b), to authorize the person served with a subpoena to object to the requested form or forms. In addition, as under Rule 34(b), Rule 45(d)(1)(B) is amended to provide that if the subpoena does not specify the form or forms for electronically stored information, the person served with the subpoena must produce electronically stored information in a form or forms in which it is usually maintained or in a form or forms that are reasonably usable. Rule 45(d)(1)(C) is added to provide that the person producing electronically stored information should not have to produce the same information in more than one form unless so ordered by the court for good cause.

As with discovery of electronically stored information from parties, complying with a subpoena for such information may impose burdens on the responding person. Rule 45(c) provides protection against undue impositions on nonparties. For example, Rule 45(c)(1) directs that a party serving a subpoena "shall take reasonable steps to avoid imposing undue burden or expense on a person subject to the subpoena," and Rule 45(c)(2)(B) permits the person served with the subpoena to object to it and directs that an order requiring compliance "shall protect a person who is neither a party nor a party's officer from significant expense resulting from" compliance. Rule 45(d)(1)(D) is added to provide that the responding person need not provide discovery of electronically stored information from sources the party identifies as not reasonably accessible, unless the court orders such discovery for good cause, considering the limitations of Rule 26(b)(2)(C), on terms that protect a nonparty against significant expense. A parallel provision is added to Rule 26(b)(2).

Rule 45(a)(1)(B) is also amended, as is Rule 34(a), to provide that a subpoena is available to permit testing and sampling as well as inspection and copying. As in Rule 34, this change recognizes that on occasion the opportunity to perform testing or sampling may be important, both for documents and for electronically stored information. Because testing or sampling may present particular issues of burden or intrusion for the person served with the subpoena, however, the protective provisions of Rule 45(c) should be enforced with vigilance when such demands are made. Inspection or testing of certain types of electronically stored information or of a person's electronic information system may raise issues of confidentiality or privacy. The addition of sampling and testing to Rule 45(a) with regard to documents and electronically stored information is not meant to create a routine right of direct access to a person's electronic information system, although such access might be justified in some circumstances. Courts should guard against undue intrusiveness resulting from inspecting or testing such systems.

Rule 45(d)(2) is amended, as is Rule 26(b)(5), to add a procedure for assertion of privilege or of protection as trial-preparation materials after production. The receiving party may submit the information to the court for resolution of the privilege claim, as under Rule 26(b)(5)(B).

Other minor amendments are made to conform the rule to the changes described above.

[B]   Purpose

FED. R. CIV. P. 45 establishes the rules for subpoenas served upon individuals and entities that are not parties to the underlying lawsuit. The function of a subpoena is "to compel the attendance of witnesses and the production of documents so that the court may have access to all of the available information for the determination of controversies before it." 9A Wright & Miller, supra note 11, § 2451, at 15.

It also governs subpoenas duces tecum for the production of documents with or without the taking of a deposition. Rule 34, pertaining to the production of documents, provides that "[a] person not a party to the action may be compelled to produce documents and things or to submit to an inspection as provided in Rule 45." FED. R. CIV. P. 34(c). One of the purposes of Rule 45 is "to facilitate access outside the deposition procedure provided by Rule 30 to documents and other information in the possession of persons who are not parties. . . . The non-party witness is subject to the same scope of discovery under this rule as that person would be as a party to whom a request is addressed pursuant to Rule 34." FED. R. CIV. P. 34 advisory committee notes (1991 amendment).

The Federal Rules of Civil Procedure provide that a court "shall quash or modify [a] subpoena if it . . . requires disclosure of privileged or other protected matter and no exception or waiver applies, or [if it] subjects a person to undue burden." FED. R. CIV. P. 45(c)(3)(A)(iii) and (iv). The rule expressly protects non-parties from incurring any "significant expense" or "undue burden" in responding to a subpoena. These cost-shifting protections are mandatory. *See, Broussard v. Lemons,* 186 F.R.D. 396, 398 (W.D. La. 1999).

Although Rule 26 refers specifically to depositions, subpoenas are governed by the same relevancy standards. *See, Syposs v. United States,* 181 F.R.D. 224, 226 (W.D.N.Y. 1998) ("The reach of a subpoena issued pursuant to FED. R. CIV. P. 45 is subject to the general relevancy standard applicable to discovery under FED. R. CIV. P. 26(b)(1)."); *Mannington Mills, Inc. v. Armstrong World Indus.,* 206 F.R.D. 525, 529 (D. Del. 2002) (detailing relationship between Rules 26 and 45).

Pending Rule 45 Amendment

The pending Rule 45 amendment pertaining to discovery from third parties conforms with the other ESI discovery rules. Specifically, Rule 45 provides:

•   For discovery of ESI similar to Rule 34(b) in the form requested. If no form is requested or the producing party objects to the form the same procedures apply as set forth in pending Rule 34 amendment.

•   That ESI does not have to be produced from sources that are not reasonably accessible because of undue burden or cost following the dictates of pending Rule 26(b)(2). The producing party has the burden of proving inaccessibility which the Court, if good cause is shown, can still require disclosure if the limitations of pending Rule 26(b)(2)(C) are met.

- That if privileged material is produced the procedure set forth under pending Rule 26(b)(5) should be followed requiring the disclosing party making that claim to give notice and the party receiving the information must return, sequester, or destroy the specified information until the claim is resolved.

[C] Reported Cases

Generally

- *S.E.C. v. Credit Bancorp, Ltd.,* 194 F.R.D. 469, 471 (S.D.N.Y. 2000). "It is not necessary that discovery materials sought by means of subpoena duces tecum from a non-party be in the physical possession of the non-party in order to compel production; rather, non-party's 'control' is sufficient, construed as the legal right, authority, or practical ability to obtain the materials sought upon demand."

- *In re Natural Gas Commodity Litig.,* No. CIV.03-6186, 2005 U.S. Dist. LEXIS 27470, at *68-70 (D.N.Y. Nov. 14, 2005) In a securities fraud action the Court granted plaintiff investors' motion to compel against a nonparty for electronic data discovery. The plaintiff agreed to pay the costs of discovery and the Court ordered the parties to negotiate a "reasonable 'sample' protocol - perhaps searching one of the 'old' computers, with leave to re-visit the burden vs. utility question based on information from that process."

- *Procter & Gamble Co. v. Haugen,* 427 F.3d 727 (10th Cir. 2005). The plaintiff's expert obtained data from a third party marketing database for use in their opinions to establish damages. The Appellate Court reversed the lower court decision to dismiss the case for failure to preserve and disclose the entire third party marketing database. The Appellate Court discussed the dynamic nature of databases and the various alternatives to obtaining the data including using Rule 45 to subpoena information directly from the third party data provider.

- *United States ex rel. Tyson v. Amerigroup Ill., Inc.,* No. CIV.02-6074, 2005 U.S. Dist. LEXIS 24929 (D. Ill. Oct. 21, 2005). The Court granted a non-party's motion to quash defendants' subpoena on the basis that discovery of one year's worth of e-mail was unduly burdensome based on the underlying computer setup of the non-party.

- *Gonzales v. Google, Inc.,* 234 F.R.D. 674, 683 (D. Cal. 2006). The Court ordered the nonparty defendant to create "new code to format and extract query and URL data from many computer banks" since the government agreed to compensate for reasonable costs of production. The Court noted that "[a]s a general rule, non-parties are not required to create documents that do not exist, simply for the purposes of discovery."

- *In re Honeywell Intern., Inc. Securities Litigation,* No. M8-85, 2003 WL 22722961, at *1-2 (S.D.N.Y. Nov. 18, 2003). The Court held that under Rule 34(b) a non-party auditor was "obligated to produce its work papers in their electronic form" as previously produced voluminous hardcopies were "essentially incomprehensible" and "insufficient because they were not produced as kept in the usual course of business."

- *Ayers v. SGS Control Servs.,* No. CIV.03-9078, 2006 U.S. Dist. LEXIS 17591, at *7-8 (D.N.Y. Apr. 3, 2006). The defendants objected to providing payroll and timekeeping records in an electronic format arguing that they should be subpoenaed through their nonparty provider. The Court did not agree and found that "this process unnecessarily delays and complicates the disclosure of these records."

- *Mazur v. Wal-Mart Stores, Inc.,* No. CIV.05-85, 2006 U.S. Dist. LEXIS 20985, at *4-6 (D. Mich. Apr. 19, 2006). The Court denied Wal-Mart's motion to compel production of the plaintiff wife's computer, who was a non-party, since it "has raised no credible reason. . . . 'to produce their computer and its storage devices for inspection.' . . . Defendant's request . . . [is] for the sole purpose of allowing Wal-Mart to engage in an invasive forensic inspection of it to obtain a copy of the summary, is an unwarranted, unnecessary and indeed, heavy handed litigation tactic."

- *Diagnostic Assocs. v. Benscome,* 833 So. 2d. 801, 802 (Fla. App. 2002). The Court ruled that the current status of the plaintiff as non-party was of "no moment in this case" where a party sought discovery from the non-party's computer system.

- *Trost v. Trost,* 164 B.R. 740, 745 n.5 (W.D. Mich. 1994). A file on a third party's laptop computer has been held to be subject to production as a document pursuant to 45(a)(1)(C).

- *Multi-Tech Systems, Inc. v. Hayes Microcomputer Products, Inc.,* 800 F. Supp. 825 (D. Minn. 1992). Court refused to quash a trial subpoena for documents sought under FED. R. CIV. P. 45.

- *Cook v. Rockwell International Corp.,* 907 F. Supp. 1460, 1465 (D. Colo. 1995). A non-party who entered into a stipulated order requiring the production of documents was held in contempt for failing to identify the computer tapes containing certain documents and failing to produce the requested database.

Costs and expenses

- *Mattel Inc. v. Walking Mountain Prods.,* 353 F.3d 792, 814 (9th Cir. 2003). The Court on appeal found no abuse of discretion when the district court awarded a non-party attorneys' fees and costs spent in opposing defendant's ex parte application to enforce an overly burdensome subpoena.

- *In re Coordinated Pretrial Proceedings in Petroleum Products Antitrust Litigation v. Kerr-McGee Corp.*, 669 F.2d 620 (10th Cir. 1982). Court in antitrust case entered a protective order wherein it conditioned discovery requested of a non-party, on payment by the requesting party.

- *Cash Today of Texas, Inc. v. Greenberg*, No. CIV.02-MC-77, 2002 WL 31414138, at *4 (D. Del. Oct. 23, 2002). The party subpoenaing documents from third party lessoned the burden of disclosure on the non-party by agreeing "(1) to accept computer disks or reports summarizing the relevant documents; and (2) to conduct an on-site, supervised inspection of the relevant documents and to copy them at its own expense. Subject to these sorts of terms, the burden of complying with the subpoena is substantially reduced such that the burden is not 'undue.'"

- *In re Propulsid Prods. Liab. Litig.*, No. MDL 1355, 2003 WL 22174137, at *2-3 (E.D. La. Sept. 9, 2003). The Court allowed recovery of reasonable costs of attorney privilege review.

- *Fed. Trade Comm'n. v. U.S. Grant Res.*, No. CIV.04-596, 2004 WL 1396315, at *4 (E.D. La. Jun. 18, 2004). The Court considered three factors in determining whether a third party should bear all or part of the cost of the expense of production. These included "whether the nonparty actually has an interest in the outcome of the case, whether the nonparty can more readily bear the costs than the requesting party and whether the litigation is of public importance."

Preservation Order

- *In re National Century Financial Enterprises, Inc. Financial Investment*, 347 F. Supp.2d 538, 540-541 (S.D. Ohio 2004). Investors brought class actions in state court alleging that defendants looted assets of Chapter 11 debtor, in violation of federal securities laws. The Court granted the plaintiff's motion to issue document preservation subpoena to a non-party.

- *In re Tyco International, Ltd., Securities Litigation*, No. 00-MD-1335-B, 2000 WL 33654141 (D.N.H. Jul. 27, 2000). Court agreed that plaintiffs could be authorized to subpoena third parties for the limited purpose of giving them notice and document preservation warnings, provided subpoenas were sufficiently particularized to note the kinds of documents at issue.

Burdensome or Overbroad

- *Theofel v. Farey Jones*, 341 F.3d 978, 981 (9th Cir. 2003), *amended by*, 359 F.3d 1066 (9th Cir. 2004), *cert. denied*, 125 S.Ct. 48. The Court ordered $9,000 in sanctions and held that a civil suit could be brought as a result of a "massively overbroad" and "patently unlawful" subpoena that was served on the opposing party's e-mail ISP.

- *Southern Diagnostic Assoc. v. Bencosme,* 833 So. 2d 801 (Fla. Dist. Ct. App. 2002). The Appellate Court reversed the lower court and quashed an order against a non-party because it was overbroad. It set no parameters or limitations on the inspection of the computer nor did it provide any plan to protect confidential and privileged information.

- *Southern Diagnostic Assoc. v. Bencosme,* 833 So. 2d 801 (Fla. Dist. Ct. App. 2002). The Appellate Court quashed an order against a non-party for electronic data discovery. The Appellate Court held the lower court's order was overbroad, setting no limits on discovery and not taking into consideration confidential and privileged information.

- *Galvin v. Gillette Co.,* 2005 WL 1476895 (Mass. Super. May 19, 2005). In a subpoena enforcement action by a state government agency investigating alleged fraud by investment banking firms perpetrated on Gillette Co., the court declined to order Gillette to pay for a vendor to access and search all of its e-mail, servers, archives, back-up tapes and other media. Noting that Gillette itself was not the target of the investigation, the court concluded that it should not enforce the subpoena because of the magnitude of the recovery effort and the fact that much of the material might include privileged or confidential trade secret information that would have to be screened out in a costly review.

Scope

- *Braxton v. Farmer's Ins. Group,* 209 F.R.D. 651 (N.D. Ala. 2002). The Court affirmed subpoena to the non-party state's insurance department for relevant data, but quashed non-party subpoena sent to the defendant's insurance agents for all documents, including e-mail and electronic documents, since the defendant said it was able to produce this data without the agent's assistance.

[D]   Interests of Third Parties to Disclosure of Electronic Information

When data is requested from third parties, it may have an effect on their right to privacy. Often, discovery of electronic data involves information that is shared by different organizations using databases, Extranets or other collaboration systems. Discovery of this information from one party may expose the other party to loss of research data, trade secrets, privacy rights, etc. If these third parties know about the attempted discovery of this information, they may try to intervene to obtain protective orders to preclude the disclosure of the information or the third party storing the information may object on their behalf.

[1]   Reported Cases

- *United States v. Bell,* 217 F.R.D 335, 343 (M.D. Penn. 2003). In this civil suit brought against a tax protestor the Court held that "[t]here is no 'right of privacy' privilege against discovery in civil cases. However, the court may take concerned individuals' privacy interests into consideration in determining whether a discovery request is oppressive or unreasonable."

- *In re Pharmatrak, Inc. Privacy Litigation,* 220 F. Supp. 2d 4 (D. Mass. 2002), *rev'd on other grounds, In re Pharmatrak, Inc.,* 329 F.3d 9 (1st Cir. 2003). The Court ruled that an Internet company had not violated privacy rights by using a "cookie" to capture detailed private information about the plaintiffs, including names, addresses, telephone numbers, dates of birth, sex, insurance status, medical conditions, education levels, occupations and e-mail content.

- *United States v. Bach,* 310 F.3d 1063 (8th Cir. 2002). In a criminal prosecution the Appellate Court held that a seizure of the defendant's e-mail by Yahoo! technician's without police being present were reasonable under the Fourth Amendment and did not violate the defendant's privacy rights.

- *Dow Chemical Corp. v. Allen,* 672 F.2d 1262, 1269 (7th Cir. 1982). The Court found that the plaintiff's need for the documents from a non-party did not outweigh the burden in producing the raw data of a research study. The non-party's study would likely be jeopardized if the raw data was produced.

- *United States v. Bailey,* 272 F. Supp. 2d 822 (D. Neb. 2003). Pursuant to an FBI subpoena an employer accessed an employee's e-mail account and found child pornography. The Court held that the defendant did not have an expectation of privacy because of his employer's regulations prescribing use of the computer. Besides posting notices on the Intranet, the company had a log-in notice that warned of possible searching and also required users to click "OK" to proceed. *See also, United States v. Angevine,* 281 F.3d 1130 (10th Cir. 2002), *cert. den.,* 537 U.S. 845.

- *Centurion Industries, Inc. v. Warren Steurer and Associates,* 665 F.2d 323 (10th Cir. 1981). Defendants' expert had access to a third party's software in writing his report and in his report concluded that the defendant did not infringe on plaintiffs' educational machine patents. The third party's software and alleged trade secrets had to be produced in discovery, so that the plaintiff's expert could utilize it to draw his own conclusions as to infringement.

- *Valley Bank of Nevada v. Superior Court,* 125 Cal. Rptr. 553, 15 Cal.3d 652, 542 P.2d 977 (1975). The plaintiff was seeking confidential bank customer information, and the bank objected on the grounds of privacy of its customer. Court granted discovery requests, with specific limitations to protect the rights of the third party.

- *Tiberino v. Spokane County*, 103 Wash. App. 680, 13 P.3d 1104 (Wash. 2000). E-mail sent by an agency employee fell within the scope of the Public Records Act. However, the e-mail were exempt from disclosure to newspapers as personal information. This employee had been terminated partially because of the excessive use of e-mail for personal use. The Court ruled that the contents of the e-mail are private, but that the number of e-mail was a matter of public information and/or interest.

[2]   Other Authorities

- Steven C. Bennett & Scott A. Locke, *Privacy in the Workplace: A Practical Primer*, 49 Lab. L.J. 781-87 (1998).

§ 7.11   SPECIAL MASTERS AND COURT-APPOINTED EXPERTS

[A]   FED. R. CIV. P. 53

Rule 53. Masters

(a) Appointment.

(1) Unless a statute provides otherwise, a court may appoint a master only to:

(A) perform duties consented to by the parties;

(B) hold trial proceedings and make or recommend findings of fact on issues to be decided by the court without a jury if appointment is warranted by

(i) some exceptional condition, or

(ii) the need to perform an accounting or resolve a difficult computation of damages; or

(C) address pretrial and post-trial matters that cannot be addressed effectively and timely by an available district judge or magistrate judge of the district.

(2) A master must not have a relationship to the parties, counsel, action, or court that would require disqualification of a judge under 28 U.S.C. § 455 unless the parties consent with the court's approval to appointment of a particular person after disclosure of any potential grounds for disqualification.

(3) In appointing a master, the court must consider the fairness of imposing the likely expenses on the parties and must protect against unreasonable expense or delay.

(b) Order Appointing Master.

(1) Notice. The court must give the parties notice and an opportunity to be heard before appointing a master. A party may suggest candidates for appointment.

(2) Contents. The order appointing a master must direct the master to proceed with all reasonable diligence and must state:

(A) the master's duties, including any investigation or enforcement duties, and any limits on the master's authority under Rule 53(c);

(B) the circumstances--if any--in which the master may communicate ex parte with the court or a party;

(C) the nature of the materials to be preserved and filed as the record of the master's activities;

(D) the time limits, method of filing the record, other procedures, and standards for reviewing the master's orders, findings, and recommendations; and

(E) the basis, terms, and procedure for fixing the master's compensation under Rule 53(h).

(3) Entry of Order. The court may enter the order appointing a master only after the master has filed an affidavit disclosing whether there is any ground for disqualification under 28 U.S.C. § 455 and, if a ground for disqualification is disclosed, after the parties have consented with the court's approval to waive the disqualification.

(4) Amendment. The order appointing a master may be amended at any time after notice to the parties, and an opportunity to be heard.

(c) Master's Authority. Unless the appointing order expressly directs otherwise, a master has authority to regulate all proceedings and take all appropriate measures to perform fairly and efficiently the assigned duties. The master may by order impose upon a party any noncontempt sanction provided by Rule 37 or 45, and may recommend a contempt sanction against a party and sanctions against a nonparty.

(d) Evidentiary Hearings. Unless the appointing order expressly directs otherwise, a master conducting an evidentiary hearing may exercise the power of the appointing court to compel, take, and record evidence.

(e) Master's Orders. A master who makes an order must file the order and promptly serve a copy on each party. The clerk must enter the order on the docket.

(f) Master's Reports. A master must report to the court as required by the order of appointment. The master must file the report and promptly serve a copy of the report on each party unless the court directs otherwise.

(g) Action on Master's Order, Report, or Recommendations.

(1) Action. In acting on a master's order, report, or recommendations, the court must afford an opportunity to be heard and may receive evidence, and may: adopt or affirm; modify; wholly or partly reject or reverse; or resubmit to the master with instructions.

(2) Time To Object or Move. A party may file objections to--or a motion to adopt or modify--the master's order, report, or recommendations no later than 20 days from the time the master's order, report, or recommendations are served, unless the court sets a different time.

(3) Fact Findings. The court must decide de novo all objections to findings of fact made or recommended by a master unless the parties stipulate with the court's consent that:

(A) the master's findings will be reviewed for clear error, or

(B) the findings of a master appointed under Rule 53(a)(1)(A) or (C) will be final.

(4) Legal Conclusions. The court must decide de novo all objections to conclusions of law made or recommended by a master.

(5) Procedural Matters. Unless the order of appointment establishes a different standard of review, the court may set aside a master's ruling on a procedural matter only for an abuse of discretion.

(h) Compensation.

(1) Fixing Compensation. The court must fix the master's compensation before or after judgment on the basis and terms stated in the order of appointment, but the court may set a new basis and terms after notice and an opportunity to be heard.

(2) Payment. The compensation fixed under Rule 53(h)(1) must be paid either:

(A) by a party or parties; or

(B) from a fund or subject matter of the action within the court's control.

(3) Allocation. The court must allocate payment of the master's compensation among the parties after considering the nature and amount of the controversy, the means of the parties, and the extent to which any party is more responsible than other parties for the reference to a master. An interim allocation may be amended to reflect a decision on the merits.

(i) Appointment of Magistrate Judge. A magistrate judge is subject to this rule only when the order referring a matter to the magistrate judge expressly provides that the reference is made under this rule.

[B]   FED. R. EVID. 706

Court Appointed Experts

(a) Appointment. The court may on its own motion or on the motion of any party enter an order to show cause why expert witnesses should not be appointed, and may request the parties to submit nominations. The court may appoint any expert witnesses agreed upon by the parties, and may appoint expert witnesses of its own selection. An expert witness shall not be appointed by the court unless the witness consents to act. A witness so appointed shall be informed of the witness' duties by the court in writing, a copy of which shall be filed with the clerk, or at a conference in which the parties shall have opportunity to participate. A witness so appointed shall advise the parties of the witness' findings, if any; the witness' deposition may be taken by any party; and the witness may be called to testify by the court or any party. The witness shall be subject to cross-examination by each party, including a party calling the witness.

[C]   Purpose

Pursuant to FED. R. CIV. P. 53 and FED. R. EVID. 706 the judge has the power to appoint a neutral expert to act as a special master or as an expert in computer-based discovery. Appointments under Rule 53 are not confined to experts; magistrate judges or other generalists may be designated to serve as special masters. Rule 53 authorizes many functions that can be assigned to a special master. The court can delegate judicial powers to preside at hearings, receive evidence, find facts, and reach conclusions of law.

Appointment of an expert under Rule 53 or 706 can assist in contentious technology disputes. A judge may appoint a neutral third party to supervise technical aspects of discovery, to act as a depository for sensitive, privileged, or disputed electronic information or assist the parties in formulating electronic discovery plans and protective orders. Because of the complexity and unfamiliarity of counsel with technology, both parties may benefit with the appointment of an expert.

[D]   Reported Cases

- *Medtronic v. Michelson,* No. CIV.01-2373, 2003 WL 21212601, at *9 (W.D. Tenn. May 13, 2003). The Court appointed a special master who was to be a neutral computer expert to assist with discovery. His duties included,

  making decisions with regard to search terms; overseeing the design of searches and the scheduling of searches and production; coordinating deliveries between the parties and their vendors; and advising both parties, at either's request, on cost estimates and technical issues. The special master shall be subject to all confidentiality requirements and protective orders set forth in this and in other orders in this cause. The special master may designate assistants with the parties' approval; if he or she does so, the same protective orders and confidentiality agreements shall apply to any assistants.

  In a subsequent order the Court in *Medtronic v. Michelson,* No. CIV.01-2373, 2004 WL 2905399, at *3 (W.D. Tenn. May 13, 2003) affirmed the special master's ruling and found that the "defendants' request for the production of deleted electronic files and e-mails is untimely as filed nearly five months after the close of discovery and unduly burdensome in light of the quickly approaching trial date."

- *Inventory Locator Serv. LLC v. Partsbase, Inc.,* No. CIV. 02-2695, 2006 WL 1646091 (W.D. Tenn. Jun. 14, 2006). The Court appointed a special master to determine the authenticity of the plaintiff's server-logs which were alleged to have been altered.

- *Gates Rubber Co. v. Bando Chemical Industries, Ltd.,* 167 F.R.D. 90 (D. Colo. 1996). The parties each appointed their own expert, with varying degrees of competence, and the results were counterproductive.

- *United States v. Microsoft Corp.,* 147 F.3d 935, 955 (D.C. Cir. 1998). "To the extent that adjudication may lead the court into deep technological mysteries, we note the court's power under Rule of Evidence 706 to appoint expert witnesses. Whether such an expert is appointed by agreement of the parties or not, the expert's exposure to cross-examination by both sides, *see* Rule 706(a), makes the device a far more apt way of drawing on expert resources than the district court's unilateral, unnoticed deputization of a vice-judge."

- *AdvantaCare Health Partners, LP v. Access IV,* No. CIV.03-04496, 2004 WL 1837997, at *9 (N.D. Cal. Aug. 17, 2004). "Plaintiffs contend that the Court should appoint a special master to oversee and ensure compliance with the preliminary injunction. Special masters are to be used sparingly and only where the use of the Court's time is not justified. (citation omitted) The appointment of a special master is appropriate where 'parties have failed to comply with Court orders, displayed intransigence in the litigation, or require close supervision.' Id. The Court is not persuaded that appointment of a special master is warranted."

- *Simon Property Group L.P. v. mySimon, Inc.,* 194 F.R.D. 639 (S.D. Ind. 2000). The Court ordered that plaintiff would appoint an expert who would serve as an officer of the court and turn over the recovered information to defendant for review of confidential information.

- *United States v. IBM,* 76 F.R.D. 97 (S.D.N.Y. 1977). In this case, the defendant was to produce information to the plaintiff pursuant to prior court orders, but production did not comport with spirit and intent of those orders and was highly technical and complex in nature. The Court determined that "exceptional conditions" existed, warranting appointment of an examiner. The examiner's duties included reporting to the court as to information that defendant possessed and produced and supervising discovery.

[E]   Other Authorities

- MANUAL FOR COMPLEX LITIGATION (FOURTH) § 11.52: "Special masters have increasingly been appointed for their expertise in particular fields, such as accounting, finance, science, and technology."

- The ABA Standards suggest that "[i]n complex cases and/or ones involving large volumes of electronic information, the court may want to consider using an expert to aid or advise the court on technology issues." ABA Standards, supra note 108, at 29 b.ii.

§ 7.12   TAXATION OF COSTS

[A]   Rule 54. Judgments; Costs

(a) Definition; Form. "Judgment" as used in these rules includes a decree and any order from which an appeal lies. A judgment shall not contain a recital of pleadings, the report of a master, or the record of prior proceedings.

* * *

(d) Costs; Attorneys' Fees.

(1) Costs Other than Attorneys' Fees. Except when express provision therefor is made either in a statute of the United States or in these rules, costs other than attorneys' fees shall be allowed as of course to the prevailing party unless the court otherwise directs; but costs against the United States, its officers, and agencies shall be imposed only to the extent permitted by law. Such costs may be taxed by the clerk on one day's notice. On motion served within 5 days thereafter, the action of the clerk may be reviewed by the court.

(2) Attorneys' Fees.

(A) Claims for attorneys' fees and related nontaxable expenses shall be made by motion unless the substantive law governing the action provides for the recovery of such fees as an element of damages to be proved at trial.

* * *

[B]   Purpose

FED. R. CIV. P. 54(d)(1) provides that "costs other than attorneys' fees shall be allowed as of course to the prevailing party" unless a statute, federal rule of civil procedure, or the court otherwise directs. Recoverable costs are listed in 28 U.S.C. § 1920:

(1) Fees of the clerk and marshal;
(2) Fees of the court reporter for all or any part of the stenographic transcript necessarily obtained for use in the case;
(3) Fees and disbursements for printing and witnesses;
(4) Fees for exemplification and copies of papers necessarily obtained for use in the case;
(5) Docket fees under section 1923 of this title;
(6) Compensation of court appointed experts, compensation of interpreters, and salaries, fees, expenses, and costs of special interpretation services under section 1828 of this title.

Courts may not award costs unauthorized by statute. *Barber v. Ruth,* 7 F.3d 636, 644 (7th Cir. 1993); *Northbrook Excess & Surplus Ins. Co. v. Proctor & Gamble Co.*, 924 F.2d 633, 642 (7th Cir. 1991).

[C]   Reported Cases

- *Summit Tech., Inc. v. Nidek Co.,* 435 F.3d 1371, 1374 (Fed. Cir. 2006). The Court found that database development costs by an outside vendor were clearly not recoverable under 28 U.S.C.S. § 1920.

- *Zenith Electronics Corp. v. WH-TV Broadcasting Corp.,* No. CIV.01-4366, 2004 WL 1631676 (N.D.Ill. Jul. 19, 2004). The Court found the following costs nonrecoverable under Rule 54; printing from electronic disks, the cost of numbering documents, the cost of a computer consultant and the cost of a consultant's work of reviewing files for privilege and preparing them for production.

- *Lanphere Enterprises, Inc. v. Jiffy Lube Intern., Inc.,* No. CIV.01-1168, 2004 WL 1080169 (D.Or. May 12, 2004). The Court denied the defendant's request for $6,325.00 for "database services" which were necessary to extract and organize data from the electronic information.

- *Mitchell-Proffitt Co. v. Eagle Crest, Inc.,* No. CIV.03-645, 2005 U.S. Dist. LEXIS 33535 (D. Fla. Nov. 28, 2005). In a copyright infringement action the Court, pursuant 28 U.S.C.S. § 1920, found that copying charges could be taxed as costs but not the costs for litigation support, scanning documents for exhibits and time-stamping of video for trial presentation.

- *In re Instinet Group, Inc.,* 2005 Del. Ch. LEXIS 195, at *9-10 (Del. Ch. Nov. 30, 2005). In a case involving the allowance of attorneys' fees and costs relating to shareholder litigation the Court stated:

> It is apparent that the plaintiffs undertook a massive document program in preparing for the preliminary injunction. As a result, they obtained several hundred thousand pages of production, from numerous sources, and devoted a very large amount of time to the review of these materials. . . . it is not unreasonable for the defendants to point out the obvious inefficiencies involved in this case, highlighted by the plaintiffs' decision to pay nearly $125,000 to convert documents produced in a digital format into a paper format. Rather than simply copying the electronic media to permit the plaintiffs' lawyers working on the case to search and review the document production on a computer screen, the plaintiffs spewed the digital production onto paper and, then, copied the paper for review. This approach both added unnecessary expense and greatly increased the number of hours required to search and review the document production. In fact, the time records submitted include a large number of hours, by multiple attorneys, spent reviewing the documents. Thus, the court must disagree with the plaintiffs' counsel's assertion that "this case was a paradigm of efficient litigation," and give less weight than customary to the number of hours expended

by plaintiffs' counsel. Additionally, it would be inappropriate to award the full amount of out-of-pocket expenses, as the very costly decision to "blow back" the digitized document discovery onto paper lacks justification.

§ 7.13   NEW TRIALS AND AMENDMENT OF JUDGMENTS

[A]   FED. R. CIV. P. 59

Rule 59. New Trials; Amendment of Judgments

(a) Grounds. A new trial may be granted to all or any of the parties and on all or part of the issues (1) in an action in which there has been a trial by jury, for any of the reasons for which new trials have heretofore been granted in actions at law in the courts of the United States; and (2) in an action tried without a jury, for any of the reasons for which rehearings have heretofore been granted in suits in equity in the courts of the United States. On a motion for a new trial in an action tried without a jury, the court may open the judgment if one has been entered, take additional testimony, amend findings of fact and conclusions of law or make new findings and conclusions, and direct the entry of a new judgment.

[B]   (Reserved)

[C]   Reported Cases

- *Wild v. Alster,* 377 F. Supp. 2d 186, 193-195 (D.D.C. 2005). The Court denied plaintiff's motion for a new trial where she argued that she was entitled to have an expert examine the hard drive of the defendants' computer to explore whether it contained the dates that photographs of the plaintiff were taken. She had alleged a doctor had altered the photographs after her malpractice claim was filed.

- *Perez v. Volvo Car Corp.,* 247 F.3d 303, 318 (1st Cir. 2001). After the Court had ruled on a summary judgment motion, the plaintiff requested relief since the defendant failed to turn over e-mail in a timely matter. The Court ruled the e-mail could be considered as "newly discovered" evidence and stated, "[a]fter all, Volvo did not produce the e-mails to the plaintiffs until January 2000 (the same month that Volvo filed its summary judgment motion) - and then only in Swedish. Given the timing, the sheer volume of documents involved in the case, and the need for translation, fundamental fairness counsels in favor of treating the e-mails as newly-discovered evidence within the purview of Federal Rule of Civil Procedure 59(e)."

- *Columbia Communications v. Echostar,* 2 Fed. Appx. 360, 368 (4th Cir. 2001). On appeal the Appellant argued as one ground for a new trial that the Appellee failed to disclose certain computer databases during discovery. The Court ruled that "[a] Rule 59 motion should be granted when: '(1) the verdict is against the clear weight of the evidence, or (2) is based upon evidence which is false, or (3) will result in a miscarriage of justice, even though there may be substantial evidence which would prevent the direction of a verdict.'" In this case the Court ruled that the appellant had failed to meet this standard since the databases, if disclosed, would have been only "marginally helpful."

• *Jinks-Umstead v. England,* 227 F.R.D. 143 (D.D.C. 2005). The Court granted the plaintiff a new trial after the defendant provided relevant database reports after the plaintiff rested her case.

§ 7.14   INJUNCTIONS

[A]   FED. R. CIV. P. 65

Rule 65. Injunctions
(a) Preliminary Injunction.

(1) *Notice.* No preliminary injunction shall be issued without notice to the adverse party.

* * *

(b) Temporary Restraining Order; Notice; Hearing; Duration. A temporary restraining order may be granted without written or oral notice to the adverse party or that party's attorney only if (1) it clearly appears from specific facts shown by affidavit or by the verified complaint that immediate and irreparable injury, loss, or damage will result to the applicant before the adverse party or that party's attorney can be heard in opposition, and (2) the applicant's attorney certifies to the court in writing the efforts, if any, which have been made to give the notice and the reasons supporting the claim that notice should not be required.

[B]   Purpose

It may be necessary to pursue a temporary restraining order (TRO) or a permanent injunction pursuant to Rule 65 to preserve electronic data or seize copyrighted computer materials. Rule 65(b) also provides the procedural framework for obtaining a TRO without notice to the opposing party.

An ex parte seizure order is a court order authorizing the seizure of relevant evidence. Rule 65 is the primary authority for issuing ex parte seizure orders. Oftentimes the order is obtained without notice to the opposing party in order to prevent the opposing party from destroying or concealing any electronic evidence relevant to the litigation. They are difficult to obtain. *See also,* § 7.3[E], *Discovery and Preservation Orders - Rule 16(c).*

[C]   Reported Cases

Preservation of computer data

- *Physicians Interactive v. Lathian Systems, Inc.,* No. CA.03-1193, 2003 WL 23018270, at *10 (E.D. Va. Dec. 5, 2003). The Court granted an injunction where defendants allegedly hacked into plaintiffs' website and stole their confidential customer lists and computer software code. The Court enjoined the defendant from using any of the information obtained and on any future attacks on the system. The Court also granted the plaintiff limited "expedited discovery to enter the sites where the computers used in the alleged attacks are located and to obtain a 'mirror image'" of the computer equipment used in the attacks. Further, the Court ruled that this discovery "must be done with the assistance of a computer forensic expert." *See also, Dodge, Warren, & Peters Ins. Servs. v. Riley,* 130 Cal. Rptr.2d 385 (Cal. Ct. App. 2003); *But see, The Gorgen Co. v. Brecht,* 2002 WL 977467 (Minn. Ct. App. May 14, 2002) (where the Court denied a TRO for misappropriation of trade secret data).

- *Henry v. IAC/Interactive Group,* No. CIV.05-1510, 2006 U.S. Dist. LEXIS 24942 (D. Wash. Feb. 14, 2006). In this employment action the Court granted defendant's preliminary injunction requiring the plaintiff to return the defendant employer's laptop and all electronic files, e-mails, etc. that she may have accessed or provided to her attorney or others.

- *Hypro, LLC v. Reser,* No. CIV.04-4921, 2004 WL 2905321 (D. Minn. Dec. 10, 2004). The Court after discussing the various factors granted a TRO granted on behalf of the plaintiffs as well as a protective order. The order covered protection of confidential business information, precluding a competing business, engaging in consulting and other activities in competition with the plaintiff and from attempting to evade the provisions of this TRO.

- *Am. Family Mut. Ins. v. Roth,* No. CIV.05-3839, 2005 U.S. Dist. LEXIS 39567, at *92-93 (D. Ill. Aug. 5, 2005). The magistrate in a detailed opinion recommended that a preliminary injunction be issued precluding the defendants from using a "customer list and [a] . . . mass of other confidential information."

- *QZO, Inc. v. Moyer,* 2004 WL 502288 (S.C. Ct. App. Mar. 15, 2004). After the Court issued a TRO to turn over a computer, a former corporate officer "reformatted" his hard drive which led the court to enter judgment for the opposing party.

- *CFTC v. Yanev,* No. CIV. 05-900, 2005 U.S. Dist. LEXIS 39304 (D. Ohio Dec. 12, 2005). In an agreed upon settlement the Court entered a preliminary injunction for the defendant to immediately cease operating specific websites.

- *Armstrong v. Bush,* 807 F. Supp. 816, 823 (D.D.C. 1992). The Court entered a temporary restraining order pursuant to Rule 65(c) requiring the preservation of current and existing computer backup tapes.

- *Smith v. Texaco, Inc.,* 951 F. Supp. 109 (E.D. Tex. 1997). A state court entered a TRO pursuant to Rule 65 preventing the defendants from deleting any electronic data relating to the plaintiff's discrimination claim. After removal to the federal court, the court modified the preservation order to permit the defendant to operate under a normal document retention and destruction policy, provided hard copies were made of all records.

- *Adobe Sys., Inc. v. Sun South Prod., Inc.,* 187 F.R.D. 636 (S.D. Cal. 1999). The Court in denying an ex parte TRO in a computer piracy suit held the preservation of computer data was not an issue since the "[m]anual or automated deletion of that software may remove superficial indicia, such as its icons or presence in the user's application menu. However, telltale traces of a previous installation remain, such as abandoned subdirectories, libraries, information in system files, and registry keys . . . Even if an infringer managed to delete every file associated with Plaintiffs' software, Plaintiffs could still recover many of those files since the operating system does not actually erase the files, but merely marks the space consumed by the files as free for use by other files."

Ex parte seizure of computers

   Under certain circumstances, which are narrowly prescribed, the computers of the opposing party may be seized without notice to the opposing party. These generally involve seizure of copyrighted materials.

- *FMC Technologies, Inc. v. Edwards,* No. CIV.05-946, 2005 WL 1312110, at *1 (W.D. Wash. Jun. 1, 2005). The court in denying a request for a TRO to retrieve computer drawings that had been downloaded set forth the factors in considering an application for a TRO. The Court stated: "In deciding whether to issue a TRO, courts generally look to the following four factors: (1) likelihood of success on the merits; (2) threat of irreparable harm to the plaintiff if the injunction is not imposed; (3) the relative balance of harm to the plaintiff and harm to the defendant; and (4) the public interest."

- *Comcast of St. Paul, Inc. v. Boyle,* No. CIV.04-4698, 2004 WL 2801588 (D. Minn. Nov. 4, 2004). The Court's opinion sets forth the content of the TRO issued pursuant to FED.R.CIV.P. 64 "directing seizure of Defendants' business records, including computers and computer accessories such as tapes and disks on which records are stored, and Defendants' inventory of 'pirate' cable television decoding equipment and any proceeds of Defendants' illegal business."

- *Microsoft Corp. v. Computer Warehouse*, 83 F. Supp. 2d 256 (D.P.R. 2000). Microsoft alleged that a retailer had sold a computer with copies of the manufacturer's products illegally installed. The Court granted Microsoft's request for an ex parte order for seizure and impoundment of copyright infringing materials.

- *First Technology Safety Systems, Inc. v. Depinet*, 11 F.3d 641, 651 (6th Cir. 1993). The plaintiffs obtained an ex parte order of seizure and impoundment of computer programs, computer printouts and documents. The Sixth Circuit reversed the ex parte order holding that it must be shown that the adverse party has "a history of disposing of evidence or violating court orders or that persons similar to the adverse party have such a history."

- *Adobe Systems, Inc. v. Ajine*, No. CIV.01-00009, 2001 WL 252916 (W.D. Va. Feb. 12, 2001). The Court rejected plaintiffs' ex parte request to seize and prevent the sale of unauthorized copies of copyrighted software and records of prior sales, since there was no showing that the defendant is likely to destroy evidence.

- *Religious Tech. Center v. Netcom On-Line Communication Servs., Inc.*, 923 F. Supp. 1231 (N.D. Cal. 1995). The Court vacated an ex parte seizure order because of the failure to show the likelihood that evidence would be destroyed.

- *Quotron Systems, Inc. v. Automatic Data Processing, Inc.*, 141 F.R.D. 37 (S.D.N.Y. 1992). In a copyright infringement and trade secret misappropriation case, the Court granted an ex parte order to prevent the defendant from destroying software before discovery could take place.

- *Sega Enterprises Ltd. v. MAPHIA*, 948 F. Supp. 923 (N.D. Cal. 1996). The plaintiff was able to seize the defendant's computer, memory devices and to copy the memory showing defendant uploaded and downloaded unauthorized versions of video games.

Prohibiting Internet activities

- *FTC v. Odysseus Mktg.*, No. CIV.05-330, 2006 U.S. Dist. LEXIS 30230 (D.N.H. Apr. 19, 2006). The Court signed an extensive preliminary injunction order precluding the defendants from conducting internet activities that violate FTC regulations.

This page intentionally left blank.

Chapter 8

Admissibility of Electronic Evidence

§ 8.1   GENERALLY

Each use of a computer (or other electronic device) results in the generation of potential electronic evidence.

Computers have changed from being used as mere depositories of information, to a myriad of other uses. For business purposes, they are used to conduct online transactions, create documents, track revenue and expenses, and to communicate with others. Personal use consists of individuals communicating by e-mail or instant messenger, paying their bills online, filing taxes electronically, keeping track of their finances and much more.

All of this electronic information may be used in legal proceedings as evidence, if relevant. Thus, electronic evidence is information existing in an electronic (digital) form, relevant to the issues in a case.

As businesses began to use computers in the late 1960s and early 1970s, the federal courts had the foresight to create a legal framework governing the discovery and admissibility of electronic information. For example, the 1970 federal advisory committee, which drafts the Federal Rule of Civil Procedure and Federal Rule of Evidence, changed FED. R. CIV. P. 34 and provided:

> The inclusive description of 'documents' is revised to accord with changing technology. It makes clear that Rule 34 [Federal Rules of Civil Procedure] applies to electronics data compilations from which information can be obtained only with the use of detection devices, and that when the data can as a practical matter be made usable by the discovering party only through respondent's devices, respondent may be required to use his devices to translate the data into usable form.

FED. R. CIV. P. 34 advisory committee notes.

Another example of this foresight is the enactment of FED. R. EVID. 1001 where Congress expanded the definitions of writing to include "computers, photographic systems, and other modern developments."

However, electronic information can pose unique and different challenges as to its admissibility. To ensure its introduction, obstacles such as authenticity, relevancy and hearsay objections must be overcome.

§ 8.2   EVIDENTIARY ISSUES

There are basic evidentiary issues that need to be addressed prior to admission of electronic evidence. Some questions to consider:

• Is the evidence relevant? (FED. R. EVID. 401-404.)

- Is there sufficient evidence for the court to grant preliminary admission of the evidence? (FED. R. EVID. 104).

- Can the evidence be properly authenticated? (FED. R. EVID. 901).

- Is the evidence hearsay and not subject to an exception? (FED. R. EVID. 801-803).

- Does the Best Evidence Rule require the original of the document to be produced? (FED. R. EVID. 1001-1003).

§ 8.3 FEDERAL RULES OF EVIDENCE

[A] Generally

The law of evidence controls the admission of facts in trial. The Federal Rules of Evidence, first adopted in 1975, apply to both criminal and civil cases in federal courts. FED. R. EVID. 101 and 1101. These evidentiary rules and procedures provide for the admission and exclusion of evidence.

More than thirty states have adopted codes that closely follow the Federal Rules of Evidence. Anthony J. Dreyer, *When the Postman Beeps Twice: The Admissibility of Electronic Mail Under the Business Records Exception of the Federal Rules of Evidence,* Fordham L. Rev. (April 1996).

[B] Direct and Circumstantial Evidence

Generally, evidence is divided into one of two categories: direct and circumstantial. A statement by a witness that he saw a particular event occur is direct evidence. "Direct evidence is evidence which, if believed, proves the existence of a fact without inference or presumption." *Scott v. Suncoast Beverage Sales, Ltd.,* 295 F.3d 1223, 1227 (11th Cir. 2002); *Caldera, Inc. v. Microsoft Corp.,* 72 F. Supp. 2d 1295 (D. Utah 1999) (court found that several intracompany e-mail offered "direct evidence" that Microsoft was trying to destroy a competitor.); *Salkovitz v. Pioneer Electronics (USA), Inc.,* No. CIV.04-344, 2005 WL 1638141 (D.N.J. Jul. 12, 2005) (court found no direct evidence of discrimination though slide show presentation had the word "retire" next to the plaintiff's name).

The proof of a fact from which the existence of a material fact is inferred is commonly referred to as circumstantial evidence. Circumstantial evidence is indirect evidence that is "based on inference and not on personal knowledge or observation." Black's Law Dictionary, 576 (7th ed. 1999). Even if a factfinder accepts circumstantial evidence as true, "additional reasoning is required to reach the proposition to which it is directed." *City of Tuscaloosa v. Harcros Chemicals, Inc.,* 158 F.3d 548, 565 (11th Cir. 1998) (citing *McCormick on Evidence* § 185 (4th ed. 1992)); *Cole v. Teel Plastics, Inc.,* No. CIV.04-633,

2005 WL 1378911 (W.D.Wis. Jun. 8, 2005) (e-mail from supervisor in employment case found not to be either direct or circumstantial evidence of discrimination).

[C]   Application to Electronic Evidence

The Federal Rules of Evidence apply to computerized data as they do to other types of evidence. *United States v. De Georgia,* 420 F.2d 889, 893 (9th Cir. 1969) ("[I]t is immaterial that the business record is maintained in a computer rather than in company books"); *United States v. Russo,* 480 F.2d 1228, 1239 (6th Cir. 1973) (noting "the extent to which businesses today depend on computers for a myriad of functions," the court stated that the FBRA [Federal Business Record Act] "should never be interpreted so strictly as to deprive the courts of the realities of business and professional practices."); *United States v. Croft,* 750 F.2d 1354, 1364 (7th Cir. 1984) (citing *United States v. Young Brothers, Inc.,* 728 F.2d 682, 694 (5th Cir.), *cert. denied,* 469 U.S. 881(1984); FED. R. EVID. 1001(1) ("'Writings' and 'recordings' consist of . . . electronic recording, or other form of data compilation."). FED. R. EVID. 1001(3) ("If data are stored in a computer or similar device, any printout or other output readable by sight, shown to reflect the data accurately, is an 'original'").

§ 8.4   PRELIMINARY QUESTIONS

[A]   Rule 104

Rule 104. Preliminary Questions

(a) Questions of admissibility generally. Preliminary questions concerning the qualification of a person to be a witness, the existence of a privilege, or the admissibility of evidence shall be determined by the court, subject to the provisions of subdivision (b). In making its determination it is not bound by the rules of evidence except those with respect to privileges.

(b) Relevancy conditioned on fact. When the relevancy of evidence depends upon the fulfillment of a condition of fact, the court shall admit it upon, or subject to, the introduction of evidence sufficient to support a finding of the fulfillment of the condition.

*   *   *

(e) Weight and credibility. This rule does not limit the right of a party to introduce before the jury evidence relevant to weight or credibility.

[B]   Generally

During trial, the judge decides questions of law and the jury questions of fact. The jury weighs contradictory evidence and the credibility of witnesses and decides the case based on the court's instructions and the facts presented. However, an important function for the judge is determining the question of admissibility of facts. FED. R. EVID. 104(a) and (b) provides that the preliminary question of admissibility and the determination of the initial relevance of evidence is a function of the court, rather than a jury. *Colorado Nat. Bank v. First Nat. Bank & Trust Co.,* 459 F. Supp. 1366 (W.D. Mich. 1978). Essentially, the court decides whether the foundational facts for evidence have been established

FED. R. EVID. 104 advisory committee notes state:

> The applicability of a particular rule of evidence often depends upon the existence of a condition. Is the alleged expert a qualified physician? Is a witness whose former testimony is offered, unavailable? Was a stranger present during a conversation between attorney and client? In each instance the admissibility of evidence will turn upon the answer to the question of the existence of the condition. Accepted practice, incorporated in the rule, places on the judge the responsibility for these determinations. *McCormick* § 53; *Morgan, Basic Problems of Evidence* 45-50 (1962).

As to matters such as authenticity of computer evidence (such as e-mail) it is up to the judge to make a preliminary decision on admissibility. The ultimate decision as to the weight to give the evidence, including its authenticity, is a question of fact, and up to the trier of fact. FED. R. EVID. 104, 901 and 1008.

In making its preliminary determination, the court is not bound by the exclusionary rules of the evidence, except those relating to privilege. FED. R. EVID. 104(a) & 1101(d)(1); *United States v. Matlock,* 415 U.S. 164, 173-174 (U.S. 1974). For example, in determining whether a witness is available to testify, the court may allow hearsay evidence as to the location of the witness. In ruling on these preliminary issues the FED. R. EVID. 104 advisory committee notes indicate the court should hear any relevant evidence in making those determinations, including affidavits.

Preliminary determinations include questions regarding the qualifications of witnesses and admissibility of evidence. *See,* FED. R. EVID. 104(a).

[C]   Reported Cases

• *American Exp. Travel Related Servs. v. Vinhnee (In re Vinhnee),* No. CIV.04-1284, 336 B.R. 437, 443, 447 (Bankr. Fed. App. 2005). The Ninth Circuit Bankruptcy Appellate Panel held that the bankruptcy court did not abuse its discretion in refusing to admit computerized records without proper authentication. In ruling upon the preliminary admissibility of evidence the Court stated, "[t]he court acts as gatekeeper on the preliminary questions regarding the admissibility of evidence. FED. R. EVID. 104. . . . Because this appeal involves a bench trial in which the roles of court and trier of fact are merged, we need not address the differences between Rules 104(a) and (b). There is authority that authenticity implicates Rule 104(b) 'relevancy conditioned on fact' as to which the court makes a preliminary ruling and leaves to the trier of fact the ultimate resolution of the authenticity question. . . . (citations omitted) Since the functions were merged and the court was not persuaded that the records were authentic, the distinction makes no difference in this appeal. . . . The admissibility of evidence is a preliminary question for the court to resolve, which may be done on declaration without being bound by the rules of evidence other than privilege rules."

- *Huddleston v. United States,* 485 U.S. 681, 689-690 (1988). "In determining whether the Government has introduced sufficient evidence to meet Rule 104(b), the trial court neither weighs credibility nor makes a finding that the Government has proved the conditional fact by a preponderance of the evidence. The court simply examines all the evidence in the case and decides whether the jury could reasonably find the conditional fact (here, that the televisions were stolen) by a preponderance of the evidence."

- *Daubert v. Merrell Dow Pharmaceuticals, Inc.,* 509 U.S. 579 (1993). In this case, it was determined that the court has the authority to determine preliminary questions of law to preclude expert testimony under FED. R. EVID. 702.

- *United States v. Nichols,* 169 F.3d 1255, 1263 (10th Cir.), *cert. denied,* 120 S.Ct. 336 (1999). The court stated, "*Daubert* challenges, like other preliminary questions of admissibility, are governed by FED. R. EVID. 104."

- *Commerce Funding Corp. v. Comprehensive Habilitation Services, Inc.,* No. CIV.01-3796, 2004 WL 1970144, at *4 (S.D.N.Y. Sept. 3, 2004). In this contractual case the Court in considering a Motion in Limine found that certain documents and e-mails met the threshold proof of Rule 104. The Court found that its decision may be "subject to change when the case unfolds . . . [and] noting that once shaky, unreliable evidence is admitted, such evidence is best challenged with '[v]igorous cross-examination, presentation of contrary evidence, and careful instruction on the burden of proof.' (quoting *Daubert v. Merrell Dow Pharmaceuticals, Inc.,* 509 U.S. 579, 596 (1993)."

§ 8.5   REMAINDER OF OR RELATED WRITINGS OR RECORDED STATEMENTS

[A]   Rule 106

Rule 106. Remainder Of or Related Writings or Recorded Statements

When a writing or recorded statement or part thereof is introduced by a party, an adverse party may require the introduction at that time of any other part or any other writing or recorded statement which ought in fairness to be considered contemporaneously with it.

[B] Generally

Rule 106 provides that whenever a conversation or writing is admitted in evidence, the opposing party may offer the remaining portion of the writing or conversation. *Beach Aircraft Corp.*, 488 U.S. 153 (1988). The purpose of the rule is to prevent a "misleading impression created by taking matters out of context." FED. R. EVID. 106 advisory committee notes; *United States v. Dorrell*, 758 F.2d 427 (9th Cir. 1985); *United States v. Rubin*, 609 F.2d 51 (2d Cir. 1979), *aff'd*, 449 U.S. 424 (1981).

[C] Reported Cases

- *Blue Cross and Blue Shield of New Jersey, Inc. v. Philip Morris, Inc.*, 199 F.R.D. 487, 489 (E.D.N.Y. 2001). After reviewing the history of Rule 106 and other authorities, the Court in tobacco litigation ruled that the plaintiff would be permitted to play deposition videotaped clips without interruption from the defendants.

- *In re Air Crash Disaster at J.F.K. Airport*, 635 F.2d 67, 73 (2nd Cir. 1980). The Court had the discretion under FED. R. EVID. 106 to order the entire tape of a cockpit voice recorder played, instead of just one voice channel.

- *Mariani v. United States*, 80 F. Supp. 2d 352, 361 (M.D. Pa. 1999). The Court allowed the remainder of a document to be read into evidence to demonstrate the overall tenor of the document.

§ 8.6 JUDICIAL NOTICE

[A] Rule 201

Rule 201. Judicial Notice of Adjudicative Facts

(a) Scope of rule. This rule governs only judicial notice of adjudicative facts.

(b) Kinds of facts. A judicially noticed fact must be one not subject to reasonable dispute in that it is either (1) generally known within the territorial jurisdiction of the trial court or (2) capable of accurate and ready determination by resort to sources whose accuracy cannot reasonably be questioned.

(c) When discretionary. A court may take judicial notice, whether requested or not.

(d) When mandatory. A court shall take judicial notice if requested by a party and supplied with the necessary information.

(e) Opportunity to be heard. A party is entitled upon timely request to an opportunity to be heard as to the propriety of taking judicial notice and the tenor of the matter noticed. In the absence of prior notification, the request may be made after judicial notice has been taken.

(f) Time of taking notice. Judicial notice may be taken at any stage of the proceeding.

(g) Instructing jury. In a civil action or proceeding, the court shall instruct the jury to accept as conclusive any fact judicially noticed. In a criminal case, the court shall instruct the jury that it may, but is not required to, accept as conclusive any fact judicially noticed.

[B]   Generally

FED. R. EVID. 201 provides an exception to the ordinary requirement that record evidence support any judicial finding of fact. Rule 201(b) permits a court to take "judicial notice" of a particular fact where that fact is "not subject to reasonable dispute in that [the fact] is either (1) generally known within the territorial jurisdiction of the trial court or (2) capable of accurate and ready determination by resort to sources whose accuracy cannot reasonably be questioned."

The purpose of judicial notice is to relieve a party from having to formally present evidence to prove a fact that is "outside the area of reasonable controversy." FED. R. EVID. 201 advisory committee notes. "The usual method of establishing adjudicative facts is through the introduction of evidence, ordinarily consisting of the testimony of witnesses. If particular facts are outside the area of reasonable controversy, this process is dispensed with as unnecessary. A high degree of indisputability is the essential prerequisite." *Id.*

A safeguard provided by the rule is that the party adversely affected by the court taking judicial notice of a fact must have an opportunity to be heard as to the propriety of that action.

[C]   Reported Cases

* *Wible v. Aetna Life Ins. Co.,* No. CIV.04-04219, 2005 WL 1592907 (C.D.Cal. Jun. 20, 2005). In this ERISA action the Court took judicial notice of website evidence from an Amazon web page and a page from the website of the American Academy of Allergy Asthma & Immunology.

- *People v. Rivera,* 182 Ill. App. 3d 33, 42, 537 N.E.2d 924, 931 (1989). The Court concluded that the trial: [J]udge correctly held that he could take judicial notice that IBM is a "standard, reliable computer," citing People v. Hendricks, 145 Ill. App.3d 71, 495 N.E.2d 85, 110 (Ill. 1986), where the Court stated: "There can be no question that computer science has created many devices, the reliability of which can scarcely be questioned. We should therefore apply the rule that its accuracy and reliability is judicially noticeable, requiring only proof of the accuracy and proper operation of the particular device under consideration. The trial court did not err in taking judicial notice that the IBM/PC is a standard, reliable computer."

- *Neal v. United States,* 402 F. Supp. 678, 680 (D.N.J. 1975). The Court took judicial notice of IRS tax refund errors citing the "GIGO Rule of Computers (Garbage In, Garbage Out)."

- *Cardiello v. The Money Store, Inc.,* No. CIV.00-7332, 2001 WL 604007, at *9 (S.D.N.Y. Jun. 1, 2001). "Indeed, we take judicial notice of the fact that a great deal of correspondence from consumer lenders is standardized, computer generated notices that are routinely issued with little or no individual review. Although automation would not excuse otherwise illegal actions, elevating routine notices to statutory violation in the absence of any harm is wholly unwarranted."

- See also cases and other legal authorities under *Specific Type of Computer Evidence* § 8.12 *et al.* for the application of the judicial notice doctrine to specific types of electronic data.

§ 8.7   RELEVANCY

[A]   Rules 401 - 403

Rule 401. Definition of "Relevant Evidence"

"Relevant evidence" means evidence having any tendency to make the existence of any fact that is of consequence to the determination of the action more probable or less probable than it would be without the evidence.

Rule 402. Relevant Evidence Generally Admissible; Irrelevant Evidence Inadmissible

All relevant evidence is admissible, except as otherwise provided by the Constitution of the United States, by Act of Congress, by these rules, or by other rules prescribed by the Supreme Court pursuant to statutory authority. Evidence which is not relevant is not admissible.

Rule 403. Exclusion of Relevant Evidence on Grounds of Prejudice, Confusion, or Waste of Time

Although relevant, evidence may be excluded if its probative value is substantially outweighed by the danger of unfair prejudice, confusion of the issues, or misleading the jury, or by considerations of undue delay, waste of time, or needless presentation of cumulative evidence.

[B]   Generally

The central tenet in the law of evidence is that of relevance. As to relevancy, FED. R. EVID. 401 advisory committee notes state:

> The variety of relevancy problems is coextensive with the ingenuity of counsel in using circumstantial evidence as a means of proof. . . . Relevancy is not an inherent characteristic of any item of evidence but exists only as a relation between an item of evidence and a matter properly provable in the case. Does the item of evidence tend to prove the matter sought to be proved? Whether the relationship exists depends upon principles evolved by experience or science, applied logically to the situation at hand. The rule summarizes this relationship as a "tendency to make the existence" of the fact to be proved "more probable or less probable." (citation omitted).

The traditional focus of relevancy is whether the offered evidence tends to establish the factual proposition for which it is offered. The test is whether the evidence has "any tendency to make the existence of the fact more or less probable then not would be without the evidence." FED. R. EVID. 401. *Residential Funding Corp. v. Degeorge Financial Corp.,* 306 F.3d 99 (2nd Cir. 2002); *United States v. Williams,* 900 F.2d 823, 826 (5th Cir. 1990).

According to FED. R. EVID. 403, relevant evidence may be excluded, however, if it's usefulness on an issue is substantially outweighed by the danger it poses of unfair prejudice, confusion of the issues, misleading or a waste of court time. FED. R. EVID. 403 advisory committee notes states:

> The case law recognizes that certain circumstances call for the exclusion of evidence which is of unquestioned relevance. These circumstances entail risks that range all the way from inducing decision on a purely emotional basis, at one extreme, to nothing more harmful than merely wasting time, at the other extreme. Situations in this area call for balancing the probative value of and need for the evidence against the harm likely to result from its admission.

Exclusions under FED. R. EVID. 403 are reviewable under an abuse of discretion standard. *Old Chief v. United States,* 519 U.S. 172 (1997). The court has the discretion to limit admissibility as to the scope of evidence and the parties. FED. R. EVID. 105.

For reported cases involving relevancy as it relates to pretrial discovery of electronic information *see* § 7.4[F], *Relevancy and Overbroad Concerns - Rule 26(b)(1)*.

[C]   Reported Cases

- *United States v. Scholle,* 553 F.2d 1109 (8th Cir. 1977), *cert. denied,* 98 S.Ct. 432 (1977). The determination of relevancy concerning printouts from a computer system was within broad discretion of the trial judge.

- *J.P. Morgan Chase Bank v. Liberty Mutual Ins.,* No. CIV.01-11523, 2002 WL 31867731 (S.D.N.Y. Dec. 23, 2002). The Court ruled pursuant to Rule 403 that e-mails sent by senior bank officials would be allowed into evidence as probative of the defendant's argument that transactions were "off-the-books" loans.

- *Williams v. Sprint/United Mgmt. Co.,* 230 F.R.D. 640, 652-653 (D. Kan. 2005). The Court ordered an employer in an employment discrimination case to restore the metadata it had "scrubbed" or "erased" from Excel spreadsheet files and "unlock" them. In denying a relevancy objection to the metadata the Court found that ". . . metadata associated with any changes to the spreadsheets, the dates of any changes, the identification of the individuals making any changes, and other metadata from which Plaintiffs could determine the final versus draft version of the spreadsheets appear relevant."

- *Daubert v. Merrell Dow Pharmaceuticals, Inc.,* 113 S.Ct. 2786, 2793, 2794 (1993). FED. R. EVID. 402 provides the baseline for determining the admissibility of evidence in the federal courts.

- See also cases and other legal authorities under *Specific Type of Computer Evidence* § 8.12 et al. discussing relevancy requirements for specific types of electronic data.

§ 8.8   TESTIMONY AND OPINIONS BY EXPERTS AND LAY WITNESSES

[A]   Rules 701 - 705

Rule 701. Opinion Testimony by Lay Witnesses

If the witness is not testifying as an expert, the witness' testimony in the form of opinions or inferences is limited to those opinions or inferences which are (a) rationally based on the perception of the witness, (b) helpful to a clear understanding of the witness' testimony or the determination of a fact in issue, and (c) not based on scientific, technical, or other specialized knowledge within the scope of Rule 702.

Rule 702. Testimony by Experts

If scientific, technical, or other specialized knowledge will assist the trier of fact to understand the evidence or to determine a fact in issue, a witness qualified as an expert by knowledge, skill, experience, training, or education, may testify thereto in the form of an opinion or otherwise, if (1) the testimony is based upon sufficient facts or data, (2) the testimony is the product of reliable principles and methods, and (3) the witness has applied the principles and methods reliably to the facts of the case.

Rule 703. Bases of Opinion Testimony by Experts

The facts or data in the particular case upon which an expert bases an opinion or inference may be those perceived by or made known to the expert at or before the hearing. If of a type reasonably relied upon by experts in the particular field in forming opinions or inferences upon the subject, the facts or data need not be admissible in evidence in order for the opinion or inference to be admitted. Facts or data that are otherwise inadmissible shall not be disclosed to the jury by the proponent of the opinion or inference unless the court determines that their probative value in assisting the jury to evaluate the expert's opinion substantially outweighs their prejudicial effect.

Rule 704. Opinion on Ultimate Issue

(a) Except as provided in subdivision (b), testimony in the form of an opinion or inference otherwise admissible is not objectionable because it embraces an ultimate issue to be decided by the trier of fact.

(b) No expert witness testifying with respect to the mental state or condition of a defendant in a criminal case may state an opinion or inference as to whether the defendant did or did not have the mental state or condition constituting an element of the crime charged or of a defense thereto. Such ultimate issues are matters for the trier of fact alone.

Rule 705. Disclosure of Facts or Data Underlying Expert Opinion

The expert may testify in terms of opinion or inference and give reasons therefor without first testifying to the underlying facts or data, unless the court requires otherwise. The expert may in any event be required to disclose the underlying facts or data on cross-examination.

[B]   Generally

[1]   Lay Witness Testimony

A lay witness's testimony must state the facts, not the inferences or conclusions that the witness has drawn from those facts. After hearing the facts, the jury or trier of fact is capable of drawing inferences from the facts. *United States v. Jackson,* 688 F.2d 1121 (7th Cir. 1982), *cert. denied,* 103 S.Ct. 1441(1983). However, this rule is difficult to apply since:

> [I]n a way, all human assertions are opinions. . . . Our whole conscious life is a process of forming working beliefs or opinions from the evidence of our senses, few of them exactly accurate, most of them near enough correct for practical use, some of them seriously erroneous. Every assertion involves the expression of one or more of these opinions. A rule of evidence which called for the exclusion of opinion in this broad sense would therefore make trials quite impossible.

Maguire, *Evidence: Common Sense and Common Law,* 24 (Foundation Press, 1947).

To solve these difficulties, FED. R. EVID. 701, entitled Opinion Testimony by Lay Witnesses, permits lay opinions under prescribed circumstances. Besides being subject to different disclosure requirements, "a witness' opinion is limited 'to those opinions and inferences which are (a) rationally based on the perception of the witness, (b) helpful to a clear understanding of the witness' testimony or the determination of a fact in issue, and (c) not based on scientific, technical, or other specialized knowledge within the scope of Rule 702.' FED. R. EVID. 701." *Morgan v. U.S. Xpress, Inc.,* No. CIV.03-88, 2006 U.S. Dist. LEXIS 7225, at *5-8 (D. Ga. Feb. 3, 2006); *Bazak Int'l. Corp. v. Tarrant Apparel Group,* 378 F. Supp. 2d 377, 392 (D.N.Y. 2005) (court noted that authenticity of e-mail could not be determined by witness affidavit where a witness was not designated as an "expert witness" and failed to meet the "lay witness" requirements set forth under FED. R. EVID. 701).

[2]   Expert Testimony

Rule 702 through 705 of the Federal Rules of Evidence governs the admissibility of expert testimony. In order to testify as an expert, Rule 702 requires the testimony satisfy three requirements: (1) the witness must be qualified as an expert "by knowledge, skill, experience, training or education," (2) the subject matter of the testimony must be "scientific, technical, or other specialized knowledge," and (3) the expert's knowledge must "assist the trier of fact to understand the evidence or to determine a fact in issue."

The United States Supreme Court, in *Daubert v. Merrell Dow Pharms., Inc.,* 113 S. Ct. 2786, 2795, 2796 (1993) imposed on the trial judge the "gatekeeping" responsibility of determining "at the outset, pursuant to Rule 104(a) whether the expert is proposing to testify to (1) scientific knowledge that (2) will assist the trier of fact to understand or determine a fact in issue." *Daubert* requires a trial judge to conduct the "preliminary assessment of whether the reasoning or methodology underlying the testimony is scientifically valid and of whether that reasoning or methodology properly can be applied to the facts in issue." *Id.* at 2796.

For testimony to be within the scope of "scientific knowledge," there must be a showing that the basis of the expert's opinion lies within the methods and procedures of science. The subjective belief of an expert witness or his unsupported speculation is insufficient to meet this standard. This gatekeeping function was extended by the Supreme Court in *Kumho Tire Co. v. Carmichael,* 119 S. Ct. 1167 (1999) in holding that *Daubert's* "gatekeeping" obligation applied not only to "scientific" testimony, but to all expert testimony.

The purpose of expert testimony is to provide evidence that will assist the trier of fact, beyond its own competence. In order for expert testimony to be admitted the court must make preliminary determination as to whether the testimony is within the common knowledge of the jury, and is the proposed witness qualified to provide that testimony. FED. R. EVID. 104; *Daubert,* supra; *Pride v. BIC Corp.,* 218 F.3d 566 (6th Cir. 2000).

See also, § 7.4[D], *Expert Witness Reports - FED. R. CIV. P. 26(a)(2)(A), Rule 26(a)(2)(B) and Rule 26(b)(4).*

The FED. R. EVID. 702 advisory committee notes provide guidance applying Rule 702. It states:

> Most of the literature assumes that experts testify only in the form of opinions. The assumption is logically unfounded. The rule accordingly recognizes that an expert on the stand may give a dissertation or exposition of scientific or other principles relevant to the case, leaving the trier of fact to apply them to the facts . . . Whether the situation is a proper one for the use of expert testimony is to be determined on the basis of assisting the trier. "There is no more certain test for determining when experts may be used than the common sense inquiry whether the untrained layman would be qualified to determine intelligently and to the best possible degree the particular issue without enlightenment from those having a specialized understanding of the subject involved in the dispute." The rule is broadly phrased. The fields of knowledge which may be drawn upon are not limited merely to the "scientific" and "technical" but extend to all "specialized" knowledge. Similarly, the expert is viewed, not in a narrow sense, but as a person qualified by "knowledge, skill, experience, training or education." Thus within the scope of the rule are not only experts in the strictest sense of the word, e.g., physicians, physicists, and architects, but also the large group sometimes called "skilled" witnesses, such as bankers or landowners testifying to land values. . . .

> *Daubert* set forth a non-exclusive checklist for trial courts to use in assessing the reliability of scientific expert testimony. The specific factors explicated by the *Daubert* Court are (1) whether the expert's technique or theory can be or has been tested - that is, whether the expert's theory can be challenged in some objective sense, or whether it is instead simply a subjective, conclusory approach that cannot reasonably be assessed for reliability; (2) whether the technique or theory has been subject to peer review and publication; (3) the known or

potential rate of error of the technique or theory when applied; (4) the existence and maintenance of standards and controls; and (5) whether the technique or theory has been generally accepted in the scientific community. The Court in *Kumho* held that these factors might also be applicable in assessing the reliability of non-scientific expert testimony, depending upon "the particular circumstances of the particular case at issue." 119 S.Ct. at 1175.

Courts both before and after *Daubert* have found other factors relevant in determining whether expert testimony is sufficiently reliable to be considered by the trier of fact. . . . Nothing in this amendment is intended to suggest that experience alone - or experience in conjunction with other knowledge, skill, training or education - may not provide a sufficient foundation for expert testimony. To the contrary, the text of Rule 702 expressly contemplates that an expert may be qualified on the basis of experience.

The need for expert testimony regarding electronic evidence may arise in different areas. *See, § 4.4, Services and Scope of Work - Forensic Specialists.*

[C] Reported Cases - Electronic Evidence Expert Testimony

Forensic Expert Credentials and Qualifications

- *Galaxy Computer Services, Inc. v. Baker,* No. CIV.04-1036, 2005 WL 1278956 (E.D.Va. May 27, 2005). The Court accepted the plaintiff's computer forensics specialist as an expert based on the facts that he had worked in the forensic field for five years and had completed between 1,600 and 1,700 forensics reports which had been accepted by various courts. The expert did not have a degree in computer science, was not an expert in a computer language, was not a computer programmer, and held no certificates in computer science. He had been, however, a member of the High Tech Crime Investigation Association and had completed three postgraduate intensive training courses in computer forensics.

- *Davison v. Eldorado Resorts LLC,* No. CIV.05-0021, 2006 U.S. Dist. LEXIS 12598, at *10-15 (D. Nev. Mar. 10, 2006). In evidentiary rulings, the Court found that plaintiff's expert was qualified as an expert even with his "reluctance to call himself an expert in forensics . . . the law does not limit expert testimony to those who are considered the absolute best in the field. (citation omitted). The law only requires that [the expert] possess 'such knowledge and experience in [the] field or calling as to make it appear that his opinion or inference will probably aid the trier in his search for the truth . . . '"

- *MGE UPS Sys. v. Fakouri Elec. Eng'g., Inc.,* No. CIV.04-445, 2006 U.S. Dist. LEXIS 14142, at *5-12 (D. Tex. Mar. 16, 2006). In a dispute over servicing of a company's computer system the Court reviewed the expert's qualifications under the Daubert standards and found the expert to be qualified.

- *Commonwealth v. Simone*, No. CR.03-0986, 2003 WL 22994245, at *1, *3 (Cir.Ct.Virg. Nov. 12, 2003). Child pornography images were found on the "temporary Internet file of the defendant's computer cache." The expert described the process of how these images are saved in the cache file. The Court found the expert qualified based on his training in computer pornography.

- *Williford v. State,* 127 S.W.3d 309, 311 (Ct. App. Tex. 2004). The Court found that a detective was qualified as an expert "to testify about mirror image of hard drive . . . that he made using specialized computer program . . . detective was computer expert for police department and was knowledgeable about program, program was generally accepted in computer forensic investigation community, detective had successfully used program in past, program had low potential rate of error, and several articles had been written about program, including one magazine that gave program five-star rating out of five stars."

Criticism of Forensic Experts

- *Gates Rubber Co. v. Bando Chemical Indus., Ltd.*, 167 F.R.D. 90, 112 (D. Colo. 1996). In this seminal case, after the defendant allegedly destroyed computer data, the Court issued an inspection order to access the defendant's computers. The plaintiff's forensic expert failed to obtain and preserve the creation dates of essential files and failed to use accepted computer evidence preservation procedures. The Court stated, "[t]o use Norton's Unerase, it was unnecessary for [the plaintiff's expert] to copy it onto the hard drive of the Denver computer. By doing so, however, the program obliterated, at random, seven to eight percent of the information which would otherwise have been available. No one can ever know what items were overwritten by the Unerase program."

- *MMI Products, Inc. v. Long,* 231 F.R.D. 215 (D. Md. 2005). The Court reversed the magistrate's proposed ruling to sanction the defendant and its counsel pursuant to FED. R. CIV. P. 26(g)(3) for failure to make reasonable inquiries into the reliability of their own expert's report. It was discovered that the laptop in question was apparently purchased subsequent to the time of the alleged misappropriation of company information.

- *Taylor v. State,* 93 S.W. 3d 487, 498-508 (Tex.App 2002). The Court in reversing the criminal conviction found several errors including,

    As previously discussed at length, [the officer] testified he had copied Taylor's hard drive. He testified the portions of the target hard drive containing the copy made of Taylor's hard drive by the EnCase program were identical. He based his testimony on his observation of two hash marks on his computer screen at the time the copying process was completed--the acquisition hash and the verification hash. Marshall made no recording of this in any form, although the EnCase software provides a verification process that would have provided written documentation of the quality of the copying procedure . . . handling of the copy of the information on Taylor's hard drive, the key physical evidence in the case, was defective, and that Taylor's hard drive was copied to a "contaminated" hard drive [officer failed to "wipe" the disk onto which the material was copied] . . . which may have already contained pornographic data . . . [also] before copying the drive, Marshall executed a format command against Taylor's drive, when he should have formatted the target drive. By doing so, he destroyed the file allocation table for Taylor's computer and there was no structure in place for the files which were copied [and] . . . the State failed to provide the defense with a copy of Taylor's hard drive and a copy of the hard drive to which Taylor's hard drive was copied.

- *In re Search of 3817 W. West End, First Floor Chicago, Illinois 60621*, 321 F. Supp.2d 953, 956 n.1 (N.D.Ill. 2004). The government sought relief from submitting a search protocol before examining computers seized in a tax fraud investigation. In ruling upon the motion, the Court observed, " . . . in one respect, the response (or non-response) by the government was quite surprising. When the Court raised the possibility of limiting the search to certain time periods, one of the government representatives stated that such a limitation would not be helpful since the file directory only shows when a document was last saved. The Court then asked the government technical expert whether that problem could not be overcome by examining the 'metadata' in the computer files, which would show not only the date a document was last saved, but also when the document was first created and (often times) the changes in the documents from the original draft to the final revision. . . . The government technical expert made no response, leaving the Court with the firm impression that he was not familiar with a term that we would expect a computer expert to know."

- *MGE UPS Sys. v. Fakouri Elec. Eng'g, Inc.*, No. CIV.04-445, 2006 U.S. Dist. LEXIS 14142, at *5-8 (D. Tex. Mar. 16, 2006). In a dispute over servicing of a company's computer system the Court held that allegations that the plaintiff's expert's opinions about "the use of six impounded laptop computers are not reliable because he used improper forensic methodology in his inspections of the computer evidence . . ." went to the weight and not the admissibility of the evidence. Defendant had argued that the plaintiff's expert had improperly "(1) used a methodology that deleted 71 files on the computers; (2) used a methodology that contaminated and altered the date and time stamps on 8,803 files on the computers; (3) did not use sanitized floppy disks to boot the computers or to copy data from the computers; (4) performed multiple forced shutdowns on the computers that may have created a number of cross-linked files found on the computers; (5) used improper ghosting procedures to image the computers' hard drives and only obtained part of the data on the computers; and (6) used computers without wiped hard drives during the ghosting procedure."

• For additional cases and other legal authorities on forensic expert credentials, qualifications and testimony *see* § 4.5[D], *Reported Cases* and § 7.4[D], *Expert Witness Reports - FED. R. CIV. P. 26(a)(2)(A), Rule 26(a)(2)(B) and Rule 26(b)(4).*

§ 8.9   HEARSAY

[A]   Rules 801 - 805, 807

Rule 801. Definitions

The following definitions apply under this article:

(a) Statement. A "statement" is (1) an oral or written assertion or (2) nonverbal conduct of a person, if it is intended by the person as an assertion.

(b) Declarant. A "declarant" is a person who makes a statement.

(c) Hearsay. "Hearsay" is a statement, other than one made by the declarant while testifying at the trial or hearing, offered in evidence to prove the truth of the matter asserted.

(d) Statements which are not hearsay. A statement is not hearsay if-

(1) Prior statement by witness. The declarant testifies at the trial or hearing and is subject to cross-examination concerning the statement, and the statement is (A) inconsistent with the declarant's testimony, and was given under oath subject to the penalty of perjury at a trial, hearing, or other proceeding, or in a deposition, or (B) consistent with the declarant's testimony and is offered to rebut an express or implied charge against the declarant of recent fabrication or improper influence or motive, or (C) one of identification of a person made after perceiving the person; or

(2) Admission by party-opponent. The statement is offered against a party and is (A) the party's own statement, in either an individual or a representative capacity or (B) a statement of which the party has manifested an adoption or belief in its truth, or (C) a statement by a person authorized by the party to make a statement concerning the subject, or (D) a statement by the party's agent or servant concerning a matter within the scope of the agency or employment, made during the existence of the relationship, or (E) a statement by a coconspirator of a party during the course and in furtherance of the conspiracy. The contents of the

statement shall be considered but are not alone sufficient to establish the declarant's authority under subdivision (C), the agency or employment relationship and scope thereof under subdivision (D), or the existence of the conspiracy and the participation therein of the declarant and the party against whom the statement is offered under subdivision (E).

Rule 802. Hearsay Rule

Hearsay is not admissible except as provided by these rules or by other rules prescribed by the Supreme Court pursuant to statutory authority or by Act of Congress.

Rule 803. Hearsay Exceptions; Availability of Declarant Immaterial

The following are not excluded by the hearsay rule, even though the declarant is available as a witness:

(1) Present sense impression. A statement describing or explaining an event or condition made while the declarant was perceiving the event or condition, or immediately thereafter.

(2) Excited utterance. A statement relating to a startling event or condition made while the declarant was under the stress of excitement caused by the event or condition.

(3) Then existing mental, emotional, or physical condition. A statement of the declarant's then existing state of mind, emotion, sensation, or physical condition (such as intent, plan, motive, design, mental feeling, pain, and bodily health), but not including a statement of memory or belief to prove the fact remembered or believed unless it relates to the execution, revocation, identification, or terms of declarant's will.

(4) Statements for purposes of medical diagnosis or treatment. Statements made for purposes of medical diagnosis or treatment and describing medical history, or past or present symptoms, pain, or sensations, or the inception or general character of the cause or external source thereof insofar as reasonably pertinent to diagnosis or treatment.

(5) Recorded recollection. A memorandum or record concerning a matter about which a witness once had knowledge but now has insufficient recollection to enable the witness to testify fully and accurately, shown to have been made or adopted by the witness when the matter was fresh in the witness' memory and to reflect that knowledge correctly. If admitted, the memorandum or record may be read into evidence but may not itself be received as an exhibit unless offered by an adverse party.

(6) Records of Regularly Conducted Activity. --A memorandum, report, record, or data compilation, in any form, of acts, events, conditions, opinions, or diagnoses, made at or near the time by, or from information transmitted by, a person with knowledge, if kept in the course of a regularly conducted business activity, and if it was the regular practice of that business activity to make the memorandum, report, record or data compilation, all as shown by the testimony of the custodian or other qualified witness, or by certification that complies with Rule 902(11), Rule 902(12), or a statute permitting certification, unless the source of information or the method or circumstances of preparation indicate lack of trustworthiness. The term "business" as used in this paragraph includes business, institution, association, profession, occupation, and calling of every kind, whether or not conducted for profit.

(7) Absence of entry in records kept in accordance with the provisions of paragraph (6). Evidence that a matter is not included in the memoranda reports, records, or data compilations, in any form, kept in accordance with the provisions of paragraph (6), to prove the nonoccurrence or nonexistence of the matter, if the matter was of a kind of which a memorandum, report, record, or data compilation was regularly made and preserved, unless the sources of information or other circumstances indicate lack of trustworthiness.

(8) Public records and reports. Records, reports, statements, or data compilations, in any form, of public offices or agencies, setting forth (A) the activities of the office or agency, or (B) matters observed pursuant to duty imposed by law as to which matters there was a duty to report, excluding, however, in criminal cases matters observed by police officers and other law enforcement personnel, or (C) in civil actions and proceedings and against the Government in criminal cases, factual findings resulting from an investigation made pursuant to authority granted by law, unless the sources of information or other circumstances indicate lack of trustworthiness.

(9) Records of vital statistics. Records or data compilations, in any form, of births, fetal deaths, deaths, or marriages, if the report thereof was made to a public office pursuant to requirements of law.

(10) Absence of public record or entry. To prove the absence of a record, report, statement, or data compilation, in any form, or the nonoccurrence or nonexistence of a matter of which a record, report, statement, or data compilation, in any form, was regularly made and preserved by a public office or agency, evidence in the form of a certification in accordance with rule 902, or testimony, that diligent search failed to disclose the record, report, statement, or data compilation, or entry.

(11) Records of religious organizations. Statements of births, marriages, divorces, deaths, legitimacy, ancestry, relationship by blood or marriage, or other similar facts of personal or family history, contained in a regularly kept record of a religious organization.

(12) Marriage, baptismal, and similar certificates. Statements of fact contained in a certificate that the maker performed a marriage or other ceremony or administered a sacrament, made by a clergyman, public official, or other person authorized by the rules or practices of a religious organization or by law to perform the act certified, and purporting to have been issued at the time of the act or within a reasonable time thereafter.

(13) Family records. Statements of fact concerning personal or family history contained in family Bibles, genealogies, charts, engravings on rings, inscriptions on family portraits, engravings on urns, crypts, or tombstones, or the like.

(14) Records of documents affecting an interest in property. The record of a document purporting to establish or affect an interest in property, as proof of the content of the original recorded document and its execution and delivery by each person by whom it purports to have been executed, if the record is a record of a public office and an applicable statute authorizes the recording of documents of that kind in that office.

(15) Statements in documents affecting an interest in property. A statement contained in a document purporting to establish or affect an interest in property if the matter stated was relevant to the purpose of the document, unless dealings with the property since the document was made have been inconsistent with the truth of the statement or the purport of the document.

(16) Statements in ancient documents. Statements in a document in existence twenty years or more the authenticity of which is established.

(17) Market reports, commercial publications. Market quotations, tabulations, lists, directories, or other published compilations, generally used and relied upon by the public or by persons in particular occupations.

(18) Learned treatises. To the extent called to the attention of an expert witness upon cross-examination or relied upon by the expert witness in direct examination, statements contained in published treatises, periodicals, or pamphlets on a subject of history, medicine, or other science or art, established as a reliable authority by the testimony or admission of the witness or by other expert testimony or by judicial notice. If admitted, the statements may be read into evidence but may not be received as exhibits.

(19) Reputation concerning personal or family history. Reputation among members of a person's family by blood, adoption, or marriage, or among a

person's associates, or in the community, concerning a person's birth, adoption, marriage, divorce, death, legitimacy, relationship by blood, adoption, or marriage, ancestry, or other similar fact of personal or family history.

(20) Reputation concerning boundaries or general history. Reputation in a community, arising before the controversy, as to boundaries of or customs affecting lands in the community, and reputation as to events of general history important to the community or State or nation in which located.

(21) Reputation as to character. Reputation of a person's character among associates or in the community.

(22) Judgment of previous conviction. Evidence of a final judgment, entered after a trial or upon a plea of guilty (but not upon a plea of nolo contendere), adjudging a person guilty of a crime punishable by death or imprisonment in excess of one year, to prove any fact essential to sustain the judgment, but not including, when offered by the Government in a criminal prosecution for purposes other than impeachment, judgments against persons other than the accused. The pendency of an appeal may be shown but does not affect admissibility.

(23) Judgment as to personal, family, or general history, or boundaries. Judgments as proof of matters of personal, family or general history, or boundaries, essential to the judgment, if the same would be provable by evidence of reputation.

(24) [Transferred to Rule 807]

Rule 804. Hearsay Exceptions; Declarant Unavailable

(a) Definition of unavailability. "Unavailability as a witness" includes situations in which the declarant--

(1) is exempted by ruling of the court on the ground of privilege from testifying concerning the subject matter of the declarant's statement; or

(2) persists in refusing to testify concerning the subject matter of the declarant's statement despite an order of the court to do so; or

(3) testifies to a lack of memory of the subject matter of the declarant's statement; or

(4) is unable to be present or to testify at the hearing because of death or then existing physical or mental illness or infirmity; or

(5) is absent from the hearing and the proponent of a statement has been unable to procure the declarant's attendance (or in the case of a hearsay exception under subdivision (b)(2), (3), or (4), the declarant's attendance or testimony) by process or other reasonable means.

A declarant is not unavailable as a witness if exemption, refusal, claim of lack of memory, inability, or absence is due to the procurement or wrongdoing of the proponent of a statement for the purpose of preventing the witness from attending or testifying.

(b) Hearsay exceptions. The following are not excluded by the hearsay rule if the declarant is unavailable as a witness:

(1) Former testimony. Testimony given as a witness at another hearing of the same or a different proceeding, or in a deposition taken in compliance with law in the course of the same or another proceeding, if the party against whom the testimony is now offered, or, in a civil action or proceeding, a predecessor in interest, had an opportunity and similar motive to develop the testimony by direct, cross, or redirect examination.

(2) Statement under belief of impending death. In a prosecution for homicide or in a civil action or proceeding, a statement made by a declarant while believing that the declarant's death was imminent, concerning the cause or circumstances of what the declarant believed to be impending death.

(3) Statement against interest. A statement which was at the time of its making so far contrary to the declarant's pecuniary or proprietary interest, or so far tended to subject the declarant to civil or criminal liability, or to render invalid a claim by the declarant against another, that a reasonable person in the declarant's position would not have made the statement unless believing it to be true. A statement tending to expose the declarant to criminal liability and offered to exculpate the accused is not admissible unless corroborating circumstances clearly indicate the trustworthiness of the statement.

(4) Statement of personal or family history. (A) A statement concerning the declarant's own birth, adoption, marriage, divorce, legitimacy, relationship by blood, adoption, or marriage, ancestry, or other similar fact of personal or family history, even though declarant had no means of acquiring personal knowledge of the matter stated; or (B) a statement concerning the foregoing matters, and death also, of another person, if the declarant was related to the other by blood, adoption, or marriage or was so intimately associated with the other's family as to be likely to have accurate information concerning the matter declared.

(5) [Transferred to Rule 807]

(6) Forfeiture by wrongdoing. A statement offered against a party that has engaged or acquiesced in wrongdoing that was intended to, and did, procure the unavailability of the declarant as a witness.

Rule 805. Hearsay Within Hearsay

Hearsay included within hearsay is not excluded under the hearsay rule if each part of the combined statements conforms with an exception to the hearsay rule provided in these rules.

Rule 807. Residual Exception

A statement not specifically covered by Rule 803 or 804 but having equivalent circumstantial guarantees of trustworthiness, is not excluded by the hearsay rule, if the court determines that (A) the statement is offered as evidence of a material fact; (B) the statement is more probative on the point for which it is offered than any other evidence which the proponent can procure through reasonable efforts; and (C) the general purposes of these rules and the interests of justice will best be served by admission of the statement into evidence. However, a statement may not be admitted under this exception unless the proponent of it makes known to the adverse party sufficiently in advance of the trial or hearing to provide the adverse party with a fair opportunity to prepare to meet it, the proponent's intention to offer the statement and the particulars of it, including the name and address of the declarant.

[B]   Generally

FED. R. EVID. 801(c) defines hearsay as an out of court statement that is "offered in evidence to prove the truth of the matter asserted." A "statement" is defined in FED. R. EVID. 801(a) as "an oral or written assertion" or "nonverbal conduct of a person." FED. R. EVID. 802 declares hearsay inadmissible.

The courts disfavor hearsay because of the inability to cross-examine and probe the quality of evidence. Cross-examination has been called the "greatest legal engine ever invented for the discovery of truth." *California v. Green,* 90 S.Ct. 1930, 1935 (1970). Cross-examination allows counsel to uncover misperceptions of an event, inaccurate or incomplete memory, credibility and sincerity of the declarant, and ambiguities in prior admissions, testimony or other out-of-court statements. Also, requiring a witness to testify allows observation as to the demeanor of the witness in gauging his credibility.

The hearsay rule applies only to statements offered to prove the truth of what they assert. The rule has no application to statements offered for other legitimate purposes. For example, words can be spoken that are offered to show their effect on a listener or reader, provide additional knowledge, that show a person's feelings or state of mind, or that has independent legal significance. *See,* Christopher B. Mueller & Laird C. Kirkpatrick, 4 *Federal Evidence* § 385-390 (1994).

The Federal Rules also exclude from the hearsay definition certain prior statements by witnesses, and certain admissions by party opponents. FED. R. EVID. 801(d)(1) & (2). FED. R. EVID. 804(b) provides five other hearsay exceptions if the hearsay declarant is unavailable to testify at trial.

FED. R. EVID. 803(7) expressly authorizes the use of evidence of the absence of an entry in a "data compilation" maintained in the regular course of business to prove the nonoccurrence of a fact unless the circumstances indicate a lack of trustworthiness.

[C] Hearsay Exceptions

Though hearsay, out-of-court statements may still be admissible under one of the listed twenty-four hearsay exceptions set forth in Rule 803 that "are not excluded by the hearsay rule." Some of the exceptions include the following.

Business record exception. FED. R. EVID. 803(6) commonly referred to as the "business record exception" excludes from hearsay: "Records of Regularly Conducted Activity. - A memorandum, report, record, or *data compilation* . . ." (emphasis added).

Present Sense Impression. FED. R. EVID. 803(1) creates a hearsay exception for "[a] statement describing or explaining an event or condition made while the declarant was perceiving the event or condition, or immediately thereafter." "The underlying theory of this exception is that 'substantial contemporaneity of event and statement negate the likelihood of deliberate or conscious misrepresentation.' Advisory Committee Note, FED. R. EVID. 803." *Booth v. State,* 306 Md. 313, 320, 508 A.2d 976, 979 (1986).

Excited Utterance. The excited utterance exception is defined by Rule 803(2) as "[a] statement relating to a startling event or condition made while the declarant was under the stress of excitement caused by the event or condition." Excited utterances are accepted from the hearsay rule because the startling event or condition "still has the capacity of reflection and produces utterances free of conscious fabrication." FED. R. EVID. 803 advisory committee's notes.

[D] Electronic Documents

Similar to conventional paper documents, if an electronic document is offered for the truth of its contents, it would be hearsay and inadmissible in the absence of an applicable exception.

See also *Specific Type of Computer Evidence* § 8.12 et al. for cases and other legal authorities regarding the specific application of the hearsay exclusionary rule to specific types of electronic data.

[E] Other Authorities

- J. Shane Givens, *The Admissibility of Electronic Evidence at Trial: Courtroom Admissibility Standards,* 34 Cumb. L. Rev. 95 (2003).

- Olin G. Wellborn III, *The Definition of Hearsay in the Federal Rules of Evidence*, 61 Tex. L. Rev 49 (1982).

- *Admissibility of Computerized Private Business Records,* 7 A.L.R.4th 8.

• *Proof of Public Records Kept or Stored on Electronic Computing Equipment,* 71 A.L.R.3d 232, 236 to 240.

§ 8.10   REQUIREMENT OF AUTHENTICATION OR IDENTIFICATION

[A]   Rules 901 - 902

Rule 901. Requirement of Authentication or Identification

(a) General provision. The requirement of authentication or identification as a condition precedent to admissibility is satisfied by evidence sufficient to support a finding that the matter in question is what its proponent claims.

(b) Illustrations. By way of illustration only, and not by way of limitation, the following are examples of authentication or identification conforming with the requirements of this rule:

(1) Testimony of witness with knowledge. Testimony that a matter is what it is claimed to be.

(2) Nonexpert opinion on handwriting. Nonexpert opinion as to the genuineness of handwriting, based upon familiarity not acquired for purposes of the litigation.

(3) Comparison by trier or expert witness. Comparison by the trier of fact or by expert witnesses with specimens which have been authenticated.

(4) Distinctive characteristics and the like. Appearance, contents, substance, internal patterns, or other distinctive characteristics, taken in conjunction with circumstances.

(5) Voice identification. Identification of a voice, whether heard firsthand or through mechanical or electronic transmission or recording, by opinion based upon hearing the voice at any time under circumstances connecting it with the alleged speaker.

(6) Telephone conversations. Telephone conversations, by evidence that a call was made to the number assigned at the time by the telephone company to a particular person or business, if (A) in the case of a person, circumstances, including self-identification, show the person answering to be the one called, or (B) in the case of a business, the call was made to a place of business and the conversation related to business reasonably transacted over the telephone.

(7) Public records or reports. Evidence that a writing authorized by law to be recorded or filed and in fact recorded or filed in a public office, or a purported public record, report, statement, or data compilation, in any form, is from the public office where items of this nature are kept.

(8) Ancient documents or data compilation. Evidence that a document or data compilation, in any form, (A) is in such condition as to create no suspicion concerning its authenticity, (B) was in a place where it, if authentic, would likely be, and (C) has been in existence 20 years or more at the time it is offered.

(9) Process or system. Evidence describing a process or system used to produce a result and showing that the process or system produces an accurate result.

(10) Methods provided by statute or rule. Any method of authentication or identification provided by Act of Congress or by other rules prescribed by the Supreme Court pursuant to statutory authority.

Rule 902. Self-authentication

Extrinsic evidence of authenticity as a condition precedent to admissibility is not required with respect to the following:

(1) Domestic public documents under seal. A document bearing a seal purporting to be that of the United States, or of any State, district, Commonwealth, territory, or insular possession thereof, or the Panama Canal Zone, or the Trust Territory of the Pacific Islands, or of a political subdivision, department, officer, or agency thereof, and a signature purporting to be an attestation or execution.

(2) Domestic public documents not under seal. A document purporting to bear the signature in the official capacity of an officer or employee of any entity included in paragraph (1) hereof, having no seal, if a public officer having a seal and having official duties in the district or political subdivision of the officer or employee certifies under seal that the signer has the official capacity and that the signature is genuine.

* * *

(4) Certified copies of public records. A copy of an official record or report or entry therein, or of a document authorized by law to be recorded or filed and actually recorded or filed in a public office, including data compilations in any form, certified as correct by the custodian or other person authorized to make the certification, by certificate complying with paragraph (1), (2), or (3) of this rule or complying with any Act of Congress or rule prescribed by the Supreme Court pursuant to statutory authority.

(5) Official publications. Books, pamphlets, or other publications purporting to be issued by public authority.

(6) Newspapers and periodicals. Printed materials purporting to be newspapers or periodicals.

(7) Trade inscriptions and the like. Inscriptions, signs, tags, or labels purporting to have been affixed in the course of business and indicating ownership, control, or origin.

(8) Acknowledged documents. Documents accompanied by a certificate of acknowledgment executed in the manner provided by law by a notary public or other officer authorized by law to take acknowledgments.

(9) Commercial paper and related documents. Commercial paper, signatures thereon, and documents relating thereto to the extent provided by general commercial law.

(10) Presumptions under Acts of Congress. Any signature, document, or other matter declared by Act of Congress to be presumptively or prima facie genuine or authentic.

(11) Certified Domestic Records of Regularly Conducted Activity. --The original or a duplicate of a domestic record of regularly conducted activity that would be admissible under Rule 803(6) if accompanied by a written declaration of its custodian or other qualified person, in a manner complying with any Act of Congress or rule prescribed by the Supreme Court pursuant to statutory authority, certifying that the record--

(A) was made at or near the time of the occurrence of the matters set forth by, or from information transmitted by, a person with knowledge of those matters;

(B) was kept in the course of the regularly conducted activity; and

(C) was made by the regularly conducted activity as a regular practice.

A party intending to offer a record into evidence under this paragraph must provide written notice of that intention to all adverse parties, and must make the record and declaration available for inspection sufficiently in advance of their offer into evidence to provide an adverse party with a fair opportunity to challenge them.

* * *

[B]   Generally

Before evidence can be introduced, it is necessary to establish that the factual information relates to the legal issues. It must be identified and linked with the relevant legal issues of the case. Otherwise, it is irrelevant. The process of connecting evidence to issues is authenticating or identifying the evidence. This is commonly referred to as "laying the foundation." Authentication of a document means to establish that a document is what it purports to be, and that there is a relationship between the document, an individual and the issues of the case. For example, in order to prove knowledge of a party regarding a specific document it is necessary to establish that the party read the document. If you wish to establish that a party made an admission about the case, then it is necessary to establish that the particular individual made or adopted the admission in issue.

Under FED. R. EVID. 901(a) documents must be properly authenticated as a condition precedent to their admissibility "by evidence sufficient to support a finding that the matter in question is what its proponent claims." FED. R. EVID. 901(b) provides a list of illustrations of authentication that would conform with the requirements of the rule. They are intended to serve as illustrations or examples, and are not exclusive. One of the illustrations provides that a document may be authenticated by "[a]ppearance, contents, substance, internal patterns, or other distinctive characteristics, taken in conjunction with circumstances." FED. R. EVID. 901(b)(4).

Pursuant to FED. R. EVID. 104, as a condition precedent, the judge must be satisfied that there is sufficient evidence upon which the trier of fact can support a finding that the evidence at issue is what the proponent claims. *See,* § 8.4[A], *Rule 104.* The court does not determine whether the evidence has been authenticated, only whether there is sufficient evidence that the trier of fact can reach a reasonable conclusion as to the authenticity of the evidence. The courts have held that a district court has discretion to determine authenticity, and that determination should not be disturbed on appeal absent a showing that there is no competent evidence in the record to support it. *United States v. Munoz,* 16 F.3d 1116, 1120-21 (11th Cir.), *cert. denied sub nom., Rodriguez v. United States,* 513 U.S. 852 (1994).

Once a judge decides that evidence meets this threshold requirement, the evidence is admissible. Determining the authenticity of the document is left to the trier of fact, who will decide the weight to be given to the evidence in support of authenticity. *Commerce Funding Corp. v. Comprehensive Habilitation Services, Inc.,* No. CIV.01-3796, 2004 WL 1970144, at *4 (S.D.N.Y. Sept. 3, 2004) (noting that once shaky, unreliable evidence is admitted, such evidence is best challenged with '[v]igorous cross-examination, presentation of contrary evidence, and careful instruction on the burden of proof.'); *United States v. Goichman,* 547 F.2d 778, 784 (3d Cir. 1976) ("The only requirement is that there has been substantial evidence from which [the jury] could infer that the document was authentic.").

Authentication of electronic records (e-mails, word processing documents, etc.) may be a problem because changes to an electronic record sometimes can be difficult or impossible to detect and uncover. *American Exp. Travel Related Servs. v. Vinhnee (In re Vinhnee),* No. CIV.04-1284, 336 B.R. 437, 443-447 (Bankr. Fed. App. 2005) (court refused to admit creditor credit card information for failure to authenticate); *See,* George L. Paul, *The "Authenticity Crisis" in Real Evidence,* 15 PRAC. LITIGATOR No. 6, at 45-49 (2004). Contrast this with paper records, where changes can usually be observed and the custodian and author of a document can be readily determined by signatures, handwriting, etc. It is difficult to trace who may have authored an electronic record. For example, electronic files can be found in a company's shared network folders for common use of all employees or in collaborative software which allows various users to create, edit and reedit data within the same project.

Authentication can be derived from direct or circumstantial evidence. For example, you may have direct evidence, such as testimony from the author of an e-mail, that they created the record. In addition, circumstantial evidence such as corporate markings, unique writing characteristics, computer audit trails and logs (§ 2.6[G], *Audit Trails and Logs*), hash values and chain of custody (§ 5.5[G], *Chain of Custody, Audit Reports and Hash Values*) or "authentication" intermediaries may provide sufficient authentication under certain circumstances.

Even though the court may preliminarily determine that the evidence is authentic, subject to cross-examination, it may still be excluded based on relevance, hearsay or Best Evidence objections.

See also, *Specific Type of Computer Evidence* § 8.12 et al. for cases and other legal authorities regarding the application of authentication requirements for specific types of electronic data.

[C]   Chain of Custody

The purpose of testimony concerning chain of custody is to prove that evidence has not been altered or changed from the time it was collected through production in court. *Gallego v. United States of America,* 276 F.2d 914 (9th Cir. 1960) (citing *United States v. S.B. Panicky & Co.*, 136 F.2d 413, 415 (2d Cir. 1943)). Chain of custody testimony would include documentation on how the data was gathered, transported, analyzed, and preserved for production. This information is important to assist in the authentication of electronic data since it can be easily altered if proper precautions are not taken.

Depending on the circumstances of the case, a chain of custody foundation will assist in the admission of evidence. When there is a chance of confusion or that data may have been altered or tampered with, evidence establishing a chain of custody is important. *United States v. Block,* 148 Fed. Appx. 904, 910-911 (11th Cir. 2005) (Court held that "challenge to the chain of custody goes to the weight rather than the admissibility of the evidence" and that copying procedure using *Bates* stamp to track origin of documents was proper.); *DeLaTorre v. Minnesota Life,* No. CIV.04-3591, 2005 U.S. Dist. LEXIS 20938, at *11-17 (D. Ill. 2005) (the Court ruled "[i]n proving a chain of custody, the proponent of an item of evidence shows that it was continuously in the safekeeping of one or more specific persons. . . . Wright and Gold, *Federal Practice and Procedure,* Evidence § 7106 at 49 (West 2000). 'It is usually unnecessary to establish a perfect or unbroken chain of custody.' . . . Rule 901(a)'s standard of 'sufficient to support a finding' is a minimal one and thus 'courts commonly tolerate gaps in the chain that might present some limited opportunity for tampering with the evidence.'"

In *Galaxy Computer Services, Inc. v. Baker,* No. CIV.04-1036, 2005 WL 1278956, at *17 (E.D.Va. May 27, 2005) the Court denied defendants' motion to exclude evidence because of alleged breaks in the chain of custody of the digital evidence. The defendant argued that the plaintiff's expert failed to follow their own internal chain of custody procedures and that the electronic evidence may have been tainted. The Court held that this allegation would not preclude admission but, instead, would go to the weight to be given the evidence. The Court stated:

> The "chain of custody" rule is a variation of the requirement under Federal Rule of Evidence 901(a) that evidence must be properly authenticated or identified prior to being admitted. *United States v. Turpin,* 65 F.3d 1207, 1213 (4th Cir. 1995) (citations omitted). The "chain of custody" rule requires that admitted exhibits "be preceded by evidence sufficient to support a finding that the matter in question is what its proponent claims." *United States v. Ricco,* 52 F.3d 58, 61 (4th Cir. 1995) (quoting FED. R. EVID. 901), *cert. denied,* 516 U.S. 898, 116 S.Ct. 254, 133 L.Ed.2d 179 (1995). However, the possibility of a break in the chain of custody goes only to the weight of the evidence. *United States v. Harrington,* 923 F.2d 1371, 1374 (9th Cir. 1991) (citations omitted). The Court will allow Taylor to testify. Defendants may, of course, cross-examine Taylor regarding the chain of custody and Taylor's inability to ascertain the exact dates of deletion and/or alteration of files or the identities of those responsible. Defendants' motion will be denied.

Oftentimes, the "chain of custody" for digital information involves the forensic acquisition methodology and its effect on admissibility and reliability. Erin E. Kenneally, *Confluence of Digital Evidence and the Law: On the Forensic Soundness of Live-Remote Digital Evidence Collection,* 2005 UCLA J. L. & Tech. 5, 26-27 (2005). This article suggests specific methodologies be employed to ensure authenticity.

> As with chain-of-custody for physical evidence, the general chain-of-custody procedures followed by digital forensic practitioners to establish authenticity for digital evidence include:
>
> • Refraining from altering the original evidence both in collection, storage and analysis (e.g. analysis performed on evidence copies; cryptographically hashing original evidence)
>
> • Documenting procedures used in the collection, storage and analysis
>
> > Specifically, the general forensic chain-of-custody procedures that control for:
> >
> > 1. What types of evidence have been collected;
> >
> > 2. Where the evidence was collected;

3. Who handled the evidence before it was collected by forensic practitioners, while it was stored, and after it was examined;

4. How the evidence was collected and stored; including what tools or methods were used to collect and/or store evidence;

5. When the evidence was collected.

• Documenting and explain any changes that may be made to evidence; establishing auditable procedures

• Maintaining the continuity of evidence

• Making a complete copy of data in question

• Utilizing a reliable copy process (e.g. independently verifiable; hashing for verification)

• Employing security measures (e.g. tamperproof storage, write protection)

• Properly labeling time, date, source (e.g. tracking numbers, tagging)

• Limiting and documenting the persons with access to data

The principles underlying these forensic procedures for ensuring reliability of digital evidence include, but are not limited to:

1. When dealing with digital evidence, all of the general forensic and procedural principles must be applied.

2. Upon seizing digital evidence, actions taken should not change that evidence.

3. When it is necessary for a person to access original digital evidence, that person should be trained for the purpose.

4. All activity relating to the seizure, access, storage or transfer of digital evidence must be fully documented, preserved and available for review.

5. An individual is responsible for all actions taken with respect to digital evidence while the digital evidence is in his/her possession.

6. Any agency that is responsible for seizing, accessing, storing or transferring digital evidence is responsible for compliance with these principles.

See also, § 5.5[G], *Chain of Custody, Audit Reports and Hash Values.*

[D]   Reported Cases

- *United States v. Scott-Emuakpor,* No. CR.99-138, 2000 WL 288443, at *13, 14 (W.D. Mich. Jan. 25, 2000). "To establish authenticity, the proponent need not rule out all possibilities inconsistent with authenticity or prove beyond any doubt that the evidence is what it purports to be. Rather, the standard for authentication is one of 'reasonable likelihood' that the evidence is authentic. Generally, Rule 901(a) is satisfied if the proponent makes a sufficient showing to allow a reasonable person to believe the evidence is what it purports to be. After the court is satisfied that this showing has been made and admits the evidence as authenticated, the jury decides what weight to give the evidence." Court allowed authentication "through the testimony of a witness who was present and observed the procedure by which the documents were obtained from Defendant's computers." *See also, United States v. Smith,* 609 F.2d 1294, 1301 (9th Cir. 1979) (court noted rule is whether "the jury, acting as reasonable men, could find its authorship as claimed by the proponent."); *United States v. Tropeano,* 252 F.3d 653 (2nd Cir. 2001) (court ruled that authentication of audio tapes by establishing a chain of custody is based on the reasonable likelihood standard.).

- *Krumwiede v. Brighton Associates, L.L.C.,* No. CIV.05-3003, 2006 WL 1308629 (N.D. Ill. May 8, 2006). The Court entered a default judgment against the plaintiff for activity evidencing the intent to destroy or hide evidence by deleting files, creating ZIP files (nesting data), moving data and multiple use of defragmentation. The Court also held that "even if the thousands of altered and modified documents located on Brighton's laptop are not actually deleted, the changes to the file metadata call the authenticity of the files and their content into question and make it impossible for [the defendant] to rely on them."

- *Davison v. Eldorado Resorts LLC,* No. CIV.05-0021, 2006 U.S. Dist. LEXIS 12598, at *26, 27 (D. Nev. Mar. 10, 2006). The plaintiff filed an ERISA complaint alleging that the defendants failed to provide her medical coverage. Defendants filed a motion to deny admission, on authenticity grounds, of nine appeal letters never received by the defendants. They were allegedly typed by the plaintiff on a computer but the "saved" dates of the files on a CD were more than 180 days after the appeal deadline. In a detailed opinion reviewing the forensic testimony the Court ruled that "considering the totality of the circumstances . . . Plaintiff has made a prima facie case of authenticity. A reasonable jury could determine Plaintiff's appeal letters are authentic . . ."

- *Williams v. Sprint/United Mgmt. Co.,* 230 F.R.D. 640, 655-656 (D. Kan. 2005). In this age discrimination action the defendant employer refused to unlock the value of cells in a spreadsheet "to ensure the integrity of the data regarding RIFs, i.e., to ensure that the data could not be accidentally or intentionally altered. . . . Defendant's concerns regarding maintaining the integrity of the spreadsheet's values and data could have been addressed by the less intrusive and more efficient use of 'hash marks.' For example, Defendant could have run the data through a mathematical process to generate a shorter symbolic reference to the original file, called a 'hash mark' or 'hash value,' that is unique to that particular file. This 'digital fingerprint' akin to a tamper-evident seal on a software package would have shown if the electronic spreadsheets were altered. When an electronic file is sent with a hash mark, others can read it, but the file cannot be altered without a change also occurring in the hash mark. The producing party can be certain that the file was not altered by running the creator's hash mark algorithm to verify that the original hash mark is generated. *This method allows a large amount of data to be self-authenticating with a rather small hash mark, efficiently assuring that the original image has not been manipulated.*" (emphasis added).

- *V Cable Inc. v. Budnick*, 23 Fed. Appx. 64, 65-66 (2nd Cir. 2001) (unpublished). The Court ruled that computer printouts of business sales records were admissible under business record hearsay exception even though the computers had been sent to an independent software company for analysis. The Appellant had suggested that the computers "from which these records were obtained, cannot be authenticated due to a break in their chain of custody" and they had been corrupted by the analysis and retrieval of documents.

- *United States v. Whitaker,* 127 F.3d 595, 601 (7th Cir. 1997). "[A criminal defendant] argues that the prosecution failed to comply with the requirements of Rule 901(a) with respect to the computer printouts because it never supplied witnesses who had personal knowledge of the computer system's operation or who could confirm the accuracy of the input to and output from the computer." The Court rejected the argument and held authentication sufficient by testimony showing agents were present when Microsoft Money was installed and when records were retrieved.

- *United States v. Bonallo,* 858 F.2d 1427, 1435, 1436 (9th Cir. 1988). In referring to computer records obtained from ATM customer affidavits and computer records, the court held, "[t]he fact that it is possible to alter data contained in a computer is plainly insufficient to establish untrustworthiness. The mere possibility that the logs may have been altered goes only to the weight of the evidence not its admissibility."

[E]   Other Authorities

- United States Department of Justice, *Searching and Seizing Computers and Obtaining Electronic Evidence in Criminal Investigations,* (Sept. 2002), available at http://www.cybercrime.gov/s&smanual2002.htm (last visited on July 27, 2006).

- MANUAL FOR COMPLEX LITIGATION (FOURTH) §11.445:

  The production of documents, either in the traditional manner or in a document depository, will not necessarily provide the foundation for admission of those documents into evidence at trial or for use in a motion for summary judgment. . . . This is particularly true when discovery involves computerized data (see section 11.446) that must be retrieved from computer systems or storage media, imaged, converted to a common format, or handled by a third-party expert or court-appointed neutral in the process of production. The judge should advise parties to agree on handling because admissibility will depend on the efficacy of these procedures.

*   MANUAL FOR COMPLEX LITIGATION (FOURTH) §11.446:

    In general, the Federal Rules of Evidence apply to computerized data as they do to other types of evidence. Computerized data, however, raise unique issues concerning accuracy and authenticity. Accuracy may be impaired by incomplete data entry, mistakes in output instructions, programming errors, damage and contamination of storage media, power outages, and equipment malfunctions. The integrity of data may also be compromised in the course of discovery by improper search and retrieval techniques, data conversion, or mishandling.

*   ABA Civil Discovery Standards (August 2004), § 29(b)(iv), "The parties are encouraged to stipulate as to the authenticity and identifying characteristics (date, author, etc.) of electronic information that is not self-authenticating on its face."

*   J. Shane Givens, *The Admissibility of Electronic Evidence at Trial: Courtroom Admissibility Standards,* 34 Cumb. L. Rev. 95 (2003).

[F]   Discovery Pointers

*   Handling of computer evidence from your client or the opposing party may raise authentication and chain of custody issues as to whether it has been altered or deleted. There are some techniques that lessen the risk of this objection from being successful. It is suggested that the evidence be copied and transferred using DVD or CD-ROM "non-rewriteable, non-erasable" technology.

*   Additional methods of authenticating computer records are using computer audit trails and logs, encryption and hashing. *See,* § 2.6[G], *Audit Trails and Logs,* § 3.5[H][1], *Encryption and Steganography* and § 5.5[G], *Chain of Custody, Audit Reports and Hash Values.*

*   Some companies will use an intermediary to "authenticate" electronic records. For example, the United States Postal Service will use auditable time stamps, digital signatures and hash codes to verify the authenticity of electronic content for parties. *See* USPS Electronic Postmark (EPM) at http://www.usps.com/electronicpostmark/welcome.htm.

§ 8.11   BEST EVIDENCE RULE

[A]   Rules 1001 – 1008

Rule 1001. Definitions

For purposes of this article the following definitions are applicable:

(1) Writings and recordings. "Writings" and "recordings" consist of letters, words, or numbers, or their equivalent, set down by handwriting, typewriting, printing, photostating, photographing, magnetic impulse, mechanical or electronic recording, or other form of data compilation.

(2) Photographs. "Photographs" include still photographs, X-ray films, video tapes, and motion pictures.

(3) Original. An "original" of a writing or recording is the writing or recording itself or any counterpart intended to have the same effect by a person executing or issuing it. An "original" of a photograph includes the negative or any print therefrom. If data are stored in a computer or similar device, any printout or other output readable by sight, shown to reflect the data accurately, is an "original".

(4) Duplicate. A "duplicate" is a counterpart produced by the same impression as the original, or from the same matrix, or by means of photography, including enlargements and miniatures, or by mechanical or electronic re-recording, or by chemical reproduction, or by other equivalent techniques, which accurately reproduces the original.

Rule 1002. Requirement of Original

To prove the content of a writing, recording, or photograph, the original writing, recording, or photograph is required, except as otherwise provided in these rules or by Act of Congress.

Rule 1003. Admissibility of Duplicates

A duplicate is admissible to the same extent as an original unless (1) a genuine question is raised as to the authenticity of the original or (2) in the circumstances it would be unfair to admit the duplicate in lieu of the original.

The contents of an official record, or of a document authorized to be recorded or filed and actually recorded or filed, including data compilations in any form, if otherwise admissible, may be proved by copy, certified as correct in accordance with rule 902 or testified to be correct by a witness who has compared it with the original. If a copy which complies with the foregoing cannot be obtained by the exercise of reasonable diligence, then other evidence of the contents may be given.

Rule 1006. Summaries

The contents of voluminous writings, recordings, or photographs which cannot conveniently be examined in court may be presented in the form of a chart, summary, or calculation. The originals, or duplicates, shall be made available for examination or copying, or both, by other parties at reasonable time and place. The court may order that they be produced in court.

Rule 1008. Functions of Court and Jury

When the admissibility of other evidence of contents of writings, recordings, or photographs under these rules depends upon the fulfillment of a condition of fact, the question whether the condition has been fulfilled is ordinarily for the court to determine in accordance with the provisions of rule 104. However, when an issue is raised (a) whether the asserted writing ever existed, or (b) whether another writing, recording, or photograph produced at the trial is the original, or (c) whether other evidence of contents correctly reflects the contents, the issue is for the trier of fact to determine as in the case of other issues of fact.

[B]   Generally

The "original writing," best or secondary evidence rule, (hereinafter Best Evidence) contained in Article X of the Federal Rules, calls for the original of a document to be offered into evidence. FED. R. EVID. 1002 states, "[t]o prove the content of a writing, recording, or photograph, the original writing, recording, or photograph is required. . . ." FED. R. EVID. 1001(3) states: "If data are stored in a computer or similar device, any printout or other output readable by sight, shown to reflect the data accurately, is an 'original.'" It is important to note that a printout of the information stored on a computer satisfies the Best Evidence rule. While other Rules mention "data compilations," the only rule in the Federal Rules of Evidence to directly mention data stored on a computer is Rule 1001(3). *See*, FED. R. EVID. 801(b)(6) and 1005.

The Best Evidence rule is concerned with the risk of fraud, misreporting, or falsification of the contents of a writing. Since this risk is not as prevalent as it was years ago, Rule 1003 provides that a duplicate to a writing, recording, or photograph is admissible to the same extent as an original unless there's a genuine question raised as to the authenticity of the original or that it would be unfair to admit the duplicate in place of the original.

Rule 1004 provides exceptions to the Best Evidence rule. Rule 1005 covers public records. Rule 1006 provides for introduction of summaries of "voluminous writings, recordings or photographs that cannot conveniently be examined in court."

Rule 1007 provides that the contents of writings, recordings or photographs can be proved by testimony, without producing the original, against the opposing party.

Rule 1007 provides that the contents of a writing, pursuant to the Best Evidence rule, can be established by the admission of the party opponent in the form of testimony, deposition or writing. An oral admission, not under oath, would be insufficient to establish the contents of the writing.

Rule 1008 is a special application of Rule 104. It provides for the allocation of responsibility between the judge's preliminary determination and the weight to be given to "other evidence of contents of writings, recordings or photographs" by the jury after it has been admitted in court.

[C]   Electronic Evidence

Under either Rule 1001(3) or 1006, challenges to electronic data under the Best Evidence rule should be overcome in most cases. Rule 1001(3) provides "[i]f data are stored in a computer or similar device, any printout or other output readable by sight, shown to reflect the data accurately, is an 'original.'" Rule 1006 provides that "[c]ontents of voluminous writings, recordings . . . may be presented in the form of a chart, summary, or calculation."

Similar to a printout, an "electronic image" (such as a TIFF or PDF replica) of electronic data should meet the Best Evidence requirements. These digitized computer files of paper or electronic data are known as "images." Imaging is a technology that converts paper or electronic data into "electronic photographs" in a computer system. Images can be generated directly from electronic information or from paper. If generated from paper, documents are scanned into a computer. "'Scanning' is the process of transforming paper copies (photos, documents, diagrams, charts, and graphs) into digital files." *In re Bristol-Myers Squibb Securities Litigation,* 205 F.R.D. 437, 439 (D.N.J. 2002). Images cannot be word searched and, generally, do not contain metadata from the original electronic file, but are a replica of a paper printout of the computer data.

[D]   Metadata and Best Evidence Issues

One of the emerging issues is whether a paper printout or electronic image of computer data is the Best Evidence, when metadata exist for electronic information. Metadata is "hidden" or "embedded" information that is stored in electronically generated materials, but which is not visible when documents or materials are printed. It is often thought of as computer information that exists beyond the visible data viewed in an application software program. This is significantly different from paper information, where all of the information is set out before you.

Metadata is automatically generated and stored when an electronic record, such as a word processing document, e-mail or a spreadsheet is created. For example a word processing document creates metadata that describes the document, its author, its date of creation and the dates on which changes were made. This metadata is never found on the printed form of the document. Spreadsheet printouts show lots of numbers, but not their "metadata" formulae. If you want to determine whether a particular person was copied on e-mail, then the metadata would disclose the persons copied as well as who was blind copied. For further discussion *see* § 3.7, *Metadata, Hidden, or Embedded Information.*

Though not characterized as such, "Best Evidence" metadata issues were addressed in *Armstrong v. Executive Office of the President,* 810 F. Supp. 335, 341-342 (D.D.C. 1993). There the court ruled that:

> A paper copy of the electronic material does not contain all of the information included in the electronic version. For example, a note distributed over these computer system includes information that is not reproduced on the paper copy regarding who has received the information and when the information was received, neither of which is reproduced on the paper copy.

In later proceedings, the court in *Armstrong v. Executive Office of the President, Office of Admin.,* 1 F.3d 1274, 1283, 1285 (D.C. Cir. 1993), held:

> [T]he mere existence of the paper printouts does not affect the record status of the electronic materials unless the paper versions include all significant material contained in the electronic records. Otherwise, the two documents cannot accurately be termed "copies" - identical twins - but are, at most, "kissing cousins." Since the record shows that the two versions of the documents may frequently be only cousins - perhaps distant ones at that - the electronic documents retain their status as federal records after the creation of the paper print-outs . . . Our refusal to agree with the government that electronic records are merely "extra copies" of the paper versions amounts to far more than judicial nitpicking. Without the missing information, the paper print-outs - akin to traditional memoranda with the "to" and "from" cut off and even the "received" stamp pruned away - are dismembered documents indeed.

See also, Williams v. Sprint/United Mgmt. Co., 230 F.R.D. 640, 652-653 (D. Kan. 2005) (Court ordered an employer in an employment discrimination case to restore the metadata it had "scrubbed" or "erased" from Excel spreadsheet files and "unlock" them. The Court noted that " . . . metadata associated with any changes to the spreadsheets, the dates of any changes, the identification of the individuals making any changes, and other metadata from which Plaintiffs could determine the final versus draft version of the spreadsheets appear relevant.")

Neither paper nor an electronic image (e.g., TIFF, PDF) of an electronic document retains the metadata of the original document. For this reason, a computer printout or electronic image is not always a complete representation of the computer-based information, and therefore, it is arguable under Article X and FED. R. EVID. 1001 and 1002 that only the computer-based versions of documents, including metadata, are "original" documents.

[E]   Reported Cases

• *United States ex rel. Magid v. Wilderman,* No. CIV.96-346, 2004 U.S. Dist. LEXIS 17494, n.5 (D. Pa. Aug. 18, 2004). The Court noted during a dispute over the admissibility of evidence that "[i]t is likely that such microfiche copies would be admissible as 'duplicate[s]' . . . [under] FED. R. EVID. 1003."

[F]   Business Record Acts

Always determine whether there is a business record act in your jurisdiction that defines documents, writings or records for evidentiary purposes.

For example the Federal Business Records Act, U.S. Code Title 28, § 1732, provides:

If any . . . department or agency of government, in the regular course of business or activity has kept or recorded any memorandum, writing, entry, print, representation or combination thereof, of any act, transaction, occurrence, or event, and in the regular course of business has caused any or all of the same to be recorded, copied, or reproduced by any . . . process which accurately reproduces or forms a durable medium for so reproducing the original, the original may be destroyed in the regular course of business unless its preservation is required by law. Such reproduction, when satisfactorily identified, is as admissible in evidence as the original itself in any judicial or administrative proceeding whether the original is in existence or not. . . . The introduction of a reproduced record . . . does not preclude admission of the original.

Specific Type of Computer Evidence

§ 8.12   E-MAIL

[A]   Generally

E-mail has been one of the most prolific sources of electronic evidence in both high profile and routine cases. From the Monica Lewinsky and Oliver North cases to employment discrimination cases, e-mail has proven to be valuable evidence.

They have become one of the most sought-after forms of electronic evidence because of their informal, casual nature and the fact that they, generally, cannot be permanently deleted. Many employees and others are often surprised to learn that their off-the-cuff remarks contained in e-mail are discoverable. Also, once an e-mail is sent, it may be stored on a variety of different computers (the senders, recipients, Internet service providers and others) as well as other storage media (backup tapes, pen drives, etc.).

E-mail can be relevant in a variety of litigation cases including business, securities and personal matters. In today's modern business setting, e-mail messages may include informal communications on business matters, status reports, inventory lists, minutes of meetings, drafts of documents, business strategies or records of important business decisions. Personal e-mail can include admissions regarding liability, injuries, damages and employment discrimination matters.

Although e-mail is obtainable through discovery, there is no guarantee that it will be admissible in court. All evidence must satisfy the threshold requirements of authentication, relevancy, hearsay and Best Evidence. For an additional discussion of e-mail, *see* § 3.8, *E-Mail.*

[B]   Definition

In *Verizon Online Services, Inc. v. Ralsky,* 203 F. Supp. 2d 601, 605 (E.D. Va. 2002), the court described e-mail as follows:

> E-mail is essentially a method of communicating and doing business over the Internet. It "enables an individual to send an electronic message - generally akin to a note or letter - to another individual or to a group of addressees. The message is generally stored electronically, sometimes waiting for the recipient to check her 'mailbox' and sometimes making its receipt known through some type of prompt." *Reno,* 521 U.S. at 851, 117 S. Ct. 2329, 2335. In addition to text, e-mail can contain hyperlinks to Web sites located on the World Wide Web. The World Wide Web is a communications platform that allows Internet users to search for and retrieve information stored in remote computers connected to the Internet.

See also, Armstrong v. Executive Office of the President, 877 F. Supp. 690, 717 (D.D.C. 1995) ("[the court described e-mail as a]document created or received on an E-mail system including brief notes, more formal or substantive narrative documents, and any attachments, such as word processing documents, which may be transmitted with the message. . . . ").

[C]   Foundation

[1]   Generally

After discovering electronic mail and other electronic data, admitting this evidence requires application of the traditional rules of evidence to a different type of information format. The evidentiary issues relating to admissibility are generally the same as with conventional paper documents, however the factual predicate for establishing authentication and other evidentiary rules will be different.

One noted commentator stated:

> The explosive growth of the Internet and burgeoning use of electronic mail are raising a series of novel evidentiary issues. The applicable legal principles are familiar--this evidence must be authenticated and, to the extent offered for its truth, it must satisfy hearsay concerns. The novelty of the evidentiary issues arises out of the novelty of the media - thus, it is essentially factual. These issues can be resolved by a relatively straightforward application of the existing principles in a fashion very similar to the way they are applied to other computer-generated evidence and to more traditional exhibits.

Gregory P. Joseph, *Internet and E-mail Evidence,* Computer and Internet Lawyer (April 2002).

Evidentiary considerations for admissibility of e-mail are set out below. In addition to these rules of evidence, one should review federal and state law for existence of statutes that may specifically address evidentiary issues concerning electronic communications. For example, many states have laws defining electronic records and provide that these records qualify as writings for evidentiary considerations. *See,* "Georgia Electronic Records and Signatures Act." §§ 10-12-1 to 10-12-5: *Transport Indem. Co. v. Seib,* 178 Neb. 253, 132 N.W.2d 871 (1965) (applying Nebraska Business Record Act).

[2]   Authentication or Identification

[a]   Generally

Computer-generated evidence, like e-mail, must be authenticated prior to admission and consideration by the trier of fact. *Uncle Henry's, Inc. v. Plaut Consulting Inc.,* 240 F. Supp. 2d 63, 71 (D. Me. 2002) ("e-mails (like letters and other documents) must be properly authenticated or shown to be self-authenticating.").

The judge, pursuant to FED. R. EVID. 104 and 901, makes the preliminary determination as to authentication. After the preliminary determination of admissibility is made, the parties can introduce evidence as to the weight to be given to the evidence in order to prove whether the e-mail is what it purports to be and whether there is a connection between the e-mail and a particular individual. *See generally,* FED. R. EVID. 104(e) (allowing parties to argue evidentiary weight to the jury); *see also,* § 8.10, *Requirement of Authentication or Identification.*

Article IX of the Federal Rules provides three rules in authenticating evidence. Rule 901 addresses the standard authentication process of requiring "evidence sufficient to support a finding that the matter in question is what its proponent claims" and provides authentication examples. Rule 902 addresses self-authentication and Rule 903 makes testimony of a subscribing witness unnecessary. E-mail is not included in one of Rule 902's ten enumerated categories of self-authenticating documents. Generally, Rule 901 provides the basis for the authentication requirements for e-mail.

Rule 901 sets forth several illustrations, which provide guidance as to authentication of e-mail.

Rule 901(b)(1) allows authentication by testimony of a witness with knowledge "that a matter is what it is claimed to be." In isolated instances, the witness may have actually observed the person creating and sending e-mail and can testify as to its authentication.

Rule 901 (b)(4) allows evidence to be authenticated by the presence of "[d]istinctive characteristics and the like." These characteristics may relate to an item's "[a]ppearance, contents, substance, internal patterns, or other distinctive characteristics, taken in conjunction with circumstances." FED. R. EVID. 901(b)(4). This is generally the illustration that is most often used in authenticating e-mail.

Rule 901(b)(10) provides for authentication by "[m]ethods provided by statute or rule." It is best to check federal and state statutes that may pertain to the authentication of writings, which may include e-mail.

Self-authentication of e-mail under Rule 902 can occur under a variety of circumstances. A common self-authenticating provision is Rule 902(7), which provides that "[t]rade inscriptions and the like. Inscriptions, signs, tags, or labels purporting to have been affixed in the course of business and indicating ownership, control, or origin." This provision is often used to self-authenticate business communications.

[b]   Factual Proof of Authentication

Set out below are several different techniques for authenticating e-mail. The quantum of proof necessary for the court to preliminarily admit e-mail pursuant to FED. R. EVID. 104 for ultimate consideration by the trier of fact will be different depending on the facts of the case and the jurisdiction of the court.

Authentication of e-mail may involve the following testimony.

Author/Recipient evidence

- Can the author, recipient or a third party identify a printout of the e-mail?

- Does the e-mail printout accurately reflect what was in the computer?

- Can someone testify as to the identity of the author/sender of the e-mail?

- Was a password required to be entered before sending or receiving e-mail by either the author or recipient?

- Did the recipient receive the e-mail?

- Describe the contents of the e-mail.

- Does the message show the origin of the e-mail – such as the author's name and/or e-mail address?

- Was the author using the computer on that particular day?

- Did the body of the e-mail contain the typewritten name or nickname of the author?

- Were the facts discussed in the e-mail only known to the individual (such as the author) that sent it or other people?

- Were there any distinguishing writing characteristics of the author? Did the author have a particular word choice or sentence structure?

- Was the purported author likely to know the information that was reflected in the message?

- Was there any subsequent conversation or action regarding the e-mail?

- After receiving the e-mail, did someone have a conversation with the author that reflected his knowledge of the contents and connection with the e-mail?

- Did the author take action consistent with the content of the message? For example, in business, this may include delivery of merchandise mentioned in the message. This type of conduct provides circumstantial authentication of the source of the e-mail.

Business evidence

- Was it necessary to enter a password to gain access to the computer or e-mail program? Also, was there a requirement that the password be frequently changed and/or a prohibition against using the same password?

- Did the body of the e-mail contain textual or graphic trademarks, signs, tags or labels? This would show a connection with a specific company, and self-authentication under Rule 902(7), Federal Rules of Civil Procedure.

- Was the identity of a business reflected in the header or in the body of the e-mail? For example an e-mail message from smith@ABCcorp.com would provide evidence that the e-mail was sent from Smith from ABC Corporation. This may self-authenticate the e-mail as having been sent by the organization under FED. R. EVID. 902(7).

- Did the customer or entity receive the e-mail? Can the e-mail be connected to the business?

- Describe the contents of the e-mail.

The reply letter doctrine

Courts have developed the so-called "reply letter doctrine." Under the doctrine, if a person sends a letter to a person, and after receiving the letter the recipient replies, the reply letter provides some evidence of authentication. For the doctrine to be established, testimony should be provided that the author prepared e-mail, the recipient received the e-mail, the recipient replied to the first e-mail and in the contents or body of the e-mail referred to the sender's e-mail. The testimony should show that the reply bore the name of the author, the sender recognizes the exhibit as the second e-mail or reply, and on what basis he or she recognizes the exhibit.

In *United States v. Reilly,* 33 F.3d 1396, 1407, 1408 (3rd Cir. 1994) the court stated,

A common aspect of authentication permissible under Rule 901(b)(4) is the reply doctrine which provides that once a letter, telegram, or telephone call is shown to have been mailed, sent or made, a letter, telegram or telephone call shown by its contents to be in reply is authenticated without more. Graham, *Federal Practice and Procedure: Evidence* § 6825 at 868-69; 5 *Weinstein's Evidence* ¶ 901(b)(4)[05] at 901-76, states, "[a] letter can be authenticated by testimony or other proof that it was sent in reply to a duly authenticated writing. A reply letter often needs no further authentication because it would be unlikely for anyone other than the purported writer to know and respond to the contents of an earlier letter addressed to him."

Expert testimony and header information

An expert may have sufficient technical knowledge of e-mail transmission and the identification process to be able to authenticate e-mail through testimony. For example, there are e-mail metadata or headers that trace its path, provide a message number ID and other information that could be used to authenticate. For an explanation of header information *see* § 3.8[J], *Metadata and Headers*.

Authentication arising from production

The court can deem documents produced pursuant to a discovery request authentic. See cases below.

Other authentication methods

- § 2.6[G], *Audit Trails and Logs;*
- § 3.5[H][1], *Encryption and Steganography;*
- § 5.5[G], *Chain of Custody, Audit Reports and Hash Values;* and
- Digital Signatures.

[c]   Challenges to Authenticity

To dispute the authentication of e-mail, the opposing party may challenge the trustworthiness and reliability of the electronic information. Such claims will generally affect the weight, and not the admissibility of evidence. *See,* FED. R. EVID. 104 and 901.

Some potential challenges:

- Were there any steps taken to safeguard the information from being falsified?
- Could the headers and other information have been altered?
- How were the contents of the e-mail transmitted and stored during the discovery process? Were they stored on read-only disks or CD-ROMs?
- Did a neutral expert retrieve the electronic information?
- On what type of system was the information stored prior to retrieval?
- How was the e-mail retrieved?
- Is there a sufficient chain of custody to eliminate questions that the information stored on a computer disk or hard drive was not manipulated, altered, replaced or spoiled in such a way that will affect its trustworthiness?

[d]   Reported Cases

Generally

- *Uncle Henry's Inc. v. Plaut Consulting Inc.,* 240 F. Supp. 2d 63 (D. Me. 2003). The Court ruled that e-mail are proper summary judgment material as long as they are properly authenticated or shown to be self-authenticating.

- *Fenje v. Feld,* 301 F. Supp. 2d 781, 809 (D. Ill. 2003). The Court ruled that "[e]-mail communications may be authenticated as being from the purported author based on an affidavit of the recipient; the e-mail address from which it originated; comparison of the content to other evidence; and/or statements or other communications from the purported author acknowledging the e-mail communication that is being authenticated. (citations omitted)."

Rule 104

- *United States v. Tann,* 425 F. Supp. 2d 26, 37-38 (D.D.C. 2006). The defendant was criminally charged and objected to the admission of a specific e-mail. The Court found that the e-mail was authenticated under FED. R. EVID. 104 since the e-mail address appeared logically connected to the defendant's place of employment.

Rule 901

- Like other electronic evidence, e-mail can be fabricated or falsified. However, in *United States v. Safavian,* No. CR.05-0370, 2006 U.S. Dist. LEXIS 32284, at *11-12 (D.D.C. May 23, 2006) the Court in responding to the defendant's motion to exclude nested e-mail the Court stated:

  The defendant argues that the trustworthiness of these e-mails cannot be demonstrated, particularly those e-mails that are embedded within e-mails as having been forwarded to or by others or as the previous e-mail to which a reply was sent. The Court rejects this as an argument against authentication of the e-mails. The defendant's argument is more appropriately directed to the weight the jury should give the evidence, not to its authenticity. While the defendant is correct that earlier e-mails that are included in a chain - either as ones that have been forwarded or to which another has replied - may be altered, this trait is not specific to e-mail evidence. It can be true of any piece of documentary evidence, such as a letter, a contract or an invoice. Indeed, fraud trials frequently center on altered paper documentation, which, through the use of techniques such as photocopies, white-out, or wholesale forgery, easily can be altered. The possibility of alteration does not and cannot be the basis for excluding e-mails as unidentified or unauthenticated as a matter of course, any more than it can be the rationale for excluding paper documents (and copies of those documents). We live in an age of technology and computer use where e-mail communication now is a normal and frequent fact for the majority of this nation's population, and is of particular importance in the professional world. The defendant is free to raise this issue with the jury and put on evidence that e-mails are capable of being altered before they are passed on. Absent specific evidence showing alteration, however, the Court will not exclude any embedded e-mails because of the mere possibility that it can be done.

See, § 3.8[N], *Falsification of E-mail* for further information.

- *United States v. Safavian,* No. CR.05-0370, 2006 U.S. Dist. LEXIS 32284 (D.D.C. May 23, 2006). In this detailed criminal case opinion the Court granted in part and denied in part the defendant's motion to exclude e-mail. The Court discussed e-mail authentication requirements pursuant to FED. R. EVID. 901-902 - specifically Rule 902(11), 901(b)(3) and 901(b)(4). The Court discussed the various hearsay exceptions and provided a chart setting forth hearsay rulings as to 260 e-mail.

- *United States v. Siddiqui,* 235 F.3d 1318 (11th Cir. 2000). The defendant falsely listed references on an application for a research grant from the National Science Foundation (NSF). Using e-mail he asked the references to tell NSF that he had their permission to use their names prior to the application being sent. In this fraud prosecution, the e-mail were properly authenticated under FED. R. EVID. 901 since they bore the defendant's e-mail address and used the defendant's nickname, and the defendant followed up with phone calls making same request.

- *United States v. Scott-Emuakpor,* No. CR.99-1382000, 2000 WL 288443, at *13, 14 (W.D. Mich. Jan. 25, 2000). In this criminal case the court held computer files (including e-mail) taken from the defendant's computer had been authenticated and stated:

  To establish authenticity, the proponent need not rule out all possibilities inconsistent with authenticity or prove beyond any doubt that the evidence is what it purports to be. Rather, the standard for authentication is one of "reasonable likelihood" that the evidence is authentic. Generally, Rule 901(a) is satisfied if the proponent makes a sufficient showing to allow a reasonable person to believe the evidence is what it purports to be. After the court is satisfied that this showing has been made and admits the evidence as authenticated, the jury decides what weight to give the evidence. . . . Thus, for example, the Government may meet the authentication requirement through the testimony of a witness who was present and observed the procedure by which the documents were obtained from Defendant's computers.

- *Massimo v. State,* 144 S.W.3d 210 (Tex. App. Fort Worth 2004). In a harassment case the Court ruled that e-mail had been sufficiently authenticated pursuant to Rule 901(a), (b)(4) where; the e-mail referred to an altercation between defendant and victim that had occurred shortly before the e-mail was sent, the victim recognized the defendants' e-mail address, the victim testified that only the defendant and few other people knew about things discussed in e-mail, the victim testified the way in which e-mail was written was the way in which the defendant would communicate, and a witness testified that she saw defendant send similar threatening e-mail to victim using same vulgarities.

- *Tibbetts v. RadioShack Corp.,* No. CIV.03-2249, 2004 WL 2203418, at *13 (N.D.Ill. Sept. 29, 2004). On a summary judgment motion the Court considered e-mails over the authenticity objections of the plaintiff. The Court held the e-mail records were authenticated under Rule 901(b)(1) since the witness himself stated "under oath that the exhibits are true and correct copies of his own correspondence, thus providing the foundation for their admission."

Rule 902

- *Superhighway Consulting, Inc. v. Techwave, Inc.,* No. CIV.98-5502, 1999 WL 1044870, at *2 (N.D. Ill. Nov. 16, 1999). The Court preliminarily decided that e-mail were self-authenticating under Federal Rule of Evidence 902(7), or since they were produced during discovery from the party's own files, that this would authenticate the e-mail.

Authentication arising from production

- *Orr v. Bank of America,* NT & SA, 285 F.3d 764, 777 n.20 (9th Cir. 2002). The court stated, "documents produced by a party in discovery were deemed authentic when offered by the party-opponent. Authentication can also be accomplished through judicial admissions such as . . . production of items in response to . . . [a] discovery request." *See also, Maljack Prods., Inc. v. GoodTimes Home Video Corp.,* 81 F.3d 881, 889 n.12 (9th Cir. 1996) (discovery documents were deemed authentic, when disclosed by party-opponent and no objection was made to their alleged lack of authenticity); *In re Homestore.com, Inc. Securities Litigation,* 347 F. Supp.2d 769, 781(C.D.Cal. 2004) (e-mails were found to be authentic since they were produced by the objecting party); *See generally, United States v. Doe,* 465 U.S. 605, 614 n.13, 79 L. Ed. 2d 552, 104 S. Ct. 1237 (1984); *United States v. Lawrence,* 934 F.2d 868, 870-72 (7th Cir. 1991); *Hood v. Dryvit Systems, Inc.,* No. CIV.04-3141, 2005 U.S. Dist. LEXIS 27055, 2005 WL 3005612 *3 (N.D. Ill. Nov. 8, 2005); and *United States v. Brown,* 688 F.2d 1112, 1114-15 (7th Cir. 1982).

Header information

- *Clement v. California Dept. of Corrections,* 220 F. Supp. 2d 1098, 1111 (N.D. Cal. 2002). In a prisoner lawsuit the Court noted that, "major e-mail providers include a coded Internet Protocol address (IP address) in the header of every e-mail. . . . The IP address allows the recipient of an e-mail to identify the sender by contacting the service provider. . . . There are, of course, means available to disguise the origin of an e-mail message."

- *People v. Downin,* 828 N.E.2d 341 (Ill.App. 3 Dist. 2005). On appeal from a criminal conviction, the defendant argued that the trial court admitted e-mails without proper foundation by not requiring evidence that the e-mails were linked to his IP address. The court held that circumstantial evidence was sufficient to establish authenticity, including testimony of the victim that the e-mails contained information known only by her and the defendant.

Residual authentication

- *Federal Trade Comm'n. v. Cyberspace.com,* No. CIV.00-1806, 2002 WL 32060289 (W.D. Wash. Jul. 10, 2002). The defendants solicited customers for its internet services by mailing "checks" to consumers. When consumers cashed the "check" to receive their rebate, they were immediately signed up for internet services with defendants. At trial, the FTC sought to introduce consumer e-mails and letters of complaint for its case. Admitting the e-mails, the court held that they showed the defendants had notice that their practice was deceptive, and that they fell under the residual hearsay exception: the e-mails were written contemporaneously upon receipt of deceptive advertising, were made available to defendants for review and were trustworthy because of the great numbers of e-mails that all relatively stated the same information.

Failure to authenticate

- *Pettiford v. North Carolina Dept. of Health and Human Services,* 228 F. Supp. 2d 677 (M.D.N.C. 2002). The e-mail exchanged between supervisors concerning the employee's complaint could not be considered at the summary judgment stage of Title VII retaliation action absent proper authentication.

- *Network Alliance Group, LLC. v. Cable & Wireless USA, Inc.,* No. CIV.02-2002, 2002 WL 1205734, at *1, (D. Minn. May 31, 2002). The Court noted authenticity problems with e-mail in denying injunction request, and stated, "C & W has noted a number of other inconsistencies within the alleged e-mail correspondence which suggest that the correspondence is not authentic. Most notably, the 'date stamp' for one of the e-mail messages is Thursday, December 6, 2002. Obviously, December 6, 2002, has not yet arrived. Moreover, December 6, 2001, was a Thursday, but December 6, 2002, will be a Friday."

- *Richard Howard, Inc. v. Hogg,* No. 12-96-5, 1996 WL 689231, at *3 (Ohio App. Nov. 19, 1996). Court excluded e-mail where the authenticating witness "was neither the recipient nor the sender of the email transmissions and he offered no other details establishing his personal knowledge that these messages were actually sent or received by the parties involved. Furthermore, the transmissions were not authenticated by any other means."

- *Internet Doorway, Inc. v. Parks,* 138 F. Supp. 2d 773 (S.D. Miss. 2001). The plaintiff alleged that the defendant falsified the "from" header to make an e-mail appear to have been sent from the plaintiff's Internet Service Provider (ISP).

Facts Supporting Authentication

- *State v. Braidic,* No. 28952-1-II, 2004 WL 52412, *2 (Jan. 13, 2004)(unpublished). The Court recounted the evidence that the defendant sent the e-mail to the victim, "J.C. testified that she received an e-mail that appeared to be from Braidic. She explained that she knew Braidic's e-mail address and sent a message to it. In response, she got the disputed e-mail from Bilbo Baggins . . . Moreover, Braidic was likely the only person with the motive to send such a message. This was sufficient to show that Braidic sent the message."

- *Kearley v. Mississippi,* 843 So. 2d 66 (Miss. Ct. App. 2002). The victim's testimony that she had received and printed the e-mail on her computer and defendant's admission sufficiently authenticated the e-mail.

[e]   Discovery Pointers

- If you anticipate authentication problems arising at trial, consider filing a request for admissions on the authenticity of documents pursuant to FED. R. EVID. 36. Under the rule you may request the opposing party to admit the authenticity of documents. If the opponent denies the request for admissions, and you have to authenticate the document at trial, you may receive costs for making the offer of proof that was rejected.

- Request a pretrial conference to resolve any problems with authentication through the use of stipulations by the parties.

- Identification and authentication of e-mail documents may also be resolved during depositions.

[f]   Other Authorities

- Mark D. Robins, *Evidence at the Electronic Frontier: Introducing E-mail at Trial in Commercial Litigation,* 29 Rutgers Computer & Tech. L.J. 219 (2003).

- Anthony J. Dreyer, *When the Postman Beeps Twice: The Admissibility of Electronic Mail Under the Business Records Exception of the Federal Rules of Evidence,* 64 Fordham L. Rev. 2285, 2305 (Apr. 1996).

- Monique C.M. Leahy, *Recovery and Reconstruction of Electronic Mail as Evidence,* 41 Am. Jur. Proof of Facts 3d 1 at § 19 (1997).

- Andrew Jablon, *"God Mail": Authentication and Admissibility of Electronic Mail in Federal Courts,* 34 Am. Crim. L. Rev. 1387-1409 (1997).

- McKeon, *Electronic Date Interchange: Uses and Legal Aspects in the Commercial Arena,* 12 J. Marshall J. Computer & Info. L. 511 (1994).

- Gregory P. Joseph, *Internet and Email Evidence,* (April 2001), available at http://www.josephnyc.com/INTERNET.shtml (last visited July 27, 2006).

[3]   Relevancy

[a]   Generally

For a general discussion of relevancy *see* § 8.7, *Relevancy.*

[b]   Reported Cases

- *Strauss v. Microsoft Corp.*, No. CIV.91-5928, 1995 WL 326492, at *1 (S.D.N.Y., Jun. 1, 1995). Defendant Microsoft attacked the admissibility of damaging e-mail messages as not relevant, unfairly prejudicial, and confusing and misleading to the jury. The court found the e-mail relevant to show a pretext for failing to promote the plaintiff and that their probative value outweighed their prejudicial effect.

- *United States v. Quattrone,* 441 F.3d 153, 165 (2d Cir. 2006). The Appellate Court reversed and remanded for a new trial the criminal convictions of the defendant based on faulty jury instructions. The defendant was aware of agency investigations when an e-mail was sent suggesting that other employees follow the company's document retention policy. On appeal the Court discussed the e-mail and applied the criteria of FED. R. EVID. 401-404 and found the e-mail relevant.

- *Monotype Corp., PLC v. International Typeface Corp.,* 43 F.3d 443, 450 (9th Cir. 1994). Pursuant to Rule 403, the Court would not admit an e-mail transmission expressing highly derogatory remarks due to prejudicial nature of the message and the fact it was not an admissible business record.

- *State v. Taylor,* 2003 WL 22966270, at *5-6 (Ohio Dec. 18, 2003). The Court found a threatening e-mail, sent after the date of the intimidation charge, was admissible under

FED. R. EVID. 404(B) as other evidence of other crimes, wrongs, or acts since its probative value was not outweighed by its prejudicial effect.

- *United States v. Sprick,* 233 F.3d 845 (5th Cir. 2000). Court ruled probative value of failed sent e-mail (e-mail was sent but it was returned as undeliverable because the wrong e-mail destination had been used) in which advisor admitted he had stolen money, was not outweighed by danger of prejudice.

- *Jamsport Entertainment, LLC v. Paradama Productions, Inc.,* No. CIV.02-2298, 2005 WL 14917, at *15 (N.D.Ill. Jan. 3, 2005). The Court denied a party's argument that "the e-mail should be excluded under Federal Rule of Evidence 403; the e-mail is probative of Clear Channel's intent, and it has identified no unfair prejudice that would result from its admission."

- *Gagnon v. Sprint Corp.,* 284 F.3d 839 (8th Cir. 2002). Court precluded e-mail because of lack of relevance.

- *Kelley v. Airborne Freight Corp.,* 140 F.3d 335 (1st Cir. 1998). Court excluded e-mail reports based on FED. R. EVID. 403, in part, because they were cumulative of other evidence.

- *JPMorgan Chase Bank ex rel. Mahonia Ltd. v. Liberty Mut. Life Ins. Co.,* No. CIV.01-11523, 2002 WL 31867731 (S.D.N.Y Dec. 23, 2002). The Court ruled that Internal e-mail evidence was probative of sureties' claim that they had been defrauded into bonding disguised loans, and such probative value was not substantially outweighed by danger of unfair prejudice.

[4]   Hearsay

[a]   Generally

The introduction of an e-mail message into evidence at trial will generally raise hearsay issues. These issues will depend upon the contents of the message, sender's identity and the availability of a witness to authenticate the document. If e-mail contains information that the sender obtained from another source, then double hearsay issues arise. Also, e-mail may contain opinion testimony that is generally inadmissible.

If these problems arise, the practitioner will have to establish that the evidence is nonhearsay or falls under one of the hearsay exceptions. The hearsay issues associated with e-mail are largely the same as those associated with conventional correspondence.

For a general discussion of hearsay *see* § 8.9, *Hearsay.*

[b]   Nonhearsay

The hearsay rule applies only to statements offered to prove the truth of what they assert. It does not apply to statements offered for other reasons. For example, words can be spoken that are offered to show their effect on a listener or reader, to show a person's feelings or state of mind, or have independent legal significance and are considered nonhearsay. *See,* Christopher B. Mueller & Laird C. Kirkpatrick, 4 *Federal Evidence* § 385-390 (1994). "There is a well established exception or departure from the hearsay rule applying to cases in which the fact in controversy is whether certain things were said or done and not as to whether these things were true or false, and in these cases the words or acts are admissible not as hearsay, but as original evidence." *People v. Fields,* 61 Cal. App. 4th 1063, 1069, 72 Cal. Rptr.2d 255 (2d Dist. 1998), quoting *People v. Henry,* 86 Cal. App. 2d 785, 789, 195 P.2d 478 (4th Dist. 1948).

[i]   Reported Cases

• *United States v. Safavian,* No. CR.05-0370, 2006 U.S. Dist. LEXIS 32284 (D.D.C. May 23, 2006). In this detailed criminal case opinion the Court granted in part and denied in part the defendant's motion to exclude e-mail. The Court discussed e-mail authentication requirements pursuant to FED. R. EVID. 901-902 - specifically Rule 902(11), 901(b)(3) and 901(b)(4). The Court also provided a chart setting forth hearsay exception rulings as to 260 e-mail and discussed the various hearsay exceptions.

• *United States v. Siddiqui,* 235 F.3d 1318, 1322-23 (11th Cir. 2000), *cert. denied,* 533 U.S. 940 (2001). The Court held that e-mail "sent by *Siddiqui* constitute admissions of a party pursuant to FED. R. EVID. 801(d)(2)(A) and those between Siddiqui and Yamada unrelated to the NSF [National Science Foundation] investigation are nonhearsay admitted to show Siddiqui's and Yamada's relationship and custom of communicating by e-mail."

• *In re Senior Living Properties, L.L.C.,* 309 B.R. 223, 229 (Bankr. N.D. Tex. Apr. 23, 2004). The Court ruled that an e-mail was admissible and stated that it "has not considered the content of an e-mail for the truth of the matter asserted, but the court does consider an e-mail as evidence of the fact of the communication."

• *State v. Braidic,* No. 28952-1-II, 2004 WL 52412, *2 (Jan. 13, 2004)(unpublished). The trial court originally allowed the admission of e-mail under the present sense impression hearsay in criminal trial. The Appellate Court reversed the basis of admitting the e-mail finding that the e-mail was not hearsay since it was not offered to prove the truth of the statements.

- *New York v. Microsoft Corp.*, No. CIV.98-1233, 2002 WL 649951 (D.D.C. Apr. 12, 2002). After discussing the nonhearsay argument and hearsay exceptions, business record and present sense impression, the court precluded the admission of the e-mail.

- *Henegar v. Daimler-Chrysler Corp.*, 280 F. Supp. 2d 680, 688 (E.D. Mich. 2003). The Court found that an e-mail that "only repeats what his subordinate supposedly told him" is inadmissible hearsay.

[c]   Reported Cases - Exceptions to the Hearsay Rule

If e-mail is offered to prove the truth of the matter asserted, hearsay concerns must be addressed. Below are methods to avoid the hearsay issue, or to admit the e-mail as an exception to the hearsay rule.

[i]   801(d) Admission of a Party Opponent

- *United States v. Tann*, 425 F. Supp. 2d 26, 37-38 (D.D.C. 2006). The defendant was criminally charged and objected to the admission of e-mail. The Court found that the four page exchange e-mail was authenticated under FED. R. EVID. 104 since the e-mail address appeared logically connected to the defendant's place of employment and fit within Federal Rule of Evidence 801(d)(2) as an admission made by the defendant.

- *Nobody in Particular Presents, Inc. v. Clear Channel Communications*, 311 F. Supp. 2d 1048, 1094-95 (D. Colo. 2004). The Court ruled e-mail messages were admissible from rock radio stations to record companies and agents of rock artists. These e-mail messages gave preference of air time and promotional support if they choose a concert promoter connected to the station. They were admissible over a hearsay objection as an admission of a party opponent.

- *In re Homestore.com, Inc. Securities Litigation*, 347 F. Supp.2d 769, 781(C.D.Cal. 2004). The e-mails written by a party are admissions of a party opponent and admissible as non-hearsay under FED. R. EVID. 801(d)(2).

- *Means v. Cullen*, 297 F. Supp. 2d 1148, 1151-52 (W.D. Wis. 2003). The Court found that e-mail sent by a state prison psychologist in which she denied telling a suicidal state prisoner that no one would care if he died, was excluded as hearsay. "The content of defendant's email does not qualify as an admission by a party opponent because it is not offered against defendant, *see* FED. R. EVID. 801(d)(2)(A), and it does not qualify as a recorded recollection because defendant has not shown that she cannot recall making the statement."

- *Perfect 10, Inc. v. Cybernet Ventures, Inc.*, 213 F. Supp. 2d 1146 (C.D. Cal. 2002). Court held employee e-mail communications were party admissions and third party nonhearsay indicating notice of infringing or potentially infringing activity.

- *Riisna v. American Broadcasting Companies, Inc.*, 219 F. Supp. 2d 568 (S.D.N.Y. 2002). Court admitted e-mail as vicarious admission of party opponent under the hearsay exception of admission of party opponent.

- *Sea-Land Service, Inc. v. Lozen Intern.*, LLC, 285 F.3d 808, 821 (9th Cir. 2002). The Court ruled an e-mail party admission was admissible, if it is offered against a party and is "a statement by the party's agent or servant concerning a matter within the scope of the agency or employment, made during the existence of the relationship." This rule "requires the proffering party to lay a foundation to show that an otherwise excludable statement relates to a matter within the scope of the agent's employment."

- *United States v. Siddiqui*, 235 F.3d 1318, 1322-23 (11th Cir. 2000), *cert. denied*, 533 U.S. 940 (2001). The Court held e-mail were admissions of a party pursuant to FED. R. EVID. 801(d)(2)(A). Other e-mail was nonhearsay and admitted to show parties relationship and custom of communicating by e-mail.

- *Vermont Elec. Power Co., Inc. v. Hartford Steam Boiler Inspection and Ins. Co.*, 72 F. Supp. 2d 441 (D. Vt. 1999). The Court held that e-mail indicating that an expert's reports were not conclusive on an issue in dispute with the insurer were admissions by a party opponent and an exception to the hearsay rule.

- *Aviles v. McKenzie*, No. CIV.91-2013, 1992 WL 715248 (N.D. Cal. Mar. 17, 1992). Court admitted e-mail under admission of party opponent hearsay exception.

[ii]   Present Sense Impression

- *Westfed Holdings, Inc. v. United States*, 55 Fed. Cl. 544 (Fed. Cl. Mar. 17, 2003). Court precluded admission of e-mail under the business record and present sense exceptions of the hearsay rule.

- *New York v. Microsoft Corp.*, No. CIV.98-1233, 2002 WL 649951 (D.D.C. Apr. 12, 2002). After discussing the nonhearsay argument and hearsay exceptions, business record and present sense impression, the court precluded the admission of the e-mail.

- *United States v. Ferber*, 966 F. Supp. 90 (D. Mass. 1997). The court refused to admit e-mail from an employee to his supervisor recounting a conversation the employee had with the defendant under the business records exception since no evidence that the e-mail record had to be maintained. The court admitted the e-mail under the present sense impression because the e-mail was prepared shortly after the conversation occurred.

[iii]   Excited Utterance.

• *United States v. Ferber,* 966 F. Supp. 90 (D. Mass. 1997). The Court refused to apply the hearsay "excited utterance" exception to e-mail.

[iv]   Recorded Recollection

• *Means v. Cullen,* 297 F. Supp. 2d 1148, 1151-52 (W.D. Wis. 2003). The Court found that e-mail sent by a state prison psychologist in which she denied telling a suicidal state prisoner that no one would care if he died, was excluded as hearsay. "The content of defendant's email does not qualify as an admission by a party opponent because it is not offered against defendant, *see* FED. R. EVID. 801(d)(2)(A), and it does not qualify as a recorded recollection because defendant has not shown that she cannot recall making the statement."

[v]   Mental, Emotional or Physical Condition

• *Meeker v. Meeker,* No. CIV.02-00741, 2004 WL 2513041, at *3 n.3 (N.D.Cal. Nov. 8, 2004). In a trademark infringement case, the court ruled that e-mails mistakenly sent to the defendant were admissible as evidence of the senders' state of mind and, thus, an exception under the hearsay rule contained within Rule 803(3).

• *New York v. Microsoft Corp.,* No. CIV.98-1233, 2002 WL 649951 (D.D.C. Apr. 12, 2002). After discussing the nonhearsay argument and hearsay exceptions, business record and present sense impression, the court precluded the admission of the e-mail.

[vi]   Business Record Exception

Though e-mail has seen widespread use in the business setting, the assumption is that e-mail generated by a business falls within the business records exception to the hearsay rule. This assumption is incorrect. The courts have been reluctant to extend the business records exception to e-mail, unless it is shown that they are kept in the "normal course of business."

• *DirecTV, Inc. v. Murray,* 307 F. Supp. 2d 764, 771-772 (D.S.C. Mar 03, 2004). The Court allowed into evidence e-mail under the business record exception for the purposes of a summary judgment motion. The witnesses' affidavit stated that the e-mails were business records of orders that were systematically retained in the normal course of business.

• *Rick v. Toyota Indus. Equip. Co.,* No. CIV.93-1331, 1994 WL 484633 (N.D. Ill. Sept. 2, 1994). In applying the test of FED. R. EVID. 803(6) to e-mail, the court implicitly acknowledged that e-mail could qualify as a record under the business records exception if the requirements of the Rule were satisfied.

• *United States v. Ferber,* 966 F. Supp. 90 (D. Mass 1997). The court refused to admit e-mail from an employee to his supervisor recounting a conversation the employee had with the defendant under the business records exception, since there was no evidence that the e-mail record had to be maintained in the regular course of business. The court admitted the e-mail under the present sense impression because the e-mail was prepared shortly after the conversation occurred.

• *Monotype Corp., PLC v. International Typeface Corp.,* 43 F.3d 443 (9th Cir. 1994). The Court rejected admitting e-mail as a business record on the basis that it is not a regularly kept record made as part of a regularly conducted activity. The court distinguished e-mail from admissible computer printouts of bookkeeping records, stating that "e-mail is far less of a systematic business activity than a monthly inventory printout."

• *New York v. Microsoft Corp.,* No. CIV.98-1233, 2002 WL 649951 (D.D.C. Apr. 12, 2002). The Court precluded several e-mail and discussed their lack of admissibility based on hearsay and the various exceptions (business record and present sense impression), which did not apply.

• *Westfed Holdings, Inc. v. United States,* No. 92-820C, 2003 WL 1398439 (Fed. Cl. Mar. 17, 2003). The Court precluded admission of e-mail under the business record and present sense exceptions of the hearsay rule.

[vii]   Residual Hearsay Exception

• *Federal Trade Comm'n v. Cyberspace.com,* No. CIV.00-1806, 2002 WL 32060289, at *3 n.5 (W.D. Wash. Jul. 10, 2002). The defendants solicited customers for its internet services by mailing checks, that when cashed, resulted in them being signed up for internet services with defendants. The Court admitted consumer e-mails and letters of complaint based on Rule 807. The Court stated, "[t]he letters were sent independently to the FTC . . . The fact that they all reported roughly similar experiences suggests their truthfulness. Furthermore, the declarants had no motive to lie [regarding their experiences and there is little risk that the complaints] were the product of faulty perception, memory or meaning, the dangers against which the hearsay rule seeks to guard."

[d]　　Other Authorities

- Anthony J. Dreyer, *When the Postman Beeps Twice: The Admissibility of Electronic Mail Under the Business Records Exception of the Federal Rules of Evidence*, 64 Fordham L. Rev. 2285, 2305 (Apr. 1996).

- Ronald L. Johnston, *A Guide for the Proponent and Opponent of Computer-Based Evidence,* 1 Computer L.J. 667, 669 (1979).

[5]　　Best Evidence Rule

See, § 8.11, *Best Evidence Rule.*

[6]　　Reported Cases

Employment Law Cases

Because of e-mail's increased usage in the workplace, more and more employment law cases turn on some form of e-mail evidence.

- *Paquette v. City of Mason,* No. CIV.01-433, 2002 WL 32060463 (S.D. Ohio Sept. 03, 2002). An employee was terminated for criticizing the administration after he sent an anonymous e-mail that was traced back to him.

- *Garrity v. John Hancock Mut. Life Ins. Co.,* No. CIV.00-12143, 2002 WL 974676 (D. Mass. May 07, 2002). Female employees were discharged for sending sexually explicit e-mail to other employees.

- *Hoffman v. Lincoln Life and Annuity Distributors, Inc.,* 174 F. Supp. 2d 367 (D. Md. 2001). Employment claim was rejected for sexual discrimination charge, since e-mail that she reviewed on behalf of her boss, were unsolicited by him from others.

- *Strauss v. Microsoft Corp.,* 814 F. Supp. 1186, 1194 (S.D.N.Y. 1993). E-mail evidence played a key role as the plaintiff offered four separate e-mail messages sent by her supervisor, containing sexually suggestive remarks. The court used the e-mail evidence to deny the defendant's motion for summary judgment, and noted that based on the e-mail messages and other evidence a jury could find, "that Microsoft's proffered reason for not promoting her is pretextual."

- *Boone v. Federal Exp. Corp.,* 59 F.3d 84 (8th Cir. 1995). The Court considered e-mail consisting of discussions regarding the plaintiff's employment and retraining. The plaintiff argued that the defendant conspired to discriminate against him by refusing to train or promote him.

- *Owens v. Morgan Stanley & Co., Inc.,* No. CIV.96-9747, 1997 WL 793004 (S.D.N.Y. Dec. 24, 1997). The Court decided that one racist e-mail was insufficient grounds for finding a hostile work environment and dismissed that portion of the employment complaint.

- *Jenkins v. Department of Veterans Affairs,* 132 F.3d 54, (Fed. Cir. 1997) (unpublished decision). An employee that had been terminated for attendance violations had been made aware of the employer's leave policy through e-mail and memos.

- *Plymouth Police Broth. v. Labor Relations Com'n.,* 417 Mass. 599, 630 N.E.2d 599 (1994). The Court affirmed the dismissal of a police officer for "conduct unbecoming a police officer" for sending an e-mail message to fellow patrolmen referring to town officials as "pigs, cheats, [and] liars."

Criminal Trials

- *Allen v. State,* 862 P.2d 487 (Okl. Cr. 1993). The Court held the defendant's e-mail messages to a woman with whom he had an affair were admissible to establish motive in his conviction for first-degree murder of his wife.

§ 8.13   COMPUTERIZED BUSINESS RECORDS

[A]   Generally

Business records are generally stored in computer files. These records can be retrieved in the form of a printout and are admissible under the business records exception provided they meet the requirements imposed by that exception and other evidentiary foundational issues.

[B]   Foundation

When introducing computerized business records, a litigant is generally faced with at least three evidentiary challenges - authentication, hearsay and the Best Evidence rule.

[1]   Authentication or Identification

Foundationally, the proponent must first show that a computer record is authentic, i.e., "sufficient to support a finding that the [evidence] in question is what its proponent claims." FED. R. EVID. 901(a).

Authenticating conventional business writing is straightforward and simple. Generally, proper custody is sufficient authorization for business records. The witness would testify that he was familiar with the business filing system, obtained the writing from the appropriate file, and that he recognizes the exhibit as the document that he removed from the file.

For computerized business records, the authentication is different since the "record" is in a computer. Courts differ as to the type and quantum of proof necessary to authenticate computer business records. Rudolph J. Peritz, *Computer Data and Reliability: A Call for Authentication of Business Records Under the Federal Rules of Evidence,* 80 NW.U.L.Rev. 956 (1986). Some courts require a more extensive foundation regarding the reliability of the particular computer, dependability of input and output procedures, and the witness's identification of that document as the printout from the computer. Others have held that if a piece of evidence satisfies the business records hearsay exception, reliability is presumed and additional evidence regarding their reliability is not required. *United States v. Moore,* 923 F.2d 910, 914-16 (1st Cir. 1991).

For a more extensive foundation, one should establish, through the testimony of the custodian of the computer-kept records or other persons familiar with the manner in which the records were processed and maintained, the following testimony:

- A computer is used in the business and the business relies on computers in the ordinary course of carrying on its activities.

- The computer is reliable, is used to keep the business records and produce the printout. This will include the type of computer, its acceptance as reliable equipment (hardware), and that it is kept in a good state of repair. (Some courts are taking judicial notice of the reliability of computers. *See,* § 8.6, *Judicial Notice.*)

- The programs and formulae used to process the data are functioning properly.

- Appropriate measures are taken to verify the proper operation and accuracy of these programs and formulae.

- The business has developed procedures designed to ensure accuracy for entering data into the computer.

- The manner in which the basic data was initially entered into the computerized record-keeping system. This includes the mechanical operation of the computer, sources of data and time of preparation.

- The data was entered within a reasonable time after the event and recorded by persons having personal knowledge of the events.

- The data was entered in the regular course of business.

- The input procedure has auditing safeguards built-in to ensure accuracy of entered data.

- The method of storing the data and the safety precautions in place to prevent its loss while in storage.

- The computer was in working order at the time the witness obtained the printout.

- The procedures or steps to obtain the printout from the computer.

- The computer accurately printed out the data in question.

- The witness can identify the exhibit as the printout.

- If the printout contains unusual symbols or terms, the witness explains the meaning of the symbols or terms.

In a recent decision the Ninth Circuit Bankruptcy Appellate Panel held that the bankruptcy court did not abuse its discretion in refusing to admit a creditor's computerized records without proper authentication. The Court still refused admission even after a post trial submission declaration tried to cure the deficiency. *American Exp. Travel Related Servs. v. Vinhnee (In re Vinhnee),* No. CIV.04-1284, 336 B.R. 437, 443-447 (Bankr. Fed. App. 2005). The Court stated:

> Authenticating a paperless electronic record, in principle, poses the same issue as for a paper record, the only difference being the format in which the record is maintained: one must demonstrate that the record that has been retrieved from the file, be it paper or electronic, is the same as the record that was originally placed into the file FED. R. EVID. 901(a). . . . Hence, the focus is not on the circumstances of the creation of the record, but rather on the circumstances of the preservation of the record during the time it is in the file so as to assure that the document being proffered is the same as the document that originally was created. . . . The paperless electronic record involves a difference in the format of the record that presents more complicated variations on the authentication problem than for paper records. Ultimately, however, it all boils down to the same question of assurance that the record is what it purports to be. . . . *The entity's policies and procedures for the use of the equipment, database, and programs are important. How access to the pertinent database is controlled and, separately, how access to the specific program is controlled are important questions. How changes in the database are logged or recorded, as well as the structure and implementation of backup systems and audit procedures for assuring the continuing integrity of the database, are pertinent to the question of whether records have been changed since their creation.* . . . Some of these questions are becoming more important as the technology advances. For example, digital technology makes it easier to alter text of documents that have been scanned into a database, thereby increasing the importance of audit procedures designed to assure the continuing integrity of the records. *See* George L. Paul, *The 'Authenticity Crisis' in Real Evidence,* 15 PRAC. LITIGATOR No.

6, at 45-49 (2004). This adds an extra dimension to consideration of whether the computer was 'regularly tested' for errors. (citation omitted) (emphasis added).

[2]   Hearsay

[a]   Generally

Computer-generated information, usually in the form of business records and reports, is hearsay and cannot be used to prove the truth of the matters asserted therein. Unless the information falls within an exception to the hearsay rule, such as FED. R. EVID. 803(6), business records exception, and authenticated, the computer records are not admissible.   Courts have regularly admitted computer printouts under the business record exception. In *Sea-Land Service, Inc. v. Lozen Intern., LLC*, 285 F.3d 808, 819 (9th Cir. 2002), the court stated, "[f]or the purposes of Rule 803(6), it is immaterial that the business record is maintained in a computer rather than in company books." *See also, United States v. DeGeorgia,* 420 F.2d 889, 893 n.11 (9th Cir. 1969). In *Sears, Roebuck & Co. v. Merla,* 142 N.J. Super. 205, 361 A.2d 68, 69 (1976) the court held that "[c]omputerized bookkeeping has become commonplace. Because the business records exception is intended to bring the realities of the business world into the courtroom, a record kept on computer in the ordinary course of business qualifies as competent evidence." *See also, United States v. Salgado,* 250 F.3d 438, 452-53 (6th Cir. 2001), *cert. denied,* 122 S.Ct. 263 (2001) and *American Exp. Travel Related Servs. v. Vinhnee (In re Vinhnee),* 336 B.R. 437, 444 (Bankr. Fed. App. 2005).

Federal courts have allowed a wide variety of computer-based information such as phone bills, banking transaction records, spreadsheets, ledgers, etc. to be admitted into evidence under the business record hearsay exception. *Admissibility of Computerized Private Business Records,* 7 A.L.R.4th 8 (1981).

In order to have these records admitted under the business record exception, one must show that they were made and maintained in the course of a regularly conducted business activity and are trustworthy. FED. R. EVID. 803(6).

The elements of a regularly conducted business activity are set forth under Rule 803(6) and allow for the admission of:

> A memorandum, report, record, or data compilation, in any form, of acts, events, conditions, opinions, or diagnoses, made at or near the time by, or from information transmitted by, a person with knowledge, if kept in the course of a regularly conducted business activity, and if it was the regular practice of that business activity to make the memorandum, report, record or data compilation, all as shown by the testimony of the custodian or other qualified witness, or by certification that complies with Rule 902(11), Rule 902(12), or a statute permitting certification, unless the source of information or the method or

circumstances of preparation indicate lack of trustworthiness. The term "business" as used in this paragraph includes business, institution, association, profession, occupation, and calling of every kind, whether or not conducted for profit.

The FED. R. EVID. 803 advisory committee notes states in part:

The form which the 'record' may assume under the example is described broadly as a 'memorandum, report, record, or data compilation, in any form.' The expression 'data compilation' is used as broadly descriptive of any means of storing information other than the conventional words and figures in written or documentary form. It includes, but is by no means limited to, electronic computer storage.

The trustworthy justification is that since the entry of information is routine, accurate, and relied on by the business to conduct its business, the guarantee of trustworthiness is present. Business entries are generally made as a matter of habit, and employees are under a duty to accurately record business data or possibly lose their jobs. Also, since there are so many business transactions, there is a necessity for business or public purposes to generate these types of reports. It would be difficult for a witness to remember a particular business entry. For that reason, the most reliable evidence available is the business record. However, courts have the power to exclude business records if their origins "indicate [a] lack of trustworthiness." FED. R. EVID. 803(6).

As an alternative, even though your records may not be admissible under the business record exception, check to determine if the records are admissible under a different hearsay exception.

[b]   Foundation

Generally, the following foundational elements must be established for computerized records to fall within the business records exception to the hearsay rule.

• The report was prepared by a person with a duty and business relationship with the company to make the report.

• The record was prepared at or near the time of the event.

• The data provider had personal firsthand knowledge or was familiar with how the facts or events were recorded.

• It was a routine practice for the business to prepare and maintain such reports.

• The report was reduced to written form.

• The report was made in the regular course of business.

- The entry is factual in orientation [or in federal court an opinion or diagnosis based on factually available information].

- The record's "source of information or the method or circumstances of preparation [do not] indicate lack of trustworthiness."

- The record has been made in a business setting (whether or not conducted for profit).

Edward J. Imwinkelried, *Evidentiary Foundations* § 4.03[1]&[2] (5th Ed.); FED. R. EVID. 803(6).

[c]   Nonoccurrence of Event – Absence of an Entry

FED. R. EVID. 803(7) expressly authorizes the use of evidence of the absence of an entry in a "data compilation" maintained in the regular course of business to prove the nonoccurrence of a fact unless the circumstances indicate a lack of trustworthiness. FED. R. EVID. 803(10) authorizes the use of evidence, in the form of a certification or testimony that a diligent search failed to disclose the entry, of the absence of a public record or entry in a "data compilation" regularly made and preserved by a public office or agency.

The foundation for absence of business records includes:

- Testimony from a business custodian or other qualified witness;

- Evidence that a matter is usually included in business records; and

- Evidence that a diligent search of the record indicates the nonexistence of any such memorandum.

[i]   Reported Cases

- *United States v. De Georgia,* 420 F.2d 889, 893 (9th Cir. 1969). The Court stated:

    Regularly-maintained business records are admissible in evidence as an exception to the hearsay rule because the circumstance that they are regularly maintained records upon which the company relies in conducting its business assures accuracy not likely to be enhanced by introducing into evidence the original documents upon which the records are based.

    In our view, this same circumstance offers a like assurance that if a business record designed to note every transaction of a particular kind contains no notation of such a transaction between specified dates, no such transaction occurred between those dates. Moreover, in our opinion, that assurance is not likely to be enhanced by the only other means of proving such a negative; that is by bringing into court all of the documents involving similar transactions during the period in question to prove that there was no record of the transactions alleged not to have occurred, and calling as witnesses all company personnel who had the duty of entering into transactions of that kind during the critical period and inquiring whether the witnesses remembered any additional transactions for which no record had been produced.

- *United States v. Cepeda Penes,* 577 F.2d 754, 761 (1st Cir. 1978). "Rule 803(10) . . . permits a 'negative certification' to be offered into evidence, and does not by its terms limit the use of such evidence in criminal proceedings."

[d]   Contesting Admissibility of Business Records

There are several areas in which one can challenge the admissibility of computer records:

- Consider cross-examining the company practices with respect to the reliability, accuracy and integrity of the computer as an accurate retriever of information.

- Challenge whether the records were of a "regularly conducted business activity" as required under FED. R. EVID. 803(6). Records that are of a personal nature do not fall within the exception. If business entries contain information other than routine business data then objections should be made as to the reliability and trustworthiness.

- Determine if there are hardware or software programming errors that may affect data calculations and analysis of the computer data.

- Were proper search and retrieval techniques used to obtain the data?

- Conduct a cross-examination to determine whether the computer system was secure. The unauthorized use of a computer system may result in false, missing or deleted information. Determine who had access to the computer system and whether they could have altered, manipulated or damaged computer records.

- Contest the error rate of the data entry and the input procedures.

- Challenge whether the entries were made near the time of the business transactions.

- Challenge the accuracy by incorrect or incomplete entry of data.

- Challenge the method of obtaining the computer printout for court and who conducted the processing of the printout.

- Determine if the storage media was contaminated or corrupted as a result of power outages or equipment malfunctions.

- Was the data mishandled by not maintaining a trustworthy chain of custody?

- Challenge output instructions, mistakes and programming errors.

[e]   Reported Cases

Business records rejected

- *American Exp. Travel Related Servs. v. Vinhnee (In re Vinhnee)*, No. CIV.04-1284, 336 B.R. 437, 443-447 (Bankr. Fed. App. 2005). The Appellate court held that the bankruptcy court did not abuse its discretion in refusing to admit a creditor's computerized records without proper authentication. The Court still refused admission even after a post trial submission declaration tried to cure the deficiency.

- *Rambus, Inc. v. Infineon Technologies AG*, No. CIV.00-524, 348 F. Supp.2d 698, 706-708 (E.D.Va. Dec. 15, 2004). In a detailed decision discussing the foundational requirements for business records the Court found that, "the goal of Rule 803(6) is to allow for the admission of business records, which would normally be excluded under the hearsay rule. The general understanding is that business records are trustworthy and therefore carry an indicia of reliability. Rule 902(11) seeks to facilitate the admission of business records by eliminating the requirement of a testifying witness. At the heart of the business records exception is a concern with trustworthiness; and the not-very-daunting requirements in Rules 803(6) and 902(11) exist to ensure that the records are in fact trustworthy. Those requirements have not been met here. Therefore, the motion in limine will be granted."

- *DirecTV, Inc. v. Reyes*, No. CIV.03-8056, 2006 U.S. Dist. LEXIS 8357, at *13-16 (D. Ill. Mar. 1, 2006). Court found that a witness declaration was not authenticated under the "requirements of Rule 902(11), namely that . . . [it] (1) was created 'at or near the time of the occurrence'; (2) 'was kept in the course of the regularly conducted activity'; and (3) 'was made by the regularly conducted activity as a regular practice.'"

- *Potamkin Cadillac Corp. v. B.R.I. Coverage Corp.*, 38 F.3d 627 (2d Cir. 1994). The Court refused to admit an insurance broker's computer printout of figures related to transactions with the insured. The court found that the broker failed to establish a regular business practice and failed to demonstrate the reliability of the information.

- *North Carolina v. Springer, Jr.*, 283 N.C. 627, 197 S.E.2d 530 (1973). The Court refused to admit printout since there was no testimony as to methods under which computer printout of credit card account was made.

- *Tomassini v. Saunders*, 274 N.J. Super. 203, 643 A.2d 665 (1994). The court denied the admissibility of the insurer's computer printout summarizing the insured's policy history. *Contra, Hahnemann University Hosp. v. Dudnick,* 292 N.J.Super. 11, 678 A.2d 266 (N.J.Super. A.D. Jun. 21, 1996).

Business records accepted

- *Hardison v. Balboa Ins. Co.,* 4 Fed. Appx. 663, 669-670 (10th Cir. 2001). The Court found that computerized records were properly authenticated and "were admissible pursuant to the business record hearsay exception of Rule 803(6). Computer business records are admissible under Rule 803(6) 'if the offeror establishes a sufficient foundation in the record for [their] introduction.' (citation omitted) . . . According to [the plaintiff, the defendant] . . . did not lay a proper foundation because [the defendant did not submit evidence of anyone who had] personal knowledge of the creation of the computer-generated documents. While it is true that a 'witness may not testify to a matter unless evidence is introduced sufficient to support a finding that the witness has personal knowledge of the matter,' FED. R. EVID. 602, 'there is no requirement that the party offering a business record produce the author of the item,' (citation omitted). Instead, a foundation for the business record hearsay exception may be established by anyone who demonstrates sufficient knowledge of the record keeping system that produced the document. Here, [defendant's witness] satisfied this requirement through her affidavit, wherein she stated she was competent to testify about the computer system that created the documents and she explained how data was entered and retrieved from the computer system."

- *AFD Fund v. United States,* 61 Fed. Cl. 540, 544-545 (Fed. Cl. 2004). In a government contractor's suit the Court found that a computer generated statements of account and account reconciliation were admissible as business records. The Court reviewed the affidavits in support of their admission and found that custodian witness provided adequate foundation for admitting the statements. The witness testified that she was the custodian, that the records were regularly made by a knowledgeable person contemporaneously with the transactions, and that the records were kept in regularly conducted business activity. In addition, the custodian witness testified that the software was capable of printing from the database records and the statement reports duplicated the relevant electronic entries.

- *Bell v. Farmer's Insurance,* No. A101246, 2004 WL 1281818 (Cal. Ct. App. Jun. 9, 2004)(unpublished). In a case involving unpaid overtime compensation, the defendant contended that the trial court erred when it denied discovery of "original time sheets" in favor of electronic records. The appellate court denied this assertion and recognized "computer generated compilations of contemporaneously recorded data entries" as the effective equivalent of the daily time sheet when supported by sworn declarations that the sources of information "were trustworthy."

- *Olympic Ins. Co. v. H. D. Harrison, Inc.,* 418 F.2d 669 (5th Cir. 1969). Computer printouts that reflected the action on the account were admitted and used as the basis for summary judgment when the agency failed to list any specific objections as to the accuracy of the printouts.

- *Kennedy v. Los Angeles Police Dept.,* 901 F.2d 702 (9th Cir. 1989). Computerized attorney time records were admissible regarding the amount to be awarded in attorney fees. *But see, Act Up!/Portland v. Bagley,* 971 F.2d 298 (9th Cir. 1992).

- *United States v. Bland,* 961 F.2d 123, 127 (9th Cir.), *cert. denied,* 506 U.S. 858 (1992). Under FED. R. EVID. 803(6) business records are admissible if they are (1) made at or near the time of the event, (2) recorded by a person with knowledge, and (3) kept in the regular course of business.

- *United States v. Glasser,* 773 F.2d 1553, 1559 (11th Cir. 1985). "Computer generated business records are admissible under the following circumstances: The records must be kept pursuant to some routine procedure designed to assure their accuracy, they must be created for motives that would tend to assure accuracy (preparation for litigation, for example, is not such a motive), and they must not themselves be mere accumulation of hearsay and uninformed opinion."

Custodian witness

- *Rambus, Inc. v. Infineon Technologies AG,* No. CIV.00-524, 348 F. Supp.2d 698, 703-704 (E.D.Va. Dec. 15, 2004). In a detailed decision the Court found that "[d]eclarations of custodians of records for computer memory manufacturers were insufficient to permit self-authentication of manufacturers' business records, and thus records were not admissible in patent infringement action, where declarations made no reference to custodians' knowledge of manufacturers' recordkeeping practices, did not state that person with knowledge made record at or near time of occurrence, and failed to assert that records were made by regularly conducted activity as regular practice."

- *State v. Veres,* 7 Ariz. App. 117, 436 P.2d 629, 637 (Ariz. 1968). Relying on the Business Records Rule court admitted bank records, even though the witness "testified that he did not prepare them, that 'it is done by automatic machine', that he did not know 'the mechanical operation aspects of the machine', that another bank employee at another bank office was in charge of that department and that the witness's only knowledge was his access to the records." *Contra, State v. Osborn,* 107 Ariz. 295, 486 P.2d 777 (Ariz. 1971).

- *FDIC v. Staudinger,* 797 F.2d 908, 910 (10th Cir. 1986). The Court noted, "there is no requirement that the party offering a business record produce the author of the item."

- *People v. Lugashi,* 205 Cal. App.3d 632, 641, 252 Cal. Rptr. 434, 441 (Cal. App. 1988). In People, a bank's loss specialist was called upon to address foundational questions regarding authenticity and hearsay. The Court held, "[an] experienced credit card fraud investigator familiar with merchant authorization terminals, counterfeit cards, credit card sales, and the manner in which sales are recorded" was a qualified witness for purposes of laying foundation for admissibility of computer evidence under business records exception to hearsay rule, even though she did not personally perform the computer functions necessary to retrieve the automatic inputs on which the computer evidence was based.

- *Dyno Construction Co. v. McWane, Inc.,* 198 F.3d 567, 575-76 (6th Cir. 1999). Likewise, "[t]o be an 'other qualified witness,' it is not necessary that the person laying the foundation for the introduction of the business record have personal knowledge of their preparation."

- *United States v. Fendley,* 522 F.2d 181 (5th Cir. 1975). A witness laying the foundation for admissibility of a document as a business record need not have been the preparer of the document.

- *In re Custodian of Records of Variety Distrib., Inc.,* 927 F.2d 244, 248 (6th Cir. 1991). The custodian of the records "need not be in control of or have individual knowledge of the particular corporate records subject to the subpoena, but need only be familiar with the company's recordkeeping practices."

- *United States v. Arias-Villanueva,* 998 F.2d 1491, 1503 (9th Cir. 1993). Business records exception applied even though manager did not know who prepared the document or whether the preparer really had knowledge of the events.

Record must be made contemporaneously

- *United States v. Russo,* 480 F.2d 1228, 1240 (6th Cir. 1973). "Since the computer printout is just a presentation in structured and comprehensible form of a mass of individual items, it is immaterial that the printout itself was not prepared until 11 months after the close of the year 1967. It would restrict the admissibility of computerized records too severely to hold that the computer product, as well as the input on which it is based, must be produced at or within a reasonable time after each act or transaction to which it relates."

- *Wheeler v. Sims,* 951 F.2d 796, 804 (7th Cir.), *cert. denied,* 506 U.S. 914 (1992). The Court held records recorded near the time of the event (11 days) were admissible.

- *Willco Kuwait Trading S.A.K. v. deSavary,* 843 F.2d 618, 628 (1st Cir. 1988). The Court rejected a record made approximately three months after an event.

- *Hiram Ricker & Sons v. Students Int'l. Meditation Soc'y.,* 501 F.2d 550, 554 (1st Cir. 1974). The Court excluded records made one week after the information contained therein was first reported, finding a lack of reliability since entries were based on the memories of witnesses.

Inaccuracies in data

- *United States v. Catabran,* 836 F.2d 453, 458 (9th Cir. 1988). "The district court recognized that the defense had brought out inaccuracies in the computer printouts but held that these inaccuracies went to the weight of the evidence, not the admissibility. This is the general rule . . . Any question as to the accuracy of the printouts, whether resulting from incorrect data entry or the operation of the computer program, as with inaccuracies in any other type of business records, would have affected only the weight of the printouts, not their admissibility."

- *Leone v. Precision Plumbing & Heating,* 121 Ariz. 514, 591 P.2d 1002 (1979). The Court ruled that even inaccurate computer printouts are admissible as an admission against a party opponent.

- *United States v. Croft,* 750 F.2d 1354, 1365 n.7 (7th Cir. 1984). The Court admitted computer evidence and stated: "In *Weatherspoon,* this court held that computer printouts were properly admitted into evidence following the Government's proof of what the input procedures were . . . that the input procedures and printouts were accurate within two percent . . . that the computer was tested for internal programming errors on a monthly basis, and . . . that the printouts were made, maintained and relied on . . . in the ordinary course of . . . business activities."

Security of computer system

- *United States v. Glasser,* 773 F.2d 1553, 1559 (11th Cir. 1985). "The existence of an airtight security system is not . . . a prerequisite to the admissibility of computer printouts. If such a prerequisite did exist, it would become virtually impossible to admit computer generated records."

Access to computer system - business records

- *United States v. Liebert,* 519 F.2d 542 (3rd Cir. 1975). In this case, the government offered to permit the defendant to run tests on its system to analyze its reliability.

- *United States v. Greenlee,* 380 F. Supp. 652 (E.D. Pa. 1974), *aff'd,* 517 F.2d 899 (3rd Cir. 1975). The defendant's request for access to IRS computers three days before trial was not timely.

Reliability or trustworthiness lacking

- *People v. Morrow,* 628 N.E.2d 550 (Ill. App. 1993). The Court found indicia of reliability lacking and ruled computer-generated attendance record inadmissible.

- *Potamkin Cadillac Corp. v. B.R.I. Coverage Corp.,* 38 F.3d 627 (2d Cir. 1994). The Court discussed the unreliability of a computer program that created the records.

- *Peritz, Computer Data and Reliability: A Call for Authentication Under the Federal Rules of Evidence,* 1986, 80 NW. L. Rev. 956, 960. "Unlike ledgers and books of payables and receivables with individual items, intermediate accounts, and scrivened entries or changes, computer printouts are not records at all, but rather neatly packaged concantations of information excerpted from numerous records in multiple files. Because program changes or data manipulations can be accomplished without leaving any trace and without affecting the day-to-day operation of a computer system, both unintentional error and intentional fraud are difficult to discover behind a perfect-looking printout."

Reliability of computers

- *People v. Rivera,* 182 Ill. App.3d 33, 42, 537 N.E.2d 924, 931 (1989). Court concluded that: "[T]he judge correctly held that he could take judicial notice that IBM is a 'standard, reliable computer.'"

- *People v. Hendricks,* 145 Ill.App.3d 71, 495 N.E.2d 85, 110 (Ill. 1986) wherein the court stated: "There can be no question that computer science has created many devices, the reliability of which can scarcely be questioned. We should therefore apply the rule that its accuracy and reliability is judicially noticeable, requiring only proof of the accuracy and proper operation of the particular device under consideration. The trial court did not err in taking judicial notice that the IBM/PC is a standard, reliable computer."

- *Perma Research and Development v. Singer Co.,* 542 F.2d 111, 121 (2d Cir. 1976) (dissenting opinion). As to the reliability of the computer, Judge Van Graafeiland of the Second Circuit has cautioned: "As one of the many who have received computerized bills and dunning letters for accounts long since paid, I am not prepared to accept the product of a computer as the equivalent of Holy Writ."

- *Neal v. United States,* 402 F. Supp. 678 (D.C.N.J. 1975). As another court has stated, "[t]he computer is a marvelous device that can perform countless tasks at high speed and low cost, but it must be used with care. This is because it can also make errors at high speed. Those who use computers for record and accounting purposes, including the government, are accordingly obliged to operate them with suitable controls to safeguard the reliability and accuracy of the information." In the same case, the Court took judicial notice of the "GIGO" principle - "Garbage In, Garbage Out."

- *United States v. Fendley,* 522 F.2d 181, 187 (5th Cir. 1975). The Court found that "a computer printout . . . [is] not intrinsically unreliable, and . . . [is] admissible as a business record" provided that requirements of the Federal Business Record Act are met.

Reports prepared for trial

- *United States v. Briscoe,* 896 F.2d 1476, 1494 n.13 (7th Cir. 1990). "We note that the fact that the actual computer printouts presented at trial were prepared specifically for this case, thus not in the regular course of Illinois Bell's business, does not preclude their admission under Rule 803(6)."

- *United States v. Fujii,* 301 F.3d 535, 539 (7th Cir. 2002). "Computer data compiled and presented in computer printouts prepared specifically for trial is admissible under Rule 803(6), even though the printouts themselves are not kept in the ordinary course of business."

Public record requirement statute - business record foundation

- *People v. Dunlap,* 18 Cal. App. 4th 1468, 23 Cal. Rptr. 2d 204 (1993). The court ruled that it may take judicial notice of the pertinent statutes that require a public employee to enter data in a certain manner.

Memoranda and correspondence under the business records exception

In addition to encompassing computer-based records, FED. R. EVID. 803(6) also apply to a "memorandum." Courts have admitted various types of correspondence under Rule 803(6).

- *Gibbs v. State Farm Mut. Ins. Co.,* 544 F.2d 423, 428 (9th Cir. 1976). Court held FED. R. EVID. 803(6) applied to an interoffice memo regarding the status of an insurance claim. It was State Farm's "regular practice" of preparing memoranda relating to a claim and of circulating them among its departments.

- *Brown v. ASD Computing Center,* 519 F. Supp. 1096 (S.D. Ohio 1981). The court held FED. R. EVID. 803(6) applicable to a warning letter from a supervisor to an employee.

Printouts prepared by other business

• *United States v. Childs,* 5 F.3d 1328, 1333 (9th Cir. 1993). The Court admitted the records, even though the information was unverifiable and completed by other businesses.

Examples of foundations

• *United States v. Russo,* 480 F.2d 1228 (6th Cir. 1973), *cert. denied,* 94 S.Ct. 915 (1974). The Court found that a proper foundation was laid for admission of computer printout and extensively discussed the mechanics of input control to assure accuracy, nature of information that went into the computer, basis of printout and that the witnesses were qualified as experts by education, training and experience and they showed a familiarity with use of particular computers in question.

• *Transport Indemnity Co. v. Seib,* 178 Neb. 253, 132 N.W.2d 871 (1965). The Court admitted computer records and noted that the foundation testimony took 141 pages of the transcript.

• *King v. State ex rel. Murdock Acceptance Corp.,* 222 So. 2d 393 (Miss. 1969). The Court discussed foundational aspects of the admissibility of computer printouts.

Computer summaries

• *United States v. Catabran,* 836 F.2d 453, 458 (9th Cir. 1988). The Court found that general ledgers are themselves business records, rather than summaries.

Computer summaries extracted from computer records

• *United States v. Russo,* 480 F.2d 1228 (6th Cir. 1973). The Court held a computer printout was not a summary, but the original record of all of the transactions. However, the witness could provide testimony that summarized the computer printout.

• *Capital Marine Supply v. M/V Roland Thomas, II,* 719 F.2d 104, 105-106 (5th Cir. 1983). The Court admitted custodian testimony that summarized computer records.

   [3]   **Best Evidence Rule**

   [a]   **Generally**

   See, § 8.11, *Best Evidence Rule.*

[b] Reported Cases

- *DirecTV, Inc. v. Reyes,* No. CIV.03-8056, 2006 U.S. Dist. LEXIS 8357, at *21 (D. Ill. Mar. 1, 2006). The defendant objected to the introduction of a computerized packing slip as not the "best evidence." The Court ruled that if the plaintiff "submits a declaration that establishes that the [packing slip is] . . . a photocopy of a computer printout of information from an electronic database, that objection will be overruled. A computer printout of information stored on a computer is an 'original' for purposes of FED. R. EVID. 1001(3) and 1002. A photocopy of the original printout is admissible unless '(1) a genuine issue is raised as to the authenticity of the original or (2) in the circumstances it would be unfair to admit the duplicate in lieu of the original.' FED. R. EVID. 1003."

- *Inventory Locator Serv., LLC v. Partsbase, Inc.,* No. CIV.02-2695, 2005 U.S. Dist. LEXIS 32680, at *28-29 (D. Tenn. Sept. 2, 2005). The Plaintiff alleged that the defendant improperly gained access to its electronic marketplace for aviation parts and attempted to solicit customers away from the plaintiff. The defendant submitted summaries and compilations from certain computer records and the Court held "these materials are admissible under FED. R. EVID. 1006 and do not violate the best evidence rule. *See,* FED. R. EVID. 1002 ('If data are stored in a computer or similar device, any printout or other output readable by sight, shown to reflect the data accurately, is an 'original.')'"

- *Cobb v. State,* No. CR.02-785, 2003 WL 22311266, at *1 (S. Ct. Ark. Oct. 9, 2003)(unpublished). The Court overruled a Best Evidence objection stating that a "computer generated time record constitutes an original under our rules because it is a printout generated from data stored in a computer that reflects accurately the data contained in trial counsel's handwritten time sheets." The criminal defendant was arguing that "alleged discrepancies in his trial counsel's time-keeping methods reflect the quality of legal advice he received from trial counsel."

[4] Other Authorities

- Medina, *The Admissibility of Computer Records as Evidence,* 14 Washington State Bar News 14-19 (Jul. 1985).

- Horning, *Electronically Stored Evidence,* 71 Wash. & Lee L. Rev. 1335-1358 (1984).

- Storm, *Admitting Computer Generated Records: A Presumption of Reliability,* 18 J. Marsh. L. Rev. 115-154 (1984).

- Bain & King, *Guidelines for the Admissibility of Evidence Generated by Computer for Purposes of Litigation,* 15 U. Cal. Davis L. Rev. 951-971 (1982).

- Rob Apgood, *Electronic Evidence: Durability of the Records and the Preservation of Trees,* Part 1 of 2, Wash. St. Bar News, Aug. 1999, 46-47.

- Mary Moreland & Steward Nazzaro, *Admitting Scanned Reproductions Into Evidence,* 18 Rev. Litig. 261-284 (1999)

- *Computer Print-Outs as Evidence,* 16 Am. Jur. Proof of Facts 273.

[5]   Discovery Pointers

- If you anticipate foundation problems arising at trial, consider filing a request for admissions as to the foundational elements of computer-based records pursuant to Federal Rule of Civil Procedure 36. Under the rule you may request the opposing party to agree to the foundational basis for the computer records. If the opponent denies the request for admissions and you have to lay the foundation for the records at trial, you may receive costs for making the offer of proof that was rejected.

- Also, during depositions or a pretrial conference you may be able to obtain testimony or agreement as to the foundational elements for computer-based records.

- Under certain circumstances, an additional method of authenticating computer records is using computer audit trails and logs. *See,* § 2.6[G], *Audit Trails and Logs.*

§ 8.14   CHAT ROOM, TEXT MESSAGING, NEWSGROUPS AND LISTSERVS

Electronic evidence can be created by using a chat room, text message, newsgroup and listserv.

[A]   Generally

[1]   Chat Room

Chat (online) is the real-time simultaneous communication between two or more participants using a computer connected to the Internet, or other electronic network. A participant types a message on their keyboard, and the people with whom they are "chatting" can see the message posted on their monitors and can respond immediately. Often these conversations are carried on in "chat rooms" and retained on storage media. These chat room postings or conversations are conducted by third parties on websites they do not own. Chat room participants usually do not use their real names, but instead use screen names or pseudonyms.

In *Cyberspace Communications, Inc. v. Engler*, 55 F. Supp. 2d 737, 743 (E.D. Mich. 1999), the court stated:

"Chat rooms" provide additional online discussion forums that allow users to engage in real time dialogue with one or many other users by typing messages and reading the messages typed by others participating in the chat, analogous to a telephone party line, using a computer and keyboard rather than a telephone. *Reno I*, 117 S. Ct. at 2335; *ACLU v. Reno*, 929 F. Supp. at 835. There are thousands of different chat rooms available "in which collectively tens of thousands of users are engaging in conversations on a huge range of subjects."

Though initially used for social interaction, chat sessions are becoming popular with business and educational institutions. Since these chat sessions can be carried on (like a regular conversation) over the Internet or on any electronic network with anyone located in the world, they have become popular and inexpensive to participate in.

Often, the chat room conversations are saved. The data (conversations) from chat rooms is generally on an Internet service provider's (ISP) storage media. However, conversations can sometimes be downloaded and saved on an individual's computer or other device. If chat room discussions are relevant to your case then discovery subpoenas to the major chat rooms (AOL and Microsoft) may prove beneficial. Also, since businesses and educational institutions are using chat rooms, discovery inquiries should include questions regarding the use of chat rooms and storage procedures regarding these conversations.

These chat rooms can also include the use of audio, graphics and video in the communication process. *See also*, §§ 3.9[C], *Internet Relay Chat (IRC), Chat Room and Instant Messaging* and 8.12, *E-Mail*.

[2] Instant or Text Messaging

Text or "instant messaging" (also known as "IM" or "IMing") is the real-time simultaneous communication between two or more people using a cell phone or other computer device. "Instant messaging permits users to exchange private e-mails in quick succession." *United States v. Root*, 296 F.3d 1222, 1224 n.3 (11th Cir. 2002), *cert. denied*, 537 U.S. 1176, 123 S. Ct. 1006, 154 L. Ed. 2d 921 (2003). One person types a message on their "keyboard" and the people with whom they are "texting" can see the message appear on their cell phone monitor and respond immediately. A user is notified of an instant message by a sound or window that indicates that someone is trying to reach them. The user can then accept or reject that message. IM allows multiple users to be online at the same time.

These text or "instant messaging" capabilities, as they develop, will include the use of audio, graphics and video in the communication process.

From an evidentiary perspective, IM resembles e-mail, except for the real-time nature of IM and its retention. Admission of IM will face similar problems as e-mail in trying to demonstrate the regularity of business practice of its use and the current disparity of practice and rationale related to retention. This will complicate the acceptance of IM as a business record. *See also,* §§ 3.9[C], *Internet Relay Chat (IRC), Chat Room and Instant Messaging* and 8.12, *E-Mail.*

[3]   Newsgroups

Newsgroups are topic specific forums on websites where people can post questions and comments and/or read and respond to such postings left by other users on the Internet or on local networks. *United States v. Hamilton,* 413 F.3d 1138, 1141, n.1 (10th Cir. 2005) (newsgroup is a "'form [sic] within the internet' that is like a bulletin board system, allowing users to read and post messages, responses, or images relating to all types of topics."); *Parker v. Google, Inc.,* 422 F. Supp. 2d 492, 495 (D. Pa. 2006). In a copyright infringement case the Court found that "Google also maintains the USENET . . . 'a global system of online bulletin boards' . . . and allows users to post and search archived messages on the system. n1 . . . USENET [is] . . . a worldwide community of electronic [bulletin boards] that is closely associated with the Internet and with the Internet community. The messages in Usenet are organized into thousands of topical groups, or 'Newsgroups'. . . . As a Usenet user, you read and contribute ('post') to your local Usenet site. Each Usenet site distributes its users' postings to other Usenet sites based on various implicit and explicit configuration settings, and in turn receives postings from other sites. Usenet traffic typically consists of as much as 30 to 50 Mbytes of messages per day. Usenet is read and contributed to on a daily basis by a total population of millions of people. . . ."

The postings are stored and available for review at later times. Participants generally use screen names or pseudonyms. To view the comments one would visit a site and enter a newsgroup area that may be protected by passwords. *See also,* § 3.9[D], *Newsgroups (Usenet).*

[4]   Listservs

Listserv is a discussion group, similar to newsgroups, where people exchange information about a variety of subjects. A listserv uses standard Internet e-mail to exchange messages. In effect, when you subscribe to a listserv, you are adding your name to a mailing list. *Rodriguez v. Maricopa County Cmty. College Dist.,* No. CIV.04-2510, 2006 U.S. Dist. LEXIS 1483, at *2 (D. Ariz. Jan. 12, 2006). When a user sends a message, it is automatically sent to everyone in the group or the messages may be sent in an aggregate format. The messages will identify the person of the e-mail, though pseudonyms may be used. Similar to newsgroups, the postings and distribution of e-mail comments are generally saved on the website. *See also,* § 3.9[E], *Listserv (Mailing List)* and § 8.12, *E-mail* (Listserv evidentiary considerations are similar to e-mail).

[B]   Foundation

[1]   Authentication

Chat room and newsgroup

Chat room and newsgroup evidence must be authenticated prior to its admission. Authentication of a chat room "conversation" or newsgroup postings raises unique issues since participants generally do not own the website where the conversations are taking place. They also use screen names or pseudonyms when conversing which makes it difficult to identify the participants. Under FED. R. EVID. 901(a), "The requirement of authentication . . . is satisfied by evidence sufficient to support a finding that the matter in question is what its proponent claims." When authenticating chat room or listserv content, focus on the following possible evidence.

- Information from the owner of the chat room or newsgroup regarding signing up or subscription to the website. Often an individual when signing up for access to a chat room will have to disclose his name, address and other personal information.

- Information pertaining to the name that the individual used while participating in the chat room or newsgroup such as "Cooldude,"etc.

- If you are inviting the person to enter a chat room, then evidence showing that a person with the particular screen name entered the room and participated in conversations. This may be relevant in a criminal or civil context involving child molesters or sharing of trade secrets.

- Evidence pertaining to other indicia such as the person using a particular screen name, real name, street address, e-mail address or other facts connecting the individual participating in the chat room or newsgroup with their identity.

- Also, the person who has been invited to the chat room or newsgroup may disclose information that had been provided by the police or business owners. This information may be unique to the police officer or business and may provide some connection to the on screen participant.

- If you have the computer that the individual purportedly used to engage in the conversations, then an examination of the hard drive should reflect the screen names used by the participant.

- Evidence on paper or in the computer showing the user ID, password and pseudonym or a screen name for the person.

Instant and text messaging, chat rooms and listservs

    See below, § 8.14[B][4], *Reported Cases* for latest evidentiary decisions on instant and text messaging, and listservs.

[2]   Hearsay

See, § 8.9, *Hearsay.*

[3]   Best Evidence

- *Laughner v. State,* 769 N.E.2d 1147 (Ind. Ct. App. 2002). The Court found that the Best Evidence of Internet instant messaging conversations were printouts of on-line instant message chats between the defendant and undercover detective posing as a 13-year-old boy. The text was not an "original" preserved and stored by an Internet Service Provider, but a copy that was cut-and-pasted into a word processing program. The detective testified that he saved the conversations with the defendant after they were concluded, and that the printout document accurately reflected the content of those conversations.

[4]   Reported Cases

Chat Rooms

- *Blakey v. Continental Airlines, Inc.,* 164 N.J. 38, 62, 751 A.2d 538, 552 (N.J. 2000). A female employee alleged her co-workers had sexually harassed her through statements made in a chat room developed by the employer. The court remanded the case to determine "whether the [chat room] was such an integral part of the workplace that harassment on [it] should be regarded as a continuation or extension of the pattern of harassment that existed in the Continental workplace."

- *Chivers v. Cent. Noble Cmty. Schs.,* 423 F. Supp. 2d 835, 842, n.1 (D. Ind. 2006). "Like a chat room, IM is used to send messages back and forth through the Internet to a specific user. It is like a chat room in the way that you can communicate, but unlike most chat room communications, the information that is being typed is sent directly to the user and is not viewed by anyone else. . . ."

- *Raytheon Co. v. John Does 1-21,* No. 99-816 (Super. Ct. Middlesex Cty., Mass. 1999). Internet users posted confidential engineering information belonging to Raytheon in chat rooms and bulletin boards. Through subpoenas to Yahoo! and other ISPs, Raytheon eventually identified the users, who were using pseudonyms, such as "Ratheonveteran," "Ditchraytheon" and "Rayman-Mass."

- *Hallissey v. Am. Online, Inc.,* No. CIV.99-3785, 2006 U.S. Dist. LEXIS 12964, at *2-5 (D.N.Y. Mar. 10, 2006). The plaintiffs claimed they were employees of AOL since they performed many duties as leaders of chatrooms. The Court denied defendant's motion to dismiss and in a detailed discussion described how chatrooms are conducted.

- *State v. Anderson,* 2004 WL 413273, *5 (Ohio 2004). The State used more than 8000 chat transcripts to convict the defendant of child pornography. In addition, testimony established that he had "accessed newsgroups associated with child pornography."

- *United States v. Harding,* 273 F. Supp. 2d 411, 427-28 (S.D.N.Y. 2003). Application for search warrant was valid even if chat transcripts may have been falsified since the agent used the information from the informant in good faith.

- *United States v. Tank,* 200 F.3d 627, 630 (9th Cir. 2000). Government "made a prima facie showing of authenticity because it presented evidence sufficient to allow a reasonable juror to find that the chat room log printouts were authenticated. . . . The government also established a connection between Tank and the chat room log printouts." Court admitted into evidence authenticated "recorded" online chat room discussions among members of an Internet club involved with child pornography.

- *United States v. Simpson,* 152 F.3d 1241 (10th Cir. 1998). The Court ruled a computer printout of a chat room conversation between an FBI agent and a defendant was admissible. Court found authentication existing since the online contact gave the defendant's name and address and the agent's e-mail and address, as given to the contact, was found on a piece of paper near the defendant's computer.

Instant and text messaging

- *In re F.P.,* 2005 WL 1399264, at * 1-3 (Pa. Super. Ct. Jun. 15, 2005). The defendant was convicted of assault and one of the links to the victim were instant messages threatening the victim. The defendant argued that the instant messages should not have been admitted without authentication evidence of their source from the Internet Service Provider or the testimony of a computer forensics expert. The court rejected this argument, stating that to do so would "create a whole new body of law just to deal with e-mails or instant messages" The Court recognized that the messages are "inherently unreliable because of their relative anonymity and the fact that while an electronic message can be traced to a particular computer it can rarely be connected to a specific author with any certainty." However, the Court found authenticity based on circumstantial evidence that the defendant had acknowledged his first name in one of the instant messages and had failed to dispute having sent the instant messages after being confronted.

- *State v. Voorheis,* No. 02-478., 2004 WL 258178 (Vt. Feb. 13, 2004). The appellate court affirmed the trial court's finding that "instant messaging" text that was saved was sufficient evidence to support the defendant's conviction of incitement and attempt of use of a child in a sexual performance.

- *Malan v. Gates,* 2004 WL 2694598, at *1 (Utah App. Nov. 26, 2004). In a stalking case the defendant objected to the introduction of a text message sent over a cellular telephone on the basis that it lacked sufficient foundation. The Court found that since the victim read the text message and the sender's name that this was sufficient foundation for its admission. The Court rejected the defendant's argument that the testimony was inadmissible opinion testimony. The Court stated that "reading a name from a cellular telephone display screen is not a skill 'so intrinsically specialized' that it lies within the exclusive domain of an expert.'"

Newsgroup

- *United States v. Hamilton,* No. CR.04-4091, 2005 WL 1519112 (10th Cir. Jun. 28, 2005). The defendant was convicted of transporting pornography in interstate commerce. On appeal he argued that computer generated header information accompanying child pornography images uploaded to an Internet newsgroup were hearsay under Fed R. Evidence 801. The Appellate Court found that "the header information was generated instantaneously by the computer without the assistance or input of a person. . . . this uncontroverted fact clearly places the header information outside of Rule 801(c)'s definition of 'hearsay.' In particular, there was neither a 'statement' nor a 'declarant' involved here within the meaning of Rule 801."

[5]   Other Authorities

- Cobb, J. Allan, *Evidentiary Issues Concerning Online "Sting" Operations: A Hypothetical Based Analysis Regarding Authentication, Identification, and Admissibility of Online Conversations - A Novel Test for the Application of Old Rules to New Crimes,* 39 Brandeis L.J. 785-846 (2001).

[6]   Discovery Pointers

- Under certain circumstances an additional method of authenticating computer records is using computer audit trails and logs. *See,* § 2.6[G], *Audit Trails and Logs.*

§ 8.15   WEB PAGE CONTENT

[A]   Generally

Corporations, government offices, individuals, educational institutions and many other entities post information on websites that may be relevant to issues in litigation. These websites are visited by customers, suppliers, and others in order to view product information, buy products, etc. At trial, a party may want to use content or assertions posted on a website as substantive evidence. *See also,* § 3.9, *Internet.*

Some courts have questioned the trustworthiness of website content. *St. Clair v. Johnny's Oyster & Shrimp, Inc.,* 76 F. Supp. 2d 773, 774-775 (S.D. Tex. 1999); *St. Luke's Cataract & Laser Inst., P.A. v. Sanderson,* No. CIV.06-223, 2006 U.S. Dist. LEXIS 28873 (D. Fla. May 12, 2006). However, the Supreme Court in *U.S. Postal Serv. v. Flamingo Indus. (USA), Ltd.,* 124 S.Ct. 1321, 1329(2004) referred to revenue and business of the United States Postal Service, as detailed on its website and in *Verizon Communications, Inc. v. Law Offices of Curtis v. Trinko, LLP,* 124 S.Ct. 872, 877 (2004) referred to a consent decree on the website of the Federal Communications Commission.

Website content is proliferating in volume and will increasingly be used in litigation. In order to have website content admitted, authentication of the information that is posted on the website must be provided to the court for purposes of FED. R. EVID. 104(B) and 901(A). Also, hearsay, relevancy and Best Evidence rules must be satisfied. The overriding concern of admitting web content is whether it meets the necessary trustworthiness and reliability requirements mandated by the Federal Rules of Evidence.

[B]   WebSite

A website is a single page or group of web pages that together represents a company or individual on the World Wide Web. *See,* § 3.09[B], *World Wide Web.* These pages are usually grouped together by topic or service.

A web server holds these web page files in a directory on a hard disk or other storage media. The hard disk or other storage media can be located on the user's machine or part of a hard disk managed by a third-party service provider such as an Internet service provider. Under the directory is a collection of web files in a HTML (Hyper-Text Markup Language) format, a web page generator or a combination of both.

[1]   Types of Web Content

Web pages may include text, photographs, graphics, illustrations, audio, video, music, animations or computer programs.

[2]   Sources of Web Content

The source of content on a web page may originate from different computer files on different directories in different locations. For example, a website may display advertisements. These advertisements generally originate and are stored on a computer belonging to the advertiser and are not stored on the same computer where the rest of the website is located. The advertisements can be changed and incorporated instantly on the web page as it is displayed. Web pages often include links to other locations in the form of hypertext, highlighted or colored text. When a user clicks on the highlighted text with their mouse, it instructs the computer to jump to the new location.

Two methods of posting web page materials are through the transfer of different types of web computer files (text, graphic, audio and video) to your website directory for display on the web. The other method is through web page generators that "refresh" or change the contents of the web page continuously. *See,* § 3.09[B][3], *Web Pages.*

[a]   Web Files

The usual method of creating web page content is to create computer files that contain images, text or other electronic information that is converted to a HTML format and then transferred to the website for viewing. Each web page is a separate HTML file. These pages may contain links to graphics, sound, video or other computer files in the same or different directories and subdirectories.

[b]   Web Page Generator

A web page translator or generator can also generate web content. A web page generator, often a software application, takes raw data from a database or other informational source file and produces a HTML file. For example, suppose an individual enters data to calculate the monthly payment for a mortgage on a website. After entering the numbers into a website page, the data is calculated on a computer web page generator and automatically converted to HTML for viewing on a website.

[c]   Internet HTML Code

HTML code is the programming language for converting computer data into a web viewable format.

[i]   Reported Case

* *ACTONet, Ltd., v. Allou Health & Beauty Care, d/b/a The Fragrance Counter, Inc.,* 219 F.3d 836, 848 (8th Cir. 2000). The court held that the HTML (HyperText Markup Language) code, the programming language that converts and produces the visual appearance of a Website, to be admissible evidence, similar to photographs. The Court found that a web browser permits a person using a computer connected to the Internet to "view" the HTML code by using a browser menu choice such as "view source" or "page source." The court equated viewing these HTML codes as similar to photographs. The Court stated: "HTML codes may present visual depictions of evidence. We conclude, therefore, that HTML codes are similar enough to photographs to apply the criteria for admission of photographs to the admission of HTML codes."

[d]   Discovery Pointer

* When discovering web page information, you need to determine whether the web data is contained in static web files or whether the data is dynamic and generated from a web page generator or other source. When requesting information on a website, request that the directory, subdirectories and files of the relevant part of the website be provided. Also, request that all raw data and any web page generator be produced. The target of your search may be the database that supplies the data for the web page generator. For further information on databases *see* § 3.10, *Database.*

* Also, see the WayBack Machine website available at www.archive.org/web/web.php if you are searching for prior web pages for different sites. The archives contain websites from early 1996 through around six months to a year ago, depending on the site.

[C]   Foundation

Litigants are increasingly offering website content as evidence. Such evidence must be authenticated, hearsay concerns considered, and best evidence objections must be resolved.

[1]   Authentication

[a]   Generally

Web page content must be authenticated prior to admission and consideration by the trier of fact. The judge, pursuant to FED. R. EVID. 104 and 901, makes the preliminary determination of authentication. After the preliminary determination of admissibility is made, the parties can introduce evidence as to the weight to be given to the authenticating evidence in order to prove whether the web page content is what it purports to be and whether there is a connection between the web page content and a company or a particular individual. *See also,* § 8.10, *Requirement of Authentication or Identification.*

Article IX of the Federal Rules provides several rules for authenticating evidence. Rule 901 addresses the standard authentication process of requiring "evidence sufficient to support a finding that the matter in question is what its proponent claims" and provides ten authentication illustrations. Rule 902 addresses self-authentication and Rule 903 makes testimony of a subscribing witness unnecessary.

Depending on the facts of the case, Rule 901 sets forth several illustrations that may assist in authenticating web content.

Rule 901(b)(1) allows authentication by testimony of a witness with knowledge "that a matter is what it is claimed to be." In isolated instances, you may have a person who has knowledge of or observes the creation of web content, such as a webmaster, who would testify as to its authentication.

Rule 901(b)(4) allows evidence to be authenticated by the presence of "[d]istinctive characteristics and the like." These characteristics may relate to an item's "[a]ppearance, contents, substance, internal patterns, or other distinctive characteristics, taken in conjunction with circumstances." A company's logo or other appearance on a web page may provide factual authentication evidence.

Rule 901(7) allows for authentication of public records or reports where there is evidence of a "writing authorized by law to be recorded or filed and [is] in fact recorded or filed in a public office, or filed in a public office, or a purported public record, report, statement, or data compilation, in any form, is from the public office where items of this nature are kept." On government websites, documents and other information may be authenticated under this rule.

The focus of laying an authentication foundation is to determine what content was on the website, does the exhibit accurately reflect it, and can it be connected to the site's owner. Generally, one will need to provide testimony that someone located, visited and viewed the website, and printed out or otherwise preserved an accurate copy of the web content.

[b]   Factual Proof of Authentication

Some of the factual testimony that should be elicited in order to lay a foundation for authentication of web content may include the following.

[i] WebSite Witness

- The witness typed in the web domain address, which is always unique for each site. The domain address is usually referred to as a uniform resource locator (URL). The site address is usually prefaced with www, such as www.aol.com.

  — The identity of the person or entity that owns and operates a website with the unique domain address or universal resource locator (URL) address can sometimes be determined by checking with a site such as Verisign (http://registrar.verisign-grs.com/whois/) and conducting a search on the domain name.

- After typing in the domain address and pressing the enter key, a web page (usually the "home page") appears.

- The witness viewed the contents of the website by using different navigation tools - such as hyperlinks and search commands.

- The witness describes the website's logos, inscriptions, labels, etc. For a business, this may self-authenticate the web content under FED. R. EVID. 902 (7).

  — The witness found and viewed specific information on the site.

  — On some sites, it is necessary to log onto the site with a password and username. This testimony should be elicited if the witness visited these "secure" areas. Also, some computers allow passwords and user names to be stored, and when one visits a "secure" web area the user does not have to reenter the password and username because it is verified automatically from data stored in the computer. These passwords are often contained in "cookie" computer files. *See also,* § 3.9[F][1], *Cookies.*

- The witness made a printout or other exhibit of what was viewed on the website.

- The printed exhibit fairly and accurately reflects what the witness saw.

  — It would be beneficial if the printout contains the Internet domain address from which the image was printed and the date on which it was printed.

- If the witness purchased an item, have the witness testify that they visited the site, ordered merchandise and received merchandise from a company. This course of conduct may assist in identifying the operator of the site.

This may be sufficient for the initial admissibility requirements under Rule 104 unless the opponent of the evidence raises a genuine issue as to trustworthiness. Even then, the court may rule that contrary authentication evidence goes to the weight, and not the admissibility of the exhibit. FED. R. EVID. 104 and 901.

[ii]   WebSite Employees

Another method of proving the content on a website is to call the owner's employee, such as a webmaster, as a witness. A webmaster is generally in charge of web content. Their testimony would be based on FED. R. EVID. 602, personal knowledge of the witness.

A webmaster can testify that a particular computer file (containing web content) was placed on the site at a specific time and remained on the site for a period of time. Sources of this testimony can be through direct personal knowledge or through documentation that may be automatically generated by software for web server auditing tools. Often, the provider of the content will not be the same individual who uploads or installs the content on the website. As the name implies, content providers provide the content of information for websites. The individual (such as a webmaster) or an entity that actually posts the content may be different from the content provider.

[iii]   Government Organizations (Self-Authentication)

Government offices publish reports, press releases and other information on their official websites. FED. R. EVID. 902(5) provides that the following are self-authenticating: "Official publications. Books, pamphlets, or other publications purporting to be issued by public authority." If the site is operated by a government organization, the documents posted there should constitute an "official publication" within Rule 902(5).

For example, the Court in *Sannes v. Jeff Wyler Chevrolet, Inc.,* No. CIV.97-930, 1999 WL 33313134, at *3 n.3 (S.D. Ohio Mar. 31, 1999) found "that the FTC press releases attached to Defendant's Motion for Summary Judgment are admissible even though they are not attached to an authenticating affidavit. The FTC press releases, printed from the FTC's government World Wide Web page, are self-authenticating official publications under Rule 902(5) of the Federal Rules of Evidence." *See also, Colt Def. LLC v. Bushmaster Firearms, Inc.,* No. CIV. 04-240, 2005 U.S. Dist. LEXIS 20874, at *19 (D. Me. Sept. 20, 2005) (court held "printouts from government web sites have been held to be self-authenticating pursuant to Federal Rules of Evidence 901(a) and/or 902(5)" (citations omitted)).

[iv]   Other Methods

• Determine whether web content and other records can be authenticated as business records. If the opposing party has implemented and maintained records of postings regarding web content changes, they may qualify as business records under FED. R. EVID. 803(6). *See, § 8.13, Computerized Business Records.*

- Determine whether there is any circumstantial evidence, such as the fact that only the person or entity who owned the site would have the information that was posted on the site.

- Under certain circumstances an additional method of authenticating computer records is using computer audit trails and logs. *See,* § 2.6[G], *Audit Trails and Logs.*

- The court can deem documents produced pursuant to a discovery request authentic. In *Orr v. Bank of America,* NT & SA, 285 F.3d 764, 777 n.20 (9th Cir. 2002), the court stated, "documents produced by a party in discovery were deemed authentic when offered by the party-opponent. Authentication can also be accomplished through judicial admissions such as . . . production of items in response to . . . [a] discovery request." *See also, Maljack Prods., Inc. v. GoodTimes Home Video Corp.,* 81 F.3d 881, 889 n.12 (9th Cir. 1996) (discovery documents were deemed authentic, when disclosed by party-opponent and no objection was made to their alleged lack of authenticity.)

[v]   Reported Cases

Judicial Notice

- *U.S. Postal Serv. v. Flamingo Indus. (USA), Ltd.,* 124 S.Ct. 1321, 1329 (2004). The Court referred to revenue and business of the United States Postal Service, as detailed on its website.

- *Verizon Communications, Inc. v. Law Offices of Curtis v. Trinko,* LLP, 124 S.Ct. 872, 877 (2004). The Court referred to a consent decree on the website of the Federal Communications Commission.

- *Nebraska v. EPA,* 331 F.3d 995, 999 (D.C. Cir. 2003). The Court found that even though "the administrative record does not contain these facts, we take judicial notice of the information on the EPA's database (citations omitted.)."

- *Town of Southold v. Town of E. Hampton,* 406 F. Supp. 2d 227, 232 (D.N.Y. 2005). In this dispute over the use of ferry terminals the Court held that, "[t]his Court may take judicial notice of the contents of a website assuming, as in this case, its authenticity has not been challenged and 'it is capable of accurate and ready determination.' (citations omitted)."

- *Lan Lan Wang v. Pataki,* 396 F. Supp. 2d 446, 458 (D.N.Y. 2005). In denying a business license, the Court, in responding to a selective prosecution claim, took judicial notice of the fact that a different listing service (citing to its website's URL) did not charge for access to its online listings.

- *N.Y.C. Medical and Neurodiagnostic PC v. Republic Western Ins. Co.,* 774 N.Y.S.2d 916, 919, 920 (Apr. 12, 2004). The Court sua sponte conducted its own research on the web regarding one of the defendants, Republic, and its sibling corporation U-Haul. The Court found that information available on a state governmental website was admissible and website content by a corporation and its sibling corporation were admissible under the party admission's exception. The Court stated that [the motion] "appears to be the first in the nation to challenge a court's use of the internet to deflate the sails of a party's arguments." The Court responded by stating that "examples of court decisions making similar citations [to the Internet] are legion. . . . For a researcher not to employ information placed on a governmental web site, by a civil servant, for the benefit of the public would, indeed, be negligent and ridiculous. For a judge to ignore these new technological changes, made available by government and encouraged by court systems, would be to blind oneself."

- *Doe v. Merten,* 219 F.R.D. 387, 396, n.28 (E.D.Va. 2004). The Court cited to a report containing statistics on a website compiled by the Bureau of Citizenship and Immigration Services of the United States Department of Homeland Security.

- *Efam Enterprises, LLC v. Travelers Indemnity Company of America, Inc.,* No. CIV.02-3854, 2002 WL 1148830 (S.D.N.Y. May 29, 2002). In determining the defendant's identity and corporate status the Court referred to both the websites of the New York State and Connecticut Departments of Insurance.

Authentication

- *Hood v. Dryvit Systems, Inc.,* No. CIV.04-3141, 2005 U.S. Dist. LEXIS 27055, at *6-9, 2005 WL 3005612 *3 (N.D. Ill. Nov. 8, 2005). The Court found website printouts were authentic for purposes of a summary judgment motion and stated that since [the plaintiff's attorney filed an affidavit] stating that he "retrieved [the documents] off the [the defendant's] . . . corporate website . . . [and that] the web addresses stamped at the bottom of each exhibit were the addresses I retrieved the exhibits from . . . sufficiently authenticates the exhibits. . . . [further] Defendant has not denied that the exhibits represent the contents of its website or argued that its own website is unreliable."

- *Ashworth v. Round Lake Beach Police Dep'.t,* No. CIV.03-7011, 2005 U.S. Dist. LEXIS 14844, at *9-11 (D. Ill. July 21, 2005). The Court found that since web documents, two training outlines from a criminal justice institute to show that there was a growing awareness of positional asphyxia, were not properly authenticated they would not be considered. In addition, the Court referenced a case holding that web documents must bear "indicia of reliability demanded for other self-authenticating documents under FED. R. EVID. 902 [to be admitted]."

- *Intel Corp. v. Hamidi,* 30 Cal.4th 1342, 1353, 1 Cal. Rptr.3d 32, 41, 71 P.3d 296, 304 (2003). The Court mentioned that a statement posted on Intel's website could be taken as an admission.

- *Inventory Locator Serv., LLC v. Partsbase, Inc.,* No. CIV.02-2695, 2005 U.S. Dist. LEXIS 32680, at *65-66 (D. Tenn. Sept. 2, 2005). The plaintiff alleged that the defendant improperly gained access to its electronic marketplace for aviation parts and attempted to solicit customers away from the plaintiff. The defendant counterclaimed alleging similar conduct on the part of the plaintiff. "In support of its counterclaims, [the defendant] offers 'web server logs,' which purport to record various unlawful entries into [the defendant's] computer system from an internet protocol ('IP') address assigned to [the plaintiff]. [The plaintiff] seeks to exclude this evidence, arguing that 1) the logs are 'incredible on their face,' 2) the logs appear to have been altered, 3) the logs have been moved and deleted, and 4) the logs are inadmissible hearsay." The Court found that the logs were properly authenticated and were not inadmissible hearsay since they were kept in the regular course of business.

- *Hess v. Riedel-Hess,* 794 N.E.2d 96, 103-04 (Ct. Apps. Ohio 2003). The Court found that for authentication purposes the "appellee testified that she recognized that the NADA guidelines submitted as evidence as the same values she had calculated herself on NADAguides.com. Appellee testimony was sufficient to support a finding that the exhibit was what its proponent claimed it to be. Evid.R. 901(A), (B)(1)."

- *State v. Blackwell,* 592 S.E.2d 701, 705-706 (Ct. Apps. N. Carl. 2004). An expert in forensic firearms identification testified on cross-examination that he obtained his information about the barrel length of an illegal shotgun from a website. The defendant contended that the testimony was inadmissible hearsay. The Court stated: "This testimony was, however, elicited by defendant's cross-examination of Nordhoff and defendant did not object or move to strike this testimony. It is apparent that defendant invited this testimony in an attempt to discredit Nordhoff's expert opinion by undermining his credibility through a showing that the only source he relied on as the basis of his opinion was an unverifiable website."

- *State v. Davis,* 141 Wash. 2d 798, 854, 10 P.3d 977, 1010 (2000). The Court refused to admit, in a death penalty case, the defendant's offer of state population statistics obtained from an official state website. The court excluded the document as hearsay, and also ruled that "[a]n unauthenticated printout obtained from the Internet does not . . . qualify as a self authenticating document under ER 902(e) [equivalent to Federal Rule of Evidence 902(5)]."

[vi]   Discovery Pointers

*   Request through a document production, true and correct copies (electronic and paper) of web content from the opposing party.

*   Investigate to determine if the opposing party may have made statements establishing their connection to the evidence, which may be admissible as admissions.

[c]   Challenges to Authentication

The opposing party will generally challenge the evidence by presenting facts that the content is not attributable to the owner of the site or that the printout does not accurately reflect the contents of a website. On some websites visitors can post messages, participate in chat rooms, and leave other "content" on the site. The owners of the site will argue that this web content has not been adopted, connected nor attributed to the business. Also, it is well documented that hackers can manipulate the content on a website, so owners may argue that they did not authorize the content to be on the site. Since a website's content is so dynamic, its content may change daily or by the minute in some instances, thus, an accurate copy of what was on the site at a given point in time may be difficult to establish.

[i]   Reported Cases

*   *St. Luke's Cataract & Laser Inst., P.A. v. Sanderson,* No. CIV.06-223, 2006 U.S. Dist. LEXIS 28873, at *5-6 (D. Fla. May 12, 2006). The Court denied plaintiff's motion to admit into evidence web pages obtained from an archiving website located at www.archive.org finding that "[w]eb-sites are not self-authenticating." The Court ruled in order to properly "authenticate printouts from a website, the party proffering the evidence must produce 'some statement or affidavit from someone with knowledge [of the website] . . . for example [a] web master or someone else with personal knowledge would be sufficient' (citation omitted)." The Court ruled in order to properly "authenticate printouts from a website, the party proffering the evidence must produce 'some statement or affidavit from someone with knowledge [of the website] . . . for example [a] web master or someone else with personal knowledge would be sufficient. (citing to *In re Homestore.com, Inc. Securities Litigation,* 347 F. Supp.2d 769, 782-783 (C.D.Cal. 2004) (website press and earnings releases not admitted))."

*   *Telewizja Polska USA, Inc. v. Echostar Satellite Corp.,* No. CIV.02-329, 2004 WL 2367740, at *6 (N.D.Ill. Oct. 15, 2004). In this contractual action, the plaintiff moved to preclude evidence establishing what its own website looked like on various dates. The plaintiff contended that the website exhibit had not been properly authenticated. The Court found that:

'an affidavit . . . verifying that the Internet Archive Company retrieved copies of the website as it appeared on the dates in question from its electronic archives' was sufficient authentication. . . . The Court further noted that [Rule] . . . 901 'requires only a prima facie showing of genuineness and leaves it to the jury to decide the true authenticity and probative value of the evidence.' (citation omitted) Admittedly, the Internet Archive does not fit neatly into any of the non-exhaustive examples listed in Rule 901; the Internet Archive is a relatively new source for archiving websites. Nevertheless, Plaintiff has presented no evidence that the Internet Archive is unreliable or biased. And Plaintiff has neither denied that the exhibit represents the contents of its website on the dates in question, nor come forward with its own evidence challenging the veracity of the exhibit. Under these circumstances, the Court is of the opinion that Ms. Davis' affidavit is sufficient to satisfy Rule 901s threshold requirement for admissibility. Plaintiff is free to raise its concerns regarding reliability with the jury.

- *Baker v. Barnhart,* No. CIV.05-3106, 2006 U.S. App. LEXIS 14404, at *23-24 (8th Cir. Jun. 13, 2006). The Appellate Court found the district court abused its discretion by taking judicial notice of an article on the Internet finding that "Gniven [sic] the limited depth of the article and the author's and publisher's interests in selling alternative testing equipment, there is no basis upon which we may conclude that the article's brief criticism of the FCE is trustworthy in the nature of an authoritative treatise."

- *E.E.O.C. v. E.I. DuPont de Nemours & Co.,* No. CIV.03-1605, 2004 WL 2347559, at *1-2 (E.D.La. Oct. 18, 2004). Dupont moved in limine to preclude admission, based on lack of authenticity, of a "printout of a table from the website of the United States Census Bureau regarding the number of persons requiring an assistive device or wheelchair." The Court found that "the EEOC has submitted evidence sufficient to authenticate the exhibit. Rule 901(a) states that the requirement of authentication 'is satisfied by evidence sufficient to support a finding that the matter in question is what its proponent claims.' FED. R. EVID. 901(a). The exhibit contains the internet domain address from which the table was printed, and the date on which it was printed. The Court has accessed the website using the domain address and has verified that the webpage printed exists at that location. The Court also notes that the webpage is maintained on a government website, and, according to Rule 902(5), 'publications purporting to be issued by public authority' are self authenticating. The Court thus finds that the EEOC has provided evidence sufficient to authenticate the exhibit."

- *Fenner v. Suthers,* 194 F. Supp. 2d 1146, 1148-1149 (D. Colo. 2002). The Court denied the magistrate's recommendations regarding prisoner litigation based on the magistrate taking judicial notice of materials located on the web. The Court stated, "[a]s defendants correctly point out, the court should take judicial notice of any fact 'capable of accurate and ready determination by resort to sources whose accuracy cannot reasonably be questioned.' FED. R. EVID. 201(b). However, defendants ignore the next part of rule 201: 'A party is entitled upon timely request to an opportunity to be heard as to the propriety of taking judicial notice and the tenor of the matter noticed.' FED. R. EVID. 201(e). These provisions of rule 201 poses three obstacles to the magistrate judge's recommendation. First, merely citing to a web site and inviting others to visit the site does not satisfy the rule's requirement that the fact be 'capable of accurate and ready determination' -- at least where the pro se prisoner is denied any access to the web site, much less 'ready' access. *Putting to one side the problem of access, I doubt that a web site can be said to provide an 'accurate' reference, at least in normal circumstances where the information can be modified at will by the web master and, perhaps, others. There is, in other words, the question of whether the defendants, the magistrate judge, the district judge, and any reviewing court are literally on the same page when they visit the site on different dates.* " (emphasis added).

• *Perfect 10, Inc. v. Cybernet Ventures, Inc.,* 213 F. Supp. 2d 1146, 1154 (C.D. Cal. 2002). The Court stated:

> The second and third categories have met the prima facie burden because the declarations, particularly in combination with circumstantial indicia of authenticity (such as the dates and web addresses), would support a reasonable juror in the belief that the documents [web pages] are what Perfect 10 says they are. *See Tank,* 200 F.3d at 630. Moreover, because computer printouts [of the web pages] are the only practical method by which the allegations of the complaint can be brought before the Court and there is generally a reduced evidentiary standard in preliminary injunction motions . . . the Court finds that, as a general rule, Zadeh's declaration is sufficient to establish the exhibits' authenticity.

• *San Luis & Delta-Mendota Water Authority v. Badgley,* 136 F. Supp. 2d 1136 (E.D. Cal. 2000). The Court refused to take judicial notice of information posted on the Fish and Wildlife Service's interagency website that posted real time data about certain endangered fish because the information was not proven reliable or admissible.

[2]   Trustworthiness

Web content presents special trustworthiness problems. Content on websites can be changed within minutes, and no audit trail may be available to chronicle the modifications. This presents an opportunity for opponents to challenge the authenticity of web content. This does not mean that the content is inadmissible, but will require the court and the parties to focus on the preliminary admissibility standards set forth under FED. R. EVID. 104 and, if admitted, the weight to be given to the evidence.

For example, in *St. Clair v. Johnny's Oyster & Shrimp, Inc.*, 76 F. Supp. 2d 773, 774, 775 (S.D. Tex. 1999), after the plaintiff was injured on a sea vessel, he sought to establish ownership of the sea vessel from evidence obtained from the web. The court rejected the trustworthiness of the data and stated:

> While some look to the Internet as an innovative vehicle for communication, the Court continues to warily and wearily view it largely as one large catalyst for rumor, innuendo, and misinformation. So as to not mince words, the Court reiterates that this so-called Web provides no way of verifying the authenticity of the alleged contentions that Plaintiff wishes to rely upon. . . . There is no way Plaintiff can overcome the presumption that the information he discovered on the Internet is inherently untrustworthy. Anyone can put anything on the Internet. No web-site is monitored for accuracy and *nothing* contained therein is under oath or even subject to independent verification absent underlying documentation. Moreover, the Court holds no illusions that hackers can adulterate the content on *any* web-site from any location at *any* time. For these reasons, any evidence procured off the Internet is adequate for almost nothing, even under the most liberal interpretation of the hearsay exception rules found in FED. R. EVID. 807. Instead of relying on the voodoo information taken from the Internet, Plaintiff must hunt for hard copy back-up documentation in admissible form.

In determining trustworthiness of web content evidence the following may be important.

• What length of time was the data posted on the site?

• How many witnesses will testify having seen the data on the site?

• Is the data still on the website for the trier of fact to view and verify?

• How skilled is the proponent of the web content in creating and modifying websites?

• Did the owner of the site, or to whom it is attributed, post the same or partial content in other locations?

• Have others republished the same data and given credit to or identified the source of the data as the website in question?

[a]   Reported Cases

• *E.E.O.C. v. E.I. DuPont de Nemours & Co.*, No. CIV.03-1605, 2004 WL 2347559, at *1 (E.D.La. Oct. 18, 2004). Dupont moved in limine to preclude admission, based on hearsay, of a "printout of a table from the website of the United States Census Bureau regarding the number of persons requiring an assistive device or wheelchair." The Court found that the web page was "excepted from the hearsay prohibition by Federal Rule of Evidence 803(8). . . . unless the sources of information or other circumstances indicate lack of trustworthiness. . . . 'Public records and government documents are generally considered not to be subject to reasonable dispute,' . . . *But see St. Clair v. Johnny's Oyster & Shrimp, Inc.,* . . . (holding that 'voodoo information taken from the Internet' was insufficient to withstand motion to dismiss because '[n]o web-site is monitored for accuracy' and 'this so-called Web provides no way of verifying the authenticity' of information plaintiff wished to rely on). The court concludes that, 'in an age where so much information is calculated, stored and displayed on a computer, massive amounts of evidence would be inadmissible' if the Court were to accept DuPont's characterization of all information on the Internet as inherently unreliable."

• *United States v. Jackson,* 208 F.3d 633, 637-638 (7th Cir.), *cert. denied,* 531 U.S. 973 (2000). The Court upheld the exclusion of certain web postings, attributed to white supremacist groups, because they were insufficiently authenticated. The criminal defendant tried to show that the groups actually posted the postings, in which these groups appeared to claim responsibility for a series of racist mailings. The court stated: "Jackson needed to show that the web postings in which the white supremacist groups took responsibility for the racist mailings actually were posted by the groups, as opposed to being slipped onto the groups' web sites by Jackson herself, who was a skilled computer user."

[b]   Other Authorities

• *Weinstein's Federal Evidence* § 900.07[5]. In considering website content authentication, the Courts consider "the length of time the particular information remained on the web site, the frequency with which the information has been republished and seen by others, the source of the information and the ability to verify the information."

[3]   Hearsay

[a]   Nonhearsay

In some cases, the content or assertion on a website may not involve hearsay. Web content may be offered not for the truth of the matters asserted, but that the evidence was published on the web and that a person relied on the information. *Ries Biologicals, Inc. v. Bank of Sante Fe,* 780 F.2d 888 (10th Cir. 1986). For example, if a customer purchases a television set from an electronics dealer on the Internet, the customer may wish to prove that he relied on an assertion (not that the assertion was true) such as a warranty that was posted on the website. In this situation the assertion would be nonhearsay and admissible since it was not the truth of the assertion, but the fact that he relied on it.

[i] Reported Cases

- *Telewizja Polska USA, Inc. v. Echostar Satellite Corp.*, No. CIV.02-329, 2004 WL 2367740, at *5 (N.D.Ill. Oct. 15, 2004). In this contractual action, the plaintiff moved to preclude evidence establishing what its own website looked like on various dates. The plaintiff contended that the website exhibit was double hearsay and had not been properly authenticated. The plaintiff had acquired the archived web pages from an Internet archive company. The Court held "[t]o the extent these images and text are being introduced to show the images and text found on the websites, they are not statements at all--and thus fall outside the ambit of the hearsay rule. . . . (citation omitted) . . . printouts of the website are admissible pursuant to the best evidence rule . . . the contents [of the] . . . website may [also] be considered an admission of a party-opponent, and are not barred by the hearsay rule. (citation omitted)."

- *Van Westrienen v. Americontinental Collection Corp.*, 94 F. Supp. 2d 1087, 1109 (D. Or. 2000). The Court stated: "The only remaining question is whether the content of the Web site is hearsay under FRE 801. . . . Here, [plaintiff], by his own account, personally viewed the Web site and submitted an affidavit detailing specifically what he viewed. Therefore, the contents of the Web site are not hearsay for purposes of this summary judgment motion."

- *Perfect 10, Inc. v. Cybernet Ventures, Inc.*, 213 F. Supp. 2d 1146, 1155 (C.D. Cal. 2002). "Cybernet objects to the printouts from third-party websites as a violation of the rule against hearsay. *See,* FED. R. EVID. 801. To the extent these images and text are being introduced to show the images and text found on the websites, they are not statements at all - and thus fall outside the ambit of the hearsay rule. To the extent that Perfect 10 relies on directories and the like as assertions that the links provided actually connect to the subject matter claimed in the link, the Court finds the hearsay issue to be a closer question."

- *Sunlight Saunas, Inc. v. Sundance Sauna, Inc.*, No. CIV.04-2597, 2006 U.S. Dist. LEXIS 22047, n.4 (D. Kan. Apr. 17, 2006). In this multiple count commercial defamation, etc. case the Court ruled that exhibits from the Better Business Bureau website which stated how long a business has been in existence and when it was started was hearsay within hearsay.

[b] Hearsay Exceptions

Website content offered for the truth must satisfy a hearsay exception.

[i]   801(d) Admission of a Party Opponent

FED. R. EVID. 801(d)(2) provides that statements are not hearsay if they are an admission by a party-opponent. Website content published by a party may be admissions of that party when offered by an opponent.

- *Van Westrienen v. Americontinental Collection Corp.,* 94 F. Supp. 2d 1087, 1109 (D. Or. 2000). "The only remaining question is whether the content of the Web site is hearsay under FRE 801. . . . the representations made by defendants on the website are admissible as admissions of the party-opponent under FRE 801(d)(2)(A)."

- *Hernandez v. AutoNation USA Corp.,* 2003 WL 22977576 (Ct. App. Cal. Dec. 2003). The Court found that they could take judicial notice of documents (press releases and an annual report) found on the defendant's web site as party admissions, and thus was admissible hearsay.

[ii]   Mental, Emotional or Physical Condition

- *Microware Systems Corp. v. Apple Computer, Inc.,* 126 F. Supp. 2d 1207, 1211 n.2 (S.D. Ia. 2000). Court found:

    As to the internet and e-mail postings . . . Microware's internet and e-mail submissions are not ideal proffers of evidence since their authors cannot be cross-examined. However, in a case involving an industry where e-mail and internet communication are a fact of life, these technical deficiencies must go to the weight of such evidence, rather than to their admissibility. . . . alternatively, under Rule 803(3) [existing state of mind hearsay exception] of the Federal Rules of Evidence, they can be offered for whatever truth they hold. (citations omitted).

[iii]   Market Reports and Commercial Publications

FED. R. EVID. 803(17) excludes from the hearsay rule "[m]arket quotations, tabulations, lists, directories, or other published compilations, generally used and relied upon by the public or by persons in particular occupations."

Cases

- *Hess v. Riedel-Hess,* 794 N.E.2d 96, 103-04 (Ct. Apps. Ohio 2003). The Court found that a used vehicle appraisal guide exhibit was properly admitted pursuant to Evid. R. 803(17) which excludes from the hearsay rule "[m]arket quotations, tabulations, lists, directories, or other published compilations, generally used and relied upon by the public or by persons in particular occupations." The Court found that the "NADA guidelines in print form and on the Internet are highly reliable and used widely by the general public."

- *Elliott Assocs., L.P. v. Banco de la Nacion,* 194 F.R.D. 116, 121 (S.D.N.Y. 2000). The Court held that prime rates posted on the Federal Reserve website satisfy the hearsay exception of FED. R. EVID. 803(17).

- *State v. Erickstad,* 620 N.W.2d 136, 145 (N.D. 2000). The Court admitted evidence from the "Kelley Blue Book internet website" as to the value of a pickup.

[iv]   Business Record and Public Records Exception

Website content may fall within the business record exception contained in Rule 803(6) or the public records and reports exception contained within 803(8), because it is "a data compilation, in any form."

For example, many businesses and government agencies publish content on websites. Since this content is generally created in the ordinary course of business, it may fall within the hearsay exception for records of a business 801(6) or public office 803(8). Foundationally, one must establish that they were created in the regular course of business and that they are reliable and trustworthy.

Both Rule 803(6) and Rule 803(8) raise trustworthiness concerns. Both rules provide for admission of content, unless the sources of information "indicate lack of trustworthiness." This trustworthiness criterion parallels the authenticity requirements of Rule 901(a) requirement of "evidence sufficient to support a finding that the matter in question is what its proponent claims." As a result, business or public records may be excluded based on untrustworthiness, either on hearsay or authenticity grounds.

Case

- *United States v. Jackson,* 208 F.3d 633, 637-638 (7th Cir. 2000). Party argued that the web content were business records of the Internet service provider. The court disagreed and stated:

    The web postings were not statements made by declarants testifying at trial, and they were being offered to prove the truth of the matter asserted. That means they were hearsay. FED. R. EVID. 801. Jackson tries to fit the web postings in as a hearsay exception under Federal Rule of Evidence 803(6) as business records of the supremacy groups' Internet service providers. Internet service providers, however, are merely conduits. . . . Jackson presented no evidence that the Internet service providers even monitored the contents of those web sites. The fact that the Internet service providers may be able to retrieve information that its customers posted or email that its customers sent does not turn that material into a business record of the Internet service provider. . . . "[C]omputer data compilations are admissible as business records under FED. R. EVID. 803(6) if a proper foundation as to the reliability of the records is established." . . . Even if these web postings did qualify for the business records hearsay exception, "the business records are inadmissible if the source of information or the method or circumstances of preparation indicate a lack of trustworthiness" Jackson was unable to show that these postings were authentic. (citations omitted).

[4]   Best Evidence Rule

The Best Evidence rule, contained in Article X of the Federal Rules, calls for the original of a document to be offered into evidence. FED. R. EVID. 1001(3) states that "If data are stored in a computer or similar device, any printout or other output readable by sight, shown to reflect the data accurately, is an 'original.'" *See also,* § 8.11, *Best Evidence Rule.*

[a]   Reported Cases

• *Perfect 10, Inc. v. Cybernet Ventures, Inc.,* 213 F. Supp. 2d 1146, 1155 n.4 (C.D. Cal. 2002). "Cybernet objects to the printouts from third-party websites as a violation of the rule against hearsay. *See,* FED. R. EVID. 801. To the extent these images and text are being introduced to show the images and text found on the websites, they are not statements at all - and thus fall outside the ambit of the hearsay rule. FN4. When used for this purpose, the Court assumes they are subject to the best evidence rule, FED. R. EVID. 1001. The Court finds that these printouts meet the Rule, for present purposes."

§ 8.16   PHOTOGRAPHS

[A]   Generally

Photographs, like other forms of evidence, must meet evidentiary requirements in order to be admitted into evidence. These requirements include relevancy and authenticity. If a photograph is relevant to a material issue and is properly authenticated, the court may admit a photograph into evidence. FED. R. EVID. 401 and 901. The authentication requirements pursuant to Rule 901, require that there be "evidence sufficient to support finding that the matter in question is what its proponent claims." FED. R. EVID. 901.

Generally, courts have admitted photographic evidence under two theories of authentication. The first is referred to as the "pictorial testimony" authentication theory. Under this theory, a sponsoring witness who has personal knowledge of the scene depicted testifies that the photograph fairly and accurately portrays that scene. *See, e.g., Simms v. Dixon,* 291 A.2d 184 (D.C. 1972). E. Cleary, *McCormick on Evidence* (3d ed. 1984) at 671. The photograph is then incorporated by reference into the testimony of the authenticating witness and is admissible as an illustration of that witness' testimony. *See, People v. Bowley,* 59 Cal. 2d 855, 31 Cal. Rptr. 471, 475 n.5, 382 P.2d 591, 595 n.5 (1963); *see generally,* McCormick, *Evidence* § 214 at p. 531 (2d ed. 1976); 3 *Wigmore on Evidence* § 790 at p. 219 (1970).

The second theory of authentication is commonly referred to as the "silent witness" theory. It allows for the admission of photographic evidence when the proponent adequately establishes the reliability of the process producing the photograph. Once authenticated it then allows the trier of fact to reasonably infer that the contents of the photograph accurately depicts the event it is offered to prove. The admission of the photographic evidence is proper, even though there is an absence of any witness verification. Admissibility under this theory is based on the reliability of photographic process. The majority of jurisdictions have adopted this theory. *Fisher v. State,* 643 S.W.2d 571 (Ark. 1982) (for a collection of state cases); *United States v. Goslee,* 389 F. Supp. 490, 493 (W.D.Pa. 1975); *United States v. Clayton,* 643 F.2d 1071 (5th Cir. 1981); *United States v. Taylor,* 530 F.2d 639 (5th Cir.), *cert. denied,* 429 U.S. 845 (1976).

In a further relaxing of the admissibility standard the court in *United States v. Rembert,* 863 F.2d 1023, 1028 (Fed. Cir. 1988) stated, "[c]onsistent with our decision in *Blackwell* and the teachings of our sister circuits and the courts of the several states, we conclude that the contents of photographic evidence to be admitted into evidence need not be merely illustrative, but can be admitted as evidence independent of the testimony of any witness as to the events depicted, upon a foundation sufficient to meet the requirements of Federal Rule of Evidence 901(a)."

[B]   Alterations to Photos

It is difficult to determine if a digital photograph (or fingerprint) has been altered or enhanced. Since "a picture is worth a thousand words," an altered piece of digital evidence can literally decide the outcome of a civil or criminal case. Black-and-blue in ones and zeros at http://www.salon.com/tech/feature/2002/07/10/digital_violence/index.html. (article discusses the various issues surrounding digital photographs used in domestic violence cases) (last visited on July 27, 2006). The field of forensics does possess tools to assist in determining digital forgeries. *Commonwealth v. Simone,* No. CR.03-0986, 2003 WL 22994245, *1, 3 (Cir. Ct. Virg. Nov. 12, 2003) (expert presented testimony that none of the images were morphed images). If the photograph or digital image is challenged on authentication or Best Evidence grounds, it may be necessary to lay a foundation through the use of metadata and other forensic tools.

[C]   Foundation

The foundational elements for photographs are as follows:

- The witness is familiar with the scene or object that is depicted in the photograph;

- The witness explains how he or she is familiar with the object or scene;

- The witness recognizes and identifies the scene or object depicted in the photograph;

- The witness identifies the photograph as a fair, true, accurate or good depiction of that scene or object at that particular time and relevant to the facts of the case.

Edward J. Imwinkelried, *Evidentiary Foundations* (5th Ed.).

[D]   Reported Cases

- *Almond v. State,* 274 Ga. 348, 349, 553 S.E.2d 803, 805 (2001). The defendant, who was convicted of murder, argued on appeal that pictures taken with a digital camera should have been inadmissible. The Court found that, "the pictures were introduced only after the prosecution properly authenticated them as fair and truthful representations of what they purported to depict. . . . We are aware of no authority, and appellant cites none, for the proposition that the procedure for admitting pictures should be any different when they were taken by a digital camera."

- *United States v. Lauder,* 409 F.3d 1254, 1265 (10th Cir. 2005). In ruling upon the admissibility of fingerprints the Court in dicta stated, "The following thought experiment is illustrative: Suppose an expert relies on photographs taken by a new digital camera in forming her opinion. A district court would not be required to perform a *Daubert* analysis as to whether the photographs accurately reflected the subject matter depicted, even though digital technology is relatively new as compared to a traditional film camera."

- *United States v. Hamilton,* 413 F.3d 1138, 1142-1143 (10th Cir. 2005). The Court affirmed the criminal conviction and found that "header" information found on computerized image or picture was not hearsay. The header information included "information regarding the person who posted the images to the newsgroup: screen name, subject of the posting, the date the images were posted, and the person's IP address."

- *Wild v. Alster,* 377 F. Supp. 2d 186, 193-195 (D.D.C. 2005). The Court denied plaintiff's motion for a new trial where she argued that she was entitled to have an expert examine the hard drive of the defendants' computer to explore whether it contained the dates that photographs of the plaintiff were taken. She had alleged a doctor had altered the photographs after her malpractice claim was filed.

- *Home Depot, U.S.A., Inc. v. United States,* 2006 Ct. Intl. Trade LEXIS 46 (Ct. Int'l Trade Apr. 7, 2006). In a tariff rate dispute, the Court found photographs, which included written content, were properly authenticated under FED. R. EVID. 901 and the written information on the grounds that it qualified under FED. R. EVID. 803(6) as an exception to the hearsay rule.

- *United States v. Maxwell,* 42 M.J. 568 (A.F.Ct. Crim.App. 1995), *rev'd on other grounds,* 45 M.J. 406 (1996). In a pornography case, the Court ruled that admission of hard copies of visual images downloaded from computers did not violate the Best Evidence Rule. The defendant argued that the images should have been displayed on the computer screen. The Court held that copies were "originals" in that they were printouts or other outputs readable by sight as allowed by Military Rules of Evid., Rules 1001(3), 1002.

- For authentication of computer files see also § 5.05[G], *Chain of Custody, Audit Reports and Hash Values.*

[E]   Other Authorities

- Guilshan, *A Picture is Worth a Thousand Lies: Electronic Imaging and the Future of the Admissibility of Photographs into Evidence,* 18 Rutgers Computer & Tech. L. J. 365-380 (1992).

- Jill Witkowski, *Can Juries Really Believe What They See? New Foundational Requirements for the Authentication of Digital Images,* 10 Wash. U. J.L. & Pol'y 267 (2002).

- Richard Kammen & Herbert Blitzer, *Ensure Admissibility of Digital Images* available at http://www.iowaiai.org/digital.htm (last visited on July 22, 2006). This article discusses standards for admissibility of crime scene photographs.

- Judge Victor E. Bianchini & Harvey Bass, *A Paradigm for the Authentication of Photographic Evidence in the Digital Age,* 20 T. Jefferson L. Rev. 303- 322 (1998).

- Christopher J. Buccafusco, *Gaining/losing Perspective on the Law, or Keeping Visual Evidence in Perspective,* 58 U. Miami L.R. 609 (2004).

Specific Computer Devices

§ 8.17   GPS DEVICE

[A]   Generally

See, § 2.5[S], *Global Positioning System (GPS).*

[B]   Reported Cases

• *State v. Andrews,* 84 P.3d 441, 444-45 (Alaska 2004). A fisherman was charged with fishing in closed waters. The lower court excluded the Loren C (similar to GPS device) tracking information based on the Best Evidence rule for failing to preserve a printout of the tracking data and lack of foundation. The Appellate Court reversed the Best Evidence ruling holding "even though this information apparently could have been stored as data, the defendants have not convinced us that the best evidence rule requires that it be so stored. Nor have the defendants otherwise convinced us that the lack of a printout should render the troopers' observations of the Loran C continuous electronic readings inadmissible." The Court also found that proper foundation was laid by testimony the "Loran C receivers were properly functioning, that proper procedures were followed, and that troopers were reasonably qualified to use Loran C technology."

• *United States v. Bennett,* 363 F.3d 947, 954 (9th Cir. 2004). The Court reversed the defendant's conviction for marijuana importation and reviewed the line of cases ruling on the admissibility of GPS evidence. In this case the defendant challenged his importation conviction arguing that GPS information taken from his boat should be excluded based on the best evidence rule and hearsay. The law enforcement agent testified that he had not taken possession of the GPS device nor obtained any record of the data contained therein. The Court found that the GPS evidence was inadmissible based on the Best Evidence rule and the court also noted that "in addition to failing to produce the GPS or its output for trial, the government did not establish that Bennett's GPS information was necessarily accurate or that the GPS itself worked properly."

§ 8.18   HARD DRIVE

[A]   Generally

See, § 2.4[B], *Hard Drive (External or Internal).*

[B]   Reported Cases

- *State v. Cook,* 149 Ohio App.3d 422, 777 N.E.2d 882 (Ohio 2002). The Appellate Court found that computer data taken from a hard drive (that had been forensically imaged) had been properly authenticated. The Court reviewed the forensic imaging process, defense expert's objections, authentication of the data retrieved from the hard drive and possibility of tampering with the data.

- *State v. Myrland,* No. CIV.03-1646, 2004 WL 1381267 (Minn. Ct. App. Jun. 22, 2004). The Court of Appeals reversed the defendant's conviction for child pornography because evidence showed that the Internet access code was the same for all the teachers on all school computers. In addition, the forensics expert admitted that all of the illegal images were retrieved from "unallocated space" on the school's hard drive and there was no way to tell who had viewed the images or if they had been viewed at all.

- *Broderick v. State,* 35 S.W.3d 67, 79 (Tex. App. 2000). The defendant appealed based on Best Evidence grounds contending that "the trial court abused its discretion by allowing the State to introduce a duplicate of the hard drive taken from his computer rather than producing the original. . . . The State's computer expert testified that the copy made of the data encoded on the hard drive exactly duplicated the contents of that drive and explained the methods used in its creation." The Appellate Court denied the appeal and also denied defendant's contentions of ineffective assistance of counsel because his counsel failed to obtain an expert to object to data retrieved from the computer.

§ 8.19   FAX

[A]   Generally

See, § 2.5[K], *Facsimile Transmission (Faxes)* and § 3.13, *Faxes.*

[B]   Reported Cases

- *United States v. Khorozian,* 333 F.3d 498, 506 (3rd Cir. 2003). The Court affirmed the defendant's conviction for bank fraud and reviewed the proper foundation to lay for admission of a fax transmission and the hearsay rule regarding the content of the fax.

- *United States v. Sattar,* No. CR.02-395, 2003 WL 22510435, at *4 (S.D.N.Y. Nov. 5, 2003). In a criminal case, the defendant argued that the government had not complied with the Best Evidence rule since it had failed to release the electronic files, only paper printouts, of faxes that were intercepted. The Court denied the motion to suppress and held that the destruction of the electronic fax files from one computer system was not done in bad faith and the fax files from the second computer were disclosed in an electronic format, though different then the original proprietary software format.

- *SEC v. Hartcourt Cos.,* No. CIV.03-3698, 2005 U.S. Dist. LEXIS 41999, at *29 n.15 (D. Cal. Jan. 24, 2005). The Court ruled that plaintiff's deposition admission that he received the fax satisfied the authenticity requirements of FED. R. EVID. 901(a).

- *Stevens Shipping & Terminal Co. v. M/V Japan Rainbow II,* 334 F.3d 439, 444 (5th Cir. 2003). The Court held that a fax confirmation sheet produces a rebuttable presumption of receipt.

- *Hill v. Citibank Corp.,* 312 F. Supp. 2d 464, 474 (D.N.Y. 2004). The Court ruled that the plaintiff failed "to authenticate the fax or the information with respect to the date and time printed on the fax, or to substantiate that the date and time were the date and time that the fax was sent to the EEOC. There is no basis for treating the 'fax header' as reliable, and it would be inadmissible at trial as hearsay--an out of court statement offered for the truth of the matter asserted--that does not fall under an established exception. *See,* FED. R. EVID. 801(c), 802 (citation omitted)."

§ 8.20   CALLER ID

[A]   Generally

See, § 2.5[I], *Caller ID Device.*

[B]   Reported Cases

- *State v. Duff,* 2001 WL 102258, at *6 (Ohio App. Feb. 08, 2001). The Court held that "other state courts have consistently held that caller ID information provided to a telephone user is based on computer-generated information and not simply repetition of prior recorded human output or observation, and thus does not fall within the scope of the hearsay rule. (citations omitted) . . . Caller ID evidence, therefore, will not be inadmissible on hearsay grounds, but may be attacked based on a lack of foundation regarding the reliability of the device, or by otherwise demonstrating the unreliability of the information disclosed by it."

- *State v. Schuette,* 273 Kan. 593, 597, 44 P.3d 459, 463 (Kan. 2002.). The defendant was convicted of the charge of criminal threat by calling the victim. The Court in a detailed decision held that sufficient foundation established reliability of victims' caller ID (identification) device and the phone number printout was not hearsay. The Court held that it was not error to admit caller ID evidence showing the number where the call originated and the name of the person to whom the phone was registered. The Court held that it could take judicial notice that the operation of a caller ID (identification) unit does not require any advanced training and that by merely pressing arrow buttons on a caller ID device, the user can review prior telephone calls that were made is so generally known or of such common notoriety within the territorial jurisdiction of the Court that it cannot reasonably be the subject of dispute.

- *State v. McGee*, 84 P.3d 690, 693 (N. Mex. 2004). The Court allowed the jury to use caller ID evidence to determine origin of harassing calls. The victim called the "police and when they arrived at her house, she showed them her caller ID that displayed the two calls that had just come from the Otero County Detention Center."

§ 8.21 CRASH DATA RECORDER

[A] Generally

See, § 2.5[U], *Vehicle Computer and Listening Devices.*

[B] Reported Cases

- *Matos v. State,* 899 So.2d 403, 405 (Fla.App. Mar. 30, 2005). The defendant appealed his conviction for manslaughter arguing that data from an event data recorder (EDR) that showed his speed at 114 m.p.h. was improperly admitted. In a case of first impression, the Appellate Court held that the ERA data from an event data recorder (EDR) was generally accepted in relevant scientific fields, and was thus admissible. In ruling upon the EDR admissibility the court noted that, "[a] 'black box' or EDR is mandated by the federal government in airplanes, ships, and trains, and more recently in buses and motor coaches. The EDR records data that can be used in accident reconstruction. . . . All vehicles with airbags have an EDR. EDRs were first used in automobiles in the 1970s, when airbags first came out. Automobile manufacturers have been using the data ever since to collect real world crash data, which they used, for example, in modifying airbag designs. The data is also being used in the medical field to compare injury forces acting on the body and by insurance companies with regard to claims."

- *People v. Hopkins,* 2004 WL 3093274, at *14 (N.Y.Cty.Ct. Aug. 30, 2004.). The Court refused the defendant's request for a *Frye* hearing and held that the "SDM (sensing diagnostic module or 'black box') modules seized from the vehicle" that showed a speed of 104 at the time of the crash would be admitted as evidence.

- *Bachman v. General Motors Corporation,* 332 Ill. App. 3rd 760 (4th Dist. 2003). The Court on appeal recognized SDM (sensing diagnostic module) data as generally accepted as reliable and accurate by the automobile industry and, therefore, admissible.

- *Lloyd v. GMC,* No. CIV.05-1495, 2006 U.S. Dist. LEXIS 4164, at *7-10 (D.S.C. Jan. 20, 2006). The defendant's expert described an SDM as "an onboard electronic module which functions to continuously monitor the air bag system in the car while the ignition is on, to deploy the air bags, and to record certain crash and air bag system data in deployment and non-deployment level crash events . . . based on her review and analysis of the SDM information, [the expert concluded] . . . that the 'air bag system was functioning properly' at the time of the accident."

- *Ray v. CSX Transp.,* 2006 U.S. App. LEXIS 12748, at *4-6 (4th Cir. May 23, 2006) (unpublished). In this discrimination case, the employer obtained information from a train's "black box" which included "the time when the train engine was operating" in order to determine whether the employees were logging off work at the correct time.

§ 8.22   COMPUTER, AUDIT AND ACCESS LOGS

[A]   Generally

For a discussion of audit and access logs see § 2.6[G], *Audit Trails and Logs.*

[B]   Reported Cases

Computers

- *State v. Bikrev,* 2003 WL 21458683 (Tenn. Crim. App. Jun. 24, 2003). In a criminal proceeding, the Appellate Court held that the government had established a proper chain of custody for a stolen computer. The defendant argued that the computers had been returned to the victim and turned on which broke the chain of custody. However, testimony was presented to establish that defendant's personal files (faxes and other files) had been created on the stolen computer a few days after the burglary and that registry files showed that the computer had not been tampered with after it was returned to the owner.

- *State v. Burrier,* 2000 WL 777855 (Ohio App. Jun. 16, 2000). In a criminal proceeding the defendant argued that his laptop should not be admitted as evidence because of chain of custody problems. The Court admitted the evidence and found that, "[a]lthough the burden of establishing the chain of custody of a particular piece of evidence is on the state, the burden in not an absolute one. (citation omitted) . . . As long as it is reasonably certain that no tampering or substitution occurred regarding the particular item of evidence, the state need not negate all possibilities of tampering or substitution. (citation omitted) Moreover, even when a break in the chain of custody is uncovered, it goes to the credibility of the evidence and not to its admissibility."

Access Logs

- *Inventory Locator Serv., LLC v. Partsbase, Inc.,* No. CIV.02-2695, 2005 U.S. Dist. LEXIS 32680, at *65-66 (D. Tenn. Sept. 2, 2005). Plaintiff alleged that the defendant improperly gained access to its electronic marketplace for aviation parts and attempted to solicit customers away from the plaintiff. The defendant counterclaimed alleging similar conduct on the part of the plaintiff. "In support of its counterclaims, [the defendant] offers 'web server logs,' which purport to record various unlawful entries into [the defendant's] computer system from an internet protocol ('IP') address assigned to [the plaintiff]. [The plaintiff] seeks to exclude this evidence, arguing that 1) the logs are 'incredible on their face,' 2) the logs appear to have been altered, 3) the logs have been moved and deleted, and 4) the logs are inadmissible hearsay." The Court found that the logs were properly authenticated and were not inadmissible hearsay since they were kept in the regular course of business.

- *People v. Hawkins,* 98 Cal. App. 4th 1428, 99 Cal. App. 4th 1333a, 121 Cal. Rptr. 2d 627 (6th Dist. 2002), *as modified on denial of reh'g.,* (July 2, 2002), *review denied,* (Aug. 28, 2002), *cert. denied,* 537 U.S. 1189 (2003). The defendant was convicted of knowingly accessing and taking data from a computer system. The defendant argues that the computer data readout of access times was hearsay and not admissible. The Court held that the readouts were not hearsay since the computer provided the readouts. The Court further ruled that the prosecutor's offer of proof that the computer clock was functioning properly was sufficient to establish the reliability of information pertaining to access times of computer files, and thus the admissibility of the printouts of those access times at trial for knowingly accessing and taking data from a computer system.

§ 8.23   VOICE MAIL

[A]   Generally

See, § 2.5[H], *Voice Mail and Answering Machine.*

[B]   Reported Case

- *White v. State,* 2006 Tex. App. LEXIS 2224 (Tex. App. 2006). The Court affirmed the lower court conviction and held that a tape recording made from the victim's voice mail was admissible because the deletions of the messages of the victim's best friend did not affect the reliability of the remaining messages on the tape. Furthermore, the messages were not hearsay under Tex. R. Evid. 801 because they were not offered to prove the truth of the matters asserted therein. Also, because the messages assisted the jury in establishing the time of the victim's death, they were relevant under Tex. R. Evid. 401.

This page intentionally left blank.

Glossary

Analog - describes the recording format of real events. Analog devices such as video and audio recording devices record real events in real time using film or audiotape. This is different from digital, where digital devices record real events in 1's and 0's for computer use.

ANSI (American National Standards Institute) - is the organization that develops standards for items like computers and software.

API (Application Program Interface) - is a term used to describe the "hooks" available to "integrate" programs with each other. For example API's are available for Microsoft Access to integrate or communicate with an image application program.

Applications Program Software - are computer programs that perform a wide range of tasks and generally designed for specific purposes. Microsoft Word and WordPerfect were designed for word processing, Summation for database and full text document search and retrieval, and Lotus 123 for a spreadsheet. They are also referred to as an *application* or *program.*

Archiving - is the process of putting data on disks for long-term storage. Backups are used to ensure data is saved in case of data loss.

ASCII (American Standard Code for Information Interchange) - is a code for representing characters as numbers.

Backups - are a duplicate storage copy of a computer program, disk or data made either for archiving purposes or for safeguarding valuable files from loss should the active copy be damaged or destroyed.

BIOS (Basic Input/Output System) - are instructions that tell the computer how to control the information between computers and peripherals.

Bit (binary digit) - is the smallest unit of measurement for a computer.

Bitmap - represents characters or graphics by individual pixels or dots. They are arranged in columns and rows and can be altered with paint programs. Bitmap graphics, also called raster graphics, are images created with pixels.

Blowback - is a slang term for printing images to paper.

Boot/Reboot - is the start-up procedure for a computer.

Bps (bits per second) - is a transmission speed between two computers.

Browser - is software, like Internet Explorer, that is used to view web pages on the Internet or Intranet. It is the user's software used to view sites located on servers running web server software.

Bulletin Board Service (BBS) - is the early forerunner to group computing systems. They permit users to exchange e-mail, retrieve files and share other computer functions between individuals who share common interests.

Byte - is the primary unit of measurement for computer storage. It denotes the amount of space needed to store a single character of text.

Cache - is a high-speed storage or memory mechanism that temporarily stores frequently used data. A computer creates cache files in order to temporarily store and efficiently reuse information about application programs and other information, such as visits to different World Wide Web sites.

CAD (Computer Aided Design) - is a computer program that assists in designing products, buildings, houses, highways and so forth.

CD-ROM (Compact Disk Read-Only Memory) - is an injection-molded aluminized disc, which stores digital data in high-density microscopic pits in a read only format.

CGI (Common Gateway Interface) - is the standard used for connecting web pages with underlying data. A CGI script has the capability of calculating mortgages, accessing databases for reports, etc.

Character Recognition - or OCR is the ability of a scanner to convert printed text into computer readable text for use in a computer program such as a word processor.

Chat (online) - is the real-time simultaneous communication between two or more people using a computer.

Client/Servers - is a type of computing that intelligently divides tasks between clients and servers. Client/server networks use a dedicated computer called a server to handle file, print and other services for client users, usually desktop computers. This system is contrasted with mainframe computers.

Communications Program – is software that controls the transfer of data from one computer to another.

Compact Flash (CF) - is a popular memory card developed by SanDisk (www.sandisk.com) and uses flash memory to store data on a very small card.

Compatibility - describes the capability of a piece of hardware or software to operate with another piece of software or hardware. For example word processing files from WordPerfect are not compatible with the Microsoft Word program, unless a conversion program is first used.

Communications Protocol - is a set of instructions, which enables two computers to talk to each other. TCP/IP is a protocol suite that is used on networks. It has become one of the key defacto standards for tying together computers. The popularity of the Internet and the communication in large part is due to this protocol. FTP (File Transfer Protocol) is a protocol for transferring files on the Internet.

Compression - is the ability of some software programs to shrink or compress graphics, images and other computer files.

Computer - is an electronic machine that enables one to input, manipulate, store and output electronic information.

Computer File - is a collection of computer commands and information stored in a file.

Computer Forensics - is the preservation, identification, extraction, documentation and analysis of computer evidence.

Computer Forensic Expert - provides expertise regarding the generation, storage, recovery, location, discovery and disclosure of computer evidence.

Cookie - is a file that is automatically created and stored on the hard disk containing information about a Web site visited.

CPU (Central Processing Unit) - is the main core of a computer. Often called the brain of the computer, it controls the interpretation and execution of computer instructions.

Cursor - is the small dash or image on the computer screen that constantly blinks and moves when the mouse or other pointing device is manipulated.

DAT (Digital Audio Tape) - is a standard medium and technology for the digital recording of audio or data on tape.

Data - is information that is processed or transmitted by a device like a computer.

Data Communications - is the transfer of data between two computer points.

Database - is simply a collection of mutually related data or information stored in computer record fields. It is data that has been organized and structured for a particular purpose such as an employee benefit system.

Database Management Systems (DBMS) - is the task of managing data in databases and retrieving information from that database.

Data Transfer Rate - is the rate of data transfer from one device to another. The higher the transfer rate, the faster the access to the data.

Deduplication - is the process of separating duplicate e-mail messages, word processing documents, and other computer files from your electronic file collection.

Device drivers - control attached peripheral devices such as a mouse, scanners and other devices.

Digital - is the recording of information in a binary manner. Information is recorded as 1's and 0's for use by a computer.

Digital Cameras - are cameras that translate real events or pictures directly into digital data.

Digitize - is the process of converting information such as a document into binary code. Documents can be converted into a digital format using a scanner.

DAT (Digital Audiotape) - is a technology that records digital audio onto magnetic tape.

Directory - is the location where files and subdirectories are located on the computer.

Disk - is a data storage media for your computer. Removable disks come in a variety of sizes.

Disk Drive - is a device that enables a computer to read and write data on a disk.

Document Retrieval - is the ability to locate, retrieve and view a document on a computer screen.

DPI (Dots Per Inch) - is a measurement of output resolution and quality. It measures the number of dots per square inch. A 600 dpi document is sharper than a 200 dpi document but requires more storage space.

Dot Pitch (DP) - is the amount of space between dots of color or pixels on a monitor. The lower the dot pitch, such as .28, the clearer and crisper the picture.

DVD (The Digital Versatile (Video) Disk) - is the next-generation optical disk standard that has a storage capacity upward of 8.5 gigabytes of data and can store two hours of movies on a side.

Electronic Discovery Software - is software that extracts application data and metadata from computer files.

Electronic Mail - systems allow you to send data (a message), attachments (computer files), and provide pointers (hypertext links to information on the Internet) to other e-mail users. Attachments can include text, sound, graphics or video.

Encryption - is the process of converting electronic information, such as messages or data, into a form that is unreadable by anyone, except the intended recipient.

Expansion Cards - are integrated circuit cards that can be added to your computer to expand its capabilities. For example, a network card can be added to your computer to give it the capability to connect it to a network.

Extranet - is a private "Internet" for two or more firms or organizations.

Fax/Modem - is a device that can send or receive faxes.

Fiber Optic Cable - is cable made from thin strands of glass through which data is transported. It is an excellent conduit to transfer data for medium or long distances, but is more expensive than normal cable.

Field - is the location on a database computer input form to collect specific data such as name, address, phone number and social security number

Field Name - is the labeled area such as "Last name," "First name," "Address" and "Social Security Number" on a database input form.

File - is a collection of electronic information in a computer file. Files are stored in directories.

Filename - is the name given to a computer file. Each computer file has a name associated with it.

Filtering - is the process of reducing the size of the electronic file population by limiting computer information to specific criteria like keywords, names, dates, etc.

File Format - defines the way the data is stored in a computer file and subsequently displayed on a screen or in print.

Firewall - is generally used to describe a security system for an Internet or Intranet web site. Its purpose is to preclude intruders from viewing or changing sensitive data.

Fixed disk - is another name for a hard drive.

Floppy - (also called a disk or diskette) is a removable storage device used to store computer files.

Forensics - *See* Computer Forensics.

Form - is a computer database input screen that contains fields where information is to be entered. After information is entered, it is called a record. *See* Record.

Fragmentation - on a disk occurs when parts or pieces of a single file are distributed to many different locations on a disk.

Full Text - is the "full" or complete text of a document. This term usually refers to a document that has been converted for use on a computer. A "full text" document can be searched for individual words, names, dates and other information in the document.

Full Text Search - is the capability of searching text files for words, phrases or patterns of characters. An image cannot be full text searched. It has to be retyped or OCR'ed into the computer.

GB (gigabyte) - is 1,073,741,824 bytes or 1024 megabytes. This unit of measurement reflects computer memory or disk storage. [In general, never use "unit of measurement; use unit of measure.]

Graphics - are primarily computer pictures and drawings. Some common graphic formats are TIFF, JPEG and GIF.

Graphical User Interface (GUI) - is a computing environment that enables one to execute commands or interact with a program using graphical symbols on the screen.

Gooey (slang for GUI) - stands for Graphical User Interface.

Handwriting Recognition - is the technology that converts human handwriting into machine-readable computer text.

Hard Drive - is a storage device generally inside the computer used to store information. A hard drive consists of a rigid circular magnetic platter that is sealed in a metal box with read/ write heads

Hardware - is the physical equipment that comprises a computer system.

Home Page - is usually the first page of a web site. It usually contains the main menu that directs the visitor to other parts of the site that can include documents, audio, video, graphics, text and other links.

HTML (Hypertext Markup Language) - is the language used to create hypertext, the language used to create Internet, Intranet and Extranet pages. HTML's commands direct a browser like Netscape how to display web pages. These commands pertain to graphics, text and links to other pages or web sites.

Hypertext Linking - is the capability to link together any two separate sources of digital information and then jump to the secondary source whenever necessary.

Hz (Hertz) - is a measurement of frequency that is defined as one cycle per second. The higher the megahertz of a computer, the faster it will run. A megahertz is 1,000,000 cycles per second. Microprocessors run at speeds that are measured in MHz or millions of cycles per second.

Image - is an "electronic picture" of a document that is in a digital format. It is not searchable.

Imaging - is the process of using a scanner to convert a paper document into a computer electronic image.

Internet - is an international network of computers linking businesses, governments, educational institutions, individual users, law firms and others.

Intranet - is a personal Internet within an organization.

Issue Code - is an enhancement code used in full text or databases to indicate a specific topic or area of interest for use within litigation reports and searches.

Java - is a programming language, owned by Sun Microsystems, that allows programmers to create web add-ons or pages that can be viewed by browsers. Generally it is used in conjunction with HTML for add-on features with web pages, though it can be used alone to create web pages.

JPEG - is a standard graphic standard for still image compression.

KB (Kilobyte) - is a unit of measurement that equals 1,024 bytes and denotes computer memory or disk storage.

Legacy Data - is generally archived electronic information that has been used in prior software and hardware configurations.

Listserv - is a discussion group, similar to newsgroups, where people exchange information about a variety of subjects. It uses standard Internet e-mail to exchange messages.

Load - is when a program is copied from the hard disk into RAM memory. This occurs whenever you start a program. When you turn on your computer, the operating system program loads.

Magnetic Tape Drives - can be external or internal and are generally used as backup devices. Magnetic tape can hold significant amounts of computer information – between 100 MB and 20 GB and higher.

Magnetic-Optic - refers to an erasable optical recording method. It is similar to a magnetic hard disk.

Menu - in a computer program is a list of options that you choose from to do different computer functions.

Megabyte - is a unit of measurement that equals 1,048,576 bytes or characters or 1,024 kilobytes.

Megahertz - *See* hertz.

Memory - is space within the computer for storing electronic data.

Metadata - is "hidden" or "embedded" information that is stored in electronically generated materials, but which is not visible when a document or other materials are printed.

Microprocessor - is the chip inside the computer that is the center of all activity. The chip controls all the operations of a computer and is used to execute program commands. It is also known as a *processor*.

MIS (**M**anagement **I**nformation **S**ystem) - is generally the department responsible for electronic information systems within an organization.

Modem - is an internal or external computer device that connects to a telephone for the purpose of sending or receiving information to/or from other computers.

Mouse - is the primary pointing device for the Windows operating system. When you move the mouse over a flat surface the cursor or arrow makes a movement on the screen and allows commands to be executed by pushing buttons.

MS-DOS (**M**icrosoft **D**isk **O**perating **S**ystem) - is a user operating system.

Multitasking Operating System - is an operating system that enables the user to perform more than one task at a time.

Multimedia - is the delivery of information in multisensory ways through the integration of previously distinct media (text, graphics, computer animation, motion video, and sound).

Network - is when two or more computers are linked together to share data, programs and hardware resources. Special hardware and software are required to network computers.

Newsgroups - are topic specific forums on the Internet or on local networks where people can post questions, news, and comments and/or read and respond to such postings left by other users.

Off line - is when a peripheral device does not have an active communications link with the computer. For example, when a printer is off line it is unable to communicate and print a document from a word processing program.

On line - is when equipment, devices and other services are in direct communication with your computer. One can be on line with a printer or the Internet.

Operating System - controls the overall operation of the computer. The operating program directs and coordinates the commands between your computer and other hardware components such as printers, video, soundboards and other components. It also coordinates the flow of commands between application programs and the computer. The most popular operating program is Windows.

Optical Character Recognition - is the process of using a scanner and software to convert paper into a searchable machine-readable text.

Optical Drive - is a storage device that reads and writes to optical disks using a laser. There are different types of optical disks such as CD-ROM which is read only storage media, WORM that can be written to once and read many times and WRRM which stands for write many, read many.

Parallel Port - is a port generally located on the back of a computer and transfers eight bits of data simultaneously through multiple wires. A printer is generally connected to a parallel port and is generally designated with the letters LPT1.

Path - is the directory sequence the computer must search to locate a particular file or directory. *See also* directory and file.

PC Cards - were formerly called PCMCIA (Personal Computer Memory Card International Association) cards and are covered circuit boards that can be inserted into special slots on laptops. PC Cards can be hard drives, modems, network adapters, RAM (random access memory), sound cards, SCSI or cellular phone connectors and flash memory.

PDF (**P**ortable **D**ocument Format) - is a document file format by Adobe Systems (www.adobe.com).

Personal Digital Assistant (PDA) - is a hand-held computer that helps with such tasks as calendaring, contact management, taking notes, paging, sending and receiving faxes and electronic mail, as well as Web access.

Pen-Based Computing - is a method of entering data into a computer using an electronic stylus or pen.

Pen Storage Drive - fits into the USB port of your computer, is the size of half of a pen, and stores upwards of 10 megabytes to 1 GB and upwards of information.

Port - is a connector to a computer that allows data to be exchanged with other devices such as a printer, mouse, CD-ROM reader or external modem.

Processor - *See* Microprocessor.

Program - *See* Application Program.

Prompt - is usually depicted as "C:\" or "A:\ " and indicates that the computer is ready to accept input.

Relational Database - stores information in a collection of tables, each table storing information about one subject. These tables can be "related" for business or other informational purposes.

RAM (Random Access Memory) - RAM is available for a user's programs and data when a computer is turned on. RAM is emptied each time you turn the computer off. RAM is generally measured in megabytes.

ROM (Read Only Memory) - is the computer memory that stores instructions permanently. The ROM contains instructions that the computer uses to run properly and is executed each time the computer is turned on.

Root Directory - is the first level directory on a computer. All other directories are subordinate to the root and are referred to as directories or subdirectories. *See also* Directory.

Record - is the name given to a database form after information has been entered into the form.

Scan - is the process of converting a paper into an image or using OCR software to convert it to machine-readable text.

Scanner - is a device that converts a document or picture into an image or machine-readable text.

Serial Port - is the connector port on a computer that sends and receives data one bit at a time. A modem, printer or mouse can be connected to your serial port. It is usually denoted as COM1. *See also* parallel port.

Server - is a computer (or computers) that control access to the network and its resources (such as hard drives, e-mail and printers).

Slack Space - is the unused space at the logical end of an active file's data and the physical end of the cluster or clusters that are assigned to an active file.

Software - is a collective term for computer programs. Programs can be application or operating system software. Software is a series of instructions to operate the computer and perform specialized tasks.

Spreadsheet Program - is a program that manipulates numbers and data in a table arranged in columns and rows. Lotus 123 and Quattro are two spreadsheet application programs.

Storage - refers to storing binary information created by the computer. The storage media stores data that is measured in bytes. Some common storage media are the floppy disk, hard drive and CD-ROM disk

Subdirectory - is a directory within another directory.

Tape Backup Unit (TBU) - is a device to back up the large amounts of data on your hard drive. It is similar in appearance to an audiotape.

TCP/IP (Transmission Control Protocol/Internet Protocol) - is the operating protocol by which all Internet and Intranet computers communicate with each other. It is the operating language directing how the packets of information will be sent over the wire or wireless network systems.

Terabyte - is about one trillion bytes or more precisely 1,099,511,627,776 bytes.

Text Search - is a technique for searching text files for occurrences of certain words or phrases.

TIFF (Tagged **I**mage **F**ile **F**ormat) - is an imaging format for storing images.

USB (Universal **S**erial **B**us) - is a standard that supports data transfer.

Virus - is a computer program that infects other programs by replicating itself. It can damage or destroy data.

Voice Recognition Technology - Refers to the capability of a computer to "hear" a word and convert the word automatically to usable computer text.

Windows - is the Microsoft operating system.

Word Processing - is software designed to create letters, briefs or other documents.

World Wide Web ("the Web") - is a massive collection of digital information resources stored on servers throughout the Internet.

WYSIWYG (What **Y**ou **S**ee **I**s **W**hat **Y**ou **G**et) - refers to a word processor or graphics program that displays images on the screen exactly how they will appear on paper.

Zip - is a compression algorithm and refers to compressing a file.

Index